Hell's Belles

Hell's Belles

PROSTITUTION, VICE, AND CRIME IN EARLY DENVER

With a Biography of Sam Howe, Frontier Lawman

Revised Edition

CLARK SECREST

University Press of Colorado

Published by the University Press of Colorado
5589 Arapahoe Avenue, Suite 206C
Boulder, Colorado 80303

The University Press of Colorado is a cooperative publishing enterprise supported, in part, by Adams State College, Colorado State University, Fort Lewis College, Mesa State College, Metropolitan State College of Denver, University of Colorado, University of Northern Colorado, University of Southern Colorado, and Western State College of Colorado.

The paper used in this publication meets the minimum requirements of the American National Standard for Information Sciences—Permanence of Paper for Printed Library Materials. ANSI Z39.48-1992

Illustration Credits

Colorado Historical Society: front cover, v, viii, x, xii, 9, 10, 11, 12, 18, 20, 21, 30, 31, 34, 35, 36, 37, 40, 41, 43, 44, 45, 46, 52, 86, 103, 112, 113, 137, 138, 140, 158, 159, 162, 163, 165, 173, 174, 175 (top), 195 (from Mazzulla, *Brass Checks and Red Lights*), 204, 208, 214 (from Miller and Mazzulla, *Holladay Street*), 221, 222, 224, 228, 234 (from Miller and Mazzulla, *Holladay Street*), 237, 238, 254, 255, 258, 260, 271, 272 (from Mazzulla, *Brass Checks and Red Lights*), 274, 276, 277, 278, 280, 281, 282, 283, 284, 285, 295, 297.

Denver Public Library Western History Department: 39, 58, 105, 142, 200, 211, 235.

Amon Carter Museum, Fort Worth, Texas: 93, 94, 209.

Colorado State Archives: 175 (bottom), 239.

National Archives: 5, 6, 8.

San Juan County (Colorado) Historical Society: 132.

Denver Firefighters Museum: 217.

Ronald W. Lackmann: back cover, 144.

Jay Sanford: 233.

Leo Stambaugh: 240.

Author's collection: 22, 79, 226–227, 231, 266, 270, 296, 312, 313.

Library of Congress Cataloging-in-Publication Data

Secrest, Clark, 1937–
     Hell's belles : prostitution, vice, and crime in early Denver : with a biography of Sam Howe, frontier lawman / Clark Secrest.— Rev. ed.
        p. cm.
     ISBN 0-87081-633-0 (pbk. : alk. paper)
     1. Prostitution—Colorado—Denver—History. 2. Crime—Colorado—Denver—History. 3. Howe, Sam, 1839-1930.   I. Title.
     HQ146.D4 S43 2001
     306.74'09788'83—dc21
                                                                        2001006523

Design by Daniel Pratt

11 10 09 08 07 06 05 04 03 02   10 9 8 7 6 5 4 3 2 1

To SAM HOWE
frontier detective

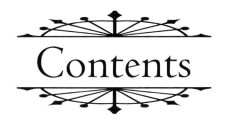

Contents

Detective Sam Howe with his scrapbooks, October 1913.

Preface

F AR BACK IN AN AISLE of the Colorado Historical Society's rare documents storage rooms, stacked to near the ceiling, rest fifty-six stately scrapbooks whose many thousands of pages offer a unique social portrait of an emerging western community. This series of books, some volumes of which are almost a foot thick, are composed of newspaper clippings detailing nearly every crime committed in Denver between 1883 and 1920.

The books were the life's labor of Sam Howe, who became a member of Denver's first police department, organized in April 1874, and was a Denver law enforcer before that. Howe served dutifully—some might say obediently, but for a stumble or two—for the next forty-seven years.[1]

For that almost half century Howe scrutinized up to five newspapers each day—precisely scissoring out every crime story, down to the tiniest suicide; consecutively numbering each clipping, indexing and cross-indexing each, and then pasting every fragment

into that year's scrapbook. Sam Howe's motive was simply to establish a data bank of crime information usable to himself and his fellow police officers. A century later, however, his scrapbooks have far greater importance: they are a vivid ongoing account of one frontier city's attempt to keep order and of those who would disrupt that order.

In an era long before sophisticated computer networks enabled law officers to almost instantly store and exchange crime data, the fame of Sam Howe's unique scrapbooks at the Denver Police Department spread throughout the United States. Lawmen, newspaper reporters, and statisticians consulted Howe's books for information on virtually every miscreant perpetrating a crime in booming Denver. Peace officers from throughout the nation traveled to Denver to marvel over Sam Howe's big books of clippings about criminals. Historian Frank Richard Prassel in *The Western Peace Officer: A Legacy of Law and Order* (Norman: University of Oklahoma Press, 1972) referred

are available for study only with curatorial approval.

When Sam Howe retired in 1921, the Denver Police Department made an effort to continue assembling the Howe scrapbooks for another decade. By that time, however, the collection and retention of criminal records were becoming more sophisticated procedures than simply cutting out newspaper clippings and pasting them in scrapbooks. Howe's labor of love consequently grew to be regarded as little but a nostalgic account of an early western town's struggle to keep order.

As time passed, the Howe Scrapbooks were seldom consulted and were consigned to a distant corner of police headquarters. After Howe's death in 1930 at age ninety-one, the scrapbooks languished for another nine years before being donated to the Colorado Historical Society. There, because of their bulk and intimidating size, the books were infrequently consulted by the curious or by social history researchers. Their pages became increasingly yellowed and brittle, and the society lacked funds to place the books on microfilm. By 1980 the Sam Howe Scrapbooks were in such delicate condition that their access to the public was restricted.

to Howe's work as "perhaps the earliest of such systems in police history" (p. 81). The *Chicago Times* on January 16, 1895, described Howe's scrapbooks as "the most valuable as well as the most complete record of a city's crime and criminals outside the department libraries of Chicago and New York." The Colorado Historical Society regards the volumes as a unique and valuable urban history resource. The fragile books are considered delicate and are maintained in a closed room under temperature and humidity controls. They

Soon after joining the Colorado Historical Society as a publications editor in 1990, I was assigned, as part of the Denver History Museum project then under way, the job of assembling basic decade-by-decade statistics regarding Denver's early organized prostitution, liquor licensing, and saloon activities. The study began with Denver's birth in 1858 and extended into the second decade of the twentieth century, when the city finally rid itself of its lengthy heritage of organized vices. Having completed that project, I realized I had scarcely begun a thorough examination of these aspects of wrongdoing in emerging Denver.

I thus faced the question of whether to end the study or to proceed by scrutinizing, page by page, all 83,500 entries in the Howe Scrapbooks. Such data assembled in one place would constitute a story of crime—particularly gambling, prostitution, narcotics abuse, and the official corruption that made them possible—in a town renowned throughout the West and nationally for such shenanigans.

I decided to proceed, and the task of examining the Howe books consumed three years. Much data not contained in previous histories of Denver were discovered and are included in these pages, augmented by supporting research from studies of sociology, criminology, and history.

The evolution of Denver's early liquor parlors has been thoroughly investigated and chronicled by historian Thomas J. Noel in *The City and the Saloon* (University Press of Colorado, 1996). Thus Denver's barroom story is not a principal focus of this book. Earlier writers such as Forbes Parkhill, Caroline Bancroft, Max Miller/Fred Mazzulla/Jo Mazzulla, and Sandra Dallas looked at frontier Denver's gambling meccas and brothels in their books, which are listed in the bibliography. Subsequently, historian Phil Goodstein's *The Seamy Side of Denver* (Denver: New Social Publications, 1993) examined those "knights of the green cloth" and *nymphs du pavé* of Market Street and the governmental and police corruption allowing their prolonged existence. Those topics are considerably expanded in these pages.

Prostitution on the Rocky Mountain frontier is a particular focus of this volume. Scholars until the 1980s preferred to ignore prostitution as a focus of research, perhaps because the topic appeared unworthy of serious investigation and the researchers had more weighty topics to mull. Until that decade the topic of prostitution, when examined at all, was left to the sociologist and the psychologist: the sociologist analyzed trends, and the psychologist pondered motives. During the 1980s, however, students of history

increasingly recognized prostitution as a social force deserving serious study. The bibliography lists such projects, including several confined to the West, such as Jacqueline Baker Barnhart's *The Fair but Frail: Prostitution in San Francisco, 1849–1900* (Reno: University of Nevada Press, 1986), Benson Tong's *Unsubmissive Women: Chinese Prostitutes in Nineteenth-Century San Francisco* (Norman: University of Oklahoma Press, 1994), and Paula Petrick's *No Step Backward: Women and Family on the Rocky Mountain Mining Frontier, Helena, Montana, 1865–1900* (Helena: Montana Historical Society Press, 1987). Additionally, I relied on important broader studies such as Anne M. Butler's *Daughters of Joy, Sisters of Misery* (Urbana: University of Illinois Press, 1985) and Ruth Rosen's *The Lost Sisterhood* (Baltimore: Johns Hopkins University Press, 1982). Timothy J. Gilfoyle's *City of Eros* (New York: W. W. Norton, 1992) is an exhaustively researched and masterfully written history of prostitution in New York City from 1790 to 1920. Nell Kimball's supposedly autobiographical *Nell Kimball, Her Life as an American Madam*, Stephen Longstreet, ed. (New York: Macmillan, 1970), is a captivating and earthy read, and in the absence of evidence to the contrary, I have cautiously assumed here that it is genuine.

A note regarding prostitutes' "recollections," however. The more deeply the researcher delves into the subject, the more suspect some of the literature becomes. That is not realized initially but slowly becomes a matter of concern. Ruth Rosen, one of the first serious scholars of prostitution, warns in her introduction to *The Maimie Papers* (with Sue Davidson) that many so-called memoirs written by prostitutes appeared during the early twentieth century. Unfortunately, they report, most of these "memoirs" must ultimately be judged inauthentic because they are typescripts with no parent manuscript. Furthermore, the authors assert, most of these memoirs were written as moralistic tracts by "purity crusaders" who wished to advance their antiprostitution movement.

Hell's Belles does not pretend to be a psycho-social analysis of prostitution in the American West. I leave this daunting task to others more qualified—the psychologist, the sociologist, and other behavioral scientists. My purpose is to present case studies of prostitution

At left: *Madam Mattie Silks, matriarch of the Denver Row, who was never observed in public without her diamond cross pendant. The photograph was taken at age forty in about 1886.* At right: *Jennie Rogers, six feet tall, statuesque, hot-tempered, and always wearing her emerald earrings.*

and its allied vices of gambling and corruption in the Rocky Mountain West and to document them in a manner enabling future scholars to conduct appropriate studies and draw whatever weighty conclusions they may.

This research encountered several popular and long-held notions regarding the Denver *demimonde* and offers accounts sometimes differing from previous conclusions. For instance, the most famous (although not the most notorious) Denver madam, Mattie Silks, did not engage in a pistol duel with her competitor Katie

Fulton over the affections of the dashing gambler Corteze Thomson. Moreover, it appears that the members of the Denver City Council did not, as has been asserted, stoop so low as to adjourn a meeting so they might attend the grand opening of a fashionable new brothel on Market Street. And when the winsome Baby Doe invaded Lizzie Preston's house of joy to gather evidence against husband Harvey Doe so Baby could divorce him and marry the silver king Horace Tabor, the whole scheme probably was engineered by Tabor. In other words, Harvey Doe was set up.

The Sam Howe Scrapbooks and other sources studied for this book offered additional disclosures regarding the urban history of Denver and of Colorado. The politically manipulated police department of early Denver was generally not one of which the citizens could be proud or in which they could have much confidence. The involvement of police officers in the "protection" (for a fee) of the gamblers and women of the *demimonde* are elaborated on in these pages. The prostitutes' flaunting of their wares is described here in a new light, and the ladies' wretched lives assume a poignancy not illustrated before. There was, for instance, the scarlet woman who entered the Larimer Street barroom and announced her intention to kill herself. "Why?" exclaimed the surprised barkeeper. "Too poor to live," was the reply. Whereupon she gulped the contents of a small glass vial and fell dead. Or the Market Street madam who reportedly concealed her occupation from her beloved and refined daughter. The daughter eventually learned of her mother's line of business and out of heartbreak and anger became one of her mother's competitors. Or the sad young prostitute who took her life after writing to her faraway father, "I have no one to love me."

This study produced additional discoveries. While examining late-nineteenth-century licensing entries at the Colorado State Archives, I came across records of liquor permits issued to the Market Street queens, such as the diamond-laden Mattie Silks and the emerald-adorned Jennie Rogers. Then Mark Shonk, a Denver policeman and avocational police historian, telephoned to say that a drawer of an old desk at downtown police headquarters had revealed twelve fragile and hitherto-undiscovered annual police reports from the early twentieth century. They are reproduced in Appendix B.

A few months later Shonk called with the exciting news of the discovery of a long-lost police census of the Market Street prostitutes, name by name, address by address. These data are retained in this second edition.

This history essentially concludes in 1915, when a rather decisive wave of moral reform effectively rid Denver of its official corruption and its old-time gambling and prostitution dens. Established traditions die hard, however, and authorities fought to suppress the prostitution vices that threatened to resurface with the influx of lonely young men inhabiting Denver's military bases during World Wars I and II.

As humanity has known all along, indulgences cannot be legislated out of existence. A *Rocky Mountain News* headline in 1991 proclaimed "Denver Police Shut Down Bordello." That sort of news does not surprise, and it certainly would not surprise Mattie Silks and Jennie Rogers if they could learn of it today.

They knew a bordello can be shut down, but vices cannot.

Notes

1. Sam Howe became involved with Denver law enforcement in 1873, a year before the first police department was formed, when he was appointed deputy city marshal. Infant Denver City's first lawman of record was Wilson E. "Bill" Sisty, named December 19, 1859. He was authorized to hire a deputy or two, which he failed to do, and he also had no jail. No wonder Sisty resigned only five months later, discouraged, and moved to Idaho Springs to prospect for gold. After Sisty, Denver had a number of marshals; one, George E. Thornton (November 1861–June 1862), was called "chief of police," although there was no police department. The 1862 *Charter and Ordinances of the City of Denver* placed many requirements on the town's earliest lawmen. They were instructed to keep enough balls and chains on hand to control prisoners on road work crews, to enforce all ordinances and election rules, to control nearly every public facility in town—including billiard tables, peddlers, public shows and exhibitions, liquor outlets, gamblers, and pawnbrokers—and to otherwise preserve the peace and quiet. Marshal Thornton doubtless ignored most such mandates, if only because he virtually worked alone. By 1873 a marshal and seven deputies—including Sam Howe—were on the street and formed the nucleus of what the following April would be designated Denver's first genuine police force. One of those first lawmen was John McCallin, who was designated chief of Denver's first real police department. The best account of Denver's often confusing procession of marshals and police chiefs—the briefest tenure was one day—is Eugene Frank Rider, "The Denver Police Department: An Administrative, Organizational, and Operational History, 1858–1905"

(unpublished Ph.D. diss., University of Denver, 1971); see also Jerome C. Smiley, *History of Denver, With Outlines of the Earlier History of the Rocky Mountain Country* (Denver: J. H. Williamson, 1903); and *Denver Police Department Pictorial Review and History 1859–1985* (Denver: Denver Police Department, 1985).

Acknowledgments

THE INCEPTION OF THIS BOOK was a research assignment in conjunction with the Colorado Historical Society's Denver History Project in 1990. Findings from that study, presented some months later to the Colorado History Colloquium, comprised a sixty-page paper on early Colorado crime.

Following that project I continued assembling data on the subject. This effort included the first-ever thorough researching of thirty-two pertinent volumes of the Historical Society's Sam Howe Scrapbooks, a massive crime ledger assembled from 1883 to 1920 by Denver's most famous policeman of the time. By 1993, a great amount of material had been gathered, and colleagues suggested that I turn it into a book.

Having written numerous articles on Colorado history but never anything so extensive as a book, I was wary and consulted experts who knew more than I about what people want to read in the realm of Colorado history. Specifically, I asked western history re-

search librarians Rebecca Lintz, my associate at the Historical Society, and Eleanor Gehres, then head of the Western History Department at the Denver Public Library, if they thought readers would be interested in a thorough book about the development of vices in nineteenth-century Colorado and particularly in Denver. They answered affirmatively, assuring me of the ongoing popularity of existing works about Colorado's prostitutes, gamblers, murderers, general rascals, and city hall crooks.

Acting on this advice, I commenced work on the manuscript, and upon completing the 160,000-word project in 1996 I set out to find a publisher. I soon learned, as other authors had before me, that hoped-for popularity on the library shelves does not necessarily translate into acceptance by a publisher. Commercial publishing houses rejected the manuscript because it was too lengthy and its nature was more appropriate, they insisted, for a university press. The university presses—by definition ever watchful of their pennies—

had a variety of excuses for turning me away. My logical first choice, of course, had been the University Press of Colorado—at that time under different management—which advised me to convert the manuscript into a "gender study," even though my preface stated that I am not a social scientist and that the book therefore was an anecdotal, rather than an analytical, history.

So in 1996 I published *Hell's Belles: Denver's Brides of the Multitudes* myself, placing it in a large format on superior paper stock, well illustrated, and even turning out 200 expensive hardcover copies for collectors. The book received an immense amount of publicity, and its reviews in the western history scholastic journals were uniformly favorable, if not flattering.

My library advisers had been right: the public welcomed an attractive, well-researched, and thorough book on the history of Colorado vice and crime. Within a year my 1,300 softcover and 200 hardcover copies were essentially gone, thanks to the Colorado Historical Society Museum Store, to Denver's famed Tattered Cover Book Store, and to libraries worldwide that wanted copies.

Next I was pleased to hear from the University Press of Colorado, suggesting that a second edition of *Hell's Belles* might be in order (and this time not mentioning anything about a gender study). But instead of a straight reprint, the University Press asked me to integrate the new research and photographs I had gathered in the intervening five years so the book would be a true revised edition. A six-week writing marathon resulted in the second edition you are holding—with 25,000 words and fifteen illustrations not in the original, printed from new plates, in a new format.

Numerous personal obligations have accrued in the preparation of both editions of *Hell's Belles*. The initial developing manuscript was read at various stages by scholars of Colorado history, including Phil Goodstein, David Fridtjof Halaas, Stephen J. Leonard, and Thomas J. Noel. My supervisor at the Historical Society, David N. Wetzel—a skilled editor, linguist, grammarian, and general all-around literate—offered patient encouragement and kind understanding through preparation of both editions.

Denver police officer Mark Shonk was active in the development of the initial manuscript, and his great contributions are detailed elsewhere in these pages. My friend Ron Samson, now retired as a sergeant from the Denver Police Department and whose collection of Denver police artifacts and history is extensive, encouraged me to continue through both editions.

Considerable effort has been expended in illustrating both editions with appropriate photographs, some unusual, many unfamiliar, and a few rare and not seen before. The preponderance of these images is from the Colorado Historical Society and the Denver Public Library Western History Department. Historian Pete Hacker researched the Fred Mazzulla Collection on my behalf at the Amon Carter Museum in Fort Worth, Texas. Mazzulla was the first person to display much interest in the early brothel queens of Colorado, and the small booklets he published in the 1970s broke the trail for this book. Fortunately, Mazzulla preserved valuable old photographs that otherwise would have been lost, a few of which are reproduced here. Betty Moynihan and Hélène Reynolds shared their knowledge of Baby Doe Tabor's invasion of Lizzie Preston's Denver bordello, and medical historian Robert Shikes, M.D., furnished books and papers from his private collection concerning Denver city physician Frederick J. Bancroft's views on prostitution.

Historian Elliott J. Gorn alerted me to published materials alleging the involvement of labor activist "Mother" Mary Jones in the Denver brothel business, and Bat Masterson biographer Robert K. DeArment reviewed the passages concerning Masterson's ten years in Denver as a sports gambler, homewrecker, and general bon vivant. James Oda of the Piqua (Ohio) Historical Society worked with me in the hopeful—but still futile—effort to locate descendants of Sam Howe. Geraldine Noble of the Warren County (Ohio) Historical Society assisted in chronicling the supposed early liaison between Denver *demimondaine* Amy Bassett and the scion of an Ohio first family of the late nineteenth century.

The considerable new material in this revision of *Hell's Belles* surfaced during the five-year interval between books, but I cannot claim credit for locating it all. Many people, upon reading the first edition and being aware that I was still collecting data, assisted greatly. Barbara Dey, a librarian at the Historical Society who regularly reviews microfilms of Colorado's early newspapers, was particularly diligent in furnishing me (right up to press time) with newly discovered accounts of our earliest prostitutes, gamblers, crooked politicians, and general scoundrels. Stan Oliner, the Society's now-retired books and documents curator, and Richard A. Kreck of Denver came up with other materials I did not have. My initial researching of the Society's Sam Howe Scrapbooks, the cornerstone of *Hell's Belles*, was made possible by Andrew Masich and Katherine Kane, both of whom have left the Colorado Historical Society for historical societies and museums in the eastern United States.

For this new edition, G. K. Elliott shared his numerous documents regarding Denver's early prostitutes, particularly their obituaries and estate records. Researcher Annette L. Student lent her valuable findings regarding Sarah "Sadie" Likens, Denver's first female law enforcer and women's and children's advocate. Student also is most knowledgeable regarding the "triplet" murders of Lena Tapper, Marie Contassot, and Kiku Oyama, whose stranglings on the same side of the same block of Denver's infamous Market Street over a nine-week period in 1894 terrified the unfortunates working there.

I thank LaVelle M. Froboese for her unswerving support and encouragement during preparation of both incarnations of this book and extend genuine appreciation to Darrin Pratt of the University Press of Colorado, who instead of doing it the easy way, advocated and shepherded this significant revision of *Hell's Belles*.

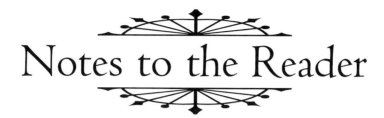

Notes to the Reader

ENVER'S LATE-NINETEENTH-CENTURY vice district was centered at Twentieth and Market Streets. Market, one of Denver's original thoroughfares, was initially (1858) McGaa Street, named for William McGaa, one of the town founders. McGaa was just one of Denver's pioneers chosen to be honored with a street name. Unlike the others, however, McGaa had a severe problem with inebriation and frequently landed in jail, thus embarrassing the new community. In 1866, therefore, McGaa Street was renamed Holladay Street, honoring stagecoach king Ben Holladay whose conveyances helped open the West. McGaa died drunk in jail the next year.

By the mid-1870s Holladay Street between Nineteenth and Twenty-third Streets had emerged as one of the notorious love-for-sale districts in the West. Not wishing to have its patriarch further identified with such goings-on, in 1887 the Holladay family petitioned the city for relief. Thus Denver's Holladay Street be-

came Market Street, named for various produce markets that lined its lower (southwesterly) reaches.

Much of this book centers on the crimson activities of Holladay and Market Streets, and those designations are utilized interchangeably in these pages according to the time frame under discussion.

About the abbreviations: This book is documented by use of chapter notes. Sources utilized in preparation of the text are listed in the Bibliography. Several frequently cited terms and abbreviations are intermingled:

Sam Howe Scrapbooks	SHS
Rocky Mountain News	RMN
Denver Times	DTI
Denver Tribune	DTR
Denver Republican	DR
Denver Post	DP
E. F. Rider dissertation	RD

A principal source was the Colorado Historical Society's collection of Sam Howe Scrapbooks. Sam

Howe was appointed one of Denver's original thirteen policemen—a chief and twelve street officers—in April 1874, but he was a Denver lawman even before that, becoming a deputy city marshal in January 1873. Howe meticulously maintained his crime scrapbooks, beginning with his promotion to detective in April 1883 and concluding with his retirement in February 1921, and others continued the Howe books for an additional decade. The scrapbooks were donated to the Historical Society by the Denver Police Department in 1939. Thirty-two of the fifty-six extant volumes (1883–1915) were utilized in this study.

Each of Howe's scrapbooks carries a volume number, beginning with Volume 1 (or, as Howe put it, "Book 1"), but his individual entries are numbered chronologically throughout the series of books, beginning with Book 1. For purposes of annotation here, "SHS 20: 23123" means Sam Howe Scrapbook, Volume or Book 20, entry 23,123. A listing of book numbers, their corresponding clipping designations, and dates of the volumes are in Appendix A.

In these pages, scholars of Colorado and Denver history will find some incidents that are new to them and other accounts familiar from previous works. In the latter case, because of additional source materials used in this study, these serious readers might find different perspectives, added details, and occasional statements that disagree with those from earlier writers. To the more casual reader, I hope she or he has a good time in these pages and learns something along the way.

First came the miners
To work in the mine.
Then came the ladies
Who lived on the Line.
—PROSPECTORS' RHYME

The miners came in fifty-nine,
The whores in sixty-one.
And when they got together,
They made a native son.
—GOLD RUSH SONG LYRIC

Oh, the lust for mountain gold dust
Brought us lusty mountain men;
Who through lust for mountin' women,
Quickly lost their gold again.
—MINERS' POEM

It is Market Street—yesterday a riotous sector of the demimonde, housing its courtesans and their ilk; bounded on the north by stumbling virtue, on the south by wrecked hopes, on the east by the miserably gray dawn of shame, and on the west by the sunset of dissipation.
—GENE FOWLER, *in a preface for a motion picture treatment of Mattie Silks's story titled* Madame Silks; *the film never materialized*

Amy Bassett reigned a veritable queen of [Market] Street. Many were the conquests she made, and the homes she wrecked. [Later], on several occasions she was implicated in brawls and was seriously injured, marring most of her noted beauty.
—ROCKY MOUNTAIN NEWS, *January 2, 1904, upon the self-immolation of Amy Bassett*

Her house is the way to hell,
Going down to the chambers of death.
—DENVER CITY PHYSICIAN FREDERICK J. BANCROFT,
in a futile plea to city council for regulation of prostitutes, 1873

These murderous traffickers [madams and procurers] drink the heart's blood of weeping mothers while they eat the flesh of their daughters, by living and fattening themselves on the destruction of the girls. Disease and debauch quickly blast the beauty of these lovely victims. Many of them are dead in two or three years. Cannibals seem almost merciful in comparison.

—ERNEST A. BELL, *in* Fighting the Traffic in Young Girls

There is something very attractive to men about a madam. She combines the brains of a businessman, the toughness of a prize fighter, the warmth of a companion, the humor of a tragedian.

—JOHN STEINBECK, *quoted by Max Miller in* Holladay Street

Here lies the bones of poor old Charlotte,
Born a virgin but died a harlot.
For eighteen years she preserved her virginity,
A damn good record for this here vicinity.

—ATTRIBUTED BY DAVE DAY, *editor of the* Ouray
Solid Muldoon, *to a gravestone in Ouray*

There were few women gamblers in those days, for women have too many nerves; there are too many temptations which make them display their emotions—feminine instinct prohibits the usual poker face. One must have a countenance that can remain immovable hour after hour. . . . At my age I suppose I should be knitting. I would rather play poker with five or six experts than to eat.

—ALICE "POKER ALICE" IVERS, *famed card dealer of Lake City,*
Alamosa, Central City, Georgetown, and Leadville

Under the Evergreens, Daisies and Dew

Think of her mournfully, sadly, not scornfully.
What she has been is nothing to you.
No one should weep for her,
Now there is sleep for her,
Under the evergreens,
Daisies and dew.

Talk if you will of her, but speak not ill of her.
The sins of the living are not of the dead.
Remember her charity,
Forget all disparity,
Let her judges be they whom she sheltered and fed.

Keep her impurity in dark obscurity.
Only remember the good she has done.
She to the dregs has quaffed
All of life's bitter draught,
Who knows what crown her kindness has won?

Though she has been denied,
The tears of a little child
may wash from the record much of her sin.
Whilst others weep and wait
Outside of Heaven's gate,
Angels may come to her, and lead her in.

When at the judgment throne the Master claims his own,
Dividing the bad from the good and the true.
There pure and spotless,
Her rank shall not be less
Than will be given, perhaps, to you.

Then do not sneer at her,
Or scornfully jeer at her.
Death came to her
And will come to you.

Will there be scoffing or weeping
When like her you are sleeping,
Under the evergreens,
Daisies,
and dew.

—Quoted by Kay Reynolds Blair
in Ladies of the Lamplight

Part I

The Policeman

I

Meet Sam Howe

"Sam Howe will get you if you don't be good."[1]

UCH WAS THE ADMONISHMENT directed toward mischievous youngsters by exasperated parents during the decades when Sam Howe was one of the two most famous "coppers" in Colorado—the other being David J. Cook. Dave Cook was daring and chased crooks and then wrote a book about his adventures, titled *Hands Up; or, Twenty Years of Detective Life in the Mountains and on the Plains*. Subsequently, Cook was the subject of a biography by William Ross Collier and Edwin Victor Westrate called *Dave Cook of the Rockies*. Sam Howe wrote no books and nobody prepared his biography, probably because he was less daring and colorful than Dave Cook. Yet Howe's long-term and lasting contribution to the history of law enforcement in the West may surpass that of Dave Cook.

Sam Howe's dedication to Denver law and order began in 1873 when there was no police department, and lawmen had to marshal the Denver streets with whatever little authority was afforded them.[2] Colo-rado was still a territory and would not become a state for three more years. Howe became among the most enduring lawmen in Colorado and the West and, some said, in the nation, retiring February 1, 1921, at age eighty-one after forty-seven years on the job. Much of that was during an era when a one-year policeman was considered an old-timer—and a lucky one at that.

Within two decades Howe saw Denver grow from a mining-supply camp full of dirty-fingernailed, ma-rauding, armed fortune seekers to a sophisticated city inhabited by the diamond-studded nouveau riche up and down the Grant Avenue "Millionaires Row."

Sam Howe was a mystery, hiding personal secrets behind his five-pointed star and copper buttons: se-crets of his Civil War record, which appears blem-ished; secrets of a change of name; secrets of a wife he virtually never discussed publicly; and secrets of a child—probably not his own—whom he reared, only to have the lad die as a teenager. Although Sam Howe was ever eager to tell reporters about himself and his recollections as a frontier detective, he did not talk about his secrets.

Regardless of his puzzling characteristics, his shy tendencies, and what some might have judged his unpolicemanlike stature—5 feet 6 and ¾ inches, 138 pounds (his first chief believed he would fail within a week)—Howe became one of America's premier crime statisticians. And with regard to his chief's prediction that he would soon give up the job, Howe recalled with a wink in 1908, "I lasted 'bout as long as the rest of that bunch had an idea *they* would last." They were all gone. He alone remained.[3]

For at least thirty-eight of his forty-seven years as a Denver policeman, detective, and detective chief, Howe tended to his scrapbooks—carefully saving an account of every crime down to the tiniest suicide, every missing person, every thief or rascal or gambler or prostitute, every suspicious incident as the squalling city grew up. (Well, *almost* every incident: Sam is known to have omitted a few stories that were unflattering to himself, but he did not exclude those that were unflattering to the police department.) Stories unkind to Sam discovered elsewhere during this study are included here anyway—with apologies to the old detective.

When an out-of-town lawman required information about a person with a Denver police record—a year, five years, or ten years after the fact—he only needed to write or telegraph the Denver Police Department, and the details could probably be found in Sam Howe's Scrapbooks. Newspapermen—Sam was fond of them because they put his name in the papers—used the Howe Scrapbooks to locate background material. Citizens, too, stopped by police headquarters in the old city hall at Fourteenth and Larimer Streets to see Sam Howe's Scrapbooks and hear the genteel, aging lawman reminisce about the old days when every bad guy packed a six-shooter—and didn't care if it was pointed toward a "copper" or not.

Sam Howe was born Simeon H. Hunt in Shelbyville, Shelby County, Ohio, on October 16, 1839.[4] He was the eldest of seven children of Ira F. Hunt, a farmer, and Rachael McVey Hunt.[5] How Simeon Hunt spent his youth is documented sparsely: he received "some education," and at an "early age" he was apprenticed to a wheelwright. Hunt completed his apprenticeship, but he disliked making wagon wheels, believing other opportunities awaited an adventuresome lad in an expanding world.[6]

By 1860, at age twenty, Simeon Hunt was practicing his trade in Louisville, Kentucky, south of his Ohio home. Every day on his way to work, Hunt passed an army recruiting station, and he discovered himself feeling "full of ginger," as he later put it. The dream of excitement rushed through him, and on his twenty-first birthday, October 16, 1860—six months before the outbreak of the Civil War—Hunt enlisted for a four-year hitch, assigned to Captain James Oaks's Company C, Second Regiment, United States Cavalry. The regimental commander was Lieutenant Colonel Robert E. Lee, who soon switched his allegiance to the Confederacy.

The Second was a proud regiment, organized by Congress in 1836 as a dragoon (horse or foot soldiers) unit.[7] The Second was immediately dispatched to guard the Mexican border and remained there until shortly before being redesignated the Fifth U.S. Cavalry on August 3, 1861. Then it was dispatched to Civil War duty.

The time was approaching when Simeon H. Hunt would cease to exist, becoming Samuel Howe, the name he used for the rest of his life.[8] Why Simeon Hunt changed his identity has not been determined, but a Civil War authority consulted during preparation of this book felt, after examining documents in the author's possession, that the name change was prompted by Howe's June 1868 desertion from the army. Howe never publicly elaborated on the name change, and he never talked about being a deserter. He left no descendants who might explain the name change.

Howe concealed his original name except on rare occasions when disclosure was necessary, such as on pension applications. Late in life, in correspondence regarding his Civil War pension, he made his signature "Samuel Howe alias Simeon Hunt." During a visit to his sisters' homes in Ohio, the *Piqua Daily Call* on September 8, 1896, referred to him as "Sam Howe Hunt." The obituary of his favorite sister, Harriet Hunt Harris Lindsley, lists as a survivor "Sim Hunt" of Denver, strengthening the notion that his name was never formally changed.[9]

Howe's various recollections, published many times in Denver's daily newspapers during his long service as a lawman, recount how the Fifth Cavalry served with Generals Wesley Merritt, John Buford, A.T.A. Torbert, and Phil Sheridan and with the Army of the Potomac; in battles such as Beverly Ford, Gettysburg, Boonsboro, Brandy Station, Todd's Tavern, Old Church, Trevillian Station, Deep Bottom, Berryville, Smithfield, the Shenandoah Valley; and during General U. S. Grant's final campaign ending with General Robert E. Lee's surrender at Appomattox, Virginia, on April 9, 1865. Howe was present at the surrender.

Sam was taken prisoner at the battle of Richmond on June 13, 1862, and was confined to the Confederacy's infamous Libby Prison, being held for only three months ("long enough," he later remarked). Upon his release as part of a prisoner exchange, Howe went briefly to Washington, D.C., and then rejoined his regiment at Winchester, Virginia.[10] In later years Howe credited his former commander, Robert E. Lee, for ensuring that Howe was a part of the exchange. When part of Libby Prison was disassembled and moved to Chicago for the 1893 World's Fair, Howe toured it and commented: "I went through Libby Prison in Chicago and had to pay 50 cents for it. The first time I went into that old prison, though, I didn't have to pay."[11]

Sam Howe's initial four-year enlistment expired in 1864, and he signed up for a second hitch at White

House Landing, Virginia, on July 11, 1864.[12] This enlistment was for three years and ended when he was honorably discharged as a corporal on July 11, 1867, in Atlanta, Georgia. This, according to all subsequent statements given by Howe, was the end of his military career. In interviews throughout his life, Howe said that after this 1867 discharge he returned to his old home in Butler County, Ohio, and then departed for Colorado in October 1868, "tempted by the alluring siren of fortune" to seek riches as a gold miner.[13]

Howe's military pension application records, now in the National Archives, disagree with his

This 1891 request for a Civil War pension is under the name "Samuel Howe alias Simeon Hunt" and lists Howe's address as "City Hall," Denver. As Howe grew older he claimed nervous debilities.

recollections. A handwritten report dated January 11, 1895, signed by War Department adjutant general George A. Ruggles and issued in response to Howe's application for an increased military pension, notes Howe's record as follows:

♦ September and October 1861: "a Private, present sick."
♦ May and June 1862: "a Private, missing in action since skirmish at Old Church, Va., June 13, 1862."
♦ September and October 1862: "a Pvt. absent sick in Hospital at St. James's College, Md., since Oct. 30/62. Joined from missing in action, Sept/62."
♦ January and February 1863: "a Private, present. Date of joining from 'absent, sick' not dated."
♦ "Appointed Corp'l, from Pvt, to date from March 6, 1864."
♦ July and August 1864: "Discharged July 11/64, by re-enlistment at Light House Point, Va., a Corporal. Re-enlisted in same Troop, July 11/64."
♦ "Roll for Nov. & Dec. '64 shows him a Private, present sick."
♦ "Appointed Corporal, May–June '67."
♦ July and August 1867: "Discharged July 11/67, by expiration of services, at Atlanta, Georgia, a Corporal."

Thus far this record agrees with the accounts Howe related all his life. There is, however, one additional entry in the official record:

Re-enlisted July 17/67, assigned to Troop M, 7th Cavalry. Rolls show him, as under: Jany & Feby '68 and

March & Apr '68 a Private, present sick in Hospital. May & June '68, Deserted, June 17/68. *A deserter at large* [emphasis in original]. He is not reported sick on any other muster rolls of the foregoing organization than as above quoted, and whether or not sickness was contracted in line of duty is not stated in any case.[14]

Thus it is recorded that Sam Howe, as he was now known, had a *third* military enlistment, into the Seventh Cavalry, made six days after his Atlanta discharge on July 11, 1867. This record says he deserted from this enlistment after eleven months of service. But as far as Howe was concerned, his military career ended honorably with the Atlanta discharge.

Given Howe's lifelong fondness for entertaining listeners with remembrances of his war years (and even his three months in Libby Prison), it is unusual that he is never recorded as having mentioned his Seventh Cavalry enlistment, if only because the Seventh had been (and was, when Howe joined) under the command of Lieutenant Colonel George Armstrong Custer. Custer was a strong taskmaster—so strong, in fact, that he could have precipitated a desertion by a soldier so inclined. The Seventh was an incongruous mixture of drunks, grumblers, and professionals, including one captain who was a former congressman. Desertion was not uncommon, as the men felt the increasingly persuasive call of the goldfields.

At the time of Howe's enlistment in the Seventh Cavalry on July 17, 1867, the regiment was exhausted and was encamped at Fort Wallace on the Smoky Hill River in extreme west-central Kansas. On July 15— two days before Howe's enlistment (at an unknown location)—Custer left Fort Wallace on a difficult 150-mile march to seek new orders, supplies, and horses. On July 20 Custer was alleged to be absent from his command, and on October 11, 1867, he was found guilty.[15]

For most of his time with the Seventh—from January through April 1868—Howe is listed as "sick in hospital," and in his later years Howe cited Civil War–contracted illnesses in applying for pensions. But the record says that by June 17, 1868, Howe was listed as a deserter. Military record keeping at times was haphazard at best, but one can only assume under the evidence at hand that Howe was not erroneously listed as a deserter, particularly since the military still carried the "deserter" notation on Howe's records thirty years later.

There is no record, however, that the army ever took action on Sam Howe's supposed desertion. He became a member in good standing of the Grand Army of the Republic veterans organization, and he drew army pensions of between six dollars a month (1899 and 1901) and eight dollars a month (1904).[16] When he died in 1930 he was receiving sixty-five dollars monthly.

Howe frequently submitted formal requests for pension increases during his later years.[17] Some of his requests are in the third person and sound almost desperate, such as "The records of the War Department must show his [Howe's] service in the Union Army in defence of the Union." In 1889 Howe and wife Helen traveled to Washington, D.C., where one of his purposes, according to the Denver press, was to "recover his discharge from the regular army, which he lost in 1864." (Howe would not likely have retained his original discharge papers if they showed a discharge that was less than honorable; indeed, of all the certificates and documents he retained about himself, no discharge papers are found.) The next year he pleaded to the government that he had "disease of the lungs, extreme nervousness and general disability." In 1897 he attested that he was "unable to [gain] support by manual labor by reason of general disability and breaking down of system, that said disabilities are of a permanent character and are not due to vicious habits." Howe made no attempts to hide his frail health, and the newspapers took note of his debilities. As early as June 1879, when he left for his old Ohio home for a visit with his sisters, the Rocky Mountain News observed that "Mr. Howe has been in poor health for some time and the trip is made for the purpose of getting much needed rest."[18]

By October 1868, five months after Sam Howe's departure from the army, he was on his way west with the hordes of other gold seekers. In an interview given to the Denver Republican on January 12, 1913, Howe sidestepped the apparent missing year from his life— when he was on the roster of the Seventh Cavalry— by stating that he was discharged in Atlanta in 1867 but did not leave for the West until 1868. He did not address what he did in the interim.

During his October 1868 westward odyssey, Sam Howe paused briefly in Ellsworth, Kansas, then the terminus of the Kansas-Pacific Railroad, which would not reach Denver until 1870. Howe recounted during the 1913 interview that in Ellsworth he met William Frederick "Buffalo Bill" Cody and James Butler "Wild Bill" Hickok, the latter the Ellsworth marshal.[19] If that encounter planted a seed that would grow into a law

War Department,

ADJUTANT GENERAL'S OFFICE,

Washington, D. C., _____ *189*

Respectfully returned to _____

It appears from the records of this office that _____
_____ *was enlisted on the* _____ *day of*
_____, 18___, *at* _____, *and was*
assigned to _____, _____ *Regiment of* _____

Roll, for Nov. & Dec. '64, shows him
a Private, present, sick."
Appointed Corporal, May-June '67.
July & Aug. '67," Discharged July 11/67,
by "expiration of service," at Atlanta,
Georgia, a Corporal."
Re-enlisted July 17/67, & assigned to
Troop" M", 7" Cavalry.
Rolls show him, as under:
Jany & Febry '68, & March & Apr. '68, "a
Private, present, sick in Hospital".
May & June '68," Deserted, June 17/68."
A deserter, at large.

He is not reported sick on any other
muster rolls of the foregoing
organizations than as above
quoted: and whether or not sickness
was contracted in line of duty is not
stated in any case.

Personal description: Born in Shelby Co: Ohio,
Age 21 years, (Oct. 16. 1860) Occupation a Wagon-
maker. Grey eyes, brown hair, ruddy complexion.
Height 5ft 6¾ inches.

Geo. S. Ruggles,
Adjutant General.
(260.)

A page of Simeon Hunt's handwritten military record from the War Department's adjutant general's office, dated January 11, 1895. The document lists Howe's reenlistment of July 17, 1867, after which he was "present, sick in Hospital." The document is specific regarding Howe's desertion on June 17, 1868—"A Deserter, at large." Throughout his life Howe never discussed this aspect of his military record, and although he was a deserter he was allowed small Civil War and Denver police pensions.

Detective Sam Howe saved this portrait of his wife, Helen M. Wright Howe, inside his sixteenth scrapbook (January–May 1897). His inscription notes the date of the photo and her date of death at age forty-seven.

46 years of age Feb 4 = 1896

Mrs Helen. M. Howe
Sept 1895
Died Sept 28 - 1897

DAILY NEWS: DENVER

enforcement career, Howe made no mention of it.

Leaving Kansas, Sam Howe drove a team to Denver and proceeded almost immediately to the Black Hawk mining district where he tinkered in the gold mines and, by his account, was "fairly successful."[20] By 1870 he was spending increasing amounts of time in Denver. The *Rocky Mountain News* observed that April 25 that "S. Howe" took the stagecoach from Denver to Central City, and on August 14 the paper published a notice that a letter awaited pickup by Howe at Denver's post office.

Howe had developed a romantic interest in Denver, and on November 25, 1871, a justice of the peace performed a wedding ceremony uniting Howe and Helen M. Wright. Born in 1850 in Troy, Ohio, near Howe's old hometown of Shelbyville, Helen was eleven years younger than Sam and had come to Denver in 1870, two years after his Colorado arrival. Although the couple was married for twenty-five years, little is known of Helen Howe. In 1889 the *Denver Times* published a one-paragraph item stating:

> A new conductor in charge of Colfax avenue cable car 36 had his heart in his mouth at 5:30 o'clock yesterday afternoon. Detective Sam Howe and Mrs. Howe were alighting from the car at Larimer street when the conductor rang to go ahead and the lady was thrown to the ground. Fortunately her injuries were not serious, but the conductor's cheeks were white as chalk.[21]

Although Howe clipped and pasted that brief news story, he almost never discussed his wife or family matters in his writings or interviews. Helen Howe is mentioned on a few government pension applications encountered during this study, and her name arises in a clipping from the *Colorado Graphic* newspaper on August 16, 1890, to the effect that Sam Howe "is married." Later in that decade Helen fell ill, and in mid-May 1897 she made her final visit to her old home in

Sam Howe and the mysterious "Master Dick" Howe, who may have been Sam's illegitimate son with Helen. This 1871 photograph, with Sam's handwriting, is the earliest known likeness of Howe.

Ohio. There, according to the local newspaper, she visited "Mrs. H. Harris of Wayne Street and Mrs. C. Rowe of West Green Street."[22] Harriet Harris and Clarissa Rowe were Sam's younger sisters. Returning to Colorado, Helen Howe died of a "protracted illness" on September 28, 1897, at the Howe residence, 1130 Eleventh Street, and was buried in Riverside Cemetery, Denver, with "Parson" Tom Uzzell, one of Denver's best-known clergymen, presiding.[23] The *Denver Times* (September 29) and the *Republican* (October 1) published brief death stories. The *Times* story contains the sen-

tence "She bore one child, a son, who is dead." The statement does not say the child was Sam's. Helen Howe is listed as survived by a sister and two brothers in Denver and a sister in Indiana. Pallbearers were detectives of the Denver Police Department.[24]

The male child reared to age fifteen by Sam and Helen Howe is a mystery. Any record of the child remains as elusive as that of Helen, because Sam never publicly talked about the boy either. The lad, as a child of age three, appears in the earliest known picture of Sam, dated December 17, 1871, only three weeks after Sam and Helen were married. In Howe's handwriting is the inscription "Richard Howe, 3 years old," and "Master Dick."[25] The only published reference to a Howe child is in a tiny, unnumbered, unattributed newspaper clipping. Under the headline "Died in the East," it reads:

> The only son of officer Sam Howe, aged 15, died on Sunday, the fifteenth instant, in Covington, Ohio, of dropsy of the heart. The deceased had been a sufferer for some years, and was taken East by his mother some two weeks ago in the hope of obtaining some relief, but with the sad result above mentioned. Officer Howe and wife have the sympathy of all who know them in their bereavement.[26]

The boy is unnamed in the clipping, which is dated in Sam's handwriting "June 1884." This newspaper notation plus the photo inscription of the lad at age three in 1871 mutually confirm that he was born in 1868—the year Sam came west to Colorado. Thus the boy was already two years old when Helen came to Denver in 1870 and was three years old when Sam and Helen married. Four possible explanations exist:

1. The child of Sam Howe and Helen Wright was born out of wedlock in Ohio in 1868, as Sam departed on his way west, and the boy was brought to Denver in 1870 by Helen.
2. The boy was born in Black Hawk in 1868 and was Howe's son but not Helen's. This possibility is unlikely because Helen's *Denver Times* obituary notes that "she bore one child, a son, who is dead."
3. The child was Helen's but not Sam's and was adopted by Sam when he married Helen in 1871.
4. The lad was adopted by both Sam and Helen.

Detective Howe took this photograph of his wife Helen's gravesite at Riverside, Denver's pioneer cemetery. Howe was put to rest next to her in 1930. In 2002, Helen's footstone, at left, is gone, and at about the location of the pine tree at left is the gravestone of Dora Barwick, in whose homes Howe resided for thirty-three years following Helen's death.

Like Sam's Civil War record, the story of "Master Dick" Howe is a mystery.

Helen Howe's death on September 29, 1897, appears to have left Detective Sam Howe with no survivors other than whatever siblings, nieces, or nephews remained in Ohio and whose paths have proved elusive nearly a hundred years later.[27] In Denver one reference has been found to Howe "cousins," Mr. and Mrs.

Lawrence C. Duncan, then of 1732 Clarkson Street, who at one point hosted a reception for Howe.[28] No other mention of the Duncans is found in Howe's writings or scrapbook entries.

Following Helen's death, Sam Howe remained a lifelong bachelor, devoting himself entirely to the Denver Police Department. He was becoming known as one of the foremost crime record keepers in the United

A dapper Sam Howe (at right) poses in September 1908 with his friends Charles and Dora Barwick in front of their residence, 1138 Eleventh Street, Denver. The Barwick home was in the block where Sam and Helen Howe resided until Helen's death in 1897. The Barwicks sold this home on February 20, 1911, and moved to the new Park Hill district of Denver, taking Howe with them. "Mr. and Mrs. White," probably neighbors, clown at left.

States, and lawmen from across the nation journeyed to Denver to view the Howe Scrapbooks.

Sam resided for the rest of his days with former neighbors of his and Helen's, Charles and Dora Barwick, first at 1138 Eleventh Street (Sam and Helen had lived at 1130 Eleventh Street) and later at 2541 Ash Street. Howe occasionally spoke of his friendship with the Barwicks—curiously, he mentioned them more frequently than he did his wife or "Master Dick" Howe. Sam took pains to save a *Rocky Mountain News* clipping of April 13, 1902, listing Dora's address, but more revealing is a photograph dated June 9, 1901, which he pasted into the inside back cover of his scrapbook number 20. The picture shows the Barwicks and Howe in front of the Eleventh Street home. In Sam's handwriting are the notations "Our Home," "Bought home and lot July 1900," and apparently a later entry: "This place sold Feb. 20, 1911."

If the Barwicks (and Sam) sold the Eleventh Street property in 1911, however, they vacated that property three or four years earlier and moved to the Ash Street home. Howe mentions the Ash Street house on the inside front cover of his scrapbook number 26, 1907–1908.

Dora Barwick, nineteen years Sam's junior, appears to have been Howe's best friend, police or not. Dora's husband, Charles, of whom we know virtually nothing, is listed in the city directories as a carpenter. The Barwicks' back bedroom at Ash Street was Sam Howe's home until his death, thirty-three years after moving into the Barwick home.

Other than playing solitaire, at which he appears to have been proficient,[29] there is no suggestion of any hobbies, although Sam did acquiesce to be third baseman for the police department's Denver Blues baseball squad in 1883. The team offered to "play any club in the state for from $60 to $100," presumably referring to winning prize money, but Sam never mentioned any baseball activities.[30] Howe appears to have had no social life following the death of his wife, although there is a notation that "Detective Howe has often been stormed by cupid, but has never capitulated."[31]

Although Howe fired up three or so cigars a day, he shed the alcohol vice, and in a reflective mood one quiet evening as Christmas approached at the police station, with an audience of newspapermen around, Howe spun the yarn of why he swore off booze. The *Denver Post* quoted the old detective:

It was a Christmas Eve in the late 1880s, and Sam was alone in the detective bureau when a man entered. "I have come to give myself up for the foulest murder that ever occurred," he announced to Sam.

"What's that?" Sam exclaimed.

"Yes sir, I am a double murderer. Yesterday I had a beautiful wife and the loveliest baby boy in the world. To-night they are both dead, dead, dead! I killed them both with these bloody hands of mine!

"Two years ago I married one of Cheyenne's loveliest girls. I had been a wild lad and one of the conditions of our marriage was that I should drink no more. I kept my vow and we flourished, but in an evil moment I sold out and came to Denver. I did well here for awhile, but bad days came upon me and soon I had nothing, save my wife and my beautiful child. Everybody was preparing for Christmas, while my wife, my wife, sir, lay dying of starvation.

"By and by someone said, 'Come and take a drink.' I drank, drank, drank, and when I was drunk I turned on my heels and left the crowd of false friends who had filled my hungry stomach with liquor instead of food. I went back home. God alone knows how I got back to the little cottage on Welton street. I sneaked into the back way and looked in through the window, and such a sight as met my gaze!

"My wife, weak and hungry, sat in the rocking chair, her big, brown eyes filled with tears as she tried vainly to coo to sleep the infant she was too famished to give nourishment. What spirit possessed me I don't know. I slipped into the wood-house, seized an axe and creeping back into the house I attacked them both furiously. I wanted to kill myself, but when the whiskey effects had died out, I could not do it. My crimes were too great already. I feared the hereafter as I had been taught to do at my mother's knee. But here I am, take me! I plead guilty to all!"

Sam Howe continued: "I stretched out my hand to catch the unfortunate devil, but he was not there. I jumped up and cried to the officers, 'Catch the murderer!' 'What murderer?' they asked, as they clustered around my chair. 'Why, the man who went out the door just as you came in. The fellow who killed his wife and child.'"

There was a general laugh as they cried: "You've been asleep, Sam, and dreaming!"

"I settled back in my chair. They were right. I went home a few minutes later and I had in my hand the one Christmas present my wife most desired, a pledge never to take another drink. If my efforts have amounted to anything, as I modestly trust and believe they have, I attribute it to stopping the use of liquor of all kinds."[32]

Christmas Eve, Denver's police mused, was the quietest holiday of the year. Again they turned to Sam

Howe for a morsel of wisdom. Pensively taking a puff on his cigar, Howe contemplated:

> People think of doing good [at Christmastime] instead of evil. There isn't a man in the world who does not remember Christmas in some way. The recollections of his home, of his mother, come back to him as clearly as though it had only been yesterday when he had hung up his stocking by the old fireplace years ago. Religious training has something to do with it, too, I believe. Every man has some religion, whether he thinks so or not, and you will see it cropping out as Christmas approaches.[33]

In addition to meticulously maintaining his police scrapbooks, Sam Howe was guardian of the police department mascot, Roxy the cat, legendary for its ability to distinguish between a policeman and a civilian.[34] The detectives had their own mascot, a dog named McGinty, which had been run over by the patrol wagon and then carried tenderly to the police surgeon's office, where it was saved. After recovering, "Officer" McGinty dutifully saw each shift off on its beat and always met the officers a block away from the station as they returned. The men gave McGinty a collar trimmed in silver, and the policemen "cheered until the corridor rang."[35] McGinty died in the line of duty when he ran beneath the wheels of the police wagon rushing to a false fire alarm at Fourteenth and Curtis Streets the night of August 8, 1894. As Sam Howe and the "boys in blue" looked on, Officer McGinty was buried on the banks of Cherry Creek, and a knot of black crepe was tied on the patrol wagon.[36]

This was Sam Howe. Diminutive, a loner, taciturn, a dedicated student of crime, and a man reluctant to discuss his loved ones or divulge the full truth about himself. A man who journeyed from the mountains to the frontier town of Denver to uphold laws barely written and who in the process earned distinction for himself and for a pioneering western law agency.

Notes

1. Sam Howe Scrapbook (SHS) 20: 23000, from the *Denver Sunday Post*, December 23, 1900.

2. *Rocky Mountain News* (RMN), February 7, 1873.

3. *Denver Post* (DP) magazine section, January 26, 1908.

4. No official record of Howe's birth has been found. Shelby County, Ohio, began keeping birth records only in 1867. The birthdate listed here is the one Howe gave throughout his life.

5. Information from James Oda, Piqua Historical Society, Piqua, Ohio, December 6, 1991; also see *Denver Times* (DTI), January 5, 1895.

6. *Colorado Graphic*, April 25, 1891.

7. *Denver Republican* (DR), January 18, 1897; also see Soldiers and Sailors Historical and Benevolent Society certificate to Samuel Howe, May 27, 1908, Denver Public Library, Western History Department document no. Minus M-371.

8. Early Denver law enforcement had two Sam Howes, which has confused historians and writers ever since. Our Sam Howe, the former Simeon Hunt, was the second Sam Howe to be a Denver lawman in the space of only thirteen years. The first Sam Howe was in Colorado by 1860 and the next year was elected sheriff of Arapahoe County, Colorado Territory (see Smiley, *History of Denver*, p. 540). This Sam Howe was an early property owner, boardinghouse proprietor, and financier in Denver. This first Sam Howe also was one of Denver's six original fire wardens, authorized on October 12, 1860, to inspect buildings and chimneys and otherwise to try to prevent the wooden hamlet from burning down (Smiley, *History of Denver*, p. 640). This Howe owned a house on the edge of town at Sixteenth and Curtis Streets. That real estate, when Howe moved to Montana, became the property of mercantile entrepreneur A. B. Daniels and later of Horace Tabor, who built his Tabor Grand Opera House on it (Smiley, *History of Denver*, p. 966).

After he moved to Montana in 1863, the first Sam Howe on occasion returned to Colorado. The *Rocky Mountain News* on November 18, 1865, published this note: "Arrived.—We were glad to take by the hand this morning our old friend and whilom sheriff of this county, Mr. Sam Howe, who has just returned from Montana. Any one can now convince himself that Sam was *not* killed by the Indians, as was reported and generally believed. He is as good as new and declares most emphatically that he is *not* dead."

Election records of October 24, 1864, include an "S. Howe" as residing in Nevada City, Madison County (information provided by the Montana Historical Society,

December 1991). On February 8, 1896, the *Madison County Monitor* in Twin Bridges, Montana, reported that "Sam Howe . . . died on December 15th, 1895, while on his return from Central America to California. . . . He was seventy-two years old at the time of his death."

It is understandable that the two Sam Howes—both early Denver law officers—were frequently confused with each other. For instance, the *Rocky Mountain News* on September 20, 1897, wrote that "Sam Howe, *now acting chief of the city detective department* (emphasis added), was the first sheriff." Our Sam Howe included this entry in his Scrapbook 17, clipping number 15134, penciling out the words italicized here, apparently aware that he could be mistaken for the earlier Denver lawman of the same name.

The confusion between the two Sam Howes led an occasional writer to emphasize that they were different men. Pioneer S. T. Sopris, in "Fifty Years Ago" (*The Trail*, April 1909, p. 8), compiling a business directory for 1859, noted that "the Sam Howe in the foregoing list was the keeper of a boarding house and sheriff of the county for one term in the early '60s. Sam Howe, the well-known detective, is another Sam."

9. Author's conversations with Jim Oda, Piqua, Ohio, Historical Society, December 6–9, 1991.

10. DR, January 18, 1897; DTI, August 17, 1901; Soldiers and Sailors certificate to Samuel Howe.

11. DTI, August 17, 1901.

12. Soldiers and Sailors certificate to Samuel Howe.

13. SHS 27: 48576, from DP, January 26, 1908.

14. Copy of Sam Howe's National Archives military pension application record in the author's possession.

15. Data regarding the Seventh Cavalry are from Robert M. Utley, *Cavalier in Buckskin: George Armstrong Custer and the Western Military Frontier* (Norman: University of Oklahoma Press, 1988), pp. 46–53.

16. Sam Howe papers, in the author's possession. See also SHS 18: 18761.

17. Pensioner Report, Certificate no. 984.728, National Archives, copy in the author's possession.

18. Howe's appeals to the government regarding his pension payments are in Sam Howe papers, in the author's possession. The account of Howe's ongoing health problems is in the RMN, June 18, 1879. Two brief clippings about his trip to Washington, D.C., to locate and retrieve his military discharge are in SHS 9: 3234, from the RMN, March 19, 1889. He and Helen Howe stopped to visit relatives in Ohio. Howe also visited the D.C. Police De-

partment, "and in his opinion Denver is as far ahead of them as it is of Cheyenne." The RMN, always eager to flatter Sam, noted when he arrived back in Denver that "nobody but the shrewdest criminals will regret Mr. Howe's return, and they will make themselves exceedingly scarce" (March 19, 1889).

19. DR, January 12, 1913.

20. DTI, January 5, 1895.

21. SHS 10: 3643, from the DT, July 29, 1889. This streetcar stop would have been but a stroll from the Howe residence at 1130 Eleventh Street.

22. SHS, 17, unnumbered clipping from unnamed Piqua, Ohio, newspaper. A copy of the same brief clipping, pasted on the inside front cover of Howe's scrapbook number 16, puts the date at May 15, 1897.

23. Ibid., 16: inside front cover. Also DTI, September 29, 1897.

24. Sam Howe preserved clippings of his wife's death on the inside front cover of his scrapbook number 16, including his personal card of thanks printed in the *Republican*, October 4, 1897.

25. The photograph is attached to the inside back cover of SHS 16.

26. SHS 2, pasted beneath clipping no. 205. Dropsy was a term for edema, a swelling of tissues or of an organ from an abnormal accumulation of fluids.

27. Author's conversation with Jim Oda, Piqua, Ohio, Historical Society, November 7, 1991. Efforts by the author to locate distant nieces and nephews of Howe have not been successful.

28. SHS 23: 33500, from the RMN, October 18, 1904.

29. The single reference to Sam Howe's fondness for solitaire is in SHS 3: unattributed and undated clipping pasted on inside front cover.

30. For a very brief organizational story and roster of the police department's Denver Blues baseball team, see the RMN, July 7, 1883. Microfilm of the story is difficult to read, but the team members appear to be pitcher, Isaac Langan; catcher, H. W. Barr; first base, Mike Schu (sp?); second base, H. Wilson; third base, Sam Howe; right field, Alonzo Pearce; left field, Henry Minart; "long field off," Gerald D. Noll; and "short field off," Richard Murphy.

31. DR, August 1, 1907. Howe was a handsome man, quiet, even shy, and debonair; it is not difficult to imagine that he would have appealed to the opposite gender.

32. DP, December 14, 1892.

33. Ibid., December 25, 1899.

34. Frank Richard Prassel, *The Western Peace Officer: A Legacy of Law and Order* (Norman: University of Oklahoma Press, 1972), p. 81.

35. Rider dissertation (RD), pp. 381–382. "Officer" McGinty was fortunate to have good friends, as Denver had a serious problem with running packs of stray dogs from the city's inception. Denver's first ordinance to control dogs was passed as early as January 16, 1862. It read that no "dog, bitch or whelp" could run at large in the city. The law was ineffective, and three decades later police officers still patrolled Denver in wagons from which they shot stray dogs. Citizens complained so vehemently of the bloody carcasses lying about that the police began corralling dogs in wire cages, which after a three-day waiting period for the animals to be claimed were submerged in a river or reservoir until all the animals were dead. RD pp. 56 ff.

36. DR, August 9, 1894.

2

A Frontier Detective

The gold stampede to the Rockies was made up of the finders and the keepers. The finders dug the gold, which too often ended up in possession of the keepers—the rakehells and rascals and renegades, the desperados, short-card artists, bunco men, gamblers, dive keepers, and the ladies devoid of virtue.[1]

IN 1871 SAM HOWE—the man with two names, sometime Civil War fighter, would-be Black Hawk gold miner, and newlywed father—moved 30 miles east to Denver to establish a home with his bride, Helen, and three-year-old Master Dick.

The only account of Howe's activities during his initial Denver years tells us that in May 1872 he became a board member of the all-volunteer fire department's James E. Bates Hose Company No. 3. The company's headquarters were at 1320 Eleventh Street, just a few blocks from Sam's residence listed in the *City Directory* as the "north side of 4th Street, between Front and Cherry streets"—today's Walnut Street between Twelfth and Thirteenth Streets.[2]

Denver in 1873 needed peacekeepers as urgently as it needed firefighters and issued a call for lawmen. Sam Howe answered the summons. Considering the rambunctious nature of the town, the occupation of peacekeeper was an incongruous choice for a reticent man of 5 feet 6 and ¾ inches and 138 pounds.

Becoming a deputy city marshal in Denver was not difficult. First, one had to be nominated or simply go to the jail and apply.[3] There is no record of any educational, physical, ethical, or moral requirements; those prerequisites came later.

Denver's early lawmen, Sam Howe often said, were equipped only with a revolver, a shotgun, a nickel-plated brass star, and the most basic territorial statutes and municipal laws. The *Denver Times* later recalled: "The town was patrolled by 'marshals,' but there was so much difficulty with the persons who were arrested on account of nothing but a badge to indicate the officers were more than ordinary citizens."[4]

The first memorandum of a required badge appears in an ordinance of August 11, 1864:

It shall be the duty of the Chief of Police to provide himself with a bright metallic star with the words "Chief of Police" indented upon the same, and to provide each member of the police of the city, whether day or night, under his control, with a like metallic

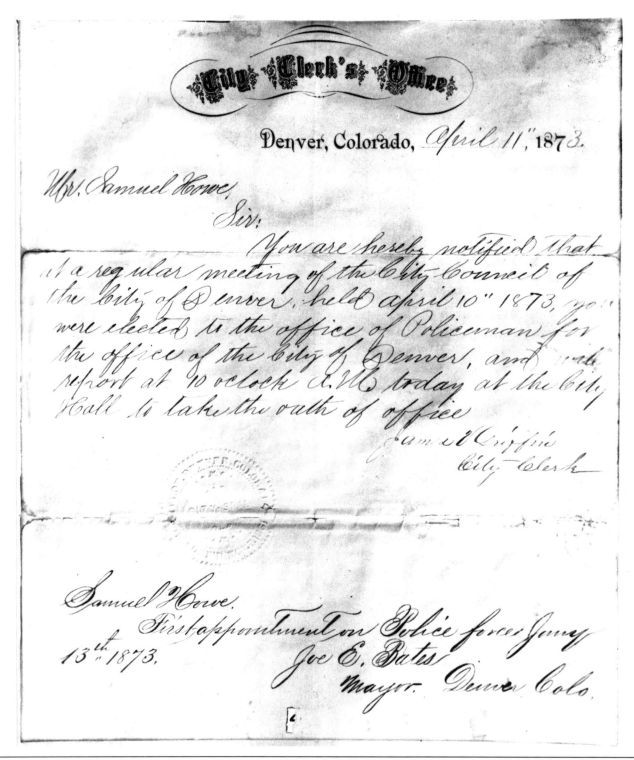

This April 11, 1873, document names Sam Howe as a Denver "policeman" although the city's first real police department was still a year hence. At the bottom the certificate states that Howe initially became a member of the "police force" the previous January 13. Denver "policemen" in 1873 were actually deputy city marshals.

star with the word "Police" indented thereon; and it shall be the duty of the police when on duty to wear such stars in a conspicuous place outside of the clothing.[5]

Denver's police came to have second thoughts about those "bright metallic stars" and at one point deduced that such badges, worn exposed on the outer coats, were a liability, particularly under the dark of night. "The fire and police board have about decided that the big silver star policemen wear on the left breast is a dangerous target at night, the bulls-eye being the officer's heart," reported the *Denver Evening Post* following the gunshot deaths of two officers. But although Denver's police occasionally and briefly were deprived of their billy clubs and even their revolvers, their badges were never taken away.[6]

Lawmen in early Denver were thankful for the arrival in early 1871 of the first gas streetlights, which they said greatly simplified night patrols and enhanced safety.[7] It became apparent during this period, however, that a marshal and two or three deputies were no longer adequate to patrol the growing town. Thus on January 13, 1873, Sam Howe and six others reported to Marshal George M. Hopkins at the "police station," today's 1530 Market Street, to become part of an expanding marshal's force. In addition to Howe, the men were John Holland (who became a longtime friend of Howe's), Ed Scholtz, Will Rhoades (also referred to as Wall Roades or Rhodes), Edward Whitney, John McCallin, and Edward Burke.[8]

At age seventy-four, on his fortieth anniversary with the department, January 12, 1913, Sam Howe told the *Denver Republican*:

On Monday, January 13, 1873, I reported to George M. Hopkins, city marshal, at headquarters, in the Crow & Clark Building on Holladay Street, which is now named Market Street. The number was 378, now 1530, between Fifteenth and Sixteenth streets. Joseph Bates was mayor. This was before we had uniforms. The first uniforms that we ever had was after Thanksgiving, 1874, and we gave them a ball [Thanksgiving night, 1874, at the Governor's Guard Hall, Fifteenth and Blake Streets, five dollars per ticket] that furnished the funds for [uniforms].[9]

Howe told the *Republican* reporter that he "found it no easier to deal with lawless characters in uniform than in plain clothes." He continued:

My first beat was on the West side. Afterward I was detailed to Blake Street, the principal thoroughfare of Denver. My partner was Ed Whitney. I traveled this post for ten long years. It was in the days when bad men from all over the world made Denver their rendezvous. There was nothing much else but saloons, dance halls and gambling resorts in this section. These were the days when there was no such thing as keys. The places of amusement with . . . attractions for men and women kept open every minute of the 24 hours. These were the days of oil lamps, gas and in some places they still used candles. Great days! And we were kept busy every minute of the time that we were on duty. When I think of the danger of those days in keeping law and order, I often wonder that I am here. Every man carried his weapons in plain sight and [it] did not take much of an argument to bring pistols into service.

Say, it was rather crude police work in those days. When we arrested a drunk he was invariably fined $12 and the arresting officer received $1 of that fine.[10]

Howe was on the job for just four days when he had a showdown with bartender Jim Morrissey in a dive on Blake Street called the Cricket, which Sam described as "not a place in which to hold religious meetings." A fight was in progress when Sam arrived with no backup, whereupon Morrissey, whom Sam characterized as "a tough killer, with many notches on his gun and knife handle," pulled a six-shooter and ordered Howe to jump through the window. Howe related that he slugged Morrissey with his .45 cap-and-ball pistol, breaking off the barrel in the process, and wrestled Morrissey to the floor and escorted him to jail.[11]

Denver's new marshal's force was only three weeks old when the *Rocky Mountain News*, on February 7, 1873, published a police payroll that included all of the names of the original men plus those of R. H. Ostrander, E. L. Thaw, E. L. Gardner, and A. H. Baker. The functions of the added men are unknown; Howe never recalled their names, and they are included on no other early Denver law enforcement lists. They might have been part-timers—Denver's police force was always

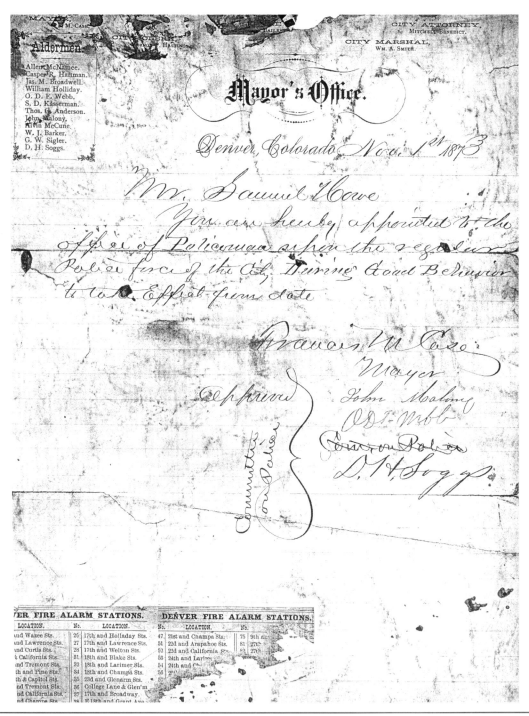

On November 1, 1873, Sam Howe received another document: "You are hereby appointed to the office of Policeman upon the regular Police force of the City, During Good Behavior to take Effect from Date." The "During Good Behavior" phrase might have meant his appointment was permanent as long as he behaved himself. Note at top right that Wm. A. "Billy" Smith is still termed "city marshal," accurately reflecting that Denver continued to have no genuine police force—no matter what Mayor Francis M. Case may have thought. The certificate became tattered in Howe's sixth scrapbook; he even pasted a listing of the city's fire alarm stations atop it.

Denver's policemen were sporty in their first uniforms. Sam Howe, badge number 5, is in the back row, second from right.

shorthanded—or independent contractors owed for some service, such as rental of a wagon to haul a prisoner to jail.

Two months later, on April 7, 1873, William A. "Billy" Smith, described by the *Rocky Mountain News* as "a thorough Republican," was elected marshal, replacing George Hopkins. Three days after Smith's election, twelve officers were appointed to assist him. Five of them—Howe, Rhoades, McCallin, Holland, and Burke—were from the original roster. An additional seven were new: James O. Moore, James Foster, H. C. Sherman, W. J. Phillips, James McCullough, D. W. Mays, and Charles Cornell.[12] The men continued to be marshals, as

Denver's first genuine police force was still a year away.

Ingenuity was often required to get a prisoner to jail in those early months; Sam Howe recalled many decades later that the only paddy wagon was a wheelbarrow.[13] On one occasion a "degraded" woman was found passed out nude in the middle of Holladay Street. Four officers were required to lift her onto a detached barn door and carry her to jail. On another occasion an officer was contemplating how to get a drunk named Nolan to jail when another drunk stumbled past and toppled over, unconscious. The officer told Nolan to pick up the second drunk and carry him to jail, and the officer thus got both drunks to jail with little effort.[14]

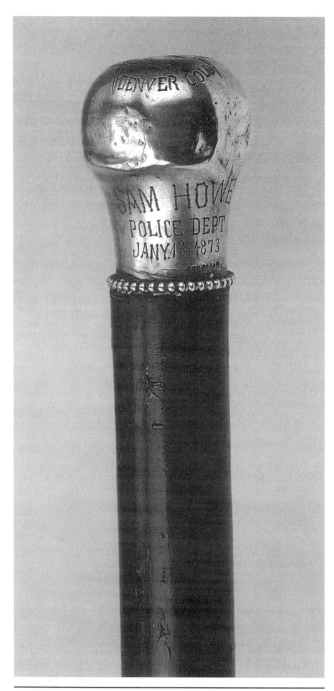

Sam Howe had his inauguration date as a Denver deputy city marshal—January 13, 1873—engraved on the sterling silver top of his Masonic Lodge walking stick. The designation "Police Dept." is not accurate; a real police department for Denver would be assembled fifteen months later. In 2000 Howe's cane top was found at a Pueblo estate sale amid a box of assorted junk metal; it was sold to a Denver antiques dealer and was acquired the following year by the author.

Officers Edward Burke and William R. Hickey (the latter later became police chief) found a 300-pound woman lying in a streetside water ditch. She was blocking the stream so water was overflowing the ditch and muddying the street. Because her nose was "above the flood" she did not drown, but it took two hours for the policemen to drag and coax her to the jail.[15]

Becoming a Denver lawman, Sam Howe would reminisce, was fairly easy: "The alderman of your ward recommended you for a place on the force, and then saw that you got it."[16] Howe told a reporter in 1897 that his job came as a result of "Alderman Hart" nominating him to Mayor Joseph E. Bates. The *Denver City Directory* of 1874 shows no Hart but an Alderman Caspar R. Hartman. Each Denver lawman received $100 monthly for twelve-hour shifts, a fairly substantial salary for the day, and had no uniform—just the star, a shotgun, and a revolver. Other men on the street had the shotgun and the revolver but not the star. The rowdy element was the principal concern. Howe later recalled:

> We had very little of the kind of crime in Denver that we now [1897] have. I mean burglary, larceny and other varieties of common thieving. The sort of crowd that does that work [e.g., commits more serious crimes] hadn't gotten here yet. Perhaps it would surprise you to hear that murders weren't very numerous either. Gambling and saloon fights were plentiful enough, but they did not result fatally [in fatalities] very often. Later on, though, big crooks who were getting away from the authorities in the East kept coming this way, and we caught a good many of them, too. Then the [police]men were allowed to hire an express wagon to haul drunken men to jail. It was found by experience that it was cheaper to own a patrol wagon than it was to hire express wagons, and one was purchased and installed in the city stable.[17]

The wagon was described:

> The latest style now in arresting a man, whether intoxicated or in an abnormal state of sobriety, is to politely persuade him to a patrol box and then pull the signal. While the victim is arguing, the patrol wagon, with its dashing horses and its brilliant lights, comes to the place with a graceful curve and a cloud of dust or splatter of mud, and the prisoner is in the jail.[18]

The *Denver Times* added on January 1, 1903:

> When an arrest was made, the prisoner would have to be walked to jail, as such a thing as a patrol wagon had not been heard of at that time. Many of these arrests were made for drunkenness and by the time the policeman got his man from the point of arrest to the jail, he was fully convinced that the life of a policeman was not a happy one. Sometimes he would be compelled to drag the man a whole block by the feet to get him to where he could be taken care of until he could sober up and pay his fine.

The customary fines for the three degrees of drunkenness—"simple drunk," "big drunk," and "drunk and disorderly"—ranged from five to twelve dollars, including court costs. In the instance of drunk and disorderly, the arresting officer was given one dollar for bringing in the culprit. The saloon owners disliked the twelve-dollar fine because it caused them to lose the "pull of twelve straight drinks."[19]

Historian Anne Curtis Knapp regards the fee-and-reward system, such as the dollar paid for the arrest of a drunk and disorderly, as a notable weakness in early Denver law enforcement. Fees and rewards were widely utilized to supplement police officers' income (see Chapter 7 of this book). Knapp wrote that everybody from policemen and deputy sheriffs to magistrates and city attorneys relied on fees and rewards to supplement their salaries or, indeed, to pay their entire salaries. This practice, unfortunately, prompted the municipal authorities to favor cases that paid elevated fees, and Denver judges bickered over which cases they would hear. In 1870 the city aldermen found it necessary to order the marshals to distribute cases evenly among the judges. One of the few blemishes on Detective Sam Howe's record, it will be seen, came as the result of the reward system.[20]

Sam Howe referred to his first beat as a deputy marshal as the "West side," probably referring to what had been Auraria. After an unstated period, Howe was assigned to what was regarded as the toughest beat in town—Blake Street—principally occupied by saloons, dance halls, and gambling hells that never closed and thus had no door keys. Howe said those that could not afford oil lamps used candles. But Howe was equal to the task: the "grim determination with which he went about everything was well-known to evil-doers," an always admiring press trumpeted.[21] Howe courted newspaper reporters, and they in turn were captivated by his stories of adventure. Howe recounted, however, that the city marshals—or "club swingers," as the Denver press delighted in calling them—lacked much authority. For fifteen months after Howe joined the marshal's force, this awkward situation existed.

Denver's policemen lacked uniforms, which except for their badges made them look pretty much like everybody else on the streets. The U.S. military had worn uniforms for some years, but the idea was not automatic as far as police were concerned. American cities did not take to the idea because uniforms were regarded as "un-American" and an "imitation of royalty." The New York City Police Department in 1860 became the first to standardize a uniform.

Denver began considering uniforms in 1873 but had no money to buy fancy blues and shiny copper buttons. A debate ensued. One alderman objected because uniforms would make it easier to "dodge a cop," but another alderman said uniforms were a good idea because a policeman involved in wrongdoing would be easily identifiable. And an abundance of Denver policemen, it will be seen, were involved in wrongdoing.

On October 23, 1873, the city drafted an ordinance decreeing that Denver's policemen—still marshals but increasingly referred to as policemen—should "dress in a uniform, including police cap, at their own expense." Mayor Francis M. Case told the men:

> Your uniform (when you get it) is sort of a letter of introduction to you for every stranger who comes to the city. Your position, gentlemen, is a very important one, as conservators of the peace, and the good name of the city. I shall expect you to be temperate and moral, active and prompt. Of course in the way of duty you will have occasion to be in saloons and houses of ill fame, but let your visits be so few that you will never be a "familiar" in either place. Another thing: Your calling brings you more or less in contact with the "roughs," the lower grades of society, but do not let this mingling in bad society ever make you forget that you are gentlemen.[22]

Because the city had no budget for police uniforms, Denver's finest might have purchased their first uniforms on credit. The new outfits, said the *Denver Tribune* on December 4, 1873, had brass buttons and were made by the Denver clothing firm of Lennon and Driscoll at the substantial cost of fifty dollars each. They were ready to be shown off at the first policemen's ball, Thursday night, December 18, 1873, which was a fund-raiser to pay for the new outfits. The *Rocky Mountain News* reported the next day:

> The policemen's ball at Turner [Turnverein] Hall last evening was a grand success. More than three hundred admission tickets at three dollars each per couple were sold, and from the crowded state of the room it was evident that the tickets were all represented. The police boys appeared in their new uniforms, which tended to make them a conspicuous body of men. The uniforms are elegantly made, and are patterned after those of the New York metropolitan police. As a result of their nobby appearance they were highly complimented on every side, which they most justly deserved.

The *Denver Times* on December 24 said the new uniforms made Denver's lawmen "look about as well as an editor or minister."

Sam Howe was a Denver lawman at the time of the December 1873 policemen's ball, but in subsequent interviews he dated Denver's first police uniforms eleven months later—November 1874. Nonetheless, by the end of 1873 Denver's marshal's force, soon to be a police department, was suitably attired. New beats were assigned; Sam Howe, badge number 5, got the day watch on Lawrence and Holladay Streets.[23]

In April 1874, Denver replaced its decreasingly satisfactory marshal system with a real police department. By this date in the West, a police department was the mark of a real city, whereas marshals were viewed as strictly rural. But despite the policemen's new title and new uniforms, Denver's abundant troublemakers still offered little respect.

Gone were the old badges that simply said "Marshal" or "City Marshal." Now, each five-pointed shield said "Denver Police" with a numeral in the center. The first chief, John McCallin, wore a badge marked "Chief." The chief was paid $150 a month; the men

got $100.[24] The new holder of badge number 5, Sam Howe, was described in newspaper clippings—which he proudly saved—as quiet and unobtrusive, slightly built, an indefatigable worker, very reserved, determined, persevering, and shunning the limelight.[25] Howe was also blessed with an almost photographic memory, which was advantageous for a man who would become one of America's first crime statisticians and chroniclers. A reporter for the *Denver Times* once accompanied Sam along a block in Denver. When they reached the corner, Sam described the physical attributes of every person they had passed along the block.[26]

Denver's law enforcement had been haphazard and unprofessional, and the establishment of a formal police department was welcomed. Nonetheless, the city's police policies and procedures remained poorly structured and ill enforced for another quarter-century. In Denver, as in other locations in the growing West, employment requirements for police were rudimentary. Toughness was necessary, and some policemen were brutal, although Sam Howe was never characterized as a head banger. To enlist bullies into the force, ethical deficiencies were often overlooked. Police misbehavior ranged from minor graft taking to drunken murder and covert alliances with criminals, which generated public mistrust of policemen at large. Cops were regarded as ruffians who constantly guzzled free beer, smoked cigars, dressed sloppily, and hung around under street lamps talking.

There must have been brave, conscientious men in the ranks, but the reputation of the force was earned by the great number of police who were inclined toward brutality and always eager for a handout. The policemen returned the scorn and often displayed contempt for the public.[27] In Denver, police antics were seldom lighthearted, and occasionally the officers were contemptuous of each other. The *Denver Republican* said, and Detective Howe duly recorded:

> Officer Stevens of the city police department was arrested last night by Deputy Constable [Charles A.] Colby on a warrant sworn out by Officer [Richard] Rutledge in Justice [F. J.] Hangs' court. The warrant charged him with assault and battery. Stevens, it is

alleged, beat Rutledge over the head with a revolver. Stevens says that while walking down Fifteenth on the way to his beat, Rutledge stepped up to him and with an oath told him to mind his own business and keep off his beat. Words led to blows and then Stevens pulled out his gun and threatened to shoot Rutledge.[28]

The equally hotheaded Ike Campbell was a Denver policeman in 1885. He had a reputation as a "clubber." Campbell also seems to have been a bumbler. On June 7 Campbell attempted to arrest Arthur Parks, but Parks managed to slip from Campbell's grasp and flee. Onlookers began laughing at Campbell, which annoyed the officer. He then tried to arrest one of the laughers, William Rathburn, whom the *Rocky Mountain News* described as "slight of stature but of jovial temperament." When Rathburn protested, Officer Campbell pulled out his club and inflicted two "ghastly wounds." The community turned against Campbell. The citizen consensus was to "turn the rascal out," but he was known around town as a "strong Democrat," which may have helped him retain his job.[29]

Patrolman F. J. Robinson got into more of a scrape the night he overdrank while on duty and wandered down Santa Fe Avenue (now Drive) at 1:30 in the morning, firing off a double-barreled shotgun at nothing in particular. Sergeants William Bohanna and R. H. McDonald were quickly dispatched to investigate, but they did not arrive until after Robinson had blown a finger off the hand of young Joseph Bierbrower, who had grabbed the barrel of Robinson's gun to keep him from killing someone. Robinson, according to the account of the incident preserved by Howe, "staggered to the patrol box at South Eighth and Santa Fe," whereupon he was intercepted by the sergeants and taken to jail "much too intoxicated to give any intelligible account of the affair."[30]

And there was Officer (no first name learned) Izett, badge number 65, who was arrested for the February 4, 1882, assault of Owen S. Owens, a crippled newsboy. Under the headline "A Brutal Policeman," the *Denver Times* related the next day:

Izett is alleged to have taken a *Times* from Owens, refusing to pay for it "because he was a policeman." As the newsboy objected, the officer slapped him upon the face and shook him by the shoulder. Officer [Axtel F.] Peterson interfered. The affair occurred at Twentieth and Larimer last night. The officer was also said to be drunk and wished to arrest Owens, although he [Izett] was not on duty at the time. Some of the crowd interfered and saved Owens from arrest and in return one of them was run in. He was, however, dismissed by Judge [Richard] Sopris this morning. Izett will be tried tomorrow morning before Justice [George] Stidger.[31]

At Officer Izett's hearing he was "thoroughly exonerated" by the Fire and Police Board—a three-member appointed panel that administered the fire and police departments—after the alleged victim, Owens, declared that the charges were made up by "a gang who have it in" for Izett. Board president Egbert Johnson said he wanted to confer with policeman Peterson "for [Peterson's] derogatory talk about Izett," and the matter was dropped after what the press suggests was a fairly superficial investigation—including no statements taken from witnesses.[32]

With regard to the unfortunate crippled newsboy Owens, in 1886 Denver had an ordinance restricting public appearance by "Deformed Persons," which by its outrageous nature deserves to be mentioned here:

Sec. 18. Any person who is in any way diseased, maimed, mutilated, or in any way deformed so as to be an unsightly or disgusting object . . . shall not expose himself or herself to public view, under a penalty of one dollar for each offense. On conviction . . . if it shall seem proper and just, the fine shall be suspended and such person detained at the Police Station, where he or she shall be well cared for until he or she can be committed to the County poor house or otherwise provided for.[33]

Today's reader will deem such an ordinance atrocious and without any possible justification, unless its purpose might have been to provide authorities with means to assist physically disabled persons by taking them to shelters and offering them ongoing care.

In June 1881 Officer Tim Ryan was accused of getting drunk, "choking three or four women, beating a cripple, [and] pounding an inoffensive citizen." The husband of one of the choked women spent several hours, shotgun in hand, hunting for the intoxicated policeman, "with vengeful purpose," but apparently did not locate him. Officer Ryan was suspended for one day, but he learned no lesson in proper police behavior. A year later, as a sergeant, Ryan became involved in what the *Denver Times* described as "an unpleasantness" with Patrolman Dick Lawrence. Ryan, known as a bully, was the largest man on the police force, whereas Lawrence was the smallest officer, which seemed not to have prevented Ryan from knocking Lawrence off a tall stool at police headquarters and onto the floor. The matter was precipitated when Lawrence called Ryan "hard names." The newspaper remarked that "it's about time for the council committee to rigidly investigate some of the numerous charges of brutality against Officer Ryan." Nothing appears to have come of it.[34]

Detectives trying to elicit a confession from four suspects in 1890 removed them from their jail cells to an adjacent room where the prisoners were threatened with death, knocked down, kicked, and beaten with pistols and billy clubs. Detectives William Crocker and George Watrous were charged with the beatings. Upon conviction, Crocker was fined forty-five dollars and given a day in jail, and Watrous was fined seventy dollars. In retrospect, if one is to heed a *Denver Post* article, it may have been unusual to find the detectives available to do anything. At this point in time, overnight officers were required to sleep at the police station, but a bell wired into their sleeping quarters from the dispatch switchboard ensured that they could be awakened for a call. At 2:30 on the morning of April 24, 1900, pharmacist Charles M. Ford of 2351 Emerson Avenue (later Street) telephoned to report that he had been robbed. The switchboard tried to awaken the detectives for ten minutes before it was discovered they had stuck wadded paper into the bell assembly so as not to be disturbed. The suitably indignant *Post* headlined its story "Sleuths Will Be Obliged if Not Awakened" and pointed out that the sleepy officers "draw salary from the pockets of the taxpayers."[35]

Drunkenness on duty was historically an affliction among Denver police and generally was forgiven,

but not in one Keystone Cops shenanigan. The *Denver Times* reported:

> A policeman under the influence of liquor and a bountiful supply of it, at that, was gyrating around and enjoying himself to the annoyance of respectable passers-by. He reached a climax when he laid hands on a woman who resisted his attack and the pair soon were rolling in the muddy ditch in a sort of cat and dog struggle. The police at the central station were informed of the affair and hastening to the scene arrested the boozy star [referring to his badge], who this morning was reported to Mayor Bates. That official at once ordered the offending officer's discharge from the force.[36]

Likewise, the *Rocky Mountain News* on July 6, 1898, reported the firing of policeman Fred Lindquist and thirty-day suspension of officer Olaf Swanson, both for drinking on duty and apparently caught in the act by Police Chief John Farley. Farley, one of Denver's few worthy police chiefs in the late nineteenth century, could be a decisive administrator. The most humiliating punishment inflicted on an erring policeman was to be stripped of his shiny brass buttons by a superior. One patrolman discovered as much:

> A [drinking] jag entered into Policeman Thomas P.S. Robinson and made him do things altogether unbefitting a guardian of the peace. After a wild and uproarious day, he wound up by arresting Alderman Thomas E. McNulty, three respectable women, a saloon keeper who refused to supply him with liquor, and then himself was stripped of his buttons and put in the bull pen.[37]

The job of a Denver policeman in the late nineteenth century could be exasperating, particularly when he had to contend with a society grande dame. Patrolman Lee Knapp, for instance, was casually strolling the 1500 block of Lincoln Street when real estate tycoon Walter Cheesman's yappy little poodle dashed out from the Cheesman mansion and bit the officer on the foot. The policeman gave the mutt a kick, which was observed from the porch by Mrs. Cheesman. "Hot words" passed between the officer and Mrs. Cheesman. Walter Cheesman went directly to Police Chief John Farley, who reported it to the

Fire and Police Board, which suspended Patrolman Knapp for six weeks.[38]

Local government officials sometimes set less than an ideal example. City license inspector Edward McCarthy, identified by the press as a former Los Angeles police chief and Denver Republican party leader, on one occasion found himself in the house of feminine delights at 1907 Market Street. There Jenny Long, alias Maggie McCarthy, was "reposing on the inspector's knee with her head pillowed on his bosom."

While the inspector was thus distracted, the "artful" Maggie relieved him of a roll of hundred-dollar bills. Instead of arresting her himself, the inspector summoned policeman James Rafferty to do the job, and Maggie was fined nineteen dollars and costs the next morning in police court. Inspector McCarthy, the *Denver Evening Post* noted, was an "especial pet" of the Fire and Police Board, whose president, the corrupt Robert W. Speer, was "very much surprised to learn that his inspector had been on such familiar terms" with the Market Street ladies the police department was supposed to control.[39]

Several days later Speer, according to a report preserved by Sam Howe, "casually remarked" at the Police Board's meeting that he "had heard charges of blackmail" involving McCarthy. Liquor dealer Racco L. Barro told the board that McCarthy "had offered to compromise a liquor license." McCarthy denied it, and no action was taken by the board. This was not surprising in any agency headed by Speer, whose subsequent mayoralty campaigns of 1904 and 1908 became notorious for their graft and financial reliance on the city's gaming, liquor, and vice interests. Inspector McCarthy was "called upon to retire" two months later as part of an "economy move."[40]

With "Boss" Speer just beginning his second term, ongoing allegations of police graft persisted. In many such instances, predictably, substantiation was not forthcoming, but on August 3, 1908, attorney E. N. Burdick attested that he had a provable case. Burdick represented Rose Wilson, keeper of a dive at 1024 Twentieth Street, who alleged that she had been shaken down for protection since the first of that year by Officer Claude Bossie at a rate of ten dollars a month

and that she had "loaned" Officers J. J. Butefish and Arthur Thompson money, which they forgot to pay back. Even worse, Wilson said, she had purchased from Sergeant Joseph McIntyre four tickets to a Democratic Party picnic, and he jailed her and her girls when she declined to buy additional tickets. The accused officers denied the allegations, with Bossie adding that it was all politics and that Wilson "simply wants to get me into trouble." Police Chief Hamilton Armstrong said that if the charges were proven in court, there would be "some vacancies in the police department." As was so often the case in matters of alleged graft, that seems to have been the end of it.[41]

Denverites since the frontier days were a thirsty lot. In 1898, for instance, a third of the 6,989 arrests were for drunkenness. The *Denver Times*, under the headline "A Year with the Bluecoats," did a story on the year-end crime statistics. The story noted that a "peculiarity of the original [Denver city] survey requires at least one officer to every thousand population," but at that time the city had one policeman for every 2,058 citizens plus twenty-two horses, three wagons, and an ambulance. In 1885, the story said, total arrests were 3,170; in 1886, 5,621; in 1887, 7,266; in 1891, 10,506; and in 1892, 8,883. In 1893, under Governor Davis H. Waite's Populist administration, five chiefs served the department during the year—one of whom was in office overnight—and 7,064 arrests were made; and in 1894, 9,748 persons were arrested in Denver.[42]

By the mid-1890s Denver's city government finally began taking the police profession seriously. In late 1896 all policemen, including commanders, were required to wear uniforms at all times when on duty, and in June 1897 Chief William H. O'Brien urged all officers to shave cleanly, get their hair cut, and "keep good company."[43]

Denver's earlier police chiefs could not have imagined the problems that would subsequently confront the police department. Chief W. A. Smith, for instance, was trying to decide if policemen should be allowed to stroll along while casually twirling their umbrellas by a cord and tassel. The chief decided it should not be permitted because it might interfere with physical activities, and, more important, he ordered the officers to wear their revolvers *outside* their uniform coats, which were of hip length. That was not standard police practice of the day, and the order was soon reversed, allowing revolvers to again be worn underneath coats. The *Rocky Mountain News* of March 25, 1874, for one, believed revolvers outside the uniforms were excessively formidable and that some officers looked like "perambulating arsenals with a revolver strapped to their belts in sight of the public." Additional rules, as drafted by Chief Smith, required policemen to be "civil and orderly," to use no "coarse, violent, or profane language," to keep a record of pertinent information about all persons they arrested, and to refrain from walking and talking with other officers unless to impart official information.

They were further instructed to stay out of politics, take charge of lost children, tend the dying and injured, arrest drunks and disorderlies (quiet and orderly drunks, if they resided in the city, were to be escorted home by the officer, who would inform the chief the next day), report all gamblers, "watch for persons of bad character," and report unlighted street lamps. They could be reprimanded for revealing orders from superior officers, neglecting to wear their badges in the proper place, maltreating citizens and prisoners, displaying laziness, disobeying orders, accepting rewards from persons arrested, entering saloons when on duty except in performance of duty, leaving their beats without authorization, becoming intoxicated, failing to wear a uniform while on duty, and exhibiting slovenliness when on duty.[++] As the reader will learn, many of these regulations were ignored for another twenty-five years.

With the formation of a real police department, the city administration ordered that the police chief each April 1 deliver an annual report listing the incidence of crime in Denver for the preceding calendar year. Whether these reports were always submitted on schedule is doubtful, as timely mention of them is seldom found in the newspapers, and the reports long ago disappeared. In data that *have* survived, no standard ongoing crime classification structure is employed, making it impossible to track trends. The numbers,

however, are effective barometers of the character of the city in the early years, and some of the later reports are included in Appendix B.

Chief John McCallin issued the first annual report of the Denver Police Department, covering the year 1874 and published in the *Rocky Mountain News* on April 3, 1875:

Burglaries, 8; larcenies (all), 163; assault with intent to kill, 6; highway robbery, 5; assault, 53; selling whiskey to Indians, 1; gambling, 3 [a low number, suggesting either the permissiveness of the times or the nebulous nature of crime statistics]; riot, 2; rape, 1; cruelty to animals [usually horses or oxen], 4; challenging to fight a duel, 1; intoxication, 712; carrying a concealed weapon, 12; vagrancy, 54; abusive language, 42; breach of the peace, 59; keeping a disorderly house, 5; fast driving, 14; leaving horses unhitched, 14; inmates of houses of ill-fame, 68; and permitting and maintaining a nuisance, 27.

Fines collected for these infractions during the year totaled $13,821, and Chief McCallin assured the community that the discipline and morale of the department were good, its efficiency was great, and its achievements were unsurpassed.

Among the procedures instituted by the new police department was the use of an "arrest book" permanently recording the name, age, birth date, trade, physical description, and reason for arrest of each offender. The statistics for the police department's first year provoke questions on several counts, and not just the fourteen arrests for leaving horses unhitched or the three for gambling. The absence of even one entry for homicide or murder is puzzling, and it is remarkable that only sixty-eight arrests for prostitution were made throughout the year. (The prostitution figure will be discussed in ensuing pages.) With regard to not one murder being recorded in a frontier town where many were armed, it is conceivable but not wholly realistic to think that the chief—following a practice in other large cities—was imposing a news blackout intended to portray Denver as more ideal than was the case.

As improbable and naïve as it sounds, gross news suppression materialized under an 1894 Denver police administration that fell under the regime of Populist governor Davis H. Waite. Waite wanted to clean up what he and others saw as Denver's wickedness, and he believed the gubernatorially appointed Fire and Police Board was shielding gamblers and prostitutes. Thus Waite attempted to remove the board, which resulted in board members barricading themselves in city hall and led to a subsequent standoff known as the March 15, 1894, "City Hall War."

Against that backdrop, Police Chief A. W. Kellogg announced to astonished reporters three weeks before the City Hall War that the police henceforth would withhold from the press whatever facts they felt the citizens should not know. He accused the papers of publishing accounts of murders, burglaries, and holdups, thus helping the criminals to escape.

The reporters could not understand the chief's logic, but the chief was not to be budged. Thus from then on, reporters could view only the initial arrest citations, and beyond that they would receive only what news the clerk and lieutenant saw fit to hand out. Even worse, they could not go behind the wood rail in the department office, which was where the records were kept.

Chief Kellogg posted a notice: REPORTERS ARE NO LONGER TO HAVE ACCESS TO ANY BOOKS OR PAPERS IN THE POLICE OFFICES EXCEPT THE RECORD OF ARRESTS. The press was outraged. The *Republican* exclaimed the next day, March 16:

> The excuse given by Chief Kellogg for shutting out the news from the press is almost too flimsy for consideration. . . . As a matter of fact, the papers give the police most of their pointers and clues. Because the taxpayers will not be able to learn that murder and robbery is rampant in their midst they will continue to pay for a police system which practically fosters such crimes.

The *Times* huffed that Chief Kellogg seemed to have become convinced he was a failure and was trying to lay the blame for his failures on the newspaper reporters.

The *Colorado Evening Sun* was calm and eloquent, stating that the chief considered secrecy necessary in the capture of criminals, although the paper said the police had scarcely distinguished themselves in that regard.

The chief had underestimated the power of an indignant press. Within twenty-four hours Police Commissioner A. J. Rogers transmitted a memo to Chief Kellogg: "You are hereby directed to give to press representatives access to all books and records of the department, as has been customary previous to this date."[45]

Perhaps the public would not have wanted to know what its police force was up to, as the department did not always project a positive public image. "There are many men in Denver and in every community," one writer observed,

> who think police duty is "a soft snap." They think that [policemen] have only to wear nice dark blue clothes with pretty bright buttons and then they walk slowly over a beat and drive accumulated boys from a street corner, help the ladies—the well-dressed ones—across the street where street cars or carriages are approaching, and grow fat; for it is a fact that very few men can remain upon a police force any length of time without growing fat.[46]

Sam Howe—who from his photographs appears to have never grown fatter than 138 pounds during his forty-seven years on the police department—walked the beats of Denver for a decade, managing to avoid mortal injuries at the hands of the roughnecks he sought to control. He also managed to avoid other sorts of notoriety. When the big cases were to be probed, Sam was rarely included in the plans. The *Rocky Mountain News* on December 21, 1878, for instance, detailed Sam's arrest of two men named Greenfall and Champion for "stealing a box of cigars from a Kansas drummer." Twenty years later citizen William Crow wearied of the presence of a dead dog, frozen solid, lying for a week at Thirteenth and Larimer Streets, only a few steps from city hall. The exasperated Crow finally strapped the carcass to his children's sled and proceeded to city hall, picking up a procession of amused passersby on his way. There Crow offered to give the carcass to Mayor Henry V. Johnson, who summoned Howe to escort Crow and the dog from the premises. Howe's fellow officers, in such instances, afforded Howe the respect due his longevity on the job, but when the major crimes needed attention, somebody else was called.[47]

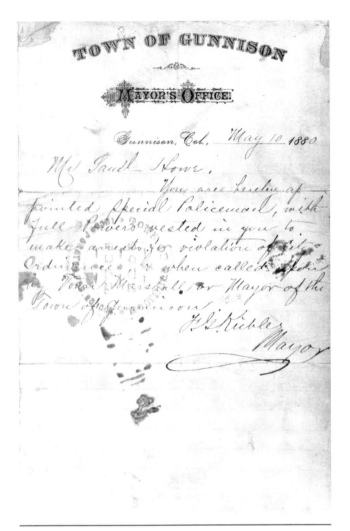

For reasons he never disclosed, Sam Howe left Denver in April 1880 to accept an appointment as "special policeman" for the new town of Gunnison, Colorado. His certificate was dated a month later, May 10.

notes in ledger books to keep track of the rascals. Sam observed as well that his newspaperman friends were diligent at preserving every newspaper crime clipping, no matter how small, for use in follow-up stories. That gave him an idea.

At the stationery store Howe purchased a standard household scrapbook. It had a fancy decorated cover and looked decidedly unbusinesslike, but it would serve the purpose. Howe began searching every Denver newspaper every day, clipping each crime story he found. Then he methodically pasted every clipping into his scrapbook.

The clippings were intended for Howe's personal use so he could keep track of what criminals were up to, but his colleagues increasingly asked to consult the book, as did reporters and occasionally a police officer from out of town or state. At the end of the first year, 1873, Howe's first scrapbook was full, so he started a new book for the next year.

Thus began Sam Howe's activities as a crime record archivist, and in 1875 he assumed the added responsibility of helping institute Denver's first rogues' gallery of criminals' photographs. He continued his news-clipping efforts during the ten years he was a patrolman, from 1873 to 1883, when he was promoted to detective.[48]

While he was still a patrolman, in 1880 a brief interval contributed to the mystery of Sam Howe. It could be called his "Gunnison interruption," and it was uncharacteristic of Howe's devotion to the Denver Police Department.

On January 5, 1880, five days after Howe was assigned to the daytime Lawrence Street beat, he quit the Denver police to become an Arapahoe County deputy sheriff (Denver was in Arapahoe County at the time). "Lack of harmony" was cited as the reason for his resignation, but escalating levels of police corruption throughout 1880 may have had a bearing on Howe's decision. Five of his colleagues soon followed him in leaving.

Nothing has been discovered regarding what Sam did with the sheriff's department for the next three months. In early April 1880, however, Howe became a "special policeman with full powers vested to make ar-

Howe moved instead toward another police function at which he would excel and which would distinguish him and the Denver Police Department nationally. Indeed, his ultimate accomplishments and lasting contributions would far surpass those of his peers who were out catching crooks.

When Sam Howe first walked the tough beats in 1873, he realized there was no system of maintaining more than the most elementary crime records. Officers relied on their memories or on handwritten pencil

On May 19, 1880, nine days after being certified as a Gunnison town officer, Howe received this appointment as undersheriff of Gunnison County, allowing him to make arrests outside the town limits. Howe was back in Denver by the end of July, however, and never again moved away from Denver. He saved his Gunnison certificates of appointment in his scrapbook number one.

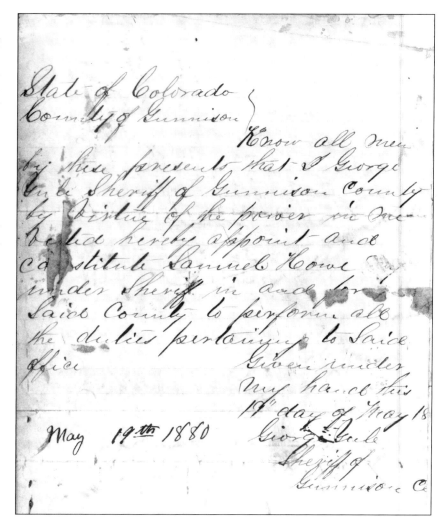

rests" (according to the wording of his appointment) in the new town of Gunnison, Colorado, 196 miles west of Denver. Nine days later he was appointed Gunnison County undersheriff, and he is also referred to in historical accounts as Gunnison's night marshal.[49]

Gunnison was a boomtown. Over a three-month period beginning May 15, 1880, 200 houses were built in the new community, which sprang up as the supply point for the developing mining camps of Pitkin, Tin Cup, Hillerton, White Pine, Gothic, and Irwin. Thousands of ore-hungry prospectors streamed into Gunnison every week.

Sam Howe's jobs as a lawman in Gunnison lasted barely three months, but they provided experiences Howe would not have encountered with the big-city police department in Denver. The *Gunnison Review* on June 26, 1880, tells that Sam Howe, identified as a deputy sheriff rather than undersheriff, accompanied by "Marshal Mr. Resner" and "Officer Roberts," traveled to the mining camp of Pitkin to arrest "Chester Gibbs" for the robbery and murders of brothers James and William Edgeley, both of Leadville. All were itinerant miners.

Longtime Gunnison County sheriff C. W. "Doc" Shores remembered the incident vividly and gave this version of the story in his autobiographical *Memoirs of a Lawman:*

Shores arrived in Gunnison in June 1880—he would become sheriff there in 1884—and was approached by a shifty-eyed individual who gave his name as "Breckenridge" and who needed help readying a pair of pack burros for a trip to the mines. Breckenridge, Shores noticed, had several bloodied blankets but explained that he had recently shot a deer and had used the blankets in cleaning up.

No sooner had Doc Shores helped Breckenridge get out of town than into Gunnison rode Marshal Reasoner (probably the "Resner" cited in the *Gunnison Review* article) from the town of Irwin. Reasoner reported that prospector Breckenridge had killed his two mining partners, the Edgley brothers (spelled "Edgeley" by the *Review*), along Indian Creek 8 miles from Irwin.[50]

31

Marshal Reasoner, Doc Shores, Sam Howe, and others got up a posse and tracked Breckenridge northeast to Pitkin, where he was arrested. On the way back to Gunnison, a lynch mob of angry miners awaited the posse, believing the law officers had captured the famous Colorado cannibal Alfred Packer. Breckenridge was terrified, but the posse assured the mob that the prisoner was not Packer.

Proceeding on to Parlin, the posse stopped for a whiskey break, leaving Sam Howe and Doc Shores in charge of Breckenridge. Shores told Howe that a full confession should be easy to elicit if they tied a rope around Breckenridge's neck and tossed the other end over a tree limb, and Sam Howe agreed. Marshal Reasoner, however, emerging from the saloon, said ample evidence was available to convict Breckenridge without frightening him into a confession, and the party proceeded to Gunnison.

Breckenridge, it turned out, was from a reputable Pennsylvania family, and he had once been a successful newspaperman at the *Philadelphia Morning Star*. Before long his mother reached Gunnison from Philadelphia, accompanied by a family friend whom Shores identifies as "Zeigfus," a Denver newspaperman. (This was probably Charles O. Ziegenfuss, city editor of the *Republican*. By 1882 Ziegenfuss apparently had abandoned the *Republican* for a try at running a Gunnison newspaper but soon abandoned that idea, returning to the *Republican*. See the *Denver Tribune*, July 19, 1882.)

In his memoirs Doc Shores wrote that Mrs. Breckenridge and Ziegenfuss were "good mixers and pretty smooth operators, and it was not long before they had won the sympathy and goodwill of many prominent Gunnison people, including the city marshal and the county sheriff." A grand jury was called into session regarding the Edgley brothers' murders, but key witnesses familiar with the case were not called to testify—not even Doc Shores, who had observed the bloody blankets, or Town Marshal Reasoner, who had inspected the crime scene.

No indictment was issued, and Breckenridge was released, escorted to the county line, and told not to come back. "To make the farce complete," Shores recorded in his memoirs, "many years later Breckenridge wrote an article for a national magazine telling how

near he came to being hanged in Gunnison County for a crime that he didn't commit."

The Shores reminiscence lists no evidence connecting Breckenridge to the Edgley brothers' murders, but Doc Shores nonetheless construed the affair to be "a sample of how justice was meted out in Gunnison County during its early boom years. All kinds of crimes were taking place, and very little was being done about it. Not only were very few outlaws captured, but those few who were caught usually broke jail or failed to be convicted." Shores became so incensed over the lawlessness that he successfully ran for sheriff, serving from 1884 to 1892, and simultaneously served as a deputy U.S. marshal for western Colorado.[51]

Sam Howe remained in Gunnison for less than a month following the arrest of Breckenridge. The *Rocky Mountain News* on July 25, 1880, carried the single-sentence note that "Samuel Howe, late of the sheriff's office [in Arapahoe County/Denver] and but recently an officer in the town of Gunnison, has returned to Denver." Neither the *News* nor any other Denver paper followed up on the story, and the *Gunnison Review* did not mention Howe's departure. It is plausible that the disappointing Breckenridge case caused Howe to leave Gunnison, as he appears to have been ever committed to the ideals of justice. Howe seldom mentioned his brief tenure in Gunnison, and he never addressed his reasons for leaving. The Gunnison hiatus was Howe's only absence from Denver in a forty-seven-year law enforcement career.[52]

When Sam Howe returned to the Denver Police Department, he found Chief David J. Cook had prepared a new set of departmental rules intended to make the operation more professional and perhaps halt or at least diminish the misdeeds of many of his officers. The entire set of rules follows:

I. Roll-call at 9 A.M. and 10 P.M.
II. Any member of the force who shall be found intoxicated or who shall manifest insubordination, or who shall be uncivil while on duty, will be discharged.
III. The use of intoxicating liquors is positively prohibited, and resorting to public houses, bawdy houses, saloons, houses of assignation, gambling

houses, or any other houses of a public nature, unless called in officially, will not be tolerated.

IV. Violence to prisoners must be guarded against. Any member unnecessarily abusing a prisoner will be discharged.

V. Under no circumstances shall a member of the force leave his beat after being duly stationed by the proper officer.

VI. Any member found asleep on his beat will be discharged.

VII. A policeman must be cautious never to interfere unnecessarily; but when required to act he should do so with discretion, decision, and boldness, and he may arrest any one who opposes him in the execution of his duty.

VIII. Officers, whether on duty or not, when applied to by the citizens for information within the line of their duty, will reply civilly, and if unable to attend to the business themselves will give the applicant the necessary information, that his business may be speedily transacted.

IX. No policeman shall accept an invitation to drink, or go into a saloon for that or any other purpose, except on official business, under the penalty of being immediately dismissed.

X. Any member of the force being cognizant of any violation of the law, without giving immediate notice to the proper authority, will be dismissed.

XI. Any officer found asleep while on duty will be dismissed [redundant, with qualification, with rule VI].

XII. Incurring of indebtedness is deprecated, but when necessitated prompt payment is required.

XIII. Being absent three times in one month from roll-call forfeits one day's pay; five times absent, dismissed.[53]

The new rules were well-intentioned, and Dave Cook was among Denver's worthiest nineteenth-century police chiefs, but as the reader will discover, many of these new regulations went unheeded. The policemen had had their way for too many years, and if they needed somebody to help protect their jobs, they had only to turn to the aldermen who paved the way for those jobs. How could policemen be expected to remain honest, sober, and upright when their city administrators were laced with graft and corruption?

Dave Cook's new rules were accompanied by a new badge, a five-pointed star instead of a shield, which the press disapproved of because its sharp points could be dangerous and the badges could be used as a weapon against the officers or against prisoners.[54]

Sam Howe walked a street beat for another three years. In 1883 he was promoted to detective and would remain in the detective bureau for the next thirty-eight years, serving as chief of detectives from 1891 to 1893 and in 1897–1898.[55]

The year 1883 was eventful for Sam Howe on two counts. First, he was promoted to detective. Second, he resumed work on his crime scrapbooks, determined to enhance their sophistication and usability. Under the new procedure each clipping was assigned a number, and each subsequent clipping regarding the same case was assigned another number that was affixed to the original clipping. Thus the reader could track an important case, for instance, from arrest to trial to conviction to imprisonment to parole. Additionally, indexes were prepared during some years that enabled the reader to access a criminal's name, locate a particular major crime, or find certain classifications of crimes.

Additionally, Howe often added the date and name of the newspaper from which the clipping came. In instances of stories from different newspapers regarding the same crime, Howe usually did not clip each story from each newspaper but selected his favorite account—not to be confused with the most lengthy, objective, or thorough account. Since the dates generally are affixed to the clippings Howe *did* include in his books, however, the researcher can consult microfilms of the newspaper accounts he did *not* include. Howe's methodology and thoroughness in early crime record keeping were unusual in U.S. law enforcement in the late nineteenth century and generally work well for the researcher a hundred years later, although sometimes that researcher must be persistent and patient.[56]

As time passed and Howe's scrapbooks became increasingly voluminous, their renown spread throughout Colorado law enforcement circles and beyond. Out-of-town and out-of-state law agencies found the books useful; in

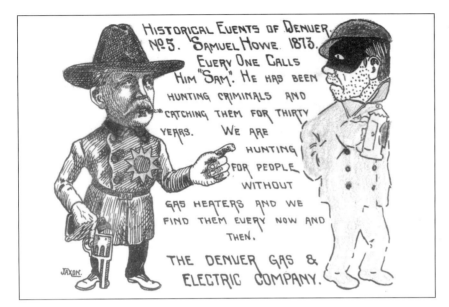

HISTORICAL EVENTS OF DENVER.
№5. SAMUEL HOWE. 1873.
EVERY ONE CALLS
HIM "SAM". HE HAS BEEN
HUNTING CRIMINALS AND
CATCHING THEM FOR THIRTY
YEARS. WE ARE
HUNTING
FOR PEOPLE
WITHOUT
GAS HEATERS AND WE
FIND THEM EVERY NOW AND
THEN.
THE DENVER GAS &
ELECTRIC COMPANY.
JAXON.

In 1903, newspaper advertisements for the Denver Gas and Electric Company utilized a series of caricatures showing "the men who have and are making history in 'The City Beautiful'" (women were excluded). So popular were the advertisements that the company reprinted them in a booklet titled A Peep into the Historical Events of Denver. *This was Detective Sam Howe's entry.*

1903, for instance, the Chicago police asked for help in locating a Peter Dahlgren, and using the Sam Howe Scrapbooks it was determined within thirty minutes that the missing man had drowned near Pueblo.[57]

Arriving promptly at his office each morning at 7, Howe spent one or two hours perusing the newspapers. Denver had as many as five dailies at a time—the *News*, *Post*, *Times*, *Republican*, and *Tribune*—plus an occasional short-lived daily or weekly Howe virtually ignored. The *Times* and *News* seemed to be his favorites; the *Republican* was the most thoughtful of Denver's newspapers of the day and thus published less blood and thunder than Howe preferred. But when the *Republican* did publish a crime story, it was well written and comprehensive and thus worth saving. The *Post* did not arrive in earnest until 1895, but its propensity for sensationalism and all-stops-out coverage endeared the paper to Howe.

In 1900, with the fame of his scrapbooks spread across the land (the *Denver Republican* called him "perhaps the best-known city official in Denver"), Howe calculated statistics regarding his long labor of love. Selecting from the various newspapers what he called the "best and fullest" accounts of crimes big and small, Sam Howe estimated that he devoted 178 hours a year to the books (a very conservative figure, perhaps designed to placate colleagues concerned that Howe was spending too much time on his scrapbooks), or a total

of 8,900 hours over "twenty-five years."[58] Each year, Howe calculated, he clipped 1,400 newspapers, and by 1900 his scrapbooks contained 161,500 column inches of type, or 21,875 linear feet, which "if placed in a line would reach over four and one-seventh miles of the streets on which Howe's detectives worked."[59]

The clippings Howe assembled were generally confined to criminal matters in Denver, but as the use of telegraphic wire services was developed, he occasionally saved important (and other times trivial) news notes from other cities, states, and even foreign countries. Accounts of momentous calamities such as earthquakes and killer fires were saved, and Howe also clipped and pasted articles about the lives, homecomings, reminiscences, and deaths of Colorado's pioneers, with whom he felt a kinship.

The inside front and back covers of his scrapbooks often were reserved for photos and newspaper articles about himself. Howe once proudly proclaimed of his crime scrapbooks, "The older these [books] get, the more valuable they grow. In a hundred years from now, they will be worth a great deal."[60] On another occasion he divulged, "[The] manager of a newspaper office offered $10,000 for them as reference works."[61] He probably was not exaggerating. A newspaper writer attested to their usefulness: "[The books] are perhaps the most valuable as well as the most complete record of a city's crime and criminals outside of the [police] department libraries of Chicago and New York. Many well-known authorities have pronounced [them] unequaled as regards [their] authenticity and systematic arrangement."[62]

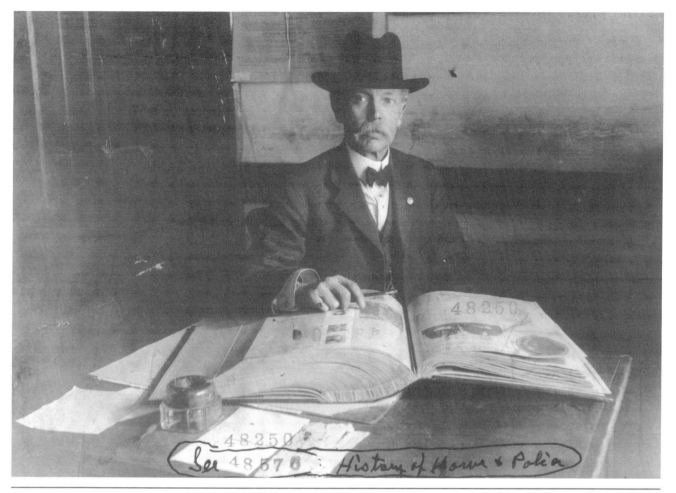

Sam Howe with one of his crime-clippings scrapbooks at police headquarters in city hall, Fourteenth and Larimer Streets. The date is 1908, and Howe was in his twenty-fifth year of daily preparation of his precious books. The markings stamped on this photograph, found in Howe's volume number twenty-seven, are representative of his system of indexing and cross-indexing by assigning a guide number to each photo and newspaper clipping. The scrapbooks have been in the possession of the Colorado Historical Society since 1939 but were never thoroughly researched until preparation of this book.

On Howe's thirtieth anniversary with the Denver police, January 13, 1903, he pondered the editor's shears long used to clip his articles and assemble his scrapbooks and lit his second cigar of the day. "Thirty years is not such a very long time," he observed, but lamented that all his old cronies from Denver's boom days were rich and he was not. The biggest change in crime during those many years, Howe said, was that the technology of safecracking had improved im-

mensely: a successful safe job once required seven men, but now one could accomplish it if he knew what he was doing.[63] Safe blowing was considered the most daring and romantic of crimes, and a good safecracker was highly regarded and aggressively pursued by a detective. But by this time, Howe attested, all robbers looked alike to him.

In addition to maintaining his scrapbooks and helping assemble the police department's growing

Chief John F. Farley, center, *examines the Denver Police Department's nationally famous "rogues' gallery" containing mug shots of around 2,000 criminals. The photo is dated January 1, 1900. In an era before fingerprinting, investigators depended on photographs, physical measurements (including skull diameters), scars, and marks. Detective Howe oversaw the so-called crime museum seen in this photograph, and he claimed to have started the rogues' gallery in May 1885, but he was far better known for his crime scrapbooks. At left is a cabinet containing safecracking tools. "Safe blowing" was the most sophisticated and daring crime of the era, and police secretly admired a skilled safecracker. In 2002 the location or fate of the rogues' gallery or other displays from the crime museum are not known. Only the Howe Scrapbooks survive, and they are unique in U.S. criminal history.*

rogues' gallery of criminals' mug shots, Howe was the Denver Police Department's semiofficial historian and curator of crime paraphernalia, including knives and guns, safe-blowers' tools, and even the rope used to hang seven convicts at the state prison in Cañon City during 1895 and 1896. Colorado enacted regulations regarding executions in 1871, and from that year until 1889, criminals were hanged in the county

where their crime was committed. From 1889 until 1897, hangings took place at the penitentiary in Cañon City. Capital punishment in Colorado was abolished in 1897 and resumed in 1901.[64]

The *Denver Times* colorfully referred to Colorado's hanging rope as "this dangling slipknot of death that has cracked the spines or squeezed the necks of seven desperate men. It is a stout and serviceable rope as

The Howe crime scrapbooks repose in 1911 in their walnut cabinet at city hall. The white volume in the middle of the bottom shelf is Sam Howe's Murder Book, *containing accounts of hundreds of Denver murders and photographs of perpetrators and victims. The* Murder Book *is the only Howe volume on microfilm.*

was ever wove in a loom, and the man who bought it took no chances of its ever proving untrustworthy or unfaithful."[65]

The rope indeed ended the earthly existence of three cop killers from Trinidad in rapid succession on the night of June 26, 1896. The penitentiary turned the rope over to Howe's crime museum when the legislature—temporarily, as it turned out—banned capital punishment effective March 29, 1897. The *Times* on December 15, 1901, spoke of Sam Howe's crime museum:

> Undoubtably [*sic*] the most interesting feature at the Denver police station and the one that leaves the greatest impression on the minds of the many visitors at headquarters is the collection of "machinery" used by the ubiquitous criminals in the perpetration of their crimes. The visitor is struck with awe when he is ushered into the room on the second floor and beholds the weird collection.

The detective bureau of which Sam Howe became a member in 1883 was a somewhat new development within the Denver Police Department. At the outset, the department had no real detective bureau, with patrolmen moving in and out of sleuth jobs on a rotating basis when required. As the 1870s progressed, however, a detective force gradually took form. Initially, the detective bureau was small, sometimes with only three or four men among a total of thirty to fifty.

Although ample investigations were available to keep the handful of detectives fairly busy, serious crimes were not complex and thus were easily solved. A notable exception was the 1894 stranglings, seemingly by the same killer, of three Market Street prostitutes. It was the biggest murder wave yet or for years to come in Denver; the Market Street vice district was transfixed in fear, and all of Denver was shocked and horrified. The detectives had no idea how to approach the matter, and despite an abundance of police blustering, no conviction was ever obtained (see Chapter 10).

A forgiving and magnanimous attitude sometimes prevailed at the police department. In 1877 a patriotic Mayor Richard G. Buckingham sent a memo to the city jailer instructing that all prisoners be released after breakfast on July 4, "because it is the day on which our whole country will celebrate the Anniversary of American Independence." The next year Mayor Richard Sopris received a letter from six short-term prisoners petitioning that they be released for New Year's Day, which the mayor allowed.[66]

The mayors might have deduced that if prisoners wanted to leave Denver's jails, they could do so fairly easily. In April 1879 six prisoners simply sauntered out of city jail, the second mass escape in a month. Two of the miscreants were found toasting each other in a Larimer Street saloon, and Sam Howe flushed out a third nearby. Police Chief William R. Hickey said that if the recaptured men would promise to leave town, he would "throw the doors of the jail open."

Five months later four prisoners departed after pulling off a bar in the old jail, climbing over the front-door transom, and walking away. And only a couple of weeks passed before two additional prisoners wriggled out of the jail, leading the *Times* to declare, "These frequent escapes from the city jail are becoming rather monotonous." No improvements were made, and soon five more prisoners, including a lad of twelve, pried aside a bar and left.[67]

Things had not appreciably improved by 1887. In that year "frontiersman and gunfighter" Newton Vorce was arrested for what his biography later described as a "minor offense" and was tossed into Denver's Arapahoe County jail. The biography added:

> Jail life proved irksome, and, besides, he had made a previous engagement to call on a girl at Deer Trail. So he kicked a hole through the jail wall, helped himself to pistols from the sheriff's office, mounted a horse, and rode away to keep his engagement. The sheriff organized a posse to escort Vorce back again. In the running battle which ensued, Vorce had two horses shot from under him, but fought off the entire posse and escaped.

Colonel [John M.] Chivington then organized another posse. Vorce knew they were coming, but declined to be put to flight. He was cornered in a prairie dugout. For hours Vorce stood off the party, until Colonel Chivington hurled a stick of dynamite on the roof of the dugout, when Vorce emerged, a gun in each hand spitting fire. But this time he was captured.[68]

In an era when an alarming percentage of Denver's policemen were drunks and grafters with no training—as evidenced by newspaper reports of their misdeeds[69]—it is impressive that during his forty-seven years on the force, only two blemishes were recorded on Sam Howe's record. In May 1879 Chief William Hickey, Howe, and five other officers were arrested and brought before an irate District Judge Victor A. Elliott "where they were severely reprimanded for not being in court when wanted to testify." Howe's second problem also involved a judge and will be related forthwith.[70]

As stated, in 1880 Howe briefly left the Denver Police Department to become a lawman for Arapahoe County and then Gunnison. Although he never elaborated much, Howe remarked on one occasion that his Denver police service had been briefly interrupted twice.[71] One of those interruptions constituted the deputy sheriff jobs, and the other, Howe conceded, was when he was given what he later described as "an enforced [five-month] vacation by one of the Populist Fire and Police boards." That incident is amusing, and it involved one of Howe's uncharacteristic confrontations with higher authority.

From 1891 to early June 1893, Howe served as chief of detectives with the Denver police, at which latter date he surrendered the job to George M. Hopkins, who had hired him twenty years earlier.[72] Howe's relinquishment of the detective chief post, according to the *Denver Republican* of January 18, 1897, resulted from a "difference of opinion" with Police Magistrate Albert S. Frost regarding the "vagrancy question":

> In the Populist magistrate's official vocabulary there was no such word as vagrant, while the particular delight of Sam Howe was to jail the "vag" element of the floating population. As fast as he locked them up, however, Judge Frost, with an accompaniment of short speeches denunciatory of police methods in this

Detective Howe preserved this photograph of himself standing before one of Denver's early jails. He identifies this decrepit structure at 1351 Thirteenth Street as serving as a city lockup from 1866 to 1883. A fuller discussion of Denver's early police headquarters and jails is in note 3, this chapter.

particular, turned them all loose. One day he charged the detectives with arresting only poor and friendless "vags" while they let [go] the gamblers and bunco steerers, who toiled not [and prowled] the city unmolested in search of prey. The next day Sam Howe sent him up 10 of the most influential bunco men in Denver on charge of vagrancy, just to vary the proceeding, but they, also, were set at liberty. Within a week or two from that date Sam Howe was laid off duty, and for five months he enjoyed an untrammelled opportunity of studying the vagrancy problem. At the expiration of that period [April 11, 1893] he was reappointed to the detective department.

But his reappointment was not as chief of detectives. Howe's cavalier attitude toward the judge and a small scandal involving the collecting of rewards, which will be related, earned him a demotion from detective chief to detective. So in the space of a few weeks, Howe went from detective chief to suspension and then back to detective, and he never again faced disciplinary action. He would, however, be detective chief again five years hence.[73] Regarding his two brief absences from the Denver police, Howe would only say, "I was out of the department for a short time."[74]

Newspapermen were among Howe's favorite people, and throughout his later career he delighted

This page and opposite: *The circumstances surrounding these two Sam Howe police commissions are not known. The* above *document, dated May 2, 1884, names Howe as a Denver "special officer" with pay; a special officer generally did not have full police powers. The second document (facing page), from October 21 of the following year, makes Howe a full policeman on the Denver force—a position he first attained back in 1874. Note the wording of the certificate, asserting "great confidence in the . . . sobriety" of the officer. As is noted in these pages, many early Denver policemen disregarded such a notion, even while on duty.*

in relating tales of the romantically dangerous old days. Too, Howe's scrapbook system was increasingly a source of background material the newsmen found very helpful, and thus they were indebted to him. The scrapbooks, one newspaper reported,

Have been at the disposal of newspaper men, day or night. Mr. Howe keeps his invaluable library in a vault at headquarters, but the key is always where the po-lice reporters can find it, and it is ever their privilege to refer to the books without asking leave. In return the reporters show Mr. Howe every courtesy, and assist him in making a thorough collection every day of all the police news published that has a bearing on a Denver criminal.[75]

The *Denver Times* explained the vault that held Sam Howe's cherished scrapbooks: "The old safe in

State of Colorado--City of Denver.

TO ALL TO WHOM THESE PRESENTS SHALL COME, GREETING:

That, Having great confidence in the ability, sobriety and integrity of *Saml Howe*, I, *J. E. Bates*, Mayor of the City of Denver, do by these presents constitute and appoint him, the said *Saml Howe*, of the City of Denver, to the office of *Policeman*, to have and to hold the said office at the pleasure of the appointing power, with —— pay as provided by Ordinance.

In Witness Whereof, I, *J. E. Bates*, Mayor of the City of Denver, have hereunto set my hand. Done at the City of Denver, this *21st* day of *Oct*, A. D. 188*5*.

Attested by the undersigned with the Corporate Seal of the City of Denver affixed thereto, this *22* day of *October* A. D. 188*5*.

_____ City Clerk.

J. E. Bates Mayor.

which Sam keeps the records would be lost without Sam, and Sam would feel lost without that safe. It is a tall, iron, fireproof safe, with the old-fashioned spring lock." The safe, the article explained, was purchased in Chicago during the 1860s and was hauled by ox team across the prairie from St. Joseph, Missouri. Its original purpose was to safeguard all of Denver's early city records, but when Howe became a policeman it was appropriated for police use exclusively.[76]

On occasion Howe modestly protested that although he never solicited attention or glorification through the press, the attention and glorification always seemed to gravitate toward him nonetheless. One announcement in the press read: "In all his years of work with the police detective department, Mr. Howe has been very close to the newspaper men. Not that he has ever sought publicity, though a great deal of that has been thrust upon him, but that he has always put himself at the service of the reporters."[77]

Although Howe never paid much attention to Denver's smaller publications, the weekly *Colorado Graphic* went out of its way to nurture Howe's ego in a short article when he was appointed assistant chief of detectives. On April 25, 1891, that paper described Howe as having "a reliable memory of faces, voices, and names . . . persevering industry, courage, and determination . . . [he is] unobtrusive in manner and [he] avoids notoriety."

At age fifty-nine, in 1898, Sam Howe was named Denver's chief of detectives for the second time. On the first occasion, 1891–1893, Howe was given the top detective task when Chief John Farley realized that William H. Loar, who had been in the post, "lacked the necessary executive ability" to carry on. An abrasiveness also surfaced between Loar and Howe—one of the very few interpersonal conflicts the mild-mannered Howe is recorded to have experienced.

So Sam Howe again became Denver's top sleuth and served in that post until December 9, 1899, when he was replaced by his old friend Hamilton "Ham" Armstrong. Armstrong became one of Denver's more noteworthy lawmen, serving four nonconsecutive terms as chief in an era when rampant politics prevented most Denver police chiefs from completing one term.[78]

Howe's replacement by Armstrong was regarded as a political move to please Thomas M. Patterson, owner of the *Rocky Mountain News*, who had once served with Armstrong in the Colorado legislature. Upon being displaced, Howe was assigned to the pawnshop detail, which appears to have been more important than it sounds because of the amount of stolen goods prevalent in the city. In July 1900, at age sixty, Howe was reassigned again, this time to the "less exhausting duty as house man and keeper of records in Chief Armstrong's office. His years of faithful service have told on his strength, and though still an indefatigable toiler, the veteran can hardly stand the strain of the daily tramp through the pawnshops."[79]

The frailties that eventually confined Howe to a succession of desk jobs, serving as a lackey to his former equals, were becoming apparent. Still, the old trouper would serve two more decades with the Denver police and was far from being forgotten by a grateful community: "He has become so well-known that nearly everybody who visits at the station asks for him, no matter what [the visitor's] business is," reported the *Denver Sunday Post* on December 23, 1900.[80]

Howe was known for his ability to settle barroom wagers about early crime in Denver. The *Rocky Mountain News* reported on October 18, 1904: "Citizens of Denver often call up Mr. Howe over the phone to settle bets that involve an event that has occurred in the criminal history of the city."[81]

As the police department's semiofficial goodwill emissary, Howe could always be depended upon to spin a good yarn for younger officers or for visitors who dropped by police headquarters to view the rogues' gallery or his magnificent scrapbooks:

As a storyteller Veteran Detective Sam Howe cannot be beaten. This is so well-known around headquarters that it keeps "Sam" busy telling about the happenings around Denver for the last quarter of a century, which time the aged sleuth has spent in serving the citizens in hunting down criminals. Today the conversation drifted to the repeal of the law [in 1897] making death the penalty for murders. Of course "Sam" had to tell about some of the hangings in the old days.

Whereupon Sam recounted how "in those days a hanging was a big event" and how 20,000 onlookers traveled miles by horses and carriages to witness the hanging of murderer Andy Green on July 27, 1886. "For fully fifteen minutes," the *Denver Times* quoted Howe as relating, "the crowd eagerly watched every twitch of the body."[82]

Howe exercised some discretion regarding the clippings placed in his scrapbooks. He omitted an 1882 incident during which he was walking robbery suspect Charles Johnson from jail to the grand jury room when at Twelfth and Welton Streets Johnson "sprang" on Howe, overpowered him, took his revolver, "sprang" into an express wagon, pulled the revolver, and said, "You git." The *Rocky Mountain News* laconically observed the next day, "The officer is a rather weak man in comparison with the desperado." Howe would rather have forgotten that occurrence, but the *News* printed it anyway.[83]

Detective Howe was age seventy-one and not considering retirement when he discovered that his professional longevity was establishing a national record. Under the headline "Denver Has Second Oldest Policeman" ran the news item:

Detective Samuel Howe, Denver's oldest police officer, both as to age and length of service, claims the distinction of being "runner up" to Edward O'Dwyer, a sergeant in the Toledo, Ohio, department, who, according to statistics gathered recently from cities throughout the country, is the oldest police officer in

Sam Howe on New Year's Day 1901 with his longtime colleague, Police Chief Hamilton "Ham" Armstrong, in Armstrong's office. Howe wears his hat indoors, as his thinning hair usually precluded him being photographed without headwear. Here he holds his spectacles, as he was seldom photographed while wearing them. An odd aspect of this photograph, which Howe preserved in his twentieth scrapbook (July–November 1901), is that Howe pasted a photo of his longtime friend Dora Barwick over the image in Armstrong's picture frame. The other two small photos are of Mr. and Mrs. Lorin Duncan, whom Howe referred to as cousins residing in Denver.

the United States in point of service. Howe is a scant year short of the mark set by O'Dwyer, [who has] forty years of police service. [Actually, Howe was nineteen months short of O'Dwyer's forty-year record.] In the matter of age, Howe has one year on O'Dwyer, who is 71 years of age. Like O'Dwyer, Howe has been eligible [for retirement on] half pay for several years, but he is still extremely active, both men-

tally and physically, and intends to stick to the police business until he has established a record for length of service that will be hard to equal.[84]

In 1913, on his fortieth anniversary with the Denver Police Department, it was observed: "Although he is 74 years old and his hair is silvery white, the veteran detective is as spry as any of the younger members of the department. . . . His chief pride is in the fact that during all the years of his service, he has not once been 'called to the carpet' for a violation of the rules of the department."[85] No departmental rules had been broken perhaps, but as the reader knows, Sam Howe had encountered at least one run-in with the judiciary and a difficulty over the collection of rewards. Still, Howe was far more ethical, far less brutal, and a much better policeman than most of his colleagues.

Sam Howe's energies were diminishing as the 1920s approached. He was a Denver lawman even before the police department was formed, and he had been a police officer in Denver much longer than anybody in history. He was eighty-one and still a cop, and in his reverie he turned to times past when Denver was a rough and tough frontier town and being a cop was different than it was today. In another year he would retire, and now Sam typed a note to one of the two men who were at his side when he first took the policeman's oath back in January 1873:

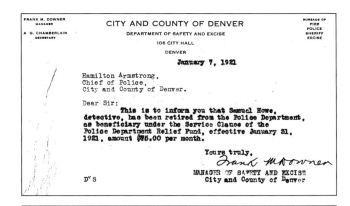

Sam Howe's long police service to Denver ended with this 1921 memorandum to Chief Armstrong from Safety Manager Frank Downer. The old detective lived nine more years, often visiting his comrades at police headquarters and discussing the exciting early days of Denver law enforcement.

> February 10, 1920
> Mr. W. J. Phillips
> 368 South Logan
> Denver, Colo.
>
> Dear Sir:—
> On the 16th of this month, the Policemen are going to give a ball at the Auditorium Building and I am writing you this letter asking you to be my guest at this occasion. You undoubtedly are aware that you and Mr. Frank Roinson [sic, Howe meant Frank A. Robinson] and myself are the three surviving members of the first uniformed police officers of this city, three of the original thirteen. Now if you can accept this invitation please let me know at your earliest convenience so that I may be able to make proper arrangements. Trusting to have the pleasure of your company on the 16th of this month, I remain, Respectfully,
> Sam Howe[86]

Howe; Phillips, age seventy-four; and Robertson, age seventy-seven, were all present at the 1920 policemen's ball. Three hundred couples had been at the first policemen's ball back in 1873, they danced to songs such as "Buffalo Gals," and the money was used to buy uniforms. This time more than 2,000 couples were there, and they danced to jazz.[87]

Sam Howe retired on a police pension at age eighty-one, February 1, 1921, but continued to visit his old comrades at police headquarters, bringing "his smiling face and cheerful disposition."[88] Although police personnel attempted to continue Howe's clipping activities following his retirement (several volumes of post-1921 scrapbooks exist, albeit lacking numbering and indexing), a departmental memo notes that "the books were discontinued shortly after Mr. Howe's retirement from the Police Department, on account of modern methods of criminal records and finger prints being established in the Department."[89]

In addition to regularly visiting his valued friends at police headquarters, the old detective maintained his affiliation with numerous organizations. He joined the Denver Masonic Lodge No. 5 on May 11, 1876, and became a life member on October 2, 1908. He was a member of the Carr Post, Grand Army of the Republic, Denver, and in November 1906 was accepted into the Sons of Colorado, an organization of "white males, of good moral character" who arrived in Colorado before it became a state on August 1, 1876. On April 15, 1908, he became a member of the Denver

Sam Howe poses formally with his best friend Dora Barwick, whom he called "Dode," October 17, 1899. He was sixty; she was forty-two and was married to Charles Barwick, a carpenter. Following Charles Barwick's death at an unknown date, Howe continued living in Dora's house until his death in 1930. She died in 1937 and is buried next to Sam and Helen Howe at Riverside Cemetery. The nature of Howe's long relationship with Dora Barwick—whether of mere friendship, one of a father and daughter, or of romance—can only be speculated upon.

Policeman's Protective Association. He was accepted into the Denver fire and police ex-chief's association on January 1, 1909, although he had never been police chief and his highest rank had been chief of detectives.[90] On March 23, 1909, he joined the Ohio Society of Colorado. Attesting to his long friendships with news reporters, on August 14, 1912, he was accepted into the rolls of the Colorado Pioneer Printers and Newsmen.[91] Howe had ample friendships to maintain and plenty of events to attend during his retirement years.

On October 16, 1928, twenty of Sam Howe's friends gathered to help the old policeman celebrate his eighty-ninth birthday. All were dressed in old-fashioned attire of sunbonnets and hoop skirts, plug hats and cutaway coats. Sam was in a vest of wine-colored velvet, with a tie to match and a high collar. A diamond scarf pin glittered in the necktie, and the *Denver Post* wrote that a "gray and black striped cutaway hugged the lines of his still supple figure." Only the day before, he had reminisced with other old cronies in the clubrooms of the Colorado Pioneer Society. A visiting reporter noted:

The veteran detective unpocketed his watch and brought it close to his spectacled blue eyes. He glanced at the door. "It's almost time for the little girl to be coming for me," he said, referring to Dora Barwick of 2541 Ash Street. Sam had made his home with Dora and her husband Charles for thirty-two years. "There she is now! Hello, Dode!"[92]

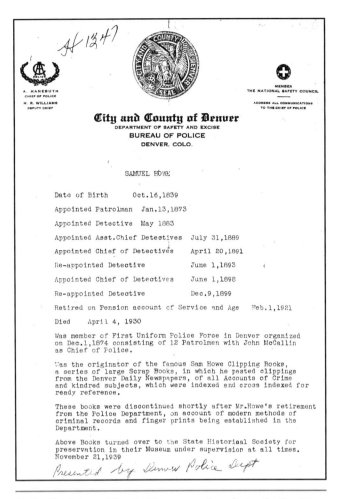

Police Chief August Hanebuth's memorandum placing the Sam Howe Scrapbooks with the Colorado Historical Society, November 21, 1939.

although they were seldom used. In 1980, because of their deteriorating condition, access to the Howe Scrapbooks became subject to curatorial permission. In the 2000s the Sam Howe Scrapbooks are maintained under temperature- and humidity-controlled conditions as funds are sought to place them on microfilm or to make them available through computer systems.

The author devoted three years to scrutinizing their pages, which comprise a cornucopia of wrongdoing and justice in one old-time western city. Part II contains some of Sam Howe's stories.

Notes

1. Forbes Parkhill in the RMN, April 19, 1959.

2. E. R. Battles, "Denver's Volunteer Fire Department," *The Trail*, two parts, January and February 1917. Sam Howe never discussed his early association with Denver's all-volunteer fire department. Howe's 1872 involvement with the J. E. Bates volunteer fire squad (named after Denver's mayor from April 1872 to April 1873) is on p. 15 of the January issue. Fire departments of this period were more interested in sponsoring dances and staging foot races than in fighting fires. Denver's volunteer fire squads disbanded between 1881 and 1885 when the city slowly converted to a professional full-time fire department; the Bates company ceased to exist on March 18, 1882, after a decade of service. There is no record of Sam Howe being with the fire department for the full period.

3. Numerous jail sites evolved in pioneer Denver. The town had its own jails, generally situated some distance from the police headquarters, and the county of Arapahoe, of which Denver was a part, maintained a jail and sheriff's facilities. The best method of locating these various lockups and their frequent relocations is to consult the *Denver City Directory*, which began publication in 1873. For particulars preceding that date, the April 1908 edition of the pioneer journal *Sons of Colorado* quotes *Denver Republican* writer Eugene Parsons as remembering the original jail in a "log cabin on the west side of Cherry Creek. It was rented by the sheriff for that purpose and prisoners were first confined in it about January 1, 1862." Sam Howe recalled that the "first jail" was at what is now 1437 Blake Street (on the east side of Cherry Creek), a leaky old structure that burned in the spring of 1863. Howe did not mention its date of origin. The next jail-

Eighteen months later, in mid-March 1930, Howe took to his bed, unable to repel an influenza attack complicated by the effects of old age and a lifetime of fragile health. His final two weeks were spent in his back bedroom of the Barwick home. The old detective murmured "goodbye" and died at thirty minutes past noon, April 4, 1930, at age ninety.[93] The only survivor was the Denver Police Department.

The Colorado Historical Society received Sam Howe's cherished scrapbooks on November 21, 1939, 100 years and five weeks after Sam Howe's birth as Simeon Hunt.[94] For the next forty-one years the books were available for consultation with no restrictions,

house, Howe said, was at the city hall in the middle of Cherry Creek, which washed away in the flood of 1864. From 1864 to 1866 the jail was in a rickety log cabin with daylight shining between the logs at what would now be 1319 Market Street. This building was an early home of William N. Byers's *Rocky Mountain News*, published there from December 8, 1859, to the spring of 1861. The Butterick Meat Market building at 1351 Thirteenth Street may have been the next jail, serving from 1866 to completion of the new city hall in 1883. The Butterick was a one-story structure that may have been difficult to leave but not to enter, as the *Daily Denver Gazette* reported on June 27, 1865: "The market of L. Butterick, Esq., was broken into on Sunday night, and about $60 in money, besides papers which are of no value to him alone, stolen. [The marshals] are after the gentleman!" The new city hall was at Fourteenth and Larimer Streets and contained the fire department, the police department, and the jail in the basement. The Rider dissertation throughout discusses the dreadful conditions within Denver's early jails.

When Sam Howe reported for duty on his first day, January 13, 1873, the city marshal's office ("police headquarters") was in the Crowe and Clark Building on Market (then Holladay) Street near Fifteenth (then F) Street, at what later would be 1530 Market Street. A year later, 1874, when the first real Denver Police Department came into being, police headquarters were "opposite the American House" hotel, which was at the northeast corner of Sixteenth and Blake Streets. In 1876 headquarters became 1517 Lawrence Street, moving across the street in 1877 to 1518 Lawrence Street where they remained until completion of city hall. Data here are from the sources cited plus Sam Howe notes and *Denver Municipal Facts*, December 25, 1909; the RMN, September 20, 1897; and the RD.

4. DTI, January 1, 1903.

5. RD, p. 65, quoting the RMN, August 11, 1864. Rider wrote that the city paid for the police stars, the only items of equipment purchased by the city. The men wore civilian clothing and carried their own weapons. Denver's police badges and uniforms are discussed in Chapter 7.

6. *Denver Evening Post*, August 22, 1899.

7. RD, p. 96.

8. DR, January 12, 1913.

9. Howe's recollection of Denver's first police uniforms and how the money was raised to purchase them may have been faulty. See this chapter, note 23.

10. SHS 32, inside front cover, and p. 1, no number assigned, from the DR, January 12, 1913. See Chapter 7 for a discussion of fees and rewards and their influences and consequences on early Denver law enforcement. An 1879 police personnel deployment list says Sam Howe was assigned to day patrol on Lawrence Street, a less dangerous detail than Blake Street. Howe is not quoted as ever mentioning duty on Lawrence Street. RD, p. 190.

11. RD, pp. 112–113, from a Howe memoir in the DR, January 12, 1913. In his many reminiscences Howe often related such tales of daring. Given Howe's physical stature and shy nature, it is difficult to envision how he could accomplish such feats, but in retrospect it is remarkable that he never is recorded as having been injured or wounded on the job. Some early West chroniclers have written that gunfighters would never deface their weapons by carving notches for each man killed.

12. RD, p. 108, quoting the DTR, April 11, 1873, pp. 2, 4. The Rider dissertation should be consulted by those seeking rosters of the ceaselessly changing Denver police personnel system and the political influences causing the constant upheaval.

13. DP, May 27, 1917.

14. RD, p. 137.

15. Ibid., p. 158.

16. DR, January 13, 1903.

17. Ibid., January 18, 1897; DTI, January 1, 1903.

18. Prassel, *The Western Peace Officer*, p. 82, quoting the *Denver Tribune-Republican*, April 18, 1886.

19. DR, January 12, 1913; Anne Curtis Knapp, "Making an Orderly Society: Criminal Justice in Denver, Colorado, 1858–1900," unpublished Ph.D. diss., University of California at San Diego, 1983, pp. 62–63. This final statement assumes that drinks were a dollar each—quadruple the cost in other contemporary accounts cited in this book.

20. Denver was not the only Colorado municipality to use the fee-and-reward system. In July 1876 the town council in Lake City set the reward rate for day officers at five dollars for each arrest and conviction. The two officers on duty at night received a flat salary of fifty dollars a month, which suggests that far more crime was perpetrated during the day than at night. See Thomas Gray Thompson, "Early Development of Lake City, Colorado," *Colorado Magazine*, April 1963, p. 98. Gunnison County Sheriff C. W. "Doc" Shores, in his *Memoirs of a Lawman* (Denver: Sage, 1962), pp. 183, 259, wrote that "a sheriff in those days had to depend on rewards to round out his

income" and recalled being paid $3,000 by the Denver and Rio Grande Railroad and an additional $1,000 by the federal government—huge amounts in the early 1880s—for helping solve an important train robbery. Shores was already on the federal payroll as deputy U.S. marshal for western Colorado. For a discussion of the fee-and-reward system's influence on early Denver justice, see Knapp, "Making an Orderly Society," pp. 55–56.

21. See SHS 27: 48576, from the DP, January 28, 1908. Howe's recollection of the saloons and gambling parlors using candles is from the DR, January 12, 1913. This article was written in the first person by Howe and is the closest document we have to an autobiography.

22. For police caps and Mayor Case's edict, see RD, pp. 115–118. The reader will learn that thirty years would pass before Denver's policemen could be described as a group as temperate, moral, and gentlemanly.

23. In the lengthy autobiography published in the DR on January 12, 1913, Howe attributed the first Denver police uniforms and funding thereof to a five-dollar-admission policemen's ball at Governor's Hall, Fifteenth and Blake Streets, on Thanksgiving night, 1874. He repeated that statement in many interviews during his lifetime; it is almost as if Howe did not attend the 1873 ball and had never heard of it. The 1873 ball was on December 18, not December 19, as announced in advance in the *Times* and *Tribune*, and $1,500 was raised. Police uniforms in the early years continued to change. When the genuine police department was founded in April 1874, Denver's police began wearing "dove-colored felt hats" followed shortly by "Panama hats"; shield-shaped badges instead of stars; and, during the winter of 1875–1876, the first official overcoats. See RD, pp. 133–135. With reference to Sam Howe's new beat, in all his reminiscences he asserted that for the ten years of 1873–1883 he walked "the tough Blake Street beat"—not Lawrence and Holladay Streets.

24. RMN, August 8, 1874. His men—and there were some new names to the roster—and their badge numbers were John Holland, 1; Ed Burke, 2; H. C. Sherman, 3; W. J. Phillips, 4; Sam Howe, 5; D. W. Mays (sometimes Mayes), 6; Joseph O. Moore, 7; Jesse Benton, 8; Charles Whitcomb, 9; Frank A. Robinson (sometimes Robertson), 10; Addison "Ad" Sanders, 11; N. W. Smith, 12; and William R. Hickey, 13. Jerome C. Smiley wrote in his *History of Denver* (pp. 632–651) that abolishing the marshal system was among several city organizational changes in 1874. Not only was the marshal's job eliminated and replaced by a chief of police, but the Arapahoe County (Colorado Territory) treasurer became ex-officio city collector, and the two police justices were replaced by one police magistrate. As early as 1861, George E. Thornton was referred to as Denver's "chief of police," and that designation was used loosely during the next dozen years, although there could be no police chief when there was no police department. John McCallin is regarded as Denver's first real police chief, 1874.

Following are the destinies of Denver's first policemen, as recorded by Sam Howe in 1903. John McCallin died in 1876. Holland, who joined the city marshal's office in 1872, a year before Sam Howe, retired as a police patrol wagon driver in about 1900 and remained in Denver. Burke moved to California. Sherman, who was Sam Howe's first patrol partner on the Blake Street day beat, was the proprietor of a hotel in Cherryvale, Kansas, in 1888—the last known record of him. Phillips was a Denver insurance agent, and Mays remained in Denver. Moore, Hickey, and Whitcomb were deceased, and Sanders was a physician in California. Only Sam Howe was still with the police department, and he remained there for another eighteen years.

25. SHS 12: 5538–5547, from undetermined newspapers April 21–25, 1891. Although Howe is described in these sources as avoiding publicity, he delighted anybody willing to hear his stories.

26. Ibid., 5569, from the DTI of June 17, 1891.

27. For a general description of policemen in the late nineteenth century, see Otto L. Bettman, *The Good Old Days—They Were Terrible!* (New York: Random House, 1974), pp. 92–93.

28. SHS 12: 5550, from the DR of May 2, 1891. Officer Stevens was a quick apparition on the Denver crime-fighting scene: no policeman by that name is listed in the city directories of 1890, 1891, or 1892.

29. RMN, June 8, 1885.

30. SHS 12: 5586, from the RMN, July 19, 1891.

31. This episode illustrates that Detective Sam Howe preserved accounts of police misbehavior, which may not have pleased the police department, but Howe seems to have proceeded undeterred. This instance of a policeman supposedly beating a crippled newsboy is in SHS 13: 6138, from the DTI, February 5, 1892.

32. DTI, February 8, 1892. It seems in retrospect that if Officer Peterson interfered with Officer Izett's slapping the crippled newsboy, witnesses at the scene would have observed it and come forth during the investigation. It is

also possible that the handicapped victim was persuaded to adjust his story. Robert W. Speer was a member of the Fire and Police Board at the time, and John F. Farley was chief of police.

33. *Rules and Regulations of the Police Department*, City of Denver, 1886.

34. RD, p. 225, from the DTR (weekly), June 8, 1881. The fight between Sergeant Ryan and Patrolman Lawrence was reported in the DTI, July 17 and 18, 1882.

35. RD, pp. 349–350. The case of the weary detectives was reported in the DP, April 25, 1900.

36. Ibid., p. 290, from the DTI, November 12, 1885.

37. Ibid., p. 409, from the DR, December 10, 1894. For John Farley, see Mary M. Farley and Marcella E. Dillon, *The Farley Scrapbook: Biography of John F. Farley* (n.d., n.p., copy in the library of the Colorado Historical Society, Denver); also see J. Anthony Lukas, *Big Trouble* (New York: Simon and Schuster, 1997), p. 191.

38. SHS 13: 7176, date and originating newspaper story undesignated.

39. Ibid., 13: 6844, from the *Denver Evening Post*, undetermined date.

40. Ibid., 13: 6906 and 7143, from unspecified newspapers and dates.

41. DP, August 3, 1908.

42. SHS 18: 17581, from the DTI, December 31, 1898. Denver police were concerned about understaffing as early as 1877. Because of political squabbling, during October of that year the regular force was reduced briefly to only two men, Sam Howe and H. C. Sherman. With no leadership, one of the men agreed to be on duty at night, the other during the day. Very quickly the town council appointed four "special" officers, including W. R. Hickey, who eventually became chief. By the following January, only seven full-time policemen, including the chief, were trying to patrol a city of 25,000. All but one of the men, however, were considered experienced and were aware of what the *Rocky Mountain Herald* referred to as the "gilted palaces of sin and shame" and the opium dens where "many an outcast sought oblivion in the deadly narcotic." See RD, pp. 168–171. Additional information regarding Denver's "Hop Alley" and opium dens will be found in subsequent chapters.

43. DR, June 30, 1897. More regarding the professionalism of Denver police will be found in Chapter 7.

44. RD, 128–129, from the RMN, March 25, 1874. Later added to these rules were provisions that officers should pay their debts, subject to forfeiture of pay, reprimand, or dismissal.

45. Police Chief A. W. Kellogg's doomed experiment in censoring the news is documented in SHS 13: 8602. Additional details regarding this odd episode are found in the newspapers cited on February 21, 1894, ff. The City Hall War of March 1894 and its causes are thoroughly discussed in all histories of Denver.

46. Prassel, *The Western Peace Officer*, p. 82, quoting the *Denver Tribune-Republican*, April 18, 1886.

47. DP, December 21, 1899.

48. Sam Howe's initial scrapbooks, 1873 to 1883, are not known to have survived, and Howe mentioned only obliquely once or twice that they ever existed. He was far prouder of his 1883–1920 series of scrapbooks, on which this book is based.

49. For Sam Howe's resignation from the Denver police force, see the RMN, January 6, 1880. This entry does not state that he was joining the Arapahoe County Sheriff's Department, but other sources identify that as the case. For Sam Howe's brief service as an Arapahoe County deputy sheriff, see RD, pp. 190, 192. In no known interview did Howe ever refer to these three months as an Arapahoe County deputy sheriff. A copy of Howe's commission as a Gunnison "special policeman" is in the author's possession. The reference to Howe being night marshal of Gunnison is in the memoirs of Cyrus Wells "Doc" Shores, Gunnison County sheriff from 1884 to 1892; see Shores, *Memoirs of a Lawman*, pp. 137–138. Howe rarely, and even then only in passing, mentioned his Gunnison service.

50. Although Doc Shores and the *Gunnison Review* are obviously speaking of the same crime, the *Review* identifies suspected murderer Breckenridge as "Chester Gibbs." The discrepancy cannot be explained.

51. For Doc Shores and Sam Howe, see Shores, *Memoirs of a Lawman*, pp. 199–200. Doc Shores's duties as a deputy U.S. marshal sometimes led him to Telluride, a fairly rough town at the time. There Shores became acquainted with Jim Clark, who was marshal of Telluride from 1887 until 1895 when he was ambushed and killed on a Telluride street. Clark was a conscientious lawman, fearless and with a lightning draw; was a crack shot; and was said to be the first to bring any order to Telluride. But Clark had a hot temper, and although he kept strict peace in Telluride, outside the city limits he would put on a disguise and participate in holdups. Nonetheless, Doc Shores

and Jim Clark became fast friends, and Shores soon noted that Clark had a special loathing for prostitutes. In his memoirs (pp. 199–200) Shores recalled the night he and Clark were walking through the red light district of Telluride: "The madam of a sporting house came outside, leading a little dog which trotted along beside her. 'Marshal,' she said, walking up to us, 'my dog here is getting to be very old, and I would appreciate it if you would take him out of town sometime soon and kill him for me.' Clark immediately jerked out his six-shooter and shot the dog between the shoulders, killing him instantly. The woman screamed, and it looked for a moment as if she was going to faint. Clark sheathed his gun and walked right along as if nothing had happened. 'Damn those women,' he said in disgust. 'I don't even like to talk to them.' I noticed that he always cut short his conversations with sporting women, and as the above incident indicated, he seemed unduly prejudiced against them. I always suspected that some tough woman had once made trouble for him to cause this deep and undying hatred for prostitutes."

52. The Breckenridge murder investigation is in Shores, *Memoirs of a Lawman*, pp. 137–139. The following October (1880), Howe was briefly back in Gunnison to testify in a murder case (see the RMN, October 27, 1880). The *Gunnison Review*, a weekly, failed to note Sam Howe's departure from town, but the *Review* seemed not greatly attentive to local news: the paper afforded only a paragraph to a Gunnison visit by General Ulysses S. Grant and a bevy of accompanying dignitaries. The RMN reference that Howe was "late of the [Denver] sheriff's office" is echoed in a subsequent clipping (RMN, October 27, 1880) also identifying him as an Arapahoe County deputy sheriff.

53. RD, pp. 216–217, from the DR, February 19, 1881. See also RD, pp. 182–245.

54. Ibid., p. 218, from the DTR, March 29, 1881. David J. Cook was a lawman known throughout Colorado and the West. In addition to serving as a Denver marshal and police chief, Cook was a territorial sheriff of Arapahoe County, a U.S. deputy marshal, and a major general in the Colorado militia. Cook also operated the Rocky Mountain Detective Association, an effective private police agency, and he was the man to whom Denver's procession of nonprofessional police chiefs turned when they needed help. See RD, pp. 182–245.

55. See the DR, January 12, 1913. Sam Howe is not listed on the police roster published on April 7, 1882, although all other evidence testifies that he was a patrolman in good standing at that time, being promoted to detective the next year. Howe's absence from this roster cannot be accounted for. See "City Council Proceedings, April 6, 1882," DR, April 7, 1882, quoted in RD, p. 240. Similarly, there appears to be no reason for the absence of Howe's name from the roster of January 15, 1884. See RD, p. 253.

56. Howe's method of indexing was inconsistent, changing in form over the years and at times lapsing altogether. See Appendix A for the listing of indexed scrapbooks. See also SHS 28: inside front cover.

57. The Peter Dahlgren matter is in SHS 22: 30366, from the RMN of an unspecified and undetermined 1903 date.

58. This reference in 1900 to the fact that Howe had maintained his books for "twenty-five years" suggests that he began his scrapbook project in 1875 (actually, probably when he became a patrolman in 1873) rather than in 1883, when he became a detective. Howe is referred to as "perhaps the best-known city official in Denver" in the DR, January 13, 1903.

59. SHS 15: inside front cover, from the DTI, January 5, 1895; see also the DTI, October 21, 1900.

60. DTI, August 17, 1901.

61. SHS 20: 23000, from the *Denver Sunday Post*, December 23, 1900.

62. RMN, February 4, 1903.

63. DR, January 13, 1903.

64. DP, February 4, 1905, contains historical notes regarding capital punishment in Colorado. A thorough discussion of Colorado lynchings is in Stephen J. Leonard, "Judge Lynch in Colorado, 1859–1919," *Colorado Heritage*, autumn 2000. The magazine also contains new data on important early Colorado criminals, including the Espinosa brothers, in 2001 still Colorado's record-holding serial murderers; Tom Horn and the 1891 Denver & Rio Grande Railroad holdup at Cotopaxi, near Salida; Bat Masterson's years in Denver; the Reynolds gang of stagecoach bandits, which struck the Fairplay vicinity in 1863; several other legendary Colorado badmen such as Jack Slade, Butch Cassidy, Doc Holliday, Bob Ford, and Jefferson Randolph "Soapy" Smith; and the surprising fate of train robber Thomas "Black Jack" Ketchum.

65. DT, April 10, 1897.

66. Mayor Buckingham's generous gesture is recorded in RD, p. 230, from the DTI, July 11, 1877. The action of

Mayor Sopris is in RD, p. 231, from the DTR, January 3, 1878.

67. *Denver Police Department Pictorial Review and History*, p. 28. For escapes, see the RMN, April 2, 1879, and RD, pp. 228–229, from the DTI (daily), November 1, 1879, and the DTI (weekly), July 20, 1881.

68. "Newton Vorce, Frontiersman, Passes Away," *The Trail*, June 1924, pp. 21–22. The article quotes Vorce's death story from the DP, date unspecified. The encounter with John Chivington's posse was far from Vorce's final confrontation with the law: several years later he shot out every new acetylene streetlight, "of which the town was very proud," in Evans, Colorado, but defied arrest by the townspeople. He also had scrapes with the law in Byers and Greeley. Vorce worked as a cowpuncher near Roggen until age ninety-one, and upon his death left a widow, Ida, whom he married when he was eighty. Chivington gained infamy twenty-five years earlier when he led a troop of Colorado Volunteers in the "Sand Creek Massacre," judged by history as a white man's slaughter of peaceful Indians.

69. Patrolman Charles Secrest (not an acknowledged ancestor of the author) in 1901 shot a citizen to death, but the killing was ruled self-defense. In February 1906, however, Secrest—drunk for days and now known as one of the "rottenest" (Sam Howe's description) policemen in the West—shot a man in the back during a barroom brawl and was sent to the Cañon City penitentiary for murder. Police Chief Mike "Third Degree" Delaney argued that he had tried to fire Secrest, but bureaucracy prevented it. Veteran officers regarded the Secrest incident as perhaps the most reckless police infraction to that time. See Denver newspapers of February 9, 1906, ff.

70. For the account of Howe and his colleagues being hauled into court, see the RMN, May 14, 1879.

71. DR, January 3, 1903.

72. Possibly because of newspaper reporters' errors or Sam Howe's confusion over dates and circumstances, contradictions exist and accounts become muddied with regard to his first term as detective chief with the Denver police and why that term ended. According to SHS 15, unnumbered clipping on page 1 from the DTI, January 5, 1895, Howe was appointed chief of detectives in July 1889 and served for two years, until July 1891. Those dates are different from those cited in the text at this point. No reason is given for his removal. The *Times* account says he was reappointed on April 11, 1893, serving two months until the following June "when he resigned, owing to a

threatened serious illness . . . which failed to materialize." A better reason for the "resignation," however, might be Howe's disapproval of the leadership of Populist Governor Davis H. Waite. See Chapter 7.

73. The story of Sam Howe's run-in with Judge Albert S. Frost was a topic Howe would rather have avoided, but it is told in the DR, January 18, 1897.

74. SHS 23: 23000, from the *Denver Sunday Post*, December 23, 1900.

75. Ibid., 27: 48576, from the DP, January 26, 1908. This feature story by Robert Emmett Harvey is the most extensive newspaper biography of Howe.

76. Ibid., 18: 16510, from the DTI, May 27, 1898.

77. Ibid., 27: 48576, from the DP, January 26, 1908.

78. Armstrong had impressive durability in a time when police chiefs were almost always selected from nonpolice sources and served political appointments at the pleasure of the mayor. Armstrong also served at the pleasure of his mayors, but he was far more resilient than most. Armstrong was police chief April 17, 1894–March 1, 1895; April 11, 1901–June 4, 1904; June 26, 1908–May 31, 1912; and May 17, 1916–January 10, 1921. When not police chief, he often was detective chief.

79. SHS 18: 19451, from the DR, December 10, 1899. Howe's difficulties in 1891 with Detective Loar and Howe's resultant assignment as detective chief are in George W. Walling and A. Kaufmann, *Recollections of a New York Chief of Police and Historical Supplement of the Denver Police* (New York: Caxton, 1887), p. 661. Howe's removal from the pawnshop detail and his new job as the chief's aide are in SHS 19: 21583, from the RMN, July 13, 1900.

80. As quoted in SHS 20: 23000.

81. Ibid., 23: 33500.

82. DTI, July 12, 1901. The hanging of Andrew Green was one of nineteenth-century Colorado's largest spectacles. Green was convicted of the May 19, 1886, holdup-murder of Denver streetcar driver James Whitnah, with the execution following only nine weeks later. Fifteen thousand to 20,000 "boisterous men, women, and children" witnessed the hanging along the south side of Cherry Creek midway between the Broadway and Colfax bridges, in the later vicinity of West Tenth Avenue at Elati Street. Green's neck was not broken, resulting in a lingering death, and the body was left swinging into the night. Green at least was afforded a scaffold rather than the cottonwood tree farther down Cherry Creek where earlier criminals swung into eternity. See William M. King, *Going to Meet a*

This remarkable assemblage of former Denver police and fire chiefs (and one distinguished old sheriff) gathered circa 1905 outside city hall, which housed fire and police headquarters at Fourteenth and Larimer Streets. The lawmen wore small, commemorative, circle-star retired badges, and the firemen pinned on a different design. Neither badge is known to collectors today. Identifications were written at some interval following the photo by a person obviously acquainted with the group. Several of those present were close old-time colleagues of Detective Sam Howe. As inscribed on the photo, the men are, standing, left to right: *Dan Mays, police chief 1877–1878; George Duggan, fire chief 1881; John L. Russell, police chief 1896; U.S. Senator Charles S. Thomas, always a supporter of Denver's fire- and policemen; Henry Brady, police chief 1887; Hamilton Armstrong, police chief 1894, 1901, 1908, 1916 (Armstrong wears a current badge rather than a retired badge); and A. W. Kellogg, police chief 1893.* Seated from left: *Phil Trounstine, fire chief 1872; William E. Roberts, fire chief April 1894–April 1895 and September 1897–April 30, 1903; John Farley, police chief 1893 (and subsequent); Joseph L. Bailey, fire chief 1873; David J. Cook, fire chief, sheriff, and interim police chief during various crises in 1867, 1868, 1869, 1880, and subsequent years; William A. "Billy" Smith, police chief 1874, 1883–1885; James Lomery, police chief 1881–1883. The photograph features the best and worst of Denver law enforcement during the final quarter of the nineteenth century. Henry Brady* (third from right, standing) *was without question the most corrupt person ever to serve as a Denver police chief, and it is surprising that he had the courage to show up for this picture, let alone stand next to Hamilton Armstrong. John Farley* (third from left, seated) *was a police chief of scruples even though he had to work under Mayor Robert W. "Boss" Speer, and Dave Cook* (third from right, seated) *was one of the great lawmen of the Rocky Mountain West. Cook advised his colleagues: "Never hit a prisoner over the head with your pistol, because you may afterwards want to use your weapon and find it disabled."*

Man: Denver's Last Legal Public Execution (Niwot: University Press of Colorado, 1990).

83. In the January 19, 1882, edition.

84. DP, August 6, 1911.

85. SHS 32: 70675, from the DP, date unspecified.

86. Letter from Sam Howe to W. J. Phillips, February 10, 1920, in the W. J. Phillips collection, box 493, Colorado Historical Society Library.

87. Unidentified newspaper clipping, ibid. Frank A. Robinson died at age eighty-four at his home at 624 West Colfax Avenue on November 2, 1927. A graduate mining engineer, he came west in 1868 to seek his fortune as an assayer. He soon became discouraged with the mining business, however, and entered law enforcement. Only Sam Howe outlived him as a member of Denver's first police department. See "The Passing of the Pioneer," *The Trail*, November 1927.

88. SHS 26: inside front cover; see also "Denver Police Bulletin," April 5, 1930.

89. Denver Police Department memorandum, copy in the author's possession.

90. On September 30, 1897, Denver ex-marshals, ex-chiefs of police, and ex–fire chiefs founded a club whose members thereafter met for social purposes on the first day of each new year. See RD, pp. 461–462, and the DTI, October 1, 1897.

91. SHS 26: inside front cover.

92. DP, October 16, 1928.

93. Ibid., April 4, 1930; see also RMN, April 5, 1930. Services were held four days later at the Olinger Mortuary drawing room, with 150 of Sam Howe's police colleagues, Grand Army of the Republic comrades, and other friends in attendance. The Reverend George Sevier said, "No one who knew him ever heard him speak an unkind word." The police traffic squad escorted the body to Riverside Cemetery.

94. Denver Police Department memorandum, November 21, 1939, copy in the author's possession.

Part II

The Indulgences

3

"Hordes of Villains and the Wages of Sin"

T HE AREA THAT BECAME DENVER was first permanently populated by whites in the autumn
of 1858. For its initial month the infant
hamlet was peaceable. This Pollyanna existence ended abruptly in late September when the
settlement's first crime of record occurred. A man
named Vincent shot a John Atwell—not fatally—and
then attempted to escape into the underbrush along
the banks of the Platte.

A group of friendly Indians intercepted the fleeing Vincent and returned him to the settlers encamped
at the Denver City site. One settler, William B. Parsons, presided at the prompt trial. The verdict, probably by a people's jury, was that Vincent must give
his horse to Atwell and would then be furnished ten
days' rations and be banished from the territory on
foot. Should he return, he would be shot on sight. He
departed.[1]

That may have been Denver's first crime, but the
initial *serious* misdeed in the Denver vicinity took place

seven months later, on April 7, 1859, when John Stuffle
shot his brother-in-law Arthur Binegraff (or Benegraff)
in the head and made off with Binegraff's small pouch
of gold dust. (These names have customarily been
spelled Stoefel and Biencroff; see note 2, this chapter.)
The incident occurred someplace west of where Clear
Creek meets the South Platte River, perhaps in the
vicinity of present-day Arvada.

It was the first recorded murder in the frontier
communities at the foot of the Rockies. Stuffle traveled to Denver, where he spent the stolen gold with
storekeeper "Uncle Dick" Wootton. Stuffle acted so
strangely that suspicions were aroused, and a search
revealed the body of the slain Binegraff. Stuffle was
arrested and promptly confessed. The next day, April
8, he was afforded a somber and orderly trial before a
"People's Court," presided over, according to some accounts, by acting county judge H.P.A. Smith. Stuffle
again admitted that he had committed the murder,
adding that he had accompanied Binegraff all the way

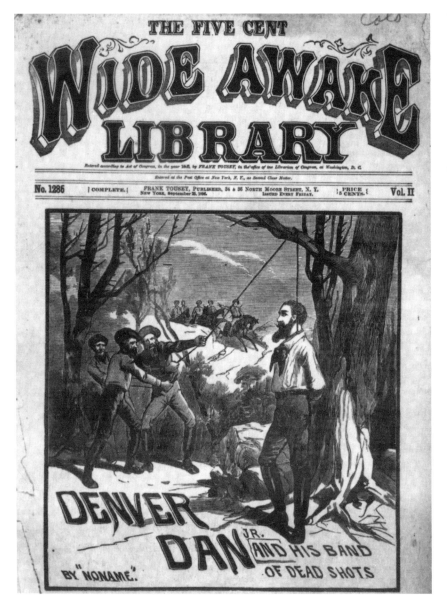

The perception of frontier Colorado as a lawless shoot-'em-up territory was reinforced by images such as this half-dime magazine cover of September 25, 1896. Here "Denver Dan Jr. and his band of dead shots" gallop to the rescue of an innocent man about to be lynched by a trio of ruffians. Despite the image projected by such illustrations, early Colorado lawmen sometimes had to wait weeks for the next serious crime.

a clergyman boarded a two-horse wagon and were driven to what today would be Tenth and Wazee (or Market) Streets. There one end of the rope was placed around Stuffle's neck and another over a tree limb. The pastor and Noisy Tom kneeled in the wagon to pray, but Stuffle did not do likewise until Noisy Tom poked the doomed man in the ribs and informed him that this was no time to "act like a heathen." The wagon was driven from under the tree, and Stuffle swung into eternity.

During the remainder of 1859, only two additional murders and one duel took place in tiny Denver City, including its equally tiny companion communities of Auraria, on the south bank of Cherry Creek, and Highland, across the South Platte River to the west. On September 8 Thomas G. Wildman wrote from Denver City to his mother and sister (cited in Hafen and Hafen):

from the states to kill and rob him after he struck gold. The verdict was "guilty," and the decision of what to do with the murderer was given to the assembled crowd. There was no jail and hence no place to lodge him. Almost in one voice the crowd chanted "Hang him! Hang him!" An old frontiersman, a well-known character called "Noisy Tom," was recruited to be the executioner.

Historian Jerome C. Smiley (pp. 339–340) wrote Wootton's recollection that Noisy Tom, Stuffle, and

There was one man killed in Auraria last week, and the people hung one night before last in Golden City [Golden], which is about 12 miles from here, for shooting at another man. There is to be a Vigilance Committee organized in town this evening. We have no jail here and no laws in fact, and the object of the Committee is to give all persons accused of crime a fair trial and punish them according to their deserts. It is thought that stabbing and drunkenness will be rampant here this winter, and we think that the row-dies and gamblers will be more careful when they find out that we are organized and that all the first men of the town are determined to punish crime. . . . Certainly, a more reckless, unprincipled set of men never got together in one place than here.[2]

And prospector William Hedges wrote of the new towns on Cherry Creek: "Denver was a most lively town, in any and all kinds of wickedness. I doubt that . . . there was ever a place on this continent, where [a] great[er] amount of evil to the square acre was so spontaneously and openly developed."[3]

As with any western frontier community, a quartet of indulgences soon surfaced in early Denver City and Auraria: overimbibing (which frequently led to the other three), homicide, gambling, and—tentatively at first—prostitution. Those four inevitably led to a fifth: local government corruption. Their interrelationships are examined in this book.

Surveyor and mining engineer Hal Sayre entered Denver in June 1859. Many years he later recalled that all the hardworking men were in the mountains, with only the slackers remaining in town:

We found here a considerable number of bustling and, for the most part, boastful men; although we soon discovered that the more enterprising members of the community had gone into the mountains. A large percentage of those remaining apparently had no other occupation than that of gambling. There were several [gambling] resorts, all of them wide open, but the largest of them was an immense hall which then and for a long time afterward was known as the Elephant Corral. In this building there were congregated several hundred men, all engaged in "bucking the tiger," vigorously and in a variety of ways. [For the Elephant Corral, also see p. 85 in this volume.]

I recall that there was immense stacks of gold on the tables, which you may believe appealed strongly to my young imagination. I wondered if all of it was Pike's Peak gold, and without a single longing for any of the treasure thus displayed, turned away from the supposed temptation there presented with a determination to go and find some of the yellow stuff for myself. In other words, I discovered nothing in Denver to tempt me to remain and, finding my compan-

ions to be like-minded, was again on the road within two or three days.[4]

When he arrived in Denver City/Auraria during mid-July 1860, Frank Hall—later a federal marshal serving in Colorado, a Colorado territorial official, and one of the state's foremost historians—gave this account of his first night on the town:

We camped over on the bottom [the Platte River bottoms] near where Daniel Witter's residence now stands. In the evening we wandered over into town. A particularly fascinating saloon and billiard room had just been opened on Ferry Street [in Auraria; later Eleventh Street], and we just strolled in. I had just one solitary gold dollar left. I need not tell you the sequel. When I walked out of that place I was a penniless orphan a thousand miles from home. The next place visited was Denver hall, on Blake street, which fairly yawned to receive us. We entered that seductive menagerie, conscious if there was nothing to be gained we had nothing to lose. Three-card monte, faro, Spanish monte, chuck a luck, and the rest of the animals were fleecing and stripping victims by the score. Men bet away upon these games everything they had in the world, but their immortal souls, on the turn of a card.[5]

When Presbyterian preacher A. T. Rankin arrived from his mission station in eastern Kansas to impart his faith to the Colorado goldfields, he recorded in his diary on July 31, 1860:

Arrived at Denver this A.M. at 4 o'clock, seven days hard staging . . . made arrangements [for] preaching next Sabbath. Went to the printing office to get my appointment announced in the paper, while there a man rushed in, caught the editor by the collar, drew a pistol, and threatened to murder him on the spot. . . . A pretty ruff [sic] introduction to Denver.

Pastor Rankin lasted only six months, writing in his diary on the following December 7: "I am now ready to be off to America."[6]

Gambling was made legal under Denver's initial city charter in 1861 and, as the reader will observe, was legal off and on for the next forty years. The charter granted the town council wide regulatory powers, including the authority to license "billiard-tables and bowling alleys, tippling houses, dram-shops, gambling-houses, bawdy-houses and other disorderly houses." The charter also gave the council the power to suppress any gambling and bawdy houses, but the city leaders exercised that power only over those games they considered specialties of confidence artists, such as three-card monte, the strap game, the thimble game, and the patent safe game. In these, neither skill nor luck increased the player's chances of winning.

For three years anyone posting a bond of $500 and paying an annual license fee of $400 could operate keno, faro, shuffleboard, bagatelle, or card games. Gambling became so popular in Denver by 1862 that walkways were sometimes blocked by the tables of traveling gamblers. Businessmen objected, leading to passage of a measure forcing gamblers behind doors and walls.

Gamblers lost their legal cover in 1864 when the town council surrendered its regulation over vice resorts to a new Colorado Territory law suppressing gambling and gambling houses and fixing the penalty for keeping a gambling house or allowing gambling on the premises at up to a year in jail and a fine of $50 to $300. Half the fine was to go to the person informing the police of the infraction and half to the public schools.

This law, wrote historian Clyde L. King, turned out to be unacceptable to Denver. Gambling and vice, after all, had lobbying powers that were put into motion, and thus the 1865 legislature passed a "special act" exempting Denver from the gambling law and restoring the permissiveness of the 1861 charter. In all other towns and counties in Colorado Territory, the law remained in effect.

As might be expected, this resulted in an awkward and unworkable situation. The gambling dens, generally located on Denver's principal business streets, enticed their customers from blocks around with brass bands and string orchestras. The town was wide open. A customer might saunter in for a dance, step to the bar for a twenty-five-cent slug of whiskey and a cigar, and wander to either side of the hall for the gambling game of his choice.

The proliferation of vice became distasteful to some of Denver's legitimate businesspersons and upstanding citizens. The city was out of control. Thus in 1866 the territorial legislature specifically prohibited Denver from licensing gambling or gambling houses, granted Denver the power to regulate "disorderly houses and houses wherein lewd persons assemble for dancing," and gave Denver the power to license its saloons. The city council quickly fixed the cost of a license at $200 yearly for whiskey and wine and $140 yearly for beer—and at the same time set a dog license tax of $8–$12 a year. Denver, as will be seen, from its inception experienced a considerable problem with packs of marauding dogs. At one point policemen rode the city in horse and wagon, blasting away at the curs with shotguns.

The council, adhering to the legislature's instruction, duly outlawed all gambling but set the penalty so low—$10 to $100 per infraction—that it virtually amounted to a license fee. The city marshal could raid a gambling house whenever he felt the action necessary or was so inclined. Thus did the legislature's antigambling statute of 1866 provide a breeding ground for police corruption.[7]

The gambling issue faded and reemerged periodically for at least a decade. The *Denver Tribune* on February 12, 1873, carried the notice that the license of any "public house" in which gambling "or any other violation of a city ordinance" was permitted would be summarily revoked, and the city marshal "is instructed to issue strict and imperative orders to every member of his police force to use extreme vigilance." As enforcement had been an ongoing problem, the notice added darkly, "Policemen [deputy marshals] failing in the performance of their duty, in any respect, will be promptly removed by the mayor." The language suggests that the marshal may not have been inclined to discharge a deputy found looking the other way, and this served as sufficient warning to Sam Howe and the rest of the newly installed marshal's force.

Into the 1870s, no territorial or state legislation was in force to control municipal vice. Denver's charter granted no power to the city to license gambling or prostitution, but the charter did grant power to prohibit them. Thus Denver made a weak attempt to eliminate such activities, but again the fines were small, ranging from $10 to $100 for gambling and $5 to $100 for prostitution. These fines were collected in lieu of licenses. In effect, therefore, charter provisions forbidding the licensing of such establishments were circumvented, which suited the city government just fine, as gambling and prostitution—kept sufficiently under control—were deemed necessary for the economy of an emerging community such as Denver.[8]

The press initially was hopeful over what appeared to be the elimination of the gaming scourge. The *Daily Denver Gazette* exuded:

> We understand that several more arrests have been made of the sports of Denver. The gambling houses are all closed, and every one found indulging in this fashionable pastime are forthwith arraigned at the bar of the District Court. Rumor says that eighteen indictments altogether have been found against the Messrs. Heatly & [Big Ed] Chase. There seems, from the general appearance of matters and things, that a general crusade has been inaugurated against this peculiar institution.[9]

Editor William N. Byers of the *Rocky Mountain News* was more circumspect. He concluded: "It is a truth, melancholy as it is true, that strong drink and 'sport,' so-called, yet rule Denver, though not with the same despotic hand that has characterized some of the bloody periods in the earlier history of the city."[10]

Nathaniel Peter Hill, who became one of Colorado's principal mining and smelting figures and served from 1879 to 1885 as a U.S. senator from Colorado, wrote to relatives back East upon his arrival in Denver in 1864:

> The notion is universal, that no man can live here without liquor. The article is to be found everywhere. Every man has it in his pocket; in his traveling bag, in the pocket of his saddle. In getting up an outfit, whatever may be forgotten, whisky is never left out. The article used is a vile compound, made of corn and full of fusel oil.[11]

Some preferred to view Denver, however, as more cosmopolitan and sober than it actually was. One such observer was the *Daily Denver Gazette*, which saw only the best. The *Gazette* exclaimed in 1865, during one period of lawlessness:

> Our youthful city has suddenly become very dignified, seemingly forgetting her formerly riotous habits. Her most uncontrolable [*sic*] member—the mllitary [*sic*]—now sets an example of order, neatness & discipline, wonderful and admirable. An ample police force preserves peace & quiet. The almost constant discharge of firearms, accompanied by the yelling of drunken soldiers which "made night hideous," has disappeared. Now our soldiers excel the citizens in neatness of dress and decorous conduct. The time has passed when a man need fear for his life or property, and security succeeds terror.[12]

The *Gazette*'s perception was as wrong as its spelling, and the editor realized as much. Three weeks later the *Gazette* did an abrupt turnaround, and the editor scolded:

> DISCHARGE OF FIREARMS: There is scarce anything which deserves more serious denunciation in our city than the constant discharge of firearms at all hours of the night. Persons who do so, thoughtlessly, are committing a terrible wrong. When the head of the family is away in the midst of business, and the house unprotected from alarm and accidents, a revolver to be fired off close to a door is very apt to occasion fright and terror to its inmates. We know of a case of that kind which has occurred within the last few days, the lady has not yet recovered from its effects, and has kept to her bed ever since.[13]

And two months after that the *Gazette* editor's patience was nearly exhausted:

> DISGRACEFUL: That person who fired the ball the other day and hit the child cannot be found. Pretty community we are in. Cannot some person come forward and testify that some poor unfortunate beef whacker fired off a gun on Saturday afternoon. The people will then get up a crowd and lynch him sure.[14]

Such was the situation in early Denver, which, according to new arrival John Scudder, had 400 "houses," 600 "regular inhabitants," 2 blacksmith shops, "grog shops without number, [and] the gamblers are very numerous, and [have] got most of the gold in their possession." Although the new town certainly had a rougher element, the gamblers—working in three eight-hour shifts—generally regarded themselves as gentlemen. Too, they contributed generously to charities—a trait the madams of Market Street soon emulated.[15]

Among the early Denver arrivals was Amos S. Billingsley, a Presbyterian clergyman who was forty-three when he arrived in town on April 26, 1861. Later he wrote that he "'put up' at the Cherokee House on Blake Street [near what became Fifteenth Street], in the midst of business and stirring music in the gambling saloons hard by. Boarding and lodging $12 a week—fare good—quite a variety." Billingsley's religious mission in a town such as Denver was not easy. Five weeks later he wrote in his diary, with some frustration: "O my God have mercy on me. *Strange!* strange that I can live in the midst of so many sinners whose 'pulses are beating the march to hell'—prominading [*sic*] the road to ruin—piling the fagots [*sic*] for their own eternal burning. (Lord God of hosts have mercy on me), and yet feel so little for their salvation."

Although he continued to preach to appreciative congregations, Billingsley's existence in Denver was an ongoing ordeal. Funds to cover his expenses did not arrive regularly from the Presbyterian Board of Home Missions, which had dispatched him to such a godforsaken place, and passing the collection plate usually resulted in only a few dollars. With winter approaching, during October 1861 Billingsley moved to a second-floor walk-up at Sixth and St. Louis Streets in Auraria (today Tenth and Lawrence Streets). He recorded in his ledger:

> Have no chair—sit on a low box with papers on top to make it soft. No Table—no bed, save a tick of hay lying on the floor—no sheet—a borrowed pillow, no blanket but use an old faded, borrowed comfort[er]. Have a broken looking glass—Borrowed stove and a borrowed bureau.—Mice bothered me last night. Cover myself nights with my over coats and usually sleep quite well. And although thus with out all these things God is here.

Billingsley performed weddings and funerals and had men die before him: he attended Deputy City Marshal

J. C. Ritchey, age twenty-two, who was mortally shot on the street the night of February 3, 1862, and lamented to his diary: "Now getting quite gray—and surrounded with troubles and trials, with my 'soul among lions,' Yet God is my *refuge* & *strength*."[16]

Within twenty years of Billingsley's writings Denver would fancy itself a city of churches. An 1886 brochure boasted that the city had sixty-two churches, second per capita only to Brooklyn, New York. Occasionally the churches became the centers of reforms that sought unsuccessfully to close the houses of prostitution and gambling dens. At the same time, many of the properties housing the gamblers and sex dens were owned as investments by stalwart churchmen.[17]

Opportunities for social interaction were available but sparse in early Denver—especially the sorts of activities that would appeal to the more "upstanding" members of the community. For others, who composed the great majority, there were only the dens of vice for entertainment. Stan Zamonski and Teddy Keller wrote of the sociological contributions of gambling resorts and liquor parlors not only in Denver but also along the Western frontier:

> These gambling halls did serve as melting pots all over the great West. Since churches and regular meeting halls were still far distant in an unsure future, and since most cabins were dirt floored, unheated, and gloomy, lonely men gravitated toward the companionship, occasional women, and relative comforts of the saloons. Here, his tongue loosened by liquor, a man's humor sharpened and his disasters were forgotten. Here the lonely man could belly up to the bar beside mountain men and prospectors and freighters and local dignitaries and catch up on all the news and gossip.[18]

Reporter Henry Villard, traveling through what became Colorado during the summer of 1859, drew a conclusion of possible interest to later sociologists:

> The virtual absence of all laws during the spring, summer and fall of 1859, together with the large number of desperados that always infest border and especially gold countries, caused a good deal of lawlessness. It was, however, confined to the towns in which many individuals, that relied on their wits more than

their muscles and sinews for a living, flourished. The mines were nearly free from it, thereby proving that remunerative employment is the best preventative of crime.[19]

After a fairly quiet beginning, a period of rambunctiousness struck Denver in 1860, with twelve homicides, "most of them cruel, wanton murders," generally resulting from ingestion of "vile liquor retailed over most of the numerous bars," as described by historian Jerome C. Smiley.[20] On September 16, 1860, Sidney B. Morrison, who with his brother John H. established a ranch on the South Platte River just north of Denver, which became the site of Riverside Cemetery, wrote to his family in Wisconsin:

[Denver] is infested with hordes of villains of the blackest dye, murderers, thieves, and blacklegs of all kinds. It appears to be an asylum for renegades and outlaws from all the surrounding regions. Nearly every day we hear of depredations being committed. Men are found murdered on the highway, others are robbed, while thefts of stock are of frequent occurrence. An old gentleman that came through with us last fall was a few days since murdered in his house and the house burned. A vigilance committee in town commenced punishing the rascals in right good earnest; they strung up a few. But what better can we expect in a community without laws? We are neither in the Union or out of it. We are not sufficiently a territory to have laws with the power to enforce them. With what shameful neglect were we treated by that august body at Washington & also by the great father J. B. [James Buchanan]?[21]

Julia S. Lambert recalled that when her family arrived in Denver in 1860, she and her father walked up Blake Street to inspect a house they had contracted to rent: "We were within a block of our home when suddenly we heard cries, saw a man start to run, another follow, shooting at him as he ran. At the second shot the man fell dead. A wild mob gathered around and we were so frightened we ran into a store for safety" (pp. 10–11). When the crowd dispersed, it was too dark for the Lambert family to inspect the new house, so it returned to its camp near town. The Lamberts reentered town the next morning, and when they finally began to move into the house, another adventure awaited. Julia wrote:

I unpacked a pair of lava vases, a present to my mother from one of her sisters. The window being open I sat them on the window-sill. We heard a commotion outside with firing of shots and we rushed to the window to see what was the matter. Mother's beautiful vases were knocked off of the window casing and had fallen to the gravel walk below. In the street below stood a man in his shirt sleeves, his long red hair and beard blowing in the wind; in his hands he held a smoking shotgun; on the ground lay a bleeding man, beside whom stood the gray horse from which he had fallen. The man with the gun was Tom Pollock, the sheriff. As the crowd gathered closer he called, "Stand back! Stand back!"

Julia Lambert identified the man on the ground as George Steel [Steele], "who had ridden up in front of the office of the *Rocky Mountain News* and shot at the proprietor, William N. Byers. Steel was taken to the hospital where he died a few days later." She continued: "These were terrible experiences to us, and we wondered what kind of a place we had come to—having seen a man killed the day before and now this one, and for six successive days after, making eight days there was a man killed within five blocks of our house." Her frightening introduction to Denver was not over. She recalled the house on Blake Street:

The stores over which we were living had no ceiling. The flooring in our rooms serving both as floor and ceiling. The cracks were wide in some places and carpets was scarce so we had none under our beds. Sometimes we heard men talking in the store below late at night. We soon learned it was the vigilance committee who were very active, in fact they were the most active of Denver's early committees. We heard the men discussing the evidence against this or that man and often in the morning the man would be found hanging to one of the large cottonwood trees back of our house. One morning when we opened the back door we saw three men all hanging on one tree. Most of these men were horse thieves and it was not considered necessary to give them a trial. We were told by our parents to keep all we heard to ourselves or it would get us into trouble, and we did so, being too frightened to mention it.[22]

The violence of mid-1860 was condemned in July by William Newton Byers's *Rocky Mountain News*, the principal newspaper in town, whose primary target was the notorious Criterion Saloon near F (later Fifteenth) and Larimer Streets, the hangout of many of the worst gamblers and desperados. The *News* editorialized:

> The rowdies, ruffians, shoulder-hitters and bullies generally, that infest our city had better be warned in time, and at once desist from their outrages upon the people. Although our community has borne their lawless acts with a fortitude, very nearly akin to indifference, we believe that forbearance has ceased to be a virtue, and that the very next outrage will call down the vengeance of an outraged people, in a wave that will engulf not only the actors, but their aiders, abettors and sympathisers whoever they may be.[23]

The Criterion's proprietor was Charley (Charlie) Harrison, the foremost gambling entrepreneur of Denver's first decade. Little is known of Harrison's background before his arrival in the Cherry Creek settlements. In *Knights of the Green Cloth*, Robert DeArment tells that despite Harrison's secessionist leanings, he was a New York (rather than a southern) gambler before drifting westward and practicing his craft in California, Montana, and Idaho and then alighting in Salt Lake City in 1859. There Harrison rescued fellow gambler Tom Hunt as the latter was about to be lynched, and together the men fled to Denver City.[24] DeArment describes Charley Harrison:

> From the day he rode into Denver and opened a monte game at the Denver House, Harrison was the undisputed leader of the gambling element. He was a clever and fearless gambler, as most of those who tried his game learned to their sorrow. . . . A compactly built, balding man with a silky, carefully trimmed beard, Harrison was about forty years of age in 1858. Always fastidious of appearance, he usually dressed in black . . . at his hips were a pair of pearl-handled .41-caliber Colt revolvers. . . . [He was] well-groomed and quiet.[25]

On July 31, 1860, the Criterion gang proceeded to the office of *News* editor and publisher William N. Byers and bodily dragged him back to the Criterion, where they decreed that he should be killed. Harrison then took Byers into a back room and told him to slip out the door and promptly return to the *News*. When the outlaw mob, led by George Steele, discovered that Byers had "escaped," the troublemakers returned to the newspaper office, where a gunfight between the two sides followed. Hearing the commotion, townspeople began arming themselves. Struck by gunfire, Steele fled to his girlfriend's brothel and then proceeded to the suburb of Highland, where he was shot by Marshal Tom Pollock. Byers always considered Harrison to have saved his life.[26]

The Trail, forerunner of the Colorado Historical Society's original journal, the *Colorado Magazine*, printed the following story in December 1922:

> Denver physicians had hard times in the early days. Dr. O. D. Cass tells of the following experience in 1860:
>
> "One evening, while sitting in my office, the door opened and in stalked a man about five feet nine inches in height, bearded like a pard, trousers in bootlegs, his dark hair covered by a black slouch hat beneath which I saw a pair of glittering black eyes.
>
> "'Are you the doctor?'
>
> "'Yes, sir.'
>
> "'Well, I want you to go and attend my woman, who's sick.'
>
> "'What's the matter with her?'
>
> "'I don't know, but I want you to go and see her.'
>
> "'Well, my fee is $25, which must be paid before I go.'
>
> "The words had scarcely passed my lips before the stranger whipped out an ugly looking six-shooter, and, thrusting it in my face, said: 'Damn your fee; follow me, sir, and be quick about it.'
>
> "Thus positively adjured, I stood not upon the order of my going, but went at once. He led me to the door of his cabin, opened it, pointed out the patient, and immediately disappeared in the darkness. I attended her for a week and cured her. I did not in the meantime see or hear of my conductor. The woman having recovered, he came again. Striding up to my desk with the air of a cavalry brigadier, he said:
>
> "'You cured her, did you?'
>
> "'Yes, I think she's all right now.'
>
> "Laying five $20 gold pieces of Clark and Gruber's

mintage [Denver's first mint] on the desk, he added in a milder tone:

"'Will that pay you for your services?'

"'Yes, sir, abundantly, and I'm very much obliged.'

"'See, here, doctor. I've taken a notion to you. There's a good many rough fellows about town, who drink and fight and make trouble for honest people. If any of 'em ever interfere with you, you send for me. My name's Charlie Harrison.'"[27]

In the article "Gun Men of the Middle West" in *The Trail*, April 1925, writer Wilbert E. Eisele quoted Bat Masterson:

There was Charlie Harrison, the most brilliant pistol handler I ever saw, and a far more deadly shot than most of the great gun fighters. He was brave, too. Yet in a fight with a man named Jim Levy, Harrison, working with all his dazzling speed, actually missed Levy six times at close range before Levy could draw a gun. Then Levy dropped him with a single shot.[28]

Assuming that the Harrison to whom Masterson refers is Denver's Charley Harrison, and considering that Masterson is not known to have arrived in Denver until the 1880s, Harrison would have remained in Denver for a quarter century following his notoriety. That is impossible, because no mention of a Charley Harrison appears in the Denver press following the mid-1860s, and he is documented to have died in the Civil War. An alternative is that Masterson is commenting on a Harrison/Levy duel in some other city.

Historian DeArment recorded that Charley Harrison left Denver on an eastbound stage on September 19, 1861, ultimately became a Confederate colonel, and in May 1863 was killed by Osage Indians in southeastern Kansas while trying to lead a Confederate raid on Denver, where he knew considerable booty could be captured. Because of his sparse hair, the Indians did not scalp Harrison. Instead, they took his luxuriant black beard.[29]

On September 3, 1860, the *Rocky Mountain News* published two adjacent one-paragraph crime stories. The first told about horse thief John B. Bishop who was chased out of town and finally captured by citizens north of Denver, near Henderson. The second article told of a late-night bullet passing through the second story of the Broadwell House Hotel, narrowly missing a pair of lodgers. "It is remarkable," said the *News*, "that where so many accidental discharges occur, so few are injured."

Next to the stories of horse thief Bishop and the Broadwell House bullet was an item headlined "Protection":

In view of the disordered condition of our municipal affairs, and the fact that property and life are without adequate protection, it has been suggested that a police force be at once organized, under an efficient head, whose duty it shall be to perform patrol service at all hours of the day and night, and guard against incendiarism, disorder, &c. The business men of our city, particularly those who own buildings on the principal streets, could contribute by monthly subscription to maintain this force, and the tax would be a very light one, if a general interest was manifested in the matter. There are plenty of good men in our midst who would be glad to become members of such a police, and who would perform their duty well and faithfully. Will our merchants call a meeting for this purpose? Delays are dangerous.

Three months later civil strife in the Denver communities persisted. Augustus Wildman, an early arrival with his brother Thomas, addressed a letter back East to his sister Lucy Starr Haskins, relating these observations on the quality of justice. The message was dated Denver City, December 16, 1860:

We are passing through exciting times in the way of murders and murder trials. No less than three murders have been committed within the last two weeks, and two others so badly wounded that the chances are against their getting well. One of them has had his trial, and been acquitted on the ground of self-defense although it was a clear case of murder; but in this country where things are so corrupt a man can find men to swear him clear and usually be able to operate on the jury so as to be able to get an acquittal. The chances are that the other two will be hung, for although they are desperate characters they are not smart enough to engineer their case so as to get clear.

Such is life in Denver.[30]

65

At one point in 1860 the lawlessness became so acute that attorney Lewis Ledyard Weld, soon the first secretary of Colorado Territory, and his fellow lawyers gave up in despair and closed their offices, proclaiming:

NOTICE: We the undersigned, Attorneys and Counsellors at Law, convinced from a long experience here, that without organized courts, either of Kansas Territory or some other Government—which certainly do not exist—the practice is worse than useless for ourselves and the public; announce by this notice, our determination to close our Law Offices after the 31st day of the present month, and thereafter our professional business ceases, until such time as regular and constitutional tribunals of Justice are established in our midst. All cases already undertaken and in our hands, we will attend to throughout. [Signed] Perkins & Weld, Beall & Conklin, N. G. Wyatt, A. C. Ford, John C. Moore, James E. Dalliba.[31]

Apparently tiring of law work, attorney A. C. Ford, a onetime Baptist preacher and delegate to one of the Jefferson Territory conventions, took charge of a horse thievery ring. Leaving his wife behind, he attempted to flee Denver on a stagecoach, which was intercepted by a much-feared posse of vigilantes called the "Denver Tribunal." Ford was removed from the coach, which was then sent on its way, its frightened passengers wondering what was going on. The posse directed Ford to a nearby gully where he was shot dead. Smiley recorded that Ford "died bravely, but without bravado."

Charley Harrison's Criterion Saloon appears to have at least once transcended its function as a nesting place for the disorderly and disreputable in pioneer Denver. Thomas G. Wildman wrote to the *Missouri Democrat* in 1859 of a social gathering there that was

One of the finest and most fashionable things which occurred in the country at large for many a day. Never since [the call of] Pike's Peak has been heard has there been a constellation of more beauty and fashion clustered inside of one room, in the border country, than was in the saloon and hall of the "Criterion," on Larimer street, Denver city, on Thursday evening last. We were literally surprised at the magnificence and interest of the scene before us. Splendid music from a

dozen or more trained musicians fell upon a gay galaxy of some eighty to a hundred couples, and bright the lamps shown o'er fair women and brave *miners!* The beauty and the chivalry of the Rocky Mountain cities and the Platte Valley were represented in their most pleasing feature on the occasion. In style, bearing, courtesy and everything else, one could not for a moment suppose but what he was in a *recherche* crowd in the St. Louis circles, or in one of the ballrooms of Baltimore. I could not do more than justice to the affair, and to the magnificent collation, were I to make use of half the complimentary adjectives in a good-sized dictionary. The writer must confess that he has felt the frost of nearly thirty winters, but nevertheless he has been affected not a little in the region of his bachelor heart upon gazing upon these Denver City adorables as they appeared in the procession before him. Their dainty mouths, their delicately arched brows, their clouds of silken curls, and the eyes, which seemed to have put on their best looks of triumph and exultation, caused him to dream of intangible visions of love and happiness in the future, and they warmed inevitably around him.[32]

Wildman's flowery jubilations over the party at the Criterion—during Denver's roughest and most inelegant period—are inconsistent with the accepted notion of the Criterion and its crowd at that time. "Dainty mouths," "delicately arched brows," and especially "clouds of silken curls" are attributes of the Denver women of 1859 that no other chroniclers have mentioned. Perhaps it had been too long since Tom Wildman had seen a woman.[33]

Nancy Fitzhugh was among the first females emigrating to Denver, arriving during the autumn of 1859, and the reminiscence she left many decades later is pertinent at this point. Her mother died shortly after the family's arrival, and Nancy wrote:

I missed Mother greatly and also felt the scarcity of members of my own sex. There probably were not to exceed a dozen women in the entire settlement and I doubt if there were even as many children as women. Most of the women were, however, of the right class, and we made the most of one another. . . . In those days there were many parties at which there were no women present; but the men liked nothing so much as dance and this they would indulge themselves in even in the absence of our sex, half the fellows tying handkerchiefs around the left arm to indicate that they were "ladies." When there was a woman present she was rushed beyond endurance.[34]

Aside from an occasional traveling stage show, public entertainment on the Colorado Territory frontier was sparse. Some of the vagabonds brought musical instruments; an occasional parlor piano was trundled over the plains, and dances were frequent. There were foot races, boxing and wrestling matches, base ball (it was then two words), shooting and hunting, horse racing against the Indians, and an occasional duel, all of which involved wagering and all of which brought a measure of excitement. Even Governor James Denver of Kansas Territory, for whom Denver City was named, had some years previously engaged in a duel in California, and nobody thought the worse of him.[35]

Clergyman Amos Billingsley appeared shocked at the spectacle of a "prize fight" between Con Oren, a twenty-six-year-old blacksmith, and Enoch Davies, forty-two, a professional boxer. The encounter was on August 27, 1861, in a ring 2 miles north of Denver, with a crowd of 1,500 to 2,000 said to have been present. After 109 rounds of about a minute each, Davies's seconds "threw in the sponge," and Oren claimed the "Championship of Colorado." Billingsley pronounced: "How brutal! Low, demoralizing, yea *humiliating*. May God have mercy on us." Why he was in attendance if he was so horrified is not explained. Pugilist Oren later became a boxer of note in Montana and New York City.[36]

Competition in boxing and other athletic activities was frequently accompanied by wagering and drinking. The betting purses sometimes ran into the thousands of dollars even for a sandlot sports encounter. When the snow came, the action moved inside. One new arrival observed: "The principal amusement during the winter has been card playing, telling yarns, and drinking the most execrable whiskey." Another man wrote, "There is more drinking and gambling here in one day than in Kansas City in six—in fact about one-half of the population do nothing else but drink whiskey and play cards." Some years afterward

one early Denver man reminisced, "We had plenty of amusements, such as they were, but they would not be called that now."

General William Larimer, one of the few 1858 arrivals to remain in Denver, wrote: "We had occasional excitements of various kinds—sometimes a dance, sometimes a free fight. Our dances were gotten up mostly by the old mountaineers and their squaws, there being but three white women in the country for a number of months."

With the scarcity of women of temperate habits, some early prospectors satisfied their need for companionship by forming secret lodges as they had back East. The first Masonic meeting in the Auraria colony was held as early as November 3, 1858. The following autumn, 1859, fledgling theatrical groups began arriving, much to the delight of a populace beginning to run out of new things to do.[37] The most important (and durable) entertainer to gravitate toward Denver in its first twenty-four months was John S. "Jack" Langrishe, a traveling showman who staged his grand opening at Denver's second-floor (above a rowdy saloon) Apollo Hall on September 25, 1860. The show was *The Youth Who Never Saw a Woman*, and the audience loved it. Langrishe and his actor wife, Jeannette, soon took over the Apollo's theatrical operations and remained welcome Denver figures until 1871, when they departed to take their shows on the eastern and midwestern theatrical circuit. Seven years later Horace Tabor hired Langrishe to run Tabor's grand new opera house in Leadville. In 1881 Langrishe returned to Denver, building a theater far uptown near Sixteenth and Welton Streets. He left Denver for good in 1885, moving to Idaho where he became a state senator.[38]

Despite the presence of stage productions, the rough prospectors visiting Denver during this time could be burdened by an overabundance of idle time and get on each other's nerves. This phenomenon affected the respectable citizens of the community as well. At a March 5, 1860, banquet at the Broadwell House Hotel attended by prominent residents, L. W. Bliss, secretary of the provisional "Territory of Jefferson," uttered remarks regarded as personally offensive by Dr. J. S. Stone, a miners' court judge from the Black Hawk district and a member of the Jefferson Territory "legislature." Bliss was ardently antislavery; Stone was "a man of extreme southern views," but the dispute centered on the workings of Jefferson Territory and concluded with a glass of wine being dashed in Dr. Stone's face. Until this time, they had been the best of friends.[39]

Stone challenged Bliss to a duel, and the showdown occurred at 3 P.M. March 7, 1860, near what is now Fifteenth Street at the South Platte River. In accordance with the gentlemen's code governing such things, Bliss was allowed to select the weapons, which he decreed to be double-barrelled shotguns with one-ounce balls, one barrel loaded in each weapon, thirty paces. As Jerome Smiley reported, Judge Hiram P. Bennet, who was in attendance, recalled:

> When I reached the appointed place Dr. Stone had just arrived in his carriage, accompanied by his seconds and surgeon. Shortly after came Bliss, walking and carrying his shot-gun carelessly on his shoulder. He mingled in the crowd, talking and chatting with his friends and acquaintances with as much apparent ease and composure. . . . Dr. Stone walked with his surgeon apart from the crowd, looking pale and highly wrought up.

After about twenty minutes the signal was given. Stone fired first without aiming but missed. Bliss then fired, and Stone, shot in the groin, fell to the ground with the cry "Killed, O my God!" Bliss, who had intended to inflict a slight wound and not to kill, walked away, his face pallid. Stone lingered with great suffering until his death seven months later. Bliss was held blameless.[40]

The communities at Cherry Creek hurtled along the path of wickedness. An anonymous correspondent, "T," wrote from Auraria to the *Missouri Republican* (St. Louis), which published the note on July 9, 1859:

> Men are perfectly wild and crazy. . . . Gambling and whiskey drinking flourish here extensively. Tanglefoot whiskey sells for 25 cents a drink, and would almost make a man shed his toenails. I find a much better town here than I expected. Denver and Auraria, taken collectively, make quite a large place. I will write you again soon, if I do not immediately come home.[41]

Many disillusioned fortune seekers—"go-backs," they were called—did indeed immediately return home to the East or Midwest, indignantly and loudly informing everybody along the way that the Pikes Peak gold craze was a humbug. Opportunistic authors of quickly published "guide books" had fooled these vagabonds into expecting gold nuggets lying about on the surface, waiting to be scooped into gunny sacks and taken back to Illinois or Indiana or beyond. Newcomer B. T. Berkley wrote back home, for instance, that "I have heard from a reliable informant that on yesterday *thirteen nuggets of gold*, weighing [worth] seventeen hundred dollars, were taken out of a gulch which had fallen in from previous excavation in Gregory's diggings [Central City]. The owner of the specimens was charging 50 cents a sight [emphasis in the original]."[42]

Promises of quick wealth appealed in particular to a class of people with little to lose, those without roots who could easily pack up a few meager possessions and begin the arduous trek westward on the gamble that quick riches would follow. Many such adventurers were scalawags and lawbreakers, and they brought their antisocial habits westward.

This phenomenon forced the responsible community to quickly enact laws and recruit vigilance committees to greet the criminal element fleeing to the "lawless" West. An "Occasional Correspondent" wrote on August 1, 1859, from Golden City (today's Golden) to the *Missouri Republican*, commenting broadly on law and order on the mining frontier. The "Occasional Correspondent" was speaking of Golden City and not of Denver/Auraria, as some of these observations, such as saloons closing on Sundays, were not the case in the Denver communities:

> Perhaps you would like to hear something about our laws out in this wooden country, it being generally supposed that in a mixed community [?] like this there is no law but force—that might is right, and that the weaker party have in all cases to submit to the power of the stronger. Such, however, is not the case here. Our laws, or rather, the laws of the miners, are so framed as to protect the innocent and punish the guilty, and that is more than you can say of those [laws] now executed and in vogue in the States. Take them as a whole, we have as good and wholesome a code of laws as ever were enacted. They are founded on jus-

tice and right, and executed with vigor and dispatch. They are not written upon parchment, nor printed in books, but they are impressed upon the mind of the miner by their daily absence, and regarded by him in all his transactions with his fellows. In a new country like this, and more particularly in a mixed community [?] the general morals of the masses are as a matter of course more or less on the loose order, but such is not the case here, as far as my experience goes. The morals of the people are generally good, in fact much better than in the generality of the cities and towns of other parts of the country. We have no Sunday laws and yet the Sabbath is more generally respected than in St. Louis. We have no laws against selling liquor on Sunday, but the shops that sell the ardent [spirits] generally close their doors on that day. We have no license laws to prevent the sale of ardent liquors, and yet there is not one-quarter the amount drank to the man here that there is in St. Louis. During the two months that I have resided here I have never seen a drunken man that I can recollect. There is some little gambling in Denver, as the people there have little else to attend to.[43]

Denver was certainly not as wholesome as the "Occasional Correspondent" proclaimed Golden to be. Not even the judiciary was safe. Police Judge Orson Brooks, for instance, was mugged by two scoundrels at G (Sixteenth) and Lawrence Streets and robbed of $100. This brash defiling of the law and of one of its prominent practitioners quickly came to the attention of City Marshal Dave Cook, who deduced that the muggers were Sam Dougan and Ed Franklin. Cook and Deputy U.S. Marshal (first name undetermined) Haskell pursued the robbers to Golden, where Cook shot Franklin to death. Dougan was captured in Cheyenne and was returned to Denver, where he was seized by a mob and hanged from a tree on Twelfth Street between Larimer and Walnut Streets. The body was left twisting in the wind until the next day as a warning to others who might rob a judge—or anybody else.[44]

As disconcerting was the experience of a woman traveling alone on a bridge over the South Platte early one morning, who looked over the railing and saw a man suspended there by the neck, his ghastly face upturned. It was a notorious horse thief who had been caught by his neighbors and summarily dealt with.

In the West, to rob a man of his horse was to rob him of his aspirations and sometimes even his life.[45]

S. Newton Pettis, appointed by Abraham Lincoln to be associate justice of the Colorado Territorial Supreme Court, wrote in flowery Victorian prose of his initial impressions of Denver's rawness:

> The presence of the government officials has not entirely intimidated these outlaws. I yesterday visited a spot upon one of our principal streets where the last murder was committed, and but a few evenings since. The blood which marks the spot is still fresh upon the threshold where it was deposited while the victim was in the last agonies of death. I am told that he was the son of kind and indulgent parents. With the exception of a few lines of care upon the brow, the face was fair and beautiful. His infancy and childhood passed leaving his heart still pure, but as he approached manhood, he turned, little by little, from the path of rectitude and virtue; a fond and loving mother prayed and wept over him, his fair young sisters strove by every allurement of affection to win him back, but to no purpose—he at last while in youth received the wages of sin, *Death*.[46]

Notes

1. The account of "the first trial ever held here" is from "The Founders of Denver and Their Doings," address by Professor Frederick J. Stanton at the first annual reunion of the Colorado pioneers, held at the Windsor Hotel, Denver, January 25, 1881, and published in *The Trail*, May 1922, pp. 3–12.

2. History has listed the identities of the perpetrator and victim, respectively, of the first recorded murder in the Cherry Creek settlements as John Stoefel and Thomas Biencroff. The murder occurred on April 7, 1859, two weeks before publication of the first edition of the first newspaper in Denver City, William N. Byers's *Rocky Mountain News*. In Vol. 1, No. 1, of that newspaper (April 23, 1859), Byers, under the heading "Murder and Execution," wrote of the killing (stating that the trial was before probate judge S. W. Wagoner), but Byers unfortunately omitted the names of the murderer and victim. Apparently, the first published account of the murder that contains the names "Stoefel" and "Biencroff" is in the weekly

Rocky Mountain News, January 9, 1878, in a retrospective headlined "'59! 'Judge Lynch' in Colorado." We cannot know how Byers arrived at those name spellings at that late date, unless they were phonetically drawn from old-timers' verbal accounts.

There the matter rested until 1995, when a New England numismatic dealer came across in Pennsylvania a tiny, ⅛-inch-thick (and only 4½ by 2¾ inches) shirt-pocket-sized diary kept by Denver City cofounder William Larimer Jr. during the town's earliest moments. The diary is now owned by the Colorado Historical Society. Larimer, whose original home was Pennsylvania, also coestablished Denver City's first burial ground, the bleak Mount Prospect Cemetery on the present site of Cheesman Park. Under the heading "Names and dates of persons buried in Mount P[rospect] Cemetery," Larimer's diary records two burials on April 9, 1859: Arthur Binegraff (or Benegraff), "German, murdered by Jn. Stuffle," and John Stuffle, "German, Hung after a fair trial." The murderer and his victim were buried on the same day, only two days following the murder and one day after Stuffle's "fair trial."

Legend has it that murderer (age twenty-six) and victim (twenty-five) were buried in the same casket to save undertaker expenses, but we cannot know as much from the Larimer diary. The author here has chosen to use the Larimer name spellings concerning Denver's first murder instead of those used nineteen years after the fact by Byers in the *Rocky Mountain News*, on the assumption that since Binegraff and Stuffle found their final resting places in William Larimer's cemetery, he probably knew how to spell their names only a few days after burying them.

Additionally, it has been heretofore believed that Binegraff and Stuffle were the first burials in Mount Prospect Cemetery. The Larimer diary discloses that they were actually third and fourth. The first burial in Denver's first cemetery, according to Larimer's handwriting, was Abraham Kay, who died March 17, 1859, of "sudden infection of the lungs" at age twenty-six and was buried on March 20; and the second was B. Marynall (spelling?), age fifteen, who died March 26 of a fall from a horse and was buried the next day. The diary lists only five burials before Larimer apparently quit making entries: Abraham Kay, B. Marynall, Arthur Binegraff, John Stuffle, and P. T. Bassett, the latter age forty-six, who died April 16 of a "shot from Jno. Scudder pistol." Bassett and Scudder were former friends and early Denver City arrivals, who subsequently had a falling-out over business matters. Scudder shot and killed Bassett when the latter attacked him with a pick handle. Scudder fled Denver and resided for a year in Salt Lake City, but in the spring of 1860 he voluntarily returned to Denver, asked to be tried, and was quickly acquitted on grounds of self-defense. See Smiley, *History of Denver*, pp. 193, 211, 250. Bassett was buried in Mount Prospect the day after he was slain, making three of Mount Prospect's first five burials either murderers or murder victims. Some years later, remains in Mount Prospect were disinterred and moved to Riverside Cemetery, but even today Cheesman Park workers occasionally unearth a forgotten grave from Denver's first cemetery.

For the hanging of Stuffle, see James H. Pierce, "With the Green Russell Party," *The Trail*, May 1921, p. 14; LeRoy R. Hafen and Ann W. Hafen (eds.), *Reports from Colorado: The Wildman Letters, 1859–1865* (Glendale, Calif.: Arthur H. Clark, 1961), pp. 59–60; Smiley, *History of Denver*, pp. 338–339. The Wildman letters are also quoted in Alice Cochran, "Jack Langrishe and the Theater of the Mining Frontier," *Colorado Magazine*, fall 1969.

Pioneer 1858er William H. "Uncle Billy" Maine, writing in *The Trail*, April and May 1926 (pp. 3–11 and 4–6), recalled the Stuffle-Binegraff affair with a few additional details. Maine said Stuffle "seemed quite ticklish" as Noisy Tom put the noose around Stuffle's neck and would not hold still. Noisy Tom "cursed him strongly, telling him he had put a rope around a dozen men's neck in California in the time it was taking him to fix this one." Maine said that "just before they pulled the wagon out from under the prisoner, another Dutchman, who had been batching with [Stuffle], came running down, and called out, 'Jake, what I do now mit the sack of flour we shust bought?' Jake replied, 'To h___ mit you and de flour.' Those were his last words spoken."

Two of Maine's recollections regarding the lynching are at odds with all other accounts. He had Stuffle killing two men instead of one and placed the hanging tree at Eleventh and Market rather than two blocks away at Tenth and Wazee, a minor discrepancy. See "'Uncle Billy' Maine: His Own Story of Experiences in Crossing the Plains in 1858 and of Coming to Denver in 1859," *The Trail*, April 1926, pp. 3–11.

The Golden City hanging to which Thomas Wildman refers was the "precautionary lynching" of Edgar Vanover, who had a habit of getting drunk and threatening the populace. Citizens decided that if something was not done he would kill somebody. At a meeting it was asked whether to deport Vanover or lynch him. The vote was for the latter, which was carried out forthwith. Also see Smiley, *History of Denver*, pp. 338–339.

3. William Hedges, *Pike's Peak . . . or Busted: Frontier Reminiscences of Wm. Hawkins Hedges*, Herbert O. Brayer, ed. (Evanston, Ill.: Branding Iron Press, 1954), pp. 24–25, quoted in Cochran, "Jack Langrishe."

4. Quoted in Albert B. Sanford, "How the Prospectors of '59 Lived," *The Trail*, December 1925, p. 11.

5. "Address of General Frank Hall at the First Annual Re-union of the Colorado Pioneers, Held in Denver, January 25, 1881," published as "Early Recollections" in *The Trail*, October 1922, p. 13.

6. Quoted in Norman J. Bender, "Crusade of the Blue Banner in Colorado," *Colorado Magazine*, spring 1970, p. 92.

7. Anne Curtis Knapp, "Making an Orderly Society: Criminal Justice in Denver, Colorado, 1858–1900" (Ph.D. diss., University of California at San Diego, 1983), contains a thorough account of early Denver's gambling ordinances, pp. 64–70. For the Denver town council's authority to regulate and grant powers within the framework of the general laws of Colorado Territory, see Clyde Lyndon King, *The History of the Government of Denver with Special Reference to Its Relations with Public Service Corporations* (Denver: Fisher, 1911), pp. 33 ff., especially pp. 52–53. For additional gambling color, see Sandra Dallas, *Cherry Creek Gothic* (Norman: University of Oklahoma Press, 1971), pp. 201–202.

8. King, *The History of the Government of Denver*, pp. 74, 108.

9. *Daily Denver Gazette*, March 23, 1866.

10. RMN, April 30, 1867.

11. "Nathaniel P. Hill Inspects Colorado," *Colorado Magazine*, October 1956, p. 261. Fusel oil was an acrid liquid resulting from poor distilling methods.

12. *Daily Denver Gazette*, June 3, 1865. With regard to the "ample police force," it is unlikely that Marshal Joseph L. Bailey had more than four or five deputies at the time, although the Rider dissertation states that nearby military camps provided provosts marshal (military police) as early as October 1863 and at least until February 1866. The soldiers encamped near Denver were notorious for their drunkenness and disturbances, a situation that continued far beyond 1865.

13. Ibid., June 27, 1865.

14. Ibid., August 31, 1865.

15. Stanley W. Zamonski and Teddy Keller, *The '59ers* (Denver: Stanza-Harp, 1967), pp. 24, 38–39.

16. Donald F. Danker and Paul D. Riley, eds., "The Journal of Amos S. Billingsley," *Colorado Magazine*, October 1963, pp. 241–270. Denver police sergeant (retired) Ronald L. Samson, chronicler of the deaths of Denver police officers since the city's inception, does not list the slaying of Deputy Marshal Ritchey as the first killing of a Denver policeman because Ritchey was off duty and strolling with a woman friend when the attack took place. Remarkably, concerning the makeup of the Denver populace, it was another twenty-seven years—July 18, 1889—before Denver recorded its first line-of-duty police death. On that date, at 12:22 in the morning, Patrolman John L. Phillips was ambushed and shot by a burglar at Fifteenth and Central Streets. Phillips dragged himself a block to the nearest call box at Fifteenth and Platte Streets and spread the alarm before he died. The murder was not solved.

17. Phil Goodstein, *Denver's Capitol Hill* (Denver: Stuart MacPhail, 1988), p. 77.

18. Zamonski and Keller, *The 59ers*, p. 39.

19. Henry Villard, *The Past and Present of the Pike's Peak Gold Regions* (Princeton: Princeton University Press, 1932, reprinted from the 1860 edition), p. 129.

20. Smiley, *History of Denver*, p. 339.

21. Sidney B. Morrison, "Letters from Colorado, 1860–1863," *Colorado Magazine*, May 1939, p. 92. The triplet towns of Denver City, Auraria, and Highland were in the faraway and thus easily ignored regions of Kansas Territory.

22. Julia S. Lambert, "Plain Tales of the Plains," *The Trail*, February and March 1916, pp. 5–12 and 6–13. She misspells the name of victim George Steele. Tom Pollock was a Denver city marshal, not sheriff, for only three weeks: October 9 to November 5, 1860. See Ronald L. Samson, "Chronological History of the Denver Police Department" (unpublished ms., Denver, 1991, copy in the author's possession). The triple hanging to which Lambert refers has not been documented in this research.

23. Quoted in Robert L. Perkin, *The First Hundred Years* (Garden City, N.Y.: Doubleday, 1959), pp. 179–180. This excellent source contains numerous accounts of wrongdoing in early Denver.

24. Robert K. DeArment, *Knights of the Green Cloth* (Norman: University of Oklahoma Press, 1982), pp. 40–41.

25. Ibid., p. 43.

26. Robert Perkin, in *The First Hundred Years*, pp. 181–182, has a colorful account of the Byers "kidnapping."

DeArment, in *Knights of the Green Cloth* (pp. 56 ff.), includes a perspective of the Byers incident. Julia Lambert remembered the shooting of Steele to have been on Denver's Blake Street rather than in the suburb of Highland.

27. Physician Cass may have learned well about gold from Charley (the preferred spelling) Harrison. Cass became a successful gold broker, banker, and Denver real estate investor, abandoning the practice of medicine along the way. See also Wilbur Stone, *History of Colorado* (Chicago: S. J. Clarke, 1918), vol. 3, p. 735. Zamonski and Keller in *The '59ers* (p. 163) identify Charley Harrison's girlfriend in this instance as Lizz Greer. See Chapter 4 for a fuller discussion of the Harrison/Ada LaMont/Lizz Greer relationships.

28. See p. 17 of the article.

29. DeArment, *Knights of the Green Cloth*, pp. 65–67. For Charley Harrison's death in the Civil War, see also Arthur Shoemaker, "Hard Rope's Civil War," *Civil War Times Illustrated*, September–October 1990, and Forbes Parkhill, *The Law Goes West* (Denver: Sage, 1956), p. 61.

30. Hafen and Hafen, *Reports from Colorado*, pp. 271–272.

31. The notice was published in the RMN, August 31, 1860, and is quoted in LeRoy R. Hafen, "Lewis Ledyard Weld and Old Camp Weld," *Colorado Magazine*, November 1941, p. 202.

32. For the fate of attorney A. C. Ford, see Smiley, *History of Denver*, pp. 346–348. Wildman is quoted in Hafen and Hafen, *Reports from Colorado*, pp. 229–231.

33. From an 1860 census of 4,749, only 790 were female, and one wonders how many frontier women would have brought along their laces and crinoline petticoats. Census figures from Stephen J. Leonard and Thomas J. Noel, *Denver: Mining Camp to Metropolis* (Niwot: University Press of Colorado, 1990), p. 12.

34. Nancy Fitzhugh Norton, "Christmas in Denver in 1859," *The Trail*, December 1920, pp. 11, 15.

35. Leonard and Noel, *Denver*, p. 23.

36. Danker and Riley, "The Journal of Amos S. Billingsley," pp. 241–270.

37. These and other examples of the diversions available to Denver's earliest citizens are in Billie Barnes Jensen, "Entertaining the 'Fifty-Niners," *Journal of the West*, January 1966, pp. 82–90.

38. Cochran, "Jack Langrishe," pp. 324–337; Virginia McConnell, "A Gauge of Popular Taste in Early Colorado," both in *Colorado Magazine*, fall 1969, pp. 338–350. Although these articles in the same edition of the same magazine are sometimes redundant, they provide a good view of early theatrical productions in Denver.

39. The unofficial "Jefferson Territory" was created by the Cherry Creek pioneers on October 24, 1859, but was never recognized by the federal government and was allowed to pass into oblivion when Colorado Territory was created on February 28, 1861. The Stone-Bliss confrontation is often written about, including in Smiley, *History of Denver*, p. 326, and with a less familiar perspective in Hafen and Hafen, *Reports from Colorado*, p. 250.

40. What might be the first duel in the Denver City communities took place on October 19, 1859, between Richard E. "Dick" Whitsett, a founder of the Denver Town Company, and Park McClure, a southern sympathizer who the next year became the first postmaster of Denver. Political disagreements were the cause. The weapons were Colt revolvers at only ten paces, and McClure was hit in the lower abdomen but soon recovered. See Smiley, *History of Denver*, pp. 302, 349; J. E. Wharton, *History of the City of Denver from Its Earliest Settlement to the Present Time* (Denver: Byers and Dailey, Printers, 1866), p. 29.

41. Hafen and Hafen, *Reports from Colorado*, p. 93.

42. Ibid., p. 137.

43. Ibid., pp. 138–140.

44. Smiley, *History of Denver*, p. 436. The attack on Judge Brooks took place on the night of November 20, 1868.

45. Grace Greenwood, *New Life in New Lands* (New York: J. B. Ford, 1873), p. 56.

46. Paul H. Giddens, "Letters of S. Newton Pettis, Associate Justice of the Colorado Supreme Court, Written in 1861," *Colorado Magazine*, January 1938, p. 8. Pettis's term on the territorial supreme court was 1860–1861, but he did not remain in Colorado long.

4

"She's Pretty Near Dead Now"

THE ARRIVAL OF COMMERCIAL SEX in the outpost of Denver was inevitable. Wherever liquor and isolated men converged, prostitutes—referred to by editor William N. Byers of the *Rocky Mountain News* as "sisters of misfortune" and "nymphs of frailty"—followed.

Far from home, faced with economic hardships, lonely, and frequently narcotics addicts, these women sold their merchandise for dozens of dollars or for twenty-five cents, depending on whether they lounged in the mirrored, velveted "parlor houses" of Jennie Rogers or Mattie Silks or squatted in the vermin-infested one-girl "cribs" a block and a half away. Historians Lillian Schlissel, Byrd Gibbens, and Elizabeth Hampsten addressed phenomena such as Denver's Holladay Street:

> Where womenless men dominated the West, prostitution and drinking were not only tolerated but were integral parts of the service structure of the community. Men without families in mining camps and cowtowns had little interest in schools and even less

in charity associations, benevolent societies, temperance reforms and churches. Most western mining camps were places of brief but intense economic exploitation occupied by highly transient males who showed open disdain for the domestic morality of the East. These men came for money, not for righteousness, and the laws they passed generally focused on economic matters and practical needs.[1]

"More than any other female occupation," historian Paula Petrik observed, "prostitution depended on the abundance of unattached men in the frontier population and the general populace's tolerant attitude toward male recreations."[2]

Some such men fled to the West from relationships, particularly marriages, considerably dampened by a persisting Victorian prudery. Physician William Acton, whose sexuality and sex advice writings were widely read during the late nineteenth century, wrote, "I should say that the majority of women (happily for them) are not much troubled with sexual feelings of any kind," adding that excessive sexual activity caused disorders of the reproductive system. Dr. Acton also advocated the regulation and licensing of prostitutes.[3]

Although a study of sexual habits beginning in 1892 by Clelia Duel Mosher, M.D., reported that many Victorian women relished sex, the survey also produced answers such as the following to Dr. Mosher's inquiry regarding what constituted an ideal sex life: "Total abstinence, with intercourse for reproduction only, until human nature is different from what it is now."[4] Under such domestic circumstances many of the male emigrants to the mineral fields of Colorado left home and made their way across the plains to the Pikes Peak country, which would become Colorado.

Soon after the initial settlers arrived, Auraria and Denver City experienced their first prostitutes. The arrival of working ladies was anticipated in the prospecting camps and supply points such as the Cherry Creek settlements. Charles Brown, a physician-turned-miner, wrote to his wife from Bonanza, southwest of Salida:

> Thus far I have seen no prostitutes in Bonanza, but I understand there will be some soon as they are looking for them every day. Wish they would not come for they are the curse of the camps. There are so many of them diseased that they set men afire [slang for venereal diseases] and many young men that come to this country with good health go back perfect wrecks to remain so for life. You [wife Maggie back home in Virginia] need never fear me having anything to do with them for if I were single even, I should avoid them.[5]

The mining hamlets even in their earliest days housed what Colorado historian Lynn I. Perrigo described in his article "Law and Order in Early Colorado Mining Camps" as "disreputable houses and obnoxious dance halls," although condemned by much of the public. Perrigo wrote that in 1860,

> Nevada [Nevadaville, near Central City] took it upon themselves [sic] to raid and "clean out" a "house of ill fame." One pioneer wrote in his reminiscences that "naturally, some notorious female characters followed the mining industry, but they were few in number and usually segregated [kept apart from public places]."

But even in the early sixties [1860s] some of the "erring sisterhood" were occasionally hailed [sic] into court, and once a group of irate citizens were called before the local peace officer because they had raided and wrecked the home of a "notorious prostitute." "Hurdy gurdy" institutions, or "brothel dance houses," seem to have been more offensive to the townsmen. In 1866 one opened across from the [Central City] Register Block, but it was promptly closed by the authorities. A den opened in 1868 met the same end.[6]

One of Colorado's first murderers, Sanford S.C. Duggan, fled to a Denver prostitute when he was being sought for a mining camp murder. Duggan, who arrived in the territory in 1861 at age sixteen, two years later cold-bloodedly killed a man named Curtis in Black Hawk. Duggan was captured but escaped to Denver, where he hid out and was supported by Kittie Wells—one of the city's initial scarlet women.[7] Sandra Dallas in *Cherry Creek Gothic* envisioned the working scenario of the earliest prostitutes in the Cherry Creek communities:

> If he wasn't too meticulous, an 1859 sourdough on Cherry Creek might find his pleasure with an amiable, unwashed young Indian woman in the privacy of a tipi thoughtfully provided by her husband, who was only too happy to collect a few coins for his wife's labor. . . . Fortunately for the first settlers—whose lust was not only for gold—where there were money and men who needed satisfaction there soon were women happy to exchange one for the other.

Some of these adventuresome "mountain men" were accompanied on their hunting and trapping excursions by Indian mates, "squaw women," who are discussed by researchers Lillian Schlissel, Vicki Ruiz, and Janice Monk:

> The standard view is that [mountain man/squaw woman] marriages were "exploitative" relationships in which mountain men took Indian women as mistresses or "wives" for a time, out of business, political, or sexual expediency, then abandoned them when they left the mountains and returned to "civilization." Certainly there can be little doubt about the exploitation of Indian women in the fur trade. Prostitution was uncommon among the Western tribes until con-

tact with [the West-moving settlers], but some of the sexual relationships between the two cultures were only slightly veiled forms of sex-for-sale.[8]

Max Miller wrote:

According to copies of old letters I have read that were written in the vicinity of Cherry Creek, Arapaho braves were at first most generous and cordial in the loaning of their squaws to those otherwise womenless frontiersmen passing through. An Arapahoe brave would also, at times, make a temporary loan of his tepee to go along with the squaw. But the squaws, when cordially being given around in this manner, gradually became smarter and wanted baubles or other gifts from the white men. The Indian men, too, got smarter and *demanded* gifts in exchange for the use of their squaws. Thus, near the junction of Cherry Creek and the South Platte, may have been created the beginning of what was soon to become Denver's famous Row or Line, and with tepees serving as Denver's first cribs.[9]

In 1859 Denver newcomer Libeus Barney wrote to his hometown newspaper in Bennington, Vermont: "There are but few *ladies* here yet, but there are females of questionable morality about town, some in bloomer costumes and some in gentlemen's attire throughout, while squaws are more than plenty. The latter seem to have no sense of shame, and live a dissolute, licentious life."[10] That June the noted traveling journalist Albert D. Richardson wrote that few "white women" had made their way to Denver. Pioneer William B. Thom quoted Richardson, adding:

It was a most forlorn and desolate metropolis. There were only five women in the whole gold region, and the appearance of a bonnet in the street was the signal for the entire population to rush to the cabin doors, and gaze upon its wearer as at any other natural curiosity. "I tell you, sir," exclaimed a lodger at the Planters House [hotel] in the sixties, "five years ago, when I first came down from the gulches into Denver, I would have given a ten-dollar piece to have seen the skirt of a servant-girl a mile off."[11]

Ada LaMont, a dark-eyed woman age nineteen, is described as Denver's first non-Indian prostitute.

Stanley W. Zamonski and Teddy Keller in *The '59ers* place LaMont's arrival at mid-1858, although at least a year following that seems more probable. A midwesterner, in 1856 LaMont married a youthful minister who became smitten with the gold bug and easily persuaded his young bride to travel west with him to Colorado.

For weeks, the story goes, their wagon train struggled across the prairie from St. Joseph, Missouri. But one night the clergyman disappeared, and it was quickly determined that a young lady of doubtful reputation who also was with the wagon train was missing as well.

The wagons stopped for a day and a search was instituted, but no trace of the absent couple was found. As the wagon train resumed its journey, LaMont was lost in silence. Upon reaching the "Indian Row" tepee neighborhood of tiny Denver City, she is recorded as proclaiming that "as a God-fearing woman, you see me for the last time. As of tomorrow, I start the first brothel in this settlement. In the future my name will be Addie LaMont."

LaMont was so successful that within the year she left her shack on Indian Row and moved to a two-story house on Arapahoe Street, where the best liquor and clean surroundings attracted a high class of clientele. There she also became the mistress of gambling entrepreneur Charley Harrison, and it is written that they made "a very handsome couple." At Ada's house, adultery and coveting were permissible, but she never stole or used the Lord's name in vain.

But tragedy, the story goes, stalked LaMont. A friend returning to Denver from Kansas in 1869 stumbled upon a human skeleton with a bullet hole in the back of the skull, and nearby was a bundle of rotting rags with a Bible containing Ada LaMont's inscription to her husband. Emotionally tortured that her husband might *not* have run off with another woman but instead been murdered on the prairie, LaMont closed her house, began drinking heavily, and fled to Georgetown where she died of starvation.[12]

If Zamonski and Keller assert that Ada LaMont was the first prostitute in Denver, Miller writes that Lizzie Preston "is generally credited with having established the first true parlor house in which men would have to watch their manners and their language, or else get put out." In his unpublished manuscript "A Salute to the Frontier Madames of Colorado," Miller says that Preston opened this classy house in 1862 or 1863 on Holladay Street (p. 5).[13] Prior to that, Miller says Preston operated "out in the open prairie, a welcoming establishment for such people as scouts, cavalry officers, early railroad surveyors, and for what few freighter drivers were then venturing the Great Plains."[14]

Denver was scarcely four years old when a series of outrages occurred that made the fearful townspeople wonder if they were back home in the urban centers of the East. On about Wednesday, November 5, 1862, arsonists tossed a turpentine-soaked ball of flaming yarn into the River House structure where Ferry Street met the South Platte River in the former Auraria neighborhood west of Cherry Creek. A dance was under way there, according to an account in the weekly *Rocky Mountain News* on November 6. Perhaps on the same evening, an incendiary device was thrown under the floor of a house near Third and St. Louis Streets, also Auraria. Because so many people were present at the River House dance, this article said, the first fire was extinguished, and for some reason the second fire failed to ignite the house.

The River House and St. Louis Street House were places of ill fame—perhaps among the earliest ones in the Cherry Creek communities. Prior to the arsons, two additional brothels had been burned, but research has not disclosed the date or circumstances.

The town with virtually no law enforcement, no courts, and certainly no firefighting abilities was alarmed. Under the page 1 headline "Incendiary," the weekly *News* on November 6 reflected the fear: "It is possible," said the newspaper, that

> the incendiaries think that they are "doing God's service" in removing these moral pests, but we beg to remind them that the penalty fixed by statute for incendiary acts is the same, whether the offense be committed against the highest or the lowest in the social scale. The city may be benefitted by the suppression of such nuisances, but the law *ought* to be sufficient to affect the case. Officials and the people may be slow to punish so long as damage is done to houses of ill

repute only, but let a fire once extend from one of those to other parts of the city, and tardiness or neglect will be forgotten. Incendiaries had better cease their operations or a startling example will probably be made against some of them. We desire in this connection to remind the authorities that a little more vigilance might effect a cure.

> If these questionable houses are a curse to the city, suppress them. If they are not, take efficient steps to stop their burning. Do not leave it for individuals to suppress a nuisance. Protect what is not a nuisance from outrage and wanton destruction. It is offering a premium for crime to wink at violations of law, and then smile at the lawbreaker who takes it into his own hands to punish the first offender.

> Denver is little better than a vast heap of tinder. A spark may destroy the entire city. Suppose a west wind had been blowing on Wednesday night last, and the River House or that other one three blocks nearer the heart of the city had once got to burning, what would have saved the heart of West Denver, including the vast Commissary stores, executive offices, and the heaviest stock of groceries in the city? It is time to think seriously about these things.

The weekly *Rocky Mountain News* in 1862 reprinted articles from the previous week's daily *Rocky Mountain News*.[15] The November 6 weekly, which carried the story reproduced here, contained a second article on the two arsons on page 2, which said the fires occurred on "Saturday evening last" and that the River House, a "crib," was destroyed. The structure, the article said, had been in place since 1859, and the occupants—"several women" and a bartender—had been warned in advance, by persons unnamed, to remove their belongings and the furniture, which they did. The article added: "There is another source of danger arising from this, besides from the actual burning of these disreputable houses themselves. It is a well-known fact that those connected with such establishments are not the most law abiding, and it would not be surprising if they should retaliate by similar incendiary acts."

Denver had another newspaper at the time, the *Weekly Commonwealth and Republican.* Its November 6 edition said numerous people "of ill fame" were in the River House when the fire was set beneath its flooring and that they managed to extinguish the fire. Then, the story said, an altercation arose between people in the building, some saying the others were responsible for setting the fire. No article explains why the concerned citizens or a marshal, if indeed the occupants had been warned to remove their belongings, bothered to interview the issuer of that warning.

A week later, November 13, the weekly edition of the *News* reported that "when fires occur with such alarming frequency as they have recently in Denver," the citizens should begin rethinking the water supply. Three small underground cistern reservoirs were in place, but they would be of use only if a fire were close by, and each of the town's wells could "be dipped dry in fifteen minutes." And there was the river for dipping the fire buckets because there was no pumping system. The article noted that the Denver Ditch and Water Company had proposed to build ditches along certain streets and that a wooden cistern could then be established at each corner. The system would cost $6,000 over five years, at 10 percent interest. The paper urged the citizens and town council to think about it, and eventually curbside ditches were established. Research has failed to reveal if responsibility for the fires was placed.

In June 1859 early western traveler and writer Henry Villard observed the scruffy and dejected inhabitants where Cherry Creek met the South Platte: "The promiscuous crowd that spent their days in gloom and distress on both banks of Cherry creek, consisted to a large extent of elements of rather doubtful morality, and hence outrages upon both property and persons did not fail to occur."[16] Denver's populace, observed chronicler George F. Willison, consisted of "large numbers of irresponsible, vicious, and lawless men. . . . Many were starving, for they had little or no money and there was little or nothing for them to do."[17] Gangs, termed "bummers," roamed the settlement, stealing and terrorizing at will.

Following Ada LaMont, Denver's first prostitutes established their business houses on the south bank of Cherry Creek just west of Larimer Street. Soon, however, they gravitated to McGaa Street (which became Holladay Street in May 1866 and Market Street in 1887), where until after the turn of the century they operated with implied municipal approval—so long as they did not attempt to expand beyond their geographic boundaries—although city hall launched an occasional obligatory raid.[18] (William McGaa was a Denver founder who died drunk in jail, and Ben Holladay was a transportation entrepreneur whose stagecoaches served Denver prior to the railroad's arrival in 1870. "Market" described several produce and crop markets on the street's lower reaches.)

Denver's bagnio district became the sanctuary for women named Lily the Fox, Hook-and-Ladder Kate, Klondike Liz, Juliette LeDue, Rotarie Rosie, Red Stockings, Liver-Lip Lou, Cattle Kate, Cock-eyed Liz, and Pancake Fan.[19] They were tolerated so long as they did not bother the decent folks. A house fee of ten dollars a week to the beat cop was a necessary business expense to keep things running smoothly, but that figure fluctuated, as did the eventual recipients of the money.[20]

Gambling was prostitution's helpmate, and although the gaming district later gravitated to Blake Street, infant Denver's initial gambling zone was along Lawrence Street. It appeared this way in late 1859:

> Lawrence Street had a few scattered buildings—a powder magazine, several stores of Indian traders, a large white house first turned into a brothel and then into a Methodist church, and the "neat Gothic cottage" where law was practiced and the affairs of the town company were managed by Secretary Dick Whitsett. . . . Every fifth building is a saloon, every tenth is a gambling hell. There are few brothels as yet. The twin camps [Denver and Auraria] together, in fact, contain scarcely a half dozen white women. In want of more the men take freely to the charms of Negresses and squaws. Altogether, it is a male society, seeking its diversions in gambling, drinking, fighting, racing and shooting.[21]

In those earliest days, before Denver's *nymphs du pavé*, or "girls of the street," were segregated into their own geographic district, they frequented the gambling halls because that was where the money was.

Although prostitution, public disrobing, and lewdness were illegal under Denver's early ordinances, fines as small as ten dollars were tantamount to licensing, and each time an arrest was made the city became a bit richer. Opponents of dance halls urged the imposition of high licensing fees to eliminate or reduce the number of such enterprises; some suggested fees of several dollars per night per girl. Occasionally, during spasms of public virtue, the police corralled all the prostitutes they could find and hauled them in simultaneously, but during those interludes the pay-offs to police and to city hall also stopped, causing official concern.

Denver's vices during the town's early years are not recorded as provoking much indignation among the citizens, and occasionally even the clergy tried to exist harmoniously with the town's boisterous goings-on. The Reverend J. H. Kehler, an Episcopalian who arrived in Denver by oxen team on January 17, 1860, became the founder of St. John's in the Wilderness cathedral and stated upon entering one of Denver's gambling infernos, "Now boys, I have never interfered with you in any way, and have come to ask a favor of you. Will you come to my church tomorrow morning?" The proprietor responded: "Boys, Father Kehler wants us to be in church tomorrow. Everyone of you be there." They were.[22]

Among the Reverend Kehler's contemporaries was the Methodist pastor J. L. Dyer, later popularly known as "the Snowshoe Itinerant" or "Father Dyer." Pioneer William B. Thom recalled this story about Dyer:

> When he first arrived at what is now Denver he saw before him a large tent, and to that, supposing a camp-meeting to be in progress, he wended his way. To his astonishment he found, not a camp-meeting, but a gambling den, with many games, including faro, poker, keno and the like, in operation. For forty-eight hours, he remained about the tent, watching the proceedings. At the end of that time he stepped upon a table and said in a voice loud enough to be heard throughout the tent: "Boys, I have looked at your games now for the past eight and forty hours. Now I ask you to give some attention to mine. Let us pray." The crowd had not before known that the solemn looking man was a minister, but at the invitation hats were removed, chips were dropped, and all bowed their heads in prayer, with Father Dyer leading. After the prayer,

which was the first uttered publicly in the Pike's Peak country, the games were merrily resumed.[23]

Skirmishes and even death visited Denver's prostitution parlors from the very beginning. James A. Gordon quickly became a desperado in a town inexperienced in dealing with desperados. On the evening of July 18, 1860, a liquored-up Gordon, known around town as a "crazy drunk," entered a "house of evil repute" on Arapahoe Street at Cherry Creek. Without provocation he shot its barkeeper, Frank O'Neill, whom historian Jerome Smiley thoughtfully described as "not an offensive man . . . despite his occupation and environments." O'Neill recovered, but Gordon eluded capture and fled east to Kansas. Denver so lacked law enforcement personnel that the frightened inhabitants passed the hat to pay volunteer William H. Middaugh to chase Gordon down and return him to Denver. He was tried and hanged October 6, 1860, from a gallows near what is now Fourteenth and Arapahoe Streets after thanking his friends and imploring the crowd: "Speak of me kindly to my mother. . . . Oh, God have mercy!" At Gordon's request, Middaugh served as executioner.[24]

The Gordon incident was not unique during Denver's bloody summer of 1860, which provoked concern among the law-abiding element. Among them was William N. Byers, founder and editor of the *Rocky Mountain News*, who on July 25 noted eloquently that "murder is murder, whether committed on the body of an unknown and unrespected human being, or that of the highest citizen of the land," continuing under the headline "Words of Caution":

> The rowdies, ruffians, shoulder-hitters, and bullies generally, that infest our city had better be warned in time, and at once desist from their outrages upon the people. Although our community has borne their lawless acts with a fortitude, very nearly akin to indifference, we believe that forbearance has ceased to be a virtue, and that the very next outrage will call down the vengeance of an outraged people, in a wave, that will engulf not only the actors, but their aiders, abettors, and sympathizers, whoever they may be. One more act of violence will [wreak] terrible results to outlaws and villains.[25]

The Criterion Saloon on Larimer near Fifteenth Street, overseen by the renowned gambling entrepreneur Charley Harrison, was among Denver's most notorious dives, but the Criterion had numerous clones, which publisher Horace Greeley visited while chronicling the emerging West for his *New York Tribune* during June 1859. The Denver House, also called Denver Hall, on Blake Street near Fifteenth, was an especially wicked place, as Greeley recorded:

Ladies of joy; from an old engraving.

> None of the earliest saloons was more iniquitous than the Denver House, although it was only slightly worse than the average Denver gambling hall. This establishment was a long, low, one-story building with log walls and a ceiling hung with white sheeting. The room was usually crowded with filthy, swarthy men who consumed enormous quantities of cigars and liquor, generally purchased at outrageous prices. The games were rough—and high; a Denver visitor early in the city's history noted that he saw the county probate judge lose thirty Denver lots there in less than half an hour one Sunday morning and later observed the county sheriff pawning his gun for twenty dollars to spend at faro. Beds were provided, and the place could call itself a hotel.

A faro game required at least three persons to operate properly: a dealer, a "lookout" who sat beside the dealer to oversee the action, and a "case keeper" or "hearse driver" who sat across the table with an abacus-like device that showed which cards had been played. At the door might stand a "steerer" inviting customers with a chant of "Faro! Faro! Faro tonight!" A "shill" was sometimes employed in games of faro and keno and was particularly necessary in con artists' specialties such as three-card monte and the thimble-rig game. Shills posed as greenhorns, hoot-ing for joy when the dealer conveniently allowed them to win.

After one look at the Denver House accommodations, Greeley sarcastically dubbed the place the "Astor House of the Gold Fields" and noted that its prices were no higher than those of a luxury hotel back East—except for liquor, "dubious whiskey, colored and nicknamed to suit the taste of the customers." One night in the Denver House was enough for Greeley, who appears to have minded sleeping on a grass mattress in one of the six sheet-shrouded cubicles or filling his wash basin from a barrel in the corridor less than he minded the constant uproar of the gamblers just a canvas sheet or two away from his room. After only a few hours Greeley slipped away to Count Henri Murat's Eldorado Hotel nearby, although not before the patrons of the Denver House had prevailed on him to give a speech.[26] General William Larimer and his son William H.H. Larimer were present with Greeley and recorded the event in their ledger:

> Greeley stood at a table placed in one corner of the hall; surrounding him were gaming tables on all sides. As he spoke, the gambling ceased and he received the close attention of all present. He was not backward about expressing himself on the liquor and gambling questions, but devoted most of his time to the discussion of agriculture, in which he had a great interest, advising the men to devote themselves to farming and not to the chasing of gold nuggets.[27]

Bulk liquor for resale had arrived in Denver City on Christmas Day 1858 when Richens "Uncle Dick" Wootton imported his first wagon load of "Taos Lightning." Wootton set up what was called a "store house" near the corner of Ferry (later Eleventh) and Fourth (later Walnut) Streets, Auraria.[28] Eighteen months later, during the murderous summer of 1860, Denver City by one account had twenty-two saloons serving a population of 5,000, and by another account it had thirty-five.[29] Whatever the tally, one writer commented: "In early 1860, by modest count, every fifth building in Denver City and Auraria was a saloon, every tenth a gambling hall, and those in between not always reputable."[30]

Uncle Dick Wootton's 1858 Christmas party for the brand-new Denver was recalled forty years later by A. E. Pierce, who was privileged to have been present:

> On Christmas Uncle Dick gave the town a blow-out. The principal refreshments consisted of one or more barrels of whisky, the [barrel] heads being knocked in, everyone helped himself freely, using tin cups. The liquid was what in those days was termed "Taos Lightning." It came from Taos, N.M., and was warranted to kill at forty yards. It is needless to say that the whole camp got hilarious.[31]

At one point Wootton tinkered with politics, elected treasurer of the provisional "Territory of Jefferson" in 1859. One observer noted that at the time of his election Wootton was a "gambling house keeper," although he was best known as a purveyor of spirits.[32]

Missourian Thomas G. Wildman wrote home to the *Missouri Democrat* in November 1859, particularly with regard to the character of Denver barrooms and the class of women in one of them:

> The leading popular saloon in Auraria is the "Western Saloon," [run] by Uncle Dick [Wootton] and in Denver, the "Denver Hall," by "Governor" Alexander Bennett, of Washington City; the "Apollo" by Barney Brothers of New York City; the "Eldorado," by J. G. Sims (colored gentleman, and wealthy, from Cincinnati); also, the "Mountain Boys' Saloon," "Stag Hall," and "The House that Jack Built," by Jack O'Neal, a good-looking, desperate character, of Troy, New York, but late of Salt Lake, who drives around his span of white mules and leads the B'hoys [?] generally. The latter is the outfit which was considered as having

more "female help" and "interesting bo[a]rders" than the common law and vigilance statutes allowed, and which at present is regulated, and we believe, "renovated." Of the sporting gentlemen, horse race managers, and speculators generally, here I have neither space nor inclination to dwell on large.[33]

The goods delivered by Wootton and available through other pioneer saloon keepers in Denver were scarcely fit for human consumption, or so wrote historian Jerome C. Smiley in 1901:

> All the early theorists, and that of practical judges, too, agreed that the whiskey Denver consumed in her youthful days was of an exceeding bad quality. It was colored and otherwise doctored to suit the fiery tastes of various grades of customers, and retailed from bottles bearing popular nick-names, one virgin barrel usually serving as the base of all these operations. The customary retail price in 1859 for all qualities— none of them good—was twenty-five cents a drink. Whiskey was at the bottom of most of the frequent brawls and fights.[34]

The public press agreed: "The high price and terrible quality of whisky and other liquors in all these distant territories," the *Daily Denver Gazette* declared, "are operating as a very effective temperance agent."[35] Early arrival Nancy Fitzhugh, one of the few women in Denver at that early time, wrote in her memoirs:

> In those days Uncle Dick Wootten [*sic*] was the connecting link between Denver and the Taos Mexican settlements of Northern New Mexico. Taos was old even then, and, according to reports, enjoyed all the most advanced features of Mexican civilization, including a special brand of whisky, which was known— widely known—as "Taos Lightning." This brand had the reputation of giving "more for the money" than any other liquor on the market and was very popular with the Mountain Men.

Taos Lightning was served at a dinner Nancy Fitzhugh attended in Denver at Christmas 1859, and nearly everybody at the dinner, including Nancy's father, promptly passed out. Remaining conscious because they had not consumed the whiskey were Nancy and the man who brought the Taos Lightning to the party. When everybody else was unconscious, the man, who had previously given Nancy unwanted attention, attempted to rape her. Her gentleman friend arrived unexpectedly to interrupt the assault and ordered the assailant to leave town and never return, at the risk of death.[36]

A fortune seeker named Andrew O. McGrew gained a measure of fame for transporting his belongings westward across the plains in a wheelbarrow during September 1858. Three months later McGrew attended, along with fifty other "fifty-eighters," an outdoor "old-fashioned Christmas" celebration in Denver City. The menu featured Taos Lightning, beef tongue, elk tongue, buffalo tongue, "grizzly bear a la mode," "mountain pig," prairie dog, mountain rat, and sandhill crane. McGrew observed that

> *Although some good things*
> *Come up from old Taos,*
> *Its whiskey ain't worth*
> *Three skips of a louse.*[37]

Drinking and gambling were not confined to the rougher characters in early Denver. S. Newton Pettis, associate justice of the Colorado Territorial Supreme Court (1861–1862), told this delightful story about Chief Justice Leavitt L. Bowen of that court, who was known as "General" Bowen:

> It became necessary for the General to come down heavily upon the practice of drinking and gambling, and although the General [himself] had a few moments before indulged and imbibed, his bursts of indignation against the vile practice [were] happy and *virtuous*, and decidedly good. After he had concluded, the eccentric [defendant] arose in anything else than a calm and dignified manner, remarking, "Jineral, I understand, indeed I am credibly informed that you are a candidate for Congress. To you I wish to say that from the tener [tenor] of your remarks and the *natur* of your discourse, I *konclude* that you are opposed to drinking and gambling, and if *so be* you are opposed to drinking and gambling, you will get *nary* a vote in our precincts!" Is it necessary to add that the house *came down?*[38]

Predictably, competition for the miners' dollars (or for their gold dust carried down from the high coun-

try in buckskin pouches) became intense in a hamlet as small as Denver. The city's earliest historian, Junius E. Wharton, wrote under the heading "The Gambling Hells of Denver":

> The pernicious practice of gambling was conducted in the most open and shameless manner. At night everything that could add attraction was resorted to in order to seduce miners and strangers into the toils of the scores of blacklegs who were the habitués of these resorts. Wine, liquors and cigars of the rarest vintage and the most costly brands garnished the splendidly furnished bars, while the best musical talent of the country was employed in entertaining with vocal and instrumental melody, the crowds of customers drawn together by these allurements. Around the walls of the room were ranged the tables of the gamblers, each temptingly displaying its piles of new and shining bank notes, besides the implements of nefarious trade, and presided over by a smiling demon, under whose blandishments there lurked a heart that considered all men his prey, and which measured humanity only by the capacity of a pocketbook and the means of getting possession of its contents. Besides these houses, of which two were located on Blake Street, the city had half a dozen more private club rooms, where large sums changed hands nightly at the games of "faro" and "monte." Indeed, the 1860 legislature of the provisional "territory of Jefferson" legalized three-card monte in Denver.[39]

In 1861, however, the new Colorado Territory legislature outlawed "Three-Card monte, The Strap Game, Thimble, The Patent Safe Game, or any other game of similar character," prescribing a five-year jail sentence or a $1,000 fine.[40]

Historian Anne Curtis Knapp identified the "vice element"—composed of prostitution and gambling—as one of three pervasive political influences in territorial Denver, the other two being the wealthy and the middle class. Those three social groups not only dominated politics but also ruled the police department and the courts:

> Between 1858 and 1889, the [Denver] vice district managed, with remarkable success, to control the extent to which its businesses would be regulated by

legislation and the degree to which its inhabitants would be harassed or left alone by public law enforcement agents. The leaders of the vice district accomplished this task by actively participating in local politics [gambler Big Ed Chase was the best example], through the outright purchase of the loyalties of street cops, and, when possible, the entire police department, and by accepting and complying with the fundamental public tenet that sin should be confined to a specific geographic district of the city. The vice district's power in local politics rose out of the willingness of wealthy members of the liquor and vice lobby to contribute large sums of money to support candidates and to use their ability to rally the transients and lower class residents of the downtown wards into a solid voting block. Because the local crime handlers had to remain, simultaneously, on good terms with all of these groups, the philosophy of criminal justice developed a social order that balanced the presence of the city's critically important vice industry with the need to establish an environment that encouraged long-term expansion and economic growth.[41]

Denver's police endeavored to balance the delicate task of dealing with vices, which some citizens wanted and others disdained. Mayor Milton M. DeLano optimistically told the city aldermen in 1867 that "we have cause for congratulations that the police department of the city has so managed during the past year . . . that almost entire satisfaction has been secured to our citizens, and crime and disorder greatly abated."[42]

Denver's sins, however, remained obvious to visitors from out of town. Abner E. Sprague recalled the culmination of his three-day trip to Denver from north-central Colorado with a wagon load of potatoes: "The only, or main bridge, over the Platte, was at the foot of Fifteenth Street. I did not gawk around town much, yet I kept my eyes open. I soon learned that a painted face was the trade mark of the women of the street; and a frock coat and silk hat that of the gambler."[43]

Sandra Dallas offered a perspective of the crude entertainments and distractions awaiting the newcomer:

The gambling halls and saloons, usually the same thing, lacked even a semblance of luxury, having dirt floors sprinkled with water to keep down the dust, canvas walls, poor ventilation and lighting, and plenty of cheap whisky. Many offered free liquor to gambling customers, and nearly all guaranteed a free funeral for a paying patron killed on the premises. . . . Three-card monte was the game that appealed to the uninitiated (since they thought the odds obviously favored the player), and to the dealer (since he knew he was nearly unbeatable); a good one might net $100 a day. Standing behind his little table, the dealer would select three cards from the deck, show their faces to the crowd, and begin his pitch: "Here you are, gentlemen."[44]

The initial task of maintaining some semblance of lawfulness in such a new hell-raising outpost fell to Denver's first formally authorized law officer, Marshal Wilson E. "Bill" Sisty. Immense confidence was vested in town marshals in the frontier West. The *Rocky Mountain News* pronounced that "there is no officer connected with our city government whose responsibilities are so great or upon whose character and qualifications the maintenance of good order so much depends" as the city marshal. To be a good marshal, according to the *News*, a man had to possess "courage, energy, and all the qualifications necessary for the duties of the office without being a rough or desperado."[45]

Marshal Sisty assumed office on December 19, 1859—the town was already more than a year old—but he was hampered by having no jail, no deputies, and little authority to enforce vague ordinances or territorial statutes. Nonetheless, the annual report of the first city administration said of Sisty and Mayor John C. Moore: "During the year they managed to get a bridge across the river, and establish and maintain pretty good order in the city—that is to say, [they] put a stop to mob violence and hung people when they needed hanging, legally and decently."[46]

Not surprisingly, Sisty quit after only five months, returning to his mining claim in the mountains. His way station there was initially known as Sisty's and later became Brookvale, 21 miles west of Morrison. Sisty eventually became one of Colorado's first game wardens.

Denver had a succession of five more marshals over the next nineteen months, and they, like their successors for the next forty years, were regularly criticized for failing to rid the town of its desperado element.[47] Horace Greeley in June 1859 described Denver as overrun with characters "soured in temper, always armed, bristling at a word, ready with the rifle, revolver, or bowie knife." Greeley was convinced there was more fighting, shooting, and general lawlessness "in this log city . . . than [in] any community of no greater number on earth."[48]

Rowdiness combined with frontier liquor and a conveniently proximate bordello led to one of early Denver's most violent episodes. The memorable headline in the daily *Commonwealth* newspaper read

A U.S. SOLDIER KILLED—
A BROTHEL and DANCE HOUSE BURNED
to the GROUND ON SABBATH!

beneath which was the story of the unfortunate William Duffield, age twenty-two, said to be the son of an Indiana legislator. Bill Duffield had pulled a handcart across the prairie from Indiana to Colorado in 1860 to find his millions in the Central City goldfields. Not only did he not find a fortune, but he was forced to retreat to Denver where he drove a vegetable-peddling wagon for businessman John Wall, an old Indiana schoolmate from South Bend.

When the call was put out to raise men for Company B of the First Colorado Cavalry at Camp Weld (at what later became West Eighth Avenue and Vallejo Street), Duffield was among the first to volunteer. Company B was shipped to Camp (later Fort) Collins, 60 miles north of Denver, where it was bivouacked when Duffield was granted a two-week furlough that returned him to Denver at Christmastime 1863.

There, with three of his fellow soldiers the night after Christmas, Duffield stopped for refreshment at the Tremont House Hotel at Blake Street and Cherry Creek. It was suggested that three of them (the fourth was too drunk to travel) visit an infamous place called Aunt Betsy's. The *Commonwealth* reported on December 30, 1863 (p. 3):

"Aunt Betsy's" is (or was) one of those haunts of vice which, during the great social change which has taken place in our city during the last six months, has left the principal streets and the most populous portion of the city, for the outskirts. It is situated in Highland, just over the Ferry Street bridge. A sign stood in front of the house, upon which were painted the words "Highland House." It was kept by one John

Kingston and a wretched woman, ripe for the bottomless pit, whose only known name is "Aunt Betsy," who not long since used to be seen dashing through our streets after the fastest horses. In her den, she kept five of the most brazen-faced journey-women harlots that ever walked the pave of any city.

Arriving at the house, they [Duffield and his friends] knocked at the door; the house watchman told them they could not come in. They then began to kick at the door, when the watchman told them that he would shoot the first man who came in. Two brickbats were then thrown through the window, breaking two lights [panes] of glass—which was replied to from the house by the firing of a pistol, also through the window.

Two of the soldiers were going off when Duffield fell, saying—"Don't run, boys, I am shot." But the boys did go. Kingston and two men inside lifted Duffield in—he tried to speak but could not. He died immediately.

One of the men (a soldier named Hovey) who was inside the house, came down town immediately to inform Mr. John Wall of the affair. Mr. Wall is an old schoolmate and friend of the deceased. Having found him, the following conversation took place:

HOVEY.—John, Bill Duffield has just been killed at Aunt Betsy's.
WALL.—Who killed him?
HOVEY.—One of the pimps.
WALL.—Where is he [referring to the pimp]?
HOVEY.—He has given himself up.

Wall immediately went to the scene of the murder, and found the deceased lying upon a bench in the bar room. Everybody in the house was up, two women were sitting over the body, weeping. His clothes were open about the neck and breast. The bullet had entered under the left shoulder but had not come out. Wall saw that he was quite dead, and went immediately away. All was quiet about the house.

At about one o'clock in the morning, the Provost's Sergeant, with two men, went to the house and took charge of the body until daylight.

By eight o'clock, a steady stream of persons set in to look at the body and to find out the facts. About ten o'clock, a large party of soldiers appeared, but with no officer in charge of them. A portion took the dead body to a private house close by, while others sprinkled turpentine about the [house] and, in a moment, it was one sheet of flame. As quietly they proceeded across the street to a barn which had been converted into a dance house—and, in a moment more, it was wrapped in a blaze. A wagon and a buggy, standing close by, were pulled away by somebody but, as they belonged to the establishment, they were speedily run back again. Nothing was allowed to be taken out of the house, except a trunk or two belonging to the wretched girls, and one feather bed. The bright light and the heavy cloud of black smoke attracted an immense crowd, which stood quietly watching the progress of the flames with evident satisfaction. There was no confusion, no noise even; everything seemed to be done "decently and in order"—also with dispatch. The crowd came away as quietly as it gathered. An ambulance having been provided, the body was then quietly taken to the barracks at Camp Weld.

The crowd proceeded to the Camp Weld guardhouse, where the shooter, Joseph Kittery (also spelled Kettry), was confined in heavy irons. There was a good deal of talk about a "hanging bee," the *Commonwealth* reported, but a Lieutenant Davidson and his troops discouraged a lynching.

Meantime, the nearby "whisky shops" kept serving their goods, and the rope talk became louder. One member of the crowd went to the Methodist Episcopal church and summoned Colonel John M. Chivington, man of God and military officer, who was unaware of the incident. He proceeded to Camp Weld where, "looking rather pale, but good-natured," the Reverend Chivington addressed the crowd. The reader will note that on the Colorado frontier it apparently was considered as shameful to shoot a man from a concealed window as it was to shoot a man in the back. Chivington said:

FELLOW CITIZENS AND SOLDIERS: Two wrongs never can make one right. A man, a comrade of some of you, was last night shot down in the prime of life, from a window. The cowardly villain who took his advantage of the man is now in this building, bound hand and foot, heavily ironed. We live in a land of Law—where every man has meted out to him equal and exact justice. It would be just as cowardly for ten, or twenty, or all of you men, to take him out from here, bound as he is, to hang him as it was for him to shoot your comrade from that window.

I did not know anything of this excitement until a gentleman called me out of church just now, else I should have been here much earlier. Now, I request you all to go home, let the law take its course, respect yourselves and do not be guilty of a row here, and to you soldiers, let me not hear that any one of you has said, "it would be a good thing to take him out and hang him"—or, "I should like to see it done" or anything of that kind for I tell you he will meet the full punishment of his crime and, if you should hang him without a trial, you would be just as guilty of a cowardly murder as he is.

Chivington's speech was heard attentively, but he was interrupted by cries of "Bring him out!" "Hang him!" and so forth. The crowd was dispersed by roving detachments of soldiers, however, and at the coroner's inquest the next day, witnesses Jackson Pollinger and Stephen D. Hovey testified that they saw Kittery shoot Duffield in the upper left back and that Duffield ran a few steps and collapsed, crying to bordello owner John Kingston, "Johnny! I am shot."

Although the six-person coroner's jury believed Duffield had been slain, the jury also believed that one kicks in the doors of brothels at one's peril. "The said jurors," concluded the jury verdict, "upon their oath, do say that Wm. Duffield came to his death by a shot from a pistol in the hands of Joseph ____." Thus the jury omitted Joseph Kittery's last name and declined to indict him. The *Commonwealth* concluded that the entire matter was a shame, adding that it would serve no purpose to moralize over the case.

The mob's torching of Aunt Betsy's place and of the dance hall across the road appears not to have been addressed by any lawman. The murder and arson occurred at midnight Saturday, the coroner's inquest was held on Sunday, and the burial was Monday.

Justice moved quickly on the Colorado frontier.[49]

Because there was no formal justice system, the dispensing of laws until the formation of Colorado Territory in February 1861 was generally done by spontaneous "People's Courts," which had a restraining influence on lawlessness. These tribunals were based on the will of the people rather than on the laws of Kansas Territory. Although there were occasional lynchings, contrary to the practices in other frontier outposts, the citizens of Denver and Auraria generally did not resort to kangaroo courts—even though the townspeople were hundreds of miles from any genuinely functioning arm of the U.S. government, whether administrative or judicial.

People's Courts did not sit on a continuing basis but were created as needed. Justice was swift. In the case of John Stuffle, the first man taken before the People's Court of Denver, the trial was held the day after the arrest, and the hanging took place right after the verdict, but nonetheless there was a trial. Early arrival Hal Sayre recalled:

> [People's Courts] were nothing more than associations of the residents. When the associations met as courts they were presided over by the chairman of the associations. Necessarily most of these men were ignorant of the law—as ignorant of it as they were indifferent to it; but there is no denying that in most cases they made an effort to do justice to all litigants. I remember John Jones, formerly a Missourian, as the presiding genius of one of these Gilpin County [30 miles west of Denver] associations, with headquarters at Nevadaville. On one occasion a party to a case to be tried before him besought the legal advice of [attorney] Henry M. Teller. When the lawyer and his client were about to enter the Hall of Justice in which the Honorable Mr. Jones was presiding, he espied them from a distance and stopping all other business called out to Teller: "See here, young man, you cain't bring no luther kivered book into this 'ere room!"[50]

Although James William Denver—governor of Kansas Territory, of which Denver and Auraria initially were a part—did designate men to run the faraway government at Cherry Creek, a criminal court was not included among his appointments, and his plan did not work well. Frustrated, on October 24, 1859, the citizens formed a provisional "Territory of Jefferson," but it was only quasi-official and it quietly slipped into obscurity fifteen months later when Colorado was granted territorial status.

Infant Denver, meanwhile, was just beginning to learn how to deal with its scofflaws. Early court records are sparse, but an 1861 police court docket

recalls that J. J. Morall, S. M. Moore, and George Truwin were fined five to eight dollars each, plus costs, for "disorderly conduct in the streets," and Ed Silsby was fined five dollars plus costs for "firing a pistol in the city limits"—a common offense, by all accounts.[51] Even a town councilman was subject to the law. In 1862, "P. P. Wilcox was then Police Judge, and was declared to be a terror to evil-doers. Among his cases was the infliction of a $50 fine on J. A. Cook, an Alderman, for breach of the peace."[52]

The People's Courts demonstrated that the citizens of Denver were eager to present an alternative to mob lynchings. Minor matters could be taken before justices of the peace; the People's Courts were reserved for serious misdeeds, such as wanton murder. When these courts operated, they did so with great decorum and careful attention to the rules of legal procedure. They also appear to have been fair. When Colorado became a territory in February 1861, the People's Courts passed from the scene, but they had accomplished a great deal in maintaining order on a frontier far away from the centers of justice.[53]

In 1861 the new Territory of Colorado established what appeared to be a set of laws, although enforcement, according to historian Jerome Smiley, was "far from efficient."[54] Denver's original set of ordinances was enacted the same year, and it addressed only four broadly defined areas of transgression:

- Offenses against good morals and decency
- Offenses affecting the public peace
- Offenses against public safety
- Offenses affecting streets and public property

Demonstrating the attentiveness of Denver's early ordinances, one such law targeted the Elephant Corral, the town's most prominent livestock corral and hostelry, which appears to have become something of a trouble spot. The city dictated:

> No person shall commit any nuisance, or indecently expose his person in the Papago way, extending through the building known as Elephant Corral, situated on Blake Street in the City of Denver, and if any person shall commit any nuisance or indecently expose his person in the Papago way aforesaid, he shall be deemed guilty of a misdemeanor.

Edward Chase
1860 328

South Platte River 1 mile upstream or downstream from Denver, at the penalty of a $10 to $100 fine.[55]

Into such a permissive environment arrived New Yorker Edward "Big Ed" Chase, Denver's most prominent gambling czar before or since. Chase was born on December 20, 1838, in Ballston Spa, New York. He attended Zenobia Seminary where he was a classmate of Leland Stanford and at age nineteen journeyed westward with his brother John and won $1,500 in a poker game. Arriving at the foot of the Rockies on June 6, 1860, the Chase brothers prospected briefly near Golden, and Ed briefly became a store clerk, small-time gambler, and prizefight promoter.[56]

The scenario was perfect for Big Ed to thrive and grow with the new town of Denver. Forty years after his arrival, Chase wrote a reminiscence that was published in the *Denver Times*, and his recollections so clearly reflect the pioneer Denver sporting climate that they are included here at length:

Denver was then a small town, bounded by Eighteenth street, Lawrence street, and the present site of the old Lindell hotel [the northwest corner of Eleventh and Larimer Streets]. On the north and northwest, beyond what is now Blake street, there was practically nothing but corrals and

The ordinance failed to describe Papago exposure, but it might have referred to a state of undress practiced by the Papago Indians of the American Southwest. A subsequent ordinance forbade nude swimming in the

stock yards. Lawrence was then the street [?] and practically all of the business of the town was located on Market, Fifteenth, and Blake. The most prominent were Denver hall, Colorado hall, "The Progressive" and Henry J. Mickley's place. Ed [Ned] Jumps had a big place on Larimer street, where Charlie [Charley] Harrison . . . killed a man named [James] Hill over a game of cards in December, 1860. [Modern historians say the cause of the shooting was a tiff with a bartender.] There were plenty of saloons scattered about the town and dance halls galore, and in these places there was more or less trouble all the time. . . .

A great many of the gamblers of 1860 were camp followers when the government sent troops to compel Brigham Young to acknowledge its authority. Camp Floyd and Fort Bridger were fairly crowded with short-card men and gamblers, who, after the Mormon leader had been conquered, cleaned out the soldiers and sent them back strapped, but victors. Then the gamblers swarmed into Denver and located. It was a common thing for some tough to ride his horse into a saloon or gambling house, just for the fun of seeing the occupants scatter. In 1861, Thad Coover, one of the gamblers of the day, rode into a saloon on Blake street, waving his gun and threatening to send everybody in the place to the happy hunting grounds. There was a rapid scattering and after he had compelled everyone to bend the knee in abject terror, Coover laughed and rode out, without firing a shot. . . .

It would be impossible to give a detailed account of the shootings and escapades in gambling houses, saloons and dancing halls of Denver's early days. Trouble for years was almost continuous, and shooting affairs were deemed of little importance. Men in those days— a certain class of men—delighted as much in fighting, carousing and shooting their fellow men as in eating a hearty meal. The coming of the railroad in 1870 was the beginning of a more civilized condition of affairs, and today there exist few reminders of the events of forty years ago.[57]

Ed Chase did more than work as a dealer in the Progressive. He and a new partner, Francis P. "Hub" Heatley, signed on to run the establishment, and Chase recalled it some years later:

The tables were the best that had been known in Denver up to that time. The entire lower floor, 25 x 100,

was devoted to gambling, with the exception of bar space. The second floor was also used by the sporting fraternity, but in a more quiet way. There were private rooms which were rented to those who could afford to pay for them. The tables were run practically without limit. When one of the big games was on, I generally sat at the head of the table, so arranging it that a customer could place as high as $200 on double cards and $100 on singles. But they never broke any bank of mine. My profits were big at times.[58]

Denver's dance halls to which Big Ed Chase referred offered customers a chance to traipse about a rough wood floor with tired and haggard women, usually paid by the number of dances they endured. Historian Elliott West wrote in *The Saloon on the Rocky Mountain Mining Frontier* that a man typically paid from twenty-five cents to a dollar per dance—a considerable amount to a prospector who had not yet struck it rich—and moreover he was expected to purchase drinks for himself and his partner. Such halls relied on dancing fees for a large part of their income, although some establishments, as Big Ed Chase will detail in the following paragraphs, were not open to women. West wrote that dance hall women, hostesses, and performers were not always prostitutes, although they often were, working out of rooms to the side or upstairs.[59]

Big Ed Chase prospered at his gambling craft and often demonstrated that he could be a good citizen as well. Chase volunteered to raise a unit of the "hundred-day" volunteer cavalry to meet the Indian uprisings in 1864, and for that civic service Chase was given the title (but not the function) of captain, Company F. Chase's unit was filled largely with recruits from Denver's gambling halls and saloons, and Company F set the record among hundred-day units for the number of deserters: sixteen.[60]

Chase's gambling enterprises brought him considerable monetary rewards. The *Daily Denver Gazette* in 1866 listed him among those earning the "highest incomes in Denver" based on tax payments. His 1865 income was $4,100, placing him among community leaders such as editor William N. Byers ($6,130), merchant Walter S. Cheesman ($5,600), and businessman David Moffat ($5,374).[61]

Chase became familiar to every gambler in the Rocky Mountain West. He was tall and lean, with graying to white hair and cool blue eyes. He dressed conservatively in dark suits, and he had little to say. He ran honest games, the thing of which he was most proud. Chase was renowned for sitting, dapperly attired, atop a high stool in his gambling parlors, shotgun across lap. He became one of early Denver's enduring personalities.[62]

On July 11, 1921, curator and historian Thomas F. Dawson of the State Historical and Natural History Society of Colorado conducted a lengthy interview with Ed Chase at his home, 1492 Race Street. After Dawson had typed the interview, he presented it to Chase. On August 11 Chase approved the manuscript, which was titled "The Sporting Side of Denver." Chase died on September 27.

A copy of the 7,500-word interview is in the Colorado Historical Society library. The preface was prepared by Dawson:

Denver was not always the staid and steady city that it is today. New precious metals strikes attracted men from all parts of the world, most of them [of] an adventurous disposition and many of them lawless. Some were cutthroats and gunmen; others mere gamblers and loafers. Gold has a particular lure for the gamester; he knows that "where money comes easy it goes easy." Therefore the gambler follows the prospector. In turn the "sports" went to Central City, to California Gulch [Leadville], to Buckskin Joe, to Montgomery, Georgetown, Cripple Creek and Creede.

While the wild life in most other localities was a comparatively brief duration it continued much longer in certain parts of Denver. Being the capital and the metropolis, all new activities, good and bad, ever have been reflected here. A complete account of the sporting life would involve tragedy as well as comedy.

Following are excerpts of the Dawson interview with Ed Chase. Statements are occasionally condensed.

I could play the game pretty well, but I did not consider, nor have I ever so considered myself, a professional gambler by any means. When I arrived in Denver [June 6, 1860] I didn't stay, but pushed on to the mountains. There I found to my surprise and regret that the yellow metal was not lying around loose. I met Hi and Billy Ford. Both were inclined to be "sporty" and they determined to open up a "joint." Golden was located at the gateway to the mountains, Golden was a great outfitting point for the mines. The Fords asked me to go with them, and I went.

There was no building available for our use so we erected a tent. Poker and whiskey were our standards, and we did a thriving business from the beginning. When fall came the Fords, not liking prospects of a winter in the tent, decided to come to Denver. There were other gaming houses in Denver. Among them was the old Elephant Corral, which was running full blast. There also was a house on Larimer street. [That] house was just as good as could be had. It helped to fix the standards for Denver houses.

Everything was open to the public. The playing was carried on on the ground floor and all the doors were flung wide. There were many idle men. There were no police to interfere—nobody to take note except the Vigilance Committee, and that organization paid little attention so long as there was a fair degree of order. They realized as well as anyone that the boys must have a vent for their speculative tendencies. I thought the boys needed me about as much as I needed them. There were many of them who just had to get rid of their surplus money at the gaming table. I thought they might as well lose to me as to some one else and did the best I could to accommodate them. But I always protected the young and inexperienced.

The courts of the day, especially the criminal courts, were mere assemblies of citizens and were generally held out of doors and in the river bottoms where there was shade and where trees for emergencies [hangings?] were convenient. If a man was guilty the fact was soon ascertained, and the chances were that his punishment would come within a day or two.

By the next spring I felt that I had sufficient experience to run a shop of my own. Blake Street was the center of life in Denver, and there I found a hall and opened up with a bar and gaming tables. I moved once or twice and went broke just as often. I opened up the Progressive on Blake street three doors from 15th. Oh, yes, we had some big games, but they never broke any bank of mine. I had the [notorious] Palace from about 1877 to some time in the nineties.

Chase conceded that "at times there was lawlessness at the Palace" and said that while he ran the place there were five murders, but he contended that any similar place that offered less personal attention would have been far worse.

> I have kept disorderly conduct down to the minimum. True, I had women liquor sellers, but I did not allow other women in the place except on some occasions. Frequently I had friends plead with me to permit them to bring their female companions with them, but I generally stood them off. In the first place it would not have paid me so well to have the place thrown open to women. Then there would have been far greater lawlessness, and in addition I knew that immense scandal would result.

Chase was renowned for his strong political connections, which ensured his four-decade career as a gambling operator.

> I did many things to help out my friends among politicians in my long career. I had to do so to keep my friends and assure a proper degree of protection. Most of the candidates sought my help, but I made it a point to be pretty sure of the success of the man whose cause I championed. Possibly I did some things in the way of getting votes that the law did not sanction.

In Denver's early years almost half of the city's homicides occurred in gambling joints and whiskey halls such as the Criterion, the Palace, Cibola Hall, the Mountain Boys Saloon, the Louisiana, the St. Charles, Adler's, and the Club House.[63] These pioneering barrooms ranged from the "fairly kept to the unspeakably vile," according to Smiley. In 1860 there were more of these "wretched blemishes" per capita—one barroom for every 135 inhabitants—than in any period of the city's history. In some localities the saloons shouldered each other in rows, wrote Smiley, "and from one week to another, through the months, night and day, their doors were never closed."[64] One visitor to Colorado preached and scolded:

> Whisky! The mystery of the age; the curse of the United States; ever the first article of commerce on the borders of civilization; the constant companion of those brave and hardy pioneers who first subdue and conquer the wilderness. Is it an agent of or an enemy to the advancement of civilization? Many here maintain that it is a stimulus that enables man to better endure the hardships of pioneer life and that without its influence man would more often be defeated in the great contest between [himself and] nature.[65]

Drinking and gambling were just two of early Denver's intensifying preoccupations. There were also the women who offered, for a price, additional diversions to the lonely men of the town. The first recorded antiprostitution laws in the United States were established in eastern cities as early as 1672, and the initial such law in Denver was published on April 12, 1862—"An Ordinance Concerning Houses of Ill Fame."[66] The first brothels were along Cherry Creek below Larimer Street, and if they attracted too much attention from the law there, the girls could quickly slip across the Platte River into the suburb of Highland—the place where William Duffield kicked in his last door.[67]

Other than a brief deathbed interview with Mattie Silks, none of Denver's early prostitutes is known to have left an account of her activities, and were it not for Denver physician G. W. Cox, today's student of vices on the Colorado frontier would have considerably less data. Dr. Cox seemed to have a special affinity for women and the prostitutes of the Cherry Creek colony, and he offered the following observation: "Women are pure by instinct and by inclination, even as they are trusting and affectionate by nature. To mention all the causes that lead to the state of harlotry would be to enumerate all the follies, freaks, eccentricities and naturally mischievous tendencies of the entire human race."[68]

Colorado historian Colin B. Goodykoontz observed: "Lonely men far from home and without women is the nurturer of rented companionship, and young upstart Denver was ripe for the occasion." In 1860 the area that would become Colorado had 2,061 men for every 100 females; twenty years later the figure was still two to one.[69] By the 1870s Denver's prostitution had gravitated uptown to a neighborhood centered at Twentieth and Holladay Streets, where it was confined for the next forty years. The attitude of police and city administrators was that what could not be eliminated could nonetheless be confined. Consequently, a visitor in 1872 was able to describe a fairly restrained Denver. The writer is thought to be Alva Adams, a future governor of Colorado:

> To a stranger acquainted with the early history of Denver, visiting there now for the first time, it will present a strange contrast to his expectation. He will look in vain for those bloody affrays, those deadly encounters which marked the daily history of its infancy. In vain will he listen for the pistol shots which harbinger another victim of lawless violence. In vain will he look for those gambling hells, and dens of infamy, which formerly obtruded themselves upon every street. Instead of those brothels, where human vice planted itself bold and defiant, Churches and Schools are now wielding a pure and civilizing influence. Instead of those gibbets, whereon criminals expiated their crimes through the instrumentality of lawless and blood-thirsty mobs, the majesty of the law prevails. Judge Lynch and the Vigilance Committees are things of the past. Justice is now administered by law-abiding, peace-loving citizens.[70]

Considerable profits were made in post-1860 Colorado prostitution, even though the front-line parlor house working women generally kept only 50 percent or less of their earnings. Much of the remainder of the income—particularly in the better houses—went for house upkeep, the bouncer, servants, the piano player, food (the girls ate well), liquor (which turned a handsome profit), maintenance, repairs, and payoffs to police and politicians. Some years later, after they received the right to vote, the women of Denver's bordellos paid another debt to the politicians: they were transported "in herds" to the polls to dutifully cast their ballots for the machine politicians to whom they owed the privilege of remaining in business. Historian Ruth Rosen wrote:

> Prostitution became a powerful political weapon in urban politics. Politicians tried to undermine an incumbent's "respectable" appearance by eagerly uncovering evidence of corruption at every doorstep. Incumbent politicians, for their part, sought to vindicate their political administrations from any connection with commercialized vice.[71]

The Women's Republican Association of Denver met at the Brown Palace Hotel on March 27, 1895, to discuss what the *Rocky Mountain News* referred to the next day as

> the method pursued . . . by the Corporation Ticket (in the recent city elections) in compelling poor creatures who live on Market street to vote the ticket. Some of the ladies said that their canvassers reported that these women said that they did not desire to go to the voting places or to take any part in politics, but that they had been notified that if they did not vote the Republican ticket, that they would be arrested. One lady said that it was the duty of the women to protect their sex even though they were fallen women.

An Association committee called on the Fire and Police Board to request that policemen be ordered not to arrest the Market Street women if they did not vote. Incredibly, the board responded that it was helpless in the matter, and if carriages were sent for the Market Street women to carry them to the polls, the board could do nothing about it.

In Denver, police and city hall accepted payments from madams and gamblers, a national practice. In what have been represented as her memoirs, the St. Louis/New Orleans/San Francisco madam Nell Kimball (written to have taken her vacations in Colorado) noted:

> The basic business is set up properly if it has official city police protection. The city officials and the police have to guarantee that in return for being paid off the house is not harassed or raided. The police alone cannot do this in any American city. They may look the other way and keep their hands out, but unless the city, and often even county and state officials, are part of the payoff, it does not make sense to spend as high as sixty thousand to furnish a house, bring in lively expert whores, set up a wine cellar, get a good cook and train maids; not unless you have that certain understanding with the law.

Kimball left New Orleans for a brief time after an unfortunate murder in her bordello led police to suggest that she go away until things cooled down. So she set up shop in San Francisco and was able to report:

The police and politicians were pressing the houses hard all the time for the boodle and the graft. The payoffs got very heavy. I paid a fixed graft for each girl I had working. I gave City Hall a cut in the likker [*sic*] sales. At one time (till I cured a political boss's son of the clap caught from a college girl by sending him to the right doctor) I had to let the police take *all* the coins from the player piano. I didn't blame them—everybody has his hand in the till in big cities. However, I knew judges and city and state capitol members; so while I paid out heavy, I didn't pay as much as some to inspectors, cops, ward heelers, night court judges, reporters (a few go for a free ride) and firemen. . . . I didn't do as well as I should have in S.F.[72]

Payments of gratuities did not give Denver's working women free run of the streets. According to an 1876 edict, the ladies "were not allowed to occupy 'undue prominence' upon the streets and in other public places; instead, they were compelled to remain inside their houses while conducting their business."[73] This was long a condition of brothel operations in Denver.

A particularly aggravated and alarming case of sexual predation became known in Denver during the summer of 1876. The *Denver Times* on July 6 explained what authorities discovered:

> A depraved creature, called "Adobe Ann," living upon Wiwatta [Wewatta] street, near McPhee's planing mill, decoyed a little white girl, only ten years of age, and the little colored girl [age thirteen] who lost both arms and a leg by being run over by the [railroad] cars three years ago, into her place, kept them more or less under the influence of liquor, and permitted a half dozen or more men to sate their passions with them during the day.

The article went on to state that the girls tried to escape, but Adobe Ann (referred to in other accounts as "Adobe Moll" but whose real name was determined to be Mary Gallaghan) caught them, beat them, and took from the African American girl $1.10 that had been paid by the men.

The incident became known, and Deputy Sheriff Joseph Arnold went to the house and discovered another girl, Laura Powell, about seventeen, drinking beer with several men while Gallaghan lay dead drunk and filthy on the floor. Police Chief D. W. Mays arrested Gallaghan the next day, July 7, and she was arraigned before Justice of the Peace O. A. Whittemore on charges of harboring young girls for immoral purposes. The evidence, stated the *Rocky Mountain News* of that date, was "unfit for publication," but the paper added that the "beastly woman," as well as the "male prostitutes associated with her in the wretched business, deserve to be lynched."

The case came to trial at the end of September, but by then the initial indignation of the newspapers and public seemed to have waned. So apparently had the interest of prosecutors and the strength of the case. The *Rocky Mountain News* on September 29 stated in a two-sentence report that "one indictment was set aside, and the prisoner [was] remanded to await a proper indictment from the grand jury and the trial proceeded on other indictments." A thorough search of Denver newspapers over the ensuing days and weeks has failed to disclose the outcome of the case.[74]

The ongoing permissive attitude exhibited by Denver's police and politicians toward prostitution confirmed that, indeed, commercial sex was good for both the city and legitimate business. Social historian Ruth Rosen wrote: "Although prostitutes were prevailingly characterized as outcasts with no place in society, in actuality they held an important place and served vital social functions. Economically, prostitution was a source of income to the police, to procurers, madams, doctors, politicians, and liquor interests."[75] Additionally, prostitution brought men to town, and men spent money in many places other than the bordellos.

Little has been discovered concerning the male clients who helped make Denver and its sin district famous throughout the United States. One sad tale, however, was of young Jacob E. Bear who arrived in Denver late in 1874, checking in to the Inter-Ocean Hotel at Sixteenth and Blake Streets. Soon it became apparent that he was experiencing difficulty paying for his lodging, although he seemed to have ample resources for recreation. The Inter-Ocean seized his belongings in lieu of payment, and Bear went to work at the dry goods shop of L. B. and Solomon Weil nearby at 377 Larimer Street (old numbering).

Before long, the Weils began missing small sums of money. One day a young woman from "up the Row" stopped by to inspect some silk. One of the Weils took down the bolt of material and thereafter noticed a piece of it missing. The girl mentioned Bear's name, making it obvious that they were acquainted. The Weils's suspicions were aroused, and upon further questioning the working girl stated that Jacob Bear "gave something to all the girls but me," naming underwear, napkins, tablecloths, and towels.

The matter was turned over to the detectives and to policeman W. J. Phillips, who began searching for Bear. The officers immediately went to "all the houses of prostitution on Holladay Street, but he was not to be found." Dave Cook, Denver city marshal, traced Bear to Zella "Zell" Glenmore's brothel at 540 Holladay Street and then to the Sargent House Hotel, where Bear was arrested. He confessed to stealing silk, kid gloves, gentlemen's suits, shirts, scissors, napkins, nightgowns, scarfs, earrings, a gold chain, sapphire studs, breast pins, an agate ring, chemise lingerie, hose, and tablecloths with a total value of $233.45. He further admitted giving all the goods to Zell Glenmore. She denied everything but later changed her story and told officers that if they would return later, she would produce the items—presumably after collecting them from her girls. She did. Sam Howe did not record Bear's fate, but it might be assumed that in subsequent dealings with the ladies of Denver's Row, he paid cash.[76]

Customers patronizing Denver's brothels sometimes departed without their wallets, jewelry, and other belongings. An example was the case of J. J. Powers, whose unfortunate experience was recorded by Sam Howe:

> A very interesting case of crime was brought to light by Detectives Watrous and Howe. James J. Powers was taking in the town a little on last Friday night and fell in with an individual named "Scotty" who escorted him to a disreputable house on lower Holladay street in West Denver. Powers there became anamored [*sic*] of a young girl, who was quite good looking, and apparently yet in her teens. Yielding to her enticements he went with her to her room. Upon de-

parture fifteen minutes later, Powers was met in the hallway by two thugs who accompanied him outside and relieved him of his watch, chain, coat, hat and eighteen dollars. Although part of the loot was recovered the next day, Mr. Powers probably thought better of making friends with young ladies on his next trip to the big city.[77]

Denver's bagnios witnessed numerous other poignant scenarios; a particularly plaintive one involved John Artman and his sickly sister Nellie. She had contracted terminal tuberculosis while working in a sweatshop shirt factory to support her aging mother and ne'er-do-well brother John. One day Artman asked his mother for whiskey money, but she said the meager funds at the family's disposal would be used to buy medicine for the ailing Nellie. Sam Howe preserved the rest of the story:

> Twenty minutes later Detectives [Leonard] DeLue and [first name?] O'Neal found [Artman] in a house of ill fame kept by a negress on Market street trying to sell a dress. The detectives suspected that the garment was stolen and asked him about it. Artman said it was his sister's dress and added, "but she's pretty near dead now and will never need it again." Sam Howe unleashed invective upon the lout, who was told "to get out of town as fast as he could go."[78]

And there was the case of Simon Goldman, teller at the German National Bank, who disappeared after work with $14,000 that was not his and was seen that evening in the gambling dens and sporting emporiums. The lure of the lights, revelry, and frivolous ladies overcame him, and in one evening, the press reported, Simon visited Minnie Hall's place, Eva Lewis's place, Jennie Rogers's place, and Ella Wellington's place, "spending money with a lavish hand." He doubtless was exhausted following the night of revelry, and we can only presume that the police finally caught up with him.[79]

Lillian "Lil" Powers arrived in Denver sometime during the 1880s and observed that being a painted lady was a tedious existence, with the dance hall girls at the Alcazar Theatre on the northeast corner of Twentieth and Market Streets making only fifty cents an evening and having to stand during their entire

Lillian "Lil" Powers, seated, *and three unidentified women. Originally a laundress, from 1903 to 1907 Powers operated a Denver bordello, the Cupola, at 1947 Market Street, thence moving her operations to the mining camps of Victor and Cripple Creek and finally to the railroad town of Salida. Laura Evens said Lillian owned fine collections of cut glass and diamonds—including Mattie Silks's diamond cross pendant. Powers boasted: "I was never legally married, never pregnant, never burned [afflicted with a sexually transmitted ailment], and I have no regrets." She died on October 22, 1960, the last of the old-time Colorado madams.*

The Club, in Cripple Creek, was the quintessential characterization of everything an Old West sin palace should have been: the musician, the madam at lower right in a striped dress, the housemaids in the doorway at left, and the ladies in their white brothel gowns hanging out of the working rooms above. In Denver, laws—which were actually enforced—prevented prostitutes from advertising their wares from windows or doorsteps. But what in the world is a baby carriage doing in a scenario such as this?

shift. Powers subsequently moved to the booming mining camp of Cripple Creek, where she became a madam; she said, "I made good right away" as a conscientious businessperson. Contrary to the practice of her neighbors, who ran men in and out of unkempt shanties as fast as they could, Lil kept her place neat and attractive, with clean linens and frilly window curtains. Her regular customers could relax and enjoy a beer and pour out their troubles to Lil's ever sympathetic ear. By her own account, she developed a loyal clientele and made more profits from tips and beer than her competitors on the block made with sex as their only commodity. Lil eventually was run out of town by a competitor named Leo the Lion and relocated to Salida, where she managed a series of cribs. In the late 1890s she opened a house nearby in Florence.[80]

Denver's prostitutes were privileged to continue marketing their wares—as long as they did not overstep their geographical boundaries on upper Holladay (Market) Street. This for many years was an ideal location, only four to eight blocks away from the growing number of hotels that accommodated Denver's many businessman visitors. It is seldom noted that the women of Holladay Street strayed beyond their designated district. If they tried to do so, the effort was generally quashed. The *Rocky Mountain News* at one point reported:

> Complaints have been received by the *News* against the practice of admitting the bawdy women of the town to theatrical and other performances at Guard Hall. Recently some of the most notorious courtesans have cut conspicuous figures in the midst of refined and fashionable audiences. They get a male to engage front seats, and by this artifice secure prominent places in the hall, and respectable folks must sit with them or go out, whichever they prefer. These complaints are not wholly unreasonable, and unless managers put a stop to this sort of thing the hall in question may degenerate into a second-class resort.[81]

Denver and the Colorado mining camps since their beginnings were populated largely by emigrants from the East or Midwest who found it relatively easy to pack up on a whim and strike out for an unknown territory where they had heard gold nuggets were scattered about the landscape, free for the gathering. When expectations failed to materialize and they became stranded far from home and without sustenance, they sometimes turned to no good. Historian Will C. Ferril was quick to blame Colorado's crime on outsiders:

> Crime is not indigenous to the West. Nearly all our criminals are sent to us from the East. Nearly one-half of all the native born Americans in the Colorado Penitentiary came from east of the Alleghenies. Of our three hundred and two American born convicts, fifty-five are native New Yorkers. Colorado has only seven native born in her total list of four hundred and five convicts. There is but little of the desperado in the native born westerner. It is a type of life sent to us. The six shooter is not the foundation of our western civilization.[82]

Notes

1. Lillian Schlissel, Byrd Gibbens, and Elizabeth Hampsten, *Far From Home: Families of the Western Journey* (New York: Schocken, 1989), pp. 22–23. Byers's nomenclature for the prostitutes is from Ann Woodbury Hafen, "Frontier Humor," *Colorado Magazine*, September 1947, p. 185. For an account of nineteenth-century prostitution and the forces that nurtured it, see Kathleen Barry, *Female Sexual Slavery* (New York: New York University Press, 1984). A thorough account of prostitution in America, particularly in New York City and dating to colonial times, is in Timothy J. Gilfoyle, *City of Eros: New York City, Prostitution, and the Commercialization of Sex 1790–1920* (New York: W. W. Norton, 1992).

2. Paula Petrik, *No Step Backward: Women and Family on the Rocky Mountain Mining Frontier, Helena, Montana, 1865–1900* (Helena: Montana Historical Society Press, 1987), p. 25.

3. Quoted in Jacqueline Baker Barnhart, *The Fair but Frail: Prostitution in San Francisco, 1849–1900* (Reno: University of Nevada Press, 1986), pp. 10–11.

4. Clelia Duel Mosher, *The Mosher Survey: Sexual Attitudes of 45 Victorian Women* (New York: Arno, 1980), p. 398. *The Mosher Survey*, believed to be the earliest American sex survey of any kind, is a unique and important document of nineteenth-century sexual mores. Mosher was a gynecologist, obstetrician, and pediatrician and studied intercourse, menstruation, contraception, labor, and delivery. Her survey of women began in 1892 and proceeded through 1920. The results were archived for the

next sixty years by Stanford University. In 1980 the survey was edited by James MaHood and Kristine Wenburg from the original 650 pages of handwritten questionnaires and was published in a 460-page volume now housed in many libraries. The text contains passages fairly unimaginable in the 2000s. A young woman answered in response to a question regarding her premarital knowledge of sexual physiology: "None to speak of . . . Miss Shepard's [book] *Talks With Girls.* So innocent of the matter that until I was eighteen I did not know the origin of babies" (p. 123). Sex researcher Kathleen Barry in *Female Sexual Slavery* (p. 31) maintains that responsibility for marital sexual "containment" rested wholly with the woman and that this sexual double standard "recognized the inevitability of male infidelity."

5. Quoted in Schlissel, Gibbens, and Hampsten, *Far from Home,* p. 116.

6. Lynn I. Perrigo, "Law and Order in Early Colorado Mining Camps," *Mississippi Valley Historical Review,* June 1941, pp. 41–62.

7. David J. Cook, *Hands Up, or Twenty Years of Detective Life in the Mountains and on the Plains* (Denver: Republican, 1882), p. 39.

8. Sandra Dallas speculated as to Denver's first prostitutes in *Cherry Creek Gothic,* pp. 200 ff. Mountain men also married "squaw women" to cement relationships with Indian tribes. See David Lavender, *Bent's Fort* (Garden City, N.Y.: Doubleday, 1954), and Lillian Schlissel, Vicki L. Ruiz, and Janice Monk, *Western Women: Their Land, Their Lives* (Albuquerque: University of New Mexico Press, 1988), pp. 206–207.

9. Max Miller, "A Salute to the Frontier Madames of Colorado," unpublished ms., Colorado Historical Society, Mazzulla Collection 1231, ff. 30, p. 4; Miller, *Holladay Street* (New York: Signet, 1962), p. 27. Miller bemoans with a straight face that the frontier madams were abjectly neglected by the creators of city monuments: "Of the many statues we have seen of Pioneer Women, usually wearing sunbonnets and with guns in hand, I have yet to see a statue of a Pioneer Madame" (p. 4 of "A Salute to the Frontier Madames of Colorado"). Miller is the only writer encountered during this study to employ the French spelling "madame."

10. Quoted in Miller, *Holladay Street,* p. 29.

11. William B. Thom, "In Pioneer Days," *The Trail,* October 1926, p. 12.

12. The relationship between Ada LaMont and Charley Harrison is from DeArment, *Knights of the Green Cloth,*

pp. 58–59. The most frequently used account of Ada LaMont is in Zamonski and Keller, *The '59ers,* pp. 14–16, 90, 116–118, 161–164, and is repeated in Dallas, *Cherry Creek Gothic,* pp. 227–228. Like some other authors writing on prostitution in early Colorado, Zamonski and Keller unfortunately did not list their sources. Historians doubt their statement that Ada LaMont arrived "in the late summer or early autumn of '58" (p. 14), noting that it is well-established that virtually the only white persons at the Denver site at that early time were the Green Russell party of gold seekers, and the personnel roster of that party does not include a woman.

13. Holladay Street did not exist until 1866. In 1863 it was McGaa Street.

14. Miller, "A Salute to the Frontier Madames of Colorado," p. 3.

15. The RMN cited here is the weekly edition, dated November 6, 1862. As stated in the text, the weekly reprinted articles from the preceding week's daily editions of the RMN. Thus the two different arson stories in this November 6 weekly, on two different pages, would have been from two different daily editions of the newspaper for the week prior. To ascertain accurate dates for these arson cases, one would have to consult the daily editions of the *News* for the seven days preceding November 6. Unfortunately, November 1862 falls within almost a one-year block of missing editions of the daily *News* at the Colorado Historical Society and the Western History Department of the Denver Public Library and, presumably, at any other repository. Thus we cannot determine precise dates for the arsonists' strikes against these early Denver dens of vice.

16. Villard, *The Past and Present of the Pikes Peak Gold Regions,* p. 27.

17. George F. Willison, *Here They Dug the Gold* (New York: Reynal and Hitchcock, 1946), p. 96.

18. Lyle W. Dorsett, *The Queen City: A History of Denver* (Boulder: Pruett, 1977), p. 29.

19. The prostitutes of notorious Myers Avenue in the mining camp of Cripple Creek had even more colorful monikers: Dirty Neck Nell, Dizzy Daisy, Goldfield Red, Tall Rose, Bilious Bessie, Slippery Sadie, Greasy Gertie, and, from the nearby mining center of Victor, the Victor Pig. See Leland Feitz, *Myers Avenue* (Colorado Springs: Little London, 1967).

20. For the cost of police protection, see Miller, *Holladay Street,* p. 45. The Denver brothels' cost in police payoffs is not known to have approached that of New York City,

where an initial fee of $300 to $500 was followed by a $30 to $50 charge per month, payable to the police precinct captain. See Bettman, *The Good Old Days—They Were Terrible!*, p. 98. Gilfoyle, in *City of Eros*, esp. chapter 12, elaborates on the cost of paying off New York City police for brothel protection. In some cases, Gilfoyle writes (p. 87), corruption extended as high as the mayor's office. As early as 1806, brothel keepers George and Amelia Benwood testified in court that "the mayor had given [them] a license to keep a whore house and dance house and tavern," and William Lowe declared that "the mayor had given him a license to keep a public whore house and given him privilege to whip or cow hide any of the girls or whores he may have in his house."

21. Quoted in Willison, *Here They Dug the Gold*, p. 75.

22. Edgar C. McMechen, "Father Kehler, Pioneer Minister," *Colorado Magazine*, May 1934, pp. 98–99.

23. Thom, "In Pioneer Days," p. 11. Thom also recalled (p. 12) that "a certain saloon in Leadville was called 'The Church' on account of its Gothic window, and one of the best known saloons and gambling houses in the city advertised its morality by distributing handbills printed as follows: 'Keno, as played at Wyman's, is a very honest, upright, and religious game. It is religious because Wyman don't allow anyone to swear or to make those vulgar expressions sometimes used in playing keno. It is respectable, because the Rev. Mr. [T. DeWitt] Talmage was in the other evening to see the game. Wyman has no noise or trouble, because he treats all his customers to the finest liquors and cigars free; also a hot free lunch three times a day. Therefore there is nothing for anyone to quarrel about.'"

As a clergyman, Talmage was not opposed to noose justice. He is quoted by Thom (p. 14) as stating that early Leadville was not as vice-ridden as reputed: "I found perfect order there, to my surprise. There was a vigilance committee in Leadville composed of bankers and merchants. It was their business to give a too cumbrous law a boost. The week before I got to Leadville this committee hanged two men. The next day eighty scoundrels took the hint and left Leadville. A great institution was the vigilance committee of those early western days. They saved San Francisco, Cheyenne and Leadville."

24. For the James A. Gordon incident, see Smiley, *History of Denver*, pp. 343–345, and especially see Calvin W. Gower, "Vigilantes," *Colorado Magazine*, spring 1964. Gower uses the Gordon case to demonstrate the judicial

and law enforcement neglect that Kansas Territory inflicted on its far western regions during the period 1858–1860. A contemporary of the Louisiana Saloon was the Blake & Williams Saloon, owned by Charles H. Blake, for whom Blake Street was named, and Andrew J. Williams, who inspired the name of Williams Street. Isaac Newton Bassett, for whom Bassett Street was named, recalled many years later regarding the Blake & Williams Saloon: "Every night there were from 300 to 400 persons in [Blake's] place, drinking or gambling. Every known game of chance was running, while miners, cowmen, Indians, business men and women [sources cited elsewhere in this study, including an interview with Big Ed Chase, maintain that women were either prohibited or discouraged from patronizing Denver's gambling parlors] were crowded around the tables, and many an exciting scene took place there. Visitors from the East used to be taken there as one of the sights of the town." See SHS 27: 50814, from the DR, September 1, 1908.

25. RMN, July 25, 1860.

26. The Greeley account is from Dallas, *Cherry Creek Gothic*, pp. 192–196. The description of the operation of faro and keno games is from Elliott West, *The Saloon on the Rocky Mountain Mining Frontier* (Lincoln: University of Nebraska Press, 1979), p. 48.

27. William H.H. Larimer, *Reminiscences of General William Larimer and of His Son William H.H. Larimer, Two of the Founders of Denver City* (Lancaster, Pa.: New Era, 1918), p. 192.

28. Although Wootton is credited with bringing the first commercial-sized load of whiskey to Denver City/Auraria at Christmastime 1858, others arrived almost simultaneously, and Wootton may not have established the first saloon in town. Also in December 1858 the Messrs. Reid and Hiffner, also spelled Reed and Hiffner, are mentioned for that honor, operating their grog shop briefly at Third and Ferry Streets, Auraria. The firm appears to have been short-lived and is absent from the 1861 Denver business directory. Historian Thomas J. Noel identified the Kansas House as Denver's first saloon, adding that many claims to "first" have been made. See Noel, *The City and the Saloon* (Lincoln: University of Nebraska Press, 1982) p. 6; Villard, *The Past and Present of the Pike's Peak Gold Regions*, pp. 14–15, quoting the RMN, January 18 and February 1, 8, 15, and 22, 1860.

29. For the smaller figure, see RD, p. 18; for the larger, see Noel, *The City and the Saloon*, p. 116.

30. Dallas, *Cherry Creek Gothic*, p. 191.

31. SHS 18: 17493, from the RMN, December 18, 1898.

32. Hafen and Hafen, *Reports from Colorado*, p. 187.

33. Ibid., p. 200.

34. Smiley, *History of Denver*, p. 293.

35. In the July 21, 1865, edition.

36. Nancy Fitzhugh Norton, "Christmas in Denver in 1859," *The Trail*, December 1920, pp. 12–13.

37. A. O. McGrew, "Denver's First Christmas, 1858," *Colorado Magazine*, January 1937, pp. 15–25, quoting a McGrew letter to the editor of the *Omaha Times*, published February 17, 1859.

38. Paul H. Giddens, "Letters of S. Newton Pettis, Associate Justice of the Colorado Supreme Court, Written in 1861," *Colorado Magazine*, January 1938, p. 10.

39. Quoted in Forbes Parkhill, *The Wildest of the West* (New York: Henry Holt, 1951), pp. 63–64. Legal gambling in Denver was an on-again, off-again phenomenon, with ordinances changed often.

40. LeRoy R. Hafen, "Colorado's First Legislative Assembly," *Colorado Magazine*, March 1943, p. 48.

41. Knapp, "Making an Orderly Society," pp. 47, 159.

42. Ibid., p. 49, quoting Mayor DeLano's statement to the Denver City Council, April 4, 1867. The term *police department* was utilized prior to establishment of a formal police department. When the mayor made this comment, Denver's law enforcement consisted only of a small force of town marshals.

43. Abner E. Sprague, "My First Trip to Denver," *Colorado Magazine*, November 1938, p. 220.

44. Dallas, *Cherry Creek Gothic*, pp. 191–192.

45. The RMN, February 8, 1887, published biographical notes on every Denver marshal and police chief between 1859 and 1887. Each biography is accompanied by a pen-and-ink sketch of the person. See SHS 5: 1179. For the importance of the town marshal, see RMN, March 13, 1861, quoted in Knapp, "Making an Orderly Society," p. 48.

46. Quoted in "The Non-academic Approach to History with Sight and Sound," ms. in Colorado Historical Society, Mazzulla boxed collection 1231, ff. 129. The source is not noted, but this would have referred to the annual report of 1860, even though Marshal Sisty served only until June of that year.

47. Dorsett, *The Queen City*, p. 30. The date on which Bill Sisty became Denver's first marshal, December 19, 1859, is from a newspaper article in the author's possession. I have been unable to determine the date and origin of the article (headline: "Denver Police Use Radio to Gather in Fleeing Criminals"), but it is believed to be from early 1923 and from the DP. The article is significant on several counts. It carries the precise date in 1859 on which Denver got its first lawman (other accounts specify only the month and year), it states that the office of chief marshal was elective instead of appointive, and it states that Sisty had "a handful of deputy marshals." The last statement contradicts other accounts, which state that Sisty served alone, a cause for grievance and his resignation. The statement in the article may refer to a few men in town on whom Sisty could call if needed.

48. For Horace Greeley, see Dallas, *Cherry Creek Gothic*, pp. 191–196.

49. The Denver daily *Commonwealth*, December 28, 1863, addressed the Duffield matter. The only other newspaper in Denver at this time was the *Rocky Mountain News*. Copies of the *News* for these dates appear not to have survived; thus the *Commonwealth* account is the sole source for the story of William Duffield and of the burning of Aunt Betsy's.

50. Quoted in Sanford, "How Prospectors of '59 Lived," pp. 18–19.

51. RD, p. 33; RMN, December 13, 1861.

52. SHS 4: 961, no newspaper cited.

53. A thorough discussion of Denver's People's Courts and their activities in maintaining justice on a faraway frontier is B. Richard Burg, "Administration of Justice in the Denver People's Courts, 1859–1861," *Journal of the West*, October 1968, pp. 510–521.

54. Smiley, *History of Denver*, p. 438.

55. John Rolfe Burroughs, "As It Was in the Beginning," *Colorado Magazine*, summer 1969, p. 185.

56. DeArment, *Knights of the Green Cloth*, p. 161.

57. DTI, July 29, 1900. In this article Big Ed Chase dispels the notion that Larimer Street, rather than Blake, was Denver's principal early business thoroughfare. On July 11, 1921, Thomas F. Dawson, historian and curator of the State Historical and Natural History Society of Colorado, conducted a lengthy interview with Ed Chase, revealing many details about early gambling and his activities in Colorado. A typescript of that interview, titled "The Sporting Side of Denver," is in the Colorado Historical Society Library, Denver (ms. IX-4).

58. DeArment, *Knights of the Green Cloth*, p. 163.

59. West, *The Saloon on the Rocky Mountain Mining Frontier*, p. 48.

60. Raymond G. Carey, "The 'Bloodless Third' Regiment, Colorado Volunteer Cavalry," *Colorado Magazine*, October 1961, pp. 279–286.

61. In the September 14, 1866, edition.

62. DeArment, *Knights of the Green Cloth*, p. 174.

63. Noel, *The City and the Saloon*, p. 13.

64. Smiley, *History of Denver*, p. 336.

65. Betty D. Freudenburg, "Overland Correspondent: Alva Adams?" unpublished ms., Estes Park, Colo., 1991, p. 15.

66. RD, p. 50. In U.S. history the first recorded legislation to control brothels was enacted in New York, Boston, and Philadelphia in 1672. "Nightwalking" was made an offense in 1699 in the same cities. Benjamin Franklin remembered seeing women "who by throwing their head to the right or left of everyone who passed by them, came out with no other design than to revive the spirit of love in Disappointed Bachelors and expose themselves to sale at the highest bidder." See Ruth Rosen, *The Lost Sisterhood* (Baltimore: Johns Hopkins University Press, 1982), p. 2.

67. Dallas, *Cherry Creek Gothic*, p. 228. Forbes Parkhill identified the location of Denver's first brothels on page 4 of his typescript of "Scarlet Sister Mattie" for *The Brand Book* of the Denver Westerners, July 1948. He expanded on the topic in the *1948 Brand Book* of the Denver Posse of the Westerners, published in 1949.

68. Quoted in Robert M. Shikes, M.D., *Rocky Mountain Medicine* (Boulder: Johnson, 1986), p. 196.

69. Colin B. Goodykoontz, "The People of Colorado," *Colorado Magazine*, September 1946, p. 251.

70. Freudenburg, "Overland Correspondent," p. 47.

71. For the expenses involved in operating a Denver bagnio, see Caroline Bancroft, *Six Racy Madams* (Boulder: Johnson, 1965), p. 7. The politics of prostitution are in Rosen, *The Lost Sisterhood*, p. 72. Many years later the *Denver Post* gave itself credit for separating the once-close relationships between politics and vice in Denver (see the editions of May 27, 1917).

72. Nell Kimball, *Nell Kimball: Her Life as an American Madam* (New York: Macmillan, 1970), pp. 67, 224.

73. RD, p. 138.

74. The alarming case of Mary Gallaghan was in the DTI, July 6 and 7, 1876, and the RMN, July 7 and September 21 and 29, 1876.

75. Rosen, *The Lost Sisterhood*, p. 6.

76. The *Denver Daily Tribune*, March 5, 1875.

77. SHS 1: 75, source unspecified.

78. SHS 18: 17123, from the *Denver Evening Post*, October 31, 1898.

79. SHS 13: 7070, from the DP, January 10, 1893.

80. Joan Swallow Reiter, *The Women* (Alexandria, Va.: Time-Life, 1978), pp. 141–142; for Lillian Powers, see Bancroft, *Six Racy Madams*, p. 47. In a biography of madam Julia Bulette, writer Hillyer Best noted that to romanticists, prostitutes were known as the fair but frail, *nymphs du pavé, filles de joie*, fallen angels, soiled doves, and calico queens. Best lists some of the girls' more interesting monikers, as they were known to clients: Cotton Tail, Little Gertie Gold Dollar, Madam Bulldog, Madam Featherlegs, Madam Mustache, Pegleg Annie, Timberline, and the memorable Velvet Ass Rose. See Hillyer Best, *Julia Bulette and Other Red Light Ladies* (Sparks, Nev.: Western, 1959).

81. From the December 2, 1875, edition. For additional examples of Denver prostitutes' unwelcome presence at theatrical events, see Chapter 10.

82. Quoted in LeRoy R. Hafen, *Colorado and Its People* (New York: Lewis Historical Publishing, 1948), p. 478.

5

"Her House Is the Way to Hell"

By 1870 Denver could count six churches, four schools, two hospitals, one library, and forty-eight saloons.[1] Despite a mining slump that lasted until the great Leadville strikes of 1878–1879, Denver and Colorado greeted the decade with a rousing "hurrah" because the arrival of the Denver Pacific and Kansas Pacific Railroads simplified reaching this outpost at the foot of the Rockies. Less frequently now did immigrants from the Midwest and East face the toilsome trek across the dreary and dangerous plains by stagecoach, by oxcart, or on foot.

Awaiting the opportunity to separate these newcomers from their remaining funds was a sporting place called the Cricket, operated by Ed Chase and his brother John. Ed Chase had been in town for ten years and was establishing himself as Colorado's foremost gambler, nightclub entrepreneur, raconteur, and cultivator of city hall politicians whose palms were not immune to greasing.

Ed Chase was trained in the New York state hotel business, and when he arrived in Denver in 1860 he was equipped with $1,500 won at poker while working as a railroad brakeman. That was a fair sum for the time but was scarcely sufficient to begin the sort of entertainment enterprise Ed wanted. Thus, with additional funds borrowed from businessmen—who sought a smart "recreation games club" for Denver—in about 1872 he opened the place called the Progressive, said to have housed Denver's first pool table, hauled across the plains in an ox-drawn wagon.

Ed Chase's Progressive was not the sort of grubby gambling den that had characterized Denver during its first decade, nor was any horseplay or funny business tolerated. The sight of Ed on his high stool with his shotgun across his lap was familiar both to Denverites and to prospectors from the mountain camps who came to Denver for a big time—which generally involved surrendering whatever hard-earned gold dust they brought down from the hills in little leather pouches.

Chase mixed well with the town's upper crust—such as it was—and he made certain the policemen, the police commissioner, the town aldermen, and the mayor were treated with the consideration their offices deserved.[2] Big Ed Chase, one of his customers noted,

> allowed no cheating in his house. It was reported that it was a common event for someone to be shot there, but he [Chase] told me that the only time a gun was discharged there was one time a drunken man dropped a gun, and it was discharged. No hungry man applied to him in vain. One day he was told that a widow and her children were cold and hungry, with nothing but rags to keep them warm. He immediately gave a friend some money and told him to go buy everything necessary.[3]

Ed Chase's Progressive outdid his Cricket, featuring a freak show, loud music, gambling, and drinks at a dime each. In 1874 Big Ed hosted a dance, and the females in attendance were Holladay Street's *nymphs du pavé*. Because the girls were seldom allowed off their block and were at least outwardly scorned, this was a bold move by Chase. The girls, he knew, would be a curiosity to the proper folks of town, who could come see the painted ladies without going to the improper part of Denver. The *Denver Tribune* reported:

> There were blondes and brunettes, and every other conceivable style of beauty that is manufactured to order. Among the most conspicuous were Belle Derring, Sadie Bent, Eva Hamilton, Elva Seymour, Kittie Wells, Laura Winner, "Gertis," "Cora," "Jennie Logan," "Emma Marsh," "Dutch Nellie," "Mormon Ann," "Frankie," "Annie." The absence of Zell Glenmore, Mesdames Praeson, Williams, French, Perry and Rhoda, was noted and much commented upon.[4]

Big Ed got the idea for his bold dance from the so-called masked balls, masquerade balls, or "French balls" held regularly in New York City since the 1840s. In that city such balls were sponsored not by gamblers such as Chase but by the more respectable madams of the district and were eventually held at an important public auditorium such as the Metropolitan Opera House or Madison Square Garden. The dress-up events were enthusiastically attended by citizens of wealth and high status, who mixed easily with prosti-

tutes, painted homosexuals, married couples, singles, and teenage girls escorted by elderly gentlemen. The French balls, with sometimes as many as 7,000 participants, tested the bounds of public morality and usually degenerated into bouts of drunken orgy.[5] Big Ed Chase's daring event at the Progressive was not that sort of frolic, but it was racy for youthful Denver.

Such goings-on notwithstanding, Denver in the early 1870s was described as "a very nice town, trees along the streets and a stream of water on each side thereof." A few business places were along Lawrence Street, but Larimer Street was the principal business thoroughfare, with stores for about three blocks off Larimer from Fourteenth to Seventeenth and a few on Blake Street.

Holladay and Blake Streets above Nineteenth were the sin centers, with parlor houses, cheap cribs, and opium dens. The residential neighborhoods in the 1870s were across Cherry Creek in the former Auraria township and northeastward from Lawrence Street in original Denver. The northeast extremity of Denver in 1873 was Twentieth Street, and the southwest boundary was in old Auraria at Larimer Street about where it met the South Platte River at Colfax Avenue. What would become Broadway was far to the east, with only about six houses on the barren rise that would soon be the site of Capitol Hill's millionaires' mansions.[6]

In 1874, Denver's first real police department was formed, and Mayor Francis M. Case was uncertain whether the first officers could deal with the temptations that surrounded them. He told the new policemen, "you will have occasion to be in saloons and houses of ill fame, but let your visits be so few that you will never be 'familiar.'"[7] Only sixty-eight prostitution arrests occurred during the entire year—a period of considerable activity in the brothels—suggesting that the eyes of Denver's new policemen were turned elsewhere, that familiarity might indeed be the case despite the mayor's remonstrance, or that the laws were so nebulous that the policemen regarded them as difficult to enforce.

Denver by this decade was notorious throughout the West for its bagnios on Holladay Street, a thoroughfare described by writer Cy Martin as "the most wicked street in the west." Martin continued:

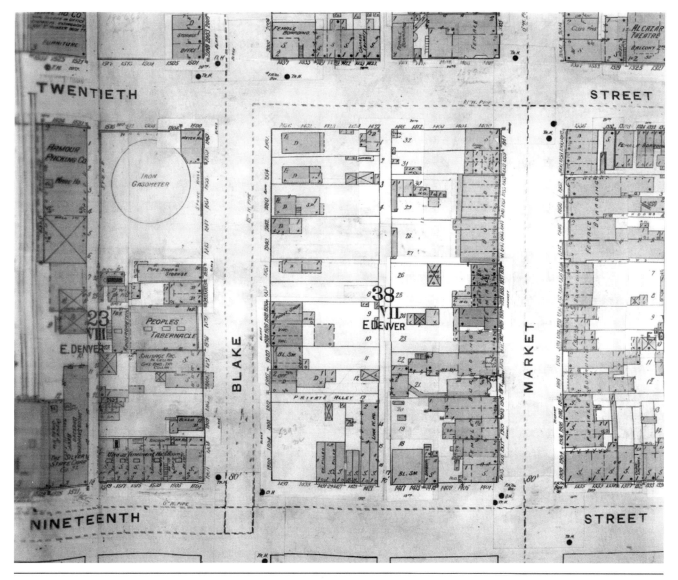

The brothel districts in large U.S. communities in the late 1800s were geographically segregated and were not allowed to extend beyond their street boundaries. The prevailing theory was that because prostitution could not be eradicated, it must be contained so as not to offend "decent folk." Nowhere is this better illustrated than on this page from an 1890s Sanborn fire insurance map of downtown Denver, displaying both sides of Market Street between Nineteenth and Twentieth Streets—the heart of the Denver bordello district. Note that the map euphemistically labels the brothels and cribs "female boarding." The same condition existed all the way up Market to Twenty-third Street, the north boundary of Denver's designated district. In the block adjacent to this one, between Twentieth and Twenty-first Streets, the map shows the brothels intermixed with structures marked "Chinese Lodging House" or the derogatory "Chine D" (for Chinese dwelling), one of Denver's two Chinatowns and also the center of the "Hop Alley" opium district.

Approximately one thousand "brides of the multitude" were available in the imposing parlor houses or lowly cribs which lined both sides of the street for three blocks. The cribs were just wide enough for a door and two narrow windows. Each crib contained two tiny rooms—a parlor in front, a boudoir in back. The rent, which ranged from fifteen to twenty-five dollars a week, was collected daily in cash. . . . Unlike the denizens of the parlor houses, the girls of the cribs made no pretense of decorum. In a costume consisting of a low-necked, knee-length spangled dress and black silk stockings, the crib girl stood in her doorway and solicited the male shoppers who were strolling down the sidewalks, inspecting the merchandise. "Come on in, dearie," was the customary invitation, but if the prospect did not respond, the girl might grab his hat and pitch it inside her room. Some of the cribs displayed signs which shocked even the hardy residents of pioneer Denver.[8]

A small corner of Holladay Street, Sandra Dallas wrote, was called "Blue Row," an assembly of crude sheds with each girl's name painted over a door. These were true discount houses—the price was ten cents.[9] The student of Denver prostitution is thankful for the surviving observations of pioneer medical doctor Frederick J. Bancroft. He was "city physician" from mid-1872 through 1876, and as such he oversaw the town's health matters. In his initial report to the city council, covering May through August 1872, Dr. Bancroft was concerned about prostitution in the young town. Stating that "the evils caused by houses of ill fame scarcely are inferior to those resulting from the intemperate use of ardent spirits," he added:

> Probably every third man who reaches the age of 25 has acquired in these places constitutional syphilis, a disease which he is liable to transmit, not only to his wife should he enter the holy bonds of matrimony, but also to his progeny. . . . While I recognize the obstacles in the way of suppressing these places, yet I earnestly recommend that they be governed by such stringent laws as to afford not only some protection of the inmates, and the wayward and thoughtless who visit them, but also to future generations, for with no other sin than with this, that the iniquities of the fathers shall be visited unto the third and fourth generations.

Bancroft's report of the following year, 1873, asserted that the prostitution scourge not only was unimproved but was worsening. He repeated and elaborated on his thoughts of 1872, pleading again that regulation be established over the increasingly notorious bordellos of Denver:

The social evil is becoming so open and bold and so pernicious in its effect on society that it cannot long go unrestrained or unregulated. No one but the physician who sees in the wives and offspring of the transgressors the corroding and contaminating effects of diseases contracted in houses of ill-fame, can form [an] estimate of the fearful consequences entailed by this evil upon the present and future generations. While I recognize the obstacles in the way of suppressing or in so regulating it as to more than partially protect the imprudent and thoughtless who visit the places of which more human wisdom has said, "Her house is the way to hell, going down to the chambers of death," I earnestly recommend that some stringent ordinance, like that passed in St. Louis [which enacted and then failed to enforce a law requiring periodical medical examinations and registration for prostitutes] be enacted here, which shall in some measure protect the unfortunate inmates of bad houses, as well as their visitors.

Another year passed, and nobody, it seemed, was hearing Bancroft's messages about a prostitution problem that was worsening with every lonely fortune seeker arriving on the new railroad line. Bancroft's message to the city council in 1874 was more eloquent, even flowery. He carried on at considerable length, citing the progress of prostitution from biblical times and its effects on humanity:

> The social evil has been one of the chief causes of the disintegration and downfall of nations, as is clearly shown throughout the pages of ancient history and the Bible. . . . Woe to the bloody city . . . there is a multitude slain, and a great number of carcasses; and there is no end of their corpses; because of the multitude of the whoredoms of the well-favored harlots, the mistress of witchcrafts, that selleth nations through her whoredoms.

Bancroft pleaded again that Denver pass a strict ordinance such as one in place in St. Louis and enforce it "and thus set an example that may be followed by every city in the union. To this end, I would respectfully recommend that some of our best legal and medical men be appointed to prepare an ordinance on this subject, and submit the same to the city council." Dr. Bancroft then decried the "murdering of the innocents" by "abor-

A demimondaine *in the customary white brothel gown and another girl in a dark hat* at far left *greet passersby along the muddy 2000 block of Market Street, 1905. The establishments in this and the 1900 block were fairly respectable, but conditions deteriorated and became increasingly dangerous as the patron proceeded up Market toward Twenty-third Street.*

tionists, male and female, some of them, I am sorry to say, attaching M.D. to their names." He was heeded on neither the prostitution nor the abortion issue.

Bancroft's observations also failed to stir Denver's populace. An 1875 letter to the *Denver Democrat* questioned why he blamed women for prostitution:

> I am somewhat surprised, I ought to say disgusted, at the supercilious arrogance of Dr. Bancroft on the Social Evil. Class legislation is contrary to the genius of American Institutions, and yet the Dr. desires women to be especially dealt with. Why? Can there be

a prostitute but what some virtuous, unsuspecting man has had a "leetle" to do with it?

A similar letter questioning Bancroft's views toward regulating prostitution was published in the *Rocky Mountain News* on May 5, 1875. Bancroft was sensitive to such criticisms and responded at length in a rambling letter to the *News*, published May 7, quoted here in small part:

> Regulation may not materially diminish prostitution, but it sensibly lessens the terrible consequences of it.

105

In the greater portion of the cities in which the social evil is regulated by law, prostitutes are forbidden to receive and entertain minors, under terms of fines and imprisonment; also if girls under a certain age are found in brothels, they are sent to houses of correction. Furthermore, it has been proved beyond controversy, that, where inspection has been vigorously enforced, contageous [sic] diseases peculiar to the evil have been very materially decreased.

Which of us may not have a promising boy, who, in the heat and indiscretion of youth, may not contract disease among harlots which will poison his blood for a lifetime, and blight the fondest hopes of his parents? And which of us may not have a daughter, pure and innocent and precious, who may be wooed and wed by one whose blood is contaminated with syphilis, who may in due time bear his ills and see her children, and children's children blighted with scrofula [swelling of the neck glands].

The 1876 *Denver City Directory* continued to identify Bancroft as Denver city physician, but perhaps he was tiring of being ignored. If he issued an annual report for that year, it is not with his papers as preserved today.[10]

Denver's bordello "Row," whether at the gilded sin palaces or the lowest cribs, was never a happy place where genuine laughter could be heard. Occasionally, however, it was the target of pranks. In 1875, on Christmas Eve—the saddest night for the girls who rented out their bodies—the mischievous lads of town dashed from bordello porch to bordello porch, ringing doorbells. A brief visit to the city jail convinced them that they should perpetrate their practical jokes elsewhere and remain away from the business ladies.[11]

In his farewell speech on April 9 that year, Mayor Case addressed gambling and prostitution in the city. His comments demonstrate a serious flaw in the city charter. And his judgment of the prostitution issue is particularly astute:

Gambling and prostitution are two evils which the experience of ages has taught us cannot be eliminated from a city the size of ours. With this experience of the past staring us in the face, what are we going to do about it? This is a problem which is agitating the people to a great extent at the present time, and which the wisest heads have thus far failed satisfactorily to solve. If our charter did not forbid the licensing of gambling houses, it might be a question whether it would not shut up some of these dens of iniquity to impose a license tax upon each establishment of from two to five thousand dollars per annum. But this is out of the question. I have tried to break up all games that necessitate the employment of "cappers" [who steered passersby into the gambling dens] upon the streets, and kept all gambling out of sight as much as possible.

With regard to prostitution, Mayor Case placed the fault less on the women or on lax law enforcement than on the bordello patrons. The mayor's assessment of the situation was one of the more socially astute evaluations of the subject quoted in print in Denver for many years to come:

In reference to the "social evil," it is difficult to discuss even in the present state of educated society. Christian women, belonging to Christian churches, associate with and admit to their family circle men who visit and contribute to the support of houses of ill-fame. The same treatment is given by Christian men to both classes; the only difference is that when the men get into municipal power they develop their treatment by raiding the poor unfortunates who are shut out from every humanizing and christianizing influence of modern civilization, while the men who patronize such places are let go scot free, because they belong to the first families, and because it is one of the sins that "society" grants absolution for. This, to my skeptical mind, seems to be all wrong, and not in accord with the religion of him who said "He that is without sin among you let him cast the first stone."[12]

Sociologist Ruth Rosen wrote that the environment of the nineteenth-century prostitute was complex. Within the red light district an entire subculture flourished, with its own values, class structure, political economy, folk culture, and social relations. Yet even though the life of the prostitute and that of the reformer seemed worlds apart, both were influenced by the increasing rationalization and commercialization of society.[13] Historians Susan Armitage and Elizabeth Jameson added: "Prostitution was a highly stratified occupation. Each woman's status was determined by a combination of race, ethnicity, education, sociability, and sexual skill, and was reflected in the place in which she worked."[14] In Denver, that meant disparities such as the seamy and squalid cribs nestled among the mirrored, satined parlor houses extending up Market Street from Nineteenth through Twenty-second Streets.

The 1870s in rowdy Denver were notable in another regard: venereal disease arrived. It doubtless had been present in Colorado for some time, but City Physician George Stover, a contemporary of Dr. Bancroft, observed now that "probably every third man who reaches the age of twenty-five has constitutional syphilis." He urged legislation to control prostitution, but none was forthcoming, and ultimately the *Denver Medical Times* estimated that half the city's prostitutes were syphilitic. Dr. Stover theorized that venereal disease was not confined to women of the cribs and parlor houses:

> Enter the palaces of the wealthy and elite, the halls of science and art, even the churches, and the scourge is there, as well as in the miserable hovels of the ignorant, degraded, or criminal. . . . No one is exempt from its menace. We are threatened with infection from the baker, butcher, barber, cigarmaker, grocery clerk, launderer, the cook who prepares our food and the waiter who serves it, in hotel, restaurant or home.[15]

Although syphilis was then regarded, according to physician Robert Shikes in *Rocky Mountain Medicine*, as "one of the most calamitous curses [and] one of the direst maladies in the world," gonorrhea was taken less seriously, and some young men even bragged about having "the clap." In the late nineteenth century a physician charged twenty dollars to treat gonorrhea, but for "curing syphilis" the cost was a hundred dollars. Since many male patients were deadbeat drifters, physicians required payment in advance.

Infection was called "being burned," and for the working girls it was bad for business. Douching between clients with potassium permanganate, carbolic acid, or bichloride of mercury was necessary. None of these treatments was very effective in eliminating the malady, but the carbolic acid had another usage: when ingested, it was an effective means to commit an agonizing suicide.

Dr. Bancroft suggested to the City Council that each Market Street lady be licensed and periodically examined and, when disease was found, that she be "sent to a hospital, where she may receive Christian influences and be led to reform." Physicians, concerned for their reputations, were careful to treat the girls within the confines of the parlor houses or cribs, and the doctors discouraged the girls from being seen entering medical offices.

Legends persist wherever there were brothels of the proverbial "whore with the golden heart." In Colorado the most famous was "Silverheels," the legendary wine hall girl who appeared as if from nowhere at Bill Buck's saloon in Buckskin Joe, northwest of Fairplay. The stories of her incredible beauty quickly traveled from mountain to mountain, and the hard-rock miners, it was said, would walk for miles just to gaze upon her smile.

Then, the story goes, a dreadful smallpox epidemic spread through Buckskin Joe, and while all the other dance hall beauties fled in terror from the disease, Silverheels—named for the sandals that decorated her dainty feet—remained behind to minister to the ailing miners. She contracted the disease, and her face was so dreadfully scarred that she was forced to dance in the cabarets of Buckskin Joe, Park City, Alma, and Montgomery wearing a heavy veil covering her countenance. One day she announced she would travel to Denver to marry an old friend. From there, the story goes, her trail disappeared, but nearby 13,822-foot Mt. Silverheels (plus Silverheels Creek and the Silverheels Mine) was named in her honor.

Historian Caroline Bancroft discovered no record of a Park County, Colorado Territory, smallpox epidemic during the 1861–1863 period in which the story supposedly transpired. Bancroft pronounced the story a lovely legend and nothing more. The yarn, however, will not go away and has been repeated in print as recently as 1963 when *Denver Post* writer Robert W. "Red" Fenwick said new evidence suggested that Silverheels was really one Gerda Bechtel, an adventuress from Pennsylvania.[16]

Colorado's prostitutes were aware of the dangers of illnesses that could interfere with their livelihoods.

One of Salida madam Laura Evens's girls, identified by interviewers Fred Mazzulla and Max Miller only as "LaVerne," recalled some years later:

> Lots of men brought their own rubbers, but if they wanted them, they could always get them from us girls, for we always kept rubbers in our rooms. Very few men came in who wanted to use them, though. One way we had of detecting if a man had a venereal disease was if, as soon as we came into the room together, he would head right out again and go to the bathroom . . . to get rid of the evidence. If the evidence was there, we'd simply say, as nicely as we could, something like, "Sorry, friend, but no go. Not this time, anyway, and maybe you'd better see a doctor." Usually the man would agree with us, if we were nice enough about it, and sometimes even apologize for having tried to fool us. But there was always the other kind of men, too—and there was always the danger of them telling other men later that they'd caught it from one of the girls at Miss Laura's place. And that would be an awful thing for anyone to say. Miss Laura was always so strict about such things—and keeping her good reputation—and she'd have us girls be regularly inspected by a doctor. As I said before, everyone loved Miss Laura. We were first-class girls in a first-class house, and as soon as a man was through, the girl he was with in a room would be sure to wash him with antiseptics. He'd know then that if he ever caught something somewhere else, he'd have no reason for trying to blame any of us. We'd wash the men first and then, when they were putting on their clothes, we'd next take care of ourselves by washing ourselves and douching, usually using a solution containing potassium permanganate. Each of us always had several douches on hand, because some had too much of a drying effect inside if used too often in succession.[17]

In her study *The Lost Sisterhood*, Rosen quoted a bordello client who attested that the girls' principal interest was getting the job done and moving on to the next customer:

> You wouldn't believe how fast those girls could get their clothes off. Usually they'd leave on their stockings and earrings, things like that. A man usually took off his trousers and shoes. New girls didn't give you a second to catch your breath before they'd be all over you trying to get you to heat up and go off as soon as possible. When it came to the actual act, though, the routine was standard. I'd say that the whole thing, from the time you got in the room until the time you came, didn't take three minutes. Then she'd wash you off again, and herself. Then she'd get dressed, without even looking at you. You could see she was already thinking about nothing but getting downstairs.[18]

Affection was pretense only. One of the prostitutes explained: "I could not make a demonstration of affection over men nor any pretense or response to their caresses. For the life of me, I could not understand why they should expect it. They had only bought my body, I could not see why they should want more. My love was not for sale, piecemeal, to every man who had the price to pay for my body."[19]

Pregnancy and disease, which the prostitute tried to avoid by douching, plus physical abuse at the hands of clients, were the great dangers awaiting the nineteenth-century prostitute. But the women knew how to take precautions. A client said: "She approached and seized my genital organ in one hand, wringing it in such a way as to determine whether or not I had the gonorrhea. She did this particular operation with more knowledge and skill than she did anything else before or after." Added another patron: "I think the girls could diagnose clap better than the doctors at that time."[20] A subsequent venereal disease study concluded:

> Nearly one-third of infected women were married and had been infected by their husbands. One doctor was led to declare that more venereal infection existed among virtuous wives infected by their husbands than among professional prostitutes. A female physician wrote that "every day, thousands of pure young women become infected in assuming what should be the most sacred relation[ship] on earth, that of wifehood."[21]

Drugs, acid solutions, and opiates used as douches by the *demimondaines* also disrupted or interrupted menstruation to prevent conceiving. It was preferable to giving birth to a child to raise in such wretched circumstances. Meanwhile, the girls also ingested narcotics and alcohol that, if they did not make life more tolerable, at least put circumstances into a haze.[22]

The Sam Howe Scrapbooks contain dozens of entries concerning young girls dying or dead from the abortion process, plus names of the physicians or midwives who were sometimes arrested and charged. "When prostitutes bore children, as they often did," historian Patricia Limerick wrote in *The Legacy of Conquest*, "their occupation made child care an extraordinary challenge and the children stood scant chance of rising to reputability. Many daughters of prostitutes followed their mothers into the business."[23] One of the saddest of such tales emerging from Denver's tenderloin, the supposed story of Lizzie Preston and her daughter Essie, is related in Chapter 10.

The Denver press avoided use of the word *abortion*, then a crude medical procedure sometimes resulting in death to the woman. Instead, the victim was said to have died from the effects of a "criminal or illegal operation." The terminology was in deference to the humiliation and social ostracism connected with becoming pregnant while unwed or, on occasion, while wed. Young ladies could not confront their condition in a social atmosphere in which a girl who had sexual relations was referred to as "ruined." Nor did such girls have much of a place to seek sanctuary and protection.

Historian Timothy J. Gilfoyle, in *City of Eros* (p. 135), characterized nineteenth-century abortion as a "controversial example of commercialized sex" whose procedures had been developed and practiced by physicians and midwives as early as the 1840s. The abortionists advertised their services, appealing to "ladies who have been unfortunate" or with regard to "diseases peculiar to females." The abortionists performed openly with little interference until the 1870s, when women's rights and purity crusaders forced them underground.

An example of this phenomenon was the case of Hilme "Helene" Haglund, a twenty-year-old Swede who worked as a maid for the wealthy Henry M. Bostwick family, 1360 Race Street, Denver. Haglund's gentleman friend was Henry Erickson, who worked with her two brothers at the big Argo Smelter just north of Denver. Hilme found herself in a family way, and she died. Her brother Emanuel, urging an investigation into the case, asserted that "my sister hid her condition from all of our own people. Not one of us ever

imagined how it was with her. She visited us last Sunday and none of us suspected there was any wrong. At one time my married sister accused Hilme, but the girl denied it in the most emphatic manner." Perhaps the last thing Hilme needed was an accusation.

Emanuel continued his statement to a *Rocky Mountain News* reporter: "However, I am told that she had previously made two visits to Dr. Vinland, 2714 Stout Street, to get medicine. She was at Vinland's place until Tuesday afternoon at 4 o'clock, when she went to 635 [615] Pearl Street," the address of the Cottage Home, one of Denver's first such social agencies.[24]

Dr. Vinland told Emanuel Haglund that he advised Hilme "that she ought to insist that Erickson marry her, and she went away saying that she would see him [presumably the doctor] again in a few days." She apparently never informed Erickson, so great was her embarrassment and shame. Vinland later suggested that Hilme may have "doctored herself," which Emanuel doubted, but whatever happened she soon was very ill with chills and violent vomiting of blood. Paralysis and unconsciousness followed, and another physician, F. G. Byles, called in Dr. T. E. Taylor. The doctors concluded, according to the press account, that "nothing further could be done to save her life." Hilme Haglund died at 1 the next morning without regaining consciousness. Authorities occasionally investigated such matters, but despite considerable newspaper coverage of the Haglund death, no inquest was called.[25]

Beginning in late 1878, Denver was greatly impacted by mining booms in the mountain towns to the west, principally Leadville, and Denver's stature as a supply center was ensured. In the 1880s Denver's population tripled from 35,629 to 106,713. Striking it rich in the mineral fields, however, eluded too many prospectors. Since a prospector was a gambler by definition, some of the unsuccessful consequently succumbed to the lure of the green cloth in their hopes to return to their homes back East as wealthy men.

Gambling was an ogre with which impressionable young men away from home and vulnerable to temptation were constantly confronted. Newcomer James Thompson wrote in his diary in 1872: "I have heard of a man working a lucrative mine here, who would lavish as much as a thousand dollars in one or two night trips to Denver, between gambling saloons & brothels."[26]

On May 23, 1881, young G. N. Scamehorn alit at the Denver train station, took residence at 1713 Larimer Street, and wandered into a gambling hall. Scamehorn was soon ensnared by the gambling demon and became compulsive. But before it was too late he saw the error of his habits, and as if to atone he penned a fervent scripture on the evils of the gaming tables, titled *Behind the Scenes, or Denver by Gaslight*. Here is an excerpt:

> The marble floors, the frescoed walls, these glittering lights, these magnificent paintings, our diamond studs, our fine clothes, our ladies' silks and satins. So with a winning of a few hundred dollars as a bait to start with I felt like thousands of other poor victims that it was an easy way to make money little dreaming of the powerful disease it was placing around me. In one short year after I commenced gambling I lost $12,000 [and] this was not all, I lost my reputation and honor as a man, the love and respect of hundreds of my best and dearest friends. Let the law be enforced by closing every gambling house in this city and close them forever. There is [sic] at this time about fifteen to twenty open gambling houses in this city these houses are running in direct violation of every principle of law and public decency, running against the will of three fourths of the people of our city.[27]

New arrival Howard T. Vaille offered a vivid picture of what Scamehorn observed in Denver at about that time:

> People of every nation and of every station in life jostled each other on its plank sidewalks, crowded its dinky little horse-cars, treading upon each other's corns in the straw which covered the floor, fought for the attention of the barkeepers and were rivals for the smiles of the dance-hall girls. The town was "wide open," as we say, no screens in front of its bars, gambling was not confined to out-of-the-way places, but poker and games of chance were played openly in every saloon; the roulette wheel was spinning everywhere and from the open doors came the caller's cry of "Keno." There were Yankee and English capitalists, professional men, miners, prospectors, mechanics, gamblers, cowboys, railroad laborers, Mexicans and Chinese. The Chinese manned the saloons, ran the restaurants, washed the clothes and solved the servant-girl problem; everywhere was youth and young manhood, and gray-haired men and women were seldom seen.[28]

Obviously among those avoiding the pitfalls of scarlet women and parlor houses were gentlemen such as W. H. Billings and Charles Edwards. Their story—unusual but not unique for the era—was told to Sam Howe, who then related it to a *Denver Evening Post* reporter. It appears here in full and verbatim:

> An infatuation of one man for another caused copious tears to flow from a deserted wife at the police station this morning. The two are W. H. Billings and Charles Edwards. Billings is a teamster and Edwards is a banjo player and acrobat. Billings lived with his wife and two children at Nederland, a small town in Boulder county. This morning Mrs. Billings arrived in Denver, entered a hack at the depot and was driven to the police station. She wanted a detective right away and she was referred to Sam Howe. She poured a tale into the veteran sleuth's ear that caused him to blush a deep crimson and refer Mrs. Billings to Detective [T. E.] McIlduff. Howe would not repeat her story, but McIlduff said that Mrs. Billings told him, among other things, that her husband had deserted her for the company of Charles Edwards.
>
> He [Billings] owned a valuable pair of horses with which he supported himself and family with ease until Charles Edwards struck Nederland. Edwards' graft was to frequent saloons where he would play a tune upon the banjo, turn a somersault and take up a collection. While he was performing these tricks Billings saw him and bought him a drink, besides dropping a quarter into the hat the banjo player passed around.
>
> After that the two men were seen in each other's company frequently, so much so that Mrs. Billings asked her husband what it all meant. In a sarcastic manner he replied that the banjo player's society was preferable to that of some women, but he mentioned no names and Mrs. Billings then thought the allusion was to a neighbor's wife who is not blessed with a surplus of handsomeness.
>
> The two men continued to go together and Billings was not happy unless he was trailing around the streets with Edwards. If his home had any charms for him,

said his wife, they had fled and all on account of the banjo player.

She said that last Saturday her husband hitched up the faithful and valuable team and started to Boulder to purchase some groceries. He did not return and the next day Mrs. Billings went to Boulder to learn what had become of him. There she ascertained that her husband had sold the team and purchased railroad tickets for himself and Edwards to Denver. She was left with very little money, she said, and has no way of providing for herself and children. Detective McIlduff is looking all over this city for Billings and the banjo player and if they are found he will land them in jail.[29]

If Detective McIlduff located Billings and his banjo-playing and somersaulting new best friend, the blushing Detective Howe did not record it.

J. B. Winslow may or may not have been of the same persuasion when he was arrested in March 1891. The *Rocky Mountain News* described Winslow as an octoroon—a person of predominantly Anglo extraction but with African American influence—which had nothing to do with his legal problems. Winslow, according to the report preserved by Detective Howe, "tried a little scheme of robbery on the innocent who go down Market Street to see life, by impersonating a female, and reliev[ing] them of their personal goods and chattels." Winslow was bound over to the district court and released on $500 bond.[30]

A notable cross-dresser of another sort in early Colorado history was Elsa Jane Forest Guerin, known in her autobiography as "Mountain Charley" ("Charles Hatfield"). Elsa's wardrobe was prompted not by sexual considerations but to facilitate her occupation as a mule and cattle herder: men's roles. Several newspaper versions of her life experiences are related in her autobiography, and they conflict in some aspects with what she wrote about herself. She may have come to Colorado in search of an errant gambler husband who ran out on her; she was at Leadville; she was in Auraria, where (as a woman) she dealt faro at Uncle Dick Wootton's saloon; and she was said to have clerked at a Central City store under the name "Charley Walworth." Guerin operated a gambling house in Cheyenne and served in the Fifth Wisconsin Infantry

as "Jackson Snow." Elsa Jane's gender was discovered by two doctors who protected her secret. An acquaintance, George West, publisher of the *Colorado Transcript* in Golden, wrote that although she was "always dressed in male attire, [she] never [made] any attempt to conceal her sex."[31]

Perhaps Guerin's motive of cross-dressing as a convenience in a man's world was the same as that of Mary E. Davis, whose brief deathbed story in the *Rocky Mountain News* on May 26, 1918, stated that she "fought side by side with men of the Sixty-eighth Illinois Infantry for nearly a year" in the Civil War: "She enlisted in the garb of a man and her identity was discovered after she had received a sword cut in the arm and was placed in a hospital." A resident of 1824 Twenty-sixth Street in Denver, the story stated that Davis "owns a war medal presented to her by President Lincoln for valor." Her funeral notice was in the *News* the following July 16.

Georgie Phillips, a young woman dressed as a man, set out on the evening of June 28, 1887, to catch the sights of Denver and headed to Big Ed Chase's notorious Palace Theater. Patrolman Dan Brady became suspicious and hauled her to City Jail, where according to the *Denver Republican* the following day, "Georgie's festive dream was rudely awakened when thrust into an iron cell." There she "carefully removed her collar and lay down on the iron couch and awaited developments." They came in the shape of a curious reporter, accompanied by a number of curious policemen. She seemed not to care, and the paper concluded that "she will tell Judge Campbell this morning what caused her to assume such an unnatural role."

A month later, July 10, 1887, Detective Sam Howe arrested a young man identifying himself as John Flesk, age eighteen, in a vacant house on Fourteenth Street near Lawrence. When they searched him at police headquarters, the officers discovered that beneath his male attire Flesk was wearing ladies' underwear, including a corset, panties, a chemise, and long hose. The officers believed Flesk—probably an alias—was a sneak thief, as valuables were found in his pockets.[32]

A deadly cross-dresser, who also may have resorted to wearing men's clothing only for purposes of disguise

at any drugstore for as little as twenty-five cents. McGinley was carrying $500.

After the murder Nina and Charles, appearing as a pair of men, fled Denver and were subsequently arrested in Rocky Ford. At her three-day trial beginning the next October 9, the newspapers reported that she wore a "neat black dress she made for herself at the county jail." It was quite a contrast, the papers said, from "the miserable creature [at Rocky Ford], disguised as a man, soiled and ragged and yelling for morphine." Charges against Charles were dismissed because of what the judge described as sloppy police work, and Nina was acquitted.

Prostitutes' thievery of clients in Denver was practiced earlier than the Patchen case. One of the first such recorded instances was on April 22, 1877, when Minnie Clark, whom the *Rocky Mountain News* said was "sometimes called Broken-nose Moll," appeared in court on charges of "feloniously making way with fifty dollars of the wealth of a young man from the country." Proper police work on this case was lacking as well, and, the paper said, "for some reason the charge failed to stick and she was discharged, no doubt considerably ahead of the game." It did not make any difference that Broken-nose Moll was adjudged innocent; the *News* was certain of her guilt and said so.[33]

Narcotic abuse was common along Denver's Row, particularly in the moderate to lower classes of brothels. Morphine, opium, and laudanum, all of which helped

and eluding capture, was prostitute and morphine addict Nina Patchen. On the night of June 20, 1895, while Nina's husband, Charles, was out of town, Nina and one Jerry McGinley ended up in a rooming house at 1734 Larimer Street. He was found dead the next day of an opium overdose, supposedly administered by Nina, who robbed him to get morphine money. Dosages of the drug were available over the counter

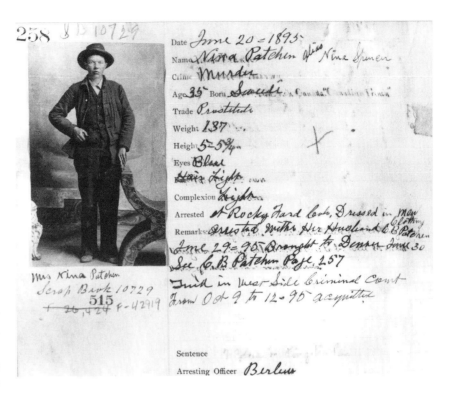

Murderer/prostitute/cross-dresser/morphine fiend Nina Patchen as a male. This is her official Denver police rap sheet as preserved by Detective Howe, in his own handwriting.

alleviate the discomforts of living in the grim outpost of Denver, were present in town by the late 1860s. The Colorado territorial legislature in 1872 and Denver's ordinances three years later prohibited the sale of opium in medicines but not in "patent" remedies that were easily available, usually in liquid form. These medicines, plus others that commonly contained alcohol, made the ill feel considerably better.[34]

Twenty-six-year-old Lizzie Desmond of Fremont County, who had never been in trouble, had a particularly disturbing experience with opiates in 1897. She stole silk cloth worth $65.90 and a dollar handkerchief, apparently intending to sell the goods to finance her opium habit. At her trial, Dr. H. H. Martin of Denver testified that in 1892 he had provided gynecological treatment for Desmond, who was pregnant at the time. The child, Dr. Martin testified, "was removed with instruments and was dead at birth." Desmond's vagina and rectum were ripped, resulting in a great loss of blood and intense pain. The doctor added that during her eight-month recovery she was often "hysterical," and he was "compelled to administer powerful opiates, almost continually."

Desmond became addicted and stole to support her habit. The jury found her guilty and recommended the mercy of the court. The $65.90 theft earned her two years in prison, served from April 20, 1897, to January 11, 1899. Her husband, W. W. Desmond, convicted on the same charges, was released eighteen months later.[35]

In 1898, a time when books on sexual matters were not commonly circulated and then only behind drawn shutters, the Vir Publishing Company of Philadelphia issued a book titled *What a Young Woman Ought to Know*, part of the company's "Self and Sex" (subtitled "Purity and Truth") series. The author was Mary Wood-Allen, identified as a medical doctor, "national superintendent of the Purity Department [of the] Women's Christian Temperance Union," and author of *The Man Wonderful in the House Beautiful*. Dr. Wood-Allen's observations on late-nineteenth-century morality and moderation deserve extended reference:

> It is a sad fact that many women, even of good social standing, are fond of alcoholic beverages. I saw a very bright, pretty young woman not long since, at a reception, refuse to take ice-cream or cake, but drink four glasses of punch, with many jests as to her fondness for the same, apparently without any glimmering of the thought that she was drinking to excess, although her flushed face and loudness of manner were proof of this to those who were witnesses.
>
> One young woman who, under ordinary circumstances, was most modest in deportment, drank at her wedding in response to the toasts to her health, and grew very jovial, until at last she danced a jig on

the platform at the railway station, amid the applause of her exhilarated friends.

What a sorrowful and undignified beginning to the duties of marriage! There is no absolute safety for either man or woman except in total abstinence. The *debauche* knows the effect of wine, and uses that knowledge to lead astray the young girl who, if herself, would find no charm in his blandishments, but who, after the wine supper, has no will to resist his advances.

Another cause of inebriety in women is found in the patent medicines advertised as a panacea for all pain, which chemical analysis shows to be largely alcoholic. Many temperance women would be horrified to know that they are taking alcohol in varying quantity, from 6 to 47 per cent, in the bitters, tonics and restorative medicines they are using, many of which are especially advertised as "purely vegetable extracts, perfectly harmless, sustaining to the nervous system," etc.

Dr. Wood-Allen proceeded to write that the result of such inebriety among parents (particularly mothers) for their children "has not been well understood in the past," but now it was deduced that the daughters of "drunken parents" were known to be

> often attractive to some men by reason of their excitable, vivacious, neurotic manner, [and they] should be carefully avoided by young men in search of wives. The man who marries the daughter of an inebriate not only endangers his own happiness, but runs the risk of entailing upon his children an inheritance of degradation and misery. No woman should marry a man who, even occasionally, drinks to excess. Further, the disposition of the sons of drunken parents ought to be investigated before any girl becomes engaged to one of them.

The Wood-Allen report decried the evil of "morphinism" and cocaine but then turned to what it considered an even more insidious drug—an issue germane even in the twenty-first century:

> The most dangerous habit of the present would almost seem to be the tobacco habit, because it is considered quite respectable and is therefore almost universal. Men who are prominent, not only as statesmen and business men, but also as moral leaders, smoke with

no apparent recognition of the evils, and lads can often sanction their beginning of the habit by the fact that a certain pastor or Sunday-school superintendent is a smoker.

> But science has not been idle in regard to the investigation of the effects of tobacco, and the discoveries made have been published, so that we are not now ignorant of the tobacco heart, or tobacco throat, or tobacco nerves, nor of the transmission of nerve degeneracy to the children of smokers.

> Girls sometimes think it is a great joke to smoke cigarettes for fun, and some grow into the habit of smoking, but the injury is not lessened by the fact that the use of the cigarette was begun in jest, nor that the user is a woman.

Dr. Wood-Allen addressed the topic of "excitable and vivacious" young women:

> There is another influence at work in causing race degeneracy concerning which the majority of girls are ignorant, and that is immorality. The prevalent idea that young men must "sow their wild oats" is accepted by many young women as true, and they think if the lover reforms before marriage and remains true to them thereafter, that is all they can reasonably demand. They will not make such excuses for themselves for lapses from virtue, but they imbibe the idea that men are not to be held to an absolute standard of purity, and so think it delicate to shut their eyes to the derelictions of young men. This chapter of human life is a sorrowful one to read, but to heed its warning would save many a girl from sorrow, many a wife from heartache. The penalty inflicted for the violation of moral law is one of the most severe, both in its effects upon the individual transgressor and upon his descendants. The most dreadful scourge of physical disease, as well as moral degeneracy, follows an impure life.

The doctor next related in some detail the effects of syphilis ("practically incurable") and concluded with this final admonition:

> A young woman of pure life married a man whose reputation was bad, but whose social position was high. To-day she is suffering from the horrible disease which he communicated to her, and her children have died or are betraying to the world in their very faces the

story of their father's wrong deeds. Truly you cannot afford to be ignorant of facts so grave as these.[36]

Dr. Wood-Allen's lecture on narcotics would have found pertinence among the influx of Chinese railroad workers entering Colorado Territory during the early 1870s, with the attendant presence of opium. The *Weekly Central City Register* in 1874 published an article titled "The Opium Pipe: The Heathen Chinese and the Narcotic of Death: How John [Chinaman] Smokes His Pipe." By 1880, Denver had seventeen opium dens, of which twelve were along "Hop Alley" on Wazee Street. The dens also bred a small number of Chinese prostitutes, or *baak haak chai* ("one hundred men's wife"), whose presence in Denver was recorded as early as 1871 when Town Marshal George Hopkins was instructed by the city government to prevent property from being rented to Chinese for "lewd purposes." The girls' earnings usually went to reimburse flesh merchants for their passage from China to the United States, but unlike San Francisco's Barbary Coast, the great majority of Denver's Market Street prostitutes were of nationalities other than Chinese.[37]

Such was not the case with opium, however. The importation of opium from the Far East remained legal until 1909, although it was subjected to such high import duties that many Chinese businessmen preferred to smuggle it into the United States. Opium was the narcotic of choice for Chinese in Colorado as well as California. The *Rocky Mountain News* reported under the triple headlines "Heathen Hordes," "The Chinese Still Crowding into the State," and "Ruining Labor and Encouraging Immorality":

A visit to the den on Arapahoe street showed it to be full of smokers, a large portion of whom were women, in the several stages of stupefaction [*sic*] produced by the drug. There seemed to be no secrecy about the matter. Any one could gain admission by knocking at the door, and once inside the Chinamen could be seen, some lazily lighting their pipes in the bunks—others enjoying the dreamy sleep produced by the opiate. Very few men were seen excepting the Chinese, but all of the women were Caucasians. It is well-known that China women do not smoke opium; that is a privilege enjoyed solely by their lords and masters. "You get more women than men here, don't you?"

was asked of the celestial who was looking after the commercial interests of the joint. "Yes, belly muchee." "How many more?" "Ten ladee one manee muchee smokee." "You mean you get ten women to one man?" He nodded his head and grinned ear to ear, saying, "Allee samee."[38]

The article was published on October 27, 1880. Three days later began the most serious ethnic disturbances in Denver's history to that date, the so-called Anti-Chinese Riots. That account is discussed later.

A physician named Gee was accused in 1883 by Hattie Jones, age twenty-one, of administering opium to her and seducing her. Jones told a *Rocky Mountain News* reporter that Gee had "asked me to be his girl . . . he said he had lots of girls," but when pressed for details Jones became vague and the newspaper observed that she was "intensely ignorant," suggesting that the matter may have been one of blackmail. Nonetheless, Gee was jailed briefly.[39]

In the mid-1880s, a vendetta developed between District Attorney LeDru R. Rhodes and the Chinese of Denver. Rhodes had a particular dislike for prostitutes, and a few months later he was caught attempting to concoct evidence against one of the most famous of them. This time, however, Gum Sing and Toy Ding, described by the newspapers as female residents of a Wazee Street "lewd house," were arrested for vagrancy. Rhodes had previously tried to prosecute Gum Sing and Toy Ding as residents of a lewd house, but the charges were tossed out when the court could not define how many residents were required to constitute a lewd house.

The district attorney was "much exasperated" by the dismissal of the charges and "vowed he would make them leave Wazee street, even if he had to arrest them for vagrancy," a catchall charge to get people off the street. Once in jail, the women encountered problems when they refused to surrender their money to other female prisoners and were beaten by cellmates. Finally released on bail, Toy Ding expressed her desire to "return to China very badly" and vowed to do just that when she could raise sufficient funds. A friend of the Chinese ladies asked indignantly, with reference to their treatment, "Is this American law?"[40]

The Chinese in Denver beginning in 1889 were involved in an imaginative scam concocted by a fast-talking Anglo swindler. William H. Hale purchased Fong Ning's laundry and installed Fong Ning as the Gun Wa of "Gun Wa's Herb Remedy Company," 1625–1629 Larimer Street. (Some have suggested that Colorado gambling king Ed Chase had a financial interest in the Gun Wa scheme.) Hale and Fong Ning gathered sage plants and "hired a negro," said the *Denver Republican*, to pound the sage and boil it in a big copper vat. The elixir thus produced was bottled and sold, the newspaper reported, "with elaborate directions as to taking it," as instructed by "Gun Wa, the celebrated Chinese doctor." The advertisements read "Weak men made strong, old men made young," and investigators discovered that Gun Wa sent illustrations through the mail of sex organs "restored" by his potion. The enterprise became enormously successful, taking in $10,000 a month with branch offices in Milwaukee, Kansas City, Detroit, St. Louis, Indianapolis, and Baltimore. Each of those cities had its own Gun Wa, an opulently dressed Chinese gentleman.

All good things must end, however, and in 1891 Hale and his Gun Was (except Fong Ning, who saw the storm clouds gathering and hid out) were arrested for mail fraud. Each of the Gun Was was fined $500. Hale was released on $5,000 bond, which he promptly jumped and fled to his home in Belfast, Ireland. After subsequent fraud arrests there and in Liverpool, England, he was extradited to Denver and sentenced in August 1896 to eighteen months in the Joliet, Illinois, federal penitentiary.[41]

Other than an occasional cry of indignation, little heed to the Blake and Wazee Street opium dens was paid by respectable Denverites, who had resolved that patrons of such hellholes deserved whatever misfortunes befell them. An exception was the aforementioned militant reformed gambler and social commentator G. N. Scamehorn, who wrote of the Blake Street fate of Hattie Caldwell:

Mrs. Hattie Caldwell's life was cut short through dissipation and she went down through the valley and shadow of death in one of the lowest dives that blots the fair name of our beautiful city. On the morning of November 21st, 1893, a fair and beautiful young girl was found cold and still in death, in a dark and dismal dive, presided over by a Chinaman, and that too beneath the shadow of our city hall [at Fourteenth and Larimer Streets, also the location of police headquarters]. After a night of dissipation and carousing, Mrs. Caldwell sought the delusive repose which habitual smokers of opium so much crave. . . . Some time after midnight they entered the notorious opium Joint of Louis Hong, at 1317 Blake street, within a stones through [sic] of City Hall. Here the party at once proceeded to enjoy the deadly drug, little did they think that the dissipated career of one of their number was to result in one of the darkest and sadest [sic] tragedies ever recorded in the dark pages of Denver's history. For, only a few hours later, Hattie Caldwell was carried from this vile den a corpse, she had succumbed to excessive opium smoking, dying in the greatest agony before medical assistance could be of any avail.[42]

To the city's distinction, Moy Gop, reportedly "the only Chinese detective employed by the United States," resided in Denver in 1900. The *Denver Post* on July 27 that year published an interview with Gop, who was thirty-seven and a naturalized American citizen. His parents had been wealthy residents of Canton but treated the lad poorly, so he stowed away on an American-bound steamer in 1875. In San Francisco he fell in with a gang of blackmailers who were subsequently arrested, and Gop became attracted to law enforcement. The article was vague as to what sort of government work Gop was engaged in or why he was in Denver, but his duties often required him to live in Washington, D.C., and sometimes included interpretation activities.

References to the Japanese are seldom found in Denver's vice annals, because immigration practices resulted in fewer Japanese than Chinese locating in Denver. An exception is this rather strong passage from the *Rocky Mountain News*. The headline read "Authorities Believe Japs Engaged in Flesh Traffic Are Responsible in Many Cases," and the story related:

For months the police have been cognizant of the existence in Denver of an underground channel of "white slave" operations, but all attempts to learn the identity of the leaders have proved futile. The foreign element residing in the redlight district are supposed to be engaged in the traffic. The police records for five months show the disappearance of twenty-one girls from their homes in Denver and towns throughout Colorado. These disappearances were due, the police believe, to the efforts of "white slavers" and other social evil influences.[43]

This period may have manifested a brief spate of xenophobia in Denver regarding the Japanese. A month later the proprietors of two Japanese restaurants were arrested after they were found to be employing "two young white girls." The vague charges seemed to be that the girls, runaways from their Nebraska farm homes, had been drinking. The city threatened to revoke the licenses of the restaurants, but nothing ever came of it.[44]

Hop Alley and its opium dens—particularly in the 2000-block alley between Blake and Market Streets and also along Twenty-second Street at Blake, Market, and Wazee Streets—were conveniently proximate to the Market Street bordellos. The dens offered morphine and cocaine as well as opium, and partaking was called "hitting the pipe" or "sucking the bamboo." On occasion, groups of "proper" Anglo young ladies and girls from Denver's respectable neighborhoods would venture to Hop Alley for an evening of giggling and dreams in the forbidden confines of the opium parlors. There they might be located by the police and returned to their shocked parents. The residents of the bordellos, also present in the dens during the young girls' "slumming" expeditions, grew to resent such intrusions.[45]

In 1908 Denver's opium joints may have established a national precedent by becoming racially segregated. One Anglo "hophead," hoping for a few puffs at his favorite establishment, went down the "dark and ill-smelling subterranean passage off Twentieth [Street], back of Blake," as described by the Rocky Mountain News on September 20, and knocked on the familiar door. "The door opened a few inches, and a weasel face peered out into the night."

"Nexit dio," the proprietor instructed. "Next door? What for?" the "hoppy" asked. "Cloled folk in here. All cloled."

The customer pushed his way in and through the haze saw, according to the paper, "that all the occu-

pants of the tier of bunks ranged against the wall were negroes."

Next door, he indeed found his old associates and his pipe. "They've drawn the color line in Hop alley, old pal," was the drowsy statement from a friend. The blind Chinese man who owned the two places confirmed as much: "No white people in the 'Jim Crow' joint and no colored people in the white 'hop joint.'" The News concluded with the sole observation that the new arrangements made "it rather inconvenient for the old-timers who have become used to a certain bunk in one or the other dens."

Five years later, Denver authorities ordered the closing of the so-called black and tan saloons, establishments frequented by both white and black women and their escorts. They seemed to be sources of ongoing trouble, and in June 1913 Safety Commissioner Alexander Nisbet ordered them all closed as part of a general "cleanup" for the upcoming Turnverein and Knights Templar conventions, which would bring hundreds of celebrating men to town. Toward the same end, Nisbet said he would also ban all street peddlers and restrict the presence of street-corner popcorn wagons. He said he wanted Denver to present a "clean front; I do not want to see the city degraded in the eyes of our visitors, but even if Denver had no conventions in sight, it is time for these plague spots of immorality to go."[46]

Denver's police seem only occasionally to have bothered with the opium dens, whose activities were openly known around town. One infrequent roundup took place just after midnight March 7, 1900, when the police raided several dope dens near Twenty-first and Market Streets. The Denver Post reported that the "hop fiends were a sorry lot this morning, as they yawned and stretched their arms while waiting for Prosecuting Attorney Adams." In the gang were two women who were dirty, their hair hung down their backs in matted strings. The women, their eight male companions, and five Chinese hosts were fined ten dollars and costs each.

The tripling of Denver's population during the great Leadville rush of the early 1880s and the attendant number of dope, vice, and prostitution dens overtaxed city services, including police capabilities. The press—particularly Thomas Patterson's *Denver Times*—pointed out the shortcomings:

> Never in all her history was Denver so at the mercy of thugs, hold-ups and professional burglars as now, and never was she in the hands of a police department with less inclination or ability to stop the lawlessness. Dozens of well-known thieves are in town, and have been for months. So well-known are they that even the captain of detectives knows them.[47]

Forbes Parkhill, who at the turn of the twentieth century was a young reporter for the *Denver Post*, later recalled Denver's vice district during those years. On the "lower side" (presumably the northwest side) of Market Street near Twentieth, a number of doorways or passageways led directly to the Hop Alley opium dens. There, Parkhill wrote:

> On either side of a dim, narrow corridor the visitor found tiny, windowless, board-partitioned cubicles, barely large enough for a cot and a taboret containing the opium-smoking layout. As a police reporter, I once took part in a raid on these firetrap opium joints. The raiders were empowered to make arrests only when they discovered a smoker in the act of "hitting the pipe." The patrolmen would boost me up to look over the transoms. If I found an addict actually smoking, he was arrested. The raid netted a number of white men, a few Negroes, two Chinese, and no women. The only woman addict I ever knew of was 22-year-old Eva Latour, one of Mattie's [Silks] girls, who killed herself with opium. Once smelled, the sweet odor of opium smoke is never forgotten. Sometimes this not-unpleasant odor seemed to fill Market Street.[48]

In late 1891 the Chinese proprietors of Wazee Street's small gambling establishments began landing in jail, all arrested by William A. Glasson, general manager of Glasson's Secret Service, a private detective agency. Private detective organizations at the time augmented the undermanned and underfunded police departments, and some agents had powers of arrest, especially in situations of interstate flight to avoid prosecution.

In the Glasson case, the *Denver Times* reported that "prominent Chinamen say that they were told that if they paid so much money to Glasson he would not have them arrested. They refused, hence their arrest." Glasson, it was discovered upon investigation by the Denver police, even drew up a contract with the Chin Poo faction of Chinese "in which Glasson acknowledges the receipt of a sum of money on condition that he will not molest any member of the Chin Poo faction between the date of contract and Jan. 1, 1892." The Fire and Police Board, Detective Sam Howe noted, quickly "commenced an investigation of Mr. Glasson's way of doing business."[49]

Chinese opium was the drug of choice among Denver's giddy middle- and upper-middle-class white women, who regarded it as daring to gather in a darkened den to smoke and doze. Opium was also particularly popular among criminals, prostitutes, and gamblers. Hop Alley became a tourist attraction. Visitor David H. Strother of West Virginia wrote in his journal that he "went with a party to visit Chinese Row. Found them playing a game like dominoes, smoking opium, casting up sums on a counting machine. Very quiet, civil, and characteristic. The girls, daughters of Ah Sin, pretty, smiling, and corrupt."[50] As will be demonstrated in these pages, easily available drugs of several sorts were the cause of many prostitutes' deaths, including suicides.

Denver endured a riot by and against its Chinese residents on October 31–November 1, 1880. Three weeks later the Chinese asked the city to pay for damage to their property, but the aldermen declined, saying they were not liable. Although the riot was serious, it was not narcotics-inspired, but the city nonetheless responded in 1881 by passing a law prohibiting "opium joints." The fine of $50 to $300 seems somewhat severe, considering that the penalty for maintaining a bawdy house was $5 to $100 and the fine for helping with a jail break was $25 to $100.

Cocaine was observed in Denver during the spring of 1885, but initially it was greatly misunderstood to be, as termed by the *Rocky Mountain News*, a "new and valuable anaesthetic [sic]." It was freely available from the pharmacy under the name "Bright Eye," was sold by the pinch in a shot of whiskey, and would become available in popular beverages such as Coca-Cola. Colorado did not restrict the unauthorized sale of cocaine until 1897, and the next year Denver passed an ordinance banning the "selling, exchanging, bartering, dispensing, and giving away" without a prescription not only of cocaine but also of morphine and opium. The fine for violation was $25 to $100.

Denver's narcotics abusers were allowed to rant and rave in their rooms or on the public streets, were committed to the state asylum in Pueblo, or were jailed. The last approach was used with regard to "Morphine Dick" Shannon, a talented young musician and graduate of the Chester, Pennsylvania, Academy of Music, who became hooked on morphine when he was injected with it after breaking a leg.

A madman without his syringe and bottle of dope, Shannon spent no more than three months out of jail during each of the eighteen years he lived in Denver, and he was reduced to playing the piano in the Market Street bordellos to feed his habit. In 1893 Denver police "gave him up as a bad job," and every time he was arrested he was sent to jail, where he was supplied with more morphine because without it he was a raving maniac.

In the midst of yet another hundred-day sentence, jail warden Albert H. Weber gave Morphine Dick a bath, clean clothing, and a good talking-to and began doling out a concoction called "squibbs," which contained a small amount of opium. The doses were gradually decreased, Shannon began to eat and exercise, his eyes turned bright, his complexion cleared up (except for hundreds of needle scars), and the county physician pronounced him cured. "Morphine ruined the best 20 years of my life," he said. "Thank God I don't want it any more. You'll never see me back here again." Morphine Dick had received the treatment most abusers in Denver either rejected or were not offered.

As early as 1883, drug and alcohol abuse was so prevalent in Colorado that the state became at the forefront in providing treatment at public expense. Friends or relatives who were unable to pay could petition their county commissioners to send the addict to a sanitarium at public expense. Treatments at such facilities often included daily injections of strychnine and atropine, which often resulted in mental disorders. The state rescinded its treatment provision two years later and began establishing standards for such centers.

Legislation, however, did not slow the use of narcotics in Denver, and abuses persisted. Still, physicians and social agencies had yet to grasp the consequences of drug abuse and its effects on the brain. Of the almost 2,000 patients admitted to the Colorado Insane Asylum in Pueblo between 1887 and 1900, authorities attributed only twenty-seven admissions to drug addiction—outdistanced in each case by liquor abuse, syphilis, "sexual self-abuse," and "religious excitement."[51]

A poet of sorts penned his impressions of an 1898 dope party attended by the *demimonde* of Butte, Montana Territory:

> All the junkies were invited
> Yes, every gink and muff,
> Not a single one was slighted
> If they were on the stuff.
>
> Invitations were presented
> To every hustler and her man.
> They even sent up invites
> To the hopheads in the can.
>
> But before they play the grand march
> Let each dancer have a shot;
> It will act as stimulation,
> And should make the dancin' hot.
>
> So from scores of hiding places
> Guests brought forth their hypo gats;
> From sleeves, brassieres and bustles,
> Some even hid them in their rats.
>
> Not all the cokies used the needle,
> Some from their opium pipes did whiff;
> Others drained their paregoric,
> A few of "happy dust" did sniff.
>
> Opium pills or hasheesh
> Came forth from many a sock.
> And some twist from China Alley
> Brought out her old yen hok.

Gink is "fellow," muff is prostitute, gat is a handgun, rat is a woman's hair ornament, a cokie is a drug addict, happy dust is cocaine, and twist means loose woman.[52]

Attempted suicides using drugs then commonly available were everyday occurrences. Rena Myers of

Denver was seventeen when she tried to commit suicide by chloroform ingestion after a disagreement with her boyfriend. The pharmacist from whom she purchased the drug said she asserted that she had a toothache, and he assured investigators that the bottle was "properly labeled."[53] Suicides crossed all social and economic boundaries. In one twenty-four-hour period in April 1889, a visiting businessman, a physician, and a druggist either hanged themselves or consumed overdoses of morphine in Denver. Indeed, the coroner's office was so full of "suicides and murdered men" that the *Rocky Mountain News* referred to it as a "Chamber of Horrors."[54]

Death from morphine was particularly disturbing. On March 6, 1892, two of madam Mattie Silks's girls, Effie Pryor and Allie Ellis, were discovered "lying on their backs, side by side, disrobed and gasping for breath, their faces black and distorted," in Mattie's place at 1916 Market Street. After drinking all night and all morning, Effie and Allie decided to end it all with morphine because Allie's boyfriend had deserted her and Effie was sympathetic. Mattie Silks told police that a young pharmacy clerk traded them the morphine for the privilege of taking pornographic photos of the two women. Dr. F. K. Dabney and police surgeon D. H. Smith used emetics and the stomach pump; Effie was saved, but Allie died a few days later after confessing her low life to "Parson" Tom Uzzell, one of Denver's best-known clergymen, and asking to be remembered fondly to her respectable parents in Greenville, Missouri.[55]

Suicides of young women of the cribs and parlor houses were further recorded in accounts preserved by Detective Howe. Sometimes the stories were three lines long; on other occasions circumstances warranted more complete accounts, particularly at Christmastime. An example:

> The room, it is said, is only a sample of the rest in the ricketty [*sic*] old row. The walls and ceiling were absolutely black with smoke and dirt, excepting where old, stained newspapers had been pasted upon them—on the ceiling, to exclude rain and melting snow, and on the walls, to cover up spots from which the plastering had fallen. The floor was rickety and filthy. Around the walls were disposed innumerable unwashed

and battered tin cooking utensils, shelves, for the most part laden with dust, old clothing, which emitted powerful effluvium, hung from nails here and there; or tumble-down chairs, a table of very rheumatic tendency, on which were broken cups, plates and remnants of food, were scattered all over its surface. An empty whisky bottle and pewter spoon or two. In one corner and taking up half the space of the den was the bedstead strongly suggestive of a bountiful crop of vermin, and on that flimsy bed lay the corpse of the suicide, clad in dirty ragged apparel, and with as horrid a look on her begrimed [*sic*], pallid features as the surroundings presented. No one of her neighbors in wretchedness had had the sense to open either of the two little windows in the room to admit pure air, hence the atmosphere was sickeningly impure and almost asphixiating [*sic*]. "My God!" exclaimed Coroner [Charles K.] McHatton, used as he is to similar scenes and smells in his official capacity, "Isn't this awful?"[56]

Ladies of the red light district were particularly dejected and introspective during the yule season. Christmas was the only holiday during which they were not busy, and they had ample time to ponder the misguided courses of their lives. Lillie, who gravitated to Holladay Street after a broken romance, ended her life in her room there, and on the bed stand were a white lily and the handwritten card:

> *Mad from life's history,*
> *   Glad to death's mystery,*
> *Swift to be hurled—*
> *   Anywhere, anywhere,*
> *Out of this world.*[57]

Pornography, to which Effie Pryor and Allie Ellis were supposedly subjected, was an unusual occurrence in Denver in the late 1880s, although it was spreading westward from the urban centers of the East. Improved printing techniques transformed pornography into a growth industry in New York as early as the 1840s, and vest-pocket books sold for a dollar at most corner newsstands and also served as guides to the prostitution districts. Sometimes they were disguised as reformist warnings to the public, as demonstrated by the title page of an 1839 booklet: "Prostitution Exposed, or, a Moral Reform Directory, Laying Bare the Lives, Histories, Residences, Seductions, &c., of the most Celebrated Courtezans and Ladies of Pleasure of the City of New York, together with a Description of the Crime and its Effects . . . and other Particulars Interesting to the Public."[58] Most early pornography consisted of more words than pictures, although imported French pornography was increasingly illustrated.

Although Denver was somewhat behind the East in pornography development, cases did exist, particularly as the processes of printing illustrations were improved. Photographer H. H. Russell, with studios at Fourteenth and Larimer Streets, along with "colored girls" Cora Thornton, Nola Jefferson, and Jessie Talbott, was arrested February 10, 1887, on charges of making and circulating obscene photographs. The evidence, the newspapers reported, displayed the "three frail maidens, each clothed in a single ear-ring and a smile." Jefferson was subsequently arrested in Denver for grand larceny and on September 21, 1888, was sentenced to the Colorado State Penitentiary. She was released on March 16, 1891. Thornton was convicted of grand larceny in Lake County and on August 20, 1891, was sentenced to the penitentiary. She was released on July 22, 1892. Each told prison authorities her occupation was "servant."[59]

A pair of publications, *Hustler* and the *Denver Sunday Sun*, became known to authorities in 1891. Nothing has been discovered about *Hustler* except that it was "perverted." Denver police in February of that year prohibited the *Sunday Sun* from being printed in the city, so the press work was done in Pueblo with plans to circulate the publication in Denver. Denver police decided otherwise and arrested principals H. D. Rucker, Frank Parks, and J. Humphrey, seizing 2,000 copies of the paper.[60]

On July 29, 1892, five men including printer C. F. Colman, whose shop was at 1838 Lawrence Street, were arrested for possession of what the newspapers described as "the most obscene literature that could be conceived by even the most diseased imagination . . . the worst products of London's printed filth and Parisian indecency." Officers estimated that about 125 of the "pamphlets" had already been sold at one to ten dollars each.[61]

The Broadway, at the upper end of Sixteenth Street, was Denver's finest legitimate theater, and on its boards trod the best traveling stage productions entering Colorado. The Broadway by the turn of the twentieth century had even supplanted the Tabor Grand, which was becoming rather seedy. In early 1895, however, the Broadway mounted a production titled *Living Pictures* that appears to have been a series of still lifes that, taken together, purported to deliver some sort of artistic and theatrical message.

Two acts were titled "The Temptation of St. Anthony" and "Truth." One of Denver's few judges of public morals at the time was the WCTU, which complained to the Fire and Police Board that the two acts contained images that were improper for public viewing. The board, accordingly, adopted a resolution prohibiting

> exposing to view the shape, private parts of nature, breasts, limbs and such parts as would be an indecent exposure of the person if exposed in the public streets, [which] is an indecent exposure, demoralizing the minds and sensual inclinations of men and women, boys and girls, and society in general, attracted to such theaters to witness such immodest, immoral, unchaste and degrading exposure.

Police Chief Hamilton Armstrong and two of his detectives attended the Broadway on the evening of January 18, 1895, to determine if the *Living Pictures* violated public sensibilities as defined by the Fire and Police Board. The officers observed that the figure of "Truth" was a woman, according to the *Rocky Mountain News* the next day, "gowned in a Mother Hubbard [robe] and small black coat, and crowned with a Salvation Army bonnet. Held high in her right hand was an electric light, while she leaned upon an umbrella held in her left. Her face was fixed in a look of determination truly heroic."

There could be nothing objectionable about such a portrayal, because word of the board's resolution had reached the producers before Chief Armstrong and his men arrived. At the foot of the figure was a sign reading: "Modified to suit the ideas of the fire and police board and the W.C.T.U." At the close of the program, however, Armstrong, perhaps to underscore his presence, informed the management that even more modifications needed to be made, although the *News* did not specify what the chief's further objections could possibly have been.

Armstrong, moreover, interpreted the board's edict as applying not only to the usually respectable Broadway but also to the various flicker grottoes up and down Fifteenth and Sixteenth Streets where, said the *News*, "young girls and men are permitted to congregate. . . . It seems to be a well established fact that the majority of the patrons of these places are minors and women of shady reputation." Armstrong pledged to keep close track of what was going on in such places.

But that was hardly the end of the WCTU's morality crusade. One member reported to Armstrong that she was, according to the *News* on January 19,

> walking along Curtis street between Fifteenth and Sixteenth when the bright light inside a saloon caught her eye. Involuntarily glancing inside she saw a sight well calculated to make the blood of a Christian woman boil. Just over the low curtains which were across the windows she could see a painting of a woman entirely devoid of costume. In order to increase the effect a number of electric lights were so arranged as to make this painting the brightest object in the place. The woman was shocked and hurried along. Next day, she told her sisters of the W.C.T.U., and they went out on an investigating tour that evening.

The ladies observed a similar picture in a wine joint on the opposite side of the street. "That was too much," the *News* continued, "and yesterday the fire and police board were told of the shame of the community. The members of the board," the newspaper reported with a straight face, "could hardly believe that such pictures were hung so as to attract the youth of the city to saloons and promised to investigate the matter very thoroughly."

In 1908 Mrs. E. T. Scott, a national lecturer for the WCTU, was horrified by what she observed in Denver. Scott was in town as an advance planner for a WCTU convention in the city that autumn and observed to the *Denver Post* that her sleep was interrupted every night by the "ribald jests" of men and women leaving the saloons. "From midnight until 4 o'clock in the morning the doors of Denver winerooms swing open for the young girls in astonishing numbers," she huffed. "I have had thrust under my observation wickedness of this sort which even New York or Chicago cannot surpass."

The naughty appeal of forbidden images was not confined to Denver's saloon customers or errant youth. At one point downtown merchants puzzled over the sudden demand for opera glasses, telescopes, binoculars, and the like. The buyers seemed to be prominent businessmen with offices in the prestigious eight-story Ernest and Cranmer office building at Seventeenth and Curtis Streets. One curious merchant sent a clerk to investigate why so many telescopes were going to one building, and the clerk observed that the building looked like an arsenal, with telescopes projecting from nearly every north-facing window. The north of the building faced a young ladies' boardinghouse whose occupants often forgot to draw their window shades. The *Denver Post* had a good deal of fun with the story, which probably reached the eyes of the wives of some of Denver's most prominent gentlemen—including City Attorney James M. Ellis and Assistant City Attorney Henry F. Jolly, particularly singled out for mention.[62]

In May 1902 the Wonderland and White House entertainment emporiums featured hand-cranked flickering picture machines that flipped a succession of cards bearing images of naked models in poses, the *Denver Times* grumped, "too bad to be described in detail." The *Times* added that compared to these girlie flicks, "burlesque shows are tasteful and artful."[63]

In 1908 Denver briefly found itself the hub of an international pornography ring with an innovative twist. Henry Goodman was a wholesale porn merchant, and his Novelty Supply House at Seventeenth and Lawrence Streets was the center of it all. Goodman's method was to obtain obscene photographs of females, paste on the pictures head shots of famous American women such as actresses or socialites, convert the altered photographs into halftone engravings, and use the engravings to print thousands of copies of the fake photos, which were marketed in small folders with suggestive titles.

Goodman advertised his product by flooding the country with brochures inviting prospective customers to "look over this list of warm subjects." In an attempt to avoid using the U.S. mails he shipped his goods via express, but the tactic did not work, despite his plea in court that "others were doing the same thing all over the country." Judge Robert E. Lewis of Denver U.S. District Court sentenced Goodman to two years in Leavenworth. Goodman's wife wailed in response: "Oh my children, my poor children! They will have to bear the hard name of it all. I have four of them and what will they do without their father?"[64]

The next year, 1909, a pornography racket invaded Denver's upper middle class. Harry Farris, age fifty-three—a prominent north Denver landowner, churchgoer, philanthropist, and upstanding father and husband—was arrested by a postal inspector and a deputy U.S. marshal for marketing what the *Denver Post* described as "the worst [photographs] that have gone through the Denver mails in many years." He advertised his wares in eastern publications such as *Marriage Bells*, and most of his customers were said to be female. His motive, he told police, was "just to make a little easy money," and he was fined one dollar and sentenced to ninety days in county jail.[65] The same year, Walter Britton, age seventeen, was nabbed by officers for handing cards "bearing indecent rhymes" to women pedestrians at Sixteenth and Curtis Streets.[66]

Lecherous real estate agent James H. Mackley and his brother John appear to have convinced authorities that their fondness for nubile young girls existed only to promote business in Colorado. The brothers inserted advertisements in newspapers summoning girls "whose figures scored perfect" to the Mackleys' civil engineering and real estate office at 1738 California Street for "measuring and photographing." Under questioning by police, James Mackley held fast to his story that the nude photos were simply for advertising. John Mackley's new seventeen-year-old bride, Matilda, told a different story: "I answered one of their advertisements. John Mackley conducted me to a rear room and mistreated me while he was pretending to measure me. I protested until he took me to the courthouse and married me. He then sent me to live on a ranch near Greeley."[67] Because of "lack of evidence," no charges were brought.[68]

In November 1899 the police were after "Jack the Hugger," who prowled the streets of old Auraria at night, giving women and girls hugs and then running away. Next he moved to the Capitol Hill neighborhood, where he operated nearly every night. Denver's street patrolmen, the *Post* remarked, received ongoing complaints but did not tell headquarters because it would look as if they weren't doing their jobs. The last straw, the officers said, was when Jack the Hugger grabbed onto a Mrs. Gordon and her daughter of 2310 Pennsylvania Avenue (later Pennsylvania Street) as they came home from church; they "screamed so badly that the whole neighborhood was aroused. The police," said the *Post*, "have had a decoy out parading the streets for this fiend, and if he grabs her it will be the last woman he ever catches hold of, as she is instructed to *shoot him dead*" (emphasis added). Meantime, Mrs. Gordon was "so badly frightened that it was thought she would have nervous prostration." Jack the Hugger appears not to have been heard from again.[69]

One night an angry and very large Newfoundland dog ran berserk through the Market Street bordello district. "The dog," reported the *Rocky Mountain News* on September 12, 1907, "was first spotted at Twenty-first and Larimer streets. It scattered the crowds clear to Market street and ran the full length of the redlight district, causing the denizens of the quarter to seek the refuge of houses and saloons and to blow their police whistles lustily." (Prostitutes and madams of the brothel district were equipped with police-issued whistles for summoning quick help.)

Sam Howe, whenever circumstances required, recorded cases of unacceptable affinities. In summer 1907 William Anderson, age twenty-nine, "believed to be a degenerate by the police" (or thus reported the *Denver Republican*), paid a dozen small girls to disrobe and "conduct a resurrection of the Grecian dance of the water nymphs" in the swimming pool at Jerome Park.

When one such resurrection was discovered, a lynch mob formed, and 500 "infuriated people from blocks around" began chasing the terrified Anderson, who found refuge in a nearby beer joint where he was rescued by policeman Christian D. Snider, who had to stand in the door with his gun drawn to keep the irate crowd away. The mob again tried to get Anderson when he was being escorted aboard the patrol wagon on his way to jail. He was charged with contributing to juvenile delinquency. In dismissing the charges, City Magistrate DeStelle B. DeLappe cited that no state statute prohibited contributing to the delinquency of a minor.[70]

Fred W. Bates, afflicted with a considerable over-imbibing problem, repaired to a saloon for another pail of beer on an autumn afternoon in 1903. Upon returning to the barn at 1116 Twentieth Street, where he had been relaxing with a drinking buddy, Bates discovered an agitated crowd demanding that he be lynched for assaulting a five-year-old girl in the barn. The *Rocky Mountain News* continued the account:

> Bates, though still very drunk, realized the seriousness of his position and dropped his can of beer and ran. [He] was arrested yesterday morning at his home, 1716 Blake Street. His wife called at the city jail. . . . She waxed indignant over the arrest of her husband on such a charge and declared that, while he is in the habit of getting drunk, he would never think of committing such a crime. When asked yesterday by Police Captain [Mike "Third Degree"] Delaney why he ran if he was not guilty, Bates replied: "Well, when I saw the crowd and heard what they accused me of, I thought it was up to me to make tracks out of the neighborhood. You know very well, captain, that under such circumstances a mob won't listen to reason, and I thought they might hang me to a telephone pole while they were in a rage, and discover when it was too late that I was an innocent man. Such a discovery, however, would not have brought me back to life, so I concluded I would get out of the vicinity."[71]

Narcotics remained more of a concern among Denver authorities during this time, however, than did pornography or suspected child assault. Denver and its public press were expressing increasing concern regarding the epidemic of dope usage and the easy over-the-counter availability of morphine, laudanum, cocaine, and even chloroform. A *Denver Times* reporter in 1900 wrote of this scenario:

> "Cocaine? Certainly."
> The druggist stepped behind the prescription counter and after dismissing the customer, heaved a sigh:

"It's funny, this cocaine business," he said.

"How did you know whether or not the man wanted it diluted?" asked a *Times* representative.

"How did I know? Why, he's an old customer. People out of the business have no idea how prevalent is the cocaine habit in Denver, and, in fact, everywhere. The man who just went out called on me a year ago for something to relieve an aching tooth. I suggested several remedies, but he shook his head at each and then asked me what I thought of cocaine. I knew it was no use to argue. I recognized in a minute that he was a cocaine fiend, and let him have it. The cocaine habit invariably starts with its use for pains and aches, and while it is a certain remedy for temporary relief, my experience is that many never stop using it, becoming so fond of it as a drug that they cannot and will not break off, and at the same time would be insulted if you were to suggest that they were slaves to the drug. You never see a cocaine fiend who uses it for other than strictly medicinal purposes. It is, in nine cases out of ten, a very convenient toothache cure. Another surprising feature is the large number of women who use it habitually. Many of them inject the solution. Some actually eat it."[72]

Eight years later Denver's narcotics abuse problem may have worsened, with the press occasionally publishing a vivid account of a particularly severe case of addiction. The following article, published in the *Denver Republican* on November 15, 1908, is repeated here nearly in its entirety and is unique in the degree of alarm it exhibits, and its relevance to a later age:

> Tearing at the bars of his cell with bleeding fingers, a boy of only 19 or 20 years of age screamed curses at officials in the city jail the other night, while across the hall in the women's department a girl of about the same age knelt and pleaded wildly, and, strange to say, neither was pleading for freedom, neither wanted friends to be notified, and, truth to tell, neither realized their position or that iron bars shut them in. A few moments later an officer hurried down the corridor with a small box in his hand. The girl seized the box with mad frenzy and tearing off the lid took a pinch of its contents, sniffing it eagerly up her nostrils. The scene was repeated on the boy's side of the corridor and the jail once more assumed the quiet

that is only broken occasionally by the mutterings of some drunken man. The box brought by the officer contained cocaine, known in police parlance as "coke," and the boy and girl, the officer would have told anyone who inquired, were "coke fiends."

Early last week F. W. Nitardy, state pharmaceutical inspector, said that 50 percent of crime in Denver and other cities of Colorado was caused by the use of such drugs as cocaine, morphine and opium. In his statement made through the *Republican* Mr. Nitardy asserted that the state pure food department would soon take up the work of securing laws to prohibit the unrestricted sale of such drugs at pharmacies or by physicians. Chief of Police [Hamilton] Armstrong and other officers of the Denver police force declare that Nitardy was wrong in his assertion that 50 percent of the crime is caused by drugs. They say he should have said two-thirds of the crime and he would have been nearer correct. . . . An average of two out of three persons arrested for misdemeanors are coke fiends. Chief Armstrong's opinion of the drug habit and the evils of unrestricted sale are expressed tersely when he says: "Take the 'coke' out of Denver and the police department will lose one of its most reliable theories of crime."

"Coke fiends" are not only watched, they are feared by police officers. They have been known to become seized with murderous fury when placed under arrest and with "coke cunning" to watch for opportunity to use a weapon upon the officer. . . . The habitual "coke fiend" known to the police does not, as is commonly supposed, use a hypodermic needle, but absorbs large quantities of the drug through his or her nostrils.

Every particle of police experience goes to prove the contention of Mr. Nitardy that the unrestricted sale of such a drug is responsible for a large per cent of the crime. Mr. Nitardy further affirms that the police department of Chicago has discovered that 75 per cent of the murderers in that city are addicted to cocaine. . . . It is the contention of the state pure food department that no person should be allowed to purchase cocaine or any other drug without a physician's prescription and that even on prescription the amount to be purchased should be limited. Mr. Nitardy has recommended that a druggist convicted of selling cocaine, opium, morphine, cannabis indica or other narcotics should have his license revoked for 30 days for the first offense and suspended altogether for any subsequent offense.[73]

The remarkably effortless access in Denver to potentially lethal narcotics is difficult to envision in a later age. Prostitutes, seeking to obliterate the conditions under which they existed, were particularly vulnerable. Sociologist Ruth Rosen wrote:

For prostitutes, having sexual relations with customers for whom they felt physical disgust was a daily fact of life. From fragmentary evidence, it appears that some prostitutes used morphine to immunize themselves against these interactions and to soften the hard-edged reality of their daily work. Morphine could be obtained through certain druggists or doctors who acted as suppliers to prostitutes. Although drug addiction among prostitutes did not receive a great deal of attention, it was probably more prevalent than realized. When arrested, many imprisoned prostitutes suddenly became seized with violent withdrawal symptoms.[74]

A forthright Denver morphine victim was Mary Gover. The *Rocky Mountain News* matter-of-factly published her death story:

Mrs. Mary Gover, who lived upstairs at 2025 Curtis street until she died there at 10 o'clock this morning, bought 25 cents worth of morphine in a drug store at Nineteenth and Curtis streets at 11 o'clock last night. A few moments later she walked into the Buckeye saloon at 2031 Curtis street.

"Hello Charlie," she said to Proprietor Walbrecht of the place; "I'm going to kill myself."

"What for?" queried the saloon keeper in some surprise.

"Too poor to live," the woman answered.[75]

Notes

1. Noel, *The City and the Saloon*, p. 116.
2. Dallas, *Cherry Creek Gothic*, p. 202.
3. Robert H. Latta, "Denver in the 1880s," *Colorado Magazine*, July 1941, pp. 131–136. Big Ed Chase was never known to have employed a female dealer, but one did exist in Leadville, perhaps the first woman dealer in Colorado.

Kitty Crawhurst, a "neat, dark-eyed, raven-haired woman" of age twenty or twenty-five, dealt cards at Winney's gambling saloon. She told the *Leadville Chronicle* that she chose to be a "rolling mustang" dealer because she did not want to work in a "dance house." She said she was in it only for the money, to support her sickly husband, and that her patrons, "rough though they are," always gave her the highest respect "when they realize they deal with a lady." Her story is reprinted in the July 28, 1880, RMN, p. 6.

4. The DTI account of Big Ed Chase's 1874 party for Denver's women of pleasure is in Dallas, *Cherry Creek Gothic*, p. 203. Chase had a discerning eye for women. At one point in 1876, his wife dashed into the "free and easy" Corn Exchange saloon dressed in men's attire, perhaps so as not to draw immediate attention inside the club, and accosted waitress Nellie Belmont, "who is alleged to have been too intimate with her husband for some time past." A few months later Mrs. Chase divorced Big Ed on grounds of adultery, charging he had kept Nellie in a love nest at one of his clubs. Chase married again the next year and once more in 1880. Dallas, *Chery Creek Gothic*, pp. 202–205, from the RMN, undated.

5. Gilfoyle, *City of Eros*, pp. 130, 232 ff.

6. Mrs. L. W. Grace, "Harry L. Baldwin," *Colorado Magazine*, November 1944, p. 208. The best explanation of early Denver's city limits, patterns of growth, street development, and evolution of neighborhoods is in Phil Goodstein, *Denver Streets: Names, Numbers, Locations, Logic* (Denver: New Social Publications, 1994).

7. RD, p. 118.

8. Cy Martin, *Whiskey and Wild Women* (New York: Hart, 1974), pp. 168–172.

9. Dallas, *Cherry Creek Gothic*, p. 229. In *The Seamy Side of Denver* (Denver: New Social Publications, 1993), historian Phil Goodstein says rates on the Blue Row ranged from twenty-five cents to a dollar (p. 29).

10. Loose newspaper clippings of the annual reports of Dr. Frederick J. Bancroft. Exact dates of the clippings are unknown, with the exception of the RMN entry of May 7, 1875. The signature of the May 7 letter is "B." Copies in the author's possession, courtesy of Robert L. Shikes, M.D.

11. RD, p. 138.

12. RMN, April 10, 1874.

13. Rosen, *The Lost Sisterhood*, p. xiv.

14. Susan Armitage and Elizabeth Jameson, *The Women's West* (Norman: University of Oklahoma Press, 1987), p. 194.

15. Quoted in Shikes, *Rocky Mountain Medicine*, p. 195.

16. The oft-told story of the "fancy lady" Silverheels [or Silver Heels, which seems to be an earlier spelling] is among the more poignant tales of Colorado history and is engagingly related in Muriel Sibell Wolle's classic *Stampede to Timberline* (Denver: Poertner Lithographing, 1949), pp. 92–96. Historian Caroline Bancroft rebuffed the Silverheels account following research conducted for the "Colorado Timeline" permanent exhibit at the Colorado Historical Society. Onetime Colorado Historical Society historian Albert B. Sanford prepared a fictional treatment of Silver Heels, listed in the bibliography under Manuscripts. In the *Denver Post*'s *Empire Magazine* on November 11, 1963, Robert W. "Red" Fenwick claimed "recent interviews" with descendants of old-timers suggested that Silverheels was Gerda Bechtel of Lititz, Pennsylvania, and that the moniker Silverheels came from the surname "Silber," which she adopted to save embarrassment to her folks back home in case she was found out. The Fenwick story relates that after Silverheels departed from Buckskin Joe to wed in Denver, she left a forwarding address of a Denver hotel. After a few letters were delivered to her there, she vanished for good. In 1938, eighty-five-year-old former miner Henry Maher of Fairplay was quoted as remembering Silverheels, apparently after her disfigurement because she was always masked. Maher termed her even then "an angel of mercy" who would nurse an injured miner back to health or grubstake a prospector in his search for precious ores (*Durango Herald-Democrat*, October 10, 1938; *Pueblo Star-Journal*, December 4, 1938; both loose clippings from the Mazzulla Collection, box 40, folder "People"; "Silver Heels," Amon Carter Museum, Fort Worth, Texas, now in the holdings of the Colorado Historical Society, Denver).

17. Miller, *Holladay Street*, pp. 172–178.

18. On p. 96.

19. Armitage and Jameson, *The Women's West*, p. 202.

20. Rosen, *The Lost Sisterhood*, pp. 95–96.

21. Ibid., p. 53. Rosen dates this study at 1907.

22. Also see Armitage and Jameson, *The Women's West*, pp. 200, 205.

23. Patricia Nelson Limerick, *The Legacy of Conquest* (New York: W. W. Norton, 1987), pp. 49–50. Timothy J. Gilfoyle, in *City of Eros*, wrote (pp. 66–67) that in New York City "some parents made prostitution a family affair" and cited numerous examples of daughters, wives, and sisters being recruited into prostitution by family

members, both male and female. For examples in Colorado, see Chapter 6.

24. The *Denver City Directory* of 1902 lists an Otto Vinland, M.D., with offices at 1705 Lawrence Street. If Hilme Haglund visited him at a Stout Street address, that was Dr. Vinland's home rather than his office. The city directory lists his home at 2724 Stout Street rather than the 2714 Stout Street reported by the RMN. The national Cottage Home program, whose mission was to "give assistance to misled, unfortunate and unprotected women and girls; to advise the untaught and motherless; to care for them if sick; to shelter those who have wandered from the right," was operated by the Women's Christian Temperance Union (WCTU) and was very active in Denver and throughout the state. The Pearl Street home opened in 1888.

25. The story of Hilme Haglund is in SHS 21: 29579, from the RMN, November 18, 1902. For the Colorado Cottage Home, see Sherilyn Brandenstein, "The Colorado Cottage Home," *Colorado Magazine*, summer 1976, pp. 229–242. The article lists the home's address as 615 Pearl Street. In 1903 the home moved to 1457 South Logan Street and in 1906 to 427 Fairfax Street. The effort was suspended because of lack of funds in March 1932.

26. K. J. Fielding, "James Thompson's Colorado Diary," *Colorado Magazine*, July 1954, p. 209.

27. G. N. Scamehorn, *Behind the Scenes, or Denver by Gaslight* (Denver: Geo. A. Shirley, 1893), pp. 10–12. The title was borrowed from New York exposé writer George G. Foster, who not only wrote *New York by Gas-Light, with Here and There a Streak of Sunshine* (1850) but also *New York Above Ground and Under-Ground* (1850), *New York in Slices, by an Experienced Carver* (1849), and *New York Naked* (1850). See Gilfoyle, *City of Eros*, p. 426. The present author assumes Scamehorn was a real person who actually experienced the happenings of which he wrote rather than the booklet being an antigambling diatribe written under a nom de plume.

28. Howard T. Vaille, "Early Years of the Telephone in Colorado," *Colorado Magazine*, August 1928, p. 122.

29. SHS 18: 16878, from the *Denver Evening Post*, September 10, 1898.

30. RMN, March 14, 1891. Gilfoyle, in *City of Eros*, esp. chapter 6, describes New Yorkers' reactions to male homosexuals. Gilfoyle also addresses exhibitions of lesbianism staged before male groups.

31. *Mountain Charley, Or the Adventures of Mrs. E. J. Guerin, Who Was Thirteen Years in Male Attire* (Norman: University of Oklahoma Press, 1968), pp. viii ff. This book contains her autobiographical accounts as well as statements by others that differ from her self-portrait.

32. The *Denver Democrat*, July 11, 1887.

33. The trial of Nina Patchen was reported in the Denver newspapers. The RMN and the DR, October 9–12, 1895, were consulted for this account. The arrest and acquittal of Broken-nose Moll are in the RMN, April 22, 1877.

34. Thorough examinations of narcotics abuse and legislation in early Colorado are in Henry O. Whiteside, "The Drug Habit in Nineteenth Century Colorado," *Colorado Magazine*, winter 1978, pp. 47–68, and particularly in Whiteside's much larger report, *Menace in the West* (Denver: Colorado Historical Society, 1997). For Denver's antiopium legislation, see Burroughs, "As It Was in the Beginning," p. 181.

35. Marjorie A. Benham, "Women in the Colorado State Penitentiary, 1873 Through 1916," master's thesis, University of Colorado at Denver, 1998, pp. 75–77.

36. Mary Wood-Allen, M.D., *What a Young Woman Ought to Know* (Philadelphia: Vir, 1898), pp. 218–231. A copy of this scarce volume is in the education department of the Colorado Historical Society.

37. See Benson Tong, *Unsubmissive Women: Chinese Prostitutes in Nineteenth-Century San Francisco* (Norman: University of Oklahoma Press, 1994), pp. 4 ff., especially pp. 20–21, for Tong's assessment of the presence of Chinese prostitutes in Denver. For Denver's edict not to rent properties to Chinese, see RD, p. 118. Prostitution by Chinese women in late-nineteenth-century Denver is discussed briefly in Patricia K. Ourada, "The Chinese in Colorado," *Colorado Magazine*, October 1952, p. 281. There were few Japanese prostitutes in late-nineteenth-century Denver, but the murder of one, Kiku Oyama, earned her a spot in the history of prostitution in Colorado. See Chapter 10.

38. RMN, October 27, 1880. Most of Denver's opium dens were near Blake and Twentieth Streets rather than Arapahoe Street. For the smuggling of opium into the United States, see Tong, *Unsubmissive Women*, p. 65.

39. RMN, August 14, 1883. The Denver city directories of 1882, 1883, and 1884 list no physician named Gee. The RMN described him as "highly esteemed among the Chinese population of the city, and [he] seems to have a pretty good knowledge of medicine."

40. SHS 3: 670, from the *Denver Tribune-Republican*, date undetermined.

41. Ibid., 21: 29758, from the DR, December 4, 1902. For an account of court proceedings on the Gun Wa medicine fraud, see the DR, March 26, 1891. Thomas J. Noel, in *Denver's Larimer Street* (Denver: Historic Denver, 1981), maintains that W. H. Hale was Dr. Gun Wa (p. 119).

42. Scamehorn, *Behind the Scenes*, pp. 68–69.

43. SHS 31: 62835, from the RMN, January 6, 1912.

44. Ibid., 63113, from the DR, February 8, 1912.

45. The *Denver Evening Post*, April 22, 1899. In *Storyville, New Orleans* (Tuscaloosa: University of Alabama Press, 1974), researcher Al Rose describes the phenomenon of "slumming" (p. 64) in that city's famed brothel district. For an additional example of Denver's "respectable" young women who were caught slumming, see Chapter 10.

46. DR, June 22, 1913.

47. The DTI, August 27, 1900, reflected back on these Denver conditions of a decade earlier. "Prosecuting Attorney Adams" could have been either J. Frank Adams or John T. Adams; inspection of city directories failed to disclose which.

48. Parkhill, "Scarlet Sister Mattie," p. 9.

49. SHS 12: 5790, from the DTI, October 6, 1891.

50. The travels of David H. Strother are in Dr. Cecil D. Eby Jr., "'Porte Crayon' in the Rocky Mountains," *Colorado Magazine*, April 1960, pp. 108–118. This entry in Strother's diary was dated August 9, 1873, somewhat early for so vivid an observation about Denver's opium joints, which were fairly new at that time.

51. See Whiteside, "The Drug Habit in Nineteenth-Century Colorado." The fullest account of Denver's Chinese-oriented disturbances on October 31 and November 1, 1880, is in Roy T. Wortman, "Denver's Anti-Chinese Riot, 1880," *Colorado Magazine*, fall 1965, pp. 275–291. The story of "Morphine Dick" Shannon is from the DR, August 10, 1894.

52. The verse and its terminology interpretations are quoted in Armitage and Jameson, *The Women's West*, p. 200.

53. SHS 22: 30005, newspaper title illegible but dated January 1, 1903.

54. Ibid., 10: 3423 and 3426, from the RMN, May 28, 1889.

55. Ibid., 13: 6200 and 6244, from the DTI, March 7, 1892. This would have been rather early for the casual use of photography.

56. Dallas, *Cherry Creek Gothic*, p. 230. Coroner McHatton himself later became a suicide victim for motives he did not specify.

57. Gene Fowler comments on the sadness of prostitutes during Christmastime in *A Solo in Tom-Toms* (New York: Viking, 1946), p. 174. As a youthful newspaper reporter in Denver, Fowler observed from close up the lives of the city's *demimonde* women. Jack Riddle wrote about Lily and her suicide poem in "The Western Gazette" in the *Denver Post's Empire Magazine*, April 3, 1960. He does not list his source, but the year would have been 1885.

58. Gilfoyle, *City of Eros*, pp. 130–131.

59. SHS 6: 1305, from the RMN, February 11, 1887. For the larceny convictions of Nola Jefferson and Cora Thornton, see Benham, "Women in the Colorado State Penitentiary," p. 69.

60. SHS 12: 5089, from the RMN, February 26, 1891.

61. Ibid., 13: 6614, newspaper and date unspecified.

62. Undated *Sunday Denver Post* clipping, copy in the author's possession.

63. Noel, *Denver's Larimer Street*, p. 20, quoting the DTI, May 13, 1902.

64. SHS 27: 50287, 50301, and 50815, from the DR, July 16, 1908; the RMN, July 17, 1908; and the DP, September 1, 1908.

65. Ibid., 28: 55981, 55989, and 56366, from the DP, September 28, 1909, ff. Why Ferris was sentenced to county jail for a federal offense is not explained.

66. Ibid., 28: 56151, from the DP, December 13, 1909.

67. Ibid., 31: 63190, from the RMN, February 17, 1912.

68. Ibid., 31: 63205, from the DR, February 18, 1912.

69. DP, November 22, 1899.

70. SHS 26: 46642, from the DR, August 8, 1907, ff.

71. SHS 22: 32984, from the RMN, November 9, 1903.

72. DTI, October 21, 1900.

73. SHS 27: 51861, from the DR, November 15, 1908.

74. Rosen, *The Lost Sisterhood*, p. 98.

75. SHS 16: 12174, from the RMN, May 6, 1896.

6

The Unlucky Pathway of Life

WHILE INDIGNANTLY CONDEMNING Denver's gambling dens and houses of commercial love, the newspapers published addresses of these establishments under the guise of warning the unsuspecting public—much as did New York's *Prostitution Exposed* booklet—of where to stay away from. It was part of being a responsible public servant, the newspapers must have asserted with a wink.

The published tourist guide in the 1870s might have led the visitor on a tour beginning with the American House at Sixteenth and Blake Streets, and then along Blake to the Corn Exchange where a glaring advertisement could have announced "Wit and Mirth" and "Free Concert" by the "Queen of Song." The visitor was then beckoned to a sign reading "Bar," toward the rear of which were any manner of gambling devices and questionable entertainments through all hours of the night and beyond.

A few more steps might have led to the Occidental

Hall. Up a single flight of stairs our visiting prospector—with a fresh bath and shave and his gold pouch in hand—entered a large hall blazing with light and flashy ornamentation. Placards of "Beer 10 Cents" appeared among gaslights, and a gaggle of "Beer Girl" waiters promenaded. He was comforted by signs proclaiming that as far as gambling was concerned, this was a "square house"—and as a bonus Miss So-and-So, the great prima donna and soprano vocalist, was appearing onstage.

The Occidental was at the corner of Fifteenth and Blake. There our visitor may have encountered not only Miss So-and-So but also a commodious bar and tables featuring a dozen games of chance. Not always rowdy, the Occidental in 1872 featured an opera concert by the exiled Baroness Stephanie of Sardinia, said to be a third cousin of Queen Victoria and a second cousin of Edward VII. She eventually married bartender Charley Tanner, and in 1904 she died destitute in a Leadville hovel.

Ed Chase's elegant (and notorious throughout the West) Palace Theater was at 1443–1457 Blake Street and entertained Denver's largest clientele. It had room for 200 players and 25 dealers and a bar with a 60-foot mirror. Midnight hors d'oeuvres included roast beef, pork, venison, antelope cutlets, breast of prairie chicken, wild turkey, quail, and salads. Not simply a gambling establishment, the Palace had a 750-seat auditorium featuring vaudevillian variety acts. The bill usually opened with songs sung by a bevy of young women seated in crescent formation, the master of ceremonies in the center, and two blackface comedians on the ends.

One by one the girls stepped to the footlights and offered their song selections, interspersed with jokes from the comedians. Many of the young women were known as seriocomic songsters, and early in the act each was dressed in skirts falling to about the knees. A man caught a cannonball shot from a cannon, the Palace performers concluded with a lively dance scene featuring the entire troupe, and the ladies' skirts went higher than the knee! And in the finale Viola Clifton sang:

> *Don't you think she's awful,*
> *Slightly on the mash?*
> *See how close her lips are*
> *To that young man's mustache.*
>
> *O heavens! He has kissed her.*
> *Her parents are away.*
> *But if they saw her actions*
> *What do you think they'd say?*

As an adjunct to nightspots such as Ed Chase's Palace, the Market Street bordello ladies prospered with the rush to Leadville's mines in 1879–1880. Demand was high, and rates escalated accordingly. The cheap crib girls now got up to two dollars, and the fancy parlor house ladies collected five dollars for a "quick date" and up to thirty dollars for a sleep-over.[1]

The rush of eager and thirsty fortune seekers through Denver and on to Leadville in the late 1870s produced many shortages, including one that was unexpected: empty liquor bottles. The solution to this serious problem was related years later by T. E. Van Evra of Marquette, Michigan, who participated in the great Leadville stampede.

Van Evra journeyed to Colorado in 1879 just to have a look around, and one day in Denver he encountered a cider factory. He thought this odd, as there were bottles of cider sitting around but no apple tree within miles.

"What kind of cider do you make?" he asked the proprietor.

"Champagne cider," replied the man in charge, whereupon he explained exactly what "champagne cider" was and how it was made.

The man took Van Evra to a back room where he displayed a barrel of brown sugar. "That's our base material," said the cider man. "A pound of sugar to a quart of water, and with a little fermenting material and some gas—that's the formula. It makes a great drink and the boys like it."

In other words, "champagne cider" was neither cider nor champagne and contained virtually no alcohol, yet there was a market for it. The cider man explained to Van Evra why the miners bought his "champagne cider" sugar water:

> We bottle it and sell it as champagne, mostly to the dance halls and variety theaters. You doubtless have noticed that there are far more men in the city Saturday nights than at any other time. They come down from the mountains Saturdays and spend their Sundays here, returning the following Monday—many of them with bigger heads but smaller purses. Most of them spend the greater part of their time in Denver about the dives on Blake and Holliday [*sic*] streets. Intoxicants flow freely and after they have swallowed a certain quantity of the liquor they get there, they will drink anything. In fact when once arrived at the proper stage they do not know what they are drinking. That's when our goods go upon the market. The girls are our agents; they know the psychological moment for disposing of the Home Brand, and they proceed to fill up their customers with our champagne at the rate of five dollars a quart.

Van Evra questioned the ethics of that, but the cider man responded that charging five dollars for a quart of fizzy sugar water was no less ethical than selling the quality of rotgut whiskey then on the Denver market.

The cider maker bemoaned that his only problem was obtaining sufficient empty bottles. He said most of his bottles were shipped full to Leadville where the prospectors "drink thousands of bottles every Saturday night and lots between times. Why, the bonanza kings set 'em up for every dance girl whose switching skirt touches them."

The cider man told Van Evra, who had a few hundred dollars to invest, to buy a horse and wagon, haul mining supplies to Leadville's hardware stores for a fee, and return with empty bottles, which the cider company would buy at seven dollars a hundred. Van Evra agreed, and when he reached Leadville with his first load of picks, axes, and shovels, he discovered a "some busy" town where the

> fair sex was but poorly represented. Indeed, most of the women in camp seemed to be leaning half naked out of the windows of houses jammed up against the sidewalk, and beckoning to the passing through to enter. I need not say that they belonged to the underworld—that is to say, that's where they belonged, the town was full of them, and I never have seen so bold and brazen a set in my life. Afternoons and evenings they were much in evidence. The gambling dens ran day and night; the hotels—but poor affairs at best—were crowded from cellar to garret; the sidewalks were jammed with men who talked nothing but prospects and sales.

As promised, Van Evra found Leadville's alleys full of small mountains of empty bottles, and his first load back to Denver consisted of 2,000 bottles for which he received the considerable sum of $140. He sold his horse and wagon for an additional big profit and never crossed paths with the cider man again.[2]

In the same year that Van Evra was engaged in his bottle-hauling venture, aspiring millionaires Charlie Hough and Fred C. Mills decided to hike from Leadville to the prospectors' camp of Magnolia 8 miles west of Boulder. But unlike the case with Van Evra, the mining camp *demimonde* ladies threatened to separate Hough and Mills from their money.

Hough and Mills, having staked their silver claims in the soon-to-be-booming Leadville, deduced in September 1879 that it might be more pleasant to winter over at the lower altitude of Magnolia rather than in 10,000-foot-high Leadville. They learned, however, that the stage or rail fare from Leadville to Magnolia was twenty-five dollars each and figured they could save about eight dollars a day by walking the 110 miles.

So with $300 apiece, the two eighteen-year-olds set off northward over Ten Mile Pass, through Robinson and Kokomo, finally stopping at what Mills later described as "the notorious Chalk Ranch, which bore an unenviable reputation." Every habitué of the Chalk Ranch way station, they knew, boasted that no man ever entered the place and left with a cent.

Charlie Hough was feeling reckless and flashed a fifty-dollar bill at what Mills later described as "one of the beautiful (?) sirens of the ranch" who "immediately fell violently in love with him." At this juncture the well-known mountain man "Colorado Charley" Utter, known to be "quick on the trigger," intervened as a friend of the two young men, and as a result "the roughnecks at Chalk Ranch were afraid to molest us." Mills and Hough proceeded over the range to Frisco to spend the night.

After losing forty dollars in a Frisco poker game ("we decided we were not as expert poker players as we imagined"), the pair proceeded to Dillon, which consisted "of two houses and a store; the store and the houses were boarded up and there was a sign on the store stating that the Utes were on the warpath and cautioning people to get out of the country."

By noon they were at the western foot of Loveland Pass, at a place kept by a man named Hayward "who was noted for his ability to separate the unsuspecting from their coin." Hough again displayed his roll of bills, whereupon Hayward suggested a card game, but instead the pair of travelers beat it over the pass to Georgetown—with Hough suggesting that the pair "could have trimmed the old man" at the card table.

In Georgetown—with most of their cash intact—Hough and Mills took a room at the Ennis House hotel and attended the local theater, where

> we were overjoyed to meet several actresses who had been infatuated with us in Leadville, especially at times when we had money. They were very glad to see us and embraced us affectionately—after Charlie had flashed his roll. As we considered that we were

The Tremont, on Blair Street in the mining town of Silverton, deep among southwestern Colorado's San Juan Mountains, was a combination saloon/brothel, with the liquor downstairs and the ladies upstairs. The madam, Matilda "Big Tillie" Fattor, is at left, and her husband, Celeste, is in the apron. "Fattor" is today believed to have been a clumsy Anglicization of the Italian Fatore. *The* Travelers' Night Guide of Colorado *lists three organized brothels in Silverton in 1893, probably about the date of this photograph: Louesa [sic] Crawford, "aided by eleven charming assistants," operated at 557 Blair Street; Cora Livingston had five girls in the "Big House" at Thirteenth and Blair Streets; and Stella Allison's place is simply listed as on Blair Street. A brothel/saloon combination was not prevalent in larger communities such as Denver, where such indulgences were generally not integrated.*

This, of course, meant more wine, for how could an eighteen-year-old miner resist such blandishments from a pretty woman and she was truly very charming in manner and appearance.

The evening ended innocently, however, according to Mills's journal of the trip, from which this account is drawn, and early the next morning the duo hiked from Georgetown to Central City. From there, traveling down the canyons toward Magnolia, they met Rocky Mountain Jim, "a four-flusher who wore his hair long, carried a big knife and had a couple of guns strapped around him." Mills recalled that they became involved in

rolling in wealth I bought wine for the lady performers which greatly surprised and pleased them, as it always had been beer on previous occasions. One of the ladies, a dancer who was glorified by being billed as "the poetry of motion" and who was at one time a star at "Perry's Palace of Pleasure" on Blake Street in Denver, confessed to me that she had always admired me from the first time she saw me at the Comique Theater in Leadville, but she never realized how extremely fascinating I was until that evening in Georgetown.

a game of euchre with Jim for a dollar a game.[3] When I produced my roll it looked like a million to him and he snatched it out of my hand and started to put it in his pocket, when Charlie Hough grabbed one of the guns out of Jim's holster and struck him on the wrist with it, which caused Jim to drop my money. Charlie took Jim's other gun and his knife away from him and told him that he would leave them at the postoffice in Magnolia. About a week later Jim came to get his arsenal, but the miners in the camp made so much fun of him that he never appeared there again.

Mills and Hough arrived back at Magnolia at 10:30 that night "but were much disappointed as the girls did not receive us with much enthusiasm and did not appear to have missed us at all."[4]

The great waves of humanity entering Denver seeking riches in the mines of Leadville taxed Denver's ability to accommodate them. At the close of 1880, police tallied the year's crime statistics: total arrests, 2,662; drunkenness, 1,058; disturbance, 200; vagrancy, 404; larceny, 252; assault and battery, 177; burglary, 11; malicious mischief, 36; threats, 20; cruelty to animals, 7; rape, 3; arson, 2; and carrying concealed weapons, 31. Inexplicably, as in the past, the serious offense of murder was excluded, as were prostitution and gambling arrests.[5]

With the dawn of the 1880s, Denver was the largest metropolis between Kansas City and the West Coast, with 35,626 inhabitants whose thirst was slaked by ninety-eight saloons. Colorado had surrendered its territorial status and become a state only four years previously; during the territorial era (1861–1876) 270 taverns were known to have existed at one time or another in Denver.[6]

By the end of 1881, Denver's population had almost doubled to 60,000, and a city never known for its moderation in alcoholic consumption recorded 1,187 arrests for drunkenness, according to the year-end report from Police Chief David J. Cook. The prostitution arrest figure of only 53 suggests that the police were perhaps less than enthusiastic about hauling in girls from the Row. Denver's position toward prostitution during this era was the same as elsewhere:

> Few western communities tried to eliminate prostitution; instead, they tried to regulate and contain it. In towns dependent on mining, cattle, or military posts, with a substantial population of male workers, prostitution was essential to the town's prosperity. The whole exercise of regulating prostitution heightened solidarity among respectable women.[7]

In an attempt to contain Denver's working girls, Police Chief Dave Cook issued orders prohibiting prostitutes from driving, riding, or making their appearance "in anyway" on the principal streets of the city.[8] Whether such a restriction could have endured a challenge on constitutional grounds is a matter of conjecture because no such challenge was mounted. The girls instead thumbed their noses at the idea, and only a few months later

> a hack full of drunken women, driven by a drunken hackman, was partially wrecked against a lumber pole [at Thirty-eighth and Blake Streets] but got away before the officer could reach them. . . . [In the meantime] Officer Sullivan captured two ladies of easy virtue who were drunk in a buggy, which they endeavored to use as a battering ram to knock down a telegraph post on Thirteenth and Lawrence streets.[9]

Denver banned prostitution—at least on paper—briefly in 1894, but the move was unpopular among the businesspeople who sought to promote visitation to the town.[10] Police Chief Hamilton Armstrong explained:

> I have tried to feel the public pulse on this question [controlling prostitution], and the traffic has been regulated and controlled to as great an extent as the manifest wishes of a majority of the citizens who have been heard would seem to justify. The fact is, the social evil [prostitution], to a greater extent than gambling, is hedged round about with influences to such an extent that the trial magistrate requires stronger evidence than the officer arresting the prisoner can produce.[11]

Toward the goal of confining prostitution within its appointed boundaries, Dave Cook assured citizens in his 1881 year-end report that the police department had "centered most of this activity in the [Holladay Street] area."[12] The segregation of prostitution within defined districts was practiced in other large cities: New Orleans's Storyville, San Francisco's Barbary Coast, Baltimore's Block, Chicago's Levee, and in New York the Bowery, Five Points, and the Tenderloin. One author vividly describes those neighborhoods:

> These sporting resorts, with their streets lined with brothels, saloons, and hotels, the air filled with the odor

of tobacco and liquor and the sounds of blaring music, windows framed by images of women making obscene gestures, gave Americans their most distasteful and frightening picture of the segregated vice districts. In many cities, regulations controlling music, lights, and stoop-calling became a common part of attempts to minimize the visibility of public prostitution.[13]

Police Chief Cook and others rotating in and out of his position during the late nineteenth century were generally successful in their efforts to confine the pleasure palaces of Denver within the four blocks of Market Street between Nineteenth and Twenty-third Streets. The chiefs knew the populace would excuse the antics of the red light ladies so long as the ladies stayed where they belonged.

There was, however, an occasional setback. In 1886 businessmen and residents in several localities near Denver's Row began complaining that the "female sporting class" was creeping beyond boundaries and too far uptown. The *Tribune-Republican* wrote:

> For a long time this class of people has been known to dwell upon one street in this city, and that thoroughfare has been tacitly given up to them. They have often gotten away from the limits prescribed, but the police have driven them back again. Lately, however, the spread of this evil has been more than usually great. There are now quite a number of these places running in full blast in Larimer and Lawrence streets, and several carried on in a most quiet manner in Arapahoe, Curtis, and Champa streets, and there is one quite notorious on Seventeenth, near Curtis street.

The *Tribune-Republican* reported that a "well-known citizen" visited the newspaper's office and suggested that "it is about time that the police used their pretty patrol wagon" to round up the girls. A reporter "looked around a little" and learned that the "rumors are true." The out-of-boundaries brothels were indeed new, but the girls were "recruited from the ranks of the fast class in the lower part of the city and that freed them from the restraints of a high-priced liquor license and the known surveillance of the police." The paper urged "an awakened police department" to "compel them to close their houses or go back where the evil has existed since the city was founded and where respect-able citizens, pure women and innocent children when on the streets will not be obliged to witness the evidence of its existence."[14] Nothing remained fixed for long, and each time the sin merchants of Denver boldly crossed beyond their long-established boundaries, an indignant public forced them back.

In 1894 Police Chief Hamilton Armstrong deduced that the girls of the street were once more becoming too bold. Under the headlines "Larimer the Limit," "Women of Ill Fame Must Move North of It," and "The Order Has Gone Forth" was this story in the *Republican*:

> Troublesome times have come for the woman of the street. Since the inauguration of the present Fire and Police board and the reorganization of the police department, her class has been harried on all sides. The raids on Market street last week, the arresting and fining of female unfortunates for publicly plying their trade, and the close nightly watch kept on the "row" by officers, have made Denver anything but an elysium for her. She is only in the beginning of her troubles, however, and yesterday the police made a new move towards regulating and keeping within bounds the women whom society has put out of its pale [boundary].

Chief Armstrong deduced that certain bawdy houses on Fifteenth Street above Larimer were masquerading as "rooming houses," and landladies of such establishments should be warned that the police were not blind to what was going on. The inhabitants of this neighborhood especially appeared to be "young girls who have run away from home and [been] installed [in the rooming houses] by male 'friends.'" Enforcement of the boundary rule appeared arbitrary, and some suspected the law to be so broad that it included any young woman living in the neighborhood, even if she was an upstanding young shop girl and not a prostitute. The *Republican* reporter recorded this exchange between Sergeant George E. Tarbox and the proprietor of one of the rooming houses:

> "Madame, I understand you have a number of women rooming here."
>
> "Yes, sir."
>
> "Well, the chief of police told me to notify you that

you must put these women out, or your place will be pulled [shut down]."

"I don't see how you can do that; I see none of my lady lodgers doing anything wrong."

"You may not see anything wrong, madame, but we know they are not proper women. Such women must stay below Larimer Street hereafter."[15]

The absence or presence of civil rights in that exchange notwithstanding, the city's love-for-sale women would thereafter confine their business activities to northwest of Larimer Street—but the girls would remain in business for another twenty-one years.

The madams of Market Street maintained an intimate and influential relationship with city fathers and municipal leaders. Whenever churches, schools, or other civic institutions found themselves in need, the madams and the pimps—or "macs" as they were called in Denver—delivered their share of the funding and more. It was considered an expense of doing business.[16]

An example of such charity was seen during the silver devaluation in 1893 and the economic depression it imposed on Colorado. Hundreds of young housemaids, particularly along the shaded and mansioned streets of Denver's Capitol Hill, lost their jobs because of the financial crash, and some found their way into the Market Street workforce. Jennie Rogers is said to have questioned each girl as to her background and moral fiber, and she sent ninety-six girls to respectable boardinghouses until she could pay their expenses back to their hometowns.[17]

The best salvation for a young girl in Denver, of course, was to resist temptation to descend into the world of scarlet sisterhood, and the best way to do that was to keep busy. In her autobiography *The Long-Lost Rachel Wild*, Denver religious missionary and counselor to fallen girls Rachel Wild Peterson wrote (p. 445) that busy hands and orderly habits would thwart the temptations of sin. "Girls," admonished Peterson,

Keep your dresser drawers and your hair ribbons clean and tidy. Everything in the house should be moved once a week, swept thoroughly and dusted. Do not wear a dress with grease spots upon it. Wash your ribbons and delicate shawls in ox-gall soap with no soda in the water. Always get taffeta ribbon, which washes well. When God uses me as an instrument in saving a soul, the first thing I think of is if the outside is clean as well as the soul.

Rolf Johnson was new to Denver in November 1879, and during that winter and the next summer he wrote to kin back East of his experiences at Big Ed Chase's Palace Theater and other impressions of Denver's nightlife and the companionship offered:

I like Denver very well. I am still staying at the Western Home, kept by Mr. Moore, and have lots of fun flirting with Jennie Chambers and Frankie Van Houghton. This evening in company with Walter During, I attended the Palace Theater, a variety show on Blake street. Among the "stars" who appeared before the footlights were Frankie Barbour, Nellie Hackett, Duncan Sisters, Minnie Farrell, John Richardson, Harry Montague, Perry Bros., Etta LeClair, Lydie Rosa, Blanche Fontainbleau, Alice Dashwood, Millie Christine. The dancing and singing of the girls who were very liberal in showing their legs and bosoms was of the most "loud" character. The place was as hard a one as I ever was in. The after piece, "The Mormons," would raise a blush on the cheek of an Indian, it was so dirty.

Johnson added that he also attended a "free fight"—probably a no-holds-barred boxing match—at the Red Light Saloon, in which the weapons used were beer bottles, and noted that

Holladay street is one of the hardest streets in Denver. It is full of bagnios and saloons and it is unsafe to venture out after dark without arms. Two blocks away on Wazee street is a row of one story brick houses occupied exclusively by Chinese courtesans and gamblers. . . . This evening as Tom Emmett, Harry Lyons and I were sitting at our window we heard three shots in rapid succession in the direction of Chinaman's Row on Wazee street. I went down to investigate and found that Yah-Ho, one of the prettiest of the Chinese girls and with whom I was well acquainted, had got shot by "Chinaman Joe," a Chinese gambler. Joe was arrested and the girl, who is shot in the shoulder, will probably recover.

A young man visiting Denver on his way to the gold or silver camps in 1881 could choose diversions of drink, women for hire, and gambling. By the spring of 1883 forty public gambling houses were operating in Denver, and estimates were that more than 5,000 people patronized them daily. The police maintained a certain vigilance over the gamblers—who had operated in Denver since virtually the day the community was founded—and the city required that the gamblers put guards at their doors and deny admission to minors, professional crooks "political or otherwise," and intoxicated persons. The *Denver Republican*, in the May 14, 1900, edition, describing the death four days earlier of former Denver police detective John Schlottman in a train wreck, wrote that "to keep the police out, most of the gambling houses built great doors, believed to be proof against any assault of the police. The chief had made a 16-pound hammer with a long handle. Equipped with this Schlottman was sent and any door that failed to open at his order was splintered with the sledge." Schlottman, on the police force in 1894 and 1895, was known around town as "Sledge-Hammer Jack."

The early Denver visitor was vulnerable to roving mobs of hoodlums. Some newcomers felt it necessary to reassure themselves and others, as did physician Charles Brown in a letter to his wife, Maggie, in 1881:

> You are always asking if I drink. No I do not, but if I want a glass of beer I go and take it. But that is very seldom. Nothing more. We have a miner's committee here [the mining hamlet of Bonanza, southwest of Buena Vista] to protect each other from what is called "the gang." In other words, bar keepers, swindlers, pickpockets. They all clog together to rob any and everyone. We will not have a drunkard or anyone that hangs around a saloon or anyone that is intimate with saloon keepers. So you see, that if I was drinking, they would not have anything to do with me. . . . You need not fear that you will have a drunken husband or one that runs after other women, for I love my wife too dearly for that, and am too hard up to gamble if I wished.

Denver's Palace Theater was condemned by Henry Martyn Hart, dean of St. John's Cathedral, as "a death trap to young men, a foul den of vice and corruption."

Hart, however, was a realist, proclaiming that it was folly to try to abolish the saloons and the bordellos, as they had always existed and always would. He said in a sermon: "Men insist on drinking and going to the tenderloin. . . . You can't cure them of the desire for those things until you breed a new race of men. That would take centuries and the thing we have got to deal with is things as they are now. Recognize facts and start your work of reform to control as far as possible what you cannot abolish."

The brothels, Hart said, should be confined to three or four blocks, and the women should be subject to rigorous medical attention and police scrutiny within their district. Abolishment, he said, would merely drive the women underground where they could not be controlled. Hart urged toughening the laws against men who forced women into prostitution: "If only the same punishment were meted out to men, if they were submitted to the same surveillance and were treated with the same social scorn, justice would be done."

The dean's condemnation of the Palace Theater was not without basis. The *Denver Republican* in 1888, for instance, denounced the Palace as a "human slaughter-house, the scene of four murders during the past 13 months . . . a thoroughly tough, hard place, frequented by a class of desperate, depraved men and women. The employes [*sic*] are, almost without exception, of the worst possible character."[18]

Consider the case of Effie Moore. Love affairs with Palace Theater showgirls were common, and at the Palace seventeen-year-old Effie met a handsome and well-off nineteen-year-old gambler, Charles E. Henry. Effie, appeared on stage dressed as a newsboy, with a bundle of papers under her arm. Part of her duties was to hustle drinks, and one night she hustled Charles Henry. Although the lothario had bedded other Palace showgirls during his two-week stay in Denver, he quickly became obsessed with Effie and asked for her hand in marriage.

She accepted, but Henry heard she already had a husband. Effie denied it; Henry got drunk and escorted her to a private box at the Palace on the night of November 13, 1887.[19] Henry pulled a .32-caliber double-action British Bulldog revolver and shot Effie four times.

Ed Chase's Palace Theater in Denver was not a brothel by definition—it was situated outside the protected brothel district—but it was the first place prospectors down from the hills or travelers up from the train station headed for feminine diversions and jollification. Famous for everything from its racy stage shows to fancy buffets to peek-a-boo bosoms to gambling, booze, and murder, the Palace was known throughout the West. The establishment was midblock on the west side of Blake Street between Fourteenth and Fifteenth Streets.

The love killing of young Effie Moore—at a tender age—became the only topic of conversation on Denver's streets for days. Around 4,500 curious "mourners"— described by a newspaper as "the very motley, loudly dressed tin-horn gamblers, actors, actresses, cowboys, bartenders"—filed past the slain actress's open casket. Effie's killer offered to bear all funeral expenses, and so did Big Ed Chase, owner of the Palace. As it turned out, Effie did indeed have a husband, whom she wed at age sixteen.[20]

Three months later Charles Henry was acquitted on grounds of "emotional insanity," "transitory frenzy," and "acting very queerly."[21] In July 1888, five months after the acquittal, he was discovered in his room at the Brunswick Hotel after having consumed a quantity of opium-in-alcohol laudanum in an apparent suicide attempt. He recovered.[22] Four years after that, Sam Howe recorded that Henry was in jail in Dallas, Texas, charged with murdering a girl with whom he was "madly infatuated," Irene Russell. She was shot

Drunk and enraged with jealousy upon discovering she was married, nineteen-year-old gambler Charles E. Henry took revolver in hand and killed Palace Theater showgirl Effie Moore (right, in a coroner's sketch) on the night of November 13, 1887. Thus Henry earned inclusion in Detective Sam Howe's Murder Book. Henry was acquitted on grounds of "transitory frenzy" and "acting most queerly." He was released, and he killed again.

through the heart.[23] Research does not divulge the ultimate fate of Charles Henry.

Theaters wherein traveling troupes presented their song, dance, comedy, and dramatic acts under new-fangled electric lights were magnets to the young people of early Denver. The matter of Effie Moore may have been the most publicized occurrence of the late-nineteenth-century Denver stage, but Denver was not unique in facing this problem. In his book *Fighting the*

Traffic in Young Girls, urban missionary Ernest A. Bell devoted a chapter to the "Peril of Stage-struck Girls":

The corruption of the present-day [1910] theater is generally admitted. . . . Low theaters exist merely to inflame those who visit them. They go to the awful length of naming the vice district as part of the merriment of the performances. Other so-called theaters are a part of the combined saloon and den of shame. I have conversed personally many times with girls who were deceived into going to such places, thinking they were going on the reputable stage. . . . Actresses of character are among the foremost to warn young women of the perils of the modern stage.[24]

The unsuspecting young women—and some may not have immediately realized it—were in the bordello district. Bell wrote of the

red-light districts, like a lake of fire, perpetually engulfing unwary and unprotected girls, along with the wilfully depraved. They are misled by crafty women and villainous young men with smooth manners and false tongues, on promises of light work, big pay, fine clothes, jewels and great happiness. The route to the abyss is commonly by way of dance halls and amusement resorts of all kinds having drinking attachments. The girl who drinks puts herself at the mercy of the young man in whose company she may be. The girl who dances is in very great peril, and she puts young men with whom she dances under greater temptation than herself. Soon after the fatal plunge a girl becomes immodest, indecent, lawless, homeless, a victim and distributor of vile diseases.[25]

In saloon-theaters such as Denver's Palace, young women—jig dancers, singers, the chorines—often were expected to mix with customers following their work shifts, even if they were not inclined to rent their bodies. Women with scruples sometimes made enough money from stage performances and a share of inflated drink prices so they felt no economic need to sell sexual favors. Townspeople considered these women a little less soiled than the standard prostitute. Hurdy-gurdy houses, as the dance halls were sometimes known, advertised that their women were dressed "in the finest clothes money can buy." Thomas Dimsdale, a chronicler of nineteenth-century Montana, wrote: "The music suddenly strikes up, and the summons, 'Take your partners for the next dance' is promptly answered by some of the male spectators, who, paying a dollar in gold for a ticket, approach the ladies' bench and—in style polite or otherwise—invite one of the ladies to dance."[26]

At 7:40 A.M., November 14, 1888 (a year and a day following the death of Effie Moore), Ed Chase's Palace was open for morning imbibing and entertainment when bartender Peter Anderson fatally shot

blacksmith R. D. Vaughn during a fight outside the front door. A general melee had started inside and spilled onto the street. Two other Palace employees were arrested, but they implicated Anderson, who had fled. Anderson claimed self-defense and said Vaughn attacked him with a 2-by-4 board. Anderson was arrested after dashing through the Palace and taking a streetcar home, and a coroner's jury indicted him for causing a death with "felonious intent."

Coroner I. N. Rogers said it was the first death attributed to "felonious intent" since he had been coroner. Anderson was acquitted, but it was not the end of violence at the Palace Theater. Three weeks later, on December 2, A. W. Munson shot and killed Thomas Gallagher in the upstairs barroom near the private boxes at the Palace. The Palace's proprietor, William Devere, testified before a coroner's jury that the parties involved and their friends had consumed great quantities of whiskey, wine, beer, and champagne but that Devere had concluded they were "not intoxicated, but were very jovial." The killing was ruled an accident, but the press was becoming exasperated at the ongoing problems the Palace spawned.[27]

Concerned Denverites occasionally questioned decisions by the police and city aldermen allowing nightspots such as the Palace to remain open at all hours, and brief, well-publicized crackdowns sometimes resulted. In 1892, for instance, a new newspaper, the *Denver Post*, asked Police Chief John F. Farley and Police Commissioner Robert W. Speer—later arguably Denver's crookedest mayor to that time—about the matter of saloons remaining open after midnight, *contrary to city ordinance*. Farley and Speer professed ignorance, blithely telling the *Post* reporter that whenever they checked, all saloons were closed tight after midnight.

The *Post* writer persisted, asking specifically about John W. "Johnny" Murphy's notorious Murphy's Exchange whiskey hall, known around town as "the Slaughterhouse," at 1617 Larimer Street. Murphy's was a favorite gathering place for pimps and scoundrels of all sorts and was a preferred hangout of Cort Thomson, who was madam Mattie Silks's husband and of whom more will be related in Chapter 9.[28]

Policemen on the beat told the *Post* that Murphy's was "not to be disturbed" and that patrons regularly

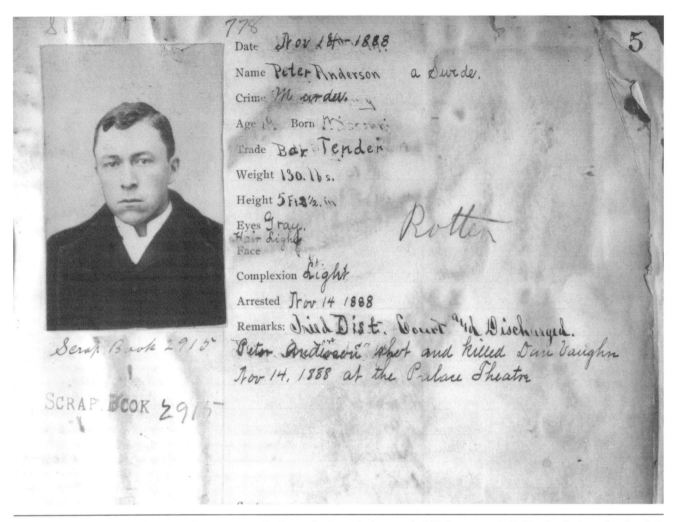

778

Date Nov 14th 1888
Name Peter Anderson   a Swede.
Crime Murder
Age 19.   Born Missouri
Trade Bar Tender
Weight 130. lbs.
Height 5 Ft 2½ in
Eyes Gray.
Hair Light
Face
Complexion Light
Arrested Nov 14 1888
Remarks: Tried Dist. Court and Discharged.
Peter Anderson shot and killed Dan Vaughn
Nov 14, 1888 at the Palace Theatre

Rotten

5

Scrap Book 2915ᵉ

SCRAP BOOK 2915

Among Big Ed Chase's murderous employees was morning bartender Peter Anderson, who killed carpenter R. D. Vaughn during a drunken fight in front of the Palace Theater on November 14, 1888. Anderson fled through the Palace back door and took a streetcar home. He claimed self-defense and was acquitted, but that did not prevent Sam Howe from placing Anderson's rap sheet in the police Murder Book, *with the added notation: "Rotten."*

entered the place "at all hours of the night after 12 o'clock." One of those questioned about Murphy's was Speer, who had become fire and police commissioner a year earlier, March 7, 1891. The following May 26 a tiny notice ran in the *Denver Republican* that effective immediately, all saloons must close by midnight, but the resolve to enforce such a rule was about as minimal as the announcement. Speer and the liquor and vice interests were intertwined and remained thus for the next twenty years. During "Boss" Speer's first two

terms as mayor, 1904–1912, he was universally recognized as a friend of saloon keepers and bordello madams, who were regularly called on for campaign contributions.[29] Speer never denied it.

The *Post*'s investigation of Johnny Murphy's "Slaughterhouse" postmidnight operation was conducted in 1892, and from that time forward midnight closings were on-again, off-again, depending on how much pressure was emanating from city hall. Nine years later, for instance, the *Denver Times* again exposed the fact that the wine rooms were operating after midnight and further that women were being allowed into such establishments, also contrary to ordinances. Police Chief Hamilton Armstrong ordered the beat cops to spread the word that the law was to be enforced, and the *Times* was able to report in its April 28 edition that "Market street was dead as a herring last night." When things cooled off, the wide-open hours would resume, as they had since Denver was founded.

Late-nineteenth-century prostitution and gambling were tied inexorably to city governments. If there had been no such working agreement, open prostitution could not have continued, which would have been detrimental to other businesses in town because visitors sought companionship and diversion—particularly in a distant, rather isolated outpost such as Denver. Historian Anne Butler analyzed the relationships between prostitutes and civic authorities at the time:

[The connection] ranged from moral rigidity to professional and personal depravity. Although the latter appeared more common to the frontier experience, both approaches created the same result for prostitutes: Their condition remained unchanged. The frontier power structure possessed the autonomy to inflict any control it wished over local prostitutes. If, in addition, judges, marshals, or mayors sought to make a personal gain off the women, no agency prevented their actions. On the contrary, communities happily charged officers of the law with the task of dealing with prostitutes if in exchange citizens could be undisturbed by the sordid realities around them. Frontier officials had free rein to set the tone for the manner in which prostitutes would be treated. Prostitutes responded by accepting this power of public officials, and, where possible, adding sexual and social intimacies to reinforce their liaison with authorities. The conduct of frontier officials helped to perpetuate prostitution, maintain the marginal existence of its employees, and further solidify the negative status of prostitutes in the community.[30]

Denver's women of the *demimonde* had less to worry about from civic authorities than from customers and agents. Some of the Market Street women were from decent families now far away, where kinfolk remained. Most such women were from working-class backgrounds, some were orphans or widows, and others were abandoned wives. The folks back home would be very sad to learn of the depths into which they had descended.

In midsummer 1882 an extortionist named Peter Morahan was charged with representing to a number of Denver's prostitutes that for a fee, he could keep their occupations out of the *Police Gazette*, a widely circulated publication akin to the supermarket tabloids of a later age. Morahan did not work for the *Gazette*, nor was he a correspondent for it. The *Gazette* covered his courtroom trial and was pleased to tell its readers on July 29 that "there was blood in the eye" of Justice of the Peace Howard B. Jeffries when Jeffries heard the girls' testimony, and he sentenced Morahan "very justly" to pay a $100 fine and spend sixty days in jail. The saga of Judge Jeffries and his impact on Denver jurisprudence, as it turned out, became more notorious than the case of Peter Morahan.

In the course of his comments on the Morahan matter, Judge Jeffries referred to the *Police Gazette* as a "vile paper." A reporter writing for such a paper, said Jeffries, "must necessarily be depraved, for that paper holds up to public view all the secret vices, sins, and crimes of mankind. By obscene and disgusting pictures it poisons and pollutes the sacred circle of the home."

This, as can be imagined, aggrieved the *Police Gazette*, which was moved to pronounce: "The snarling of this hound can do us no harm, and in fact we are proclaiming [Jeffries] as the *Police Gazette* champion liar. We are ready to back our new champion for the championship of the universe in lying—barefaced lying, covert lying, sneaking, brazen, roundabout or any other style."[31]

Justice of the Peace Jeffries may or may not have been a barefaced, covert, sneaking, brazen liar, but he did turn to the publishing business and used it to turn a confidence game. In 1888 Jeffries was arrested for larceny and obtaining money under false pretenses for allegedly swindling $4,300 from Maggie Horan, a onetime washerwoman who had made some fortunate real estate investments. He collateralized the loan with

"If one girl is a good money-maker, they make her take one of those men [pimps] to support. They take all those poor girls' money every night, and they send them back to work the next day penniless. If they should not make enough for them they are beaten, and sometimes killed." Such was the confession of a white slave victim in Ernest A. Bell's Fighting the Traffic in Young Girls *(p. 78).*

valueless stock in a newspaper he supposedly owned, *Denver Afternoon,* and fled to San Francisco. When he finally returned to Denver to face charges and avoid a grand jury indictment, Jeffries said it was all a misunderstanding.[32]

Also attempting—and failing—to pull a fast one was the *demimonde* entrepreneurship known as "Mamma and Baby," a couple who in 1895 maintained a luxurious parlor far uptown at 1717 Tremont Place, convenient to the Brown Palace, the ritziest hotel in the

Mountain West. "Mamma," the brains of the operation, was Marie Devere, described by the *Denver Republican* as "well along in years," and "Baby" was May Oleson, still under twenty-one. Baby was falsely represented to clients as Mamma's daughter.[33]

Mamma and Baby had been hauled into the courthouse numerous times on soliciting and prostitution charges, on each occasion emerging with the usual light fine. Police were curious as to how the pair could afford such unusually nice quarters, even with a prostitute's earnings, until the officers discovered that the ladies were blackmailers as well.

Their scheme was simple. They would select a man's name at random, Mamma Marie would compose a handwritten letter claiming he had patronized her house, and she would demand hush money. The cunning pair signed the letters "Mamma and Baby." Very often payment would be forthcoming from men who had been somewhere else but could not recall where.

Mamma and Baby slipped up, however, when they dispatched a letter to an employee of Denver's city health department who knew he had not visited Mamma and Baby and who reported the matter to the police, who turned the case over to postal inspector William M. McMechin, who in turn placed a hold on the women for an appearance before the U.S. commissioner. The *Republican* speculated that Mamma and Baby would soon be taking "a lengthy sojourn in the Federal prison in Detroit."[34] As was typical of the Denver press, the story was not followed up, and we do not know the fate of Mamma and Baby.

Eight years later Maud Niggel of Denver was charged with dressing up her daughter, not yet sixteen, and dispatching the child out onto the sidewalks "for the vilest of purposes," proclaimed Deputy District Attorney William J. L. Crank. A young man named Lloyd Newcomb was determined to have "disgraced" the girl, who was unnamed in a *Denver Post* article and who then found herself involved with sixteen-year-old Earl Burroughs. Burroughs, in turn, was ordered by juvenile court officer John Phillips to marry the girl. Burroughs complied, and Maud was found guilty of neglect when Crank told the court: "Better to have our children in the orphans' home or have the coroner take them to the potters' field than have them presided over by such mothers. The people of Denver want her to know that she cannot sell the young girls of this country on the streets of this city."[35]

Mamma, Baby, and Maud Niggel had been independent operators, atypical of the standard sex-for-sale business in Denver. Most Denver prostitutes fell into one of three categories: the fancy women of the parlor houses with cigars and brandies, the wretches of the nearby vermin-infested cribs, and the prostitutes loosely masquerading as barroom girls. In the last case saloon owners gave each girl a small commission for the drinks she peddled, and sometimes the saloon men received kickbacks from nearby "hotels" to which the girls took their clients. The saloon keepers often conceded that they made their greatest profits from drinks bought by customers who accompanied prostitutes to the nearby hotels, rear booths, or upstairs rooms.[36] All this despite a Denver ordinance that women were not to be employed in saloons: "Any person who shall employ any woman in any liquor or beer saloon as a waiter or bartender, or who shall, for the purpose of attracting customers to any liquor or beer saloon, permit women to assemble, shall be deemed . . . guilty of a misdemeanor." As has been shown, however, fines for such infractions were so low they were laughed at by defendants.[37]

Prostitution and the dispensing of liquor became so intertwined that historian Lawrence H. Larsen discussed them in tandem. In his book *The Urban West at the End of the Frontier* Larsen includes a table enumerating the number of Colorado bordellos and saloons "admitted [to] officially by local authorities" in 1880. By this surprising count Denver had a meager 7 bordellos—a figure so low it apparently addressed only the fancy parlor houses and excluded the nearby independent cribs. The listing credits Denver with 200 saloons, a sizable number. Leadville is listed as having 100 bordellos and 150 saloons. Larsen noted: "Only twelve cities in the United States claimed more or as many 'resorts' as Leadville's 100." By comparison, the numbers for all of Los Angeles were 12 bordellos and 70 saloons and for San Francisco no bordellos but an astonishing 8,694 saloons. Different standards, it appears, were applied in arriving at the various statistics.[38]

Big Ed Chase's Palace Theater and saloon was the most renowned in Colorado during its heyday, 1870–1890. Near the end of this period, with the Palace firmly established as a center for violence and murder, Chase and his partners sold the establishment to Canadian-born Bertholomiew "Bat" Masterson, one of the most notable gamblers and boxing entrepreneurs in the West. Masterson, a onetime lawman in Dodge City, Kansas, and Trinidad, Colorado, found Denver

The reckless life of the bordello woman is illustrated in this almost comical photograph from within a parlor house. When joining the flesh trade, such women traded in their standard wardrobes for white brothel gowns—used fairly universally in organized prostitution throughout the United States in the late nineteenth century. Along Denver's Market Street Row, young habitués could be big drinkers but were often even bigger consumers of morphine, opium, or especially laudanum.

to his liking, making the city his home beginning in early 1880 but frequently traveling wherever he could make book on prizefights or other athletic contests. Masterson was described by an acquaintance as a "compactly built man with grayish hair and a serious countenance . . . carrying two valises and decked out in patent-leather shoes, a plug hat, and a sealskin-trimmed chinchilla ulster that almost reached the ground."[39]

Masterson downplayed his successes in Denver. After residing in the city for ten years, he wrote to a friend:

I can't say that I have been prosperous, although I have not suffered much from adversity. I have been connected nearly all the time since coming here in the gambling business and have experienced the vicissitudes which has always characterized the business. Some days—plenty, and more days—nothing, this may all be greek to you. I came into the world without anything and I have about held my own up to date.[40]

Masterson's fondness for wagering led him into all the gambling dives in Denver, but he particularly liked the notorious Palace—so much so that he purchased the place in about 1888 from Big Ed Chase and Ed Gaylord. Masterson enjoyed the establishment's traveling variety shows, its 60 feet of mirroring, its gigantic sparkling chandelier, and its gambling room that accommodated 25 dealers and 200 players. The adjacent theater held 750, and private boxes were hidden behind tapestries and velvet.[41]

Masterson, observed the *Rocky Mountain News*, was "a handsome man, and one who pleases the ladies." At one point, probably in the early 1880s, he wed song-and-dance girl Emma Walters, of whom little is known other than the fact that she influenced Masterson to remain in Denver for her health. Masterson had other female friends. One was Nellie McMahon Spencer, who when she arrived in Denver in 1886 had been married for three years to Lou Spencer, "the negro comedian, who has been convulsing the audiences at California hall [Hall] for a week past."[42] On Saturday night, September 18, 1886, Lou Spencer was thus convulsing the audience when he looked up and saw Nellie, as Lou later told a *News* reporter,

> sitting on Bat Masterson's knee in a box during the performance. I went to the door and called her out, and asked her what she was doing. Masterson spoke up and said that if I had anything to say to the lady I might tell it to him. I reminded him that the lady was my wife, when he struck at me with his pistol, and I struck back with my fist. Then we were arrested and taken down to the station, where we were both released and I went back to work.

The next day, Lou told the reporter, Nellie "called me to her a dozen times and asked me to forgive her, after the affair, and I told her there was nothing to forgive." Nellie remained in town Sunday and Monday, and on Tuesday she and Masterson disappeared. The press theorized they were headed for Dodge City; he, at least, is recorded as arriving there.

On Wednesday Nellie's lawyer filed a divorce suit in Superior Court, alleging nonsupport, brutality, and "habitual drunkenness." Lou Spencer responded that the charges were false, that she was unemployed (she had formerly appeared in Denver as a vocalist with the Kate Castleton Opera Company), and that he had supported her for five months when she was without employment.

Lou Spencer was sufficiently distressed over his wife's "elopement" that he repaired to an opium den, where he was arrested. He was bailed out of jail by a friend named Bagsby. Masterson (and presumably Nellie) came back to town and became irritated when he learned of Bagsby's rescue. Masterson tracked down Bagsby at Murphy's Exchange saloon—the establishment police had been ordered not to disturb. Masterson confronted Bagsby and struck him over the head, opening a bad gash and blackening Bagsby's eyes.

According to a *Rocky Mountain News* reporter who overheard the fracas, Masterson accompanied the blow with "an oath and a vile epithet," and then a shot was heard. The *News* reported that Bagsby pleaded, "I never did anything to hurt you, Bat."

The gunshot struck Masterson in the leg, and he was carried into the saloon's back room, to which Dr. W. W. Anderson was summoned. The place was in chaos, with Bagsby in the front room mopping his head and "swearing profusely" while Bat was being tended to in the back room. Policemen Snyder (first name not listed in city directories) and Lew S. Tuttle quickly arrived and called for the paddy wagon, but as neither Masterson nor Bagsby wanted to pursue the matter further, no arrests were made. That seems to have been the end of it.[43]

Masterson sold the Palace at some point, and it closed in 1889, doubtless to the great relief of citizens who wanted peace and quiet. Masterson briefly ran a Larimer Street saloon and in 1891 moved to the new silver boomtown of Creede to operate the Denver Exchange saloon, restaurant, and gambling hall—and to referee boxing matches. He was known as the coolest and nerviest man in the camp. By 1893 Masterson was back in Denver, but its citizens, conservative gambling habits, police department, and general demeanor increasingly annoyed him.[44]

Masterson spent the next few years operating a succession of gambling houses up and down Seventeenth, Curtis, and Larimer Streets, with frequent trips out of state wherever a notable prizefight was being staged on which Masterson could make book. Masterson's friend Wyatt Earp occasionally dealt faro alongside Masterson in Denver, and the confidence man Jefferson Randolph "Soapy" Smith set up his shell game outside Masterson's gambling parlors. Masterson knew Smith and his troublemaking brother Bascom from Leadville and later Creede, and he liked Smith. Masterson wrote a letter to Soapy Smith, after the latter had been run out of Denver and was swindling miners in Skagway, stating that Bascom Smith seemed always to be in trouble in Denver: "He has been arrested twice of late for disturbance and for discharging firearms down in the neighborhood of Twentieth and Market streets, and you know the kind of people who frequent that locality."[45]

For a time during the mid-1890s, Masterson managed Denver's long notorious Arcade saloon and gambling parlor. From there—or so went the story published in the *Denver Post* years later—Masterson escorted out by the nose an unnamed Denver police chief (or the mayor, depending on the version).[46]

Masterson's most notorious Denver escapade—and one of the most colorful shooting incidents in the history of Denver law enforcement—took place on election night, April 6, 1897. Masterson was hired as a special deputy sheriff to help oversee the election and was stationed at Precinct 3, Third Ward, 1837 Arapahoe Street. Also present was police Patrolman Timothy Connors (also spelled Connor). Masterson had campaigned against city alderman James Doyle, and when the polls closed, Masterson was asked to leave while the votes were counted. He refused and was ejected by Officer Connors. Masterson promised to return and said that if the vote count began without him, he would "use my gun."

Masterson soon reappeared, drew his .45, and fired at Connors. The officer grabbed Bat's arm, and the bullet hit precinct election clerk Charles Louderbaugh in the left wrist, grazing the bone and passing into Louderbaugh's hip pocket where it lodged against a penny in his coin purse. Masterson fled during the ensuing melee. Nothing seems to have come of the matter other than Louderbaugh threatening to sue Masterson for damages to the purse and contents, all of which became keepsakes of the Louderbaugh family. Connors was indicted three months later in conjunction with an investigation of election fraud. It appears he was not convicted, and by 1905 he was the Denver Police Department's captain of detectives.

At a major prizefight in Carson City, Nevada, on February 8, 1897, pitting Ruby Bob Fitzsimmons against Gentleman Jim Corbett, the stage was set for Masterson to encounter the man who became his mortal enemy, sportswriter Otto Floto. At the fight Harry H. Tammen met and hired Floto to report sports for the *Denver Post*, the scandal sheet co-owned by Tammen and Frederick G. Bonfils.

Masterson and Floto had similar backgrounds and interests and initially were friends. When Floto double-crossed Masterson in a business venture, however, Floto may have not understood that whereas Masterson could be intensely loyal to friends (e.g., the no-good Doc Holliday), he was an unforgiving enemy. Thus began a feud—usually conducted in print—between Masterson and Floto that reached its crescendo in 1899 when the two accidently encountered each other in front of Bert Davis's cigar store at Sixteenth and Champa Streets.

Gene Fowler witnessed the brouhaha, which he said "stirred up more wind than the town had felt since the blizzard of 1883." Masterson, 200 pounds, swung his cane, and Floto, at 250 pounds, retreated, outrunning Masterson, leading the latter to later confess: "He is the best runner I ever saw."

Masterson's disenchantment with Denver was growing. In 1898 he took it out on the Denver Police Department:

> The police department of Denver is now and has been for ten years a political machine. You cannot expect much of a police department that is run strictly along political lines. It would not do any good to increase the police force. If the force was increased to twice

its present size you would simply have a political machine twice the size of the present one—nothing more.[47]

In 1900 Masterson pledged to put as much distance as possible between Denver and himself, and that September he sold his interest in a boxing facility he owned, the Olympic Club, and left town with a parting shot:

This town is the worst in the country. There ain't a sport in it. It is actually the cheapest town I was ever in. It is filled up with a whole lot of bluffers and hoodlums and robbers and fakirs, and everyone is trying his best to skin his neighbor. Nothing is done on the square if there is a crooked way to do it, and the man who skins his neighbor oftenest during the year is a great man in the community. . . . Why, the town is known from one end of the country to the other as the greatest town for fakes in the world. . . . [Denver] is a great hospital in which are gathered more old, broken-down fossils, fakirs, and bunks than can be gathered up with a fine comb by dragging the country. I hope nobody thinks I have been living in this rotten place because I loved it or was making money here. . . . I would not have stayed here over twenty minutes if it had not been for my wife's health.[48]

Masterson returned to Denver one last time, an event residents talked about for years. He had long maintained a legal residence at 1825 Curtis Street and in 1902 came back to vote in a school board election in which one of the candidates was a woman. Masterson believed women not only should not be running for office but should not be voting.

Masterson sauntered to the nearby polling place, where a handful of stern women stood guard to intercept people they knew were not authorized to vote or who tried to vote twice in different precincts. Politicians often used prostitutes in such voting frauds. As Masterson approached the polling place, one of the women challenged him, and when he asked why she felt he should not vote, she rapped him across the neck with her umbrella.

That was enough. Masterson, never known as much of a drinker, had had it with Denver and, it was subsequently written, went on a drinking binge. Word

of Masterson's disruptive behavior quickly reached District Attorney Harry Lindsley, who asked Police Chief Hamilton Armstrong to remove Masterson from Denver. Armstrong enlisted Jim Marshall, an old acquaintance of Masterson's who was a fearless officer in Cripple Creek. Chief Armstrong sent a telegram asking Marshall to confront Masterson and escort him to the city limits.

Masterson learned all of this and sent word for Marshall to meet him at the Scholtz drugstore at 10 A.M. Marshall did not show up. Masterson waited an hour and then strolled to the saloon across the street for a morning nip. As he lifted his glass Marshall's low voice announced, "Sorry I was a little late, Bat." Masterson's gun hand was poised in midair, holding the whiskey glass. Marshall's gun hand was poised in midair, holding a revolver pointed straight at Masterson.

Masterson considered this predicament for a moment and then inquired, "If I leave, how soon do I have to go?"

"Could you make the four o'clock Burlington, Bat?"

"I reckon so."[49]

Bat Masterson was among the well-known gamblers wandering Denver's streets in the late nineteenth century and whose visits were observed and recorded by Detective Sam Howe. Cebert A. Trease, a surveyor who had known the James family back in Missouri, saw Jesse and Frank in Denver one day and recalled many years later:

I thought them as fine men as I ever met. They seemed quiet and unassuming. Both Frank and Jesse were expert shots with rifle and revolver. I saw the James boys in Denver on Larimer Street . . . and asked Charley Conners, who was a policeman at that time, if he knew who they were. He said, "Yes, but I never lost anything over there [on the other side of the street]." I crossed over to speak to the [James] boys and they said Conners was safe as long as he stayed on his side of the street.[50]

Boomtown Denver also beckoned Wyatt Earp's good friend and nonpracticing dentist John Henry "Doc" Holliday, a onetime Tombstone, Arizona, lawman and former U.S. deputy marshal. The tubercular and homicidal Holliday had been in Pueblo, where he ran a gambling concession, and in the summer of 1875 he arrived in Denver to make a fresh start under the alias Tom Mackey. He went to work as a dealer at John Babb's Theatre Comique, 357 Blake Street (old numbering). Holliday was unable to stay out of trouble and got in a knife fight, among other skirmishes. From Denver it was off on a rambling excursion back to Pueblo and other points.

Pueblo's dance halls arrived in 1872, and prostitution was close behind; Mollie May worked there before moving on to become the best-known scarlet woman of Leadville. The *Pueblo Chieftain* on August 10, 1872, under the headline "Disgraceful," wrote:

> A couple of abandoned women at the Hotel de Omaha had a misunderstanding that culminated in a regular street fight. They rolled and tumbled in the mud, pulled hair, fought, bit, gouged and pommelled each other and filled the air with blood-curdling oaths. None of the police officers were on hand to interfere. It was a disgraceful spectacle, and a strong illustration of the morals on the banks of the Arkansas.

Pueblo's first antiprostitution ordinances were passed on January 14, 1875, setting a complete schedule of fines. The *Chieftain* observed that "our city fathers have suddenly awakened to the fact that lewd women are to be found in Pueblo" but added pointedly that "the effect of prohibitory legislation upon these things is simply to make the carrying on of them rather more secret, and hence less under the control of the police. We must conclude then that the ordinance is passed for the purpose of revenue."[51]

Doc Holliday's health was continuing to decline. By August 4, 1886, he had slipped so far into the depths of debauchery that police in Denver hauled him in for common vagrancy with a gaggle of his ne'er-do-well pals. The Denver *Tribune-Republican* reported (confusing the spelling of Doc Holliday's name with that of stagecoach entrepreneur Ben Holladay for whom Holladay Street was named):

> The notorious Doc Holladay was arrested last evening by the police for vagrancy. . . . His only means of living [is] gambling in its worst form and confidence

work. Three weeks ago, he left town on a penalty of being arrested, but returned a few days ago, so the police say, in company with a score of other confidence men, thieves and sure-thing workers. Last evening Holliday [and companions] were standing on Sixteenth street, when officer Norkott [the city directory lists a policeman Michael B. Norkett] called up the patrol wagon and they were gathered in.[52]

Denver indeed did not appreciate the presence of Doc Holliday. The *Republican* said on one occasion and with considerable exaggeration, which Holliday might have appreciated:

> Doc Holliday, the prisoner, is one of the most noted desperadoes of the West. In comparison, Billy the Kid or any other of the many Western desperadoes who have recently met their fate, fade into insignificance. The murders committed by him are counted by the scores and his other crimes are legion. For years he has roamed the West, gaining his living by gambling, robbery and murder. In the Southwest his name is a terror.[53]

Fifteen months later, in a desperate search for a tuberculosis cure, Holliday took the stagecoach to the mineral waters of Glenwood Springs, Colorado, where he died at age thirty-seven on November 8, 1887. He is buried in an unrecorded plot in the Glenwood Springs cemetery. Nearby, the city has erected as a tourist attraction a granite monument to the memory of Doc Holliday, the stone decorated with engravings of pistols and poker hands.[54]

Historian Phil Goodstein has written of a Denver visit by Robert Leroy Parker, better known as Butch Cassidy, who stood lookout at Seventeenth and Larimer Streets on March 29, 1889, when a man wielding what he represented as a bottle of explosive nitroglycerine swindled $21,000 from the First National Bank of Denver. The robber identified himself to bank president David H. Moffat as C. J. Wells, but in retrospect he was believed to have been Thomas C. McCarty, an associate of desperado Cole Younger. McCarty escaped and was never caught, and there is no indication that Cassidy was questioned either. The "nitroglycerine" bottle was discovered discarded on Larimer Street and contained a harmless oil.[55]

While the Denver police tried to keep track of Bat Masterson, Jesse and Frank James, Doc Holliday, Butch Cassidy, and dozens of lesser-knowns, Denver's home-grown gambler, Big Ed Chase, became involved with the Arcade sporting house, next door to the feared Murphy's Exchange on Larimer Street. Before Chase purchased the Arcade, it was just another gambling joint. A favorite anecdote involved two gamblers, the second the one-eyed Deadeye Dick. The first man quietly pulled his revolver, laid it on the table, and announced: "I ain't mentioning any names, but if someone does any more cheating while I'm here, I'll shoot out his other eye."

Unlike the Palace—and certainly unlike Murphy's Exchange—the Arcade under Ed Chase was primarily a restaurant, and one of its early chefs was John Elitch, who with his wife, Mary, later built an amusement park. The Arcade became a first-class establishment with mahogany furniture, chandeliers, and a leaded glass skylight depicting a tiger.

Sam Howe, detective and crime statistician, kept a running total of the problems caused by places such as the Palace and Johnny Murphy's Exchange. Howe assembled the monthly data for July 1886, for instance, and found that of the 431 arrests, 25 percent—or 151—were for drunkenness. Nearly every drunk—147 of the 151—was tossed in jail; the other 4 were hauled home by sympathetic policemen. (A newspaper reporter quipped that those taken home to their wives may have faced a fate worse than jail.)[56] Other figures for that month included 25 arrests for being an inmate of a house of prostitution, 1 for keeping a disorderly house, 1 for keeping a house of prostitutes, and *none* for gambling.[57] Clearly, the payoffs were in full force.

Of all the wicked nightspots that plagued Denver, the G.A.R. Saloon on Larimer Street joined the Palace on the list of the worst. Further, the G.A.R. was an embarrassment to men of the Grand Army of the Republic, for which the nefarious place may have been named (although the *Rocky Mountain News* speculated that the letters stood for "Great African Resort.") The G.A.R. was particularly a gathering spot for African Americans. The *Rocky Mountain News* on June 21, 1886, described the G.A.R. as a "dive and den of vice and crime, said to be a resort for the very worst cutthroats, thieves, burglars, gamblers, prostitutes, and vagrants, white and colored." The "colored murderers [Andrew] Green and [first name?] Withers," said the *News*, patronized the G.A.R., but the "honest, hard-working colored men of the city, who have families growing up, and who desire to see their own race relieved from pitfalls of the devil and temptations to crime, are very earnestly demanding that this hellish plague-spot of iniquity shall be wiped out."

Only a month earlier the G.A.R. had been linked to the robbery-slaying by African American Andrew Green of streetcar driver Joseph C. Whitnah, who was white. Prior to the murder Green had visited the G.A.R. and, in his own words, also patronized "Eva Catlin's house on Holladay street, a colored dive." The Board of Aldermen revoked the G.A.R.'s liquor license, but the next step appears to have been for the city supervisors to shut the place down. Supervisor Thomas Nicholl seemed to be blocking the closure, and no record has been located of the G.A.R. being closed. The G.A.R. is not mentioned in Denver crime annals subsequent to the summer of 1886, so probably the place was closed by public sentiment, and neither it nor its supposed proprietor can be located in city directories of the day.[58]

Two hundred persons were employed in Denver gambling houses as 1886 began; the town had six "square" games in operation, the remainder being crooked—or "brace"—games. Faro dealers were paid five dollars a day for a six-day week. The elite and wealthy patronized private gambling rooms in the Tabor Opera House building (where H.A.W. Tabor often played and usually lost). Denver had one female gambling house operator, Belle Siddons, but her place of employment is not recorded.[59]

Honest games were not the norm in Denver, but they did exist. For instance, no evidence has come to light about Big Ed Chase ever swindling a customer, and indeed he stated that he never did. Chase considered himself above such shenanigans, and that sort of behavior would have tarnished the business and political interests he labored so long to establish.

The same appears to be true of Bill Cate, who in the late 1880s ran a "palace of fortune" on the second floor of the old Walhalla Hall building at Sixteenth and Curtis Streets. Curtis increasingly became a gambling center through the 1880s. When the structure was demolished during the summer of 1916—it was then known as the Church Building—the pioneer-oriented journal *The Trail* remembered Cate fondly as "for many years one of the best known and squarest of gamblers that ever controlled a faro layout or keno game." The article, quoting Sam Howe, continued:

> Cate was of the West. Rider of the Pony Express, when every minute was fraught with peril; prospector for gold and soldiers of fortune when off the long ride from Fort Leavenworth, Cate was all that appealed in the days when money was easy come, easy go, and his resort, because of his reputation for fair play, soon became a rendezvous where the sudden millionaires of Georgetown and Central and Leadville and Aspen took their fling—not to gain more wealth but to win the excitement that was denied them in other ways.

Sam Howe remembered a murder in Cate's club room. Tex Iager and a man named Weiderman were playing cards when a dispute over alleged cheating arose, Howe recalled. Weapons were drawn, and "when the finish came, Weiderman lay on the floor. It was a 'justifiable' killing, according to the verdict, for in the code of those days the use of the word 'cheat' was a warrant for a shooting."[60]

Although the police were not inclined to do much about Denver's gambling establishments, the newspapers were beginning to grouse about these business places and their clientele:

> The town is full to overflowing with vagrants and other disreputable characters. The great majority will take anything that is not nailed to the floor. Said one of the detectives yesterday: "From now on we expect to have more trouble with the gamblers than all the other classes put together. They are a bad lot through and through, and will do anything from picking a pocket to burglarizing a store."[61]

As 1887 turned into 1888, the town recorded 7,266 arrests: 1,002 for vagrancy, only 57 for gambling, 2,472 for drunkenness, and, the *Denver Republican* indignantly reported, "179 women ranging in age from the young girl of 14 who had taken her first downward step to the gray-haired harridan of 50, were held in durance vile for being inmates of houses of prostitution."[62]

To G. N. Scamehorn, Denver's gambling addict–turned–antigambling crusader, the palaces of the green cloth, which had stolen his money and dignity, continued to be purgatory personified. In *Behind the Scenes, or Denver by Gaslight*, Scamehorn wrote of dens such as the Leadville Club on Curtis Street where

> William R. Perry, late clerk of the county court lost hundreds and thousands of dollars, [where] Mr. Quinn, late county treasurer at Grand Junction lost hundreds and thousands of the tax payers money, but the bloated proprietor remains as cold and distant as the arctic icicle. Many a poor fellow after losing his last cent has asked for twenty-five cents, then we see the poor fellow stumbling down the stairway, thinking what he must tell his wife and family when he gets home. Oh how I do wish every gambling hell was burned up.

Scamehorn continued his tirade, listing the Capitol gambling hall on Curtis Street, Billy Leese's Colander Club at 1626 Curtis Street, Bill Cate's Club at Sixteenth and Curtis (the one Sam Howe pronounced fairly harmless), and the Jockey Club on Sixteenth Street where "thousands and tens of thousands was lost. . . . Scores of once prosperous business men are today nothing more than beggars, wandering along what they call the 'unlucky pathway of life.'"[63]

The gamblers, prostitutes, and corrupt politicians did not listen to Scamehorn and his ilk, and Denver hurtled onward down its path of wickedness. On the horizon, though, a Populist reform wave would try to clean up Denver.

Notes

1. These and other descriptions of Denver nightspots of the period are in Dallas, *Cherry Creek Gothic*, pp. 203–215, and Thom, "Stage Celebrities in Denver Theatres Forty Years Ago." Also see Bancroft, *Six Racy Madams*, pp. 5–6.

2. "One Man's Experience in Early Leadville," as related by T. E. Van Evra, *The Trail*, December 1918, pp. 20–23.

3. Euchre was played with thirty-two cards, all below seven with the ace removed. It involved two, three, or four players, and as with bridge it was played with trumps and tricks.

4. Fred C. Mills recalled the trek he and Charlie Hough made from Leadville to Magnolia in "A Boy's Hike in the '70s," *The Trail*, October 1924, pp. 17–18.

5. DTR, January 1, 1881; RD, p. 223.

6. Noel, *The City and the Saloon*, pp. 20, 116.

7. Limerick, *The Legacy of Conquest*, p. 51. The 1881 Denver year-end population figure of 60,000 is from that year's *Colorado State Business Directory*.

8. RD, p. 223.

9. Ibid., p. 244.

10. See Ordinance 99, Section 9, city council proceedings of 1884, quoted in Burroughs, "As It Was in the Beginning," p. 186.

11. Quoted in RD, p. 410.

12. Denver Public Library, Western History Department, loose newspaper clippings file of police chief reports. Clipping unidentified as to originating newspaper and date.

13. Rosen, *The Lost Sisterhood*, p. 79.

14. The *Denver Tribune-Republican*, April 18, 1886.

15. DR, April 25, 1894.

16. R. L. Hanna, "The Art of American Policing, 1900–1930," unpublished master's thesis, University of Colorado at Denver, 1990, p. 44.

17. Eve Bennett, "Shady Ladies of the '80s," *Rocky Mountain Life*, April 1947, pp. 12–13.

18. For the forty gambling houses operating in Denver in 1883 and their clientele, see RD, p. 334. For the various descriptions of Denver at night, see SHS 8: 2597, from the RMN, July 19, 1888; SHS 8: 2280, from the DR, February 26, 1888; SHS 7: 1969-1971, from the DR and *Denver Evening Times*, November 16, 1887; and SHS 9: 2962, from the DR, December 4, 1888. See also Thom, "Stage Celebrities in Denver Theatres," pp. 12–15. Rolf Johnson's views of Denver's Holladay and Wazee Streets are in Don Bloch, "The Saga of the Wandering Swede," *1954 Brand Book* of the Denver Posse of the Westerners (Boulder: Johnson, 1955), pp. 271, 277, 279. Charles Brown's comments regarding the imbibing habits in the mining camp of Bonanza are from Schlissel, Gibbens, and Hampsten, *Far from Home*, p. 116, and further observations regarding the Palace Theater are from the DR, December 4, 1888. Henry Martyn Hart's views on prostitution are from George N. Rainsford, "Dean Henry Martyn Hart and Public Issues," *Colorado Magazine*, summer 1971, p. 208–210.

19. The location of Effie Moore's violent death at Denver's Palace Theater could be equated to the so-called third-tier private boxes in New York City's "concert saloons." The third tier was above the main floor and balcony seating and consisted of secluded, semiprivate box seats where male theater patrons could rendezvous with willing women—prostitutes or not. The third tier was the only part of such halls where prostitutes were permitted, and they and their customers were allowed to remain as long as they were reasonably quiet. Some of the New York girls, however, were ejected after leaning over the railing, wrote historian Timothy Gilfoyle, exposing their breasts and urging men to come up and have some fun. In some concert saloons female performers and waitresses doubled as prostitutes. This mixture of stage show, liquor, and sex was new in the business of prostitution and competed with parlor houses and cribs. Gilfoyle in *City of Eros* (chapter 11) discusses at some length concert saloons and their related "French balls."

20. SHS 7: 1969–1971, from the DR and *Denver Evening Times*, November 16, 1887; see also SHS 9: 2962, from the DR, December 4, 1888, and Thom, "Stage Celebrities in Denver Theatres," pp. 12–15.

21. SHS 8: 2280, from the DR, February 26, 1888.

22. Ibid., 2597, from the RMN, July 19, 1888.

23. Ibid., 13: 6318, from the DR, April 22, 1892.

24. Ernest A. Bell, *Fighting the Traffic in Young Girls, or War on the White Slave Trade* (n.c.: G. S. Ball, 1910), p. 230.

25. Ibid., pp. 282–283. The Market Street bordello district in Denver never experienced the presence of red light lanterns, a practice said to have existed in some towns when railroadmen hung their work lanterns outside brothels as they entered.

26. As quoted in Reiter, *The Women*, pp. 141–142.

27. The slayings of R. D. Vaughn and Thomas Gallagher at the Palace Theater are in SHS 9: 2917, from the DR, November 15, 1888; 9: 2955, from the DR, December 4, 1888. The "felonious intent" indictment against Palace bartender Peter Anderson is from SHS 9: 2919, clipping dated November 16, 1888, newspaper unidentified.

28. The Murphy's Exchange saloon was overseen by sportsman, practical joker, and bon vivant Johnny Murphy

(1848–1902) who came west in the 1870s and settled in Fairplay, Colorado, where he became the manager of boxer Billy Coleman. On Murphy's 1878 arrival in Denver, he was briefly a fight manager before opening the saloon where he announced that no Negroes were welcome. Prizefighter John L. Sullivan always stopped by Murphy's when he was in Denver. See SHS 21: 29717, from the DTI, December 1, 1902; Dallas, *Cherry Creek Gothic*, pp. 203–215.

29. SHS 13: 6773 and 12: 5566, from the DR, May 26, 1891. Charles A. Johnson, *Denver's Mayor Speer* (Denver: Green Mountain, 1969), is among the works examining Robert W. Speer.

30. Anne M. Butler, *Daughters of Joy, Sisters of Misery* (Urbana: University of Illinois Press, 1985), p. 76.

31. Gene Smith and Jayne Barry Smith, *The Police Gazette* (New York: Simon and Schuster, 1972), p. 34.

32. SHS 9: 2947, from the DTI, November 28, 1888. *Denver Afternoon*, if indeed it was ever published, was such an obscure newspaper that city directories do not mention it among dozens of big and small publications in Denver in the late 1880s. Nor does *Denver Afternoon* appear in the findings of the Colorado Historical Society's "Colorado Newspaper Project," a comprehensive survey, completed in 1991, of all newspapers ever published in the state. The 1888 *Denver City Directory* lists Jeffries not as a lawyer or a judge but as a "journalist."

33. Experienced prostitutes even in their twenties, hoping to appeal to male fantasies for young sex partners, sometimes disguised themselves as schoolgirls, earning the designation "buzzards in doves' plumes." See Gilfoyle, *City of Eros*, pp. 285–286.

34. In the September 22, 1895, edition.

35. DP, July 3, 1908.

36. Rosen, *The Lost Sisterhood*, p. 77.

37. Cited in Burroughs, "As It Was in the Beginning," p. 185. The date of the ordinance was 1884.

38. Lawrence H. Larsen, *The Urban West at the End of the Frontier* (Lawrence: Regents Press of Kansas, 1978), p. 87.

39. Quoted in Robert K. DeArment, *Bat Masterson: The Man and the Legend* (Norman: University of Oklahoma Press, 1979), pp. 292–293.

40. Ibid., p. 293.

41. Ibid., pp. 328–330.

42. RMN, September 18, 1886. For Emma Walters Masterson, see ibid., p. 330.

43. Bat Masterson's imbroglio in Murphy's Exchange as the result of his friendship with Nellie McMahon Spencer is told in SHS 4: 949, from the RMN, September 22, 1886, and SHS 4: 879, from the RMN, October 5, 1886. DeArment in *Bat Masterson* tells of the Masterson-Spencer affair on pp. 326–327 but does not write of the subsequent Bagsby gunplay. See also James D. Horan, *The Authentic Wild West* (New York: Crown, 1980), pp. 22–52.

44. Masterson's brief term as a gambling entrepreneur in Creede is told in DeArment, *Bat Masterson*, pp. 330–338.

45. Ibid., pp. 344–345.

46. In the October 25, 1921, edition.

47. Masterson's flare-up as an election guard is in SHS 17: 14102, 14105, from the DR, April 7, 8, 1897. The fate of Tim Connors is in SHS 17: 14672, quoting the DR, July 1, 1897, and SHS 27: 37983, from the DTI, unspecified date but probably March 13, 1905. For the Masterson-Floto grudge match, see DeArment, *Bat Masterson*, pp. 352–357. Masterson's evaluation of the Denver Police Department is from SHS 18: 17362, quoting the DP, December 1, 1898. Students of the political influence imposed on the Denver Police Department during its formative years should consult the RD.

48. DeArment, *Bat Masterson*, pp. 361–363.

49. A concise account of Bat Masterson's years in Denver is Robert K. DeArment, "Bat Masterson and the Boxing Club War of Denver," *Colorado Heritage*, autumn 2000, pp. 28–36. The story of the Jim Marshall–Bat Masterson confrontation was told by *Denver Republican* reporter (and later novelist) William MacLeod Raine, citing an unpublished manuscript prepared by District Attorney Harry Lindsley; quoted in DeArment, *Bat Masterson*, pp. 364–367. As DeArment suggests in the *Colorado Heritage* article, the Marshall-Masterson confrontation story might be true—but even if not, it is too good to omit from any story about Bat Masterson's years in Denver.

50. James R. Harvey, "Cebert Alexander Trease, Engineer," *Colorado Magazine*, November 1939, p. 222.

51. Joanne West Dodds, *What's a Nice Girl Like You Doing in a Place Like This? Prostitution in Southern Colorado, 1860 to 1911* (Pueblo: Focal Plain, 1996), pp. 7 ff. A young Damon Runyon, when a newspaper reporter in Pueblo, established a rapport with the commercial women of the town. His experiences are related in Ed Weiner, *The Damon Runyon Story* (New York: Longmans, Green, 1948); Edwin P. Hoyt, *A Gentleman of Broadway* (Boston: Little, Brown, 1964); Jimmy Breslin, *Damon Runyon* (New York: Ticknor and Fields, 1991).

52. SHS 4: 762, from the Denver *Tribune-Republican*, August 4, 1886. DeArment in *Bat Masterson* includes an informative chapter on John H. "Doc" Holliday, "The Deadly Dentist" (pp. 218–231). Masterson did not like Holliday but tolerated him because he was a friend of Wyatt Earp's, whom Masterson respected. DeArment quotes Masterson writing of Holliday (p. 226): "Holliday had a mean disposition and an ungovernable temper, and under the influence of liquor was a most dangerous man. . . . Holliday had few real friends anywhere in the west. He was selfish and had a perverse nature—traits not calculated to make a man popular in the early days on the frontier. Physically, Doc Holliday was a weakling who could not have whipped a healthy 15-year-old boy, and no one knew this better than himself. He was hotheaded and impetuous and very much given to both drinking and quarreling and, among men who didn't fear him, was very much disliked. It was easily seen that he was not a healthy man for he not only looked the part, but he incessantly coughed it as well."

53. Quoted in DeArment, *Bat Masterson*, p. 229.

54. A recent worthwhile addition to the expansive John Henry Holliday literature is Karen Holliday Tanner, *Doc Holliday: A Family Portrait* (Norman: University of Oklahoma Press, 1998). See Horan, *The Authentic Wild West*, pp. 251–259, or the abundant additional studies of the life of Doc Holliday.

55. Goodstein, *The Seamy Side of Denver*, pp. 224–225. Students of Colorado law enforcement history should acquaint themselves with events of November 5, 1898, at Paddy Maloney's White Dog Saloon in Kiowa, a hamlet on the high plains 50 miles southeast of Denver. There, twenty men and half-grown boys were discussing current events. Lone Jim, the holdup man, was said to be headed this way from Denver, and there was comparison of the three candidates for sheriff: "Curly," "Ten-Cent Charlie," and Bob Steele. Curly and Ten-Cent Charlie were favored because they were local boys, but Bob Steele was not from these parts, and some said he was a coward anyway.

A stranger rode into town and swung open the door to the White Dog. He could have posed for Frederic Remington.

"Cold out, Pardner?" asked Paddy, sensing a whiskey sale.

"Rather. Gentlemen, have something." Paddy scurried to behind the bar.

Kiowa had a strict etiquette. All glasses remained untouched until the stranger took his in one gulp. Then all simultaneously raised glasses toward lips. With one hand of each man thus occupied, the stranger spoke, low and quiet: "Hands up."

He held a matched pair of short-barreled .45-Colts at full cock. "I'll bore the first man who makes a break."

"A-a-are you Lone Jim?" asked Spud Tommie, barely eighteen.

The stranger ordered Paddy's customers to face the bar; he slipped one of the Colts into a waistband and relieved each one of his belongings. Then he ordered: "Gentlemen, have one, same as before."

The stranger then astonished everyone by laying his artillery on the bar and handing Paddy a five-dollar gold piece. He said: "My opponents have been telling you that I lack nerve. Gentlemen, drink to the health of Bob Steele, the next sheriff of Elbert County."

He was, too.

See Chauncey Thomas (ed.), "Sheriff of Elbert," *The Trail*, November 1927, pp. 18–20.

56. Denver's jail earned a measure of world renown when an eccentric named Rocco Dianovitch came through town. Dianovitch had traveled the globe for thirty-four years, intentionally getting tossed into jails as he went along. He inspected jails in Belgium, France, England, Italy, Spain, Greece, Australia, and the United States. In a book on the subject he voted the one in "Denver, America" the "pleasantest." The worst were in Australia. In response, Denver's humorless head jailer William H. Conley said he regretted "the popularity of the Denver jail [and] having entertained Rocco Dianovitch." Generally, throughout the late nineteenth century Denver's jails were regarded as hellholes. See SHS 17, from the DR, February 25, 1898.

57. SHS 4: 760, from the RMN, August 3, 1886.

58. For the G.A.R. Saloon, see the RMN, June 21, 1886. The establishment is also mentioned in King, *Going to Meet a Man*, pp. 34, 87. The G.A.R., however, is not listed in the Denver city directories of 1885 or 1886, and neither is a man named "Hagar," its supposed owner.

59. Parkhill, *The Wildest of the West*, pp. 70–71.

60. "An Old Landmark Disappears," *The Trail*, August 1916, p. 28.

61. SHS 7: 2179, from the RMN, January 7, 1888.

62. Ibid., 8: 2342, from the DR, April 5, 1888.

63. Scamehorn, *Behind the Scenes*, pp. 13–14.

7

The Recording Angel Gave Them One White Mark

ENVER'S TENDERLOIN ACTIVITY BY THE 1880S was said to be third only to San Francisco's Barbary Coast and Storyville in New Orleans. Leadville was booming as no mineral camp in Colorado ever had, and most of the prospectors headed there passed through Denver first. Many had their last fling with female companionship before embarking for the mountains.

Much of Denver winked at its love-for-rent district, viewing it as a thriving, profitable industry that drew men to town where they might remain an extra night or two. The only thing the aldermen asked was that the girls stay in their place, along the upper reaches of Holladay Street. Regular payoffs to the police and city hall ensured that Denver's bagnios could remain in business fairly unhindered by officialdom.

The *Rocky Mountain News* on August 21, 1880, supposedly reported that the city council was unable to meet for lack of a quorum because of the opening of a "newer and fashionable den of prostitution on Holladay Street." That is an oft-told story, and although it probably did not happen quite that way, the report may have carried a morsel of truth.[1]

Three years later, on April 6, 1883, the *News* told of a routine city council meeting during which a proposed new bridge over the South Platte River at Fifteenth Street was discussed at length and finally voted on, whereupon

> the clerk read a petition from one Mattie Silks requesting the change of a liquor license. He began, "A petition from Mattie Silks—." Alderman [George W.] Armstrong, who was busily engaged in fixing up some papers, raised his head when the name was read and exclaimed, "What?" Everybody laughed while the mayor pounded with his gavel and Alderman Armstrong bent to his work on the papers with an energy both surprising and praiseworthy. But he blushed.[2]

In harmony with the city council's apparent familiarity with the sisters of Holladay Street, the Denver

Police Department's procedure for dealing with the city's pimps, prostitutes, and gamblers was fairly well-established by this date: collect payoffs on behalf of city hall, skim off a bit for yourself, remain reasonably sober, and wink at much of what you see.

Denver's growth during this period was remarkable, from 4,759 in 1870 to 35,629 in 1880. As discussed earlier, Denver was the principal supply depot for the thriving mining enterprises in the mountains to the west, particularly Leadville. The great wave of fortune seekers severely challenged Denver's social services, including the police department, particularly since the department had twelve men when it was founded in 1874 and still had twelve when the boom began in 1879.

Later that year, however, police manpower was doubled to twenty-four, and by 1881 the number totaled thirty-nine. Citizens appeared satisfied with the protection provided by that many officers, and so long as the vice zone remained where it was supposed to be, the citizens were fairly happy, and the police appeared comfortable. A reporter wrote:

> There are really no hard beats in the city. The officers on the more vicious localities have occasionally a tough customer to handle, but the occasion will not average once a week. Denver is far ahead of the older cities of the country in its good behavior. . . . This has been explained from the fact that the reputation of the frontier cities of the West established some years ago acts as a preventive of rowdyism now.[3]

Although the levels of gambling and prostitution may have been temporarily under control—or at least tolerable—the principal ongoing problem was alcohol. Denver's streets were continually plagued with drunks, and if the inebriates had not been present the police would have had considerably more free time—although, as will be demonstrated, the police were frequently drunker than the citizenry and were considerably more dangerous when thus afflicted. One newspaper viewed the drunks with a philosophical eye, proclaiming them to be more an inconvenience than anything else:

> The fact is that Denver is for its size and its youth and rapid growing qualities, a remarkably good, or-

derly city, not only for a western municipality, but taking it in comparison with other cities in the country. The major portion of lawbreakers are taken at once to the jail. While the patrol wagon makes many trips through Denver streets every week, and while it clears the streets of objectionable persons, nine out of every ten of the offenders are arrested for merely being drunk; and of the Denver drunkards there is scarcely one out of every hundred arrested whose inebriety is a menace to anybody, and his arrest is generally as much a favor to himself as to the community at large.[4]

In 1885 Chief William A. "Billy" Smith tried to improve the image and respectability of his police department. Smith disliked the practice of smoking on duty, and he demanded a good appearance from his sometimes slovenly men. He ordered them to button their coats, wear belts, and not have cigars hanging from their mouths. The coat-buttoning order provoked the cops to complain that it interfered with access to their revolvers, but the *Rocky Mountain News* commented that the men did not use their guns anyway.[5]

In April 1885 Chief Smith—after lasting in office a respectable two years—stepped down, as Denver chiefs of police were wont to do. At a city hall ceremony, Alderman E. J. Brooks (who once ordered Smith to shut down the gambling joints) said Smith had been "kind and firm and always strictly impartial" and that because of his presence, 70,000 Denverites slept nightly "in sweet security." Smith was given a gold "presentation badge" depicting a ruby-eyed gold eagle holding in its talons a heart-shaped shield. Fancy gold, sterling, and gem-encrusted badges were often presented to Denver's police chiefs—whether they deserved them or not.[6]

On February 19, 1886, the police department felt it had matured when it acquired Denver's first real patrol wagon. It was difficult to determine whether the policemen or the populace were more excited. A team of horses pulled the glossy black new "prisoners' chariot" up to city hall, accompanied by a special guard of policemen with "drawn clubs," followed by yelping dogs and hundreds of youngsters "of all sizes and color." As the procession went past the fire station—which already had its own fancy red wagons—

the firemen saluted and rang the firehouse bell. The police wagon had red wheels, a gas headlight, and a gong to warn all ahead to get out of the way. It had first aid equipment and a booklet that told the driver and attendant how to deal with broken limbs, slit throats, fits, frostbite, shock, and chest wounds. It also had leg irons, chains, handcuffs, and other "gentle restrainers."

On March 1 the wagon was inaugurated into duty, along with thirty call boxes on various street corners, enabling patrolmen to summon the wagon and give hourly reports. At the same time, the department concentrated on upgrading its photo gallery of criminals. Chief Austin Hogle put Captain Wilson Swain and Detective Sam Howe in charge of that project.

In July the department installed what was known as a "patrol box jail," the first of several, at Nineteenth and Market Streets next to the bordello Row. It was a steel cage capable of holding three arrestees. The policeman tossed the prisoner inside, and when he closed the door the patrol wagon was automatically summoned over a series of telegraph wires. Atop the box was a green electric light that could be activated from headquarters. When the patrolman saw the light glowing, he was to call in.[7] Some years later, in 1898, Chief John Farley bought two carrier pigeons and pronounced that no longer would any of his policemen, especially those on the fringe of the city, have an excuse for not staying in touch.[8] The carrier pigeon experiment was not mentioned again.

The department still needed to make improvements regarding the treatment of female prisoners, who were lodged so near the men that the women were subject to constant harassment, ogling, and vile language. Finally, in October 1888 the mayor was empowered to hire the city's first police matron, Sarah "Sadie" Likens, at a salary of sixty-five dollars a month. She was in charge of all women and children in jail and gave them an advocate when behind bars in the filthy lockup.[9] In July 1894 Sadie Likens was removed from her job because her views clashed with those of the Fire and Police Board of Populist governor Davis H. Waite. She was reinstated after the administration left office and remained in the position until August 22, 1895, when she accepted a position as superintendent of the State Home and Industrial School for In-

corrigible Girls.[10] Likens established a worthy record of assistance to Denver's women and youngsters in a sometimes inhospitable environment. For more information on Sadie Likens, see Chapter 10.

A police matron, a shiny police wagon with red wheels, and a rogues' gallery of criminals' photographs, however, could not check a growing malaise afflicting Denver's police system. So pervasive was the police-politics interrelationship that in October 1883 Denver's policemen were issued the astonishing order by Chief William A. Smith that they were not to discuss political issues with anyone, especially while on duty. One policeman described the reaction to the chief's instruction:

> It was a paralyzer. You see there are several old ward politicians on the force, and they have been known to do some good work for the party. They are always talking politics and chip in their share for campaign purposes from pure loyalty. The order made them sick at first, and such men as Tim Ryan and Sam Dorsey and Sam Howe actually turned pale with rage.[11]

A year later, on November 21, 1884, Chief Smith shut down every gambling joint in town. Up and down the streets or in the newspapers, nobody seemed to understand initially what precipitated the raids, whether an order of the chief (unlikely), the mayor, the city council, the Arapahoe County sheriff, or the grand jury.

As it happened, the written order came from E. J. Brooks, mayor pro tem, citing the police department's failure to enforce city ordinances regarding gambling. Denver's old-time gamblers said that because of the "unsettled condition of affairs," which they did not explain, they knew something was about to happen. As had been the case with other quickie reforms made to placate the public and politicians, the gamblers were back in business within a month. One gambler, referring to the shutdown as a "spasm of virtue," told a *News* reporter that it was nice to have a short vacation and added:

> This fight is not [a matter of] good morals and decency as many would have you and others believe. It is a Republican move, rather. You see, the Republican party of Arapahoe [County] is divided into two factions. Each trying to get the better of the other, and we, the innocent parties, have to suffer for their foolishness.[12]

By 1886, Denver's on-again, off-again attention to the city's bordellos was off again. That year the annual report of Police Chief Hogle noted that of the 5,353 total arrests, 17 madams and 117 of their girls were hauled in during the entire twelve months. The figure becomes even less impressive when it is recalled that Denver was in the midst of a boom in the mid-1880s, and the Market Street Row had never been more active. And despite Chief Hogle's token arrests, business remained active.[13]

Kitty Robbins may have been Denver's first "outcall" girl of record. One of her initial adventures led to the death of, according to the newspapers, "one of the leading colored men of the city." The victim was A. E. Nickens, a barber at Seventeenth and Holladay Streets who was "quite intelligent." Nickens became infatuated with Miss Kitty, who was white. After learning that Kitty was "partial to colored men," he wrote her a note inviting her to the barbershop he shared with Charles Green. Miss Kitty responded with a note:

My Dear Friend:—I received your note this evening and it is impossible for me to meet you this evening, as Miss —— would like for me to stay at home this evening, as it being New Year's evening. I would rather meet you some other place, but if you cannot arrange, I will meet you there. I would like to see you to-morrow afternoon. Kitty.

Sarah Jane Morehouse Washburn Likens, as Denver's initial police matron, was the city's first jailhouse champion of women's and children's rights. Before "Sadie" Likens joined the jail staff in October 1888, incarcerated women were under the supervision of male jailers. Six years later, however, Likens became mired in the political bog that had long encumbered the Denver Police Department, and she left to superintend the state girls' reformatory. She was a longtime friend of Detective Howe's, and he preserved this photograph of her in his twelfth scrapbook along with a clipping bearing the date of Christmas 1890. An old commemorative monument dedicated to Sadie Likens remains today at the southeast corner of Colfax and Broadway, near Colorado's capitol building.

Kitty Robbins indeed met Nickens—and his partner Green—in their barbershop, but it would be Nickens's last encounter with Kitty or anybody else. After a night of drinking by the trio, Green slit Nickens's throat and left him lying in the barbershop. Green was arrested; Kitty briefly went back to work and forthwith left town. Green was acquitted after testimony that Nickens came at him with a hatchet in a jealous rage over the attentions of Kitty Robbins of Holladay Street.[14]

The police department's 1890 accomplishments in controlling vice were no more impressive than the arrest figures of four years earlier, when police took in eighty-seven prostitutes for soliciting, arrested seventy-six gamblers, and made sixty-seven arrests for "violating the red light ordinance," a terminology not seen before but that meant either maintaining or patronizing a brothel.[15] As the 1880s turned into the 1890s, the police department's structure and cohesiveness eroded, as did the Denver city government in general. Glaring frauds were becoming known; saloon fees and other licensing proceeds did not find their way to the city treasury. Even the dog licensing money was missing, and duplicate dog tags were issued to cover the thefts. It was charged that city officers engaged in sideline businesses for the sole purpose of furnishing goods and services to the city at exorbitant prices and that the entire corrupt administration of Mayor Wolfe Londoner

ONE OF THE FINEST!

The New Woman Policeman "Pinches" a Brutal Husband.
—*Denver Republican*

(1889–1891) "had been organized for the purpose of robbery, which the mayor was powerless to prevent."[16]

But even a decade before the Londoner city hall, the Denver police were being suspected of inefficiency, lax leadership, and outright dishonesty. Under the two-year regime (1878–1880) of Chief William R. Hickey, the press reported, a mere fifty dollars would buy an appointment as a policeman. Hickey's officers, moreover, were told to be diplomatically selective as to whom they arrested so that they did not accost any friend of city hall. Local arrestees were to be afforded more courtesies than visitors or itinerants. An official order said:

> Patrolmen will be careful and judicious in making arrests of business men whom they may find on the streets in an intoxicated condition or creating a disturbance by fights or noisy quarrels. It will be the duty of the officer on the beat to quiet the disturbance and notify the offender to appear in police court the next morning, rather than to excite attention and create a scandal by making an arrest and summoning the patrol wagon.[17]

The *Rocky Mountain News* on October 19, 1880, published an interview with an unnamed "man who has held high positions in eastern cities in connection with police and detective work." He said of the Denver police system:

> It is the worst, most loose and corrupt that ever came under my observation. I am conversant with the police system of all the large cities of the Union, but I have never met with anything so careless and reckless as the police system of Denver. To begin with, it is supposed that the police, or a certain portion of them, are on duty all night. I know a case where a certain officer has gone to bed every night at a certain hotel, instead of remaining on his beat. They are either in their own or somebody else's bed. Denver

would be the very paradise of thieves if they only knew it.

One policeman, whose last name was Merrill, told the *News* (also reported in the October 19 edition) that neither Chief Hickey, Mayor Richard Sopris, nor the town aldermen ran Denver but rather "the sporting fraternity has the most to say about what should be done. Bill Hickey belonged to the prostitutes and gamblers and he had to do about what they wanted him to." The interviewee, however, said the corruption went beyond Chief Hickey, right to the doorstep of Mayor Sopris: "He gets twenty per cent of the bunko and gambling profits. I was told so by a bunko steerer himself." Hickey, who had just been removed from office, responded:

> I have been between two fires all the time; have asked the old man [Mayor Sopris] over and over again if I should close up the dens around town and he wouldn't give me permission, therefore I couldn't do it, and the next thing I was blamed for not doing it. There was eight or ten men on the force I wanted to discharge long ago for being corrupt. I knew they were getting money from bunko-men and acting crooked all through, but he wouldn't let me discharge them, each one of them was the pet of some particular alderman and had to be protected.

The *News* editorialized:

> As long as the police force is under the control of the council, it will be like its controlling power, corrupt. When one makes a haul the others have to wink at it or be exposed themselves. They are like a lot of school boys. One says if you tell on me I'll tell on you, and so to preserve peace in the family and plenty in the pocket they are blind to each other's offenses. The only struggle they have is to see who can make the most.[18]

The year 1887 was particularly noteworthy with regard to wrongdoing by Denver's police. By this date, historian Anne Curtis Knapp wrote, the department was in such a mire of corruption and brutality that officers and supervisors seemingly spent the majority of their time systematically deriving revenue from notorious houses, stealing money from arrestees, organizing votes for the Republican machine, collabo-

rating with pawnbrokers who were involved in receiving stolen property, and accepting bribes from gamblers and tavern keepers in exchange for protection and favors. Knapp wrote that the underpaid, often bellicose patrolmen and detectives frequently refused to work unless they received extra pay, beyond salaries, for their services.[19]

The practice of giving Denver policemen private rewards for performance of public duties wreaked immeasurable damage on the police department. The first mention of the "fee-and-reward" system in Denver law enforcement was made as early as 1862, when the town council authorized such fees to supplement a monthly salary of $48.[20] Within weeks the city decided to save a "snug little sum" by suspending salaries and paying only fees and allowing for rewards. The officers refused to work under such conditions, whereupon the city agreed to pay $30 a month.[21]

The fee-and-reward system continued, and by the 1880s, fees could supplement a policeman's salary of $100 a month (the chief made $250) by $40 a month. But this system also led to selective enforcement of the law: the policeman was far more inclined to chase a well-known criminal whose apprehension would pay an extra $50 than to spend his time on an arrest that would go unrewarded. Not only did businesses and private detective agencies pay such rewards, but so did the city. In 1880 a policeman was paid $2.50 in city funds for each arrest. For that sum he was expected to take the prisoner to jail, for which he received no extra pay. If, however, the policeman could find a constable, who was a court employee, the policeman would turn the prisoner over to the constable, who would collect $5 to take the prisoner to jail and split it with the policeman. Sometimes late at night, the policeman and prisoner would go to a constable's home (or the courthouse) and wake the constable, who would book the prisoner into jail. The practice cost the city government thousands of dollars a year.[22]

Earlier, in 1874, just before the Denver Police Department was formed out of the marshal's force, the city marshal was collecting a salary of $1,200 a year plus $200 a month in fees from the city. He could earn an additional $6,000 yearly as a constable in county matters.[23]

One Denver officer, Knapp wrote, asked for reimbursement of expenses incurred in capturing a thief and returning stolen property, and when the merchant responded that that was what a policeman was supposed to do, the merchant was sent a formal billing. This prompted a Denver newspaper to remark that Denver's "detectives seldom detected anything unless a reward were offered."[24] For additional discussion of Denver's fee-and-reward system, see Chapter 2.

An exasperated *Rocky Mountain News* commented on August 21, 1880: "The rapid increase of crime in this city must be very encouraging to our grand army of detectives. Has it come to this, that our noble detectives can not find an atrocious murderer until a reward is offered?" The paper was probably referring to the slaying of merchant M. Marburger two days earlier in a Holladay Street brothel. The suspect, Harry Travilla, stole money from his girlfriend, madam Carrie Smith, and fled to Cheyenne.

The Fire and Police Board in 1897 directed that no policeman could accept a reward without the board's approval and that any rewards thus accepted must be placed in a fund to be used for expenses incurred in extraditing prisoners back to Denver.[25]

Pickpocketing was another means through which a Denver policeman could augment his salary. Patrolman John Bell and pawnbroker H. Solomon were inspecting Capitol Hill real estate when Bell removed what was described as an 18-carat, $150 stickpin from Solomon's shirt bosom. When the loss was discovered, Solomon offered fifty dollars to Detectives Howe and John Connor for the return of the pin. Patrolman M. M. Burnett also knew of the loss, and five months later he was approached by Officer Bell, who admitted it was he who had relieved Solomon of the diamond pin as a joke. Burnett, the *Rocky Mountain News* reported, "told Mr. Bell that he must be a slick one to take a pin from as slick a man as Mr. Solomon, and Mr. Bell replied that he was a slick one." Bell further added that he had sold the pin for seventy-five dollars.

Burnett eventually told Lieutenant Samuel T. Inman of the incident. Inman reported the matter to Police Chief Henry T. Brady who told Mayor William Scott Lee, who demanded and received Bell's resignation on the spot. The mayor then fired Burnett for knowing about the theft and not immediately reporting it.[26]

An additional example of police thievery in late-nineteenth-century Denver, one that had important repercussions, occurred a year following the Solomon incident. On this occasion, city jailer Charles Delmege alleged that Sergeant David J. Ellsworth, when booking prisoners into jail, would remove "money, often in considerable amounts," from their clothing, conceal it in the palm of his hand, and slip it into his pocket. The jailer said he had suspected as much for some time but finally witnessed such an incident. He reported it to Lieutenant Inman who told Chief Brady, but nothing was done. When the matter was drawn to the attention of the press, the Fire and Police Board conducted a hearing and took testimony, whereupon Sergeant Ellsworth resigned.

Under the leadership of Chief Brady, the Denver Police Department endured its worst years. For instance, two of Brady's top officers, Detective Charles Connor and Lieutenant James Connor, cousins, in collusion with a James Marshall—a close friend of Chief Brady's—planned a train robbery along the route of the Denver & Rio Grande Railroad. That remarkable episode is related in Chapter 7.[27]

The matter of Sergeant Ellsworth slipping prisoners' funds into his pocket was important because it cast an even broader shadow across Brady's corrupt police administration. In commenting on the Ellsworth situation, the *Rocky Mountain News* said:

> When Chief Brady reads this [account of the Ellsworth case] over his coffee this morning, he will doubtless realize that his official career is at an end, and that in his capacity as chief of police he will no longer be able to bulldoze registration boarders [prostitutes who were registered to vote in several different precincts], threaten gamblers, or assess courtesans for the benefit of the Republican campaign fund.[28]

Henry T. Brady was inarguably the most unethical chief in the history of the Denver Police Department, before or since. Brady joined the department as a patrolman in 1881, became city jailer, and in early 1886 was appointed lieutenant. The following April

HENRY BRADY, Chief.

It is difficult to imagine a worse police chief than Denver's Henry C. Brady, before or since. His two-year term beginning in 1887 was marked by unprecedented laxity, corruption, and turmoil. Only the subsequent tenure of the brutal chief Michael "Third Degree" Delaney approached the decay of Brady's time in office. Delaney was so unmanageable and explosive that even the corrupt mayor, Robert W. "Boss" Speer, could not tolerate it and kicked him out.

he was made chief. Conditions within the department immediately plummeted. Great laxity developed in the ranks; many semihonest policemen departed and were replaced by political appointees. During this time an

inquisitive reporter set out to search lower downtown for a policeman. He looked for two hours before finally locating one in a bar in the center of the Holladay Street bordello district.

Brady was indicted by a grand jury during the spring of 1889 on charges of accepting a bribe and "levying contributions from the gambling houses and houses of ill fame." He was said to have accepted a $300 payment from a Chinese man named Chin Poo in return for guaranteeing Chinese gamblers immunity from prosecution. During the trial, however, Chin Poo—supposedly after being talked to by Brady's attorneys—testified that the money had been a contribution to the Republican Party coffers. On the basis of that testimony, Brady was acquitted and resigned, declaring:

> I have had enough of the business. It is a very difficult, thankless position to fill, and one that brings you nothing but worry and trouble. Unless you please everybody, which is an impossibility, you are sure to be censured and talked about. I am mighty glad to be out of the position and never want to hold such a one again.

Chief Brady was not acquitted by history, however. Eugene Frank Rider, whose Ph.D. dissertation is the definitive history of the Denver Police Department, terms the Brady regime an "interlude of decay," and the book *Denver Police Department Pictorial Review and History* (1985), the official history of the department, talks about Brady under the headline "Decay and Corruption" and asserts that "it can truthfully be said that there were no significant accomplishments" under Brady.[29] Indeed, Sam Howe recorded an observation from the *Cincinnati Enquirer* in 1889 that Denver police corruption was so permeating that it was difficult to get arrested.[30]

Denver did not rid itself of Henry Brady. In 1896 he was on the payroll as city license inspector, at the same time diligently serving in the political campaign of Colorado U.S. Senator Edward Oliver Wolcott. Historian William L. Hewett, in his article "The Election of 1896: Two Factions Square Off," later observed that Brady was working "so hard for Wolcott that he did not even have time to attend to his official duties."[31]

Denver's policemen had such a reputation for drunkenness on the job that the Denver Republican *poked fun at the situation. Despite the officers' attempts to stifle their whiskey breath with cloves, Police Chief Ham Armstrong vows here to add a breath test to the daily inspection.*

ENFORCING THAT POLICE DEPARTMENT TEMPERANCE EDICT.

Chief Armstrong will add breath inspection to the daily routine of police headquarters.

The Denver police in 1889, the year Henry Brady departed as chief, made another token raid on the brothel district—a regularly predictable occurrence designed either to offer the illusion that morality reigned or to enhance the city treasury. The prostitutes again were told they could not solicit openly or "hail persons with vile and indecent remarks," and the police wagon made five trips to Twentieth and Market Streets, transporting "lewd women" to jail. The first load consisted of French women and the fifth of Negro women.[32] The "decent" ladies of Denver were so pleased at this show of morality that they presented the police department with a silk flag decorated with the image of an eagle and yellow stars, emblazoned "Denver Police Department." The "loyal matrons" said it was for the policemen to carry whenever they led a parade.[33]

Despite such occasional public showiness, however, corruption, disorganization, and poor leadership persisted within the Denver Police Department. For these and additional political reasons, in 1889 the state seized control of the Denver Police and Fire Departments, and that was still the status of these city agencies in 1892 when Aspen newspaper publisher Davis H. Waite, a radical reformer and Populist, was elected governor and pledged to do something about vice, crime, and crooked cops. Sam Howe, no supporter of the Populists, resigned from his two-year position as

detective chief on June 1, 1893, although he remained on the detective force. In a cleanout of non-Populists, Howe and five others, all Republicans, were dismissed from the force in August 1893. He was reinstated the following April.

On April 20, 1894, the *Denver Republican* was able to announce that the new Populist Fire and Police Board had ordered that every gambling house in town be shut down by the following Monday. "Such an order," the *Republican* explained, "did not occasion surprise. The new board was pledged to this policy. The order removing the old board signified that it was because it permitted or encouraged gambling that such action was taken." The order elaborated that "the old fire and police board recognized gambling and gambling houses, and kept special policemen to superintend, watch over and protect gambling houses and gambling places."

Police Chief Hamilton Armstrong, respected for his long terms of service despite his reputation as a city hall lackey, assured the populace that the closure rule would be adhered to by the larger and leading gambling houses and that "those who refuse to obey will be promptly dealt with." Policemen or detectives not enforcing the new guidelines, the *Republican* said optimistically, also would be dealt with, and the police judge had agreed in advance to prescribe severe fines. Included along with the gambling parlors in this latest crackdown—and perhaps the target of it—were "the confidence men and swell vagrants that infest Seventeenth street and the lower portion of Larimer street. It is the intention to force them out of town."[34]

But the new Fire and Police Board saved its biggest announcement until the day after the confidence-man crackdown. The board, over the signature of Fire Commissioner Dennis Mullins, announced that the police department was so undisciplined that policemen on duty were drinking free liquor and smoking free cigars in saloons; were neglecting to arrest prostitutes and "low women" soliciting on the streets, from windows, and from the front steps of Market Street; were winking at cases of indecent exposure; were allowing saloons to run all day and night every day and night, even Sundays; were "frequenting houses of prostitution and dens of low resort, and participating in the advantages carried on in the same"; and were "receiving blackmail and hush money from the unfortunate victims of prostitution and from saloons and dives to allow them to continue their unlawful and demoralizing trade." In other words, the Denver Police Department was doing what it had been doing for years.

The new board concluded that as a result of this chicanery, the department was in "a very demoralized condition" and was a "shame and a disgrace and an outrage not to be tolerated under any circumstances." Thus the board ordered the police to stop doing these bad things, and it specifically prohibited policemen from visiting brothels "under any pretext, except to make arrests and detect crime, under penalty of instant discharge for a single offense, and from having conversation with lewd women or girls of the streets while on duty, or soliciting blackmail or hush money." Patrolmen were further ordered to "discontinue unnecessary conversation with citizens while on duty, and must give their attention to the details of their beats." Saloon closing hours must be enforced, the board said, adding somewhat lamely at the end of its long pronouncement that "the board has no intention of modifying the order against gambling." That was of no great consequence, because the order against gambling said merely that gambling halls must close on Mondays. It was fairly obvious where the Fire and Police Board's interests lay.

Finally, the board abolished the office of chief of detectives, asked for and immediately received the resignation of detective chief H. M. Behymer (who had been in office for five weeks), placed the detectives under direct command of Chief Armstrong, and named Sam Howe, "who was in the detective department for many years, and who has been a most efficient servant, to look after the routine of the [detective] office under the direction of the chief." Armstrong, who had political alliances with Governor Waite's Populists, emerged unscathed and was not even mentioned in the board's stay-away-from-the-prostitutes-and-keep-out-of-the-bars regulations. Neither was Police Commissioner A. J. Rogers. Additionally, firemen were prohibited from visiting saloons while on duty.[35]

Conditions were deteriorating a month later, and in fact, Denver was becoming increasingly noted for its con men and bunco artists. L. B. Casebier, a visiting schoolteacher from Kansas, and two other tourists, Solomon Corell and James Mills, complained to Armstrong of being befriended and then robbed in a Denver vice and gambling den. Casebier, who was knocked unconscious during the assault, alleged that Jefferson Randolph "Soapy" Smith, Denver's famous confidence man, was in on the caper, and Soapy was arrested under the catchall charge "disturbance." Casebier indignantly announced, "I shall never speak to another stranger while I am in this city unless

Although they were always ill trained, too often drunk on duty, unashamedly careless with human rights, and forever unsupervised, Denver's policemen of the period 1873–1915 sometimes had well-founded complaints. This Denver Republican *cartoon of August 17, 1912, for instance, lampoons a directive prohibiting the carrying of nightsticks—but not of handguns. "A cop shot me," a citizen complains to the police commissioner in a caption that accompanied the cartoon. "Never mind, I'll take his club away," responds the commissioner, to which the citizen responds: "He didn't shoot me with a club." On another occasion the city ordered that policemen wear their revolvers* beneath *their long woolen overcoats, making the weapons virtually impossible to reach quickly.*

WHEN THE GRAND "DISARMAMENT" TAKES PLACE.

he is properly introduced to me." Armstrong, as a result of this flurry of fleecing tourists, boisterously announced "a general war on suspected poker clubs," which was a hollow threat and the gamblers knew it.[36]

Following the failed Populist antivice and good police crusade, conditions in Denver did not change perceptibly. Policemen continued along pretty much as they had for years, drinking and reveling on duty and chumming with the gamblers and women of the *demimonde.* In this regard, Denver seemed to be conforming to a nationwide trend. Throughout the country during the 1880s and 1890s, vice was booming as the urgent demands of lust and money proved irresistible. Laws were on the books, but they were largely unenforced in Denver and elsewhere.[37]

Nonetheless, in April 1894 Denver's police again announced a crackdown on saloons and gambling houses and the corruption that protected them. These dens of badness, city hall said, would now would be required to close at midnight and, in just a few days, to close forever. "This," the newspapers reported, "is the first time that such orders have been given in a long time."[38] The headlines shouted: "Gamblers Count Their Last Hours of Existence," "Infamous Charac-

ters, Male and Female, Will Be Compelled to Respect the Law—Extortion and Blackmail Formerly Practiced by Patrolmen and Higher Officers Will Not Be Countenanced," and, sternly, "Gambling Houses Ordered to Close at Noon Monday."[39]

Despite the hopes of Governor Waite, however, vice had not disappeared from the city during his Populist regime, and the Denver Police Department had high personnel turnovers, including six chiefs in the year beginning March 1893. As was customary, Denver police chiefs, with the exception of Dave Cook and Hamilton Armstrong, historically had been civilians with friends at city hall and no law enforcement knowledge. In July 1893 mining engineer Aaron W. Kellogg became chief, succeeding businessman James Veatch. Kellogg was followed by furniture dealer/police lieutenant John F. Stone, and then came meat dealer D. C. Oswald, undertaker H. M. Behymer (who served one day), and then Armstrong. Armstrong—who always said what he thought—reflected later: "After a little more than nine months' experience as chief of police, I am clearly of the opinion that the police force will never reach a high plain of usefulness until proficiency in politics is eliminated from the list of accomplishments an applicant for appointment must possess."[40]

By March 1894 law enforcement in Denver was in chaos and deteriorated further when policemen, firemen, and underworld characters defended two members of the Fire and Police Board who barricaded themselves in city hall at Fourteenth and Larimer Streets, resulting in what was called the City Hall War. Governor Waite wanted to clean out police and other city officials who shielded prostitutes and gamblers, and the governor ordered a militia march on city hall. The matter was solved when federal intervention prevented gunfire and the Colorado Supreme Court ruled that Waite was empowered to remove the police and fire commissioners.[41] Sam Howe, uncharacteristically, omitted accounts of the City Hall War from his scrapbooks, although on other occasions he did not hesitate to include articles unflattering to the police department.

As historian Eugene Frank Rider reported in his dissertation (p. 421), in late 1894 the Populists were turned out after one chaotic term, Waite was sent back to Aspen, and even more shakeups occurred within the heavily political police department. George Goulding became police chief, and among his initial requirements was "a perfect crease in every officer's blue trousers." Goulding further described the ideal Denver policeman: "In my judgment, a policeman should be brave, alert, honest, gentlemanly, and as good-looking as you can get them. It is just as easy to have a well drilled and soldierly-appearing force as one that is not." Goulding named William R. Farrington, who had been a volunteer fireman, detective chief. Rider wrote that Farrington's detective squad consisted of the following:

- Sam Howe, "oldest, and by general consent the best-informed detective in the West"
- Dave Cook, a "terror to the crooks"
- H. E. Burlew, who "knew by sight every man who had been in the penitentiary"
- John J. Leyden, "dogged, keen, and seldom without equal when a difficult case had to be tracked"
- Al Moore, "a born detective"

- John S. Gardner, with a "cold keen eye that read a man through and through"
- John Connor, the "ideal policeman"
- William Reno, who had been a detective before "the Populists displaced detectives with farmers"
- H. C. Chambers, qualifications not listed

Chief Goulding also, according to the press, "notified the inmates on Market Street [that] if they wanted to stay out of jail, no soliciting was to be permitted on the streets; the prostitutes were to refrain from going outdoors in their 'house costumes' and all window curtains of bordellos were to be kept shut." Those edicts had been tried before.[42]

Gambling became the object of yet another police crusade. Policemen, "on advice of the district attorney's office," during a spring evening in 1894, raided dozens of "saloons, club rooms, and cigar stores," seizing a number of "nickel-in-the-slot" machines. The move puzzled some citizens who took the inoffensive one-armed bandits for granted. The *Denver Republican* also was somewhat bewildered and wrote:

> It is not known who is at the bottom of the move. It is rumored in semi-official circles that the departure [of the machines] is but the initial movement in a general round-up of all the gambling houses in the city, and that yesterday's raid will be followed by an onslaught on every room where faro, roulette, or craps is in the game.[43]

The police were embarrassed to the extreme four days later upon discovering that all 120 machines had been jimmied open while in the detective department and the money removed. Detective Chief Leonard DeLue confessed to being "deeply puzzled" over this development, and the machines—broken locks and all—were returned to the gambling halls and cigar stores.[44] There were no more raids for a while.

Because Denver had most other classifications of crime and vice, it was no surprise when phony cash showed up, too. Generally, only paper money was vulnerable to counterfeiting, but during the winter of 1896–1897 an unusual pair of criminals tried something difficult. Sam Howe recorded it as one of Denver's odder crimes. On January 10, 1897, Agent Joseph A. Walker of the U.S. Secret Service apprehended a gang of two in the act of manufacturing pennies out of lead and solder and then depositing their booty in the town's slot machines, where sometimes they won and sometimes they lost. The culprits were school-boys in the suburb of Highland, and they learned how to make their plaster-of-paris penny molds from a newspaper article and several helpful chums. The matter came before U.S. District Judge Moses ("Moses the Meek") Hallett who, according to the press, "decided that the boys could properly be sent to the reform school at Golden," but because they had not known they were breaking the law (or so they asserted), the judge ruled that "the vigorous use of the switch by the parents" was all the correction needed. Secret Service Agent Walker, meantime, was searching for another gang of boys doing the same thing with nickels.[45]

Of more serious potential consequence was the 1896 federal grand jury indictment of William J. Van Horn, son of Denver mayor Marion D. Van Horn (1893–1895), for passing a counterfeit fifty-dollar bill taken from a collection of phony bills the senior Van Horn had amassed as a Secret Service agent. William Van Horn submitted the fake bill in exchange for gambling chips. He was acquitted on a technicality because his indictment was obtained under a wrong section of the applicable statute.[46] The *Rocky Mountain News* and the *Denver Republican* harped constantly that lawlessness and corruption were out of control, but the rival *Denver Times* proclaimed in August 1895 that Denver was relatively free from open vice—cleaner, that is, the *Times* said, than when the Populists were in office. The *Times* sent secretary William G. Latze of the Denver YMCA and a committee of his YMCA colleagues on a one-night fact-finding investigation of the gambling and prostitution neighborhoods to determine whether the *News* and *Republican* accounts were valid. Latze made the following report, which includes some qualifications:

> They are lies, all lies. I never saw the city of Denver as clean as it is under the present police administration. Compared to what it was a year ago, or compared to any other city I have ever visited, Denver is morally a paradise. The first place visited was Curtis street, once the gathering place of gamblers of all degrees of life. We found the gambling devices in the different rooms covered with accumulated dust. On Larimer street we found the same condition of affairs. Not a gambling game of any kind was found running.
>
> On Market and other down-town streets where vice is said to be rampant, we found things to be most orderly and quiet, *considering the nature of the traffic that is carried on there* [emphasis added]. Not a single woman was found in the saloons of the district. Unfortunately, there were a good many men hanging about, but there were no women.
>
> We walked from one end of Market street to the other and saw one lewd woman on the street outside of the houses. That was in the French colony. The blinds were all down, the curtains drawn and the doors closed tight. There was little noise or boisterousness from within. We visited two of the houses and found eighteen women within. Of these only one could possibly have been under 23 years of age. We made diligent inquiry to ascertain whether there were any girls underage on the street, but we were unable to find any.[47]

Only a skeptic would suggest that the gamblers and bordello queens had been tipped off that the YMCA was on the way. Nonetheless, the *Times* blamed the hullabaloo on the "malicious and utterly baseless attacks" by the other two newspapers.

Economic conditions faltered in Colorado through the mid-1890s, following the 1893 collapse of the silver market. One result of the business recession was that any efforts to shut down gambling and prostitution were opposed vigorously by business leaders, who argued that such actions would be "a detriment to the business interests of the city of Denver" and added that if these entertainment enterprises were closed, "many buildings and parts of buildings would be rendered tenantless and bring in no rent to the owners thereof." In addition, "A large amount of money would be kept from coming into the city of Denver and being put into circulation."[48]

In this sort of civic climate the reader must empathize with City Alderman John D. "Mac" McGilvray. He represented what the press termed the "gallant Seventh" Ward across Cherry Creek from Denver City Hall, the old Auraria neighborhood. McGilvray, a stone contractor by trade and a blustery sort given to stentorian tones, was not a friend of the police department. Eight years earlier, in 1880, McGilvray, "in his rugged and forcible manner" (as the *Rocky Mountain News* termed it), referred to the police department as "a set of bushwhackers" and added that the department had three chiefs, and the men did not know from whom to take orders. Alderman C. H. McLaughlin seconded McGilvray's thoughts, referring to Police Chief Bill Hickey as unfit for the job and guilty of dereliction of duty, incompetence, and inefficiency.

Sensitivities were particularly heightened because the city had just endured the anti-Chinese riot, and the Chinese were leaning on the city to help with reparations for their damaged property. The city responded that the riot was not its fault and declined to pay. Nonetheless, Chief Hickey was soon out, and Dave Cook would soon be in.[49]

During the riot a mob raided Chinese laundries, looted Chinese homes, injured some Chinese, and killed one. In a remarkable case of the downtrodden aiding the downtrodden, however, the Chinese found support among the ladies of Denver's *demimonde.* In his study of the riot, historian Roy T. Wortman wrote:

> At Seventeenth and Holladay Streets, Liz Preston, a madam of a local brothel, was protecting four cowering Chinese with a shotgun. According to fireman William Roberts, a force of "ten Amazonian beauties" armed with champagne bottles, stove pokers, and high-heeled shoes, backed up Miss Preston. The crowd finally retreated when Roberts—who was by this time in the riot [and was] made a deputy sheriff—and his men arrived. The four Chinese were placed for protection in the side parlor of Miss Preston's brothel. By the end of the riot the madam and her colleagues had sheltered thirty-four Chinese. Recalling the role of the prostitutes in the riot, Roberts said: "That day the pariahs, the outcasts of society, the denizens of Holladay Street, the center of the red light district, put themselves in the hall of fame. And perhaps the recording angel gave them one white mark."[50]

Eight years later the feisty antipolice Alderman McGilvray decided to rid Denver of gambling. This did not make him popular among the business community, and neither did it endear him to the police department, whose members enjoyed certain financial benefits from the gambling enterprise.

On the evening of November 21, 1888, a righteous and indignant McGilvray confronted the operator of the Arcade gambling parlor, and as a city officer he demanded that the place shut its doors forthwith. McGilvray met with decided opposition, the proprietor openly refusing to recognize his authority.

The thwarted alderman summoned from a nearby street corner policeman John Connor (the same John Connor Chief Goulding referred to as "the ideal policeman") and said to Connor: "John, there's gambling going on on your beat. I wish you would seize the gambling articles in the Arcade." Officer Connor refused, whereupon an "angry quarrel ensued," concluding with Connor arresting the alderman. "This was the unkindest cut of all," the *Denver Times* observed, "and bitterly did the gentleman from across the placid waters of Cherry Creek resent it." McGilvray was spared the humiliation of being tossed in jail (after all, he was a member of the city council's police committee, fire committee, and judiciary committee), and instead he was released on his good name pending trial the next morning.

Fully 250 people jammed into the courtroom of Police Judge Charles M. Campbell. The defendant, the press noted, was "clean shaven and wore an air of bravado, one of his most distinguishing characteristics." He acted as his own attorney.

The first person to testify was Police Officer Connor. "The sight of his captor," the *Times* reported, "enraged Mr. McGilvray very perceptibly; he changed color and acted quite like a man struggling to suppress great mental excitement." Connor testified that after refusing to close down the Arcade at McGilvray's insistence, he told McGilvray to move along, and when McGilvray refused, Officer Connor shoved him down the street. McGilvray shoved Connor back, and the officer fell into the gutter, which was highly embarrassing since a crowd was gathering. Connor grabbed McGilvray by the collar, but getting him to the patrol call box was another matter, with the crowd jeering and hooting and McGilvray ranting and raving "during which he damned the entire city administration in a most emphatic manner," according to the *Times.*

At this point, the officer testified, he drew his gun, "as much for the purpose of protecting his celebrated prisoner as anything else." Four witnesses then testified in support of Officer Connor, particularly with regard to Alderman McGilvray's defiant demeanor. The witnesses particularly described the scene at the police call box during which the alderman let forth with "a string of profanity not quite in accordance with one who seeks fame as a reformer of the city's morals."

One witness testified that Connor threatened onlookers with the drawn gun and called the city alderman a "___ ____ cur." McGilvray took the stand and, as the newspaper reported, was "extremely indignant, but managed to suppress his rage fairly well." He said he had informed Mayor William Scott Lee of his views on gambling and, armed with his authority, had started out the day with the intent of doing something about it. First, he visited the gambling rooms of Clifton Bell, next the Missouri House, and finally the Arcade.

After demanding that Officer Connor close the place, McGilvray testified, the policeman responded, "___ ___ you, I don't recognize your authority. I'm working for Mayor Lee and Chief Brady." At the hearing, McGilvray produced a copy of the city charter and read the antigambling ordinances at length while the courtroom audience, composed mainly of gamblers, laughed heartily. After due consideration the judge found the councilman innocent of resisting an officer and of causing a disturbance. The judge ruled that Connor and McGilvray were both city officials, and each thought he was doing his duty. The legality of gambling was not addressed. The matter was closed.[51]

Patrolman Connor, like many Denver policemen before (and after) him, also became involved at least once in election improprieties. A one-paragraph newspaper clipping encountered in this study, from an unknown newspaper but probably from November 1899, stated that Connor, along with Officers Coleman Bell, Leonard De Lue, and Ed Carberry, was arrested by court officers. The arrests were made on the "complaint of Billy Arnett and Tom Clark [who themselves] were again arrested yesterday for intimidation at the polls."

Denver's gambling parlors throughout the second half of the nineteenth century were viewed with considerable tolerance. Said Police Chief Hamilton Armstrong, "Gambling is starting up again, but it seems to be what the people want. Their votes show that."[52]

The resurgence of gambling during the 1890s would not have earned the vote of Charles E. Baker, a stenographer in the Denver city clerk's office. He wrote a series of bad checks, and when finally arrested he broke down and confessed, according to the *Colorado Sun* on July 9, 1892, "that he was led into gambling and a fast life by people pretending to be friends. He wanted more money and they easily enticed him into wrong-doing. He gave as an apology the old story of wine, women and cards."

A sadder testimony of the ruinous aspects of open gambling in Denver was the case of Douglas Mitchell, age forty-seven, a civil engineer from Grand Junction who came to Denver in late April 1907 to visit his wife, a patient at St. Joseph Hospital. Mitchell fell in with a group of old-time friends who led him, according to a news report, "to make his home in gambling houses and saloons." On May 30 he was arrested on a street corner for writing bad checks, and at police headquarters he confessed:

> I have been drunk here in Denver more than a month and as I am returning to my senses it is with the shocking realization that I have gone through more than $1,500 during the terrible four or five weeks that have just passed. I was not conscious of what I was doing. What will my poor invalid wife think when she hears of my predicament![53]

As Christmas approached eight months after the unfortunate Mitchell presumably returned to Grand Junction, George Yawitz of 2349 California Street in Denver, who ran the coat-check stand at the Brown Palace Hotel, had lost everything including his wife's family jewelry to the gambling tables of Big Ed Chase, Vaso Chucovich, and Ed Gaylord. Yawitz borrowed a dime for a vial of carbolic acid, swallowed it, fell writhing, and died. "My husband was the best of husbands until he took to gambling," the prostrated widow, Fanny Yawitz, said the next day. "The gambling den keepers are his murderers. His blood is upon their heads." Ed Chase responded, "I will contribute liberally to a fund for the support of his family." Chucovich asserted that Yawitz was not known in any of the city's gambling parlors but that horse racing was actually the problem. Mayor Robert "Boss" Speer was called on to close the gambling parlors once and for all, but since the gamblers were principal contributors to his political activities, he could not do so.[54]

The gambling parlor, dance hall, saloon, and brothel, wrote sociologists Schlissel, Ruiz, and Monk, were viewed by men

> as necessary adjuncts to [the community.] If [males] supported moral reform, they did so cautiously and hesitantly and justified such reforms in economic terms. To these men, prostitution was not the target. [The target] was the wide-open bawdy house that gave the town a bad name to visitors and future settlers; gambling per se was not evil, only gamblers who cheated naive outsiders of their money, thereby discrediting the town and hurting future economic growth. Thus it was women who dominated the ranks of those opposed to drink, gambling, and prostitution. Local authorities considered prostitution a necessary social service. The arrival of families, however, challenged this vision of prostitution. With the advent of more even sex ratios, a sharp increase in the number of children, and the rise of respectable, middle-class occupations, women (and some men) called for the strict regulation or abolition of brothels. After all, prostitution was an affront to women's moral sensibilities and to Victorian ideas about sexual exclusivity, emotional intimacy, the sanctity of motherhood, and the importance of domestic life. To virtuous women, prostitution degraded men and women and threatened the sexual integrity of husbands and sons.[55]

In return for its financial contributions and help at the polls, the vice industry continued to receive concessions from Denver's city hall and courts. Police Chief Armstrong observed in 1894 that gambling and prostitution had been "tolerated . . . fostered . . . and protected by various state and municipal officers who regarded gambling as the hub around which all other interests of the populace revolved."[56]

Concerns about police corruption came and went. The press would complain loudly; next the mayor,

police commission, and police chief would indignantly assert that the final straw had been reached and something would be done about it, and nothing ever was. A good example was the arrival and prompt failure of the Populists. A typical case was H. M. Behymer, a real estate dealer whom the *Denver Republican* proclaimed to have been an "applicant for everything in sight since the Populists got into power." When Behymer was appointed detective chief, the newspaper sarcastically added that "the sleuths of history will bow their heads in recognition of the distinguished acquisition to their ranks."[57]

The Behymer appointment was an example of political patronage at its extreme, and the people could only wonder how long it would persist. Several years earlier the Fire and Police Board had approved resolutions dictating that (1) no Denver policemen could smoke on the streets or drink intoxicants in uniform on or off duty, and (2) no policeman or fireman was allowed to take any active part in politics, including attending political conventions or "advocating the cause of" any candidate.[58] The rule excluded the act of voting, but it suggested two things: (1) policemen were spending a good amount of time drinking in uniform on or off duty, and (2) they could affect the direction of the department by allying with political candidates.

Riding the wave of permissiveness in Denver as the 1890s arrived was Big Ed Chase, now in almost his thirtieth year of accommodating the city's gambling fraternity—a remarkable run. But Ed and all "respectable" gamblers knew how to avoid controversy and generate good publicity. This lesson went all the way back to 1859 when a three-card monte dealer at the Denver House announced, "I take no bets from paupers, cripples, or orphan children." In 1895, however, the *Rocky Mountain News* headlined: "Gamblers Fleece a Crip [Cripple]. Invalid Loses His Little Pile." This was a public relations misstep for the Denver gambling industry.[59]

By the late 1890s Ed Chase was operating what was perhaps the most sedate gambling emporium Denver had ever seen. It was the Inter-Ocean Club at 1422 Curtis Street, which Chase managed fairly successfully to keep out of the headlines. A notable exception was when Big Al Hoffses killed James Thornton in Ed Chase's office. That notwithstanding, Chase was the king of the Denver gamblers, not even equalled by the wealthy and politically powerful Vaso Chucovich. In 1899 Chucovich and Chase became partners in a takeover of the old Brinker's Collegiate Institute, a private boarding school at Broadway and Tremont Place. In it they installed the fanciest gambling parlor in Denver's history.

When the city fathers determined that the place was attracting undue public attention, Chase and Chucovich downplayed the gambling, installed a restaurant and bar, and renamed the establishment the Navarre—with games of chance still upstairs. The location—barely a block from Henry C. Brown's upscale Brown Palace Hotel—could not have been more advantageous. Only Chase and Chucovich, both suave and well connected at city hall, could have made it work because vices were uncommon so far uptown.

Under their stewardship the Navarre became a premier gambling mecca of the West. Nothing was overlooked, from the life-sized painting *After the Bath* over the crystal bar to the Renaissance-style upstairs dining room, with a discreet private entrance for use, as a brochure explained, "if Madame is with you."[60]

In 1908 Arthur Bawdin came to Denver from the Cripple Creek District and went to work chauffeuring Ed Chase, then age seventy. On February 3, 1967, volunteers Elinor Kingery and Nancy Denious of the Colorado Historical Society visited Bawdin at the Primrose Apartments, 1720 Logan Street, where he resided, and tape-recorded his recollections, including these memories of Chase:

> Ed Chase owned the Tramway Company [an erroneous statement]. He was a very wealthy man. He had a Thomas Flyer [automobile], two passenger. . . . Yes, he could drive. He drove so much and I used to ride with him. He was an old man, seventy years old. He wasn't active [in the gambling business] then. He used to go up [and visit] this police station on Seventeenth. He didn't really run the Navarre, he just controlled it. And he owned all that property on Market Street, all them little houses down there.
>
> QUESTION: *You seem to sort of equate the gambling business with the prostitution business. Were they the same thing?*

They were two different things, but they did kind of go hand in hand.

> QUESTION: *You seemed to think that it was better to have a red light district.*

Sure, I think so. Well, when you have a red light district, men has some place to go to satisfy whatever they got. They used to go down there, you could pay a dollar, two dollars, five dollars, or as high as twenty. All depends on whatever woman you had picked out. Now you don't have red light districts. Now women go into a bar, take a few drinks, pick up a guy, take him out to wherever she's going to take him, come back . . . and two days later the guy wakes up with the syphilis, or the clap, or the gonorrhea. [Formerly] down there a police surgeon examined those women twice a week. . . . Madam Silks, I knew her. [Anna] "Goldie" Gould, there's another one I used to know. You see, I used to do a little bit of that on the side. I used to know a lot of them and a lot of rich men. I used to know one of the biggest guys in the Public Service [utility company]. I used to call up a lady for him.

Kingery added to the typescript:

> When I went to see Mr. Bawdin to make arrangements for the tape recording, he told me that Mr. Chase's wife was a prostitute, that Mr. Chase had picked her up out of one of the houses on Market Street. At that time Mr. Bawdin told me also that Mr. Chase didn't get along with his wife. These two things he would not repeat on tape. I think we also erased unintentionally the part where Mr. Bawdin said that Mr. Chase would come out to the garage to talk to him, the garage at 1492 Race Street, smoking his big cigar, that he was seldom without a cigar in his mouth. I remember that the implication was that when things got too much for him with his wife, he would do this.[61]

Reverberations of police involvement with vice, gambling, and liquor rumbled loudly all the way up Sixteenth Street to Colorado's new capitol building, where on February 7, 1901, a Senate resolution was introduced seeking a legislative investigation of the Denver police. Becoming increasingly nervous, the city's Fire and Police Board—headed by the urbane Robert W. Speer, eventually the crookedest mayor in Denver history—quickly decided to conduct its own investigation. Six policemen were fired; none was charged with corruption. City hall watchers cried "whitewash."[62]

Occasionally, one of the steady succession of police chiefs—seldom law enforcement professionals, still recruited from the ranks of civilian friends of the mayor—would weakly try to upgrade law enforcement in Denver. Chief William H. O'Brien suggested in 1897 that a policeman should adhere to certain character traits, appearance codes, and degrees of honesty. He urged all officers to shave cleanly, get their hair cut, and "keep good company," delivering the following lecture at roll call:

> Do not forget that in this business your character is your capital. Deal honorably with all persons, and hold your word sacred. If you are intrusted [sic] with the care of a beat, do not play the loafer on it by lounging in doorways or on corners, or by leaning against lamp posts, but patrol your beat continually. Make it your business to know what is going on on every part of it, let no person or circumstance escape your notice. Lend a willing ear to all complaints made to you in your official capacity. The most unworthy have a right to be heard, and a word of comfort to the afflicted, or of advice to the erring, may do much good. You must, when on duty, be neat in person, and have your clothes and boots clean.[63]

Chief O'Brien may have been best known for purchasing a trunk full of disguises for nine dollars from the Pinkerton private detective agency and dispatching Detective Samuel H. Emrich, wearing a set of fake whiskers, to capture a gang of chicken thieves. All Detective Emrich accomplished was to be arrested as a suspicious character by Detective Willis A. Loomis, who himself was wearing a false nose and whiskers and was looking for an arsonist. Two months later the Fire and Police Board requested and received Chief O'Brien's resignation. Observed the board, "You do not possess the judgment or discretion to successfully manage the police department."[64]

Sam Emrich, who at about five-feet-five was even more diminutive than Sam Howe, was the smallest member of the police department. Emrich enjoyed a certain measure of fortitude, however, and on November 18, 1901, he shot and killed robber and child assaulter Robert Butler as Butler fled from officers near Thirty-third and Wynkoop Streets. By 1904, however, Emrich's fortunes had plummeted. Emrich and a Mike Ryan became involved in an altercation in the saloon of William Malone, and when Malone tried to eject Emrich, the detective shot him dead.

Emrich appealed for a new trial all the way to the Colorado Supreme Court but was refused. His old friend, Denver police chief Hamilton Armstrong (at this time Arapahoe County sheriff), accompanied Emrich to Cañon City to begin a fourteen-year term, nine years with good behavior. Emrich said that inasmuch as Ryan and Malone both had criminal records, he regarded his sentence as too severe. He blamed his troubles on a "superabundance of booze," adding, "I will be a good detective when I get out. I will be with all the criminals there and will know them all." No record has been discovered as to what Emrich did after he was released from the penitentiary.[65]

There were limits to the attentions a policeman was expected to devote to the public, especially certain members of the public, and these guidelines were addressed by the venerable Chief Hamilton Armstrong as the new century was under way in one of the most eloquent manifestoes ever delivered by a Denver police chief. It was quoted in the newspaper:

> Six handsome young policemen who have been on six months probation in the department are not to be enrolled on the permanent force, because, according to Chief Armstrong, any pretty woman can make them go over the jumps, roll over, play dead, or any other one of the numerous foolish things a woman can make a susceptible man do. "I want coppers on this force," said the chief, "not candidates for a masculine beauty show. How can I put a stop to the masher nuisance with six brass-buttoned flirts on my staff setting a bad example? I want men to look neat and keep clean, but when they get to wearing bunches of violets to hide their stars [badges], just because some dame gave them the flowers, and taking Florida water [perfumed] baths and manicuring their finger nails, there's nothing for 'em in this business. What I want on this department is big, husky young fellows who can drive a nail with their bare fists, and live [as]

Although the detective force of 1901 had increased in numbers, the community appeared not appreciably more trusting of the beleaguered Denver Police Department. Two particularly bad cops are in this photograph. Seated, from left: George Sanders, Sam Howe, Samuel Emrich, Detective Captain Michael A. Delaney, and Tom Connor. Standing, from left: A. F. Peterson, John J. Leyden (whose image appears superimposed on the photograph), Ed Carberry, Thomas Brown, Pete Koehler, Frank Leary, and John C. McNeill. Mike Delaney, a henchman for the corrupt Mayor Robert Speer, would become police chief and a poor one at that, nicknamed "Third Degree" Delaney for his brutal propensities. After Delaney beat up an innocent citizen, Speer had to ask him to leave. Worse, Detective Sam Emrich went to prison in 1906 for a drunken murder committed while off duty.

close to nature as is proper for their health—officers who can look one of these foolish flirts in the face without batting an eye, and shame her into running home, where she belongs.[66]

Gambling, corruption, and manicured policemen wearing violets were accompanied by a still-thriving prostitution business in the new century. The bagnios and cribs of Market Street had seldom been busier—nurtured by the agreed-on payoffs to city hall and an ample clientele of portly businessmen and miners, ranchers, and farmers from the mountains and plains. Accordingly, the women of Market Street determined it prudent to project an image of good citizenship. When forger and perpetual prison escapee James K. Stratton broke out of the Cañon City penitentiary in October 1899, he quickly gravitated, as might be expected, toward Market Street to relieve the tensions of confinement. After his departure the "negress" (the newspaper's term) resident of the house, Ida Jones (more familiarly known, and feared, as "Black Ide"), and her next-door neighbor, Lena Martin, promptly informed police of his presence at their establishments. It did no good, and Stratton made good his getaway.[67] Perhaps the only regrets were felt by prison warden C. P. Hoyt, who was held negligent by the penitentiary commissioners for allowing conditions permitting Stratton to escape. The warden was remonstrated, but that was the end of it.[68]

Two years later Black Ide clubbed "colored" Jennie Thompson with a baseball bat wielded "with all the strength which has made her a reputation," according to an account of the incident preserved by Sam Howe. Black Ide, the press reported, was "one

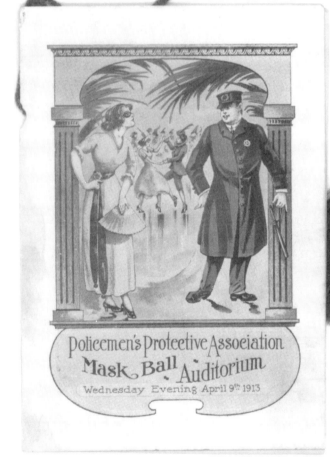

Policemen's Protective Association
Mask Ball Auditorium
Wednesday Evening April 9th 1913

of the most dangerous in the city. She has a reputation as a desperate fighter. On August 1, 1890, she murdered Steve Zimmer on Market street. She followed him and stabbed him to death." For this Black Ide received a fifteen-year penitentiary sentence and was released after eight years.[69]

In August 1901 Ida Mae was arrested for "choking and pounding" Jessie Smith in a jealous rage. "The negro population of Market street from Nineteenth to Twenty-first streets is terrorized by Ida Jones," it was reported in police court.[70] Not a quick learner, eight weeks later the fearsome Ida, now released, pulled a gun on miner Charles Peterson after he, upon leaving her rooms, noticed that his money pouch containing $275 was missing and protested. Whether he found the pouch is not recorded, but the press again pronounced Ide "the most vicious and dangerous woman in Denver."[71]

Another of Black Ide's victims was Henry Fitschen, about sixty, of Rosette, Wyoming, who reported to police that Black Ide had robbed him of $105, whereupon he went to a serene spot above Golden and hanged himself from a tree. A larceny conviction earned Black Ide a return to Cañon City, March 23, 1902. This time she got five-to-ten and was pregnant. A brief note in prison records states that the baby was born, but what became of it is unknown. Of the 299 female prisoners enter-

Police Chief Hamilton Armstrong publicly berated what he termed "brass-buttoned flirts" who wore "posies" over their badges and splashed on colognes. One such dandified officer is pictured on the cover of this tassled dance card from the 1913 Policemen's Ball. The dances included the waltz, schottische, lancers, two-step, and, as the finale, a waltz to "Home, Sweet Home." Although city bigwigs and police and fire commanders were present, the beat cops may have been discouraged from attending: "I want coppers on this force," huffed Armstrong, "not candidates for a masculine beauty show."

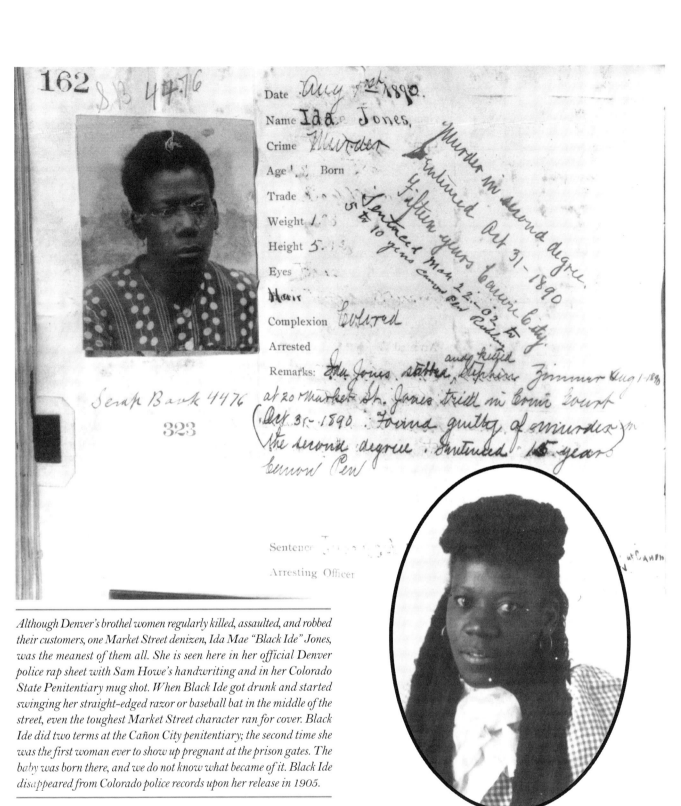

162   SB 4476

Date Aug 1st 1890.
Name Ida Jones,
Crime Murder
Age   Born
Trade
Weight 1
Height 5.
Eyes
Hair
Complexion Colored
Arrested
Remarks: Ida Jones stabbed Stephen Zimmer Aug 1-1890
at 20 Market St. James tried in Criminal Court
Oct 35-1890. Found guilty of murder in
the second degree. Sentenced 15 years
Canon Pen

Murder in second degree.
Sentenced Oct 31-1890
Fifteen years Cañon City.
Sentenced Mar 22-02 to
5 to 10 yrs Cañon Pen Robbing
and killed

Scrap Book 4476
323

Sentence
Arresting Officer

Although Denver's brothel women regularly killed, assaulted, and robbed their customers, one Market Street denizen, Ida Mae "Black Ide" Jones, was the meanest of them all. She is seen here in her official Denver police rap sheet with Sam Howe's handwriting and in her Colorado State Penitentiary mug shot. When Black Ide got drunk and started swinging her straight-edged razor or baseball bat in the middle of the street, even the toughest Market Street character ran for cover. Black Ide did two terms at the Cañon City penitentiary; the second time she was the first woman ever to show up pregnant at the prison gates. The baby was born there, and we do not know what became of it. Black Ide disappeared from Colorado police records upon her release in 1905.

Ida Jones. 2388

ing the Colorado State Penitentiary between 1873 and 1916, Ida Mae is the only one reported to have been pregnant. In many other jurisdictions, babies born in prison were usually retained there until age six months and were then sent to relatives or placed for adoption. Ida Mae was paroled on December 30, 1905, and we hear of her no more.[72]

Life, dangerous as it was, struggled forward up and down notorious Market Street. Its cribs, more than its fancier parlor houses, were scenes of debauchery:

> Each crib was cheaply furnished with a washstand, an iron bed spread with a gaudy coverlet, and sometimes the homey touch of a few religious pictures on the wall. Generally, a girl solicited from the door, although sometimes she left the curtains open so that an interested customer willing to wait his turn could window shop while she was working. . . . Rickety steps led up from the street to a squalid hallway so narrow that two persons could barely pass, and in case of fire a rush of three or four would have blocked escape. Between what an early newspaper called its "insect-haunted walls," wretched creatures operated in dank rooms, selling their squalid selves for paltry sums to men grim enough to enter, debased enough to need what those pitiful creatures sold. This was not the expensive, glittering life of the demimondaine, so popular in later historical accounts, but the sordid, wretched existence of a prostitute. The cubicles were rank and stale from smoke and liquor and lust. The girls were onerous and weak from too much drink or dope or just depravity. By the time a prostitute reached the cribs, she usually was unfit for anything but prostitution.[73]

The woman known as Josie Washburn endured the brothels beginning in 1871 at age seventeen and in 1925 prepared her reminiscences, which she titled *The Underworld Sewer.* "At the bottom of the underworld," she wrote,

> can be found the lowest type of poverty stricken humanity; it is composed of all shades, grades and colors huddled together. These places of existence are called cribs, dives, dens, holes and nests. These hellholes catch all kinds of girls on the drift, who do not realize their fate, or that they are with the scum of the earth, until too late. It would not be possible to escape even had they a desire to do so. It is where male and female lie around everywhere stupefied with dope and liquor; the house is blue with smoke and profanity, and reeking in filth, disease and degradation . . . dwarfed in body and mind, they are disqualified to earn a living except by vice.[74]

They were truly Hell's Belles.

Notes

1. The RMN report that the city council could not meet because its members were visiting a new pleasure house is a well-known story surrounding the Denver *demimonde.* It appears not to have happened that way, however. The *News* on August 21, 1880, wrote that the DR had reported that the councilmen were at the bordello, adding, "A mob may take that council in hand yet." An examination of the *Republican* of the day before, August 20, disclosed that all it said was: "No surprise was caused by the absence of the Aldermen last night, when a quorum could not be obtained. They had been invited elsewhere." One suspects, however, that the *News*'s interpretation had some truth to it. The *Republican* that week was particularly on an antiprostitution crusade because of the August 19 fatal shooting of a prominent merchant, M. Marburger, in the Holladay Street house of madam Carrie Smith. The *Republican* editorialized the next day: "We read that men with wives and families are frequenters of these dens of sin and shame, and under cover of night disgrace their good name by such vile associations. They trust it will not be discovered and continue to frequent these disreputable haunts, which, but for their support, would sink into the lowest dens of crime and be wiped from the face of the earth."

2. Historian Robert L. Perkin, in *The First Hundred Years,* p. 371, lists this RMN report as being published on April 16, 1883. Forbes Parkhill, in "Scarlet Sister Mattie," correctly dates the article to ten days earlier.

3. Knapp, "Making an Orderly Society," p. 124, quoting SHS 2: 311, newspaper unnamed but dated January 4, 1886.

4. SHS 5: 1103, newspaper unnamed but dated November 10, 1886.

5. RD, p. 254.

6. For Chief "Billy" Smith's departure, see the RMN, January 14, 1885. The first known "presentation badge"

awarded in Denver went to Andrew J. Snyder, who was elected city marshal in April 1862 and remained in office for a year. This marvelous gold and sterling silver badge was donated to the Colorado Historical Society in 1953. A fancy badge was given to William R. Hickey when he became chief in October 1878. It was customary to award a presentation badge to a chief upon his departure; the badge given to Hickey was in honor of his eleven years of service. Hickey's badge was described as "pure gold and very large." See the DTR, October 20, 1878. Two years later Dave Cook, high on the list of Denver's most able police chiefs of the late nineteenth century, was given an elaborately engraved solid gold five-pointed star, three inches from tip to tip. Some expressed skepticism about the stars, which had sharp points and might be turned against the officer. See the DTI, March 3, 1881, and the RD, p. 218, quoting the DTR, March 29, 1881. After patrolmen Thomas Clifford and William E. Griffith were slain on August 13, 1899, it was noted that each had been shot near the heart, and some officers began wondering if large shiny badges might make a good target. Chief John Farley decided instead that the policemen were terrible shots and needed firearms training. See RD, pp. 496–499. For a few years beginning in 1862, the Denver mayor and city aldermen had badges similar to those worn by policemen but smaller. They were engraved *Mayor of Denver* or *Alderman* (followed by the Ward number). See RD, p. 178, quoting Alfred C. Phelps, comp., *The Charter and Ordinances of the City of Denver* (Denver: 1878), p. 137. Henry Brady, the most corrupt nineteenth-century Denver police chief, was given a gold, silver, and enameled badge with a silver wreath encircling a shield when he became chief in August 1887. When he stepped down, the grateful businesspeople of Denver were so thankful he was gone and that they finally had a reasonably honest chief that on Christmas Eve 1889 they presented Brady's successor, John Farley, with an impressive gold "suspension badge," meaning the badge had several components, each suspended by a gold chain. For the presentation to Farley a "general alarm" was sounded for every policeman on the night shift to report to the mayor's office. The officers thought a riot had broken out but discovered they had been summoned to observe the badge presentation. For the Brady and Farley badges, see RD, pp. 300–301, 335. On Christmas morning 1895 Chief George Goulding was given an eight-pointed gold star inscribed with his name and a diamond in the middle. It cost $500. See RD, p. 430.

7. RD, pp. 274–277, 425. Police Captain Wilson Swain, variously of the Thiel Detective Service and the Denver Police Department, in 1905 was imported to Caldwell, Idaho, to help investigate the assassination of that state's former governor, Frank Steunenberg. See Lukas, *Big Trouble*, p. 72.

8. Ibid., p. 469.

9. Ibid., pp. 315, 320.

10. RMN, August 23, 1895. See also RD, pp. 407–408.

11. RMN, October 8, 1883.

12. Ibid., November 22, 1884. The gambler interviewed here acknowledged that some Denver gaming houses deserved to be shut down because they were operated by "thieves and tin horns" whose only intent was to "skin suckers." That sort of operator could not afford, said the gambler, to be out of work for more than a week, "and in that way [the shutdown] will be beneficial."

13. SHS 6: 1279, from the DR, January 15, 1887.

14. Ibid., 6: 1231, from the RMN, January 4, 1887; book number 7: clippings 1925, 1926, 1927, from the RMN, November 3, 4, 6, 1887.

15. Ibid., 12: 4855, from the DR, January 1, 1891.

16. R. G. Dill, *Political Campaigns of Colorado with Complete Tabulated Statements of the Official Vote* (Denver: Arapahoe, 1895), pp. 161–162.

17. RD, p. 332.

18. RMN, October 19, 1880.

19. Knapp, "Making an Orderly Society," pp. 169–173.

20. RD, p. 34.

21. Ibid., p. 42.

22. RMN, October 19, 1880.

23. RD, p. 125.

24. Knapp, "Making an Orderly Society," pp. 170–171. The reward incidents in the preceding paragraphs are from SHS 10: 3494, unlisted newspaper but dated June (?), 1889, and SHS 13: 7822, unnamed newspaper but dated August 30, 1893.

25. RD, p. 460.

26. SHS 8: 2251, from the DR, February 16, 1888, and 8: 2252, from the RMN, the same date. The victim of the diamond stickpin heist, H. Solomon, is not listed by a full first name in the 1888 *Denver City Directory* and is one of several Solomons in either the pawnbroking or haberdashery business in Denver that year.

27. We do not know whether this is the same Jim Marshall who prompted Bat Masterson's quick exit from Denver (see Chapter 6), but inasmuch as both seem to

have been familiar with Denver police chiefs, the possibility exists. For the other misdeeds under Henry Brady, refer to RD, pp. 321, 346–347, and the RMN, November 28, 1888.

28. SHS 9: 2873, from the RMN, October 24, 1888, and 2876, from the DR, October 26, 1888.

29. For Henry Brady, see RD, pp. 321–325, 335; also the *Denver Police Department Pictorial Review and History*, p. 34; SHS 10: 3503, 3579, 3580, from the RMN, June 12, 1889, and DTI, July 12, 1889.

30. Knapp, "Making an Orderly Society," p. 160, quoting SHS 10: 3555. Students of Denver police corruption in the 1880s and 1890s should consult the RD throughout and the Knapp dissertation, especially pp. 160–179.

31. Hewett's article is in the *Colorado Magazine*, winter 1977: 44–57.

32. RD, pp. 333–334.

33. Ibid., p. 340.

34. For Sam Howe's resignation as detective chief, see RD, pp. 367, 404, 407. Sam Howe's job assignments during the summer of 1893 are muddied, and accounts are contradictory. Consult note 72, Chapter 2. For the Populist Fire and Police Board, see the DR, April 20, 1894. Police Chief Hamilton Armstrong is listed as unfailingly obedient to city hall by District Attorney Philip S. Van Cise in *Fighting the Underworld* (Cambridge, Mass.: Riverside, 1936), pp. 18–22.

35. DR, April 21, 1894. The massive Denver Police Department shakeups of March and April 1894 and their links to the Populist-inspired City Hall War on March 15 are the subjects of studies of their own. See, for instance, the RD, pp. 364–417; Goodstein, *The Seamy Side of Denver*, pp. 119–121; Smiley, *History of Denver*, pp. 921–927.

36. DR, May 11, 1894. The remarkable accomplishments of confidence man Jefferson Randolph "Soapy" Smith are not elaborated on here because he has been the object of several studies, including two full-length books: William Ross Collier and Edwin Victor Westrate, *The Reign of Soapy Smith: Monarch of Misrule* (Garden City, N.Y.: Doubleday, Doran, 1935), and Frank C. Robertson and Beth Kay Harris, *Soapy Smith: King of the Frontier Con Men* (New York: Hastings House, 1961). Far lesser known but at least as erudite is Barkalow Barnacle, "'Soapy' Smith, the Gambler," *The Trail*, January 1920, pp. 5–11. The article elicited follow-up comments published in *The Trail*, June 1920, pp. 10–13.

37. Bettman, *The Good Old Days—They Were Terrible!* p. 98.

38. SHS 14: 8856, from the RMN, April 18, 1894.

39. Ibid., 14: 8858, 8859, 8860, quoting the RMN, April 19–21, 1894.

40. RD, pp. 389–413. The political influences felt by the police department were still present in 1896 when J. L. Russell was chief for a year, and a good chief at that. Said Russell after he had survived allegations of impropriety: "I have, at least, learned enough to know that politics is the curse of the department, and that so long as the men are subject to removal to make places for the friends of every new governor, or to please this or that political organization, there never will be an efficient force. With every change in administration the men become uneasy and the force becomes demoralized. This will always be true until merit and efficient service govern appointments and promotions" (RD, p. 446).

41. The so-called City Hall War of 1894 is a well-documented episode in Colorado history. A thorough account is in Smiley, *History of Denver*, pp. 921–927. Also see Leonard and Noel, *Denver: Mining Camp to Metropolis*, pp. 105–107.

42. RD, pp. 421–422, 428–429.

43. SHS 14: 8792, from the DR, April 7, 1894.

44. Ibid., 14: 8817, from the DR, April 11, 1894.

45. Ibid., 16: 13531, from the RMN, January 13, 1897.

46. Ibid., 16: 13595, 13596, from the DR, January 20, 1897.

47. DTI, August 19, 1895.

48. Quoted in Knapp, "Making an Orderly Society," p. 134.

49. Tensions between Alderman John D. McGilvray and the police department as a result of the anti-Chinese riot are detailed in the RMN, November 19, 1880.

50. Wortman, "Denver's Anti-Chinese Riot, 1880," p. 283, quoting the reminiscences of fireman William Roberts; papers located in the Denver Veteran Volunteer Firemen's Association Papers No. 5, Western History Department, Denver Public Library.

51. SHS 9: 2931, from the DTI, November 22, 1888.

52. Knapp, "Making an Orderly Society," p. 134, quoting SHS 15: 9710, newspaper unnamed but dated November 10, 1894.

53. RMN, May 31, 1907.

54. For George Yawitz, see the RMN, December 18, 1907. Follow-up articles and indignant editorials were printed on December 19, 24, 25, 26.

55. Schlissel, Ruiz, and Monk, *Western Women*, pp. 23–25.

56. Knapp, "Making an Orderly Society," pp. 159–160. Hamilton Armstrong was notable for his durability as a Denver police chief, but he had his oddities. Former crime-busting district attorney Philip S. Van Cise, in his classic *Fighting the Underworld*, said of Armstrong (p. 20): "[He was] a square shooter if ever there was one, and an able and fearless officer, but [he] had to take his orders from upstairs. Armstrong called everybody younger than himself 'son,' and could hardly say a sentence without cussing."

57. DR, March 11, 1894.

58. Ibid., March 26, 1891.

59. Quoted in Dallas, *Cherry Creek Gothic*, p. 216.

60. Ibid., pp. 217–220. For a detailed account of the Brinker's/Navarre, see Minnie Hall Krauser, "Brinker Collegiate Institute–Navarre Cafe," *Colorado Magazine*, March 1947, pp. 79–85. The popular myth persists that the Navarre was at some time a brothel. The Navarre was far outside the designated Market Street brothel district, and no exception would have been made for a location so close to the Brown Palace Hotel—the West's classiest. Nurturing the myth was the fact that the Navarre featured private, closed-off dining booths and was indeed a place to which a gentleman could safely escort to dinner a woman not his wife.

61. Transcript, Elinor Kingery and Nancy Denious interview with Arthur Bawdin, Denver, February 3, 1967, Colorado Historical Society, oral history interview number 119. For Ed Chase's wives, refer to note 4, Chapter 5. We do not know the identity of the wife referred to here.

62. Hanna, "The Art of American Policing, 1900–1930," pp. 45–51.

63. SHS 17: 14649, from the DR, June 30, 1897.

64. RD, pp. 455–457.

65. For Detective Sam Emrich's shooting of Robert Butler, see the DTI and RMN, November 19, 1901. For Emrich's conviction for murder, see the DR and DTI, August 1, 1904, and the DP, August 2. On November 10, 1901, Emrich and other Denver principal police officers were interviewed by the DTI with regard to their favorite cases, and Emrich chose his capture in Denver of post office robber and cop killer Harry Crawford, an escapee from Ohio, on February 13, 1897. The article suggests that Emrich was dispatched alone to capture Crawford. The *Times* article of November 10, 1901, relates a series of exciting adventures undertaken by Denver's best-known police heroes and is recommended for any student of Denver police history. Only eight days after the account of Emrich's showdown with Crawford was published, Emrich faced Robert Butler—which would have given him a new number-one adventure.

66. SHS 29: 56707, from the RMN, January 31, 1910.

67. Ibid., 18: 19107, from the RMN, October 13, 1899. According to somewhat sparse existing data on the subject examined in this study, African Americans appear to have made up only a small percentage of the late-nineteenth-century prostitute population of Denver. In his *Murder Book*, however, Detective Sam Howe left evidence that the African American prostitutes exceeded their Anglo counterparts in the use of violence and the number of homicides committed. Historian Benson Tong in *Unsubmissive Women* (pp. 14–15) states that in the western United States, African American prostitutes primarily set up shop in communities with a sizable population of black cowhands or black soldiers. Denver and Colorado did not fit either of those categories. Tong adds on p. 127: "Prostitutes of all racial origins, despite being a minority group within the female population, accounted for most of the brute force and lawlessness committed by or directed at women" in the small frontier town of Bodie, California, and on p. 140 Tong discusses violence directed toward prostitutes by their patrons.

68. Ibid., 8: 19300, from the DR, November 17, 1899. The activities of two-term penitentiary warden C. P. Hoyt and other Colorado prison activities are in Julie Whitmore, *A History of the Colorado State Penitentiary, 1871–1980* (Cañon City, Colo.: Printing Plus, 1984).

69. SHS 20: 23864, possibly from the DP, April 7, 1901.

70. Ibid., 20: 25308, from the DR, August 30, 1901.

71. Ibid., 20: 25816, from the DR, October 24, 1901.

72. For Henry Fitschen, see SHS 20: 25999, from the RMN, November 15, 1901. For Ida Jones's pregnancy and final prison term, see Benham, "Women in the Colorado State Penitentiary, 1873 Through 1916," pp. 79–80, 109–110.

73. Dallas, *Cherry Creek Gothic*, pp. 229–230. For an additional description of the pleasure spots of Holladay and Market Streets, see Goodstein, *The Seamy Side of Denver*, p. 30.

74. Josie Washburn, *The Underworld Sewer: A Prostitute Reflects on Life in the Trade, 1871–1909* (Lincoln: University of Nebraska Press, 1997), pp. 159–160.

8

"Here She Is. Now Give Me the Five Dollars."

EMPLOYMENT OTHER THAN MENIAL LABOR was scant for the women of Denver during the final quarter of the nineteenth century. The help-wanted advertisements in the city's newspapers revealed a virtual absence of professional positions. Only the most fortunate young women had education beyond high school; the remainder were forced by family economic necessities into whatever jobs could be located.

Among the few choices were opportunities as store clerks (called "shop girls"), milliners, dressmakers, and positions rolling tobacco leaves at the cigar factories. The largest number of employed young women worked as nannies and housekeepers for the families that struck it rich in the gold or silver fields and built fancy new homes along Denver's Grant Avenue ("Millionaire's Row") or elsewhere on Capitol Hill.

Low wages for female workers were a principal factor in inducing young women to sell themselves. A six-dollar weekly shop girl's salary was often insuffi-

cient to pay for a suitable room and meals—even at the YWCA. Thus in 1898 three philanthropic Denver women—Mrs. Dean Peck, Agnes Hart, and Mrs. S. F. Lord—established the Home for Working Girls in a large rented house at 808 Thirteenth Street. There, low-paid women or those searching for a job could get room and board at three dollars a week—or a dollar fifty if they couldn't afford three dollars. The rules were to be "on time for meals" and "in at 10 P.M." In the twelve months preceding July 1898, the home had 518 total admissions and an average nightly population of twenty-four. Collected fees met $1,887 of the $2,587 annual operating costs, with the remainder made up by donations.

As teenage women increasingly moved to Denver from outlying farm and mining towns beginning in the late 1870s, a large pool of cheap labor formed—far too many workers than the market demanded. Dr. William Sanger's national study of prostitution observed that male employers "drive a woman to starvation by

181

refusing her employment, and then condemn her for maintaining a wretched existence at the price of her virtue."[1]

Almost all female occupations historically offered low pay. Big-city seamstresses prior to the Civil War earned 37½ cents per day. By 1870 the pay was $6 to $12 per week. In contrast, a Denver parlor house girl could keep $30 a week for herself, even after splitting the take with her madam.

Nationally, there were many sorts of seamstresses, and a considerable percentage worked part-time as prostitutes, as calculated by Dr. Sanger: umbrella sewers, 79 percent; fur sewers, 67 percent; "tailoresses" and cap makers, 58 percent; upholsterers, 57 percent; and sock makers, 50 percent.[2]

The millinery shop girl or department store sales-girl was generally regarded at the turn of the century as on a certain path to prostitution. As is detailed elsewhere in this study, the shop girl was exposed to fancy dress and opulence she could never hope to attain for herself; she was continually reminded that other women had money and means, and she did not. The department store was the hangout of the young and snappily attired "cadets," or pimps, who traded on the weaknesses of these poor girls. Such young men constantly reinforced to the five-dollar-a-week salesgirl that she could earn three times that in just an hour, wear fancy satins, and sip champagne with wealthy clients in the process.[3]

Many of Denver's young women came to town with their families whose males were eager to hit the big time in mining or to live well from the support industries the busy town had to offer. The great majority of these immigrating families realized successes in neither, and the women and their kin teetered on poverty. In too many cases young females of such families either gravitated or were pushed toward commercial sex, for which there was a sizable market.

Among the most revealing documents discovered during preparation of this book was an address delivered by Denver physician George W. Cox before the twelfth annual convention of the Colorado State Medical Society in Pueblo, June 1882. Dr. Cox titled his speech "The Social Evil," a nineteenth-century euphemism for prostitution. It is remarkable for its forth-

rightness and insight, as well as its occasional naivete, reflective of the age.[4]

Dr. Cox's best estimates at the time of his study were that the United States held about 200,000 prostitutes, or one for every 250 population, and that 480 prostitutes were active in Denver, a ratio of 1 to 110. He prefaced his address to the medical society with a broad statement of premise:

> The vast majority of women are pure by instinct and by inclination, even as they are trusting and affectionate by nature; but the devices for their ruin are so numerous and so cunning that even before they are aware of danger, they are often hurled into the depths of sin and disgrace. They fall innocently, unwittingly and unwillingly. Just where men acquire all these habits of deviltry it would be impossible to say.

His study of the prostitute's environment convinced Dr. Cox that although some such young women came from impoverished and abusive home situations, others were from a middle-class upbringing and turned to prostitution because it was a convenient profession in which they did not have to work very hard. He told the medical society:

> From [the impoverished] class we find the greatest number of those [prostitutes] who have suffered bodily injury at the hands of cruel parents, and the few who have been led into lives of sin by an unnatural mother. And just here I would mention the fact that one of the largest bawdy houses in Denver was recently kept by a woman who had for her star boarders her own daughter and two of her own nieces. But it is rather from the middle classes that the ranks of prostitution are principally kept full. Shop girls, milliners, dress-makers and all those who, by force of circumstances, are compelled to earn their own living are easily induced to yield to the temptations that are daily held out to them by unscrupulous men and unprincipled women. Girls of this class must do long hours of hard work for small pay, and when the evil one comes with his patronizing smiles and fair promises, it is not strange that so many of them should hesitate, and falter, and fall. On one of my tours of discovery I was informed by a landlady that I need not look beyond the limits of her home to find education and culture of a very high order; and in proof of her

assertion she called in and introduced one of her boarders. The young woman seated herself at the piano, and from the manner in which she rendered selections from the ancient and modern masters, it was evident that the musical part of her education, at least, had been carefully and patiently attended to. She had spent several years in travel through the different quarters of the globe; could speak three languages with fluency and grace. . . . The parents of this child of misfortune are among the wealthiest and most highly respected of one of the cities of the Atlantic coast.[5]

The topic of male influence on women vulnerable to the lure of commercial sex was examined by the U.S. Senate, whose members received testimony from a woman of the *demimonde*:

Girls don't go wrong because they are hungry or because they need clothes. They go wrong because they are tempted by lies and overpowered by the evil in men. They listen to the fair and pretty things that men tell them and they fall because they think they can trust themselves and trust the tempters. I was a good girl and I worked in a store. I didn't get that much money, but that didn't matter. I lived on $8 a week and would be living like that now—but I met men. They seemed to consider me their prey.

Another woman of the bordellos told the senators:

You're looking for the things that made such women as I. Low wages! Dance halls! Hunger! Cold! They all helped a bit, but they didn't turn the trick themselves. You're all a bunch of hypocrites, afraid to look the thing in the face and afraid to learn the truth. I don't know any girls who sold themselves for money to buy bread or clothes, but I do know lots of us who hit the road for hell because a lot of blackguards kept hounding us with their rotten "attentions." God help the men and not us. We're all right when we start— all we need is to be let alone. There are hundreds and hundreds of kids and sports who hang around State street [Chicago] and wait like wolves for the tired girls to leave the stores.[6]

The motivations to turn to prostitution during the last half of the nineteenth century have been examined by several writers, including "Madeline," whose memoirs were originally published in 1919, detailing her activities in Chicago, St. Louis, and Kansas City. Historian Marcia Carlisle, who wrote the introduction to a 1986 reprint of *Madeline, An Autobiography*, referred to the book as the first "personal document of any significance" written by a prostitute. The writer, "homeless, defenseless, hungry," unmarried, and pregnant at age seventeen in about 1887, wrote that her dilemma offered three choices: prostitution, life in a home "for fallen women," or suicide: "I had no choice between the course I took and the Mississippi River [brothels]," she wrote (pp. vii, ix).

Chicago was notorious for a prostitution industry that grossed $15 million a year and employed 5,000 women, not counting part-timers. Vice there was far less controlled than in the other notorious sin capital of mid-America, New Orleans. Having learned little from New Orleans, Denver, or New York City, which were fairly successful in controlling their bordellos, the city commissioned a thorough study whose findings were published in 1911 as *The Social Evil in Chicago: A Study of Existing Conditions, with Recommendations by the Vice Commission of Chicago*. The research found numerous contributing factors, not all of them the fault of the women. Civic hypocrisy was one, a condition that permitted and applauded dances by women almost naked in certain public places under the guise of art and condemned dances no worse before audiences from less prosperous walks of life. Women, the study found, were drawn to prostitution by want of necessities of life, by a desire for some simple luxuries, by ignorance, by vain hopes, by broken promises, and by the deceit and lust of men. When the researchers polled prostitutes about their motives for entering the business, half listed "for money" (average: five dollars weekly), followed by "seduced and violated," "to support others," and "bad home conditions," among other reasons. One respondent answered "better than ruining eyes sewing." Samuel Paynter Wilson, in *Chicago and Its Cess-Pools of Infamy* (p. 47), blamed much of the problem not on greed and bad fortune among the women but rather on procurers who promised lives of glamour, only for the girls to realize "their awful fate with scalding tears and moans of horror."

Researcher Anne M. Butler, in *Daughters of Joy, Sisters of Misery*, described the typical bordello inmate as homeless and youthful—ages fifteen to thirty. Some houses, Butler reported, prided themselves on offering young virgins for defloration, but other madams were just as proud to boast that a young girl had never been ruined in her house. These young girls were generally either runaways or expelled by their parents. Compounding this dilemma facing a poor, ignorant girl were the exciting tales of glitter and glamour portrayed by the madam: parties, liquor, wealthy gentlemen, and morphine and opium to deaden the physical pain.[7]

Denver's Row witnessed occasional displays of welcome humor. On a December evening in 1877, for instance, Fannie Gray, a lady of color, rampaged through the streets announcing loudly that her name was "Susan Snowdrop." As she did not, in the arresting officer's words, "bear the remotest resemblance to a snow drop," he took her in "for telling stories." Not amusing was the subsequent incident in which Detective John Holland discovered Fannie—or Susan—beating her daughter with a lead-loaded stick. The daughter, Holland noted, was "undoubtedly an unconscionably bad girl," but he nonetheless took the weapon from Fannie and "instructed her to treat the girl properly."[8]

In April 1882 the British dramatist, essayist, apostle of aestheticism, and poet Oscar Wilde, a delicate and sensitive sort, was invited to be a distinguished guest of Denver, speaking on the topic of "Decorative Arts." The town, whose growing affluence in the early 1880s made it thirsty for culture, did not know quite what to think.

Wilde had a fondness for sunflowers and lilies, which the Market Street girls gleefully interpreted as sissyish. On April 5 madam Minnie Clifford, described by the *Rocky Mountain News* as "a woman of the town, in anticipation of the coming of Oscar Wilde," dressed herself and her girls in lilies and sunflowers, "determined not to be outdone in estheticism by any of her fair sisters of either the social world or the *demi monde*." Minnie herself wore a sunflower "the size of a dinner plate" on the back of her new spring bonnet. She was quoted as exclaiming, "I know what makes the wildcat wild, but who makes Oscar?"

City hall huffily considered this a slight against Wilde, and policeman Thomas O'Connor tossed

Minnie and one of her girls (who was wearing a giant lily) in jail on the charge of "meretricious display on the public streets." The *News* ran two paragraphs on the incident under the memorable headline "Arrested for Estheticism."[9] Three days later the same paper published a poem titled "Ascerbated [*sic*] Esthetics," subtitled "A tale which shows the wisdom of crushing the sunflower in the bud," which began:

> Oh, Oscar! Oh, Oscar
> Pray take a hos'car
> And hasten to aid us;
> Aid or we're busted.
> No daffydowndilly
> No sunflower or lily
> In Denver is trusted.[10]

The sale of virginity earned the greatest amount for a young girl or her madam. Figures for Colorado were not included in contemporary accounts, but Timothy Gilfoyle cited several examples from late-nineteenth-century New York, including that of wine merchant John Ryan who paid fifty dollars—a year's wages for a teenager—to deflower fourteen-year-old Ann Kerrigan and then paid her twenty dollars a week for almost two years to continue as his mistress. The age of consent was ten.[11]

An occasional madam boasted (advertised) that no young girl had ever been deflowered under her roof, a claim that demonstrated an empathy toward young girls entering a life of sin. The Sam Howe Scrapbooks contain an entry from 1898 illustrating this phenomenon. The clipping, excerpted here, carries the headline "Saved from a Life of Vice." Verona Baldwin was a Denver madam.

A pretty, blue eyed young woman arrived in the city last Tuesday night [from Wyoming], intending to seek employment. At an employment office she met a woman who advised her to adopt a course of vice. The girl was exceedingly pretty. She had large blue eyes, a great abundance of brown hair, her features were regular and her face as innocent as that of a little child. About 9 o'clock Tuesday night the woman, called "Mary Anderson," in company with a notorious procuress, rang the bell of a brothel, where she was referred to another dive. At the latter place arrangements were quickly completed. In less than a half hour the landlady was informed that the girl was innocent. Verona Baldwin, the landlady, was quickly convinced that the statement was only too true. A chance had come to warn an innocent beginner of the error of her ways, and Verona was not slow to avail herself of it. She pleaded with the girl for the sake of mother and family to return to her home. Verona Baldwin called the police, and Detectives McIlduff and Burlew took "Mary Anderson" to police headquarters and later to Union Station to catch a train to relatives' home. The police paid for the ticket.[12]

Marriage, regarded by some as an alternative to the *demimonde* life, was often entered into too early by young female émigrés to Denver from the small towns and farms of the West. History questions whether marriage was an advantageous alternative. Parents of these young women were sometimes happy to see them depart from the meager home. Their leaving lightened the family burden and meant one less stomach to fill.

The husbands they could find in Denver, however, were young and with little promise of a future, and life for the young couple was grim in second- or third-floor Larimer Street walk-ups. Drugs such as laudanum (sold by mail through the 1897 Sears Roebuck catalog) or morphine became effective means through which these unfortunates could obliterate their grief over their separation from a real home, friends, and family. Divorces frequently followed, and at age eighteen or nineteen a young woman with perhaps an eighth-grade education and no promise for the future found herself abjectly alone.

Child prostitution was a major cause of concern in large eastern urban centers as early as the 1830s. Reformer Stephen Allen, a onetime New York mayor, told the Society for the Reformation of Juvenile Delinquents that most such girls "have fallen from the combined influence of poverty, neglect, ignorance, and bad company, rather than because of individual or voluntary depravity." A decade later dozens of child prostitutes regularly lounged around New York's city hall at night. Conditions were worse by midcentury, when lawmen estimated that 380 "juvenile harlots" were present in one police precinct.[13]

Laudanum was the solace of the *demimonde* and a fixture of the Denver crib. When she had a headache, the girl had her laudanum. When overburdened with too many customers, the girl had her laudanum to appear bright and eager. When dejected over absence of family, love, and home, the girl had her laudanum. When mustering courage to confront the pimp who beat her and took her earnings, the girl had her laudanum. At Christmas—the worst day in the bordello—the girl had her laudanum to keep from being engulfed in sorrow. Her vial of laudanum was as essential as her douche of mercuric bichloride, mercuric cyanide, potassium permanganate, or carbolic acid.[14]

A convenient solution for a bewildered girl new to town or just divorced was prostitution, which at least initially lent the illusion of a life of luxury, doing no work but draped in velvet gowns and sipping brandies and smoking cigarillos and lounging in mirrored parlors with a helpful madam to play the mother role, fawned over by gentlemen of means and stature who ordered a cognac and cigar before retiring upstairs. Perhaps she even might find a husband.

Many immigrating future prostitutes of Denver and Colorado during the late nineteenth century came from outlying rural towns or from the Midwest, beckoned by the lure of job opportunities the burgeoning new mineral prosperity might offer. The recruitment of girls through national white slave rings, particularly in New York City and Chicago, was not evident along Denver's Row. Perhaps it was not necessary. An abundance of procurers patrolled Denver's streets, soda fountains, and employment agencies; its courthouse, seeking the just divorced; or its train depot to intercept unsuspecting new arrivals to the big city. In *Fighting the Traffic in Young Girls* (1910) Ernest A. Bell offered a typical scenario of a country girl's arrival:

> She had hardly stepped from the train into the big station when she heard a man's voice saying: "Why, hello, Mary!"
>
> "My name's not Mary, it's Nellie."
>
> "You look the very picture," he responded, "of a girl I know well whose name is Mary—and she's a fine girl, too! Are any of your folks here to meet you?"

[Over lunch], he asked her if she would not like to find a place at which to work. "I know of a fine place in Blank City," he added. "The woman is looking for a good girl just like you."

He paid the unsuspecting girl's fare to Blank City, gave her carriage money to the brothel, and she was virtually kept prisoner until she succumbed.[15]

In a particularly aggravated case, Denver Juvenile Court officer John Phillips arrested eighteen-year-old Alma Godswin for trying to recruit her cousin, Bessie Thompson, fifteen, into what the newspapers termed a "life of ruin." Godswin, originally from Colorado Springs, had always been incorrigible and was confined to the girls' reformatory at Morrison for two years. She was paroled on May 8, 1909, and proceeded directly to Helen Bennett's bordello in Cheyenne. From there, she mailed a letter to Thompson in Denver, "detailing in glowing terms life in the tenderloin." Phillips extradited her back to Denver where she was lodged in the city jail matron's quarters while he searched for two of Godswin's accomplices in a developing gang of procurers.[16]

Girls were kept in the brothels until their spirits were broken. Whatever apparel they could wear on the street was taken from them until they were deemed trustworthy to return if let out, and in some locales their windows were barred—ostensibly to keep out "burglars." (This was particularly a Chicago phenomenon, and no such instance is recorded to have taken place in Denver.) As will be seen, the brothel girl was often kept so financially indebted to her madam that she would not be allowed to leave until the obligation was satisfied, and doing so was impossible.

Ice cream parlors and sidewalk fruit stands, innocent as they might sound, were important recruiting sources for the dapper, properly dressed, and sincere-sounding pimps—"cadets" they were called—because they were natural and seemingly safe places for a young girl to stop during her first days in a new city. Even in small communities, the ice cream parlor was a haunt for procurers from out of town. At the turn of the twentieth century and with the growing popularity of amusement parks, cadets found good picking at locales such as Mary and John Elitch's Gardens in Denver, where young single girls went to escape the stifling closeness of small, hot rooming house quarters.

The homesickness of a country girl, alone in the big city, could be profound. Bell (p. 109) observed that "in a brothel one night I was talking with a girl who was playing with a little pet dog. As I continued to talk to her, all at once she said looking into the dog's face, then into mine, 'This is the only friend I have and if I feel blue and discouraged, he will climb into my lap and try to comfort me.'"

In memoirs attributed to madam Nell Kimball, who kept houses in St. Louis, New Orleans, and San Francisco, it was written: "Hookers are mean but sentimental. They cry over dogs, kittens, kids, novels, sad songs." As will be related elsewhere, Denver's brothel women were particularly fond of white poodles—to the extent that "respectable" women avoided owning the breed.

Divorce court was a productive source for the madams of Denver because alimony was rarely asked and even more rarely granted. A penniless young divorcee (or a girl just off the farm) was certain to be approached by a procurer. His fee for each new girl was five or ten dollars, depending on her age, personality, and appearance.[17]

Here is one procedure described for obtaining new inventory for the brothels. A presentable young cadet would routinely strike up an acquaintance with a girl and court her, just as an ordinary young couple would conduct itself. Eventually, she would acquiesce to accompany him to bed, but depending on her character or her upbringing he might have to first promise marriage. Infrequently, a bogus marriage ceremony would be performed. Thereupon the couple would retire to a "hotel" for their "honeymoon," but when she awoke in the morning she would discover that her suitor was gone and she was actually in a brothel room. She would be virtually kept prisoner there, cajoled, and sometimes drugged and raped until her spirit was broken and she agreed to work as instructed.[18] Any family values or moral scruples were often fairly easily dismissed. One young prostitute said it this way: "I know what making money is, sir. I am only fourteen, but I am old enough. I have had to take care of myself ever since I was ten years old, and I have never had a cent given to me. It may be a sin, sir, but God will forgive. The rich do such things and worse, and no one says anything against them."[19]

Well-meaning Samaritans sometimes tried to prevent young women from being tricked or kidnapped into prostitution. In Chicago, Francis Kellor launched a campaign to identify "unsavory" employment agencies and rooming houses that attempted to recruit prostitutes, and in Denver, women's organizations such as the YWCA or the WCTU offered aid to women new to town.[20]

Procurers were usually snappily dressed, smooth-talking young men, but mercenary women were involved as well. In Denver, Mrs. Diana Howard, age about sixty, was charged during summer 1894 with "enticing reputable unmarried women into houses of ill fame for immoral purposes." The *Rocky Mountain News* on June 8 explained:

> It is said that an extended traffic of this nature is being carried on in the city, and that girls of tender age are placed in houses where necessarily their moral character is wholly ruined. Police Matron Frincke [probably Mrs. Otto Frincke] says that in certain bagnios on Market street little girls of 12 and 13 years of age have been placed, but owing to the almost perfect manner in which the traffic is covered up, it is almost impossible to secure a conviction.[21]

Shipping clerk T. H. Trailor experimented briefly that summer as a one-man procuring ring. The lumber yard at which Trailor worked was near the home of Lena Ceccarilli, age eighteen, of 1735 Wynkoop Street. Trailor often observed Lena and theorized that her dark, Italian good looks might have commercial value. Aware that she earned only fifty or seventy-five cents a day at the Union Cigar factory, he mailed an unsigned letter "in seductive words," according to a police account of the incident recorded by Sam Howe, describing a plan whereby she could easily make from twenty-five to fifty dollars a week with scant effort.

Ceccarilli would retain two-thirds of her earnings, and the letter writer would keep a third. In return, he guaranteed to conduct the business so that no suspicion would be cast on her name. He also guaranteed that all her patrons would be gentlemen, to whom

twenty-five to a hundred dollars was nothing. The letter writer stated that many young girls in Denver made their livings in a similar manner at his house, and all were "decent" girls on whom no cloud of suspicion had fallen.

It was a bold try, but Ceccarilli went immediately to the police. Trailor was charged with sending obscene literature through the mail for the purpose of "ruining young girls." He pleaded guilty and was locked up.[22]

Denver became a recruiting center for proprietors of out-of-town bordellos, run by men a bit craftier than Trailor. The brothels of Leadville during its post-1879 boom were infamous for their profusion and brashness, and their procurers competed with Denver's Market Street madams for the best new talent. When Michael Annacito was arrested in Denver in the company of young Mary Jenkins and Lucy Schroeder, the detectives found in his pocket a set of instructions from bordello keeper Ben Loeb, whose Leadville establishment at 126 State Street was described by a newspaper as "one of the most disgraceful of its kind in the state":

> Leadville, Colo., Dec. 11, 1895
> Mike Annacito, Denver:
>
> Worthy Friend—I received your dispatch and have answered the same. You want to be very careful what girls you select—some that have sense, that are good dancers and not bashful to sell drinks. Send them just the way you get them, one or two at a time. . . . Look out for good lookers and well dressers. Telegraph at any time for tickets and as soon as the girl is ready, bring her trunk to the depot where she gets her ticket. Hoping that you be successful, try and secure the address of a good man there, which can send me girls if I pay him a commission. I shall send you your commission if you come across some good lookers, that I don't want to come now, secure their addresses. Don't mention anything about advancing fare as some of them got money.[23]

The notorious brothels of Leadville, one of the great boomtowns of the West, were little discussed prior to the 1996 publication by the Colorado Historical Society and the University Press of Colorado of Don and Jean Griswold's massive 2,347-page, 1.3-

million-word *History of Leadville and Lake County, Colorado.* In its pages are the interesting stories of "ladies of the crimson cohorts" such as Mollie May—the most famed Leadville had to offer—plus "Festive Fanny" Benton, Ellen "Forty But Anything But Fair" Smith, Mollie Gorman, Sallie Purple, and the rest. Although a thorough discussion of Leadville's vices is beyond the scope of this study, the following can be reported.

Quickly and inevitably after the town's inception in 1878, Leadville became known for its bordellos and saloons. The better class of Anglo girls and their madams—Mollie May, Winnie Purdy, Sallie Purple, and Molly Price—mainly inhabited the finer houses along West Fifth Street, although there were ethnic cribs in the older part of town, too, known as French Row and Coon Row.

Leadville was in its infancy and perhaps not accustomed to such antics when the *Chronicle* reported the case of Julia Stanton, who first raised the question of whether sin could be excused by the payment of a fine. Stanton tested the willpower of a Leadville policeman as well:

> The trial of Miss Julia Stanton, the young woman arrested yesterday and who deposited her jewelry with the court for her reappearance this morning, is attracting unusual attention in the city court to-day. The testimony . . . tends to the conviction that the young prisoner is not in Leadville to win fortune either by taking in washing or making dresses for the toned. She was found in a house of ill-fame, without having paid the required license or fine of five dollars per month. Whether this is imposed by the City Council or how, does not clearly appear. Prostitution can no more be licensed than can pickpocketing or house breaking. Under the general law, prostitution is a crime, and cannot be licensed by any special legislation. It would appear from developments of the trial, that the city of Leadville has permitted this crime to be carried on within the city limits upon each guilty person paying in to the city treasurer five dollars per month. Of course the revenue from this source is very large.

The policeman found Miss Stanton "luxuriously reclining on a palatial couch at one of the many well-known fashionable houses of prostitution in the city," reported the *Evening Chronicle:*

> The room was gorgeously furnished, and the officer as he entered the presence of so much beauty, ease, and apparent wealth, paused, and, for a moment, seemed to hesitate. But there was the stern arm of duty, and he entered. Miss Stanton motioned him to a five-hundred-dollar rocking chair by the richly damask curtained window and then resumed her reading. The officer, still nervous, tried several times to say something. His embarrassment being noticed by the reclining beauty, she pleasantly inquired what he wished.
>
> "I came for your fine, madam."
>
> "For my what?"

Thereupon ensued a discussion between the officer and the "Jezebel" (as she was referred to by the *Chronicle*), he alleging that she was in a house of ill fame without paying what amounted to a license fee, and she responding: "How do you know the fame of this house is ill? What business have you coming here to insult a lady by such language?" She refused to pay, whereupon the stalwart officer "took the frail and heavily-jeweled beauty by the arm and by the strength of the law led her from her luxurious apartment to the portals and dismal cell of the Pine street tombs [jailhouse]. The frail Miss weakened on seeing the interior of the wretched place." The judge the next day, after listening to much testimony, found Miss Stanton guilty and fined her twenty-five dollars. She appealed to County Court, where she was acquitted by a jury.[24]

The powers for a purer Leadville put the town's brassy *demimonde* on notice that the war was yet to be staged. Within four days they had the mining camp's notorious madam, Winnie Purdy, before the bar of justice. The *Chronicle's* articulate and observant reporter again was present, and it was a sight to which not even rambunctious Leadville was accustomed:

> At two o'clock and thirty minutes this afternoon the case of Miss Winnie Purdy was called before Justice [J. B.] Stansell. The defendant, a comely woman of about thirty summers, sat at the elbow of her attorney, Judge A. W. Rucker, and at her left sat Miss Molly [spelled in some accounts as Mollie] May, modestly

dressed in black. Round about the court room sat sixteen girls ranging in age from perhaps seventeen to thirty-five. They looked quietly on the proceedings as they progressed. Taken as a whole, if these auditors and prisoners in the case were met in parlor or waiting room, not one man in a dozen would guess their calling. Neither their dress nor faces gave in evidence that they were women of the town, that they had fallen from the high pedestal of womanhood to the brothel. Their conduct was, if you please, lady-like. . . . The world readily recognizes these outcasts, but further than this recognition they seem to have no place.

A jury unfamiliar with Miss Purdy or the case could not be seated until seventy-five minutes had passed. Prosecutor L. R. Thomas—"a good talker," the *Chronicle* observed—told the jurors that if they found the charges substantiated, they must convict Purdy even though she was a woman. The jury must return a conviction, he stated, if it were proved that Purdy enticed young men to her house or tempted married men from their families to her brothel.

Defense attorney Rucker responded that the women would not appeal to the jury's sympathies. Assistant defense attorney J. M. Murphy added that the entire matter was persecution. At four o'clock the trial began.

Curiously, that was the end of the *Chronicle*'s coverage, and the paper did not present the scandalous testimony. Two days later the *Chronicle* gave a one-sentence report that the court had dismissed the charges, "and the girls are again jubilant."[25] The Leadville gendarmes persisted, but the girls were realizing that it was easier to cooperate with the lawmen, whose protection made their business activities run more smoothly. The following autumn Police Captain John Fraser proceeded to the Coliseum Theater on Chestnut Street and approached Alice Franklin, "heavily jeweled and in a state of delicious coquetry with her lover." Fraser said he had a warrant for her arrest for supposedly stealing a silk dress and cloak from Mollie May, and Alice responded, "All right, I'll go."[26]

A year later, in 1880, Leadville was no less boisterous, and the flashy girls of the town were still stealing from each other. When Mollie May purloined a $135 silk dress from Emma Little, the *Chronicle* reporter covering the event ended his article with a police report indicating that one-fifth of the robberies perpetrated in the city "are done at the notorious bagnios on Fifth street."

Early Sunday morning, September 26, 1880, showgirl Laura LeClair—or as the *Leadville Chronicle* described her, "one of the fair ones, who place themselves on exhibition for the few dollars they derive therefrom and the fawning adulation of degenerate humanity"—became irritated with Lillie Vane, a "box girl" who entertained men in the box seats above stage. As soon as Laura finished her clog dance—dressed in tights that enhanced her mobility—she bounded up the stairs muttering "damn you, I'll give you hell" and thumped Lillie over the head with a lead-loaded billy club. Leadville's railroad men joined the fray, and considerable blood was lost in the ensuing melee. Laura was apprehended and ordered to show why she should be allowed to carry a billy club and was required to put up bond guaranteeing her future good behavior. The *Chronicle* reported the whole hoorah the next day. LeClair (later Mrs. Charles Reynolds) moved on to become a showgirl in Denver and died there of heart disease at age thirty-eight on August 26, 1889.

Leadville's "French Row," consisting of a half-dozen or so small cubicles along State Street near the Grand Central Hotel, was increasingly attracting the attention of civic officials. In September 1880 a new immigration of French ladies arrived, and a *Chronicle* reporter (probably Orth Stein), accompanied by a friend who spoke "excellent Parisian French," went on a tour of French Row and reported his findings in the September 30 edition. Curiously, he found Leadville's French ladies to be decidedly the opposite of their counterparts in Denver, who were well-known as the sleaziest the profession had to offer (see Chapter 11).

The *Chronicle* reported that each house along French Row was occupied by only one woman, and each consisted of two tiny six-by-ten-foot rooms and an even tinier kitchen. Most of the women spoke no English. Defying Frenchwoman prostitution as it existed over the mountain range in Denver, Leadville's French ladies did not consume alcohol and seldom permitted clients to enter their houses carrying liquor. They detested profanity, they did crochet work when business was slack, and, said the *Chronicle* in a statement defying credulity, they were "disgusted with the degraded conduct of both men and women in Leadville." Stein and his interpreter first visited the house of Madame Margueritte, "a stately brunette of commanding appearance, with a plentiful growth of rich black hair done up in what is known as the turban style, beneath which she sported a mass of coquettish curls; large brown eyes, a well-shaped mouth, and a Grecian nose."

Margueritte's house was disguised from the outside as a cigar store, and within, the writer found it to be neat and tidy, with a lace curtain leading to the boudoir. Stein's companion interviewed the lady in French, during which she made these observations:

- With regard to Leadville: "Bad country for women; bad men; drunk all the time; Merican [*sic*] women just do same, dey shoot de man for nothing. Not much money. I go way again in a few days."
- On her previous workplaces: "Been in Montana and Utah. Dis [Leadville] de worst country for women. All whisky here and women good for nothing."
- End of interview: "Bon soir, Messieurs, I go see my child, two year old, whom I keep outside."

From there the duo proceeded next door to the place of

Empress Eugenie; a lavender negligee covered her well-rounded body. A jaunty snow-white hat and feather was carelessly tipped to one side of her head. A pair of keen quick coal-black eyes bespoke the devilment within and "gave away" the saucy temperament of the woman. A graceful Grecian nose and a puckered little mouth made up what would be termed regular and handsome features.

The interview, which seemed doomed from the outset, began:

How do you like Leadville? "I do not like it at all. This is a queer country. Woman in this country [Leadville] are not thought much of. You see where we come from the woman are more ladylike, are better behaved,

and consequently are more respected. But here the American woman drink too much bad whisky, and then they fight or do anything desperate. They will take a pistol and order a great big man out, and if he don't go, shoot him like a dog."

During the interview Eugenie, the reporters observed, "made use of rather an inelegant expression" for which she was scolded by Margueritte, "who seems to act as a sort of guardian over her fair sisters in crime."

"Don't you know these are newspaper men?" whispered Margueritte in French.

"I don't know it," replied the haughty Eugenie flippantly.

I don't know, and much more I don't care; beezness is beezness. I have sufficient of the Yankee in me to know that I didn't come to Leadville for fun. What impudence this man has. He is in my house, and he talks as though he paid the rent. I shall call a policeman. Now, Messieurs, as I told you before, beezness is beezness, and if you spend nothing please go away, so somebody else will come in and do a little beezness.

From there the newspapermen proceeded along with their investigative tour to the place of Miss Camille (tall, dark, but not handsome—not from France, from Belgium)—and visited Miss Martha (280 pounds and deaf). All despised Leadville and pledged to leave at the first opportunity.

The so-called Coon Row was not the subject of such a tour, possibly because of the dangers involved. The following December 22 the *Chronicle* told of a brouhaha along Coon Row, whose activities the reporter found less amusing than those on French Row. Under the headlines "Razors in De Air" and "An Awful Fight in An Awful Locality" was the crude report:

Coon Row was shaken from center to circumference last night. Coon Row, for the benefit of those who are not familiar with the lower stratums of Leadville, is a section of frame houses near the Grand Central Theatre and back of the notorious French Row, occupied by colored ladies whose virtue is ten shades blacker than their cuticle. These erring children of Africa are noted for their ugliness, big feet, and disposition to fight. . . . Last night, the biggest kind of row took place. Razors cleft the startled air, and some say the wool on the floor was three inches deep. Words fail to picture it in its awful awfulness, and at the end of the fray the only thing in the house with a whole nose was the teakettle. The ringleaders were four dusky *nymphs du pavé* named Ellen Smith, Georgia Cox, Lizzie Archer, and Lou Campbell. They are bold, bad women and care neither for God, man or the Police Court. They will look nice in the County Jail.

The next day all were in court, and each filed assault charges against the others. Eventually, all were convicted and fined.[27]

Across Independence Pass from Leadville was the much smaller (and much poorer) Aspen—much less rip-roaring and much less bawdy. There was, however, the matter of Mary Murphy who on March 2, 1897, overimbibed and decided, according to the *Aspen Weekly Times*, to disrobe and "exhibit herself on the streets as a living picture." Police Magistrate Sharp fined her five dollars and costs, of which she had neither, so she went to jail. There she told police that surely somebody in town owed her five dollars, but the officers found nobody. So she served her time, and the last she was seen, according to the paper, "Mary now is in her right mind, as well as in her ordinary wearing apparel, and is sorry that she looked upon the wine when it was red."[28]

A hundred miles or so distant, the brothels of Denver continued to search for new talent. The *Denver Times* told of the pathetic case that began with Mrs. F. C. Probasco of 1920 Lawrence Street, who

> got hard up for money. Knowing no place else to borrow, she went to Nellie White, keeper of a bagnio on Market street, and asked for a loan of $5. Nellie White was willing to advance the money, but demanded security. The sort of security troubled the woman, but finally Mrs. Probasco went away from the Market street house, back to 1920 Lawrence street. She soon returned, accompanied by a 16-year-old girl, Florence Loew. "Here she is," she said to the other woman. "Now give me the $5."

Florence ran away from the brothel within a week because, to quote the newspaper account, the existence there was "so utterly repugnant," and in that regard

the matter turned out happily. Police learned of the transaction, and Mrs. Probasco's husband, who appeared to be the architect of the scheme, was arrested. Florence had been a family friend of the Probascos.[29]

Denver physician George W. Cox commented on the character values of the Denver prostitutes with whom he was professionally acquainted during the 1880s:

> Generally speaking, the behavior of a "thorough-bred" prostitute is of the most vicious and disgusting character. Influenced by their associates and surroundings, they very soon lose all the native modesty they may have possessed, and acquire habits of indolence, filthiness, dishonesty, and intemperance. Smoking, chewing, dipping snuff, drinking, eating opium and fighting all seem to follow as natural consequences of their depraved manner of living. Almost without exception they are of a roving disposition—moving about from city to city, and from house to house in the same city—and part of their religion seems to be to cut on a board bill or to leave an unliquidated debt at the dress-maker's. This last named trait may be partly owing to the fact that they are always bankrupt.[30]

Not surprisingly, therefore, Cox also determined that Denver's prostitutes failed to achieve a full life expectancy. Dr. Cox's colleagues elsewhere reached the same conclusions. Dr. William Sanger of New York said earlier that four years was the maximum career span of a prostitute; in 1868 researcher James D. McCabe Jr. solemnly reminded women that "the wages of sin is death. Once entered upon a life of shame, however glittering it may be in the outset, her fate is certain—unless she anticipates her final doom by suicide. She cannot reform if she would." The next year researcher George Ellington wrote that the careers of 99 of 100 prostitutes followed a steady descent to death.[31]

Denver's Dr. Cox agreed with McCabe that it was difficult for such women to reform and placed their life span at eight to fifteen years after commencing their career. Historian Richard White, in *It's Your Misfortune and None of My Own*, asserted that "many" prostitutes managed to marry and even have children while working in the profession but that few succeeded as wives or mothers. It was possible but not probable for a working girl to change her name and reappear in another city as a young, respectable widow who could then marry and take up a normal nineteenth-century existence. Dr. Cox, however, offered an observation that no more striking examples of inborn goodness of heart or of the lasting effects of early training were ever witnessed than were found among fallen women. In that regard, he wrote, they only carried out that principle of extreme habit that was so characteristic of their lives.[32]

For the former prostitute known as "Josie Washburn," reformation was possible under the sympathetic eye and active help of the community. "Should the good people conclude that the time is ripe for the removal of the underworld," she wrote (p. 344),

and have decided to permit us to reform, a comprehensive view should be taken of our helplessness, and be well considered as there are several millions of us, and places must be provided and put in condition for the accommodation of such a vast number, when you think it is worth while to send us to a respectable place, instead of the jail, or treat us with kindness instead of brutality. The city, county, state, and nation must furnish schools, hospitals and homes, conducted under good management and moral influence, to which our girls may go, and from which they may graduate to respectability and ability to support themselves.[33]

When prostitutes endeavored to establish a measure of security through marriage, historian Patricia Limerick wrote, "they found their partners in an unpromising pool of saloon owners, pimps, and criminals, men who were often violent and who were neither inclined nor able to rescue their spouses from their rough lives."[34]

Physician Cox's address contains important insight into the interactions he observed between Denver's prostitutes and madams and their male hangers-on:

[The women] nearly always have a worthless, trifling, vagabond of a husband or "lover" to support, [rendering] it impossible for them to save anything out of their unholy earnings. [The women] are extremely jealous in their disposition, selfish in a very high degree, and superstitious beyond endurance. It

is nothing for one of them to spend an entire night at some chance game at cards to ascertain whether the object of her affection is true in his devotion to her. If the cards happen to speak in the young man's favor, the moments are eagerly counted till he comes, so anxious is she to lavish her blessing and caresses upon his devoted head. But if the cards happen to tell an adverse story, the remainder of the interim will be spent in tears and debauchery, and the innocent swain will receive such a tirade of contumely and abuse as is never witnessed outside the circles of lewdness. The wrangle continues till the adorer becomes exasperated; and then, in order to prove that his affection is of the truest and noblest type, he proceeds to mutilate the countenance, and demolish the bones of his frail companion till she looks and feels as if she had just emerged from an engagement with an Old Jerusalem battering-ram.

This evidence of faithfulness on his part is invariably conclusive and satisfactory; the girl hands over the few dollars she may have earned during his absence; and the grand finale is sure to culminate in one of three ways. The most frequent sequel to such scenes is for the girl, out of remorse for having caused her noble lover so much unhappiness, to take a dose of morphine and end her earthly existence. Next to this course, she would most likely devote the next two weeks to administering to his comfort in every possible way—pawning her jewelry or clothing, if necessary, in order that he should be well supplied with currency. And last of all, she might possibly conceive the idea of blowing his brains out; but this generally follows only when she finds out who his other girl is, and that her money had been used for his other girl's support or comfort.

This is a fair, and not overdrawn, picture of the life and habits of a typical, representative prostitute. The exceptions are the "tit bits" [young, new prostitutes] who are just entering upon their life of shame, and who are not conversant with the ways of the "thorough-bred," and a few of the older ones who cannot forget the principles they held and the precepts they were taught at a mother's knee.[35]

A "rich man" from northern Colorado asked a girl of Mattie Silks's named Dollie to marry him, but Dollie was not so inclined. Mattie's housekeeper Janie Green told Dollie, "Honey, you got a chance to grab a perma-nent man, you do it." Dollie took Janie's advice and every four or five years returned to Denver to visit with Janie.[36] Some in Denver's *demimonde* managed to balance marriage and a career with the full approval of a husband. Such was the case with newlywed Goldie Chiles, age seventeen and from a prominent north Denver family. Goldie was married to I. V. Chiles, who made a small salary driving a laundry wagon. When Goldie wanted new clothes there was no money, so I. V. told her to go out and earn it. She hit the streets and several weeks later was arrested, soliciting in front of the Albany Hotel at Seventeenth and Stout Streets. Her fine of $60 would be suspended if she ceased her activities "and stayed away from other men." I. V. was also charged with encouraging his wife into a life of shame and was fined $160.[37]

Just as sinister was the case of Robert Goodman who "went wrong" and forced his wife into business as a boarder at 2061 Market Street while he lived from her earnings, even though his family was very successful in the meatpacking business. Robert was slain by his wife's brother, George Cohen, who had little to lose in vindicating his sister's honor because he was dying of tuberculosis (and did indeed die only a month into a twelve-to- eighteen-month sentence for voluntary manslaughter). Two years later Robert's younger brother, Ima, was arrested as a procurer.[38]

Laura Allman was an orphan who journeyed to Denver at age seventeen and found work in the Over-land cotton mills along what became West Evans Av-enue. Fred Arnold, a laborer at the nearby brickyard, wooed and won her, but she soon discovered he was a no-account who expected her to support him at what-ever moral cost. They moved to a room at 2438 Walnut Street, where they were reduced to poverty. "Some-thing had to be done to keep us from starving," she later sobbed to Police Chief Hamilton Armstrong, so Fred forced her to eke out what the *Rocky Mountain News* called "a miserable existence at 2111 Market Street, one of the lowest cribs on the row."

"Between her sobs" to Chief Armstrong, the news-paper said, "she then related her life to date; how she loathed and despised it and how she would have com-mitted suicide time and again but for the hope that

she would soon leave it." Unlike some of her sisters in shame, Laura's salvation arrived quickly. Fred and two of his drinking pals were arrested for murder, and she was placed in the care of the police matron "until arrangements to rescue her from a life of shame [could] be made."[39]

The possibility of marriage was not wholly alien to the denizens of Denver's bagnios. In fact, one work-ing woman, Jennie DeFres, pleaded with officers to allow her to wed while in jail as a suspected illegal alien. She was taken from a Market Street house and incarcerated with her boyfriend/procurer, Gordon Parham (or Parlian). "I want to marry Gordon," she told the jailer, "if they will allow a ceremony to be performed in jail. He has the license in his pocket and I know he loves me. I don't want to go back to Ger-many."[40] Jennie's real name was discovered to be Nellie Sikkema, most recently from Rawlins, Wyoming. Parham was arrested by federal authorities for white slavery; the outcome was not recorded by Detective Sam Howe.[41]

Catherine Lajoanio alleged in a divorce suit that she followed a life of shame for eight years and in the process saved $10,000 to buy a home on Denver's swank Capitol Hill, where she "expected to live in peace the remainder of her days." She charged that her hus-band, Joseph, whom she referred to as "the white slave owner" and who she said had not earned a cent the whole time she was working, deeded the property away just as she was retiring from the business. She prevailed in the divorce and regained the house. The 1909 *Den-ver City Directory* lists a Joseph LaJoanio residence at 1933 Market Street—the middle of the bagnio district.[42]

Even the churches and clergy, lamented Dr. Cox, would turn away the prostitute attempting to extri-cate herself from her profession, and any attempts at reform would be viewed as futile by her former friends. Dr. Cox preached this fiery condemnation:

> It can be truly said of them as a class that they are of few days and full of trouble. Their average longevity has been variously estimated at from eight to fifteen years after they have become properly installed in their new mode of living . . . considering the great number of accidents to which they are exposed, their irregu-lar habits, their liability to disease and their tendency

to self-destruction. There are few of these women who abandon their evil ways and return to the paths of virtue. When a woman has once yielded up her virtue, and it becomes known to her old associates, she is at once and forever abandoned by them, and it is impossible for her ever to work her way back into their confidence and respect again. No matter how circumspect her after conduct may be, her name will be a by-word, and her one mistake a target for the poisoned arrows that are sent forth by the prejudices of the human heart. Then again, her progress in the downward direction is so rapid that she soon loses all her self-respect and much of her desire to be anything but that which she already is.

And even when she has finally determined upon reform, the obstacles in her way are so numerous and so grave that it requires a character of giant strength to carry out her designs. If she seeks for honorable employment where her history is known, her petitions are invariably spurned or ignored; and if she goes among strangers and asks for servitude of the most menial character, she is expected to furnish references that would entitle her to a place in society.

When one of these unfortunate women does reform, from what source does she receive encouragement to do so? There is not a church door in the land but that would close at her approach; not a minister of the gospel who would dare to publicly appeal to the throne of grace in her behalf, and not a sainted sister but who would imitate the example of the priest. There are no Samaritans in our day to stretch forth the hand of assistance. . . . A doting mother will defend her profligate son against the demands of justice with her very life itself, and at the same time heap maledictions upon the head of a young and innocent girl who has fallen a victim to his villainy.[43]

Whether "fallen women" could indeed be rehabilitated—and Cox suggests that even the church would turn its back on them—was a concern in Denver even before Cox began analyzing the dilemma of rescuing prostitutes. In 1874 the *Denver Times* pondered:

It has long been a serious subject in the minds of the philanthropist how women may be rescued who have fallen into a course of life which ostracizes them from society. Every one bewails their fate and the state of society which renders their reformation practically

so nearly impossible. All admit that things ought to be different, but when asked to put their shoulders to the wheel they shrug their shoulders and say it is impractible [*sic*].

Making kind or pitying remarks will not do it; prayer without works will not do it. The present stand taken by the city government in enforcing the law regarding these and kindred vices will have the tendency to cause suffering among those who though not sinless are human, and perhaps more sinned against than sinning. There are many women of this class in Denver who doubtless could be made useful in and to society, could the proper course be pursued and influences brought to bear.

Many of these women are yet young, and are not bad at heart. Circumstances in their lives have led them to this life of folly, and which they bitterly rue, but can find no door of escape.

The *Times* continued by saying that although the prostitutes of Denver's Row

held up [the city] in public disgrace, the keepers of the houses [would] turn them into the streets moneyless and friendless. They would gladly adopt a different mode of life, but where can they go? What man dares take them into his family with his wife and children, and if he dares, where is the woman who would not feel that the touch of their skirts was contamination in her own home, and yet some of these women have been tenderly reared by loving parents and loathe their present mode of life, but how can they escape the deadly tolls and snares which are about them. They can be reclaimed by proper effort, but it is no way to commence by calling them great nuisances, telling them they ought to go to hell.

The *Times* concluded that the problem should be addressed but offered no solutions.[44]

Rachel Wild Peterson, the late-nineteenth-century Denver social worker and street-corner missionary, visited a Market Street brothel and in her autobiography wrote her observations:

Telling of one house we went into, where there were five girls and the madam, we had taken our seats in the parlor, the girls being up and dressed. They generally

Fred Mazzulla, an early researcher into Denver prostitution, identified this photograph as taken at Mamie Darling's brothel at 1959 Market Street, date unknown. As was customary nationally, most women of organized Denver prostitution dressed in white smocks called brothel gowns. Darling, who never became a principal Denver madam, is probably the woman in the dark dress, and the man seated on the floor beside her would have been the piano player, the bouncer/bodyguard, or a pimp.

get up at 1 o'clock in the afternoon. . . . [During a] homey chat we had with the girls, [we discussed] the cause of their downfall, and . . . our talk brought back to them their young lives, with dear old mother around the fireplace in the old homestead. Some of their mothers had gone on to receive their reward. One by one [they] in tears told their stories, and how they had drifted into the life of death. . . . As I went on telling them of dear Mollie Hill [a Denver prostitute who had died] and others, I could see one by one reach for their handkerchiefs until I do not believe there was a dry eye in the house.[45]

Women in the fancier parlor houses often slept until 2 P.M., then shouted downstairs to the housekeeper ("usually an old dyke," as Nell Kimball recalled) for coffee. At Kimball's establishments the *demimondaines* were expected to be washed, with their hair done up and clean robes, for the principal meal at 4 P.M. At 9 P.M. the piano player began to play, and business would be fully under way by midnight. By 2 A.M. came the peak of client turnover, Kimball recalled in her memoirs (pp. 5–8), "and the girls would sort of slide downstairs again, their faces refreshed and their hair combed." By 3 A.M., Kimball wrote, the

> all-night tricks were tucked away, and on the third floor there might be a show going on—naked or in frilly underwear . . . two or three of the girls doing a dance, just enough to set up the clients who could join in as a group or a solo. Unless a special guest asked for a little voodoo, I hardly went in for group orgies.

The working girls of Denver's Market Street died young but not without experience. And there seemed nowhere to turn. Even though the city directories in the 1880s and later contain listings of a few social agencies that might have consoled the remorseful prostitute or prevented her from falling in the first place, no accounts discovered describe the effectiveness of these agencies.

Secretary E. K. Whitehead of the Colorado Bureau of Child and Animal Protection suggested that one way to deal with the initial temptation toward prostitution would be to close the dance halls:

> We are told by the wayward girls who fall into our hands that one of the most common causes of their getting into mischief are the dancing halls of the cheaper and lower class. Young toughs go there for the express purpose of meeting girls, getting acquainted with them and following up the acquaintance in any way in which they are able. In my opinion these dancing places are the first cause of most of the young girls going wrong. I know many young girls who got their start in sporting that way. I know a considerable number from 14 to 17 years old who live in first one and then the other of the disreputable blocks around town. Some of them have gone to dance halls in the mountains. I know girls who frequent the first-named place from 9 years old up. Another especially dangerous influence on innocent but foolish girls is association with older girls who are already bad.[46]

Physician George Cox of Denver subscribed to Whitehead's assessment of the city's dance halls:

> I would abolish dancing—or at least that part of it which has been so happily described as "hugging set to music." It is without doubt the most senseless, vulgar, harmful and indecent practice that is tolerated by refined society. Without stopping to analyze, I would simply ask any fair minded person to step into a ballroom for five minutes and watch the hideous contortions that are going through within the new "Society."[47]

Instead of dancing, Cox suggested that young people be guided toward literary pursuits, musical societies, and reading clubs.

Social agencies to which the prostitutes of Denver could turn for help were so scant that even Police Chief Austin Hogle could not arrive at a recommendation. The *Denver Times* wrote in September 1886 that Hogle found it

> surprising how many girls of tender age seek a life of shame in the city. Within a few weeks he [Hogle] has been called upon to search for about half-a-dozen, not over thirteen years of age, who had left comfortable homes, and had gone to houses of infamy or had been led astray by libertines and had been hidden away by them. One of these children had been hunted down and restored to her parents three times, and had become so absolutely depraved, that she boasted of it in disgusting terms. The worst of it is that there is no institution to which such children can be committed.

Two days later the editor of the *Times* received a letter from a reader advising that the chief must have overlooked one sanctuary for the girl gone astray. The Home of the Good Shepherd, the reader wrote, "presided over by the good sisters in South Denver is just the place of which you say we stand in need. This home provides for wayward women and girls, and helps them back into the right path. It also cares for children of wayward, worthless parents."[48]

The Home of the Good Shepherd was an offshoot of Denver's growing conscience about its bordello women. "There are in Denver," observed the *Rocky Mountain News* when the home was announced, "large numbers of that peculiar class of unfortunates known as fallen women. How these shall be cared for is a vexed question in every community." The newspaper continued:

> Society has one way of dealing with them, which is to ignore them entirely as too degraded for the hand of

sympathy and help to aid them. . . . There have been from time to time [in Denver] suggestions made by the Ladies' Relief society, the Humane society, the Woman's Christian temperance union [*sic*] and other charitable and benevolent organizations as to what should be done to check the social evil and reform the poor creatures who are so fast going to destruction in the great city. But the movement has been found to be a little outside the recognized sphere of any of these societies and none of them have the money or influence necessary to successfully carry it forward.

Thus it was announced that the Right Reverend Joseph P. Machebeuf, Roman Catholic bishop of Denver, had assumed responsibility for the salvation of Denver's women of joy and that the Sisters of the Good Shepherd would establish a sanctuary "especially designed as a house of refuge for fallen women and which shall have connected with it a school of preservation for young girls of from 8 to 15 years who are children of vicious and dissipated parents, or who have been abandoned by their parents." The Sisters of the Good Shepherd, a St. Louis, Missouri, order, obtained 5 acres near West Ellsworth Avenue and Elati Street for the facility.[49]

The Home of the Good Shepherd struggled on a limited basis until it achieved some success as a children's shelter, but that was not until the early 1910s. The Florence Crittenton Home, originally with links to the Women's Christian Temperance Union, was a refuge for mistreated waifs around the turn of the twentieth century and later became a well-known facility for unwed mothers. Churches appear to have not had active programs to rescue young girls from prostitution, and psychiatry and psychology were barely known and crudely practiced in Denver. A Sam Howe 1887 scrapbook refers to a "House of Refuge" for abandoned infants.[50] In Denver the Humane Society existed for the "aid of animals and children" and sometimes helped in cases of abject child abuse, but not until the 1890s.

Recalcitrant juveniles, especially females, were a constant concern. The *Denver Times* wrote in 1886:

[Police Chief Austin W.] Hogle says he proposes to ask the coming state legislature to make an appropriation for the erection and maintenance of an insti-

tution of a reformatory character in which to place girls of a tender age arrested for crime [or] rescued from houses of infamy. The institution, he says, should be conducted similar to the one at Golden [the state reform school] to which the girls should be sentenced for a term of years and there receive good moral training and taught methods of earning an honest livelihood. He also proposes to submit to the legislature a proposition in the shape of a stringent law with severe penalties attached, for the benefit of human wretches who inveigle young girls into places of infamy. He says that his discoveries in this respect, since he has been chief of police, have been shocking in the extreme, and that the men and women engaged in the horrible traffic go unpunished for the need of adequate laws. He says that in nearly every instance wherein young girls have been reported by their parents to have left their homes mysteriously, it has been discovered, after investigation, that such has been at the instigation of men and women who, holding up before their victims' mental vision pictures of a free, careless and luxurious life abandoned women are supposed to enjoy, overcome the girls' scruples and lead them into dens of iniquity and lives of degradation and misery.[51]

By 1895 the State Home for Incorrigible Girls was operational, with Sadie Likens as its superintendent.

Brothel keepers seldom expressed concern over the ages of their "boarders." The *Rocky Mountain News* in July 1894 reported under the headlines "Ruined for Life: Wrecked Homes and Heartbroken Parents/Sequels to a Night in the Notorious Resorts/Which Chief Armstrong Is Trying to Uproot":

In the notoriously low dive run by Jim Meskew near Manhattan Beach [an amusement park near present Sloan Lake] on Sunday night were three young girls who did not look to be over 14 or 15 years of age. They wore short dresses and that flippant air which implies incorrigibleness. Yesterday they told their story to the chief of police. As a result he caused the arrest of Lulu Livingstone on the charge of being a procuress of Mme. Duval of 1808 Champa street, [and] on the charge of running an assignation house and of Wayne Hogben on the charge of seduction. The first named enticed one of the small girls from her home to the rooms of Mme. Duval where she was forced to lead a life of shame.[52]

Sociologist Ruth Rosen in *The Lost Sisterhood* observed, however, that most teenage girls or young women entered prostitution "more or less willingly":

[They] viewed the trade as an "easier" and more lucrative means of survival than the other kinds of jobs open to them. Although in general sexual and economic exploitation may be considered the preconditions of prostitution, a complicated web of particular economic, social, and family difficulties led individual working-class women to choose prostitution as a survival strategy. . . . Although some reformers called prostitutes the "lost sisterhood," the women did not in fact accept this view of themselves. They were not "lost" within their own communities, where they played an integral and highly visible role in shaping the character of many urban neighborhoods. Nor did prostitutes generally view themselves as morally "lost," as pathological or fallen victims of sinister forces. Their life was grim and frequently degrading, but prostitutes were actors in history who understood that they made choices, even when those choices were severely constrained by painful social relations, demoralizing economic circumstances, and limited alternatives. . . . All too often, a woman had to choose from an array of dehumanizing alternatives: to sell her body in a loveless marriage contracted solely for economic protection, to sell her body for starvation wages as an unskilled worker, or to sell her body as a "sporting woman." Whatever the choice, some form of prostitution was likely to be involved.[53]

In the matter of Lulu Livingstone and her teenage boarders, Police Chief Hamilton Armstrong may have been grandstanding when he took a reporter to Jim Meskew's place near Manhattan Beach, as Sam Howe kept no record that Chief Armstrong did more than bring about the arrest of Lulu. On occasion, however, even the tolerance of a permissive police department and court system was tested to the limits, and they were forced to do something. One of those occasions came when madam Fourchette was arrested three times in one week with teenage girls in her bordello. The *Denver Times* covered a hearing into the matter, wherein the frustrated judge decided that what had

been Denver's problem should be passed along to some other town, and reported:

Again she was fined $100 and costs for keeping a house of prostitution. This time the fine was suspended upon the promise that she would dispose of her furniture and leave the city inside of forty-eight hours. Four of her girls were also fined $10 and costs, but the fine [was] suspended on the promise that they would immediately leave the house and not return to it. This afternoon B. R. Imhoff, who is the alleged power behind the throne at this house of prostitution, was arrested on a charge of being an inmate. [The 1891 *Denver City Directory* lists a Benjamin R. Imhof, watchmaker, residence 1921 Lawrence Street.]

Some very damaging charges are made against him by the three little girls who were found in the house, and he will be given the extreme penalty of the law when his case comes to trial. President [Egbert] Johnson of the police commissioners said to-day: "We have determined to rid the city of houses of this character if it takes every police officer and detective on the force to do so. Numerous complaints have come to us of girls of 14 years of age and under being found in houses of ill-fame on Market Street, and crimes which are entirely too revolting to be mentioned being committed daily."[54]

Police Commissioner Johnson's indignant and boisterous pledges were as hollow as those of his police chief, and after this little brouhaha conditions along Market proceeded on their merry way. Under the headline "Swarming with Harpies" the *Rocky Mountain News* reported:

George Green, a railway man living in Colorado City, was robbed of $175 last Monday night in a saloon at Twenty-first and Market streets. Green, it is said, stepped into the saloon on the suggestion of one of his friends, when a woman threw her arms around his neck and took all his cash. At least a dozen robberies of similar nature, all committed by women, have been reported to the detectives within the past two weeks. Detectives Burlew and McIlduff arrested Gladys Raymond of 1955 Market street last night. The prisoner is known as "Queen Bess" and came to this city about two months ago from St. Paul, Minn.[55]

Denver police historian Eugene Frank Rider wrote:

> It was alleged that the police, obviously under orders from the Fire and Police Board, were used to intimidate brewers, saloonkeepers, gamblers and the denizens of Market Street to contribute money and votes to the success of the Democratic ticket. In return, saloons were allowed to remain open all night and some on Sundays, public gambling was sanctioned, and ladies of scarce virtue were permitted to extend their operations gradually over the central part of the city. Carriages were even sent through Market Street where they collected "disreputable women" and carried them to the polls.[56]

Politics indeed. The *Denver Republican* on December 12, 1897, documented Fire and Police Commissioner Robert W. Speer's laissez-faire attitude toward prostitution: "It can hardly be expected that the Fire and Police Board of Denver can do in a short time what other boards and governments have failed in. As far as I am concerned, I do not approve of a change in policy [regarding prostitution.]"

Rider wrote that Denver exhibited "a display of vice not to be seen in any other city in the country" and that some of the brothels flaunted suggestive signs and names. The "brazen women" were permitted to keep doors and windows open day and night, and they also "could appear half-clad on the sidewalks and were allowed to call out to pedestrians."[57]

The *Denver Post* on July 10, 1901, reported that in return for immunity, the gambling dens, saloons, and brothels made payoffs to the Democratic Party campaign chest. The *Post*'s rival, the *Times*, agreed in an unusual burst of harmony between Denver's warring newspapers. On March 28, 1901, the *Times* proclaimed:

THE POLICE FARCE
Criminals Rule the City
No Arrests Will Be Made Because Every
Lawbreaker Jailed Means One Vote Less
For the Democratic Party

The story characterized Hamilton Armstrong as "an inefficient political chief" [scheming] to "keep the public in ignorance of the true state of affairs in Denver." The *Times* story was prompted by an incident involving a "colored man" who followed a nine-year-old girl down the sidewalk (and that appears to have been the end of it), plus an incident in which a "feeble-minded man" was "horribly beaten" by a policeman, and the fact that no police report was made in either instance.

Despite such opposition, Armstrong is regarded as having brought many innovations and much-needed discipline to the Denver Police Department. On occasion he would change into civilian clothing and travel the streets to observe his men. A favorite story was his encounter with a Patrolman Gibbons, who after only three days on the force was paying his respects at Big Emma's establishment on Market Street. Upon departing with a bottle, Patrolman Gibbons encountered Chief Armstrong, who delivered the most humiliating and final retribution to which a police officer could be subjected: Armstrong brought out a pocket knife and cut Gibbons's copper buttons from his blue uniform. Gibbons was finished.[58]

Patrolman Thomas Robinson suffered a certain ignominy on December 10, 1894. He got drunk on his way to work and for no apparent reason arrested Alderman Thomas E. McNulty and three innocent women merely because they were in his way, whereupon he kicked in a saloon door while looking for more whiskey. He, too, was stripped of his buttons—while en route to the drunk tank.[59]

In August 1895 Patrolmen Louis Lipschitz and A. C. Watson, described as "walking arsenals," were arrested for assault after they "unmercifully," according to the *Rocky Mountain News*, clubbed a pedestrian, Frank Simmons, about the head when he was on his way to seek work extricating victims from the Gumry Hotel explosion. Simmons apparently failed to obey Lipschitz's order not to proceed down an alley. Witnesses told police commanders that the "exhibition was by no means a credit to the policemen."[60]

Occasionally, problems of a more serious nature arose. Although the incident was not flattering to the police force, Detective Sam Howe preserved notice of a grand jury report of October 14, 1890, accusing Detective Chief William H. Loar and Detectives William Crocker, G. F. Watrous, W. H. Ingersoll, and C. E. Clark of false imprisonment, assault to kill, assault and battery, blackmailing prostitutes, and "complicity

A brothel-gown-clad demimondaine *of the Denver Row solicits from the doorway of 2130 Market Street in 1905 as another girl leans against the windowsill. Three men* at left *proceed on their way. Few photographs exist of Denver's brothel district; this old glass negative discloses a dirt street and litter. The fanciest of Denver's parlor houses were in the next blocks to the right, out of this view.*

with criminals." The jury described the police detective bureau as the "most vicious, corrupt administration which ever cursed Denver" and accused police of "threats to murder, backed by drawn pistols, by knocking the victim down and each detective taking his turn at kicking him while down, by striking him over the head and face with pistols, clubs and billys until he was senseless." The jury concluded that "said depart-

ment utterly lacks system, efficiency, integrity, and any degree of devotion to the public welfare."[61]

Much of the criticism fell on Loar, an adversary of Detective Howe. This conflict may have prompted Howe to put the grand jury's account in his scrapbook. Howe was Loar's assistant, but Howe a few days earlier had audibly addressed Loar as a "pinhead" (or "block-head"; see the quotation below). *The Road,* a

Denver business journal, reported such a conflict in its May 31, 1890, edition.

> Chief Loar and Detective Howe had a grand round up in the presence of Chief Farley, Wednesday last. Mr. Howe failed to confine himself to the language used by "our very best society" in paying his compliments to Loar, and intimated that he [would] as soon be found dead in a nigger's den as to be found walking on the street with such a block-head as Loar, and there will be razzers [razors] flying in the air.

This may be the only incident of gross insubordination during Howe's forty-eight-year record as a lawman.

The matter was indeed serious. Ten days after the grand jury report, District Attorney Isaac N. Stevens charged Loar with aiding accused murderers James Cummings, Hugh Johnson, Frank Edwards, and Charles Johnson in a successful escape from the county jail. Detectives Watrous and Crocker were convicted of extortion and assault, and Detective Chief Loar resigned.[62] Watrous was fined seventy dollars and returned to service; Crocker was fined forty-five dollars and sentenced to a day in jail.[63]

It became inevitable that recurring periods of corruption and aloofness would eventually overtake the Denver Police Department. A situation developed that reverberated to the highest echelons of city hall. The scandal was nurtured by the quarter-century-long practice of shaking down vice establishments for protection money. This was the beginning of it.

The name of Detective T. E. McIlduff is frequently encountered in a study of vice in early Denver. McIlduff was a nephew of President Robert W. Speer of the Fire and Police Board, later a three-term Denver mayor and a dedicated ally of the city's gamblers, madams, and liquor interests. They were expected to help out when the city needed money and when Speer needed a friend.

The police with considerable fanfare conducted periodic raids of the vice dens to lend an appearance of upholding civic morality. Perhaps the most flamboyant such cleansing took place on the afternoon of May 3, 1889. Market Street from Eighteenth to Twenty-third Streets was the scene of great excitement as thirty lawmen in two large covered coaches each pulled by six white horses raided the bordellos armed with 110 warrants for "Mary Doe," each alleging the keeping of a bawdy house and of a disorderly house to the encouragement of drinking and fornication.

Many of the girls, still drunk from the night before, scurried from room to room in an attempt to escape, and one even hung a "for rent" sign on her door and hid in her trunk. Newspaper accounts said Market Street and the side streets were thronged with "the rough, the tough, the vags [vagrants], the tin-horn gamblers, the Chinese, negroes and whites, all mixed together" to observe the spectacle.

The entire third floor of the Arapahoe County Court House at Sixteenth Street and Court Place was required for a temporary jail. The women—many of them French—babbled nonstop, others laughed and cried and shouted and danced. All wanted beer and cigarettes. The *Denver Republican* wrote the next day:

> There was every style of dress. Some were richly clad and others were almost in rags. Coarse and vulgar in appearance and talk, they formed a disgusting instance of the depth to which women can sink in vice and crime. "Woman" is too sacred a term to apply to them. Their painted faces, disheveled hair, coarse talk, jeerings and ribaldry made a sad and striking scene.

Reinforcing the legacy of the "whore with a heart of gold," each woman who had a cot for the night offered to give it up for "Little Annie," a compatriot who was very ill. We do not know her fate.

The menu consisted of sandwiches with coffee or water, which immensely displeased the ladies. Then, as if on cue, the best delicacies from the fine restaurants of Denver began to arrive by deliveryman at the courthouse doors. Silver urns held delicious teas and coffees with sugar and real cream; included were the juiciest tenderloin steaks, asparagus, and delicate and costly desserts. Wicker baskets held apples, oranges, and other fruits. One can only hypothesize whether such delicacies were sent by benevolent and sympathetic patrons.[64]

At the turn of the twentieth century, Denver's Fire and Police Board was still firmly under state control as a result of the City Hall War several years earlier.

Although the terms of Governors Charles S. Thomas (1899–1901) and James Orman (1901–1903) featured two comparatively able police chiefs, John Farley and Hamilton Armstrong, the police department remained dominated by political machinery because the governors did not insist otherwise. Especially under Governor Thomas's administration, Denver remained what the press declared a "wide open city" with few restraints against gambling, saloons, prostitution, and con artists. In a long-prevailing atmosphere of corruption and crime, Chiefs Farley and Armstrong sometimes were powerless to act for the public good.

Against this background, in November 1899 Sam Howe, who had been acting chief of detectives since 1897, requested to be relieved of that job and became a staff detective once again. And at this time a vigilante committee was formed—not to string up bad men to cottonwood trees on the banks of Cherry Creek, as had been done forty years before, but rather to hand the criminals over to the police.[65]

By 1901 gambling was flourishing virtually unchecked in Denver, and that February an incident at "Three-Finger Jim" Marshall's gaming parlor at 1861 Larimer Street outraged the public and led to renewed indignation. Marshall (perhaps the same Jim Marshall who supposedly expedited the removal of Bat Masterson from Denver) had a reputation for being particularly mean, and that may have prompted the Larimer Street landlord to seek Marshall's removal from the gambling property. A six-man private posse was retained to accomplish the eviction. Predictably, gunfire ensued, and one of the posse members was shot and seriously wounded.

The shooting was less regrettable than the permissiveness of city hall in allowing Denver to breed such problems, or such was the opinion of the *Denver Republican*. Under the headline "Human Life Will Be the Cost of Open Gambling," the newspaper editorialized that the shooting at Three-Finger Jim's was the direct responsibility of the Fire and Police Board, Robert W. Speer, president. The *Republican*'s scolding went unheeded. Bob Speer's friendship with the vice lords of Denver was just beginning.[66]

Forces, meantime, were at work that culminated in what would be called the Denver Police Scandal of 1901.

During late spring of 1900, Hamilton Armstrong, serving as detective captain, arrested Mollie Kenney, Ruth Stanton, "Klondyke [*sic*] Liz," Effie Ellsler, and their pimps, Frank Moore, Clint Clewell, George Clayton, and "Kid" Burns—all proficient at robbing drunks and bordello customers.

Kid Burns was a dope addict and associate of the by-then-deceased Cort Thomson, Mattie Silks's husband. Ruth Stanton and Effie Ellsler were two of the *demimonde*'s best-dressed habitués; Stanton, during a court appearance on March 6, 1900, wore an ostrich-feather hat as big as a parasol and an abundance of rouge and other facial decorations. They were acquitted of stealing ten dollars from clients when it was disclosed that the men had enjoyed "many a Larimer Street cocktail."

After the arrests, Captain Armstrong proposed that the eight offenders be run out of town. In the course of the investigation, however, Detective T. E. McIlduff (who, it will be remembered, was a nephew of Fire and Police Commissioner Robert W. Speer) alleged that Sergeant Michael Mahoney, Patrolmen S. B. Engle and John Slack, and Detectives G. W. Sanders and Edward Carberry routinely kept half the loot of the thieves they caught and were shaking down gamblers and prostitutes (which had been standard procedure for years). Moreover, it was learned and reported in the newspapers that Police Captain Arthur Martyn supposedly was a partner in two gambling establishments "and also got money from the divekeepers on Market street" and that the remainder of the police department was mired in corruption.

A large and noisy investigation ensued, with Police Chief John Farley and his top commanders maintaining they had heard rumors of graft but were unable to pin down any wrongdoing. A gambling house bookkeeper testified that Captain Martyn received 10 percent of the establishment's earnings in exchange for protection and that Martyn shot at a bordello girl when she refused to give him $100 of the $150 she had stolen from a customer. Such stories were reported continually during the course of the investigation. Martyn denied everything, but street talk held that most of his "take" was passed along to city hall "to be used for political purposes."

Not surprisingly, Commissioner Speer's Fire and Police Board dismissed most of the charges as "minor irregularities" born of jealousies and bickering within the police department and brought no charges. District Attorney Henry A. Lindsley, however, pronounced the whitewash "unsatisfactory." He added that if justice were to be accomplished, Detectives Carberry and Sanders would be declared innocent, McIlduff—who finally blew the whistle on his Uncle Robert Speer's corruption—nonetheless would be guilty of shielding fellow officers, Engle and Mahoney would be guilty of extortion, and Captain Martyn would be guilty of running a protection racket.

Two months later Chief Farley resigned, as did Speer's Fire and Police Board. As if to thumb their noses at the district attorney, their final act of business was to fire Detectives Carberry and Sanders, whom the district attorney had proclaimed innocent.[67]

John Farley, however, is regarded as one of the more honest and level-headed of Denver's nineteenth-century police chiefs, and much can be learned of his career through a privately printed book—a copy of which is in the Colorado Historical Society library—prepared by his descendants. Farley's presence was particularly welcomed because it followed the term of Henry Brady, inarguably the most corrupt police chief who ran the most corrupt police department in Denver's history. Citizens and business owners alike embraced Farley and contributed to the purchase of the fancy gold chief's badge he treasured for the remainder of his life. (Brady, it must be acknowledged, also received a fancy going-away badge.)

Farley, however, did not enjoy trouble-free tours of duty. In *Recollections of a New York Chief of Police, and Historic Supplement of the Denver Police*, writer A. Kaufmann addressed Chief Farley's budgetary restraints:

The city of Denver is fortunate in the possession, at present, of a Chief of Police who is essentially a gentleman, as well as a man of excellent judgment and of vast experience as a detective officer. It must be a source of regret that Mr. Farley's usefulness has been greatly handicapped by conditions that ought not to exist in that class of cities among which Denver ranks. The fault-finders and grumblers, who are as numerous here as elsewhere, are encouraged in their favorite pastime by the false and mistaken notions of economy that prevail. . . . The department must be sustained and supported with all the moral and financial aid of which this community is capable.[68]

Absent from the accounts of the police scandal was the name of Sam Howe who, except for a skirmish or two with a judge, appears to have managed his career with great propriety. In March 1893, however, Howe made a misstep that caused momentary embarrassment to both himself and the police department.

As has been discussed, Denver lawmen from the earliest days supplemented their salaries by accepting fees and rewards for the arrests they made. In the early 1890s the Fire and Police Board drafted a policy whereby all rewards thus collected were to be turned over to a widows and orphans fund. Private detective services, such as the famous Pinkerton agency, however, would be permitted to keep such rewards.

Against that backdrop, an unusual controversy enveloped Sam Howe. On March 18, 1893, city detective Edwin D. Currier arrested one J. E. B. Mordaunt, a suspected embezzler who had fled from Chicago to Denver. Mordaunt was taken to police headquarters, but before he could be jailed a Pinkerton detective showed up and indignantly protested that city police had arrested a man whom the agency had been hired to find and whom agents had been following.

Sam Howe, then detective chief, released Mordaunt to the Pinkertons, who immediately returned the suspect to Chicago. Word immediately was out on the street that the Pinkertons had split a reward with Howe, and the *Denver Times* fanned the fire by suggesting it had been "common talk for years" in the police department that Howe "was not there for his salary alone."

Howe was called up before the Fire and Police Board, an action the press noted "was such as to almost take the breath of the chief [Howe] away." The press noted, however, that Howe, "in addition to being a good thief catcher, is as smooth as oil in other respects."

The next day Superintendent James McParland of the Denver Pinkerton office did much to defuse the situation by issuing a statement to the newspapers that the Pinkerton agency and its employees had a

"ARE YOU WID US OR AGIN US?"

POLICE CORRUPTION

CORRUPT BALLOT

PROTECTED CRIME

The police department shakeups of 1901, prompted by allegations that the department was in cahoots with organized vice and gambling, were fueled by cartoons such as this from the March 28 Denver Times, depicting "Police Corruption" strolling hand-in-hand with "Corrupt Ballot" and "Protected Crime." The police department had been essentially crooked for so long that reforms could not be instant. It would be another dozen years before corruption, organized prostitution, and protected gambling would be effectively restrained.

policy of not accepting rewards. What took place behind the closed doors of Sam Howe's hearing before the Fire and Police Board was not reported by the press, but Howe was soon demoted from detective chief to detective. He never discussed the reasons, and neither did the newspapers. Nonetheless, Howe enjoyed another twenty-seven years with the Denver police and was again promoted to detective chief in 1897—the same year the police established a rule that all rewards received were to be placed in a fund to pay for extraditions.[69]

In the wake of payoffs, corruption, and improper rewards, the old standbys—gambling and prostitution—continued to thrive up and down Market Street, although now and again it was suggested that prostitution should be outlawed. But those of good judgment knew such an attempt would be folly. Even George W. Cox, the feminist-leaning Denver physician who was the first of his profession to survey Denver's prostitution climate, attested that outlawing

commercial sex would not succeed, and he heaped guilt on his fellow males:

The reason [prostitution cannot be legally prohibited] is plain. Laws are made by men; made in the interests of men; made so as to protect men and punish women for the sins of men; and so in the enforcement of such one-sided rules we offer a premium on our own guilt without a corresponding recompense for any good that may abide in the female. . . . We can not eradicate it; and past experience gives us such small encouragement that we even hesitate to hint at means to modify it. The passage of certain laws would, if properly enforced, be of some service. For instance, I think a law making the land-lady of a house of ill fame responsible for every theft or other outrage committed under her roof, would have a tendency to check this particular class of their many vices. License none who could not give bonds for the fulfillment of this clause. Do not impose an outrageous tax upon them; do not revive the almost forgotten custom of weekly examinations, and do not fine or imprison a woman simply because she is a prostitute. This is inhuman; and a manly dignity should condemn the practice to eternal oblivion. Wait till she does something one-half as mean as the man did when he seduced her. In short, let all laws be tempered with simple justice; and let them be executed in the name of equity and humanity.[70]

Notes

1. Sanger is quoted in Gilfoyle, *City of Eros*, pp. 60–61. Gilfoyle focuses on the motives of women entering prostitution in nineteenth-century New York City; many of his conclusions apply to locales elsewhere. For Denver's Home for Working Girls, see the RMN, July 6, 1898.

2. Gilfoyle, *City of Eros*, p. 345.

3. Ruth Rosen and Sue Davidson, *The Maimie Papers* (Old Westbury, N.Y.: Feminist Press, 1977), pp. xiv ff.

4. Dr. Cox's paper is unusual if only because it approaches the subjects of male prostitution, masturbation, and perversion—topics so taboo they were largely avoided by early behavioral researchers. He describes male prostitutes as "specimens so peculiar, so unique, and withal so degraded in their lives and conduct [that they] are intimately associated with the social evil in general." The doctor characterizes masturbation as "another form of prostitution . . . a filthy and harmful habit . . . generally confined to young boys and men of rather a weak mind." Under perversions he describes a man, married and a father, an upstanding business leader, whose "peculiarities are absolutely unrivaled." Once a week the man would visit a brothel, where he would employ two or three of the heaviest women in the house, require them to disrobe, and instruct the women to walk over him, digging the sharp heels of their boots into his flesh. At times one woman would stand on one heel on his chest, and the other woman would spin her around. During two or three hours of such activity, he would order a "dozen or more" bottles of wine for himself and his tormentors. Completed, he would dress, pay his bill, and return to "the marts of trade, only to return and repeat the strange entertainment in about one week" (quotes on p. 67).

5. George W. Cox, M.D., "The Social Evil," address delivered to the twelfth annual convention of the Colorado State Medical Society, Pueblo, Colorado, June 1882. A transcript was published in *Transactions of the Colorado State Medical Society at Its Twelfth Annual Convention* (Denver: Edwin Price, June 1882), pp. 67–68. Copy in the periodicals department of the Stephen H. Hart Library, Colorado Historical Society, Denver.

6. The Senate hearings were held in Chicago during mid-March 1913. This testimony is from SHS 32, number not assigned but quoting a telegraph report in the DR, March 13, 1913.

7. Butler, *Daughters of Joy, Sisters of Misery*, pp. 1–2, 15–16, 89.

8. RD, pp. 160–161.

9. Parkhill, "Scarlet Sister Mattie," p. 6. The story is repeated, probably with embellishment, in Perkin, *The First Hundred Years*, pp. 372–373. The RMN story and its marvelous headline are in the April 6, 1882, edition.

10. RMN, April 9, 1882. In Denver at the same time as Oscar Wilde was Charles "Doc" Baggs, one of the greatest confidence men ever to visit the city. One of Wilde's favorite sayings was "too, too divine," which prompted the *News* to observe:

> If thou dost boast of being too, we will
> Produce Charles Baggs, M.D., who is as too
> As thou art, and a durned sight tooer.

See DeArment, *Knights of the Green Cloth*, p. 353.

11. Gilfoyle, *City of Eros*, pp. 68–69.

12. RMN, April 28, 1898.

13. Gilfoyle, *City of Eros*, p. 63.

14. Miller, *Holladay Street*, pp. 58–59.

15. Bell, *Fighting the Traffic in Young Girls*, pp. 121–122.

16. DP, July 16, 1909.

17. For "Nell Kimball," see *Nell Kimball: Her Life as an American Madam*, p. 5. Kimball's summer vacations were spent in Colorado with other madams from New Orleans. She wrote on p. 205: "We'd meet and dine and talk shop in Denver at the old Windsor [Hotel]—all mirrors and ormolu and fine plush, like any high class cat house, or we'd hire a fancy rig and go down to Louie Dupuy's Hotel de Paris in Georgetown, the Teller House in Central City, Haw Tabor's Vendome in Leadville. The food was good, and I was gambling." For the recruiting opportunities at Denver's divorce courts, see Miller, *Holladay Street*, pp. 172–176.

18. Barnhart, *The Fair but Frail*, p. 68. Some young women might not have been so naive as to find themselves in the predicament described here. The fake marriage phenomenon and similar scams employed in luring prospective young prostitutes are examined at length in Bell, *Fighting the Traffic in Young Girls*; see, for instance, pp. 50–51 and 126: "Let every mother teach her daughter that the man who proposes an elopement, a runaway marriage, is not to be trusted for an instant, and puts himself under suspicion of being that most loathsome of all things in human form—a white slave trader! . . . The mother who has allowed her girl to go to the big city and work should find out what kind of life that girl is living and find out from some other source than the girl herself. . . . Do

not trust any man who pretends to take an interest in your girl if that interest involves her leaving her own roof. Keep her with you. She is far safer in the country than in the big city."

19. Gilfoyle, *City of Eros*, p. 60.

20. Rosen, *The Lost Sisterhood*, p. 58.

21. From SHS 14: 9034.

22. Ibid., 15: 9177, newspaper and date unspecified.

23. Ibid., 15: 11344, newspaper and date unspecified.

24. *Leadville Evening Chronicle*, July 14, 1879. The material covered by notes 26–29 is from editions of the *Chronicle* as cited and recorded in Don and Jean Griswold, *History of Leadville and Lake County, Colorado* (Denver: Colorado Historical Society and University Press of Colorado, 1996).

25. July 18 and 20, 1879.

26. September 15, 1879. This edition of the *Leadville Chronicle* reported under the headline "Riot at Mollie May's" that two men entered and tore up the place and that Miss May was "knocked down and kicked all around the room. She was very much battered and bruised." As seen elsewhere, such a "brothel riot" occasionally took place in the bordellos of New York, but this is the only similar incident discovered during this study to have taken place in Colorado. Brothel riots made it necessary for pimps to be on the premises of many bordellos to provide protection.

27. September 30, December 22 and 23, 1880. For Laura LeClair, see the Mazzulla Collection, box 48A, ex–Amon Carter Museum Collection, now at the Colorado Historical Society, Denver.

28. The *Aspen Weekly Times*, March 6, 1897. Available Aspen city directories and Colorado business directories fail to disclose the first name of Magistrate Sharp.

29. SHS 16: 13023, from the DTI, October 20, 1896.

30. Cox, "The Social Evil," p. 68. With regard to Dr. Cox's observation that Denver's prostitutes ran out on a dressmaker's bill, it is known that many madams paid for their girls' wardrobes, docking the girls' earnings until the bill was settled, if ever. The madams used the debt to keep the girls in line and, they hoped, from quitting. In her memoirs, Nell Kimball, however, wrote on p. 5 that "I paid the girls one-third of what they earned and never held back, and I didn't shark them with interest on loans I made them, or get them on drugs or have them [wooed] by fancy men like some houses did. I never cottoned to the sweet daddies that attached themselves to a girl's earn-

ings and lived off her twat. There is nothing lower in life than a pimp, unless it's some politicians I've known."

31. Gilfoyle, *City of Eros*, p. 156.

32. Cox, "The Social Evil," pp. 69–70; Richard White, *It's Your Misfortune and None of My Own: A History of the American West* (Norman: University of Oklahoma Press, 1991), pp. 304–307.

33. Washburn, *The Underworld Sewer*, pp. 336–371.

34. Limerick, *The Legacy of Conquest*, pp. 49–50. This overlooks the possibility that in any town there might have been at least a few decent, marriageable men. Also see Petrik, *No Step Backward*, pp. 33, 49. Joan S. Reiter in *The Women* wrote that the typical late-nineteenth-century prostitute in Kansas was in her late teens and rarely worked past her early twenties. Some fell victim to the hazards of their trade: venereal disease, a crude abortion, too much to drink, an overdose of laudanum, or an assault by a jealous man (pp. 141–142).

35. Cox, "The Social Evil," p. 69.

36. Parkhill, "Scarlet Sister Mattie," p. 12.

37. SHS 27: 48811, from the DTI, February 14, 1908.

38. Ibid., 27: 51951, from the RMN, December 9, 1908.

39. RMN, February 2, 1904.

40. SHS 31: 63830, from the RMN, April 26, 1912.

41. Ibid., 31: 63844, from the DR, April 28, 1912.

42. Ibid., 29: 57637, from the DP, April 30, 1910.

43. Cox, "The Social Evil," pp. 70–71.

44. DT, August 15, 1874.

45. Peterson, *The Long-Lost Rachel Wild*, pp. 213–214.

46. SHS 22: 31223, from the RMN, May 7, 1903.

47. Cox, "The Social Evil," p. 79.

48. DTI (daily), September 4 and 6, 1886. The Home of the Good Shepherd was active in rescuing fallen women in Denver, but the facility may not have enjoyed a high profile. Also see discussion of the Denver Cottage Home in Chapter 5.

49. RMN, August 14, 1883.

50. SHS 7: 2212, originating newspaper unspecified. Christopher B. Gerboth (ed.), in *Address Unknown: The Face of Homelessness* (Denver: Colorado Endowment for the Humanities, 1995), mentions several agencies (pp. 15–17) active in social programs in the late nineteenth and early twentieth centuries. The Cottage Home (1886) cared for unwed mothers and placed unwanted children; the Day Nursery (1888) was a Center Christian Temperance Union facility and provided day-care services; the Ladies Relief Society began in 1874. The Denver Orphans Home was in

operation by 1881 and became the best-known such relief organization. Add to the list at various times the Byers Home, Catholic Orphanages, and the Colorado Christian Home. Others were the Newsboys and Bootblacks Home and the Working Boys Home and School (both 1882), the Denver Jewish Sheltering Home (1907), and the tax-supported State Home for Dependent and Neglected Children (1895). Others, such as the Brightside Industrial School for Boys, the Foundlings Home, the Children's Home of Cripple Creek, and the Fries Orphanage of Pueblo, were poorly administered and sometimes attracted scandal.

51. Ibid., 5: 990, from the DTI (daily), November 4, 1886.

52. SHS 15: 9160, from the RMN, July 17, 1894.

53. Rosen, *The Lost Sisterhood*, pp. xiv, xvii.

54. SHS 12: 5549, from the DTI, May 1, 1891. Egbert Johnson had been a trapper, prospector, and surveyor near Georgetown, moving to the Denver vicinity in about 1870. He was a cattle raiser, mining speculator, and in 1895 was appointed a land appraiser for the state. He died at his Denver home on July 12, 1897. See Mort Stern, "In Search of Major Anderson" in *mem-ber-a-bil-ia* (Georgetown, Colo.: Historic Georgetown, August 1997).

55. Ibid., 19: 20064, from the RMN, January 10, 1900.

56. RD, p. 486.

57. Ibid., p. 517. More regarding the blatant advertising practiced by Denver's crib girls can be found in Chapter 9.

58. Hanna, "The Art of American Policing, 1900–1930," pp. 68–69.

59. SHS 15: 9849, no newspaper cited.

60. In the August 23, 1895, edition.

61. SHS 12: 4617, from the RMN, October 15, 1890.

62. Ibid., 12: clippings 4653 and 4658, the latter from the DR, November 1, 1890; the former undetermined.

63. Ibid., 12: 4770, newspaper undetermined.

64. DR, May 4, 1889. This account includes reference to intoxicated prostitutes. In her reminiscences (p. 5) Nell Kimball had this observation about intoxicated employees: "A drunk is no good as a whore. You can't hide her breath, and she doesn't do her work in style."

65. RD, pp. 479–480. For Sam Howe, see RD, p. 490, quoting the RMN, November 23, 1899. For particulars regarding the political influences exerted on Denver police through this period, consult the RD, pp. 478–484.

66. SHS 20: 23353, from the DR, February 14, 1901. For a favorable Speer biography, see Johnson, *Denver's Mayor Speer*.

67. The Police Scandal of 1901 was amply covered by Denver's daily press. Consulted here were the SHS 19: 20926, from the DP, April 21, 1900, and 21221, from the DTI, May 26, 1900. See also the DP, DR, and RMN, February 8–15, 1901, and the RMN, February 20, April 10, 1901. The RD, pp. 475 ff., contains many particulars of the police department's difficulties during this turbulent period. For a sketch of Ruth Stanton and her ostrich-feather hat in court, see the DP, March 6, 1900.

68. See pp. 637–639.

69. DTI, March 20–21, 1893.

70. Cox, "The Social Evil," pp. 73, 79–80. Dr. Cox's earlier counterpart, prostitution researcher Dr. William Sanger of New York, said as early as 1859 that it was a mere absurdity to assert that prostitution can ever be eradicated.

Mattie Silks.

9

Mattie Silks and Jennie Rogers: Queens of the Denver Row

Jennie Rogers.

IEWING WITH restrained amusement the corrupt Denver city administration and its directionless police department were the nationally notorious Colorado madams Mattie Silks and Jennie Rogers. Each was a savvy business-person, wisely and dutifully submitting her protection payments to the police and thus avoiding bothersome questions and unnecessary inconveniences. Scandal in Mattie's or Jennie's place was infrequent, and the reputation of each for attentive customer service was widespread. A good madam exercised total discretion in handling both police and clients. Even the girls often did not know their patrons' names.

Mattie's and Jennie's ladies were of the highest class within the profession between St. Louis and San Francisco. In Jennie's houses, historian Caroline Bancroft suggested (pp. 7–8), each room had an enamel or brass bed, a dresser, commode, slop jar, rocking chair, straight-back chair, rug, lamp, and lace curtains; some even had a writing desk. Mattie's and Jennie's employees had the prettiest faces, the tiniest waists, the creamiest bosoms, the daintiest giggles, the best conversational skills, the most imaginative techniques, the perkiest personalities (their sparkling eyes resulting from the use of belladonna and its dilation of the pupils), and the best acting abilities (leading the customer to believe she really cared). As important, none is ever recorded to have stolen from a client.

Mattie and Jennie called their places "young ladies' boardinghouses." This was an apt description, since the girls were required to pay for their room and board, ranging upward from five dollars a week, and were further obliged to split 50 percent of their earnings with the house. The boarders were required to dress fairly attractively and could be encouraged to charge clothing to the madams' accounts at the local stores. This threatened to keep the girls constantly in debt, affording the madam another means of control. Kickbacks from dressmakers to the madams were common.

Aside from the madams and property owners, nobody realized significant earnings from the Denver bagnios. The better-class parlor houses employed a male piano player (usually called "the Professor") who played for a small wage plus tips and drinks. In 1911, when the city government ordered closure of Market Street's smaller brothels, newspapers reported that "during the next few days more than 150 pianos will be hauled away" (doubtless a considerable exaggeration). "It has been estimated that there were $50,000 worth of pianos alone in the Denver cribs. These will be thrown on the market."[1]

The madam paid all expenses of running the house, hiring domestics, bouncers, the piano player, and a kitchen staff in the fancier places; making payoffs to the police; and obtaining the required liquor and gambling licensing. The better accouterments applied only to the nicely appointed parlor houses, not to the despicable filthy cribs a few doors up Market Street.[2]

Unfortunately, no Denver bordello proprietor or prostitute of the late nineteenth century left a diary. In St. Louis, however, a person identified as madam Nell Kimball did write an account of her business experiences. In the morning, she wrote,

I always had plenty to do, getting the police and the city hall cut of the night's take put in envelopes, inspecting the laundry with the housekeeper, [paying] the cleaning bills, replacing busted chairs, lamps, linens. The house in the morning was still a bit strong. Body powder, Lysol, dead cigars, the woman smell of it always heavy; sweat, scent, piss, body powder, arm-

pits, medical douche, and spilled likker [sic]. After awhile to me a house wasn't a good house unless it had that musk smell in the morning. Lacey Belle, the cooks, and me would drink our coffee in the kitchen, all the girls sleeping, and I'd read the paper and see who was at the good hotels and make bets with Lacey as to who would show up that night going down the line.[3]

A successful madam, especially one who managed a classy sporting house, had to be both charming and a capable, ruthless businessperson. The madam set the tone for her house, and the tone determined the quality of her customers. She had to be adept at public relations and be the epitome of discretion. To recruit and retain a staff that was volatile by nature, she had to be at once tough and motherly.

The madam also faced occasional legal difficulties. Despite the gratuities distributed regularly to the policeman on the beat, his captain, or city hall, a pesky justice system—such as it was—occasionally required attention. If an outright charge of prostitution was not brought, the girls could be run in for drunkenness (drinking with clients was part of the job, although Nell Kimball proclaimed a drunk girl could not do her job properly) if they wandered outside their workplace or especially if they went beyond the boundaries of their appointed district. They might be arrested for disturbing the peace, for swearing in public, for vagrancy, indecent exposure, or public fighting. These sorts of entanglements, however, generally afflicted the crib girls in their rookeries rather than the silk and satined young ladies of the mirrored sporting houses.

In its management of organized and controlled prostitution, Denver took a somewhat different approach from other large communities. In St. Paul, Minnesota, for instance, each madam was required to appear at the police court each month. There she was arrested, charged, convicted, fined, and released to return to her brothel, only to repeat the process the next month. Such hypocrisy was tantamount to licensing.[4]

In Denver as elsewhere, the denizens of the parlor houses had to be of the highest class, beautiful, and, ideally, of some cultural or educational accomplishment:

A visit to a perfectly managed parlor house was much like a visit to a private home, and the prostitutes in

One of the finer establishments of the Denver Row was Belle Birnard's place at 518 Holladay Street, which became 1952 Market Street following the street redesignations in the late nineteenth century. The photograph was taken in about 1885. Note the young lady at the window. The 1892 Denver Red Book brothel guide carried Birnard's advertisement for "12 Boarders, 14 rooms, 5 parlors, Music and Dance Halls, Strictly First-Class in Every Respect. Choice Wines, Liquors and Cigars. Strangers Cordially Welcomed."

residence resembled, in decorum and dress, the daughters of the house. Some [asserted] that the only difference was that the prostitute was more attractive, more intelligent, and more accomplished than the young society lady.[5]

The guest was conducted into the velveted parlor by the madam, and he might encounter business acquaintances chatting with attractive women. Following a glass of brandy, the patron was invited to a fine room for activities of his pleasure. The madam collected the fee in advance, which was considered better manners than having the girl do it. The madam of a sophisticated house infrequently or never practiced prostitution herself, as that would put her in direct competition with her boarding girls.[6] There is no direct evidence such as an arrest record or even a newspaper account that Mattie Silks or Jennie Rogers was a prostitute.

None of these rules of propriety and good manners applied to the seamier houses or cribs, where there was no madam, the girl accepted her own payment, and the quantity of customers took precedence over the quality of service. In 1913 onetime newspaper reporter Forbes Parkhill recalled the Market Street cribs of twenty-five years earlier:

[They were] just wide enough for a door and a single window. Each contained two rooms; a parlor and a boudoir. At that time they rented for from $15 to $25 a week, payable daily. In the white section the cribs were known as "dollar houses," but in the "black belt" beyond Twenty-first [on Market] they were "two-bit houses." Prices in the parlor houses ranged from $5 up. No matter how many partook, a round of beer, served in containers only slightly larger than a shot glass, was always $1. At this time a nickel would buy a schooner of beer on Larimer street so large it almost took two hands to lift it.

In the old days [probably the 1880s and 1890s] the crib girls, wearing low-neck, knee-length dresses and black silk stockings, were permitted to stand in the doorways to solicit business. Sometimes they would snatch hats to induce customers to enter. At one period they used placards that finally became so crude that an ordinance was passed to regulate their wording. A card that complied with this ordinance was passed and the city censors [approved], "Men taken

in and done for." Successive reform waves compelled the girls to abandon open soliciting. Curtains were required on the windows, but nothing in the law prohibited the accidental punching of peep holes in the curtains. A typical night scene would reveal throngs of males strolling along the sidewalks, stooping at each window to peer through the peep hole. There was none of this peeping at the parlor houses, which were conducted with dignity and restraint.[7]

Such were the lowly cribs of Denver. The well-appointed parlor house, however, according to author Joan Swallow Reiter, was generally

fussy Victorian, unrestrained by any semblance of good taste, lavishly adorned outside [generally not the case in Denver], inside overflowing with a preponderance of bad design—mirrored walls and ceilings that reflected rich woodwork, grand pianos, and Louis XIV furniture with ottomans for the girls. The finest rooms in the houses were the downstairs reception rooms where the girls gathered to meet their callers. Some of the houses featured banquet rooms which doubled as dining rooms for the girls during off hours, along with kitchens, wine cellars in the basements, and of course a multitude of bedrooms on the second floor. The boarders' rooms were fitted with iron or brass beds, dressers, commodes and slop jars, the girl's private trunk, and sometimes dolls, holy pictures, and photographs. . . .

[The bordellos were] where a man's comfort was of prime importance, where he could remove his coat and relax among women who offered a kind of entertainment not to be found at the opera house. It was these women to whom men turned for less constrained diversions.[8]

In Colorado, one of Laura Evens's girls, LaVerne, offered insight into the etiquette and manners expected of a lady in one of the proper houses on Market Street. Probably dating to the twentieth century, it is the only statement discovered during this study—other than a deathbed interview with Mattie Silks—attributed to a Market Street woman:

Miss Laura never wanted us girls to talk loud, and we were always taught to watch our language. We parlor house girls never used four-letter words. Miss Laura would tell us never to come in the parlor with a gingham dress on—that's what a man sees all day at home. . . . Under our evening clothes, we first-class girls always wore panties and a bra. This was because—after we were inside our room with a man—if the girl took off her dress and had nothing under it, the shock would probably kill him. I don't mean it might *really* kill him, but it might be too much for him all at once.

We'd take our evening gowns right off soon as we could. We didn't want them to get messed up or torn or anything, for sometimes a man, first of all, would try to start taking off our gowns himself, and we'd have to beat him to it, for he really didn't know the right way to take off a gown usually, and the more excited he'd get whenever he tried, the clumsier he'd get. There was no telling what might happen to our dresses if we didn't take them off by ourselves as soon as we could.

We girls took our own panties off, too, for they might get torn if a man took them off. Most men usually got a kick out of seeing us girls take our panties off. That is, unless the man was too busy taking his own pants off. . . . And it had this advantage, besides—the more steamed up and excited the man got while watching us take our panties off, that would usually save us girls from just that much more work later.[9]

In 1951 Laura Evens told researcher Fred Mazzulla that she became a prostitute in Leadville in about 1894 and was told that the mayor, Samuel D. Nicholson, would be up to see her and that she should be on her guard. Indeed he showed up and during the evening "proceeded to bite a piece out of her thigh about the size of a quarter." Subsequently, she was arrested for an unstated offense, and as the policeman was escorting her and another woman to jail, the mayor approached. He recognized Laura and asked the policeman what the problem was. Mazzulla wrote: "Laura said that she reached down and felt the inside of her thigh and said: 'I think I hurt myself here a little bit.' The Mayor complimented the officer on his efficiency, and took the girls off of his hands." Then he whispered to her, "Get going and don't get into a mess like this again. I'll come up and see you soon and teach you a few things." He never returned.[10]

With the Professor at the keyboard and customers in a reflective mood with cigar, brandy, and pleasant (albeit commercial) companionship cuddling nearby, the favorite parlor house songs were usually sad—reminiscent of mother and father and faraway family homes and happier times and goodbyes. "Silver Threads Among the Gold" was an example, as were "On the Banks of the Wabash," "Good-by, My Lady Love," "In Zanzibar," "Down on the Farm," "Lady Lou," "Call Me Back Again," "Just a Dream of You, Dear," and "The Longest Way Around Is the Sweetest Way Home." Mattie Silks always said a lonely out-of-town businessman or a homesick hardscrabble miner would spend more money if surrounded by tenderness and memories. Her favorite song was "Humoresque."[11]

Mattie Silks of Denver—the name reverberated like the ring of fine crystal wherever womenless men congregated. Jennie Rogers was Mattie's friend, colleague, and competitor. Rogers was classier than Silks, but Jennie's name was not as catchy as Mattie's, and Jennie had not been in Denver as long. Thus she was less famous. Together, however, Silks and Rogers were among the acclaimed love merchants of the frontier West.

Chubby and curly-locked, Mattie Silks was an enduring businessperson in an era when few women embarked on any sort of business venture. She was successful in an enterprise other women frowned on outwardly but looked upon privately with some curiosity: Mattie Silks was a bordello madam and a good one—famous throughout the West. Plus, she never apologized for it.

There were flesh merchants, and then there were *accomplished* flesh merchants, such as Mattie and Jennie. They might have prospered in legitimate entrepreneurships. The successful madam had many responsibilities. Sociologist Ruth Rosen writes in *The Lost Sisterhood*:

> Running a house with four to twelve inmates required skillful management. In a sense, the madam managed a small business; she checked on the servants who prepared meals for the inmates and herself, made sure that sheets in all rooms were changed several times during an evening, maintained an adequate supply of fine wines and liquors, and oversaw repairs. In addition, the madam interviewed, hired, and fired servants,

Authors Max Miller and Fred and Jo Mazzulla reported in their book Holladay Street *that this is an 1866 photograph of Casey Silks, first husband of Mattie Silks. Copied from* Holladay Street; *an original print of this photo has not been located.*

book to make revisions and, for reasons unexplained, burned it. His notes remained, however, and in the 1970s the writings were loosely consulted by Fowler's son Will and by attorney/historian Fred Mazzulla to prepare a film script titled *Madam Silks.* The movie idea never went anywhere, possibly because it was highly fictionalized.[13]

Forbes Parkhill became the principal biographer of Mattie Silks. Parkhill was a Denver native and a police reporter for the *Post* in 1913; thus he observed the final years of the Market Street Row, and he knew Silks toward the conclusion of her career. Parkhill subsequently worked for the *Rocky Mountain News* and for newspapers in New York City; he wrote fiction and nonfiction and then became a screenwriter for Paramount Pictures. Historians today place credibility on Parkhill's accounts of Mattie Silks because they were contemporaries.

For the two manuscripts he prepared regarding Mattie Silks (note 7, this chapter) Parkhill talked to policemen on the Market Street beat, to businesspeople who knew her, and to Janie Green, who in late 1912 was a cook and maid for Mattie Silks and who survived to relate her memories, although some of Green's recollections may have been mistaken. Parkhill also consulted documents at the Colorado Historical Society and the Denver Public Library. The result is the most complete data

maids, musicians, and prostitutes who worked in her house. Since local patrons always demanded "new faces," a good businesswoman always sought new prostitutes.[12]

Gene Fowler once wrote a full-length book on Mattie Silks's life, submitted it to his publisher, and was accepted. A few days later Fowler withdrew the

available on the life and career of Mattie Silks, but many questions remain that may never be answered. Nonetheless, if Parkhill had not done his work—which has been generously borrowed upon and dressed up by later writers—we would know little about Mattie Silks.

Mattie Silks is thought to have been born in Terre Haute or Gary, Indiana, 1846 to 1848, and to have run away from home at age thirteen. Her given name is not recorded, but on certain documents pertaining to her, including her death certificate, the first name "Martha" was used. An envelope found under the flooring of one of her Market Street houses was addressed to "Miss Maté Weinman," but she is not known to have ever used such a name. Mattie claimed she never communicated with her family, whose members may have been unaware of her career. The death certificate asserts that the names of her father and mother are "unknown."

At age nineteen in Springfield, Illinois, she became proprietor of her first "sporting house." Mattie Silks always asserted that she had never been a prostitute, and she bragged that she was unique in that she entered the ranks of management without ever having served as a "boarder."

Leaving Springfield, Mattie worked briefly as a freighter on the wagon trains traveling between St. Joseph, Missouri, and Colorado. This experience rendered her fond of horses for the rest of her life; indeed, Mattie Silks owned racing steeds that ran at Denver's Overland Park, and she had a horse and stock ranch 18 miles northeast of Wray, Colorado.

Janie Green recalled that Mattie told her of recruiting three girls from Abilene, Kansas, and one from Dodge City, and heading west, with Mattie's new employees working in a tent along the way. The fivesome stopped briefly in Denver at the Elephant Corral where they behaved with the "utmost decorum" before progressing into the mountains—still with the tent as their traveling bordello and including the first portable canvas bathtub to enter the mining camps. Jamestown, northwest of Boulder, was their initial stop.[14]

Holladay Street author Max Miller prepared an undated article titled "A Salute to the Frontier Ma-

dames of Colorado," which was found in 1995 in Mazzulla's papers at the Colorado Historical Society. Quoting "Fred Mazzulla and his tape recordings with oldtimers," Miller says Mattie referred to her mountain tent as a "first-class boardinghouse for young ladies" and that she always preferred to establish her tent brothels below a camp "because prospective patrons would more willingly walk down a mountainside than climb it."[15]

Next, Mattie proceeded to Georgetown, where she may have married a Casey Silks or a George W. Silks. Historians generally have accepted the notion that railroader Casey Silks became her husband, but a professional gambler named George Silks is said to have arrived in Georgetown shortly before Mattie in 1875 and to have departed for Denver just after Mattie did, in the spring of 1877. Mattie Silks's name can be found today on county records.[16]

The marriage to Casey Silks or George Silks, if it occurred, did not survive, but it was the source of the surname she carried for the rest of her life. Writer Caroline Bancroft in *Six Racy Madams* (p. 37) quotes Janie Green, who was interviewed four decades later, as recalling that Mattie had a child by one of the Silkses. The intriguing notion persists that Mattie Silks had a natural daughter, stepdaughter, or adopted daughter, and this will be discussed at length later.

At some point following Mattie's brief relationship with Casey or George, she met a handsome, swaggering young athlete-gambler-raconteur from Texas named Corteze "Cort" D. Thomson. Thought to have been born on March 15, 1847, in Huntsville, Alabama, Cort said he served in the Civil War with Quantrill's Raiders and briefly emigrated to California as a gambler before coming to Colorado. With an affinity for foot-racing competitions, popular among volunteer fire departments of the day, Thomson was a sprinter for the Silver Queen volunteer fire laddies of Georgetown, on which large sums of money were bet during competition with squads from other towns. Cort took up with Mattie, and together they relocated to Denver.

When he met Mattie Silks, Thomson was married and the father of an infant, possibly a girl. The presence of this child, if she existed—and repeated evidence suggests she did—became an important although shrouded factor in the life of Mattie Silks. Cort and Mattie embarked upon a lifelong relationship from which Mattie could not or did not extricate herself and Cort would not because Mattie supported his degenerate habits. On at least two occasions Cort beat Mattie unmercifully, but he was her man.[17]

Friends described Mattie as short, with curly blonde to light brown hair, attractive with a tilted nose and protruding ears, "well-upholstered and an accomplished hell-raiser." Cort was as diminutive as Mattie and was a snappy dresser, uncommonly good-looking, mustachioed, and lithe. He was a likable fellow when sober and carried a small handgun in each hip pocket. Mattie as well often carried an ivory-handled pistol and fancied herself a good shot, which she was not. Thomson's athletic specialty was the 60-yard dash, at which he was invincible, but he also was known to have "thrown" foot races.

Cort and Mattie arrived in Denver probably in early 1877. We know she was in Denver by March 1877, because on the 28th of that month the *Rocky Mountain News* reported that "Madame Silks was fined $12 for drunkenness, and paid it like a little woman. She ought to play it finer when she gets on a spree." It is hasty to assume that the French usage *madame* signified that Silks was a brothel madam at the time (although she probably was); Denver's newspapers often preceded women's names with the title *madame*. The non-French spelling *madam* was more often applied to entrepreneurs of the *demimonde*.

The skirmish with the law over a matter of inebriation appears not to have deterred Silks from her carefree ways. The following August 24 (1877), Mattie was involved in an altercation with rival madam Katie Fulton in a cottonwood grove called Denver Park, also called Denver Gardens, also called Olympic Gardens, on the west side of the South Platte near the junction with Cherry Creek. This fairly routine confrontation has, over the years, escalated into the most famous woman-against-woman battle in Colorado history—more famous for what it was not than for what it was.

Denver Park was just beyond the city limits and had become what the *Rocky Mountain News* termed "a resort for fast men and for fast women," a place the

police found it impractical to patrol. Earlier on Friday, August 24, Cort Thomson had defeated the noted Sam Doherty in a 125-yard dash, winning at least $2,000 bet on him by Mattie Silks. The victory called for a celebration that evening at the park. At least a half-dozen revelers were present, including Mattie, Cort, Katie, and Katie's man, Sam Thatcher. In the course of the evening Mattie and Katie got into a tiff, whereupon Cort stepped in and slugged Katie in the face, knocking her down. Sam tried to intercede but was knocked to the ground. Katie was knocked down a second time and kicked in the face, breaking her nose. Then Cort was knocked down, whereupon he dropped a pistol he had drawn. The pistol disappeared, and the fight broke up.

Cort (and presumably Mattie) returned to his buggy and started for town when another buggy pulled alongside (presumably carrying Katie and Sam). A shot was fired; Cort was hit, incurring a minor neck wound; and that was the end of it, except for the myths that developed around the incident.

The *Rocky Mountain News* and *Denver Times* learned of the incident, as did authorities. The *News* on August 26 reported that during the fight between Mattie and Katie, Cort and Sam Thatcher stepped in—which was true—but the *News* unfortunately used the word *seconds* in referring to Cort and Sam. *Second* then and now conventionally refers to a person designated to back up a combatant in a pistol duel.

There the matter rested for seventy-three years until one day in 1951 when Forbes Parkhill noted the word *seconds* in the *News* story and deduced that the fight *must* have culminated in a gun duel and, further, that the duel *must* have been prompted by Mattie's and Katie's mutual attentions to Cort. That is the way Parkhill wrote it up in *The Wildest of the West*.

There the matter remained again until 1962, when novelist Max Miller, with encouragement from Fred Mazzulla—the latter known to exaggerate the truth now and then—embellished the story further in *Holladay Street*. This time the authors had Mattie and Katie dressed for their "duel" in their best Victorian dresses, jewelry, and ostrich plumes, and the men in top hats and with pearl-inlaid canes. Miller and Mazzulla even speculated in print that Mattie and

Not fond of working, Cort Thomson drew on Mattie Silks's money and patience to nurture his activity of engaging in (and wagering on) foot races. He also organized and conducted foot-racing contests between teams from volunteer fire departments, called "hose companies," throughout Colorado. This photograph of Denver's James E. Bates Hose Company, taken in 1877 at the time of Cort and Mattie's arrival from Georgetown, shows the handsome Cort (middle row, left, seated, without striped stockings) and his running teammates. Front row, from left: J. W. Scott, Hugh Duggan, George Duggan (a Denver fire chief in the 1880s). Middle row, from left: Cort D. Thomson, James Duggan, George Graham, James Canavan. Back row, from left: *J. W. Sutterlin, Burt Colborn, T. E. Walsh, Sam Pedgrift, R. L. (or R. F.) Arrington.* The original of this photograph is with the Denver Firefighters Museum.

Katie might have stripped to the waist to facilitate their pistol aim—but then the authors conceded that such a suggestion might be a bit outrageous, although they printed it anyway.

Writers have had fun over the Mattie-Katie "duel" ever since; the yarn is simply too good to die and is more romantic and exciting than the truth. In 2001, for instance, the western history buff magazine *True West* placed an image of a determined-looking Mattie Silks on its cover; she is firing a pistol and is unclad above the waist except for her bonnet. The marvelous old myths of western history can never die.

The day after the shooting of Cort Thomson, Katie Fulton left on the next train to Kansas City; Cort recovered quickly, and the *Denver Times* proclaimed that Denver Park was a trouble spot in which "no woman who does not desire to risk her reputation and perhaps her honor should be willing to be seen." The *Rocky Mountain News* added that the Denver Brewing Company owned the park and ought to do something about it. Katie Fulton soon returned to Denver, where she and Mattie had another confrontation on September 3, 1877, with Mattie knocking Katie down, further injuring her nose. Katie was charged with threatening Mattie, but the allegation was dismissed.[18]

For the rest of their lives together, Mattie gave her love to Cort and her fortunes to the support of his wild ways. If she felt guilt over the bullet wound he suffered following her fisticuffs one drunken night, that could have been part of their bond. But Cort would forever be Mattie's first love and the second of her three husbands (assuming she married Casey Silks).

Following the melee in Denver Park, Mattie continued to run her business and Cort continued to foot race and gamble. When paying off one of his gaming debts Mattie once said that if Cort wanted to continue playing cards, she wished he would learn how to do it effectively but that she guessed he never would. In November 1880 Cort lost a $250 race in Greeley, and the following August it was suspected that Cort participated in a rigged race. He was arrested and Mattie bailed him out of jail, but the resolution of that matter is not recorded.[19]

As mentioned, Cort Thomson left a wife and infant daughter behind in Georgetown. On July 2, 1884,

Cort learned of the death of the woman he had abandoned. Records say Martha A. Silks and Cortez [*sic*] D. Thomson were married four days later in Peru, Indiana, where Mattie had friends. Performing the ceremony was the Reverend W. H. Daniel. The earnings from Mattie's successful enterprises from then on supported Cort's foot-racing contests and his drinking and gambling. Further, the proceeds from her business activities financed the 1,400-acre ranch near Wray in northeastern Colorado that Mattie purchased for Cort's benefit. She hoped the wide-open plains would help Cort repel the evil influences and his disreputable pals in Denver.[20]

Cort Thomson's interests ranged from participating in foot races to organizing and promoting races among individuals, lodges, and the early volunteer fire departments. Thomson had been a member of Denver's Woody Fisher Hose Company fire squad; such cadres of firemen were dedicated more to athletic competitions and socializing than to fighting fires: much is recorded about their athletic contests, fancy outfits, trophies, and leather belts and little about their efforts at extinguishing fires.

Thomson arranged firemen's foot races throughout the West. Most were betting events—and Cort was one of the principal bettors. In August 1881 he promoted a foot race in Denver that offered $1,000 in prizes and accepted $9,000 in side bets. Cort bet $2,000 on the runner he had trained, and newspapers reported that "a woman of the demi-monde" bet an additional $3,000 on the same racer. The affair was a disaster for Cort and Mattie: their racer not only lost, but somebody skipped town with the prize money and the betting proceeds. Cort was tossed into jail, but Mattie got him out again.

When Mattie Silks arrived in Denver in 1877, she established her first bagnio at 501 Holladay Street (old numbering, near Twentieth Street). The *Rocky Mountain News* reported on July 15, 1878, that Mattie paid $13,000 ($3,000 down and the balance in two years) for Nellie French's house "on Holladay Street," and Silks subsequently moved among 500, 501, and 502 Holladay until 1887 when she paid $14,000 for a place at 1916 Market Street (formerly Holladay). There she prospered and continued to invest in one property and then another. Real estate transfer records in the Colorado State Archives show Martha A. Silks buying two parcels in August 1879, a third in 1880, another in 1884. She applied for a permit to build a $3,000 brick home, and she petitioned for an additional permit to build a carriage house. Mattie's friendly competitor Jennie Rogers was buying properties as well; the *Denver Times* on October 4, 1888, told of Rogers's litigation with Albert H. Myers over "valuable lots located at Twentieth and Holladay streets." Jennie won.[21]

Mattie Silks, meantime, oversaw her business, according to the only good photograph of her that exists, attired in a skirt with tiers of lace flounces and sometimes with white gloves covering the diamond rings of which she was fond. Her trademark became a diamond-encrusted cross worn at the neck; the eleven-diamond, $900 necklace originally belonged to Lizzie Preston, and Mattie bought it at Lizzie's estate sale. When driving her buggy, Mattie carried a lace parasol and a frilly hankie to wave at friends. Jim Ridell, a Denver man who had seen Mattie Silks many years before, told Max Miller and Fred Mazzulla in the early 1960s that Silks was finely attired in a different dress every day and that she reminded him of photos of Baby Doe Tabor, "that same round, smooth face, and that same way of doing their hair—curly like."[22]

Cort hung out at the Murphy's Exchange saloon with his sporting cronies. On one occasion Cort was at the saloon with friends Bill Crooks and Cliff Sparks. The latter was a St. Louis gambler who wore a $2,500 diamond stud in his shirt. In walked Jefferson Randolph "Soapy" Smith, Colorado's most noted confidence man, with a cohort, Tom Cady. Cort's group made a derogatory remark about Soapy's shell-game frauds, and Soapy and Cady responded with a few comments regarding men who subsisted on the charms of Market Street women.

This led to gunfire. Sparks fell mortally wounded, and Crooks burst into tears and flung himself across the body of his dying friend, lifting the diamond stud with his teeth. Nobody was convicted of the murder, but Cort Thomson may have been so impressed with the technique of biting the diamond that he told Mattie about it. Soon the Market Street ladies employed the

same trick on occasion when hugging their clients, and a Denver dentist was said to have attracted a considerable clientele by fitting removable steel "biters" to the girls' front teeth. In 1884 one Minnie Darley was arrested for thus lifting a diamond pin from her client Frank LeFebre.[23]

The women of Denver's *demimonde* had additional clever methods of increasing their earnings, and these procedures usually involved subcontractors called "panel workers," "creepers," and "hook artists."

The working girls of Denver's Row preferred that their clients keep their clothes on—except their hats. It was a time-saving consideration, important especially during rush periods when fast turnover was needed. On particularly busy payday nights the girl would lay a strip of canvas over the coverlet at the foot of her bed to prevent the customer's heavy boots from ripping or muddying the linens. The girl did not inform her customer that she was rushing him along so she could welcome the next patron. Instead, she expedited matters by fondling and groping and cooing that he was so exciting that she just could not wait.

Such flattery was generally successful, and it was one manner of increasing the business flow. Sometimes a girl did have the gentleman disrobe—after he paid in advance—whereupon the helpful girl volunteered to fold his shirt and trousers neatly and hang them in the closet. The closet had a convenient rear sliding panel, behind which was the girl's confederate. The "panel worker" would not remove anything such as a wallet, which could immediately be missed. Rather, the accomplice carefully went through the billfold, removing some of the contents before replacing it in the proper pocket. It was important that the girl make certain the accomplice had sufficient time. One of Detective Howe's scrapbooks carries a newspaper sketch of a successful panel layout police had discovered.

The "creeper" had to move faster than the panel worker and needed to possess great skill and judgment, crawling at just the right time across the floor to the chair where the pants were hung while the girl kept the customer busy as long as she could. The creeper had to leave the room promptly. If the customer discovered he had "lost" his gold watch and it was nowhere to be found he could hardly blame the girl, as he knew what she had been doing, and they were the only two in the room.

The "hook artist" extended a rod—much like a fishing pole—through a transom, hooked the trousers, drew the garment outside, removed the valuables, and quietly lowered the trousers through the transom back onto the floor. The customer might be irate at finding his rumpled trousers and might discover a twenty-dollar gold piece missing, but the girl would be just as mystified as he was.[24]

Such antics were not permitted in the honest houses of Mattie Silks or Jennie Rogers, which depended on good word-of-mouth, on keeping the police away, and on repeat business. After all, their places were respectable.

Mattie's business prospered, and she often carried a pocketful of ten- and twenty-dollar gold pieces. "The sweetest sound in the world," she said, "is the jingle of gold coins." Following Colorado's economic crash of 1893, Silks supervised a campaign among her Market Street friends to provide food for the mountain men who drifted back to town. Additionally, in River Front Park she supposedly set up her big tent—reportedly the one used in the mountains as her first "boardinghouse for young ladies"—as a shelter for the down-and-out miners, many of whom Mattie had known in better days.[25]

The ranch near Wray, in addition to attempting to keep Cort out of trouble in Denver, was a good place to pasture Mattie's twenty-one race horses, of which she was very proud when they competed at Denver's Overland Park race course. Few in Denver were aware that the Mrs. C. D. Thomson of Wray whose horses ran and were shown so often was Mattie Silks.[26] Cort spent much time at the ranch, occasionally rustling livestock. Mattie was usually in Denver, and when Cort came to town from the ranch he would demand money, which she usually furnished. When Mattie refused his pleadings on one occasion, he rode a horse through the door and into the velveted parlor of her house. Rather than see the dance floor ruined, she gave Cort $500.

Mattie Silks was involved in one of the most plaintive episodes involving a Market Street bordello, that of little Jennie John. The case was recorded by Detective Sam Howe. On the evening of July 17, 1895, Detectives Leonard DeLue and Benjamin F. Finch received a tip that a little boy living at Mattie's place at 1916 Market Street was actually a little girl. On rare occasions a child would reside briefly at a Denver bordello because of circumstances the child's mother found herself in.

The detectives entered Mattie's place and removed the child. At the police station the child insisted that his name was Willie Evans, but the face and voice were not those of a boy. "Willie" finally broke down and confessed that he was a girl, Jennie John. Jennie sobbed out a story of child abuse the likes of which the officers had never heard and which incriminated her cruel stepfather, fifty-four-year-old Thomas Sutton of Rock Springs, Wyoming.

Sutton, the officers learned, apparently paid off Jennie's father to disguise her as a boy and spirit her away to Denver, thus preventing her from testifying against Sutton, who was under investigation for assaulting Jennie's thirteen-year-old sister, Hannah. Indeed, without Jennie's testimony Sutton was acquitted and fled to Mexico. The detectives located Jennie's father, William Evans John, who told them he had brought Jennie to Denver and hid her for "safe keeping" among the women of the *demimonde* not to prevent her from testifying but to spare her the disgrace of being involved in a sex matter. Police Matron Sadie Likens reunited Jennie with her tearful mother.

The newspaper report of Jennie John had an intriguing sidelight. At the end of a very long story about Jennie John's plight, the *Denver Republican* included a paragraph stating, incidentally, that the Jennie John matter had resulted in the discovery of another child living at Mattie Silks's place. She was only five, her first name was listed as "Theresa," and her surname was spelled by the newspaper as "Thompson." That is all the article says of her, and no subsequent mention of this little girl has been located by the author.[27] Given the dates involved here—Cort leaving his wife and small daughter in 1874 and the discovery of the five-year-old Theresa Thompson in 1895—Theresa could not have been Cort's long-lost daughter but could have been his granddaughter. Or could

Theresa Thompson have been the daughter of Cort and Mattie? There were later suggestions that Mattie had a daughter, but we do not know for certain.

Mattie Silks shipped Cort Thomson to the distant ranch near Wray to remove him from his evil companions in the saloons and gambling halls of Denver, but Cort found he could drink just as much in Wray. And he got into other mischief as well, as related by the *Rocky Mountain News*:

> Court Thompson [*sic*], who stood well in the community and was popularly supposed to be well known, concluded some time ago that cattle stealing was more profitable than cattle raising. He is accused with two or three other men of stealing several car loads of cattle and shipping them to Kansas city where they sold them at a handsome profit.

Cort was detected in this scheme, however, and fled to Texas, pursued by the Julesburg sheriff. The *News* said the sheriff returned Cort to Colorado where he "is in jail counting up the wages of sin."[28]

Mattie is said to have had, during this approximate interim, a gentleman friend who was not Cort Thomson. A wealthy and socially prominent New York railroad president reportedly became enamored of Mattie during a Denver visit and asked her to accompany him on a business trip to California for a month. She declined, explaining that she must remain in Denver and attend to business because she had a $5,000 note falling due.

He wrote out a check for $5,000, and they departed. On their return trip they stopped for another month at a Wyoming ranch of the Potter Palmers, members of New York's Sacred 400 society circle, where the railroad man introduced Mattie as his wife. Mattie thought it amusing that during the entire month the New Yorkers had no suspicion as to her identity and line of work. For a moment she felt totally respectable; she boasted of the event for the rest of her life.

Through city administration after city administration, police administration after police administration, Mattie prospered in a business known for its nomadic nature and short-lived entrepreneurships.

Mother Ryan's kid, and it's nobody's business where she's brought up," was the brazen answer given when inquiry was made. "The child is fed, clothed and has a home," said another. And such a home and the having of such a habitation was "nobody's business."

To those who ask, Mother Ryan gives answer that the child is hers by adoption. Where she got it or whose

BABY'S VILE HOME.

it is she will not tell. To-day the police will investigate and endeavor to find out where it came from, and an effort will be made to take it from the "hovel" to some home where vice and dissolute women do not reign supreme.

THE D. A. C. DANCE.

An Enjoyable Evening with a Large Attendance.

The Rocky Mountain News *decried the presence of a child in a Market Street bordello, January 6, 1894.*

Liquor licensing and real estate records show Mattie constantly adjusting and refining her ventures; she and Jennie Rogers, for instance, alternately with Ella Wellington, owned the famed House of Mirrors at 1942 Market Street. On July 8, 1892, the *Colorado Sun* published a note that Mattie Silks's petition for a bottled liquor license was denied because the aldermen wanted her to get a regular saloon license instead. Under ordinary circumstances that might have been just a pesky delay for Mattie, but in this instance the timing was particularly bad: the big Knights Templar convention was coming up in a month, and Silks had to get ready.

The houses of Silks and Rogers were well-known among a highly placed clientele, including city authorities and state legislators. Mattie, Jennie, and the other madams of Market Street were generally friendly toward each other and cooperated for mutual benefits, safety, and aid.

Only 30 miles away in Boulder, such was not the case with that city's two leading sex merchants, Susie Brown and "Madam" Day, who amused themselves and the community by engaging in fistfights and setting each other's bordellos afire. That was enough to give the business a bad name.[29]

The most tragic story of downfall in Boulder concerned pretty Annie Blythe, by all accounts a happy girl of a good family until her mother horsewhipped a young man who had paid her attentions. In 1886 in Boulder Annie married railroader Sam Speas and the couple moved to Como, the rail center of South Park. The couple had three children, each dying in infancy, and these tragedies plus the isolation of Como appear to have driven Annie over the brink and into self-loathing. She developed a fondness for liquor and fast company, and on the night of April 6, 1894, while Sam was on a freight run to Climax, the Como town marshal was shot dead while investigating a party Annie was attending.

Annie was arrested as an accessory, but Sam hired the best attorney in town, and Annie was acquitted. Before the year was out, Sam divorced Annie and she moved to Denver, where the depths of her degradation defied the understanding of those who had known

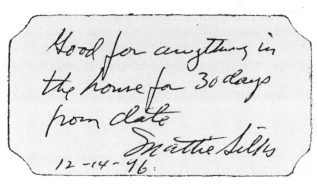

Researcher Fred Mazzulla saved this Mattie Silks business card, interesting because of the handwritten inscription on the reverse: "Good for anything in the house for 30 days from date, 12-14-96." The "Gent's Furnishings" (gentleman's clothing) inscription was to allay any wife's suspicions should a card be found in her husband's pocket.

her—"the vilest dissipation," wrote the *Boulder Daily Camera*, "being her constant occupation." "She had been mingling with negroes and degraded whites ever since," wrote the *Denver Times*. Annie's mother, Mary, traveled to Denver to accompany her to Boulder, but Annie fled back to Denver where she moved into what the *Denver Post* described as a "hovel" at 2143 Lawrence Street. "The shack," continued the *Post*, "was occupied by John C. Motley and family, colored, and Annie Blythe lived in the upper story [with] Andrew Lyles, colored." "Bo" Lyles beat her the night of July 5, 1898, and again the morning of the 6th, and she asked neighbors what to do, but nobody wanted to become involved, and at about noon on the 6th she died at age twenty-six. She had been drunk for three weeks.

Lyles and Motley were detained for questioning. The autopsy showed an abscess from an injury, but the ruling was death from pneumonia and alcoholism.

The heartbroken Mary Blythe made a final sad trip to Denver to return Annie home. Motley and Lyles were released, but Lyles was quickly rearrested on suspicion of assaulting his ten-year-old stepdaughter. The *Rocky Mountain News* headline was "Down the Chutes to Death."[30]

Like her friend Jennie Rogers, Mattie Silks was a businesswoman who knew which strings to pull at city hall and police headquarters. Each woman enjoyed fine horses and dandyish gentlemen friends; each was loyal to her longtime customers and reasonably kind to her boarders. There were numerous other madams along Market Street, several of whom advertised in a small 1892 vest-pocket publication titled the *Denver Red Book*. It was the social register of the Denver *demimonde*, issued in conjunction with the national convention of the Knights Templar fraternal society—the biggest assemblage of out-of-towners the city had ever seen. The *Red Book*, subtitled "A Reliable Directory of the Pleasure Resorts of Denver," promised "All the Pleasures of Home" and "A Cordial Welcome to Strangers." Coincidental with the *Red Book*'s appearance was the opening of the Brown Palace, the ritziest hotel yet seen in the mountain West.

The eighteen-page (including covers) *Red Book* contained advertisements for restaurants and a few civic attractions in addition to the notices regarding Denver's bordellos. There were ads for Jennie Holmes, 2015 Market Street; Blanche Brown, Twentieth and Market Streets; Belle Birnard, 1952 Market Street; and Ella Wellington, 1942 Market Street. Some of the entries listed the number of boarders and other attractions such as the availability of the "finest wines, liquors and cigars." Also advertised in the booklet were five "club rooms" (gambling parlors), plus a handful of legitimate enterprises such as Schlitz's Famous Milwaukee Beer, the New Broadway Theatre, the Alhambra vaudeville hall, and even H.A.W. Tabor's opera house.[31]

The 1892 *Denver Red Book* did not carry Mattie Silks's advertising. Her business was doing well despite a statewide economic slowdown, and Silks must have thought it unnecessary to advertise. She had all the business she and her boarders could accommo-

date. Her employees regarded her as an "awful kind and generous lady," housekeeper Janie Green recalled years later.

To keep her mind clear for business, Mattie now drank sparingly—a touch of champagne or a sip of beer when necessary. Long gone were the reckless days when she would be fined twelve dollars for public drunkenness and hell-raising. "Madam Silks," Green remembered, would talk about her long-ago feud with Katie Fulton and say it was over a man—Cort Thomson. Mattie still liked to think she was a crack shot, and occasionally she would travel to the Wray ranch, where Cort was supposedly drying out, to practice shooting. She told Denver friends her destination was in the San Luis Valley because she did not want the people around Wray to learn she was a sporting lady.[32]

Mattie, Green said, allowed her boarders to keep half their earnings, but out of that half they had to pay room and board. She served two good meals a day—breakfast at 11:30 A.M. and dinner at 5, before things got busy for the evening. Janie also told writers Forbes Parkhill and Fred Mazzulla—and this would have been an unusual practice for the time—that Mattie maintained two or three "call girls" who resided at the uptown hotels and kept appointments Mattie made for them. All of Mattie's girls were required to dress very nicely, and her boarders generally were in debt to her for their outfits.

Mattie told Janie Green she had "made a million dollars, maybe two million," but most of it was gone "'cause she had taken too many chances. She was a betting lady, and lost lots of money on the races at Overland Park. She said she would have been better off if she hadn't been such a fool for good-looking men." Janie heard Mattie repeat this story.

> She had been a landlady since she was 19, and never "hustled" for herself. Said the man didn't live who had money enough to buy her, and claimed she never had anything to do with any man, except [if] she loved him. Sometimes she would cry a little and say she was sorry she was a sporting lady, and if she had her life to live over she would go into some other line, because running a sporting house was a very uncertain line of business, what with the law and all.[33]

The Denver Red Book, *a guide to prostitution services in the city, was published coincidentally with the opening of the Brown Palace Hotel and with the huge 1892 Knights Templar convention in Denver. The book is conveniently pocket-sized for the gentleman to tuck discreetly into his vest pocket for quick consultation. This is one of five early photocopies researcher/author Fred Mazzulla allowed to be made of the* Red Book. *In the 1960s he furnished one copy to the Colorado Historical Society and another to the Western History Department of the Denver Public Library. Mazzulla related that pages 13 and 14 were missing when the book was found on the floor of a streetcar, and thus the contents of those pages are unknown. The book has 16 surviving pages. Location of this original book is not known, and no other original copy of the* Red Book *is known to exist.*

Denver's *Red Book* and the recently discovered *Travelers' Night Guide to Colorado* were similar to prostitution guidebooks in other states. The New Orleans Storyville *Blue Book* appeared in 1895 and was distributed until 1915. Its motto was "Order of the Garter: *Honi Soit Qui Mal y Pense*" (evil to him who evil thinks). Storyville was New Orleans's designated bordello neighborhood.[34] In New York City, guidebooks with titles such as *Prostitution Exposed* existed as early as 1839, disguised as public "warnings" of which neighborhoods to avoid. The vest-pocket books were a dollar each and were available to the gentleman visitor at many corner bookstalls. Guidebooks were just one method of advertising, augmented by business cards plain and fancy (Denver's Mattie Silks utilized both), and even newspapers.

The *Denver Red Book* advertisement of Ella Wellington at 1942 Market Street—an address more closely identified with Jennie Rogers and Mattie Silks—calls for an explanation. Wellington has been described as Jennie Rogers's bookkeeper, and it has been suggested that in the *Red Book* advertisement Wellington was simply "fronting" for Jennie at the 1942 Market address.[35] Ella Wellington was not an employee of Jennie Rogers but was a Market Street businessperson in her own right who was eclipsed by the fame of Mattie and Jennie—as were all the other madams up and down Market Street. Ella Wellington purchased the House of Mirrors from Jennie Rogers and became the center of one of the most plaintive stories to emerge from a Market Street brothel.

Ella Bowse (or Bouse) was a respectable wife and mother in Omaha when the western wanderlust hit her and she ran off to Salt Lake City with the dashing Sam Cross, who was not her husband. Sam disappeared, and by 1889 Ella found herself in Denver, running with a fast crowd. Saving money given her by gentleman friends, in 1891 Ella was able to make a down payment with a two-year note on the $25,000 House of Mirrors at 1942 Market Street, the famous *mansion de joie* built by Jennie Rogers in 1889. The House of Mirrors, as we shall see shortly, was not kind to Ella Wellington.

Working at the House of Mirrors at about this time—under whose ownership we are unsure—was Laura Evens, eventually a madam in Salida. She recalled:

> There was a birds-eye maple grand piano in the mirrored parlor. The piano was in the southwest corner of the room, and to the left of the fireplace as you entered. There was a tête-à-tête chair, being a chair shaped like the letter S, in the middle of the room under the chandelier. This S-shaped chair was covered with white velvet with big embossed red roses with green leaves. It matched the satin carpet on the floor. The woodwork on this chair, and some of the other furniture, was imitation of gold. There were two big arm chairs in the room at the front; one in each corner. There was a settee in the other corner in the southeast corner of the room. The beautiful crystal chandelier hung from the middle of the room. Directly south [Evens must have meant east] of this parlor was the ballroom. There were mirrors about three feet wide that went from the ceiling to the floor. These mirrors were in oval frames. The frames were carved with figures of nude women.
>
> There were electric lights all around the ballroom. The five-piece colored orchestra sat on an elevated platform. There were high-backed carved gothic styled chairs around the room. The chairs had big stuffed arms. There were Ottomans on each side of the chairs. The girls were permitted to sit only on the Ottomans. They were not permitted to sit on the chairs, or on the laps of the gentlemen guests.

These observations were delivered to researcher Fred Mazzulla, who suggested that Laura Evens was describing the house's appearance prior to Silks's purchase of it on January 16, 1911. Wrote Mazzulla: "Later on [under Mattie Silks's ownership?], Mattie's place lost some of its glory. Laura emphasized that later on the girls were old and fat, and the place was known as the old ladies' roost."[36]

The "five-piece colored" music group was probably George Morrison and his Jazz Orchestra. Morrison was a violinist who initially played engagements in Boulder, recalling many years later, "In a little old town like Boulder, we didn't have many Negroes, and so I used to come down to Denver" where he met his soon-to-be wife. His recollections to jazz historian Gunther Schuller offer a new perspective on the brothels of Denver's Market Street:

TRAVELERS' Night Guide OF... COLORADO

Traveler's NIGHT GUIDE Of Colorado

ALL RESORTS

(Except those that may be stamped dangerous in Red Ink) mentioned in this guide are guaranteed strictly first-class and absolutely safe (financially and otherwise.)

COLORADO CITY

"You'll be a Long time Dead"

.... Enjoy life while you can.

My Entertainers are Dispensers of Pleasure.

Will be pleased to have you call. ♫ ♫ ♫ ♫ ♫

Miss Lucille Deming,

222 WASHINGTON AVENUE, COLORADO CITY.

INSPIRATION POINT
On Long Top, U.P., Denver & Gulf Ry.

CRIPPLE CREEK

"The Curfew will not Ring To-night."

But our lunch bell rings at 10.30 every evening. All are cordially invited. Ten attractive entertainers attired in white will wait upon you at

Pearl Devere's,

329 MYERS AVENUE.

PALISADES.

DOME ROCK.

DENVER

To the Gentlemen:

KINDLY REMEMBER

THE YOUNG AND POPULAR LANDLADY OF DENVER

Assisted by ten brilliant entertainers. Grand Musicale every evening.

GEORGIE A. BURNHAM,

. . . 2036 Market Street.

DENVER

WILL BE PLEASED TO ENTERTAIN YOU AT THE

STONE FRONT

Jennie Rogers.

1942 Market Street———————— •←

Mt. HOLY CROSS.

ESTES DOME.

DENVER

 Will be pleased to discuss with Yourself and friends the Political Aspect Of the Day

MALVINA,

Cor. 20th and Market Streets.

Unique in the history of vice in Colorado, the Travelers' Night Guide of Colorado *was a directory of certain Colorado brothels ("resorts") at the close of the nineteenth century. The* Guide *included houses of joy in nineteen communities; the names of the "proprietresses" (madams) and some of their interesting advertising slogans are included in the following listing. The guide's title page includes the advisory that all of these brothels, except those "stamped in red ink," were "guaranteed [to be] strictly first-class and absolutely safe (financially and otherwise)," which meant the patron (it was hoped) would not be assaulted, robbed, or murdered while on the premises. None of the entries in the book is stamped in red ink.*

Alamosa: Tsing Toya and China Pete. Aspen: Lizzie Gordon, "smooth and pleasing." Buena Vista: Lizzie Marshalls [sic]. Breckenridge: Molly McClarren, "Latest Parisian and German musical Productions every evening." Central City: May Martin. Colorado City: Bell Bristol; Lucille Deming, "You'll be a Long time Dead. . . . Enjoy life while you can; My Entertainers are Dispensers of Pleasure." Cripple Creek: Pearl Devere, "The Curfew will not Ring To-night." Denver: Georgie A. Burnham, "Grand Musicale every evening"; Minnie Hall; Malvina (no surname), "Will be pleased to discuss with Yourself and friends the Political Aspect of the Day"; Belle Bernard [sic; the correct spelling was Birnard]; Emma English; Rena Powers; and Jennie Rogers. Durango: Rose Mays, "Racy Entertainment." The silver camp of Georgetown: Frankie Hatch, who would not entertain customers who supported the gold rather than silver monetary standard. Glenwood Springs: Nellie Otis; Maud Bannister, whose establishment featured "lady impersonators"; and Abbie Kingsley, whose advertisement included a Grover Cleveland riddle. Grand Junction: Nellie Clark. Idaho Springs: Florence Leland, "Life Is Short; While pleasure is within reach—GRASP IT." Lake City: Clara Ogden, "High-Class Musical and Literary Entertainment"; May Thomas, "Pleasant Dreams"; and Annie Blanchard, "Nine of Those Sweet Dreamland Faces." Ouray: Carrie Linnell, "Interesting and instructive entertainment every evening"; Lola Singleton; and the Bon Ton Dance Hall with no madam listed. Pueblo: Mabel Miller. Salida: Ida Brooks. Silverton: Louesa [sic] Crawford; Cora Livingston; and Stella Allison. Telluride: Gussie Grant. Trinidad: May Phelps and Mrs. S. W. Cunningham.

Glaringly absent is the silver camp of Leadville—then indisputably the sin capital of Colorado. A logical explanation is that Leadville felt it deserved its own brothel directory. If one was issued, a copy has not been located.

The publisher of the Guide *is unlisted, but inasmuch as the book utilizes stock photographs of various Colorado towns and scenic attractions, it could have been issued surreptitiously by the same print shop that issued railroad touring booklets and timetables familiar to museum curators and collectors today. The vest-pocket-sized* Travelers' Night Guide *is 66 pages in length, 3 inches by 4¾ inches, the pictures are black-and-white, and the type is a dark blue. Only this copy is known to exist.*

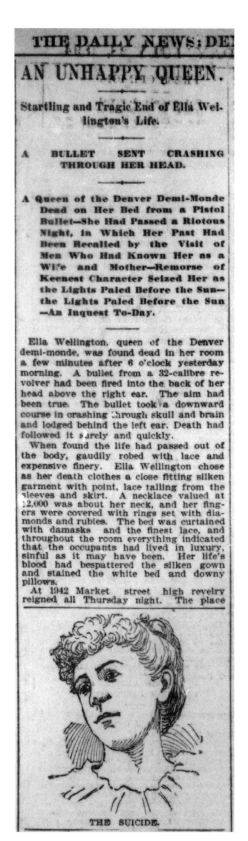

THE DAILY NEWS; DE

AN UNHAPPY QUEEN.

Startling and Tragic End of Ella Wellington's Life.

A BULLET SENT CRASHING THROUGH HER HEAD.

A Queen of the Denver Demi-Monde Dead on Her Bed from a Pistol Bullet—She Had Passed a Riotous Night, in Which Her Past Had Been Recalled by the Visit of Men Who Had Known Her as a Wife and Mother—Remorse of Keenest Character Seized Her as the Lights Paled Before the Sun—the Lights Paled Before the Sun—An Inquest To-Day.

Ella Wellington, queen of the Denver demi-monde, was found dead in her room a few minutes after 6 o'clock yesterday morning. A bullet from a 32-calibre revolver had been fired into the back of her head above the right ear. The aim had been true. The bullet took a downward course in crashing through skull and brain and lodged behind the left ear. Death had followed it surely and quickly.

When found the life had passed out of the body, gaudily robed with lace and expensive finery. Ella Wellington chose as her death clothes a close fitting silken garment with point, lace falling from the sleeves and skirt. A necklace valued at $2,000 was about her neck, and her fingers were covered with rings set with diamonds and rubies. The bed was curtained with damasks and the finest lace, and throughout the room everything indicated that the occupants had lived in luxury, sinful as it may have been. Her life's blood had bespattered the silken gown and stained the white bed and downy pillows.

At 1942 Market street high revelry reigned all Thursday night. The place

THE SUICIDE.

Of all the Market Street prostitute suicides—and there were many—that of madam Ella Wellington was newsworthy only because of her social stature up and down the street and in town. Other girls who killed themselves had their own tragic stories that could have been told, but the newspapers usually wouldn't bother. This article is from the Rocky Mountain News, *July 28, 1894.*

We married in 1911 and I moved to Denver. It was in those years that I started working in the parlor houses, for Mattie Silks, one of the famous madams. That was around 1913 and 1914. Some people might think that my wife minded my working in the parlor houses. My gracious, I was trying to make a living in music any way I could. Of course, when we played the parlor houses, they wanted mostly kind of quiet music. And they didn't want any long pieces. Short, very short, maybe two choruses. And no rest, for us.

Their philosophy was to get the customers to buy a drink. They almost never allowed the girls to dance, you know. The music was there for music lovers that wanted to hear some nice numbers and maybe once in a while dance one number. And it was not noisy music. We had no drummers, for example—never—in the houses. Just violin, piano, and guitar. We'd play pieces like "Blue Bell"—that was a waltz. And "Red Wing"—that was a two-step. As a specialty we'd do "Silver Threads Among the Gold" for them, or "Goodbye, My Lady Love," and "Down on the Farm," "Lady Lou," "Call Me Back," and "Just a Dream." All those old numbers. We'd also play pieces like "Darktown Strutters' Ball"—pretty fast and lively.[37]

But back to Ella Wellington's fatal experience at her House of Mirrors. During the evening of July 26, 1894, Wellington's splendorous rooms at the House were the scene of merriment and orgy. The party had been going on for several days. Ella was draped in her finest jewels and laces. Then into the establishment came an old Omaha friend of Ella and Fred Bowse.

Ella had long pined for Fred, the husband she abandoned, and she asked the visitor about Fred's health and well-being. When told of Fred's happy remarriage, Ella was taken aback, and next she asked about the little boy and girl she and Fred had adopted.

On being assured that they, too, were happy, Ella exclaimed, "I too am happy, Oh so happy!" and she sank into a melancholy, from which she had suffered previously, over her wasted life.

Ella retired upstairs to her lavish boudoir, babbling, "Oh I am so happy! So happy that I'll just blow my god-damned brains out." And at age thirty-one Ella Wellington sent a .38-caliber bullet crashing through her head, and blood oozed over the $2,000 ruby necklace she wore and saturated the fluffy white pillows.

In her bed at that moment—and it was not his first visit—was William R. "Billy" Prinn, deputy county clerk and family man. Considerably startled by Ella blowing her brains out in front of him, Prinn's initial inclination was to get his trousers on as quickly as possible and vacate the premises through the convenient back door. Prinn remained in the house, however, and subsequently testified before a coroner's jury. He resigned from his public office a week later.

The ladies of Market Street enlisted every available carriage to give Ella Wellington a suitable procession to Riverside Cemetery. Weeping every day at her grave was another of Ella's suitors, Frederick N. Sturges, age thirty-one, who even spent several nights sleeping atop the freshly filled mound. Three weeks following Ella's suicide, Sturges swallowed twenty grains of morphine and died. In his pocket was a photograph of Wellington, and in Sturges's hand was written "Bury this picture of my own dear Ella beside me." His plot was next to hers at Riverside; he had purchased it only days after her burial.[38]

One of Ella Wellington's girls, thirty-year-old Emma McDonald, alias Emma Moore, had been keeping company for five months with faro dealer Abe Byers, age sixty, but they broke up in mid-May 1891 after he beat her up. He began writing her letters, one suggesting that she obtain a dog for companionship because "when I get done with you, no man will want you."

At 7 P.M. on June 10, Byers entered Wellington's place at 1942 Market Street and proceeded with Emma to her room, where he threatened to kill her and himself. She fled to the downstairs reception parlor, to which Wellington had summoned Patrolman H. V. Cornell on report of a disturbance. Byers followed, opened fire on Emma and Cornell with a .44-caliber

Colt, but missed. In the ensuing melee Byers beat the officer with the gun butt, inflicting head injuries. Byers was jailed for assault with intent to murder.[39]

Following Ella Wellington's death, the House of Mirrors at some point revolved back into the hands of the structure's builder, Jennie Rogers. But the days of the free-wheeling Denver sin palaces were soon to end. Mattie Silks, the final person to operate the House of Mirrors as a brothel, had built a residence at 2635 Lawrence Street, which she maintained for a number of years as she phased out her business interests.[40]

Throughout the story of Mattie Silks and Cort Thomson, the matter of a girl child resurfaces. Sometimes, as mentioned, she is a daughter of Cort's by his first marriage, sometimes she is a daughter of the daughter. Sometimes a daughter was supposedly adopted by Mattie, and sometimes that daughter is instead a granddaughter. It has even been said that Cort and Mattie had a daughter of their own. Janie Green related that Mattie often talked of an adopted daughter who did not live in Denver. Green believed Silks gave this daughter gifts of jewelry. Green said Silks would occasionally relate that she was going to an uptown hotel for a day or two, because her daughter was coming to Denver for a visit.

The reader will recall the mysterious "Theresa Thompson," age five, mentioned by the *Denver Republican* in July 1895. One again wonders if "Theresa Thompson" or the "adopted daughter" mentioned by Janie Green might have been the granddaughter of Cort Thomson by the wife he left in Georgetown to run off with Mattie or, indeed, might have been a daughter of Mattie and Cort's, which seems unlikely because there is no record of Mattie Silks ever being seen pregnant. Parkhill, writing about Mattie Silks in the *Rocky Mountain News* on April 19, 1959, asserts that the adopted girl was Cort's granddaughter, whom Parkhill calls not "Theresa" but "Rita."

Further muddying the waters, Detective Sam Howe's books contain a fascinating one-sentence clipping from the *Rocky Mountain News* on September 4, 1887, inexplicable given present knowledge of Mattie Silks's personal circumstances: "Nettie Silks, an adopted daughter of the notorious Mattie Silks, was taken from Mrs. Seymour's house of ill fame by the officers yesterday and sent by Judge Campbell to the Home of the Good Shepherd until April 22 [1888], when she will have attained her majority."[41]

If Nettie Silks reached her "majority"—age sixteen or eighteen—in 1888, she would have been born in 1870 or 1872, some half-dozen years before Cort Thomson abandoned his wife and small daughter in about 1877 to run off with Mattie. A search of newspaper microfilms of April 22 and 23, 1888, reveals nothing of a Nettie Silks being released from the House (Home) of the Good Shepherd, although such routine releases were rarely reported.

Several possible explanations exist with regard to the mysterious Nettie Silks. She could have been Cort Thomson's five- or seven-year-old daughter at the time Cort abandoned her. Or Nettie could have been adopted as a child by Mattie when Mattie was conducting wagon trains across the plains to the Colorado frontier in the early 1870s. Or Nettie Silks could have been wrongly assumed by the *Rocky Mountain News* reporter to have been adopted by Mattie. Perhaps someday the reports of a young person in Mattie Silks's life will be resolved.

At the Yuma County ranch near Wray, meantime, Cort Thomson continued to get drunk, rustle cattle, and generally thwart Mattie's efforts to make him respectable. Longtime Yuma County judge Irving L. Barker of Wray recalled that Cort was reputed around town

> to have killed a number of men, but nothing was ever proved on him. He always dressed in the latest clothes and always was spending and gambling his money. [Mattie Silks] furnished most of the money for his different ventures including the ranch. He gambled most of it off, either that or drank it. He was noted for being a cattle rustler, but then it was not uncommon for anyone if he found a stray, to put his own brand on it.[42]

Enter Lillie Dab, a friend of Mattie's who had worked at the Red Light Hall on State Street in Leadville. The Red Light Hall, according to its advertisement in the *Leadville Democrat*, was "the place to go for standard amusement. The girls are rounder,

rosier, and more beautiful than elsewhere and will take you through the mazy waltz in refreshing movements." Lillie and Cort may have known each other before his marriage to Mattie, as a court proceeding detailed that Cort had once tried to kill himself in a jealous fit over Lillie. On March 14, 1891, after catching Cort and Lillie together, Mattie sued Cort for divorce, charging that he was a drunk, a wife beater, and a philanderer and that he had been living with Lillie Dab for six months and with other women at various times.[43]

Cort beat Mattie when she protested too much. Her divorce papers contended that

> without fault on her part, [Thomson] assaulted, struck, beat and bruised Plaintiff in the most cruel, barbarous and inhuman manner to her great physical pain and harm and so as nearly to endanger her life. . . . Plaintiff endured this treatment as best she could until the night of March 13th, 1891, at their residence in Denver, the said Defendant, without any fault on her part, or any real provocation being given, assaulted this Plaintiff, knocked her down, blackened her eye, beat her face and body and kicked her while she was lying on the floor in a most cruel and brutal way that it is impossible for Plaintiff to further endure such conduct and actions on the part of her said husband.

Perhaps anticipating Cort's questions regarding her sixty-day jaunt with the railroad president, Mattie added to the divorce filing: "Her conduct during her said married life with Defendant has ever been such that any acts she may have committed that were in any wise inconsistent with her marriage vows were directly sanctioned, connived at and condoned by said Defendant."[44] She said that although three parcels of land in Yuma County were in his name, they had been purchased with her money. Mattie successfully petitioned the court to restrain Cort from selling the land. She said

> that at the time of her said marriage Plaintiff was worth a large sum of money and had valuable properties . . . that at various times since such marriage Defendant has spent and squandered in gambling and riotous living her money derived from rents of property, sales of property and from other sources at least a sum equal to between forty-five thousand and fifty thousand dollars.

An artist imagined the manner in which Mattie Silks corrected the erring ways of her longtime man, the sodden, no-good, mooching philanderer Cort Thomson, her second husband. The researcher is hard-pressed to discover any redeemable values in Thomson, but Mattie stuck with him until the end.

To conciliate, Thomson agreed that the ranch property should be converted to her name, and on March 25, 1891, Mattie dismissed her divorce petition.[45]

Cort and Mattie lived happily again, and in 1897 they enjoyed a trip to Great Britain, returning later that year. The Klondike was booming, and the next spring they embarked for Alaska where Mattie opened a house. The weather did not agree with her, and they returned to Denver only three months later, but Mattie said that even with having to pay the Northwest Mounted Police $50 a day in protection money, she cleared $38,000 during those ninety days.[46]

In spring of 1900, Cort was spending most of his time in Wray and Mattie most of hers looking after business affairs in Denver. Finally, the press reported:

> To celebrate his fifty-third birthday, on March 15, Thomson drank to excess. He came to Denver three weeks ago and ran across "Kid" Burns. Later they

cashed a $55 check at Pennington's saloon. The checks [*sic*] were drawn upon a bank at Haigler, Neb. [17 miles east of Wray], on funds deposited there by Mattie Silks. Burns announced that he and "Cort" were going to the ranch, sell out the cattle and start for the Klondyke [*sic*]. Burns packed away an opium lay-out in his grip before his departure from Denver. Mattie Silks left the city [Denver], intending to cause the arrest of her husband and Burns. Sheriff Tuttle of Yuma county served the warrant last Wednesday, but Thomson and the prisoner, it is reported, induced him [the sheriff] to get drunk with them. On Thursday they all went to Wray and Thomson celebrated their arrival by riding up and down the sidewalks and announcing that if he had his 45-caliber revolver he would clean out the town. The sheriff slept.[47]

Thomson fell violently ill from general debauchery, and Mattie was summoned from Denver. On April 10, 1900, she met Cort seated in his rocking chair at the Commercial Hotel in Wray. "Damn you, Mattie," old-timers around Wray quoted Cort as saying. "You hired that fellow to poison me. If I had a gun I'd kill you." Mattie supposedly responded, "All right, Cort," drawing the pistol she always carried and placing it in his hand. "If you're going to die, I don't want to live." He did not shoot but died in his rocking chair, supposedly from eating spoiled oysters, but the *Rocky Mountain News* attributed the death to whiskey and opium. Said the *News*, "His wife, *daughter* [emphasis added] and landlady of the hotel were with him at the time."

Mattie, described by the newspaper as a citizen of the "half world," returned his body to Denver and buried him in an unmarked grave in Fairmount Cemetery. It was then, asserts Parkhill, that Mattie adopted Cort's granddaughter Rita.[48] A footnote exists to Cort Thomson's degenerate life: in the course of research for his Bat Masterson biographies, historian Robert K. DeArment located an obscure note from the April 14, 1900, edition of *George's Weekly*, a small periodical published in Denver. It gives the first evidence that Thomson, in his less sober moments, had occasionally gunned for the famed Masterson:

"Court" [*sic*] Thomson is dead. This may be good news for Bat Masterson and it may not be, but for

years every time "Court" got full of "hop" he borrowed a gun and started out to kill Bat, fancying it would shred much glory upon [him] to kill a man of Masterson's worldwide reputation. Bat breathes easier though we believe he never feared him.

Fred Mazzulla obtained court documents listing Thomson's assets and liabilities at the time of death. He had four assets: a fifteen-dollar saddle, a five-dollar brass watch, a two-dollar overcoat, "and a lot of wearing apparel" valued at twenty-five dollars. Among his unpaid bills were

Hot whiskies, $1; Underwear, $1; 1 Gal. Whisky, $4; 1 pr. suspenders, 40¢; 4 demijohns Whisky, $6; Crackers, 10¢; 1 can B'lk Berries, 10¢; Bar, $5.70; Horse doctoring and medicine, $1.30; Pr. Overshoes, $1.50; Balou Gal. Whisky, $1.80; Bar, 50¢; Bread Pan, 30¢; ½ Gal. Whisky, $2.50; 1 s'ck meal, 25¢; Whisky and Cigs, $1.35; Whisky, $3; Lunch, 15¢; 1 Hd'k, 15¢; shoe strings, 5¢; 1 Qt. Planet Whisky, $1.50.[49]

After Mattie buried Cort, she took a sweetheart named John Dillon Ready, a redheaded, 250-pound native Nova Scotian who had been the foreman at the Wray ranch. In Denver, Ready became known up and down Market Street as "Handsome Jack" or "Handsome Jack Kelley." Mattie hired Ready to be her bookkeeper, bouncer, and general helper. The always smiling Jack, a former telegrapher, was considerably younger than Mattie and wore a Prince Albert coat and carried a cane. Janie Green remembered him as very good-looking but bossy toward Mattie but says Mattie did not seem to mind. Jack told Janie he had to take care of Mattie "because she [was] getting old." Jack prided himself on his boxing abilities. In the ballroom of Mattie's house he fought an opponent bare-knuckled for an hour with no stopping. Janie said the opponent almost killed Jack.[50]

During World War I Mattie Silks became a patriot, and under the name Mrs. C. D. Thomson she was awarded a certificate of merit by Treasury Secretary William Gibbs McAdoo for selling Liberty Bonds. Mattie converted her property at 1916 Market Street into the "Silks Hotel," and on November 18, 1919, she sold her 1942 Market Street property to Japanese interests, which used it as a Buddhist temple until 1948.

Denver Tribune.

DENVER, COLORADO. MONDAY, JULY 17, 1882.

Death of Mattie Silks

A private dispatch received in Denver last evening announced the death in St. Louis of the notorious woman of the town, Mattie Silks, who was proprietress for a long time of a place on Holladay street. No particulars were given, but the news was not altogether unexpected, as she had not been well for some time past.

Forty-seven years before her actual demise in 1929, Mattie Silks must have had a chuckle over this phony story published in the Denver Tribune *on July 17, 1882. In that year Silks would have been in her personal and professional prime, and the article probably caused some alarmed concern around Denver—especially among her many loyal clients. The* Tribune *never followed up on the story, and it was published in no other Denver newspaper. Today the article smacks of a practical joke planted by a friend—or enemy.*

The 1921 *Denver City Directory* lists John D. Ready, telegrapher, as residing next door at 1922 Market Street. The 1923 directory lists John D. Ready and Mattie Silks as living at her bungalow at 2635 Lawrence Street. The 1924 directory shows John D. Ready, livestock dealer, and his new wife, Martha, at the Lawrence Street address. Mattie Silks was age seventy-six or seventy-eight—assuming birth years of either 1846 or 1848—when she married Jack Ready.

In 1926 Mattie broke a hip and was confined to a wheelchair. During autumn 1928 the *Rocky Mountain News* dispatched an intern reporter to Mattie's cottage to conduct an interview, which was never published lest it offend the paper's readers. Thirty-five years later Max Miller contacted the reporter, who preferred that her name not be mentioned, and asked her to recount the interview. She wrote to Miller, in part:

There in a bed over which was hanging a crucifix on a chain was lying a frail, tiny old woman with transparent skin, faded watery eyes, a kindly expression. She answered questions without any restraint or holding back. Looking back at it now I can understand that she was a most unusual woman with humor and detachment about a phase of life she had once known and left—and with humor and detachment about the whole of life which she was soon to leave. She defended calmly but without emotion the life she had led. And she said at the first:

"I went into the sporting life for business reasons and for no other. It was a way for a woman in those days to make money and I made it. I considered myself then and do now—as a business woman. I operated the best houses in town and I had as my clients the most important men in the West.

"I kept the names of my regular customers on a list. I never showed that list to anyone—nor will I tell you the names now. If a man did not conduct himself as a gentleman, he was not welcome nor ever permitted to come again. My customers knew I would not talk about them and they respected me for this. This was good business. My houses were well kept and well furnished. They had better furnishings than any of my competitors; gilt mirrors, velvet curtains.

"I never took a girl into my house who had had no previous experience of life and men. That was a rule of mine. Most of the girls had been married and had left their husbands—or else they had become involved with a man. No innocent young girl was ever hired by me. And they came to me for the same reason I hired them. Because there was money in it for all of us.

"Some of my girls married the customers. And [and this was the only part of the interview where Mattie Silks became the least bit defiant] my girls made good wives. They understood men and how to treat them and they were faithful to their husbands. Mostly the men they married were ranchers. I remained friends with them, and afterwards with their husbands, and I got reports. So I knew they were good wives."

That was the substance of the interview, the reporter told Miller, adding:

Mattie Silks's third spouse was the always snappily dressed John Dillon Ready, known throughout the Denver tenderloin as Handsome Jack Kelley. Upon Mattie's death in 1929, however, she was laid to rest next to Cort Thomson. Further, Mattie saw to it that when Handsome Jack died two years later, he was buried far away from her in Fairmount Cemetery. Here Kelley is seen with madam Sadie Doyle, who became one of the more durable (albeit low-profile) women of Market Street. Indeed, up to a year before her death in 1950, "Blind Sadie" Doyle continued to pimp, even as she became almost totally sightless. She was an ongoing consternation to the police and courts, both of which tried to treat her with some deference.

Fearful of nothing, as her maid Janie Green later put it, Mattie got out of her wheelchair at a Christmas Day party in 1928 and fell, breaking the hip again. She was taken to Denver General Hospital, where the next day she made out a will on hospital letterhead. She died January 7, 1929, at age eighty-three (again assuming an 1846 birth date).[52]

Services were held at the Hofmann undertaking parlors without benefit of clergy. Pallbearers were informed it was a Quaker service. There was no music, no flowers, and few mourners. Three or four friends followed the hearse to Fairmount Cemetery. There, without prayers and under the name of Martha A. Ready, Mattie Silks was buried beside the unmarked grave of Cort Thomson.

She left an estate of but $4,000 in real estate—consisting only of her cottage on Lawrence Street—and $2,500 in jewelry, composed of two diamond rings and the diamond cross necklace that had once belonged to Lizzie Preston. Some said Cort Thomson gave her one of the rings and Handsome Jack Ready the other and that the cross was a symbol of something life had withheld from her.

She smiled kindly at us [the reporter and a photographer] as we left. There may have been a little contempt in her smile and I felt there was—but it was good humored contempt mixed with a little pity—the look of a woman who believed she knew a great deal more about this world than we did. It was with a definite feeling of disappointment I left the premises and not without a certain amount of scorn. For I asked myself what right had that old woman to have a crucifix over her bed? To be lying there so sweet and clean and serene when so close to her end?—and to have caused me for a few minutes actually to like her?[51]

An elderly Mattie Silks is at left. Silks admired a good steed and owned racehorses from the time she came to Denver. This horse was named Jim Blaine. The woman in the white blouse has never been identified. This photograph may have been taken at a suburban house Silks owned in far rural Wheat Ridge, but no corroboration can be found that she was involved in such a real estate holding. Silks's home was at 2635 Lawrence Street—now a parking lot—and whether horses could be kept on that property at the probable time of this photo, 1910–1915, has not been determined.

Mattie Silks was said to have given numerous jewels to the mysterious adopted daughter (or granddaughter) called Theresa, who, it was whispered, was college educated and once played the piano in Mattie's house. In Wray, people said Theresa was indeed the offspring of Cort Thomson; in her obituaries, "adopted daughter Mrs. Theresa Thompson" was mentioned as residing in Selah, Washington. The "Mrs." designation suggests that Thompson was a married name, further adding to the mystery of this supposed person. The mysterious Theresa or descendants are not known to have ever come forward.

Mattie's estate was divided equally between Theresa and "Handsome Jack Kelley" Ready. He died May 23, 1931, and is buried at Fairmount in an unmarked grave, far away from a stone marked "Martha A. Ready."[53]

Jennie Rogers was Mattie Silks's competitor and friend. Mattie was short, plump, creamy complected, and a

235

fairly good businessperson with the exception of her tendency to gamble, and she was fond of diamonds. Jennie Rogers was a six-foot brunette, statuesque and uncommonly attractive, hot-tempered, authoritative, skilled in business dealings, well-spoken, and not given to profanities. Whereas Mattie was seldom seen without her diamond cross pendant, Jennie Rogers was seldom seen without her emerald earrings. And Jennie wanted to replace Mattie as Denver's Queen of the Row.[54]

The *Denver Times* on September 25, 1886, published an article concerning the filing of larceny charges against one "Edward Washington (colored)" for stealing "some diamonds from Jennie Rogers, on Holladay Street." Edward Washington was probably Jennie's houseman, and the theft charges are less important in retrospect than the manner in which Rogers's identity was tied to a street: "Jennie Rogers, *on Holladay Street.*" Like New York's Tenderloin or New Orleans's Storyville, the prostitutes' protected neighborhood—their island of sin—was their scarlet letter.

Jennie Rogers's true name was probably Leah (or Leeah) J. Tehme, born July 4, 1843, in Allegheny, Pennsylvania. Her father's name was James Weaver, and as a young girl she associated with farm produce peddlers. Because of her beauty, she entertained many offers of matrimony. Her biography in the Office of History at the Colorado Historical Society says Jennie was married in about 1860 to a physician, perhaps named Fries, but soon ran away with a steamboat master named Rogers whose craft, the *Jennie Rogers*, ran between Pittsburgh and Cincinnati. They did not marry, however, whereupon Leah J. (for Jennie?) Fries subsequently became "housekeeper" for "a Pittsburgh mayor." The ensuing scandal prompted her departure from Pittsburgh with enough hush money to establish in St. Louis her first "fashionable resort"—as it was termed in one of her obituaries. She advertised by driving her finely attired boarding girls about town in a coach with four horses, and Jennie was a superb horsewoman.

Enthused over business opportunities in booming Colorado, Jennie Rogers arrived in Denver just after Christmas 1879, as the city was experiencing the first rush toward the newly discovered Leadville silver strikes. Jennie found that Mattie Silks had been in town for at least three years. On January 15, 1880, scarcely two weeks after her arrival, Jennie purchased her first Denver house, at 527 Holladay Street (later 2009 Market Street) from Mattie for $4,600. The purchase was made under the name Leah J. Fries.

She was arrested, the Colorado Historical Society biography says, in March 1880 in the company of madam Eva Lewis for "unladylike conduct in the streets," the result of showily riding their steeds through town. The following winter, when her horse slipped on a frozen street and spilled her on Holladay Street, the *Rocky Mountain News* delicately described her only as "well-known in this city." Her equestrian display through town notwithstanding, Jennie was generally discreet. Whereas other Holladay Street madams may have paid to get their names *into* the gossipy *Police Gazette* tabloid, Jennie was said to have paid to keep her name *out* of the *Gazette*. A Jennie Calvington, identified by the *Rocky Mountain News* as an alias of Jennie Rogers, was arrested on July 28, 1884, for vagrancy and "being a professional morphine taker" and was sentenced to ten days in jail. This characterization does not fit the pattern of Jennie Rogers, but the episode is attributed by history to Rogers.[55]

Detective Sam Howe preserved accounts from autumn of 1886 regarding a lewd house case in which Rogers was the defendant.[56] What probably was intended as a routine court matter became unusual when Jennie's defense attorney, not named in the stories, disclosed to the court that District Attorney LeDru R. Rhodes had paid twenty-five dollars to two men, including Police Lieutenant Henry W. Barr, to snoop around Jennie's place, inside and out, and "lay traps for their victims, and then go before the grand jury and the criminal court and testify as to what they saw and heard."

Upon hearing that evidence, which suggested lazy investigative work, the newspaper said courtroom spectators "expressed themselves in terms of considerable disgust and said that the present means adopted to prosecute the Holladay street women was but little less than blackmail and under the circumstances they would be glad if every one of them were acquitted." Jennie, however, was convicted by Judge Platt Rogers (no relation) and fined seventy-five dollars.

Jennie's best friend in St. Louis was said to have been the chief of police, who occasionally journeyed to Denver for a stay On one occasion, Forbes Parkhill related, the chief helped Jennie raise the $17,780 to construct the House of Mirrors at 1942 Market Street by blackmailing a prominent Denver businessman. Rogers hired architect William Quayle (who also designed the First Congregational Church and, later, West High School) to design 1942 Market, installing along the cornice five carved stone faces depicting persons who were supposedly the principals of the blackmail story—including Jennie. It was the fanciest such business establishment in town—far fancier than anything Mattie Silks owned.[57]

On August 13, 1889, Jennie wed John A. "Jack" Wood (sometimes "Woods"), a wagon driver fourteen years her junior who had been a bartender at the Brown Palace Hotel. Jennie subsequently financed Wood in the saloon business in Salt Lake City and then Omaha. On one occasion she paid an unannounced visit to Salt Lake City, finding him in the company of another woman. Jennie is said to have whipped out a pistol and shot him through the arm. The police inquired why, and legend records the immortal words of a woman scorned: "I shot him because I love him, damn him!"

When Jack was running the Omaha saloon (again with her money), she heard he was consorting with a Mollie Gibson. Jennie traveled there and at first insisted on being smuggled into Gibson's rooms but decided instead to meet Wood at an attorney's office. "There was a scene that cannot be described," the *Denver Times* later reported. "For nearly an hour the storm raged, and when at last the clouds of battle began to clear away a contract securing to Miss Rogers her financial rights in the business was drawn up and signed, and she returned to Denver."[58]

A savvy businessperson, Rogers built a fine parlor at 1950 Market Street in Denver with fifteen bedrooms and one of the first centralized furnaces in town. At the zenith of her career, she employed twenty-two "boarders" at one time.

Jennie's brothels were only about five blocks from the meeting places of the Colorado legislature during

JACK WOODS.

The Rocky Mountain News *obituary sketch of Jack Wood, Jennie Rogers's one and only, February 29, 1896. On one occasion the hot-tempered Jennie shot Jack and then is said to have blurted to police: "I shot him because I love him, damn him!" Today they rest together in fashionable Fairmount Cemetery—near many of her influential clients.*

the 1880s and much of the 1890s. David Mechling's drugstore was between Jennie's establishment and the legislative rooms, and he observed that when the senators and representatives were in session, each afternoon about three o'clock the lawmakers would retire to Jennie Rogers's and there amuse themselves. Nothing was thought of that sort of thing in those days, Mechling said.

In October 1902, pestered by anti-brothel crusades, upset over the death of her pet dog—which she was said to have buried in a golden casket—and afflicted with Bright's disease, which stole her youthful attractiveness, Jennie temporarily relocated to Chicago where she bought a parlor house and a suburban home. At the brothel she met contractor Archibald T. Fitzgerald, and they were wed on April 26, 1904, in Hot Springs, Arkansas.

She journeyed to Denver immediately after her marriage to Fitzgerald to attend the funeral of Lizzie Preston, and while in the city she looked after business affairs and installed madams in properties she still owned. Upon her return to Chicago she heard Fitzgerald was already married when she wed him, and in 1907 Jennie Rogers came back to Denver.

Rogers moved into the House of Mirrors and resumed its management. She left town again and returned to Arkansas with Fitzgerald, coming back to Denver for good early in 1909 at age sixty-five. She was increasingly short of cash, depending on small loans from her old business associate Leona de Camp. During October 1909 she fell ill, and at 1 A.M. on the 11th she summoned her attorney, Stanley C. Warner, to her residence at 1950 Market Street to prepare a will in which she left everything to a sister, Annie Smith; a niece, Annie Prestle; and a nephew, Marsh Mariner.[59]

Rogers grew increasingly ill and breathed her last on Sunday, October 17, 1909. She was buried next to

Jack Wood died of heart disease on February 28, 1896, and although Jennie was not mentioned in his published obituary, she erected a 5-foot monument over his grave at Fairmount Cemetery.

Jennie's business interests expanded beyond the Row; she bought water bonds in Logan County, purchased land in the Denver suburbs near Sloan Lake, and bought uptown properties along Sixteenth and Nineteenth Streets.

Jack Wood in one of the most dignified areas of Fairmount Cemetery as the remaining madams, girls, pimps, and assorted characters of Market Street looked on.

Archie Fitzgerald challenged Jennie Rogers's estate, and her attorneys in response alleged that they had never legally married.[60] On September 20, 1910, the House of Mirrors at 1942 Market Street passed briefly into his hands. One of the claims against the estate was an invoice from private detective Harry E. Burlew, a onetime Denver police investigator who specialized in vice matters, for following Archie.

Mattie Silks acquired the House of Mirrors on January 16, 1911, and had "M. Silks" inlaid in tile on the front doorstep. The days of the Market Street brothels were fading, but once again and finally Mattie was Queen of the Row.[61]

Mattie Silks and Jennie Rogers were the most renowned women of the Denver *demimonde*, and the fame of their parlors spread throughout the West. Market Street, however, was the business address of other women whose entrepreneurships helped meet the growing consumer demand.

Among these was Verona Baldwin, once described by a California newspaper as "the most beautiful girl on the Pacific coast." Baldwin's name was frequently mentioned in the Denver press, but her life in Colorado was uneventful compared to the publicity she received in California after she shot her multimillionaire gambler cousin, E. J. "Lucky" Baldwin.

Lucky Baldwin made his fortune as a Nevada mining speculator. Moving to San Francisco, he built the opulent Baldwin Hotel, established a stable of racing horses, and invested in real estate. In the early 1880s he was said to have won $200,000 on the turn of one card at the El Dorado gambling saloon in San Francisco, but he may have been best known as a womanizer who, it is written, was named more than any other defendant in seduction and breach-of-promise suits.

Verona, age twenty-three in 1883, claimed to be of British royalty; was tall and very slender; possessed huge, hazel-colored eyes; was trained as a school-

It is said that some Denver houses of joy issued advertising tokens such as this nickel-sized "Compliments of Miss Olga" example, shown above front and back. This token is believed to be genuine, but most other "brothel tokens," readily available to collectors today, are not. The Colorado Historical Society possesses records of historian/author Fred Mazzulla that detail his contracts with Chicago firms to reproduce old-looking brothel tokens during the 1960s. Almost certain to be of that ilk are tokens marked "Silver Dollar Hotel, Ruth Campbell, prop., Good for One Screw." The die and particularly the lettering of the Miss Olga example appear old, with lettering raised above the surface, as opposed to the "Silver Dollar Hotel" tokens, which are stamped. We do not know who "Miss Olga" was. Courtesy, Leo Stambaugh.

teacher; and spoke with a cultured English accent. She taught and resided at Lucky's ranch.

On January 4, 1883, Verona shot Lucky as he left his private dining room in the Baldwin Hotel. Reuben H. Lloyd, his attorney, said during the investigation that the shooting followed her dismissal from the staff by Lucky after a servant discovered her in a compromising position with a guest of Lucky's—a physician—in a ranch house room. The bullet she fired at Lucky produced a slight wound to the arm. When asked by police why she did it, Verona answered: "He ruined me in body and mind. That is why I shot him. I ought to have killed him." He responded through the attorney that she had threatened to kill him if he did not give her money.

Lucky declined to testify at her trial, and prosecutors were left without a case. Funds that were quickly provided for her immediate removal to Washington Territory might have been interpreted as a settlement. Three years later she reappeared and demanded maintenance of a child she said was Lucky's. We do not know whether he acquiesced, and again she vanished.

Then came word that Verona Baldwin had been adjudged insane and been institutionalized. Horace Bell, a Los Angeles attorney who was familiar with the case, commented afterward that "our hellish statutes protected him [Baldwin] and enabled him to send his victim to an insane asylum."

Verona Baldwin's next stop was Denver, where she displayed no symptoms of insanity upon arriving in town in the late 1890s. From 1903 until a wave of morality finally closed Denver's Row a dozen years later, she operated the house at 2020 Market Street. Following the shutdown, she lived in an apartment

240

on Denver's fashionable Capitol Hill and operated a tavern called the Baldwin Inn. She died in the 1940s. Lucky Baldwin's hotel burned and he lost most of his fortune, although he retained some of his landholdings, which produced little revenue.[62]

There were players on the Denver *demimonde* stage other than Ella Wellington, Mattie Silks, Jennie Rogers, and Verona Baldwin. These women may have been sadder or more obscure or less successful, but they had stories too. Some of them are related in Chapter 10.

Notes

1. Dawson Scrapbooks 36, p. 357, Colorado Historical Society, Denver. Dawson's identification of this clipping appears to be the DR, October 22, 1911, but examination of *Republican* microfilms of the 22nd and several adjacent dates fails to produce the clipping. Interestingly, the clipping reveals that closure of the smaller brothels between Eighteenth and Twenty-third Streets was ordered because "with the opening of the Twentieth street viaduct it became certain that some changes would be necessary," adding that "the larger houses will not be bothered for the present." The clipping adds: "The news that Market street was to be closed was well circulated and hundreds of curious spectators thronged to the street last night. Numbers of big automobiles, many of them containing fur clad women, dashed rapidly down the street." Actually, full shutdown of Market Street did not occur for another two years. For the furnishings of Jennie Rogers's parlor houses, see Bancroft, *Six Racy Madams*, p. 7. Bancroft also characterized (pp. 7–8) the girls as frequently not knowing their customer's identity. For further descriptions, see Reiter, *The Women*, p. 141; Dallas, *Cherry Creek Gothic*, pp. 225–235.

2. Bancroft, *Six Racy Madams*, pp. 7–8; Reiter, *The Women*, p. 141.

3. Kimball, *Nell Kimball*, p. 9.

4. For the Minnesota system, see Joel Best, *Controlling Vice: Regulating Brothel Prostitution in St. Paul, 1865–1883* (Columbus: Ohio State University Press, 1998), p. 4.

5. Barnhart, *The Fair but Frail*, pp. 26–27.

6. Ibid., p. 27.

7. Parkhill, "Scarlet Sister Mattie," p. 21; also see pp. 1–15. Two versions of this article exist, differing in composition and content. The first and original version is an obscure bound typescript dated July 1948. The second version is the *Brand Book* account. Each is in the library of the Colorado Historical Society. In 1951 Parkhill included some of the information in his popular book *The Wildest of the West*.

8. Reiter, *The Women*, pp. 141–142.

9. Miller, *Holladay Street*, pp. 172–176. This statement was one of several obtained by researchers Fred and Josephine "Jo" Mazzulla and shared with coauthor Max Miller. Mazzulla complained in a 1968 letter that "these bastards" (publishers of *Holladay Street*) "managed things so that I got exactly nothing out of *Holladay Street*. By 'exactly nothing' I mean, up until now, I am out of pocket about $1,500 . . . and in return I am promised big movie profits etc. etc." A motion picture dreamed of by Mazzulla and Hollywood writer Will Fowler never materialized. (See correspondence of Fred Mazzulla, Colorado Historical Society collection 1231, especially file folders 14–17.)

With regard to the spelling of Laura Evens's surname, Caroline Bancroft in *Six Racy Madams* (pp. 40 ff.) and other writers have preferred the spelling "Evans." The Mazzullas, in *Brass Checks and Red Lights* (Denver: the authors, 1966), spell it "Evens" (pp. 36–41) and show a photograph of her gravestone (p. 39) that carries the unconventional spelling. Collection 1231, file folder 132, contains the following statement in a letter to Miller from Fred Mazzulla, dated January 5, 1967: "Many, many years ago Laura Evens had confided in me the true spelling of her name. Her husband was a member of the Evens Tile and Brick Company family of St. Louis, Missouri. She changed the (e) to (a) and it remained Evans so far as I was concerned until my last trip to Salida [site of Laura's final bordello] when I noticed the true name was put on the tombstone."

DP writer Earl Pomeroy commented to Mazzulla in 1951 that Laura Evens once boasted that "if all the male sex appendages she personally harbored during her career were laid end to end, such a chain would girdle the earth." Pomeroy assumed Evens was referring to the circumference of the earth at the 39th parallel, the parallel nearest Leadville, where she had worked, and calculated the earth's circumference at that point to be 19,522.7 miles, or 101,906,160 feet. Pomeroy researched physiology journals and concluded that the "dimension of the phallus of the average adult human male" was fourteen to sixteen centimeters ($5\frac{2}{3}$ to $6\frac{1}{3}$ inches) in a nonrelaxed state, "and so, to circumscribe the earth at 39th parallel, the phallic requirement would have been 203,812,320 individual links." Through a complicated series of formulas, Pomeroy calculated Evens's maximum work year at 3,900 hours and deduced that if she began her apprenticeship at age eighteen and ended at age sixty, at four engagements per hour, thirteen hours a day, the total over forty-two years would have been 655,200. That, said Pomeroy, would have amounted to only 327,600 linear feet of phallus, not even close to the 101,906,160 feet of which Evens boasted. "Therefore," concluded Pomeroy, "I say that some of the testimony supplied by Laura should be discounted, and some of the other reopened for analysis." See Pomeroy to Mazzulla, May 11, 1951, Collection 1231, ff. 140.

10. Four-page undated, uncatalogued manuscript by Fred Mazzulla, Mazzulla boxed papers, Colorado Historical Society, Denver, pp. 3–4. The manuscript contains numerous interesting observations about Laura Evens, Jennie Rogers, Lillian Powers, and Mattie Silks. The manuscript is an ex–Amon Carter Museum holding, now at the Colorado Historical Society; copy in the author's possession.

11. Miller, *Holladay Street*, pp. 181–185.

12. Rosen, *The Lost Sisterhood*, p. 87.

13. Script treatments and correspondence between Will Fowler and Fred Mazzulla survive in the Mazzulla Collection (no. 1231) of the Colorado Historical Society. See particularly ff. 20 and adjacent folders. Additionally, the present author wrote articles for the DP regarding the proposed Mattie Silks movie in the editions of January 26 and February 6, 1973. For the account of Gene Fowler burning his manuscript on the life of Mattie Silks, see Fred Mazzulla to Mrs. Louise Auer, February 15, 1968, Collection 1231, ff. 140. Mazzulla wrote: "As you must know, it was Gene Fowler who discovered Mattie Silks and first put her in print." Mazzulla's basis for this statement is not known. Mazzulla further stated that *Holladay Street* was a credible account of the Denver bordello district and was "based on tape interviews of many people who knew Mattie."

14. For thorough discussions of Mattie Silks and her activities in Colorado, see Miller, *Holladay Street*, pp. 21 ff., and Parkhill, *The Wildest of the West*, pp. 207–286. Her death certificate under the name Martha Ready lists registration number "511"; a copy is in the author's possession. Historian Phil Goodstein in *The Seamy Side of Denver* says Silks's first bordello was in Springfield, Missouri, rather than Springfield, Illinois, and dates her arrival in Georgetown, Colorado, at 1875 (pp. 35–36).

15. Miller, "A Salute to the Frontier Madames of Colorado," pp. 6–8; Miller, *Holladay Street*, pp. 24–36. Fred Mazzulla died in Reno, Nevada, on January 28, 1981. He earlier sold the bulk of his remarkable collection of Colorado photographic negatives to the Amon Carter Museum in Fort Worth, Texas, but most of these materials have been returned to the Colorado Historical Society. Mazzulla is remembered for publishing several small booklets on the early prostitutes of Colorado. Each copy of one of the books, *Brass Checks and Red Lights* (1966), was accompanied by an old-looking brass token inscribed "Silver Dollar Hotel, Ruth Campbell, prop.—Good for One Screw." Business correspondence between Mazzulla and the manufacturers of the coins (or "restrikes," as Mazzulla termed them) are included in the Mazzulla document collection of the Colorado Historical Society.

16. The Georgetown/Silver Plume National Historic Landmark District has located Mattie Silks on the handwritten Clear Creek County property tax rolls of 1876. The entry gives no occupation but lists ownership of a hundred dollars' worth of furniture. An additional entry shows that on March 25, 1875, Silks borrowed from (or owed to) carpenter/undertaker Henry Boyer the amount of $133.75 and that she put up her furniture as collateral. She had paid off the loan by May 10. See Mort Stern, "Mattie Silks in Georgetown," *Georgetown/Silver Plume National Historic Landmark District Journal*, April 1996: 1–11, which also contains the reference to George W. Silks. Caroline Bancroft in *Six Racy Madams* (pp. 37–38) writes that Mattie may have taken her surname either from railroad man Casey Silks or from George W. Silks, a card dealer in Colorado mountain towns during the 1870s and early 1880s. Or, Bancroft suggests, Casey Silks and George W. Silks may have been the same person. Bancroft quotes Mattie's servant Janie Green (referred to as Hattie Green by Forbes Parkhill and Jannie Green by Max Miller) as saying Casey Silks and Mattie were common-law husband and wife for thirteen years and that Mattie knew Casey in Missouri as early as 1866 (p. 37).

17. Miller and Goodstein spell Thomson's first name "Cortez." His birth date of March 15, 1847, is calculated through the knowledge that shortly before his death he celebrated his fifty-third birthday on March 15, 1900. Goodstein says Cort and Mattie became engaged in August 1877, he at age thirty and she at either thirty-one or thirty-three. (If she was born in 1848, however, she would have been twenty-nine when she married Cort.)

18. For Cort Thomson "throwing" foot races, see DeArment, *Bat Masterson*, p. 248. DeArment spells Thomson's name "Thompson," a common error. The true account of the Mattie Silks/Katie Fulton/Cort Thompson/Sam Thatcher brouhaha is from the DTI, August 25, 1877, and the RMN, August 26. If a Mattie Silks/Katie Fulton duel was held, neither of these accounts mentions it. See also Parkhill, *The Wildest of the West*, pp. 210–213; Miller, *Holladay Street*, pp. 99–108. For Katie Fulton's return to Denver and the second fight between Mattie and Katie, see Goodstein, *The Seamy Side of Denver*, p. 37; Miller, *Holladay Street*, p. 103. Goodstein is the first historian to point out that no evidence is known to support the colorful myth that Mattie Silks and Katie Fulton were involved in a duel (pp. 36–37). Parkhill in *The Wildest of the West* has a fairly detailed description of Cort Thomson on pp. 235–236.

19. Miller, *Holladay Street*, pp. 72–73. For Mattie's wish that Cort would learn to play cards properly, see p. 67.

20. The July 2, 1884, marriage date and place for Mattie Silks and Cort Thomson is from Parkhill, *The Wildest of the West*, p. 261, and additional details are in Miller, *Holladay Street*, p. 109. Miller lists the marriage as entered in Marriage Record No. 7, p. 268, Miami County Circuit Court. The Mazzulla papers, Box 48B, file 13, Mattie Silks folder, ex–Amon Carter Museum, Fort Worth, Texas, contain a typewritten transcript, probably done by Mazzulla, of the "Martha A. Thomson vs. Cortez [*sic*] Thomson" divorce action; hereafter cited as "Mazzulla/Thomson divorce papers." Copy in the author's possession.

21. The Denver city directories throughout the late nineteenth century list the various address changes of Mattie Silks, Jennie Rogers, and their contemporaries. Mattie is first listed in 1878 at 501 Holladay Street, although she may have entered business the year before. Jennie Rogers is initially listed in 1881 at 304½ Holladay, approximately today's 1700 block of Market Street, which might have been her residence address since it was rather far southwest for a bordello to have been permitted, particularly as late as 1881. In 1882 Jennie's address was 527 Holladay Street, within the *demimonde* district.

22. Parkhill, "Scarlet Sister Mattie" (typescript), p. 13. The matter of Mattie Silks's diamond-studded cross originally belonging to her friend and competitor Lizzie Preston is in Miller, "A Salute to the Frontier Madams of Colorado," p. 10, and Miller, *Holladay Street*, p. 92. Jim Ridell's recollections of seeing Mattie Silks are in *Holladay Street*, pp. 105–106.

23. For "biters," see Parkhill, *The Wildest of the West*, p. 26.
24. Miller, *Holladay Street*, pp. 62–63.
25. Miller, "A Salute to the Frontier Madames of Colorado," p. 11.
26. For particulars about Mattie Silks's horses and Cort's barroom escapades, see Parkhill, "Scarlet Sister Mattie" (published version), p. 32.
27. SHS 15: 10806, 10807, from the DR, July 18–19, 1895. The fleeting reference to "Theresa Thompson" is near the end of the story dated July 19.
28. Ibid., 12: 4641, from the RMN, October 25, 1890.
29. For Mattie Silks, see Dallas, *Cherry Creek Gothic*, pp. 232–242. The antics of Susie Brown and Madam Day are from Sanford Charles Gladden, "Ladies of the Night," *Early Boulder Series No. 5* (Boulder: n.p., 1979), pp. 2–8. For the Colorado legislators' visits to Jennie Rogers's House of Mirrors, see Reiter, *The Women*, p. 143. Denver's madams, especially the principal ones, were generally conscientious about attending to the details of proper liquor licensing; it was a small effort for large returns. Some minor denizens of the *demimonde*, however, were not so careful. The DTI, September 25, 1886, records that "the ancient and notorious" Julia Mullins pleaded guilty and was fined forty dollars plus costs for selling liquor without a license but requested a court appearance on the charge of keeping a disorderly house, as did her colleague Annie O'Donnel.
30. For Annie Blythe, see the *Fairplay Flume*, April 12, 1894; the DTI, July 6, 1898; the DP, July 6 and 7; and the *Boulder Daily Camera*, RMN, and DR, July 7; also Margaret Coel, *Goin' Railroading* (Boulder: Pruett, 1991).
31. See Fred and Jo Mazzulla, *Brass Checks and Red Lights* (Denver: the authors, 1966), p. 15. With regard to the *Denver Red Book*, in a letter to Will Fowler, son of Gene Fowler, dated April 14, 1972, Fred Mazzulla stated: "I made five of these [Xerox] copies [of the *Red Book*] and sold one of them to the NY Public Library, another one to the Denver Public Library. I gave one of them to [former governor] Ralph Carr and I think I gave one of them to your Dad. This is the fifth and last one. It is your property." The Colorado Historical Society owns a photocopy of the *Red Book*, but it is not known which of the above-mentioned copies it is or, indeed, whether it is a copy of a copy. In the letter to Will Fowler, Mazzulla noted that "pages 13 and 14 are missing from my original," accounting for those missing pages in the copies. *Brass Checks and Red Lights* stated that only one original example of the

Red Book was known to exist. The April 1972 Mazzulla letter said he obtained this original edition of the *Red Book* from "Gene Kaiser who worked for (the) Burt Davis Cigar Store in Denver for many years. Notice the two little black spots in the upper right-hand corner of the booklet. That was punched in there by a street car conductor. Gene said he picked it up on the floor of a street car during [the] Knight Templars [*sic*] [convention] in Denver in 1892." Mazzulla stated that he paid Gene Kaiser $100 for this only known original copy of the *Denver Red Book* and that at that time (1972) he valued the book at $600. What became of the original when Mazzulla died is not known. Many of his materials were purchased by the Amon Carter Museum in Fort Worth, Texas, but the *Denver Red Book* was not included in the inventory. For the Fowler letter, see Colorado Historical Society, Mazzulla boxed collection 1231, ff. 19. The Mazzulla Collection, ex–Amon Carter but now at the Colorado Historical Society, contains a copy of an article by Alson J. Smith from the February–March 1966 issue of *Frontier Times*, a magazine of popularized western history. In it the author states: "[Market] Street was well organized, and its attractions were duly advertised in an annual guide called *The Red Book, or Gentleman's Guide to Denver. Listing the Principal* Masions de Joie. *Names of Madames, Angels, and Nymphs by Color and Nationality.* The 104-page 1907 edition listed twenty-two parlor houses." That is the only reference found during this study of a 1907 edition of the *Denver Red Book*. Moreover, the present author is unaware that the *Red Book* was ever an annual publication, as stated in the Smith article. If indeed it exists, the 1907 *Red Book* with its 104 pages would be even rarer than the 1893 edition.

Brass Checks and Red Lights was a "quickie" volume the authors sold in great quantity, according to Mazzulla's correspondence now at the Colorado Historical Society, for three to five dollars each. Every book was accompanied by a newly made "Good for One Screw" "brothel token." Fred Mazzulla had these tokens manufactured by the thousands by an Illinois token-making company. Several varieties of the tokens exist. The only distinguishing characteristic of *Brass Checks and Red Lights* was a series of bordello and prostitute photos from the Mazzulla collection. The text was scant on solid historical research. Although the book sold readily to bordello and Old West buffs and Mazzulla's many friends, it was not well reviewed. The historian Caroline Bancroft was asked by editor Palmer Hoyt of the DP to review the book, and she responded to

Hoyt on August 8, 1967: "There are countless statements that they [the Mazzullas] have made in that book and other places that I KNOW to be wrong and can so document. . . . There are also a couple of photos in 'Brass Checks and Red Lights' that are very likely complete misrepresentations—Mr. Mazzulla has been caught in misrepresentations before."

Bancroft declined Hoyt's invitation to review *Brass Checks*, and another reviewer noted with regard to the Mazzullas' previous book, *Outlaw Album*, that the text was so brief and legend-laden that "the pictures make you forget the text." Mazzulla preserved the Bancroft/Hoyt letter and the *Outlaw* review among his materials now at the Colorado Historical Society, collection 1231. Mazzulla's papers suggest that *Brass Checks* received at least one additional unfavorable review, but it is not included with the papers. For the above-mentioned Mazzulla correspondence, see Colorado Historical Society, Boxed Collection 1231, ff. 141.

32. Parkhill, "Scarlet Sister Mattie," article version, pp. 11–12.

33. Ibid., pp. 12–13.

34. Rosen, *The Lost Sisterhood*, p. 81.

35. Parkhill, *The Wildest of the West*, p. 22; Bancroft, *Six Racy Madams*, p. 23.

36. Mazzulla four-page manuscript, circa 1951, Colorado Historical Society, Denver. Copy in the author's possession.

37. Gunther Schuller, *Early Jazz: Its Roots and Musical Development* (New York: Oxford University Press, 1968), p. 362.

38. The RMN, DR, and DTI, July 27, 1894, ff.

39. Unspecified newspaper clipping headlined "An Unsteady Aim: Abe Byers Tries to Kill Emma Moore and Officer Cornell," George Watrous Scrapbook, Denver Public Library, Western History Department. The typography identifies this clipping as being from the DR, and two dates are affixed: April 25, 1890, and June 11, 1891. The author could locate the clipping in neither of those editions nor in editions on adjacent dates.

40. Parkhill, "Scarlet Sister Mattie," article version, p. 9.

41. Clipping found in SHS 6: 1768. No other newspaper of the day carried a story regarding "Nettie Silks." Judge Campbell was Police Magistrate Charles M. Campbell. Although Denver's madams are sometimes listed in the city directories, the 1887 Denver directory contains no entry for the brothel of "Mrs. Seymour."

42. J. T. Kearns interview with Yuma County judge Irving L. Barker, 1935, Colorado Historical Society Pam. 352/23.

43. Parkhill, *Wildest of the West*, p. 273; Miller, *Holladay Street*, pp. 110–117. Both sources say the divorce petition was a result of the Cort Thomson–Lillie Dab affair, but the DR, March 15, 1891, suggests that the divorce action was prompted the previous evening when "Con Thompson [*sic*], husband of Mattie Silks, [drew] a revolver on her, threatening to kill her. There was no bloodshed." The divorce papers contain the language included here.

44. Miller, *Holladay Street*, pp. 115–116; Silks/Thomson divorce papers, preserved by Fred Mazzulla. Max Miller collaborated with Fred Mazzulla in the preparation of *Holladay Street*, and this document could have been one obtained by Mazzulla, who was an attorney, in his study of early Denver prostitutes and madams.

45. Parkhill, *Wildest of the West*, pp. 261–262; Miller, *Holladay Street*, p. 116. The RMN, March 15, 1891, says that on the day prior, Mattie filed for divorce from Cort and restrained him from disposing of or encumbering "his ranch" or other property. The author has been unable to locate any newspaper account of March 25 or thereafter stating that the divorce suit was withdrawn.

46. Parkhill, *The Wildest of the West*, pp. 267–270.

47. SHS 19: 20894, from the RMN, April 11, 1900.

48. Parkhill, "Scarlet Sister Mattie" (published version), p. 32; Miller, *Holladay Street*, pp. 163–166. Data regarding Cort's death and Mattie's supposed adoption of his granddaughter Rita are from Parkhill, *The Wildest of the West*, pp. 272–274. The story of Cort's final drunken spree is in the RMN, April 11, 1900.

49. Miller, *Holladay Street*, p. 166.

50. Parkhill, "Scarlet Sister Mattie" (typescript), p. 13, and published version, p. 32.

51. Miller, *Holladay Street*, pp. 212–215. For the account of Mattie Silks's activity selling World War I Liberty Bonds, see Forbes Parkhill in the RMN, April 19, 1959.

52. Mattie Silks had been proclaimed dead by the media once before. The front page of the DTR, July 17, 1882, carried a one-paragraph story:

DEATH OF MATTIE SILKS

A private dispatch received in Denver last evening announced the death in St. Louis of the notorious woman of the town Mattie Silks, who was proprietress for a long time of a place on Holladay street. No particulars were given, but the news was not altogether unexpected, as she had not been well for some time past.

No other Denver newspapers carried the story. The *Tribune* did not retract the story or mention it again.

53. Material regarding Mattie's final months is from Parkhill, "Scarlet Sister Mattie" (typescript), pp. 13–15, and the published version, pp. 33–36.

54. In Mazzulla and Mazzulla, *Brass Checks and Red Lights*, p. 20, former madam Laura Evens is quoted as saying on tape in April 1950 that Jennie Rogers was six feet tall and "could barely read or write. A Georgia girl—and she was gorgeous, perfectly beautiful." The same book on the next page, however, shows Jennie's handwritten will, finely scribed (we assume by her) and perfectly literate. This plus the fact that Jennie Rogers is not reported to have been in Georgia raises questions about the reliability of Laura Evens's recollections or of Fred and Jo Mazzulla's account of Rogers. Gene Fowler in *A Solo in Tom-Toms* (pp. 211–226) recalled Jennie Rogers's real name as "Sara Jane Rogers"—the only such reference located in this study—and remembered Mattie Silks as particularly foul-tempered. Bancroft in *Six Racy Madams* (p. 5) insisted that Jennie made her signature as "Leeah" J. Fries. Bancroft's lengthy (pp. 5–33) portrait of Rogers is thorough and detailed. Unfortunately, like Forbes Parkhill before her, Bancroft documented none of her sources. Bancroft believed she bore a physical resemblance to the statuesque Rogers.

55. Differing from the RMN account, the DR identifies the arrestee as "Jennie Calmonton," does not identify her as Jennie Rogers, and omits mention of morphine addiction. No other sources suggest that Jennie Rogers was a narcotics abuser, and the names Calvington and Calmonton appear nowhere else in Rogers's biographies. "Vagrancy" was a catchall charge employed by the Denver police. Both accounts of this arrest were in the newspapers the next day, July 29, 1894. Jennie's arrest for "unladylike conduct in the street" is in Reiter, *The Women*, p. 142. The account of Jennie Rogers's years in Denver is from several sources. A biography of Jennie is in the files of the Office of History at the Colorado Historical Society. Additional materials are from Parkhill, "Scarlet Sister Mattie" (typescript and published versions), and particularly from Parkhill's *The Wildest of the West*, pp. 44–49. The Howe citation regarding Jennie's trial for keeping a lewd house is listed in the text. See also Fowler, *A Solo in Tom-Toms*, pp. 217–220, and Goodstein, *The Seamy Side of Denver*, pp. 38–41. Biographical notes on Jennie Rogers are in Bancroft, *Six Racy Madams*, pp. 5–32; Dallas, *Cherry Creek Gothic*, pp.

234–237; Reiter, *The Women*, pp. 142–143; and the SHS 16: 11789, from the DTI, February 28, 1896.

56. SHS 4: 901, 904, newspaper unidentified, dated October 13 and 15, 1886.

57. Press accounts of the investigation of Jennie Rogers by Henry W. Barr identify him as a former Denver police lieutenant, but the *Denver City Directory* of 1886 lists him as an active policeman. In 2001 the House of Mirrors has been lovingly restored by owners who appreciate the building's history and the structure serves as Mattie's House of Mirrors restaurant. The locations of three of the five stone faces are known, and two have been faithfully copied and placed high above Market Street on the cornice. (The third face was found too late in the restoration project to be included but may be copied someday and placed in the restaurant entry.) The House of Mirrors building has been designated as a contributing structure to Denver's Lower Downtown Historic District.

58. The Rogers-Wood confrontation in Omaha is from the DTI, January 6, 1885, four years before the couple's marriage.

59. Data regarding the relatives to whom Jennie Rogers (named Leah J. Wood) left all her properties are from notations concerning her estate, Denver County Court file 12912 (2171-528 and 1948-133) from Box 48B, Prostitution: Jennie Rogers, Mazzulla Collection, formerly at the Amon Carter Museum, Fort Worth, Texas, now housed at the Colorado Historical Society, Denver. Copy in the author's possession.

60. The will and papers of the estate of Leah J. Wood (Jennie Rogers), probate case 12912, Denver County Court, recorded January 16, 1911, are on file in box 53293, Colorado State Archives, Denver. They include depositions regarding the legality of the marriage; the transfer of Lot 6, Block 50, Denver (1942 Market Street), to Martha A. Thomson (Mattie Silks); records of various debts; and, most interesting, communications from Leah to Archie Fitzgerald, dated 1907–1908, and some written on stationery of the St. James Hotel, Denver. They are variously signed "L. J. Fitzgerald" or "L. J. Wood." One letter is signed "Love and a hundred kisses and one hundred hugs." The letter of January 1, 1907, addressed to Fitzgerald in Goldfield, Nevada, states: "There was several balls last night and most of the folks on [Market] street was there, I staid home and took in 75.00."

61. Fred Mazzulla told the author in 1966 that he had obtained the tile entryway lettering from the House of Mirrors on which was inscribed "M. Silks." A photograph of the entryway tile is in Mazzulla and Mazzulla, *Brass Checks and Red Lights*, p. 19. Parkhill, Fowler, Bancroft, Dallas, and Mazzulla, unfortunately, do not list sources.

62. For Verona Baldwin, see Parkhill, *The Wildest of the West*, pp. 50–59.

10

"I Have No One to Love Me"

The Denver demimonde produced many tales, comic to melancholic to tragic. Some of them are written here.

DETECTIVE SAM HOWE preserved the story of Lillie DeMorris, the wayward daughter of a well-known Philadelphia physician. What path led her to Denver we cannot know, but under the name of Ruby Gray she worked Market Street before moving on to Butte City, Montana Territory. There, sadness and loneliness overwhelmed her. She drank a morphine potion and died at age twenty. On her dresser was found a note:

> DEAR FATHER—I cannot live any longer. I have no one to love me. Pity me.
> Your only child,
> *Lillie DeMorris*[1]

The ingestion of an opium solution called laudanum or of morphine or of a fearsome household product called "Rough on Rats" was the preferred method of self-destruction in Denver in the late nineteenth century. All caused agonizing deaths.

The preparations were used frequently for suicide by a variety of citizens—rich or poor, prostitute or not—and were so readily available that one must wonder why their sale was not controlled. Ten cents over the counter would buy ample morphine for a quick exit from life's oppression in the dismal, dirty, faraway, friendless outpost of Denver.

Suicide in the town occasionally approached epidemic proportions. Detective Sam Howe's scrapbooks contain hundreds of such accounts. Denver in the nineteenth century could be an unpleasant place for those without means, and many of its habitués were unhappy. Alternately dusty or muddy and always far from loved ones (especially before the arrival of the railroad in 1870), the naïve emigrants flocking westward seeking a quick fortune saw their hopes dashed while others around them grew wealthy. Unable to return home to old friends and families, some turned to alcohol and drugs—both plentiful—worsening their dilemmas.

247

The girls of Holladay and Market Streets were even more deprived. For some, the only escape was death. The *Denver Times* wrote in 1886:

SUICIDE BY POISON

A Fallen Woman Ends Her Day with Morphia

West Holladay street was this afternoon the scene of a suicide which threw the inhabitants of that part of the city into a frenzy of excitement and caused nearly all the women in the neighborhood to emerge from the humble tenements which line the greater portion of either side of the thoroughfare, and stand, bareheaded, with arms akimbo gossiping about the event. Between Twelfth and Thirteenth streets stands a long row of two-story, very rickety frame tenements. The place is inhabited by people, many of them of the lowest stripe, several of the apartments, or more properly speaking, dens, being occupied by fallen women and low lived males who consort with them.

To-day at two o'clock a policeman paced up and down in front of the entrance . . . his every move being watched eagerly by a curious crowd of hangers-about who heard that one of the wretched inmates had committed suicide. The coroner had been called for and soon arrived, and proceeded up stairs. There in a small room, black with smoke of ages and the air of which was overpoweringly unpleasant, lay stretched on a bed, a woman, dead. Her name was Mrs. Wringer. The story was she had been drinking heavily; her "husband," a Frenchman, had deserted her, and last night she swallowed a big dose of morphine. On the bed beside the dead woman lay a terrier, her pet, whining piteously.[2]

Among the scarlet women to die of morphine ingestion was Mrs. C. B. Flynn, more popularly known in the West as Pearl DeVere, who was not Colorado's average *nymph du pavé*. DeVere practiced her trade in Denver before moving to booming Cripple Creek, where she superintended the famous Old Homestead parlor house on Myers Avenue. There in June 1897, after "a night's carousal," she went to bed at 7 A.M. after swallowing a quantity of morphine "to produce sleep," as it was reported. By 3:30 P.M. all efforts to revive her had failed. The *Denver Republican's* headline proclaimed "Close of an Erratic Life."[3]

Denver's brothel district was a block or two from the opium dens, which were in a neighborhood bounded by Twentieth, Twenty-second, Blake, and Market Streets. The greatest fear of Denver's drug addicts was being sent to jail because of the deprivation—although some addicts were administered narcotics while incarcerated to keep them calm and quiet.

Among the provocative documents discovered during preparation of this book was an unsigned letter to the editor of the *Denver Post*, which published it in the Sunday edition on February 25, 1900. The letter apparently was prompted by an article detailing an investigatory visit to the Market Street netherworld by a group of civic-minded local women. Under the headline "Problems of a Great City" was the following, sufficiently significant to be excerpted here at length. Its intent was to emphasize the great economic chasm between the haves and the have-nots of Denver and the men and boys who patronized women of the brothels and wine parlors:

Some women visited the lower part of town and reported that they were surprised at the condition of things and did not dream that such things were going on in Denver. I wonder if they stopped to think who made it possible for them to exist? We notice that they all live well, dress elegantly, have diamonds and horses and everything they desire. Their expenses for living alone are often $100 or $150 a month.

As I sit here writing, I stop to think, and I remember my son went out tonight. It is now 12:30 and he has not returned. Where is he? If I were to ask him he would say: "Oh, out with the boys. We took in the town." And where was my husband last night? He said he was going to lodge. Sometimes I think I will join the lodge myself, because my husband seems to take so much interest in his.

We are all careful of our daughters, but what good will that do if we neglect our husbands and sons? Girls as well-taught as ours are walking the streets of Denver tonight. Until the standard of our brothers, sons, and husbands' morality is raised, we may hope in vain for the purity of our city.

If our daughters are accused of unchastity, we are horrified, and well we may be. But if our son or brother is so accused, we smile and say: "The young man must sow his wild oats." Wild oats! Yes, and maybe the one who reaps the harvest was somebody's daughter or sister who but yesterday said her prayers at her mother's knee and lay down to dreams as pure as those of an angel's.

Of course, ladies, there are other reasons why these things exist. I have mentioned one reason. The next reason is the lack of good Christian people to work for. Outside of housework, where one is expected to do cooking, waiting on table, chamber work, washing and ironing, answering door and tending the furnace, all for $20 or $25 a month, with only one afternoon out, and then one is expected to hurry home and get dinner, what can the girls do? Yes, there are the stores, the overall factory, the cracker factory, the cotton mills, the paper mills, the box factory and the telephone where one can work, and these places employ thousands of girls and women. What wages do they earn? They earn from $3 to $5 a week, ten hours a day of steady, confining work. I know even if a girl got $6 a week, it will cost her each month $13.50 for her food alone, $7 for a room, and a dark little hole at that. She then has $3.50 left for clothes and washing and other little things she needs. That's the honest labor that was open to those girls if they choose it.

Some of *you* started with $5,000 twenty years ago, and some of you now are worth hundreds of thousands, have splendid homes, costly furniture, horses and carriages, bank stocks, real estate, in short all that you could desire.

The offenses which are committed day after day in this city go hand in hand with poverty. Drunkenness is not uncommon. Theft is of daily occurrence and often you hear of some sad accident happening to some little one while the mother is engaged as your employee. You will say you surely don't blame us for that? I am blaming nobody; I am just thinking. There are those girls and here are your workers with just as pure a heart as any of our daughters. What are we doing for them? What is the use of worrying with them after they have gone so far? Let us keep the others from following their example.

The letter writer's words were not heeded, and conditions may have even worsened. Seven years later the *Rocky Mountain News* (September 9, 1907) headlined "Whose Daughters in Winerooms? Yours," adding the warning of the Reverend J. L. Blanchard of City Park Congregational Church, who told his flock:

Do the people of Denver want the town wide open? It is wide open now. Saloons run all night and Sundays, winerooms are scattered all over the city from the depot to the statehouse, and they are patronized by all sorts of women and men, from the demi-monde to the society belle, and from the hanger-on of disreputable houses to the worthless rake of a Capitol Hill millionaire family. Dozens of gambling places are wide open and patronized day and night by men and boys. Hundreds of thieves make Denver their headquarters. Ballot boxes are stuffed or stolen at the behest of men who call themselves good citizens.

And two years after that, traveling evangelist Gipsy Smith told 12,000 sinners assembled at City Auditorium to shed tears for what he termed the "woman of the Tenderloin." He shouted scornfully:

You spurn her, you kick her down a little lower. But listen! If your friend who ruined her, if he can dress well, and ride in an automobile and live on Capitol Hill; you mothers who take communion, you members of churches, let that fiend into your home, you give him a seat at the table, you let him meet your daughters and play cards with them and dance with them! You talk about your fallen women. Where are the fallen men? I tell you, for every one fallen woman in your tenderloin, you have twenty men in your city who keep them there.

You women who take communion are partly to blame. You never speak to the woman that steps down and try to lead her to purity. You would not invite her to your house for a cup of tea. If you saw her in a store, you'd pass her by without speaking. There's only one way for that woman and that is the death way!

Smith converted 300 followers after that one revival session alone.[+]

Denver's young women were attracted to Market Street by a set of circumstances, generally but not always related to earnings. When police raided 1921 Market Street on its "opening night" in 1890, sixteen-year-old Bessie King told them: "I worked at Price's and other [restaurants]. It was while I was there a girl who lived at 2111 Market Street told me I could make more money. So I went. I never had any clothes or anything else, and I didn't think it made much difference, anyhow." King said she had been mistreated at home: "I never got up in the morning without having to hear some slur."[5]

In addition to the potential for earnings, complicated by poverty, girls of the Row could have been attracted by early sexual experiences, alcoholism and drug addiction, emotional deprivation, keeping bad company, a wish for adventure, despair over life, or—less often than one might believe—unhappy romantic experiences.[6] In an 1859 national study, one of the first such to be conducted, physician William W. Sanger questioned 2,000 prostitutes about their reasons for selecting their profession. Five hundred responded "destitution" and "inclination," whereas 258 said "seduced and abandoned"; 181 blamed their drinking habits; 164 cited ill treatment by parents, relatives, or husbands; and 124 listed "an easy life." Eighty-four blamed "bad company," 71 were persuaded by other prostitutes, and 29 cited laziness. Twenty-seven listed "violated," 16 said they were "seduced aboard emigrant ships," and 8 said they were seduced in emigrant boardinghouses.[7]

An unlikely woman perhaps to become involved with Denver prostitution was Mary Harris Jones. She was born Mary Harris in Ireland on May 1, 1830. Her family emigrated early in her life, and Mary found sympathy with the U.S. laboring class—miners in particular—and became an organizer of the Western Federation of Miners. By the 1890s social zealot "Mother" Jones ("Get it right. I'm not a humanitarian. I'm a hell-raiser") was a pro-labor agitator of national note. She drifted in and out of Colorado, focusing particularly on the coal fields around Trinidad, and according to the *Pueblo Chieftain* she "kept pretty busy stirring things up . . . never advocating peace nor arbitration; but always being for strife and war."[8] Mother Jones was in Colorado stirring things up prior to the "Ludlow Massacre" on April 20, 1914, in which the state militia faced off against a tent city of striking coal miners and their families. Five miners, one militia man, two women, and eleven children died.

A decade earlier, however, Mother Jones is said to have encountered perhaps her most serious Colorado crisis—one of a personal nature that followed her for the rest of her life. The flamboyant sob sister Polly Pry (nee Mrs. Leonel Ross Campbell O'Bryan) was a pulp fiction writer and a favorite staff columnist of Frederick G. Bonfils and Harry H. Tammen, proprietors of the sensationalist muckraking *Denver Post*. In February 1903, while still writing for the *Post*, Pry started her own sensationalist muckraking weekly titled *Polly Pry*, devoted to "society, politics, theaters, racing matters, the newest books, the latest fad in furious fiction, the last new drink, personalities; in fact, life in Colorado as it is, and not as it ought to be."[9] In her January 2 and 9, 1904, editions, Pry undertook an exposé of Mother Jones. The fact that Pry was fervently against organized labor must be remembered when considering her comments about Jones. The January 2 article introduced Mother Jones as a woman "who is always to the front when there is strife, with her battle cry of 'We'd rather fight than work!' 'Mother' Jones, who gets $5 per day and expenses as there is trouble brewing . . . is said to be worth any five men as an agitator."

Then Pry got to the point. At the Denver office of the Pinkerton private detective agency, she alleged, were documents describing Mother Jones as "a vulgar, heartless, vicious creature, with a fiery temper and a cold-blooded brutality rare even in the slums." Pry quoted the Pinkerton files as describing Mother Jones as a "well-known character" of the bordello district not only of Denver but also of Omaha, Kansas City, Chicago, and San Francisco. Pry added specifics, including the accusation that Mother Jones was a pimp:

> [Mother Jones was] an inmate of Jennie Rogers' house on Market street, Denver, some twelve years ago [that would have been 1892, when Mother Jones was sixty-two]. She got into trouble with the Rogers woman for bribing all of her girls to leave her and go to a house in Omaha—for which she [Jones] was paid a procuress fee of $5 to $10 apiece for the girls. She was a confidential servant in Rose Lovejoy's private house on Market street, Denver, and [was] with her several years.
>
> [Jones] was well known to Annie Wilson, another Denver woman who ran a place on Market street, afterward had a place in Cripple Creek, and now lives in Kansas City. Known to Lola Livingston, with whom she went to San Francisco. Lived in Eva Lewis' house

on Market street at the time the Coxey Army passed through here, and took a prominent part in the Denver preparations for their care.[10] Is known to Harry Loss, a piano player at 1925 Market street, who says he knew her first in Omaha in 1894, when she lived in a house at Tenth and Douglas. She was then selling clothes to the girls.

A sewing woman for the sporting class living on Lawrence street—name withheld—knew her twelve or fifteen years ago, when she lived with Minnie Hall, and afterwards with Jennie Rogers; says it was commonly reported that she was a procuress by trade.

A week later, on January 9, 1904, Pry reported in her newspaper that Mother Jones had not shown up for a scheduled speech at Denver's Coliseum Hall the previous weekend (when Pry's initial article appeared). Jones had traveled to Denver from Trinidad for the appearance. Jones, said Pry, instead of making a "rip-snorting" speech, went to her room at the Oxford Hotel, from which she departed the next morning "and since that time not a trace can be found of her." Polly Pry unleashed additional salacious material about the Denver activities of Mother Jones:

"Mother" Jones always was a changeable being, ever since she was known as "Mother" Harris, in May 1889, when she leased the house then standing on what is now 2114 Market street between Twenty-first and Twenty-second streets. She refurnished it from top to bottom, and soon opened it as a "house" that afterwards became one of the most notorious in the city. Had seven inmates, who were known as the "best-looking girls on the row." For several months took great pride in the character of her house and the class that patronized it. At that time was the most exclusive "house" on Market street.

Made a specialty of midnight lunches and social card games, at which unlimited gambling was indulged in. Catered entirely to the "gang" then in control of the city, county political machines and a few wealthy mining men. Four months after opening the house, had over $15,000 on deposit in city banks. Had a "friend" at that time, called "Black-leg." He deserted her in September and went to New Mexico with an inmate of the house.

After that "Mother" went to the bad. Took to drink, and was arrested several times on the charge of drunkenness and disorderly conduct. Left her "house" to manage itself, and in a short time it became one of the typical dives of Market street. By November 15th she had spent the $15,000 she had on deposit in the bank only a few months before, and borrowed $2,500 from S. H. Engel, a loan broker, giving a chattel mortgage on the furniture in the "house."[11]

On December 20th, 1889, the mortgage was foreclosed, the furniture sold and the house closed. "Mother" Jones then became an inmate of the "Minnie Hall house." Then came the record as I told it last week. And this is the woman the wives and children of the deluded miners call "Mother." Interesting, isn't it?

Pry's articles were picked up and printed by other newspapers, but the most damaging consequence came when Colorado's pro–mine owner congressman George Kindel read the *Polly Pry* writings of ten years earlier into the *Congressional Record* of June 13, 1914, two months after the Ludlow strife. As a result, labor advocate Terence Powderly, a Mother Jones supporter, wrote to Kindel stating that he (Powderly) became acquainted with Mother Jones at the time of her alleged brothel associations and that he was certain she was not a "keeper, inmate, or procuress" of such places, adding that Kindel should be ashamed of himself for assailing "a white-haired, aged, defenseless woman."

Mother Jones never denied the charges that she was involved in bordello activities in Denver or elsewhere. Indeed, her biographer Dale Fetherling quotes Jones as essentially confessing to her past life when she asked her union friend Duncan McDonald, "Don't you think whatever my past might have been that I have more than made up for it?" Fetherling also quotes Upton Sinclair as stating that Jones told him that the stories stemmed from her earlier days as a seamstress for prostitutes.[12]

In her 1905 autobiography, *The Long-Lost Rachel Wild, or Seeking Diamonds in the Rough*, Denver neighborhood missionary Rachel Wild Peterson wrote of visiting a "fallen girl" named Mollie Hill, dying of tuberculosis in a Denver "sporting house." Peterson and a friend rapped on the door lightly, and a faint voice said: "Come in." I shall never forget the sight that met my eyes. There in the middle of the room, in a large rocking chair, with pillows all around her, she sat, but oh, so pale! Nothing but a skeleton she seemed, and her large, sad, blue eyes only gave her a more deathly appearance, and such a place made it that much more solemn to me. I went to her side and took her hand [and she said], "I always did believe in God, for my mother was a Christian. I was only seven years old when mother died." Her voice trembled all the time she was telling her sad story. "If mother had lived I would not be where I am to-day. I was nine years old when I went out to work, and at eleven years of age I was a bad girl. I went from bad to worse, and it was not long till I was living a life like this. There is no hope for me. I am too far away from God, too deep in sin."

The two missionaries and Mollie prayed for strength. In a few days the madam evicted Mollie because she could no longer work, and the madam needed the room Mollie was occupying. Peterson helped her find a room in a "recruit house" where "sick or broken down or diseased" prostitutes went to recuperate until they were able to resume their bordello duties. The other girls gathered around "on their tiptoes, still as mice" to listen as Peterson and Mollie prayed every day until Mollie died. Among Mollie's statements to Peterson, whom she called "mama," was the following.

> I cannot remember the time I was ever loved by anyone except you and mother. I never loved but one man in my life. I did not intend to give up all hope and go to the depths of sin. I was yet in my teens when I met this man and I believed in all the promises he made me. Oh, how I did love him. My foolish young heart could not dream of such a thing as doubting him, mama, and yet he left me. Yes, he went away and left me. Do you know what it means to be out in this cold, friendless world without one soul to go to when your heart is breaking?[13]

The funeral of the forlorn Mollie Hill, who could scarcely remember ever being loved, was conducted by missionary Rachel Wild Peterson at the Miller undertaking parlor because, Peterson decided, her (Peterson's) own church was populated by a "heartless, thoughtless, selfish crowd" who regarded Mollie

as a "poor, fallen outcast, [and] despised." Mollie's funeral, however, *was* faithfully attended by what Peterson described as "those women." She added:

> The madam of the house in which she was taken sick paid for the carriages and coffin and shroud. I never before attended a service like that, where there were so many tears shed as there were that Sunday morning. The Lord led me to talk very plain to those girls. As we all stood there to look on one that death had fastened his clutches upon, not knowing who would go next, oh, how I was led to warn them, and try to pursuade [*sic*] them to be ready!

Reactions from relatives of Market Street's prostitutes are as scarce as recollections of the girls themselves. Detective Sam Howe preserved one such account, however. Mr. and Mrs. H. E. Hammond of Omaha, Nebraska, sent their daughter Edna westward to Colorado's healthy mountain climate for her lung condition, regularly mailing her money for living expenses. She wrote them often, telling them of her health improvement, and one day they journeyed to Denver for a surprise visit.

Nobody at the Colfax Avenue address she was using had ever seen such a person, and the parents traced her to a Market Street establishment. "She was broken-hearted at seeing her horrified parents," the *Denver Republican* reported, "but she refused to return with them, saying she had nothing to live for."[14] Or, as a man named A. B. Kahny wrote before hanging himself at the Victor Hotel, Eighteenth and Larimer Streets: "I owe no one a cent—my rent is paid. Too honest to steal, too poor to beg."[15]

The women of Denver's Market Street occasionally indulged in uncharacteristic high jinks. For instance, in 1883, when black was the standard women's garb from nape to ankle, a Market Street inhabitant was arrested for "meretricious display . . . flaming red silk dress, red hat, red shoes and stockings, carried a red fan in her hand, and led a white poodle dog colored red with a red string." On another occasion, longtime fire chief John Healy, responding to an alarm, wrecked the fire department's first automobile while trying to avoid a Market Street poodle. The breed became so identified with prostitution in Denver that no respectable female would dare own one.[16]

Pets were frequently kept in bordellos, in Denver and elsewhere. Storyville was New Orleans's *demimonde* district, and E. J. Bellocq's hallmark photographic study of the Storyville prostitutes illustrates several girls with their treasured pets—perhaps their only friends.[17]

The actions of Market Street's prostitutes in rescuing victims from Denver's anti-Chinese riot in 1880 were discussed in Chapter 7. Another "whore with a golden heart" episode affected Denver's gambling neighborhood. When gambler James W. Hogue was discovered beaten to death in his quarters at the Alta Furnished Rooms, 1754 Lawrence Street, Eva Marshall, one of Mattie Silks's girls at 1922 Market Street, composed a note to Police Captain Frank W. Lee: "Let me know promptly if relatives of James W. Hogue cannot be located and I will bear all of the expenses of a respectable funeral for him. He was kind to me and I will never forget him." Eva had met Hogue in Kansas City, and he accompanied her to Denver, paying all expenses, and saw to it that she did not go wanting until she found work at Mattie's. "I was never in love with Hogue and there was never anything to our relations save friendship," she wrote. "Yet he showed me every kindness. . . . I could not bear to think of his being buried in the potter's field [cemetery sections for the indigent]." An additional sympathetic press notice concerns a pair of "God's own girls" in a Florence, Colorado, brothel who rescued birds flying into telegraph wires and nursed them back to health.[18]

When cleaning her wardrobe with gasoline on January 1, 1904, Amy Bassett, employed in the house of Jennie Rogers at 2015 Market Street, became enveloped in flames. Policeman George Kaylor rescued Amy from the burning room and carried her across the street to Lillis Lovell's bordello, from which she was taken to the hospital and quickly died. Amy, whose real surname was Vamberger, was pronounced by the *Rocky Mountain News* to be "long known as the most beautiful woman in the half world of Denver." She was thirty-four and was said by the *News* to have once been married to Duke Corbin, son of former Ohio governor Thomas Corbin. (The *News* misstated the surname, which is properly spelled Corwin.) The student of prostitution in early Colorado and elsewhere notes that often at times of death and tragedy the biographical data become tender and flattering (and exaggerated, if not concocted): whores with hearts of gold, harlots who at one time were happily married mothers, girls rescued from their scarlet existences by soft-hearted (preferably wealthy) clients, boys introduced to sex in a local brothel, prostitution as a result of seduction and abandonment, women who disgraced the name of their prominent family back home, madams who amassed fortunes in jewelry, girls who were educated in the finest schools and then went wrong. An interesting twist on the latter was the *Rocky Mountain News*'s statement that Denver's Lillis Lovell had been a "concert singer." Such stories have a name: "whorehouse tales"—overstatements or outright untruths far more often than not and detectable by their abundant use, with variations.

At the time of Amy Bassett's marriage into the governor's family, said the newspaper, she already had a somewhat notorious reputation and subsequently was driven from the family by the governor. A son of Corwin and Amy Bassett's remained in Cincinnati and had no idea of his mother's occupation in Denver, said the newspaper. In whorehouse tales the errant disgraced woman often retreats into anonymity, lest the innocent child be devastated by the knowledge that mother was impure.

Amy's funeral a week later, the *News* reported, was attended by her grieving husband, George Converse, and women "who had probably never uttered a prayer since their childhood [and who] joined in the Lord's Prayer with tears in their eyes." They included

from Chinatown, Yee Lung, in a clean new blue blouse, with shining brass buttons, and "Smoke" Wing, from the opium dens, dressed for the first time anyone could remember, in American garments. Even "Chiny Annie," lavishly painted and powdered, hobbled in before the conclusion of the service, and from the other end of the row came half a dozen colored women. On the way [to Fairmount Cemetery] they told stories of the dead woman's striking generosity to her more needy companions in the scarlet life.[19]

Jennie Rogers's girl Amy Bassett, said to have once been the scion of an Ohio gubernatorial family, met death by flames in a Denver brothel. She had, lamented the Rocky Mountain News *(January 2, 1904, p. 5), once been so fortunate and so beautiful. "Many were the conquests she made," said the* News, *"and the homes she wrecked." But more recently, "On several occasions she has been implicated in brawls and seriously injured, marring most of her noted beauty." This is a retouched version of the coroner's postmortem photograph.*

woman, who placed the wreath on the coffin, will mourn for a lost daughter. To them she will be missing only. Of her death they probably will never hear. That her funeral was attended by no one save the scarlet women, the expenses met by their subscriptions and the services held in the rear room of a coroner's office, they will never know. That much is spared them.[20]

The girls of Denver's Row did not always coexist well. As the *Denver Republican* reported in 1884: "Louise Carlin and Maggie Wise, who are both Holladay Street women, paid fines of $10 and costs each at the police court yesterday, for the Sunday pastime of scratching each other and tearing hair."[21] "Holladay Street" women: like the Scarlet Letter, it was their burden to bear.

Some men were nurtured from the proceeds of the illicit district. Denver's male procurers were called *macs* rather than the cruder term *pimps*. "Mac" was an alliteration of the French *maquereau*, translated as "brothel keeper" and almost always misspelled by the Denver press as *macquereau*. A mac who took his profession seriously could skim a handsome living from the services of the girls (*les chevaliers d'amour*—literally a low-ranked girl of love) he oversaw. Madam Nell Kimball, however, wrote in what are represented as her memoirs (p. 5) that she had a difficult time accepting the "sweet daddies that attached themselves to a girl's earnings and lived off her twat."

Kathleen Barry in *Female Sexual Slavery* (p. 86) views procurement by men as "perhaps the most ruthless display of male power and sexual dominance" and

A similar farewell was afforded "Clara Smith" who burned to death when her gown caught fire from a stove in the house at 1938 Market Street. The *Denver Republican* eloquently described the spartan service:

A charwoman, faded, bent and broken, stood silently beside the coffin of a woman of the underworld yesterday afternoon in the dim light of an undertaker's chapel. Beyond, in a little group, sat a dozen more women from the restricted district. The new plot out at Riverside [Cemetery] will be marked by a plain slab bearing the name "Clara Smith" and the date of her death. That is not her right name. What her name really was, who were her parents and where they lived, are things not known. In the underworld no one knew. There she was simply Clara Smith. Somewhere a mother and father, possibly as old and feeble as the old char-

Pimps and brothel owners were the scourge of the city, and Jack Maynard (real name: John Mahan) and Billy Wheeler were two of Denver's worst in 1908 and 1909. Wheeler went to jail for ninety days and was fined $200, whereas Maynard jumped the district attorney's dragnet and disappeared before reconsidering and turning himself in. Maynard subsequently graduated from pimping and became a New York dealer in stolen gems. In 1923 he returned briefly to Denver to stash $86,200 in hot jewelry in Denver's Chinese district, but he was eventually caught.

2   THE DAILY NEWS: DEN'

ADMITS THAT LARGE FORTUNE CAME FROM FALLEN WOMEN

"Billy" Wheeler Confesses to Shame on Witness Stand and Jury Confirms Jail Sentence.

crib for a home. Wheeler replied "I live there because it is quiet and retired."

"Do you consider it a fit place for your wife to live?"

"Oh, yes; there are lots of respectable people living all around me."

"Do you consider the morals of the community good and the business your neighbors engaged in legitimate?"

"Well, you see, I am broad-minded on questions of that kind and never gave it much thought."

Pressed to state how he made a living, Wheeler replied that he didn't have to work for a living as he was retired, merely raising dogs and keeping a garden for pastime.

When the laughter that this answer evoked had subsided, the district attorney asked him point blank if he collected rent from any of the cribs.

"No, sir, I do not."

"Does your wife?"

"Well, that's her business. If she does I never interfere."

"Does your wife collect the rent?"

"Well, yes, I guess she does, but I don't have anything to do with it."

JACK MAYNARD   BILLY WHEELER

grancy charge at the time of the roundup last week, surrendered yesterday after-noon and gave a cash bond of $400 for

refers to pimping as "the oldest profession"—a term long associated with prostitution itself. In Chapter 5 Barry examines what she describes as five alternative "patterns," or avenues, of procuring: (1) by becoming a friend or lover; (2) through gangs, syndicates, and organized crime; (3) through employment agencies; (4) by purchasing women for cash (principally a foreign phenomenon); and (5) by kidnapping.

America's original pimps came about as a result of the so-called New York brothel riots of the 1830s. In those disturbances hoodlum intruders would raid a brothel—terrorizing, raping, looting, vandalizing. Thus pimps were hired for protection. They served other functions as well: shopping, repairing the house, attending to city hall and payoffs, recruiting new talent, and making themselves otherwise useful. Soon their presence—whether in the highest parlor or alongside the lowest streetwalker—became indispensable. The report of the 1911 Vice Commission of Chicago described the pimp, or "cadet," as

> averaging from eighteen to twenty-five years of age, who, after having served a short apprenticeship as a "lighthouse" [?] secures a staff of girls and lives upon their earnings. He dresses better than the ordinary neighborhood boy, wears an abundance of cheap jewelry, and has usually cultivated a limited amount of gentlemanly demeanor. His occupation is professional

seduction. . . . He is the lowest specimen of humanity, and whenever apprehended should be dealt with to the fullest extent of the law.[22]

Pimps were often the girls' lovers, and they could brutalize the prostitute who did not promptly turn over her night's earnings.[23]

Denver's police conducted a roundup of sex purveyors in late March 1908. Among them was a keeper of the filthy cribs—the lowest sort of mac—William "Billy" Wheeler. During his trial for vagrancy—a catchall charge filed when the prosecutor did not know what else to do—Wheeler conceded that he had no job but had amassed "considerable money loaned out at good interest, had $9,000 at the Colorado National Bank, and owned real estate in Canada." The newspaper reporter editorialized that these assets were "bought with the price of women's shame . . . most of it secured from the poor, miserable, painted creatures in the Market Street cribs."

Wheeler told the judge his wife collected rents on their six cribs, that he and Mrs. Wheeler resided in a house behind one of the cribs, and that he was "broad-minded" about community morals. He was fined $200 and given ninety days in jail, a sentence also given to Market Street property owner John W. Mahan (Mayhan), better known to police as Jack Maynard.[24]

Maynard was a major marketer of Denver prostitution from about 1906 to 1914. He owned at least one brothel, near Twentieth and Market Streets; was well-known to the police; and maintained a reputation as a conniving loan shark. To keep his girls from undercharging favorite clients, thus depriving him of his proper percentage, Maynard installed cash registers in each crib, which earned him national publicity.[25] Demonstrating Maynard's insolence, not to mention his political clout, the *Rocky Mountain News* quoted him as commenting to an officer arresting him for disturbance: "Who are you, you big roundhead? I am just the man from Market Street, but I can get your job. Those stiffs down at city hall will fire you if I say the word." The article added, significantly: "Maynard has been a faithful worker for the Speer machine, and has occupied the post of precinct committeeman for the city hall organization. He is also known as the 'king of the macquereaux [*sic*].' "[26]

Despite his city hall connections, Maynard realized in 1914 that Denver was finally serious about shutting down the Row and concluded that this would be a good time to relocate. In Denver he had been involved in small-time loan sharking and prostitution. New York City offered more opportunities for professional growth, so Maynard opened a jewelry business on Broadway in Manhattan. Stolen jewelry, that is.

We do not know how long Jack Maynard got away with fencing stolen gems, but his downfall finally came ten years later at the hands of Irene Schoellkopf, a reckless and fun-loving young matron from Buffalo, New York. Irene was married to the wealthy Hugo Schoellkopf, but on New Year's Eve 1922 she was accompanied by another man—her "traveling companion and dancing partner" (as the newspapers delicately put it) Frank Barrett "Barry" Carman—to a raucous party at the West Fifty-second Street apartment house where Carman resided. The gathering got rowdy; Irene entered a hallway, was grabbed, and was dragged inside another apartment where her jewelry was sto-

len and she was beaten. The loot was subsequently estimated as worth $238,000 to $300,000.

Police immediately suspected an inside job or setup. Carman was arrested but was released at Irene's insistence. The police began looking for two renters of the apartment where Irene was assaulted, Eugene Moran and Albert Hurwitz who, as it turned out, had sold $86,200 of the loot to Maynard for $37,000.

The following August, Maynard transported at least some of the gems to Denver where he sealed them in a fruit jar and buried them somewhere in "Chinatown," the by-then decrepit old Hop Alley neighborhood northwest of Twentieth and Market that had been Jack's old stomping ground.

Maynard became a suspect in November, and on the second of that month he offered to cooperate with the district attorney in exchange for leniency. That same day Maynard's business partner, Harry Hirsch, committed suicide. Two months later Moran and Hurwitz were arrested in New Jersey and further detailed Jack Maynard's involvement in the Schoellkopf jewel heist.

In return for possible leniency, Maynard agreed to lead New York detective Martin S. Owens and E. J. Harris, secretary to Hugo Schoellkopf, to the gems' hiding place. The secret three-day train trip westward began without Maynard revealing the eventual destination to Owens and Harris. Harris—who was along to possibly identify the jewelry—and Owens were skeptical, but the trio arrived in town on January 20 and checked in to the Oxford Hotel. Maynard contacted some of his old cronies and reportedly even attended the National Western Stock Show. Then he led the detective and Harris straight to the buried jar, which reportedly contained a $41,700 pearl plus rings, bracelets, and bar pins. The trio never contacted the Denver police, instead proceeding with the gems directly to Union Station and departing for New York. Denver's newspapers learned of the scenario over the wire services several days later and never published the location of the buried loot. In New York, Maynard disclosed the whereabouts of another $75,000 of Schoellkopf's loot.

Maynard had made these confessions and disclosures not out of guilt or regret but rather because he felt he had been jinxed by the Schoellkopf gems. Once a robust and handsome 200 pounds, since the robbery he was down to 150 pounds and was suffering from a heart ailment, high blood pressure, and paralysis. He had been told by a religious adviser that it was all because "jewels taken from a body of a woman bring trouble" (Irene Schoellkopf had not been killed in the robbery). Furthermore, Jack pointed out, his business partner Hirsch was dead because of the gems, and of the eight people who had been at Barry Carman's New Year's Eve party, three were dead.

After confessing and surrendering Irene Schoellkopf's jewelry, Jack Maynard began to feel better and was sorry he had opened his mouth. "I'll get every damned stone and pearl back," he grumbled, "if only I can live to do it." Moran and Hurwitz went to prison; Irene presumably got at least some of her jewels back; and there the saga of Jack Maynard appears to end, as no further accounts of him have been discovered.[27]

Much was reported through the years on the political wooing of liquor interests, madams, and prostitutes whose votes at election time were eagerly sought. In his article "Dirty Tricks in Denver" (p. 225), historian Elliott West wrote that during the municipal elections of 1889,

> rumor had it that the liquor dealers of Denver had raised $20,000 to pay for [escorting saloon customers to the polls] and to reward the mobs at the polls at a rate of two dollars a vote. . . . Policemen and bartenders reportedly made sure the flow of ballots for [mayoral candidate Wolfe Londoner] remained smooth and uninterrupted. Occasionally a poll watcher complained, only to be ignored or physically abused.

When the official canvassing was completed, Londoner had defeated Elias Barton by 377 votes, but Londoner's election triggered two years of turmoil rarely equaled in the political history of Denver. Londoner was charged with packing city departments so full of political cronies—including Police Chief Henry Brady, police officer and henchman Sam Emrich (later imprisoned for murder), and Lieutenant James Connor—that the city was almost forced to declare bankruptcy. Months of scandals culminated in a trial that included

testimony that Connor, Emrich, confidence man Jefferson Randolph "Soapy" Smith, and Bat Masterson had compiled voter registration lists naming persons who were dead or out of town or who were simply fabricated. The courts ordered Londoner removed from office, something that had never happened in Denver mayoral history.[28]

There can be little doubt that prostitutes were paraded to the polls. In 1906 reporter Lawrence Lewis, who had been the *Rocky Mountain News* correspondent in Pueblo, wrote a statistical article titled "How Woman's Suffrage Works in Colorado" for *The Outlook*, a national magazine. Lewis concluded that Colorado brothel precincts showed higher proportions of women voters than did nonbrothel precincts.[29]

In an extreme incident during May 1908, Mayor Robert Speer's protection of Denver's pimps was blamed for two deaths. City fireman Burton Koch shot and killed his ex-wife, Louise, accidentally shot and wounded her mother, and then killed himself after it was disclosed that Louise had been working for *maquereau* Bert Lustig, with whom she apparently was infatuated. Koch had gone to his wife to plead with her to leave the pimp and return to Koch and their four-year-old son. "The double tragedy," said the *Rocky Mountain News*, "reverts back to the protection extended to macquereaux [sic] by Mayor Speer and his former chief of police Michael A. Delaney. Had it been impossible for men of Lustig's ilk to traffic in women in Denver, the misguided Louise Koch, her friends declare, would have been living with her husband and would have been a good wife and mother." In a jailhouse interview with the *News*, Bert Lustig showed the reporter "the loud and expensive clothing of his unnatural profession. Turning up his trousers and displaying a pair of hose which were wonders for color and design," Lustig said, "I did my best to keep her away from me, but there was no use. She, like lots of others, was crazy about me and I couldn't fight 'em off."[30]

Following the Billy Wheeler and Jack Maynard *maquereau* incidents, Denver's police made yet another public show at pursuing the dandies who were profiting from the activities of the Market Street women. A newspaper reported in 1908:

THE DAILY NEWS: DENVER, COLORADO, WI

Triple Tragedy Due to Police Protection Given to Macquereaux by Order of Speer

BERT LUSTIG GRINS AT MURDER THAT HE CAUSED

Blames Dead Girl, Ignorantly Infatuated With Him, for Husband's Acts.

OUT of the protection accorded the macquereaux by Mayor Robert W. Speer grew the tragedy of yesterday morning, when Burton Koch, city fireman, shot and killed his divorced wife, Louise Perry Koch, accidentally shot and seriously injured Mrs. Matilda Motley, his mother-in-law, and committed suicide by shooting himself.

Albert Lustig, confessed proprietor of women, who was arrested in District Attorney George Stidger's raid on the tenderloin, and who was convicted on the testimony of Mrs. Koch, who admitted that he had sold her to men from whom he collected the money, yesterday talked freely of the murder case and the disgraceful liason which existed between him and the murdered woman prior to his arrest.

In his cell in the county jail Lustig insisted that he had been given the worst of it in the case which was brought against him. He laughingly said that he was glad he was in the county jail when Koch started out with his gun.

"I was lucky," he said, "that he didn't get me too, but on the level, she chased me and I had to stand for her."

Baby With Father's Parents.

Valentine Koch, the 4-year-old child, who was made an orphan as a result of the murder and suicide is with Mr. and Mrs. Alois Koch, his grandparents, at their home, 1432 Downing avenue, and will be cared for by them.

Mrs. Matilda Motley, mother of the murdered woman, is at the county hospital suffering from a gunshot wound in the leg, inflicted while she was trying to save her daughter's life.

Mrs. Motley, although very weak, is able to talk and blames both Koch and Lustig. Her mother-love asserts itself and she cannot hold her daughter to blame for the terrible results of her infatuation for Lustig.

Reasoning the case from all of its phases the cause of the double tragedy

BERT LUSTIG,
The Macquereau Who Brags That Women Adore Him, and Who Was the Cause of the Koch Tragedy.

"Macquereau" (pimp) Bert Lustig told Denver police it was not his fault that divorcée Louise Perry Koch was so infatuated with him that she allowed him to sell her favors to other men. (Lustig kept the money.) Louise's anguished husband, city fireman Burton Koch, discovered as much and killed her and himself. Showing a Rocky Mountain News *reporter his fancy silk socks during a jailhouse interview, Lustig said: "I was lucky that he didn't get me too, but on the level she chased me and I had to stand for her" (May 6, 1908, p. 4). Stretching things a bit, the* Rocky Mountain News *blamed the whole tragedy on "the protection extended to [pimps] by Mayor Speer and his former chief of police Michael A. Delaney." As difficult as it is to defend much of what Mike Delaney did, it is difficult to pin this murder-suicide on him or Speer.*

member of the macquereaux colony, was arrested. Ormsby has been known as the best friend of [madam] Mrs. Verona Baldwin [see Chapter 9] . . . hat and cane in hand and his generous chest swelled out like that of a pouter pigeon, Baldwin strutted up and down in [Police] Captain [Frank] Lee's office and attempted to secure clemency. At last report, Ormsby had discarded a Newmarket overcoat, hat, gloves and cane, and under the guidance of two drunken tramps was vainly attempting to send a telephone message for aid out of the "bull pen."[31]

Like rats rushing from a sinking ship, Denver's population of macquereaux [sic] are hurrying from the city. When Chief [Hamilton] Armstrong declared that he was going to purge Denver of this loathsome species of mankind many said it was only a bluff. But last night, when Detectives [Peter J.] Carr and [Coleman] Bell arrested a half dozen of the most notorious and influential of the macquereaux and placed them in jail as vagrants, fear gripped the denizens of the redlight district like palsy. Gossip was rife last night when the word was passed down the line that Edward Ormsby, 57 years old, the most debonair and well-groomed

The French influence on Denver's *demimonde* was considerable during the last two decades of the nineteenth century. For example, the circa 1900 prostitute census of 2134 Market Street included *desmoiselles* Lucile [sic] Lacourt, Blanch [sic] Laduc, and Bertha Delacroix, all listed as natives of France, and a Jeanne Kaundolf. These *filles de pavé* held a special attraction for Denver customers. Romance seemed attached to these women's very names, but often, as will be seen, they attracted the attention of the police.

In 1904 it appeared federal immigration officials in Denver were finally attempting to discourage the importation of French prostitutes. On December 3 Immigration Agent Louis Adams and Denver policemen Francis J. Carney and Clarke (possibly Culver E. Clark) arrested Juliet Beaudert, twenty-one, and Bertha Beaudert, twenty-five, who had been enticed from France with the promise of good employment in America. After being "subjected to most shameful treatment" in Texas, they were shipped to the Denver brothel at 1920 Market Street, where they were arrested pending deportation to France. The madam at 1920, Esther Paisson, also known as Esther Alexander, was also arrested. The scenario, reported the *Rocky Mountain News*, had sent Denver's *maquereau* pimps into hiding.

The Denver Police Department at the turn of the twentieth century was maintaining a periodic vigilance over what was happening on the Denver Row. If the occasional saber rattling of Police Chief Hamilton Armstrong was not sufficient to provoke the Market Street set, the 1908–1909 legislature decreed that "women who receive money from any woman inmate of houses in the redlight district are liable to prosecution and penitentiary sentences. Any man who places a woman in such a house will be equally guilty with the man who lives from the earnings of the unfortunate woman." The result, the *Rocky Mountain News* reported, was that "Market Street was in a state of consternation. There will be an exodus of macquereaux [*sic*] today."[32]

Prostitutes' or madams' lovers were not always pimps. Historians Susan Armitage and Elizabeth Jameson, drawing a vague line between the prostitute/pimp relationship and the possibly more caring madam/boyfriend association, wrote:

> The relationship between prostitutes and pimps was the most complex in the demimonde. Some prostitutes considered pimps parasites and would have nothing to do with them. Pimps unquestionably exploited prostitutes, living off their earnings and often treating them viciously, but some women willingly allied with pimps. Whatever emotional support, physical protection, sexual satisfaction, or illusion of romance these men "of fancy dress and patent leather shoes"

provided seemed to offset the abuse with which they treated their lovers. Many prostitutes demanded faithfulness from their paramours, and when they suspected infidelity, they took action. One night at a party, [Colorado's] Laura Evans [Evens] decided that her beau was dancing too frequently with another woman and knocked him through a plate-glass window. . . . Pimps violated every tenet of nineteenth-century manliness. Pimps did neither "honest" nor "manly" work. They were supported by women; worse, they exploited women's virtue.[33]

As the new century arrived, the daring among Denver's "respectable" young ladies came to regard the naughty tenderloin neighborhood as an outlet for their blithe spirits, venturing downtown to visit the wine rooms, dance halls, and theaters and maybe sneaking off toward the Market Street brothels to peek at the unfortunates living and working there. For some months during autumn of 1907, Denver experienced what the newspapers viewed as "a rapid fall in morals" among otherwise respectable, well-bred, and educated young ladies. This situation, in the view of the police, had become so dangerous by September that officers raided the wine rooms and beer joints and hauled twenty presumably naive young ladies off to jail to teach them a lesson. "Slumming," it was called. "We have got to do something to prevent these young girls from experimenting with places that are dangerous for their future welfare," said Police Chief Michael A. Delaney. "Show none of those we arrested mercy, make it a real lesson, don't let any of their friends see them tonight."

The jail was full of sobbing young women while fancy carriages pulled up in front of police headquarters at Fourteenth and Larimer Streets, carrying well-heeled and indignant mothers and fathers demanding to visit their offspring. "Nothing doing," responded Captain Lee. "If your daughters take the chance of entering wine rooms, which a distinct ordinance prohibits, they must expect to take consequences."

The chief and captain, to their probable chagrin, were informed the next morning by Mayor Robert W. Speer—a politician never oblivious to the influences of Denver's movers and shakers—that they had arrested the wrong people. Speer said the barkeeps rather than

TEMPTING TO RUIN!
HOW GOTHAM'S PALACES OF SIN ARE GARRISONED OUT OF THE HOVELS—
THE GAUDY SPIDER SPREADING HER WEBS FOR THE FLIES WHO
MAKE HER LOATHSOME TRADE PROFITABLE.

This engraving from the Police Gazette, *a sensationalist but popular tabloid of the time, was titled "Tempting to Ruin!" The image at* lower right *shows a woman recruiter enlisting two innocent schoolgirls for prostitution.* At the top *is a view of what shortly would come of the unsuspecting young girls.*

had been to both affluent city leaders *and* Denver's liquor interests. In this case, the booze faction had to concede.

Denver's jail was no place for a lady, as the *Denver Post* later related. The paper reported in a 1917 retrospective: "Many a woman suffered indignities unspeakable in the 'bull pen' of the city jail until *The Post*, voicing the sentiment of the women in Denver, demanded the appointment of a police matron and the segregation of women and girls charged with crime." Possibly in 1888 on a provisional basis, Sarah "Sadie" Morehouse Likens became the first matron, and her appointment was made official on July 1, 1889.[34]

Sadie Likens is an important figure in early Denver law enforcement. She was not Denver's first policewoman, as is often said (that honor fell to Josephine Roche more than a dozen years later), but the diminutive (five-foot-two) Likens was Denver's first police *matron* and is said to have been the second such matron in the United States.[35]

Sadie Morehouse was born in Trenton, Ohio, on July 14, 1840 or 1842, the youngest of six children. Approaching adulthood, she moved to Wisconsin where she married David Washburn, a Union soldier who died during the Civil War. After the war Sadie relocated to Mineral Point, Wisconsin, where she married lawyer William Likens. The couple had four chil-

the customers should have been charged. The girls were released, and nine wine room owners were cited to appear before the police and fire board for "serving liquors to women." This case was particularly perplexing for Mayor Speer, whose political allegiances

dren. William Likens was a crook and fled to California to avoid arrest for forgery. The family reunited and in 1881 relocated to Boulder, Colorado, where William Likens again practiced law—and again faced forgery charges. Convicted, he was sentenced in May 1885 to four years in the state penitentiary in Cañon City. Released in July 1888, he fled to Washington state and then Wisconsin.

Sadie and the children moved to Denver in 1886, and she became matron for a Women's Christian Temperance Union home, which led to the police matron's job with the city—a new position paying sixty-five dollars a month. Her daughter Belle was hired as assistant matron on May 6, 1891. Prior to Sadie's presence, women and children in custody of the law had never had an advocate and were overseen by male guards. In July 1894 Likens was caught up in a political shakeup and left the matron's job, becoming superintendent of the state home for incorrigible girls. She died in Denver on July 30, 1920.[36]

Only a few weeks after the wine parlor roundup of Denver's young, daring, and misguided blue-blooded women, the Speer administration renewed its on-again, off-again tough stance regarding females in saloons. This began when the Fire and Police Board revoked the liquor license of Frank Morrato's establishment at Twenty-second and Curtis Streets for remaining open after hours and allowing a woman on the premises.[37]

The notoriety of Denver's wine rooms persisted, however, with the disclosure that they were being used as meeting places for "orgies" between young girls and older men. Such discoveries began with the arrest of Olive Mayhew, nineteen, of 1529 West Third Avenue, who was procuring young girls and steering them to the wine rooms where they were introduced to men. "This is the worst case of juvenile delinquency and depravity it has been my fortune to handle during the four years I have been connected with this court," said Special Officer John S. Phillips of Denver Juvenile Court. The offenses were conducted in the saloons themselves, in cheap rooming houses, or in the homes of the men involved.

Nine persons, including the men, were arrested in the Mayhew incident, and the Fire and Police Board revoked two saloon licenses. Among those arrested was Mrs. Carrie McDowell on charges of "enticing her daughter [age fifteen] to error." Two of the girls were fifteen, the other was fourteen. Olive Mayhew pleaded guilty to a charge of juvenile delinquency. The newspapers reported that one of the customers, Bert Chase, an iceman, said in his defense that he spent his days on the ice wagon shouting "'Ice! Ice! Ice!' and didn't have time to chase around with girls, and was a Y.M.C.A. man." Another defendant, Fred Roberts, said he, too, "worked too hard to fool around with girls all night and was a member of the Y.M.C.A." Apparently the YMCA defense had worked before in court. Perhaps it did this time. After squabbling among the attorneys, "the case was continued for further hearing," said the *Denver Republican*, and all indications are that it was never pursued.[38]

The matter of Mrs. A. E. "Bessie" Horney resembled that of Olive Mayhew, with the important exception that Bessie found herself before the well-known judge Ben Lindsey of Denver Juvenile Court, a founder of the juvenile court system in the United States. From her Denver home at 221 Fourteenth Street, Bessie procured young girls for what the *Denver Times* called "debauchery shocking in the extreme. Nightly orgies participated in by men of 40, 50, and even older in years are said to have occurred in the house, which is situated within almost a stone's throw of the courthouse, the mint and the public library."

The authorities charged Horney with procuring, but Judge Lindsey went after the men who frequented the house. "It is the men that are higher up whom I am after," said Lindsey. "I want to get the names of those scoundrels who have gone to this house and have been guilty of immoral conduct with girls of tender years. I would far rather have them than to have this woman punished."[39] Horney was acquitted by a juvenile court jury, largely because it was discovered that the prosecution's principal witness, teenager Pauline Herring, had been promiscuous in Kansas City before moving to Denver. There is no record of any attempt to prosecute the male patrons of the house, despite the judge's condemnation, although Lindsey ultimately became a well-known protector of child rights and family matters.[40]

The big city could be frightening and dangerous for a young lady from outstate alighting from the train at Union Station. A sixteen-year-old girl from Greeley entered Denver in June 1906 to look for work and was "attracted by the music" in the Mills Edisonia flickering movie parlor near Sixteenth and Curtis Streets. There one Samuel Miller enticed her to his room with a promise of employment, and she was forced into prostitution by Miller and by his friends Charles Cutter and wife, Ida. They were arrested, and the girl was remanded to a detention home.[41] In a separate incident, Jennie Kubler told police she was an immigrant who could not speak or understand English when her husband, in addition to administering daily beatings, forced her to work in a house at 2148 Market Street. She finally summoned the courage to file for divorce.[42]

Instances are recorded of policemen being more closely involved in the *demimonde* district than simply looking the other way. Antonio Santopietro (Tony Sanders), whose troubles will be cited later in this chapter, is a good example. Additionally, the district attorney's (DA) office during summer of 1908 investigated whether Denver police—Detective Billy Green in particular—were directly benefiting from the earnings of fallen women. When the DA's probers arrested "Little Ruth" Campbell, known up and down Market Street as Billy Green's girl, Green was observed scurrying around on city time until late at night trying to raise her $400 bond. Little Ruth was released, but he left in jail four others apprehended with her in what was said to be Billy's bagnio. The district attorney's men told the *Rocky Mountain News* that "other police officers are in the crib business, and we promise to make further and more sensational raids." There is no indication that they did, and perhaps the episode of Little Ruth was meant to put corrupt policemen on notice that they were being watched. Little Ruth showed her appreciation by skipping bond, which was forfeited. Billy Green had considerable influence along Denver's Row. He escorted the brothel ladies to the polls on election day, just to make sure they got there safely and voted correctly. During such times the Row was known in political circles as "Green Country."[43]

How Denver police detective Green could have so continually and openly operated with impunity as a keeper of prostitutes is a curiosity, but the case of Deputy U.S. Marshal Benjamin M. Borland was at least as surprising. As Christmas 1899 approached, Eva Walker, eighteen and without friends and homeless, ended up in federal custody for claiming and cashing a fifteen-dollar U.S. money order addressed to another Eva Walker in care of the Denver post office. Several nights later Borland called at the county jail and asked to remove Eva. The jail matron, knowing the young woman was a federal prisoner, complied. Eva was sobbing when she left. The next morning Eva, unaccompanied, returned to the jail—drunk.

An investigation disclosed that Borland had apparently told Eva, in the words of the *Denver Post*, that "if she would comply with his wishes he would assist her in her trouble with the government. If she would not go with him he could send her to the penitentiary."

At this point the Humane Society, at the time one of the very few child social service agencies in Denver—and which was also responsible for domestic-animal abuse cases—attempted to interview Eva but "was denied access because Government authority exceeded theirs," according to the newspaper. Eva was removed from the jail again "by the marshal's office representative and also by a guard at the jail. It seemed to her that anything was better than going to the penitentiary. It was a jail scandal, and other prisoners talked about it."

Finally, Eva disappeared permanently from confinement and could not immediately be located by the press. There had not been a hearing, and no bail was posted. The *Post* reported that the marshal's office had exerted sufficient pressure on the U.S. Attorney's office to get rid of the matter. Within forty-eight hours Eva, who looked older than her years, was located in a brothel at 2120 Market Street in company with Lillian Gardner, a "dance hall woman" who did not know who Eva was. Gardner told the Market Street beat patrolman that Eva had been handed over "by a deputy United States marshal, and that it was all right." A Humane Department official observed: "It looks very much as though this poor, homeless, friendless and penniless girl has been driven to a life of shame by the marshal's office. Now she is in a resort on the Row and her life has been ruined, and by a man who is supposed to be a protector."

Walker had been in jail pending a federal grand jury indictment for stealing the fifteen dollars. On January 30, 1900, she appeared in Denver U.S. District Court, where Judge (first name?) Riner instructed a twelve-man jury to issue a verdict of innocent, which they did without leaving the jury box. The grand jury returned indictments accusing Benjamin M. Borland, now a *former* deputy federal marshal, of feloniously permitting Walker to escape. The girl, described by the *Post* as "well formed, blue eyed, comely, and blushing," testified before the jury that she and Borland had walked the streets—she begging him not to return her to jail—and that she spent the night "with a friend on Larimer Street."

Before her acquittal Walker married Peter Schalk, a killer she met in jail. Judge Riner immediately granted Borland's attorney's motions arguing that the indictment was faulty and insufficient evidence of an escape existed.[44]

Young Eva Walker alone and on the streets—a circumstance common and acceptable among ragamuffin boys of the late nineteenth century but not among the girls. New York children's advocate Charles Loring Brace, when asked to comment in 1872 on Stephen Crane's novel *Maggie: A Girl of the Streets*, wrote (p. 65) that with a small boy "one always has the consolation that, despite his ragged clothes, he often has a rather good time of it, and enjoys many of the delicious pleasures of a child's roving life. The oaths, tobacco spitting, and slang, and even the fighting and stealing of a street-boy, are not so bad as they look." With a female—Eva Walker being this Denver example—the situation as Brace saw it was not so simple.

> With a girl-vagrant it is different. She feels homelessness and friendlessness more; she has more of the feminine dependence on affection; the street-trades, too, are harder for her, and the return at night to some lonely cellar or tenement-room, crowded with dirty people of all ages and sexes, is more dreary. She develops body and mind earlier than the boy, and the habits of vagabondism stamped on her in childhood are more difficult to wear off. The sin of the girl soon

becomes what the Bible calls "a sin against one's own body," the most debasing of all sins. She soon learns to offer for sale that which is in its nature beyond all price, and to feign the most sacred affections. She perverts a passion and sells herself. This crime, with the girl, seems to sap and rot the whole nature. She loses self-respect, without which every human being soon sinks to the lowest depths.[45]

Forbes Parkhill reported that Denver at one point required "public women" in the city to wear yellow ribbons on their arms when on the streets as a badge of the profession. The edict was no match for the madams of Market Street: they dressed their girls in yellow from slippers to bonnet and ordered them to swarm through the restaurants and other public places where "respectable" people gathered. There were hundreds of them, Parkhill wrote, and apparently they were disregarding the city edict that they should not travel outside their district. To the visitor it must have appeared there was not a chaste woman in Denver. It was all the idea of Mattie Silks and Jennie Rogers. They thought it a hoot. The rule was repealed.[46]

Evalyn Capps Walker, whose family arrived in Denver in 1863, recalled many years later that her mother and aunt, as young girls, peeked at the hanging of two men and were scolded by their parents. The aunt, indeed, was locked in her room on a diet of bread and water, and the young girls were warned that they were not to view what their parents prohibited, including "girls in yellow."[47]

If such carryings-on of Denver's yellow-clad red light businesswomen seemed frivolous, more so were the antics of bordello queens to the north in Helena, Montana, where townspeople complained about the "indiscriminate seating of members of the demimonde in the dress circle and parquette" of the local opera house. The theater manager informed the women of the *demimonde* that although they would still be admitted, their chairs would be confined to a less conspicuous area. Whereupon five of the ladies purloined habits from the Sisters of Charity and presented themselves at the opera house door. Even though the manager denied their entry, the community was outraged at such a display of sacrilege.[48] Much the same thing happened in Denver. An 1878 review of *Il Trovatore* at Nate Forrester's opera house, printed in the *Rocky Mountain News*, commented on the presence of prostitutes in the audience.[49]

The Holladay Street ladies had endured enough oppression and restriction at the hands of authorities and concluded that there was strength in numbers. The *Denver Times* in 1886 explained what followed:

> Bell Bernard [her advertisements list her as Belle Birnard], Gussie Grant, Lizzie Preston, Jennie Caylor, Clara Dumont, Jennie Rogers, Bell Jewell, Eva Lewis, Mattie Silks, Emma Smith, Rosa Lee, Mary Smith, Anna Gray, Minnie Palmer and Clara Hayden, a lot of the "giddy girls" of Holladay street, charged with keeping lewd houses, and who gave bond in the District court last week for their appearance in the Criminal court, were arraigned to-day before Judge [Platt] Rogers, and pleaded "not guilty." The girls have formed a pool to test this matter, and if they are convicted in the Criminal court they will enter a plea to the jurisdiction by way of abatement, and carry the cases to the Supreme court.[50]

Verdicts in this case ranged from dismissals to guilty. Jennie Rogers was found guilty—despite testimony that the district attorney had employed "stool pigeons" to gather evidence—and was fined seventy-five dollars plus costs. Two days later her attorney moved that the fine be set aside since Rogers would take the matter to the Colorado Supreme Court. Caroline Bancroft said that during the court's December 1886 term, Rogers lost and forfeited the seventy-five-dollar fine.[51] The working women of Denver's Row, however, continued to tweak the law, as when Belle Jones, Daisy Smith, and Annie Griffin were overtaken with high spirits and danced nude at Nineteenth and Larimer Streets, for which they were arrested and fined for "naughty capers."[52]

Lizzie Preston (real name Hannah E. Foster) was one of the "giddy girls of Holladay Street," and two remarkable stories emerged from her house. One involved Colorado's famous Tabor family. The other, a tragedy, involved the madam who could no longer hide her deepest secret from her unsuspecting daughter.

Elizabeth B. McCourt married William Harvey Doe Jr. in Oshkosh, Wisconsin, on June 27, 1877, when she was only seventeen, and the young couple moved west to Colorado. "Babe" Doe, as Harvey called her, had the face of a cherub, hair like spun gold, a peaches-and-cream complexion, an hourglass figure, and a restless nature.

None of that escaped silver millionaire Horace Austin Warner Tabor when he observed young Harvey and Baby Doe strolling through the lobby of Larimer Street's Windsor Hotel, Denver's swankest. Tabor, it was said, offered Harvey Doe a thousand dollars for an introduction, and soon Tabor—who was married to the rather severe (albeit devoted) Augusta Tabor—and Baby Doe were Denver's favorite subject of whispered titters.

On the night of March 2, 1880, Baby Doe waited with policeman Edward Newman across the street from Lizzie Preston's bordello at 433 Holladay Street (later 1943 Market). Baby Doe and the lawman observed Harvey entering the establishment with another man, whereupon Baby and Newman went onto the porch of the house of ill fame and knocked on the door.

A woman, perhaps Lizzie Preston, answered and asked Baby her business, and Baby replied that she had just seen her husband enter and wanted to follow him. The woman at the door warned Baby Doe and policeman Newman that they were about to enter a house of ill fame, whereupon they proceeded inside and saw Harvey, as Newman later testified, "sitting on a lounge in one of the rooms." They departed, and two days later Baby filed for divorce, alleging adultery and nonsupport, stating she had to sell her jewelry to pay family expenses.

Understandably, Harvey Doe was unnerved. A month later he wrote to her parents, stating that he had entered the brothel only to try to find a purchaser for a mine he wanted to sell. The spellings, punctuation, and capitalizations are his.

> My Dear Father & Mother:
> You have of corse herd before this of my sad sad loss in loosing my darling Babe I am heart broken about it I shal go crazey about it I know I shal for my dear Father & Mother it was not my fault that I went into that parlor house. Let me tell you all about it and then I hope you will not blame me there is a man in this town who was trying to sell my mine for me. We had been looking all over town for a man who said he

could sell it so we hunted all over for him so this man said let us look in Lizzie Preston's for him I told him I did not go into such places as that Well he says if you want to sell your mine to this man we have got to find him tonight for he is going away in the morning so I told him if he would not stay in there I would go in and right out again So I went in and who should be a cross the street but Babe and saw me going in there I did not stay I did not stay in there only long enough to see if that man was in there just as I was going to go out Babe came there and caught me and she did act like a perfect lady and conducted herself so nicely in such a place as that. Now my dear Father & Mother do not blame me I went in there on business of great importance to me I can assure you. I was so hard up I did not have any money nor nothing to eat in the house and I thought if I could find this man I might get some money from him to help me out I did not go in that place with any bad intentions no no I love my darling wife babe to much ever to disgrace her in that manner I have been as true to her as any man could be to his wife so I went into that parlor house thinking I might get some money to help us along in the world. . . . I hope and sincerely pray my dear parents you will not blame me and do try and get babe to come back to me for she is all I have got in thes world do try and pursuade her to come back to me for with out her I am a miserable man and am nearly crazey abot the affare. . . .

    Loving Son
    Harvey

By this point Baby Doe's money woes had been relieved by her new best friend, Horace Tabor. In retrospect it appears suspiciously coincidental that Baby Doe and a police witness were lurking across the street from Lizzie Preston's just as Harvey and his business companion entered. A cynic might suggest that the companion steered Harvey into Lizzie's place and that Tabor had retained the companion to entrap Harvey Doe and fabricate evidence to be presented in the divorce action.[53]

Baby Doe got her divorce from hapless Harvey; she and Horace Tabor married and became principals in the most famous love story in Colorado's history.

Lizzie Preston's house was also central to one of the most plaintive stories to emanate from the Denver Row. In Washington, D.C., in 1874 Lizzie and her husband adopted a girl, Essie May, age fourteen months. The family emigrated to Denver to seek its fortune. Lizzie's husband died of tuberculosis, but Lizzie, a woman of will, decided to try to make it on the Western frontier. With a small savings she purchased what she understood to be a lodging house at Twenty-third and Lawrence Streets. It was actually a bordello.

Encouraged by the house's earnings, she remained in the business, leading a double life as a secret madam and a single parent to Essie May. Lizzie and the child lived the quiet life at 3051 Stout Street, an upscale residential neighborhood.

When Essie May reached thirteen, Lizzie knew her secret could not be kept much longer, and she enrolled Essie in an expensive Catholic convent in the East. Five years later the happy and refined Essie returned to Denver unannounced and proceeded from the train station to the Stout Street home, where she was told her mother was at work and was given the location. Anxious to see her mother, Essie skipped to the front door, which upon being opened, instantly disclosed Lizzie Preston's dark secret.

Essie was beyond consolation and, according to Forbes Parkhill in *The Wildest of the West* (p. 57), screamed at Lizzie: "All right, if this is the truth, I'll work beside you! You have ruined my life!" I've gone to hell! All I can do now is follow in your footsteps! I'll be a whore like you!"

Lizzie Preston pleaded for Essie to flee Denver and go where nobody knew the family's shame. Essie dashed from the porch and stood frantic in the midst of Denver's sordidness. Soon she was across the street, working for one of Lizzie's competitors. She never spoke to her mother again.[54]

Preston died in 1904 at age sixty-five, and the next year Essie May, now thirty-three, brought suit seeking Lizzie's estate of $25,000 in real estate and jewelry. The family court judge Ben Lindsey, who later became famous, ruled that although Essie May had maintained she was the "daughter" of Preston, there was no evidence that Essie May was legally adopted by Preston; thus Essie was not an heir and had no right to the distribution of the estate.[55]

On New Year's night 1913, with the temperature at minus twenty-one, police received a sick call from the house of Mattie Silks. The police ambulance was busy elsewhere, so police reporter Forbes Parkhill and a policeman drove to the call in a touring car. The men found Mattie standing at the top of the narrow staircase leading to the second-floor rooms. Parkhill recalled later:

> She was short, quite fat, and wore spectacles. She looked like a kindly grandmother, but I recall that she still wore several diamond rings and at her throat, a diamond cross. Without a word she led us to the room where the girl, named Stella, wearing only a pair of black openwork silk stockings, lay "sobbing and praying and wretching [*sic*] and writhing and dying, alone, in agony from the poison she had swallowed. The thump-thump of the piano came from downstairs."

The men lifted Stella from the bed. Halfway down the narrow stairs she threw up and ruined Parkhill's suit. They loaded her into the open car and hauled her to the county hospital. She died the next day and earned a three-line notice in the *Denver Post*. Suicide attempts by Market Street girls were fairly common—perhaps two or three a week—and seldom rated more than a line or two in the newspapers.[56]

Author Gene Fowler was reared in Denver. Just after the turn of the twentieth century he was a delivery boy for what he identified in the autobiographical *A Solo in Tom-Toms* as the Grand National Market, which supplied groceries to Market Street's sex palaces. The following account of his experiences among the red lights—and of his first true love—is from that book:

> I had daily contact in the red-light district with the people of a forbidden world. Alive as I was to the savage hungers of adolescence, I escaped seduction in the brothels. Contrary to legend, these women were not the cunning agents of a boy's depravity. I believe that any man's vice is of his own making, be he young in blood or an old rake flying the remnants of his passion like a riddled banner.
>
> The Grand National Market seemed to me to have been transported from Bagdad [*sic*]. Its shelves held

OUR SUICIDES ARE MANY

In 1871 seventeen-year-old Josie Washburn joined the Omaha brothel of Anna Wilson. At age fifty-three Washburn wrote about her long experiences as a flesh merchant in The Underworld Sewer: A Prostitute Reflects on Life in the Trade, 1871–1909. *Among the illustrations was "Our Suicides Are Many," reproduced here, showing prostitutes shooting themselves and otherwise plunging into a pond in which float the bodies of other victims. Washburn wrote: "We attempt to retain our self-respect, the only trait that may be used as a stepping-stone to redemption. When pride and hope cease to be a domineering feature of the underworld woman, she commits suicide. Marvel not that so many take this step, but rather marvel that many more do not go that way" (p. 264).*

merchandise seldom heard of by ordinary Westerners, or tasted by them. These expensive goods were imported for the epicureans of the red-light district, many of whom were continental Europeans. The panders of "The Row" spared no expense on self-indulgence in wine cellar, wardrobe, or at table. I have long observed that the worse off a man's morals are, the better he dines, drinks, and clothes himself.

Grandpa was [an employee of the Grand National]; they called him "Dad." He would not, however, permit the men customers to call him that. Whenever one of the male habitués of Market Street became so familiar to address him as "Dad," the old gentleman would say frigidly, "The name is Wheeler." . . .

A commotion at the front part of the store interrupted the conversation. [We] hastened to the grocery department to find Grandpa hurling cans of French peas and crocks of goose liver at a male customer, then grappling with him. Grandpa's antagonist was a procurer known as Diamond Louie, so called because of the numerous gems he wore, including a diamond set into an upper front tooth. "Here, now," said Uncle Dewey [the owner]. "What's going on?"

"I'm beating the hell out of this pimp," Grandpa said from a clinch. "That's what's going on." Diamond Louie was yelling, "Get this crazy old bastard off of me!"

It was [in a bordello] that I first met Trixie, and although she never knew a thing about it, I saw in Trixie the successor to the fabulous and beautiful darling of the pioneers, Sarah Jane Rogers, known to the generation before mine as Jennie. Madam Rogers had built this house and long reigned in it. . . . Jennie Rogers employed twenty-four girls at her mansion during the early days, it was said, but I doubt if ever she had one as beautiful as Trixie. I first saw Trixie [in autumn of 1905] in the kitchen of 1942 Market Street. The basket of groceries was heavy on my shoulder. . . .

As I went inside the kitchen to lay down my burden on a table, a woman's voice said, "Don't look!" Other than a pair of high-heeled slippers, she had on no clothes. I did not know what had brought her to the kitchen, and I was not the kind of person to ask idle questions. Of one I was certain, and that was the way Keats felt when he first saw the Grecian urn.

Trixie hastened out of the kitchen, and I went to the back yard, completely forgetting to take the bas

ket with me. I made it my business to learn the girl's name. She was beautiful and dark, and she had a way of walking into my skull at night. I could tell whenever she was coming into my skull long before I would see her in the moonlight. I could hear the sharp rapping of her slipper heels on the floor of my head.

All night long I would dream of Trixie, and all day long think about her. In the slender hope that I might come upon Trixie somehow during my deliveries, I resorted to such subterfuges as neglecting to take a whole order to her house on one trip. I would leave behind at the store or in the wagon a loaf of French bread, then go back to the mansion on the pretext of delivering the mislaid package.

I had almost despaired of ever seeing Trixie again when one day I was driving my grocery wagon and crossed the path of a smart carriage in which Trixie was riding with her madam, Leona de Camp. I lived upon this vision for a week. I became indifferent to the sordid aspects of the red-light district, so occupied was I by my dreams of Trixie.

Of Trixie I dreamed through the long white winter, then on St. Valentine's Day of 1906 my plight became downright hazardous. I had wanted all along to send her a note, a poem even. On Valentine's Day I bought a somewhat ambitious creation with a winged cherub framed in a mat of paper lace and an outer ring of heart design sprinkled with flecks of gypsum. I did not sign my name to this token, to be sure. Instead, I printed the magic word, "Trixie," on the back of the valentine. I waited until after Mr. Ott had checked the basket that was to go to the mansion. Then I surreptitiously placed the valentine among the articles ordered for Trixie's house.

I hoisted the other baskets and boxes onto the wagon, then returned to get the one that contained my gift. I was unprepared for what I now saw. Mr. Ott was standing over the basket, the valentine in one hand, an ear lobe in the other. "Oho!" he all but shouted. "A walentiner it is!"

"I better get started," I muttered over the basket, and my voice seemed to come from a far-off cave of despair.

"Hah!" Mr. Ott snorted. "Started at vat? Started at funny business! Ve vill look into dis t'ing." Then he said insinuatingly, "Tell me all about it, you and Trixie. Everyt'ing. Begin at de first."

"There's nothing to tell," I objected. "What would there be to tell?"

"Aha!" he exclaimed. "Noddings to tell, he says! . . . Ve vill let de walentiner tell it."

"Mr. Ott," I almost howled. "It's the truth. I just bought a valentine, and that's all. Trixie doesn't even know I'm alive!"

He came back to where I stood. He studied me closely, then said impressively: "I haff only dis to recommend, and it is for you to learn dat until you get old enough to wear long pants and go in de front door of a fancy place mit five dollars in hand, don't go in de back door mit only walentiners. Yah!"

"I won't," I said, putting out an unsure hand toward the valentine. "Will you give that back to me now?"

"*Nein* . . . I will just keep dis walentiner someplace. And for my saying noddings about it, you vill show me how good a grocer clerk you can become."

In this manner I was blackmailed into becoming an alert, industrious, efficient, and capable grocery clerk as well as a dependable delivery boy. I learned to be polite even to Mattie Silks, the most testy-tempered of the madams. And all these labors were as nothing whenever I thought of Trixie—or remembered that Mr. Ott held over me the weapon of a winged cherub framed in a mat of paper lace and an outer ring of heart design sprinkled with flecks of gypsum.

Then one day I learned that Trixie had vanished from the mansion. Had she died?

One afternoon I set out to deliver an order of goods to the home of a Mrs. Blank in South Denver. I found a small cottage that lay in a respectable although unpretentious part of the city. . . . Mrs. Blank turned out to be Trixie. . . . She was plainly dressed in a calico wrapper, and she seemed extremely contented and housewifely. Trixie had on no rouge, and there were no high-heeled slippers on her feet. But Trixie was Trixie, dressed no matter how. It occurred to me that she now was married. A great, aching resentment boiled inside my breast. I felt that Trixie had been grievously unfaithful to me. Moreover, as she directed me where to set down the order of groceries, she gave no evidence of ever having seen me anywhere before, or caring to do so ever again.

Years afterward, my uncle happened to say, in discussing the matter of courtesans entering wedlock, that Trixie had stayed happily married. I should imag-

ine that in a world of change we never should be astonished or amazed at anyone's change of profession. Change also has come upon the old mansion built by Jennie Rogers, in the kitchen of which I saw my love. That great house now is a Buddhist temple, where gongs sound and incense is burned. *Auf Wiedersehen.*[57]

In a similar regard Max Miller, in *Holladay Street*, quotes Fred Mazzulla, who as a youngster in the railroad town of Salida delivered laundry along that town's well-established Line:

I was paid five cents to deliver a load of laundry, consisting of three or four parcels. . . . What Mollie [Mollie Alexander, the laundress who did washing for the girls along the Line] didn't know was that the girls were always good for at least a ten-cent tip, and most of the time a twenty-five-cent tip, for each bundle of laundry. The deliveries were always made at the back door. Sometimes I had to wait.[58]

The Denver love-for-sale establishments of Mattie Silks and her colleagues were central to a somewhat brash, and in retrospect even comical, counterfeiting scheme smashed by Detective Sam Howe during summer of 1885. It was one of Howe's earliest "big" cases—as big as Sam was ever assigned—and thus earned a sizable space in his scrapbook.

During summer of 1883 several hundred-dollar-bill printing plates were stolen somewhere in the East by three counterfeiters whose names were Doyle, Brockway, and Foster (first names unknown). Although the first two were captured and convicted, Foster made his way to Greenland, Colorado, south of Denver. There he was arrested, extradited to the East, and convicted.

Two years passed until one day counterfeit hundred-dollar bills began surfacing in Denver. In the first incident, a delivery boy was given one of the bills with a note addressed to a cigar dealer, ordering a hundred cigars worth $9.50, with the cigars and the $90.50 in change to be returned to the sender via the same delivery boy. The cigar dealer detected that the bill was fraudulent and dispatched a note back to the sender that delivery could not be made. The same trick was tried twice more in quick succession, with one of the attempts successful.

The bill passer shaved off his moustache, substituted his brown felt hat with a sportier white straw hat, and headed for Holladay Street. His first stop was the parlor of Mattie Silks, where he offered a bogus hundred-dollar bill for a five-dollar bottle of wine. The assistant madam on duty could not change the hundred and sent to a nearby bar for the cash. The perpetrator received the $95 and left without drinking the wine or showing any interest in the main attraction of the place.

He then proceeded to Minnie Clifford's house and from there to that of Eva Lewis, neither of which could make change for the bill. By this time Officers Howe and Martin "Mart" Watrous, accompanied by Captain Wilson S. Swain, were in pursuit by foot. They followed the trail to the home of Frank A. Gulden, 504 Arapahoe Street (between Fourteenth and Fifteenth Streets), where they were told by Mrs. Gulden that her husband was not there. That was false; he was inside frantically packing his trunk, intending to take the first train out of town, presumably without Mrs. Gulden. Mattie was out $90.50, and Gulden got five years in prison.[59]

In Denver the love-for-sale situation had worsened by December 1883, when Police Chief W. A. Smith conceded to the *Rocky Mountain News* that he had identified 275 houses of prostitution, "including alleged cigar stores [with] brazen women sitting in the windows." Circumstances did not improve: two decades later the cigar store women were still present, and the Fire and Police Board announced it would henceforth disallow so-called cigar girls—described as "women employed at cigar stands, located at or in the entrances of saloons and billiard halls"—because "young women should not be employed at saloons and pool rooms, because it is against public policy and morality for people passing by on the street to glance into the entrances and see girls throwing dice with a crowd of young men hanging over the counter." These women's salaries were high: ten to twelve dollars a week in pay and five to eight dollars a week in tips.[60]

The advertising practice of stationing women in bordello windows was long established elsewhere by the time prostitution arrived in Denver. In 1830 New York, for instance, homeowner George Chapman protested that from his front window he could see females across the street "parading in a state of nature, with the front window open to the street." Other times the girls would call out to passersby, inviting them inside. Later, pictures or drawings were displayed in windows.[61]

Denver's Police Chief Smith acknowledged that he had been the object of "no little abuse" over the "failure to attempt to close the houses of prostitution," supposedly "carried on more openly and shamelessly than in any city of the country." The chief had been training a special ten-man squad to "rid the city of this evil."[62] Nothing appears to have come of Chief Smith's indignation; indeed, in all of 1883—when prostitution in Denver was at a zenith—only *one* officially recorded arrest was made for prostitution and *none* for gambling, if the reader is to believe a report issued to the press.[63]

As discussed in Chapter 9, the women of Denver's *demimonde* enlisted the skills of a friendly dentist to install removable steel "biters" on their teeth, used to snip diamond stickpins from the vests of wealthy clients. Many other sorts of nefarious activities were common on Market Street. Robert Goge, a traveling salesman, reported to police the theft of a hundred dollars' worth of velvet cases and fancy parasols from his room at 1534 Larimer Street. Several days later at 4 A.M., police raided Lizzie Arbor's place at 2026 Holladay Street, seized the stolen goods, and hauled the house's occupants off to jail. The suspects, the press reported, "were confirmed morphine and opium fiends. . . . One of the prisoners took two hyperdemic [*sic*] injections of morphine in his arm before he left the house." Five men and three women were jailed.[64]

Lillis and Lois Lovell were said to have been blood sisters in sin who conducted business at Jennie Rogers's place at 2020 Market Street. Lillis was born Emma Lillis Quigley on October 4, 1864, probably in York County, Nebraska. She was a cabaret girl in Leadville beginning circa 1882, moving ten years later to Creede ("It's day all day in the daytime, and there is no night in Creede"), the silver and gold camp in southwestern Colorado's San Juan mountains. There she was known as "Creede Lil."[65]

Emma Lillis Quigley was new to the big city of Denver from her family's Nebraska farm when she had this proper studio card view taken by photographer W. H. Demaree. Quigley soon discovered that gentlemen would eagerly pay for certain of her favors, abandoned her outward respectability evident in the photograph, and relocated to the boomtown of Creede.

As the citizens formed a bucket brigade, Majors's husband called to her that they must save what they could. They stacked prized possessions in a hallway, ready to be carried out to safety. Majors continued:

> Then came a never to be forgotten surprise. The street door swung open and three women of the demimonde came up the stairway! The one who first reached the top addressed me by name, and said it would be impossible to save our building, and that they had come to help me, to forget who they were and tell them what to do. When told the things in the hall were ready to be taken, they carried them [out], even the heavy trunks, then stood guard over them. The street was filled with swearing men and weeping women, some with babes in arms, little children carrying favorite toys and dolls. . . . But the fire was finally under control. Then those women carried our belongings back. I felt most grateful to those poor outcasts, and would gladly have treated them with kindness, but they never saw me again. [They] gave me no chance to speak to them.

These people of the half world were never presumptuous, loud or boisterous in public places. They visited the stores to do their shopping, but never in an intoxicated condition, or smoking. It was only the women of the half world who smoked in those days.[66]

In 1945 Mrs. A. H. Majors of Creede wrote a reminiscence in which she discussed a rash of fires in Creede sometime after 1893. Majors recalled hearing the railroad locomotive's whistle in the middle of the night, a call for all townspeople to turn out and help fight a fire. The blaze was in a building a short distance down the narrow street, with a breeze fanning it in her direction, jumping buildings as it went.

In Creede, Emma Lillis Quigley decided her real name and photograph-parlor image were too stodgy for her new profession and became "Lillis Lovell," posing in her svelte new gown. Business increased proportionately with her new identity, and Lillis returned to Denver where it was said she wore $6,000 in jewels during strolls down the avenue. When she died in 1907, the Denver Republican *proclaimed her to have been a woman of superior intellectual attainments.*

Lillis Lovell came to Denver from Creede in 1901 at age thirty-six. The *Denver Post* wrote about her with undisguised admiration (and probably some exaggeration):

[Lillis Lovell] was one of the wealthiest women of the tenderloin. Whenever she appeared on the streets she wore between $6,000 and $10,000 worth of diamonds, and her resort [brothel] was one of the most lavishly decorated in the entire country. The decorations were in white and gold. Not gilt, but pure gold leaf, was used on the furniture and walls of the parlors, and this represents an expenditure alone of $10,000.[67]

In March 1907, the month of her death from pneumonia, Lovell was still running 2020 Market and making purchases at the upper-class Daniels and Fisher store. Her bill that month amounted to $158.58. Lillis died on March 22, and cremation took place at Riverside Cemetery. Her one-paragraph obituary in the March 25 *Denver Times* said:

Her funeral was largely attended. For years [she] conducted resorts in the tenderloin districts of Denver, Leadville, and Creede. The woman was said to be a concert singer before she deserted the stage to lead the life of the demimonde. She had been known in the half-world for twenty-five years and during

Before she left for Denver, Lillis Lovell— "Creede Lil"—may have worked alongside these four women and their "Forget Me Not" pillow and morning-glory phonograph horn. Researcher Fred Mazzulla identified this picture as "Bob Ford's Girls" in Creede in 1892. Ford, who owned a dance hall/saloon/brothel in Creede, was the assassin of Jesse James.

that time had amassed a fortune said to have exceeded $50,000.

The *Denver Republican*, whose sober appearance belied its ongoing attention to racy items from the Denver *demimonde*, elaborated on the *Times's* fleeting "concert singer" reference. The *Republican's* headline pronounced Lovell a "former opera singer," stating:

This afternoon the body of Lillis Lovell, once a grand opera soprano of prominence, will be laid in its final resting place. Lillis Lovell, under another name, was at one time prominent in grand opera and concert circles, both in this country and abroad, but through some incident in her life which she never chose to divulge even to her intimate associates, she left the stage some 15 or 20 years ago and has since been a figure of the half world here and in other cities throughout the country. A woman of superior intellectual attainments, Lillis Lovell was much above the ordinary woman of the class to which she descended.[68]

Prostitutes' obituaries often asserted that the deceased at one time had been rich, famous, talented, well-bred, happily married, a loving mother, an accomplished musician, or otherwise respectable. A recapitulation of Lillis Lovell's estate, dated April 29, 1907, valued her belongings not at $50,000 (the *Times*), not at "$50,000 to $60,000" (the *Post*), and not "between $50,000 and $100,000" (the *Republican*), but rather at $16,076, of which $12,000 was in real estate.

Lovell's will, dated June 23, 1905, suggests she may not have been on friendly terms with most of her siblings. One dollar each was left to four brothers, a sister, and various nieces and nephews; $3,500 was left to sister Martha Albine Quigley McKillup of Kansas City, Missouri; 320 acres in Red Willow County, Nebraska, was willed to brother T. K. Quigley of Indianola, Nebraska; $500 was left to her longtime lawyer, James D. Pilcher of Alamosa (60 miles southeast of Creede); and the remainder of the estate went to Lillis's husband, Clarence J. Trimble, who, she wrote, "has done much to assist me in accumulating my property, and has aided and assisted me in a great many ways." The *Post* was less kind to Trimble (March 26), dismissing him as "a Market street habitué."

The inventory of her property was not representative of an ordinary household. It lists 33 cuspidors valued at a total of $9.50; 3 pianos totaling $225; 1 brass bed and 12 iron beds for a sum of $41; 14 dressers at $70 for the lot; 35 nightstands at $17.50 total; 14 rocking chairs and 56 other chairs for a total of $27; many mattresses, blankets, bedspreads, pillows, sheets, and pillowcases; 44 doorway curtains; 1 bird and cage; 6 diamond rings; and a Bible.

Lillis Lovell's supposed sister and fellow prostitute, Lois Lovell, is more of a mystery. Lillis's will mentions only one sister residing in Denver, and that was Mary Nirene Quigley Wilder (who could have used the pseudonym Lois Lovell). If that is the case, it is doubtful whether the two sisters could have been partners in crime (let alone friends), because Mary

was left only a dollar in Lillis's will. In any event, Lillis's death left Lois alone and in grief (or so wrote Forbes Parkhill), but the next year she fell in love with a young Denver businessman who asked her to marry him. She declined, telling him her profession might bring him into disrepute.

He pleaded in vain, the story continues, and after being rejected he descended the brothel staircase as Lois cried after him with one of the great remonstrations ever to echo along Market Street: "No, darling, I won't marry you, and the reason I won't marry you is because I love you so." It recalled Jennie Rogers's statement to police after she shot Jack Wood in 1889: "I shot him because I love him, damn him!"

Lois Lovell's true love left Denver on the next train, and at the sound of the locomotive whistle fading into the distance, Lois fatally shot herself in her bordello room. A week later her lover returned to Denver, jubilant with the new idea that they could wed and take up residence in another city or state and nobody would know her past. When informed that Lois had killed herself, he insisted on being taken to her grave at Riverside Cemetery, where, gazing upon the newly dug mound, he drew a pistol and blew his brains out.[69]

Sadness up and down Market Street surrounding the Lois Lovell matter was intensified by the ill-worded send-off given to Market Street resident Emma Goodrich, alias Hattie Griffin, who worked at madam Eva Lewis's place. Griffin's death, or the demise of any girl of Market Street, was inherently unfortunate, but the *Rocky Mountain News* obituary writer bombastically ensured that Griffin was as disparaged in print as she had been in life—and her colleagues were slighted as well. The notice, obviously written by a person repulsed by prostitutes, was published in the July 27, 1887, edition:

A SAD ENDING

The end of Hattie Griffin's wayward life was as sad as the last few years of it had been, as a great number of her unfortunate companions gathered to pay the last tribute which even a fallen woman receives. Six of her companions in immaculate white dresses that seemed a travesty on purity and truth, bore her remains to the hearse and a hundred other cyprians brought floral arches . . . even though she had been

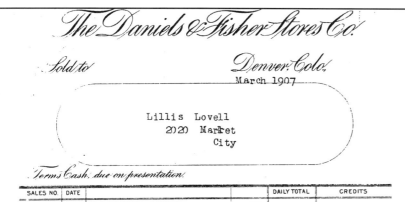

The Daniels & Fisher Stores Co.

Sold to   Denver, Colo.
                           March 1907

Lillis Lovell
2020 Market
City

Terms Cash, due on presentation.

SALES NO.	DATE				DAILY TOTAL		CREDITS
503	1	1	Pillow Top	35			
		2	Dz Silk	1 00	1 35		
504	7	1	Pillow Top	35			
		1	Pillow	1 75			
		2½	Dz Silk	1 25			
		1	Ruffle	45	3 80		
260	9	8	N Shirts	5 20			
704		6	Combn Suits	21 00			
		8	Gowns	8 00			
		1	Kimona	2 75			
		1	"	2 50			
212		3	Hose	1 00			
303		2	Dz Towels	5 70			
		4	"	2 00			
212		1	Hose	1 50	49 65		
112	12	5	Yds Ribbon	2 50			
		5	" "	1 88			
703		1	Corset	4 00			
		1	Lace	50	8 88		
260	13	1	Suit Pajamas		4 00		
1204	15	3	Pr Curtains	5 25			
210		6	Hose	9 00	14 25		
210	16	1	Hose	1 50			
503		3	Pillows	3 00			
		1	Ruffle	45			
		1	"	50			
503		3	Pillows	3 00			
		2	Tops	70			
		2	Cords	70			
		1	Ruffle	45	10 30		
703	20	1	Corset	15 00			
		1	Pr Supporters	60			
			Altering	50			
			Steel In Old Corset	25	16 35		
Miller	20	1	Garment		50 00		
					158 58		

Lillis Lovell was charging silk pillows, bed ruffles, corsets, ribbons, and nightshirts for her girls right up to her death in 1907. But her estate was worth far less than the starstruck newspapers had estimated—and one wonders whether she had ever been a "grand opera soprano," as stated in her death story. That may have been a "whorehouse tale," as madam Nell Kimball characterized such exaggerations: every fallen angel once had been so, so much more.

of their nightly revels was forgotten. "Hattie was a good girl," said Miss Eva Lewis last night. "Hattie had been sick a long time. She just faded away and died. It was a sad ending," and the woman went up the stairs to the rooms from which came the sound of music and laughter.

The ladies of the Market Street parlor houses entertained dozens of strangers weekly (the wretched girls of the sleazier cribs could accommodate a dozen in an evening), and some of the customers were the ne'er-do-well riffraff a western outpost might attract—those who had more finances than good behavior. Such clientele made the girls vulnerable to physical dangers. Fights, drunkenness, and mayhem filled the air of the brothel—although less so in the more respectable parlor houses than in the lower places or the dreadful cribs. Even the most harmless-appearing patron might unexpectedly turn on a prostitute, or an unsuspecting girl could get caught in the crossfire between feuding customers. The most routine encounter could unpredictably erupt into murder or maiming.[70]

For instance, Agnes Kelly, known on Denver's Row as Edna Miller, told Police Chief Hamilton Armstrong that "I had to shoot him or he would have killed me,"

nothing but a woman of the town. The six pall-bearers [were] pretty and young looking girls, upon the faces of whom the taint of a wrecked life had not yet begun to cast its shadows. For once the tawdry glitter

regarding traveling salesman August Schramm, who got drunk, refused to leave, and was slugging Agnes and her coworker Goldie Stanley. Schramm was critically wounded but survived, and Agnes was arrested on charges of assault with intent to kill.[71] The saloon hostesses in Cripple Creek formed the Dance Hall Girls Protective Association and called a strike to underscore their concerns, including their percentage of the take from hustling drinks to customers.[72]

A boarder of Laura Evens's, whose name was LaVerne, recalled some years later the perils of the job:

> We girls never locked the doors to our rooms. We kept them unlocked, so in case the man started getting too rough with us—biting us, twisting our breasts too hard, clawing us with his fingernails right down there where they hurt us the most, well, a girl who was starting to get that treatment would yell for help. Someone would be sure to come to help—and maybe quite a few would come. We had no man bouncer at Miss Laura's. But what chance would the customer have if, say, for instance, eight other girls came running into the room to protect her? If a man tried to hurt me, I'd knock his head off—or try to. I've had to slap the hell out of a lot of them—that's how some of them got their satisfaction, though. You run across all kinds in that business, and you might as well go along with them if it doesn't hurt you. You just close your mind to it.[73]

On October 24, 1886, Bessie Livingston, a boarder at 529 Holladay Street, was entertaining a client named Hutton when gunfire was heard. Other girls rushed to Bessie's door to find her badly wounded by a bullet in the side. Hutton told officers that Bessie had been playing with a gun. The outcome of this matter is not recorded, but similarly, madam Della Thompson was shot in the arm at her Market Street bagnio on the night of July 11, 1889, by her "discarded lover" Ed Hendershot, who then "blew his brains out."[74]

The most frightening series of events on Denver's Row was the so-called triplet murders that occurred on September 3, October 28, and November 13, 1894. Lena Tapper, age thirty-seven, German; Marie Contassot, age twenty-three, French; and Kiku Oyama, age variously given as nineteen and twenty-four, Japa-

nese, were strangled to death, respectively, at 1911, 1925, and 1957 Market—all in the same block on the west side of the notorious street. The Row was now referred to as "Strangler's Row" as the newspapers breathlessly reported the murders, theorized as to the perpetrators, and published long, flowery accounts of what had brought the unfortunate victims to their ruination and ultimate deaths. The *Denver Evening Post* referred to the "moneyed men [property owners], who have large interests in that quarter [of the city, who] have combined and offered a reward of $1,000" for capture of the killer or killers. That was a sizable sum, which brought out every private detective in town and prompted the police detectives to make wholesale arrests, all to no avail.

The women of Market Street, understandably, were terrified—they were afraid to sleep, the *Post* reported later, and were "apprehensive that they should awaken and find fierce fingers grasping their throats, choking out the lives of wretchedness to which they cling as ferociously as if their paths were strewn with roses instead of thorns."

Lena Tapper was the first to be murdered, choked to death with a part of her skirt, whereupon the killer stole away undetected. All of the victims were left lying on their beds, nothing was stolen, no sex involvement was detected. Signs of struggles were few; little was disturbed in the rooms. The police developed no mutual—or even individual—motives, although a valid speculation was simply that somebody hated prostitutes.

A grand jury indicted brothel district hanger-on Richard Demady in the Lena Tapper death. Lena had been Richard's longtime on-again, off-again lover. Five months after her death, Lena Tapper appeared as a ghost to Diana Fouchet, who was Demady's sister and a proprietor of 1949 Market Street. On March 14, 1895, Fouchet was jailed as mentally deranged, and when jailer Hugh Smith entered her cell, Fouchet—who had been raving violently—was standing stone still. "Monsieur," she said over and over again, "I see Lena Tapper," to which the *Rocky Mountain News* quoted her as adding, "Ze crime, ze terrible crime. Richard was not guilty—he was in hees bed when ze crime was committed."

The approaching client is eyed by the not shy demimondaine *working out of her doorway at 2032 Market Street. If he does not stop in, he may be taunted, and she might even snatch off his fedora, tossing it inside so he must enter to retrieve it. That mistake could cost him his life, as the ladies of Denver's Row were not above robbery by murder.*

that Marie and her sister Eugenie had immigrated to Denver from France in 1890, specifically to enter the flesh business. Frenchwomen were popular among Denver bordello customers. Eugenie did not remain a subordinate for long, being promoted to the madamship of 1905–1907 Market Street. At the time of Marie's death, her policeman-boyfriend, Antonio Santopietro, also known as Tony Saunders, was establishing her as a madam at 1925 Market Street. It was not uncommon for policemen to be directly involved in the business aspect of prostitution in the American West.

Two weeks later and only a few doors farther north in the same block of Market Street, number 1957, Kiku Oyama was found by her lover and pimp, Imi Oyama, dead on her bed, strangled by a piece of toweling. Again, no clues. Oyama had come to the United States the year before as part of her country's involvement in the Columbian Exposition in Chicago and apparently had met Imi there; together they journeyed to booming Denver to set up shop. Kiku Oyama, a tiny person at barely 90 pounds, had been a novelty on the Row because Denver had few Japanese prostitutes. Imi Oyama (they shared the same surname) was never suspected in her murder. Within an hour of discovery of her body, however, police detectives had questioned Imi and the only other Japanese prostitutes on Market Street: C. Minayawa;

An admitted consort of the French *demimondaines,* Demady was promptly acquitted. His sister Diana was not consoled by the acquittal. By the time of her brother's trial, Diana was described by the press as a "raving maniac."

Seven weeks later, on October 28, Marie Contassot was discovered murdered on her bed at 1925 Market, just a few doors north of the Tapper slaying site. Contassot apparently had been strangled with a length of cord found nearby. The *Denver Republican* wrote

LENA TAPPER

FOR WHOSE MURDER RICHARD DEMADY IS BEING TRIED

Market Street was tossed into a panic with the 1894 murders of Lena Tapper, a German, and two other prostitutes—Marie Contassot, a Frenchwoman; and Kiku Oyama, a Japanese. What had simply been "the Row" was now "Strangler's Row," as frightened denizens of the street huddled in clusters on sidewalks fearing for their lives. The police bumbled and stumbled, and finally Tapper's boyfriend, Richard Demady, was charged—and promptly acquitted. The Market Street murders were never solved. Detective Sam Howe preserved these photographs of Lena Tapper (left) *and Richard Demady* (next page) *in his* Murder Book. *Contassot is remembered today through a large and elaborate grave monument—topped by an angel—in Denver's Riverside Cemetery.*

N. Noyama; Hannah Ito; and Mary, Mabel, and Isiko Torni were arrested for their own safety.

The Strangler's Row murders stopped. Nobody was ever convicted.[75]

Frenchwoman Jennie LaTainge kept a place called the Fashion at 2036 Market Street, where she engaged in sexual practices regarded as extreme even among the Denver *demimonde*. LaTainge was made aware of her transgressions by the moralistic *Denver Evening Post*, a new paper seeking to make its influence felt in 1896. It pronounced:

> Convinced that [Police Chief George] Goulding will no longer tolerate such a vile den of iniquity as she has long conducted at the Fashion, a notoriously abhorrent resort, Jennie LaTainge, the outlaw French woman, better known to police as Melvina Davis, has expressed her desire to quit Denver forever. The vile wretch was conclusively convinced that the police were after her in earnest when her infamous den was raided last Wednesday. On that occasion Madame Davis and five female creatures too depraved to be characterized

nearby peddler and not a prostitute. Brown's murder appeared to have been a strangulation, but the autopsy revealed a considerable amount of water in her lungs—either because someone had held her head under water or from water being poured down her throat in an effort to revive her.

Mabel Brown's family had moved from Chicago to Denver, and her mother died when Mabel was young. Her father, a notorious saloon keeper, was ordered out of town by the police. Brown fell in with unsavory friends. She was seeing a Samuel Holzsweig, who owned a wine hall in the heart of the bordello district, 2201 Market Street, and then she was said to have been seduced and aban-. doned by a wealthy young man who had given her a taste of what it was like to have a few dollars—money easily available by selling herself. Meantime she befriended a bartender named Harry Challis, who was reportedly quick-tempered and strong. And she incurred the wrath of a French pimp who wanted to recruit her and got into an argument with another prostitute.

Thus the police had several possibilities when Mabel's body was found. Challis, who had discovered the crime scene, became the chief suspect, but evidence was sparse. Police bumbled, a judge dismissed the weak case, and Challis was freed. Like the earlier Tapper-Contassot-Oyama murders, no conviction was ever obtained.[77]

Following the Mabel Brown murder, the Market Street habitués recalled the Demady case of eight years earlier, and those who did not remember were quickly told of it. The press reported:

as women were arrested, and certain apparatus confiscated which were presumed to exist in only remote localities outside of the slums of Paris. Another girl, a recent accession of the Madame's, who revolted at the infamous practices indulged in at the Fashion, and who had expressed a sincere desire for reformation, was rescued from the clutches of the French harpie.[76]

The professional women of Market Street held to supernatural beliefs, particularly regarding murders occurring in their neighborhoods. On July 5, 1903, Mabel Brown, age twenty, was found dead in her brothel room at 1931 Market Street, only a week after the same fate befell Mrs. Antoine Kenhan, who was a

A shudder of horror swept through the ranks of the scarlet women of the half-world when they learned of the mysterious crime. Market Street is superstitious. There is a belief that one such murder is bound to be followed by two others in rapid succession. Every woman in the quarter believes this as firmly as she believes death is inevitable. Convinced of this fact, the half-world is in a state of excitement bordering on panic that nothing will assuage. . . . A hush fell upon Market Street. Women awakened from their sleep by the first alarm dressed partially and hastened in silence to the scene of the crime. In the dim light from the street lamps they stood about in groups before the door of the house of death and talked in whispers of the tragedy.[78]

The Brown and Kenhan killings were never solved.

The bordellos of Market Street presented dangers to customers as well. Prostitution then, as well as later, was considered a "victimless crime," but such was not the case for William Joos, among others. Joos, a brewery worker from Golden, came to Denver for recreation and relaxation on May 27, 1891, and his revels led him to the doorstep of Blanche Morgan, alias Pearl Smith, at 2235 Market Street, well north of the better houses. The story was best told by the *Denver Republican* the next day. The multiple headlines said:

MURDER BY MORPHINE
William Joos doped to death in a house of ill-fame.
Put to sleep and robbed
Arrest of Four Colored Denizens of the Place
Where the Crime Was Committed.

Joos, variously spelled "Joas" and "Jous," age about thirty, entered the bordello in the afternoon and retired with Ardell Smith—a "bushy haired mulatto"—to her room for a half-hour. While he was thus engaged, madam Blanche Morgan dispatched a passerby to a nearby saloon for a bucket of beer. Into it Blanche mixed the morphine, and it was given to Joos, who drank it, became ill, and was briefly unconscious. The women robbed him of fifty-five dollars in gold pieces and tossed him out the back door. Regaining his senses, he summoned police but subsequently was discovered dead by Detective Chief Sam Howe. Arrested were Smith, Morgan, and Mattie Fisher, all of the Morgan

address, and Mollie White of 2242 Market Street, who had furnished the morphine. Smith and Fisher were convicted of involuntary manslaughter and were "led away weeping" to county jail, where they were confined for a year.[79]

Blanche Morgan, the madam, appears not to have been charged and was released, but scarcely ten days later she was in trouble again. Along with Lillie White, "another black-skinned harpy," she snatched a silk handkerchief from the coat of one J. Craft, who was passing by their Market Street brothel, thus luring him inside where four of the residents relieved him of forty dollars and then "kicked him out the back door," according to the newspapers. It was back to jail for Blanche.[80] In Chicago on June 19, 1893, she was sentenced under the name Emma Ford to five years in the Joliet penitentiary for "highway robbery."[81]

Although the upper reaches of Holladay (and later Market) Streets were the most life-threatening on the Row, perils also lurked at the far classier Nineteenth Street intersection that housed the bordellos of Jennie Rogers and Mattie Silks. Even Eighteenth Street, at the extreme south boundary of the vice district, occasionally experienced an incident. The girlfriend of gambler Charlie Stanton worked at a house there, and on the evening of January 7, 1883, Stanton, his lady, and pal George Bunch went out on the town, returning to her room at about 10 P.M. An argument over splitting her money ensued, and Stanton pulled the hair of the "frail miss," not otherwise identified in a *Rocky Mountain News* account of the incident the next day. She pulled a knife from her dress and began slashing at Charlie's face. Bunch took Stanton downstairs to the saloon, where strong whiskey was administered as a disinfectant and Charlie's cheek was sewn up. It was a domestic affair, so the frail miss was not arrested.

A Holladay Street sporting house was the destination of John H. Fitzgerald, who on March 20, 1884, entered Belle (sometimes spelled Bell) Warden's establishment at 578 Holladay Street, where he met Mattie Lemmon, one of Belle's girls. Police Lieutenant John E. Phillips recalled in 1890 that Fitzgerald was a barber from Leadville who was traveling east and carrying "considerable money." Lemmon and Fitzgerald, Phillips said, went to a "dance at City Hall" and then

Madam Blanche (or Blanch) Morgan, alias Pearl Smith, was among the last to see a visiting reveler, William Joos, alive. Morgan's brothel was at 2235 Market Street, at the far northern reaches of the Denver tenderloin—a dangerous block of the most dreadful cribs Denver had to offer. While Joos was engaged with Blanche's girl Ardell Smith, Blanche mixed morphine in his beer. African American women did not dominate Denver prostitution in the late nineteenth century, but they seem to have murdered their customers with little thought. In his book Fighting the Traffic in Young Girls, social reformer Ernest A. Bell, under the headline "Negro Girls Driven to Evil," wrote (p. 160):

> In addition to [a] proximity to immoral conditions, young colored girls are often forced into idleness because of a prejudice against them, and they are eventually forced to accept positions as maids in houses of prostitution. Employment agents do not hesitate to send colored girls as servants to these houses. They make the astounding statement that the law does not allow them to send white girls but they will furnish colored help! The apparent discrimination against the colored citizens of the city in permitting vice to be set down in their midst is unjust and abhorrent to all fair-minded people. Colored children should receive the same moral protection that white children receive.

returned to Belle's place, where he was murdered. On May 18 his body, its throat slit, was found half buried in the Cherry Creek sands under the Colfax Avenue bridge. Arrested were Warden, Lemmon, and their respective lovers, Charles "Nigger Charley" Smith (who was white and whose real name was Tony Delph) and Barry Gates. Gates was the actual killer; Smith was a wagon driver who had carted the deceased to his final resting place. Detective Sam Howe and his colleagues determined that robbery was the motive, although all four suspects proclaimed innocence at the December 26, 1884, sentencing before District Judge Victor A. Elliott. Each was given ten years of hard labor in the state penitentiary at Cañon City.

After the sentencing, the four were briefly interviewed by a reporter from the *Denver Tribune-Republican.*

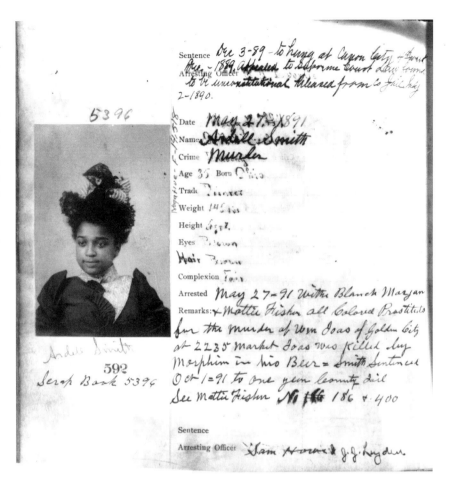

Ardell Smith's entry in Detective Howe's Murder Book tells of the morphine poisoning of William Joos, for which Smith received a year in county jail for involuntary manslaughter. Blanche Morgan appears to have been released. The four handwritten lines at the top of Smith's sheet relate to a crime on a previous page. The center portions of Smith's entry seem to have been partially obliterated and are not descriptive of her physical characteristics, suggesting the page had once been used for another person. Note that Sam Howe and his longtime colleague John J. Leyden made the arrests in the Joos murder.

Warden said she did not know what she could do in prison because she had never performed work of consequence. Lemmon told the reporter she had always wanted to be a chambermaid: "Do they have chambermaids in the penitentiary?" Smith said, "I would like to drive a cab, if they have one down there." Gates said he would pursue his trade as a blacksmith. Gates was eventually released and was known to be residing in Salt Lake City in 1895. Lemmon died of unknown causes in the Cañon City prison on May 8, 1887; she was twenty-five. The fates of Warden and Smith are not known. Belle Warden and Mattie Lemmon were not the most ferocious prostitutes on the Market Street Row. That honor went to the murderous "Black Ide" Jones, who struck terror in the most hardened of Denver's bordello women (see Chapter 7).[82]

The *Rocky Mountain News* editorialized on the perils of visiting a Denver brothel:

> It is fearfully rough on any man to get killed in a den of prostitution, for it advertises the fact that he has been to such places. If after such revelation he could come to life he would keep away the rest of his days. If the dens were raided in good faith and the respectable citizens caught there could be fined and [their names] published, it would doubtless cure them of

the vice. A house of ill fame is veritably an alluring gateway to hell.[83]

Mr. and Mrs. John Shields of Brooklyn, New York, would discover as much, although their experiences in the Denver netherworld proved more humorous than life-threatening. Having heard that Denver was a "wicked town," they set out to explore the nightspots—he wearing a revolver and she a $1,000 diamond pin. The *Rocky Mountain News* told how they "descended into the forbidden parts of the city" and entered a "resort, where they were royally entertained." Things were fine until Shields "began to 'jolly' the girls whose acquaintances he had made," which did not meet with the jollification of Mrs. Shields, and after a tiff they departed.

A thug grabbed her pin, and she screamed. Mr. Shields fired a shot, whereupon the police arrived. The couple was taken to the police station but was released

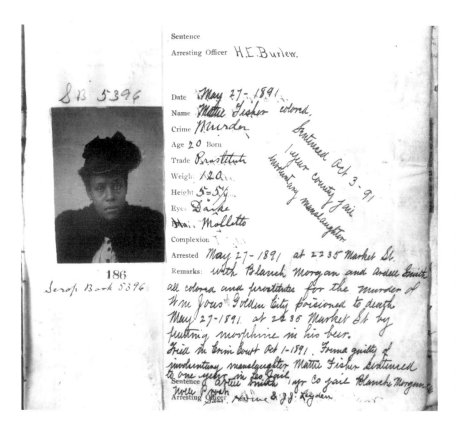

Mattie Fisher, coworker of Ardell Smith and Blanche Morgan, was twenty when she was jailed with Smith for the poisoning murder of brewery worker William Joos of Golden City.

Doe" and alleging the keeping of a lewd house. The next morning, as the ladies were counting the receipts from the evening before, they doubtless did not notice an unusually large number of horse-drawn streetcars making their way toward Market Street. Once the officers appeared and made their business known, however, the word spread quickly up and down the alleyways. According to the *Rocky Mountain News* on May 4, 1889, some of the habitués attempted to flee, only to find

the strong and capacious arms of the law ready to embrace and carry them off captive to the county building. . . . Oaths, mellifluous in tone but vile and profane in their signification, were launched at the officers in the manner of a deluge. On the other hand, a good majority of the women treated their arrest as a good joke, poked fun at the officers, and after donning their Sunday "don't-go-to-meeting" clothes, submitted to the inevitable.

Back and forth to the courthouse went the wagons, as their occupants launched into "snatches of French songs interspersed with jeers and shouts." The last of what the press described as "frolicsome doves" was at the county jail by 5 P.M.—"over 100 representatives of frailty in its worst form." Curious citizens heard the news and crowded around for a close-up glimpse of ladies they had heard of only in whispers. The women appeared at the open front windows of the jail, and "Romeo and Juliet scenes were enacted with their lovers below," reported the *News.*

Laughter and shouting emanated from the incoming horse-drawn cars, followed by vile and ribald jokes

with the advice that the West was not Brooklyn and the next time they descended into such neighborhoods they were to leave their diamonds and revolver in the hotel safe.[84]

In 1889 Denver's crib girls of French ancestry were the object of perhaps the most outrageous spectacle ever witnessed along the Denver Row. For some weeks prior to May of that year, the grand jury of Arapahoe County had been looking into the worsening prostitution situation along "Frenchwoman's Row," a section of Market Street. Citizens and police were willing to tolerate the prostitutes in Denver as long as they remained in their proper place along the Row, but there was a growing problem with the mademoiselles spilling into adjacent neighborhoods. These were not the gowned and bejeweled ladies of the parlor houses. The newspapers described the Frenchwomen as the "most vicious and depraved to be found in the ranks of femininity."

Late on the night of May 2, 1889, the grand jury issued around 300 indictments, most naming "Mary

Belle Warden and Mattie Lemmon received considerably more severe sentences than did Ardell Smith and Mattie Fisher —but Warden and Lemmon slit their customer's throat and buried him in Cherry Creek instead of merely lacing his beer with a lethal dose of morphine. Warden (whose first name is spelled "Bell" by Detective Howe) received ten years in the Cañon City prison.

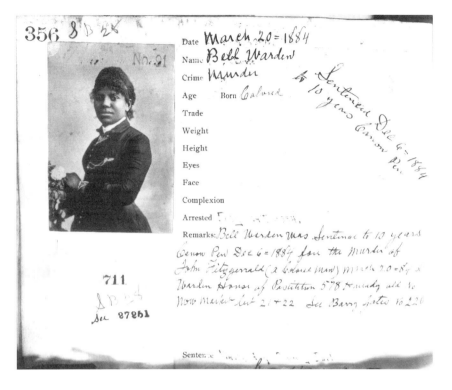

Mattie Lemmon was sentenced to ten years in the penitentiary with her friend Belle Warden for the murder of John Fitzgerald, but Lemmon died in prison after only two years, at age twenty-four. These are studio photographs rather than police mug shots; Sam Howe must have obtained the photos from Warden and Lemmon.

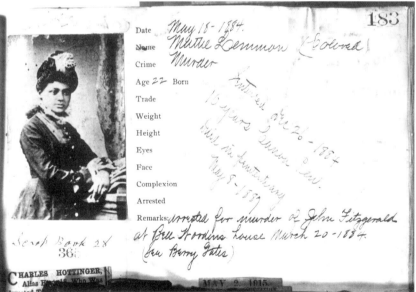

to the chorus of "Oh Girls, Why Won't You Try to Be Good." Balding, paunchy gentlemen friends and admirers lined up to post bail. Scarlet sisters waved and winked from upper-story windows to the crowd below. The notorious "Big Em," all 310 pounds of her, described in the press as "so black that charcoal would make a white mark," was in her cell playing pinochle, and all of the women chattered "in the heathenish jargon which is only heard in the lower quarters of Paris," the *News* continued.

Every time the door opened the cry went up: "Beer, beer, bring us beer!" Everybody in town who had wanted to see the girls of the Market Street Row but had been afraid to visit there turned out in front of the Arapahoe County Courthouse. Denver had not had

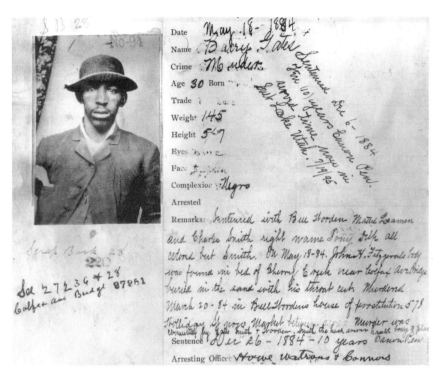

Barry Gates helped dispose of John Fitzgerald's blood-drained corpse under the sands of Cherry Creek and got a ten-year prison sentence for his trouble.

such a distraction in years. And in the corner of a jail cell, a baby was being born.

District Attorney Isaac N. Stevens was not amused. He said:

> These French women are the worst nuisance in the city, and they have got to go. The public has no idea of the demoralizing practices of these French women. Their places are the hotbeds of disease of the worst character, and their actions are disgraceful to any civilized city. They are in the habit of enticing young boys into their places, and have ruined hundreds of them during the four years they have been allowed to be in the city.

The district attorney said some of the most upstanding men in Denver leased houses to these dregs of womanhood. Stevens did not pledge to go after the slumlords, but he did say the women would be given no mere slap on the wrist, as reported by the *Denver Republican* on May 5, 1889:

> There are 125 of these houses, and as there are about two women on an average to each house, you may count on about 250 French women in the city altogether. I

shall accept no pleas of guilty in any of these cases with any understanding that only a fine sentence shall be imposed, and all parties who stand trial, I am satisfied, will receive the full limit of the jail sentence imposed by law.

The night of the raid, a reporter visited Market Street. The cribs were closed because all of their girls were in jail. But in the fancy parlor houses of Jennie Rogers, Mattie Silks, and the others, behind the "heavy folds of sweeping curtains, were sounds of music, of jingling glasses, and of merry laughter." Denver did not treat all of its scarlet women equally.[85]

Notes

1. SHS 9: 3119, from the DT, January 28, 1889.
2. DTI, December 13, 1886. The terms *West Holladay Street* and *between Twelfth and Thirteenth Streets* indicate that a brothel neighborhood was operating in 1886 nine blocks southwest on Holladay Street (near Cherry Creek) from the designated and protected red light district, which extended from Nineteenth to Twenty-third Streets. No other mention of a brothel district so far down Holladay Street in 1886 has been encountered during this study, and the author suspects these two designations are in error.
3. SHS 17: 14471, from the DR, June 6, 1897.
4. *Farmer Lawton Scrapbooks*, Western History Department, Denver Public Library. Entry from unidentified newspaper dated March 16, 1909. For the opium district, see RD, p. 528.
5. SHS 7: 4450, from the DTI, July 24, 1890.
6. These motives were not exclusive to Denver and are listed in Armitage and Jameson, *The Women's West*, p. 199.

The two faces of Jenny Shears. Why Shears elected to be photographed in such stark contrasts cannot be determined, but perhaps one image was for the folks back home and the other was for whatever business purposes Shears deemed useful. These glass plate images were taken by the pioneering photographer O. E. Aultman of Trinidad, a town that in the late nineteenth century had an active brothel district along Santa Fe Avenue. The circa 1893 Travelers' Night Guide of Colorado *(see pp. 226–227 of this book) lists May Phelps's rooms at 228 Santa Fe Avenue and Mrs. S. W. Cunningham's place at 335 Santa Fe Avenue as recommended bordellos. Research has failed to disclose any details about Jenny Shears, but the era of these photos suggests she could have worked for Phelps or Cunningham.*

7. Martin, *Whiskey and Wild Women*, p. 24. Martin does not list the full range of responses to Dr. Sanger's survey. Historian Timothy J. Gilfoyle, however, frequently refers to the Sanger study in *City of Eros*. Sanger had a good vantage point for the study of midcentury prostitution: he was a staff physician at New York City Hospital.

8. In the July 28, 1914, issue.

9. DR, February 30, 1903.

10. Elements of "Coxey's Army" of the jobless passed through Denver during June 1894. See Leonard and Noel, *Denver: Mining Camp to Metropolis*, pp. 104–105.

11. The 2100 block of Market Street, as cited here by *Polly Pry*, was never a locale where one could expect to find the classiest bordello on Denver's Row. That far north on Market was the site of ramshackle cribs, and it is doubtful that a person of the stature of Mother Jones would have established a bagnio there. A "Samuel Engel, money broker," is listed in the 1889 *Denver City Directory*.

12. *Polly Pry*, January 2 and January 9, 1904, editions, are in the Western History Department, Denver Public Library. See also Dale Fetherling, *Mother Jones: The Miners' Angel* (Carbondale: Southern Illinois University Press,

1974), pp. 134–137. Fetherling's statement that Mother Jones leased the Denver bordello at 2114 Market Street in 1899 disagrees with *Polly Pry*'s account of January 9, 1904, which puts the date at 1889. This discrepancy probably discounts Fetherling's defense of Mother Jones (p. 137), stating that she could not have been in Denver in 1899 because she was aiding coal miners in eastern Pennsylvania. For Mother Jones also see the *Pueblo* [Colorado] *Chieftain*, July 28, 1914; "Polly Pry Did Not Just Report the News; She *Made* It," *Smithsonian*, January 1991, p. 10; and the DR, February 30, 1903. No record of Mother Jones's presence in Denver has been found in the Denver city directories, in contemporary accounts of prostitution in Denver during the last two decades of the nineteenth century, or in records of liquor license transfers in the Colorado State Archives. Colorado historians Thomas J. Noel and Phil Goodstein, and perhaps others, discount the *Polly Pry* exposé as little but an antilabor smear on the reputation of Mother Jones. Historian Elliott J. Gorn, who has assembled new biographical material on Mother Jones, told the author that the truth about her alleged Denver prostitution involvements may never be learned but stated that *Polly Pry* cited enough specifics to warrant attention.

13. Peterson, *The Long-Lost Rachel Wild*, pp. 98–103.

14. SHS 26: 47589, from the November 18, 1907, edition. Ernest A. Bell in *Fighting the Traffic in Young Girls* wrote (p. 50): "Practically every girl [interviewed] begged that her real name be withheld from the public because of the sorrow and shame it would bring to her parents. One said: 'My mother thinks I am studying in a stenographic school'; another stated, 'My parents in the country think I have a good position in a department store.' . . . There are, to put it mildly, hundreds—yes, thousands—of trusting mothers in the smaller cities, who believe that their daughters are 'getting on fine' in the city."

15. SHS 28: 53166, from the DR, March 2, 1909.

16. Parkhill, *The Wildest of the West*, p. 25.

17. Rosen, *The Lost Sisterhood*, p. 106. In 1970 the Museum of Modern Art published *E. J. Bellocq: Storyville Portraits, Photographs from the New Orleans Red-Light District, Circa 1912*, a remarkable series of photographic studies taken from a cache of glass negatives discovered following Bellocq's death. That volume was followed in 1996 by the expanded companion volume, *Bellocq, Photographs from Storyville, the Red-Light District of New Orleans* (New York: Random House). Al Rose, *Storyville, New Orleans*, is an informative account of prostitution's heyday in that Louisiana city.

18. SHS 27: 50487, from the RMN, July 31, 1908. The entry regarding the Florence prostitutes is in the *Denver Evening Post*, February 20, 1897.

19. RMN, January 2, 5, 7, 1904. Governor Thomas Corwin had one son, William Henry Corwin, born January 3, 1829; died March 12, 1880, following a stroke, in Lebanon, Ohio. William Henry Corwin was a longtime homeopathic physician and was secretary to his father's legation as U.S. minister to Mexico in 1861–1864. The younger Corwin remained in Mexico until 1866, whereupon he returned to Ohio. His death story in the *Cincinnati Times*, quoted in the Lebanon (?) *Western Times*, March 18, 1880, stated that he "had an inate [*sic*] abhorrence of all that was low and base." No reference has been found that William Henry Corwin was referred to as "Duke." No surviving family members (and no son) are mentioned in his death story or biography. See correspondence to the author from the Ohio Historical Society, April 28, 1995, and from the Warren County (Ohio) Historical Society, May 17, 1995.

20. SHS 31: 65350, from the DR, October 5, 1912.

21. DR, July 29, 1884.

22. *The Social Evil in Chicago: A Study of Existing Conditions with Recommendations by the Vice Commission of Chicago*, pp. 185 ff.

23. Gilfoyle, *City of Eros*, pp. 88–89, 175.

24. SHS 27: 49294 and 49314, from the RMN, April 2, 1908, and the DR, April 5, 1908.

25. Ibid., 27: 51415, from the DTI, October 29, 1908. The account of Jack Maynard and the cash registers is from Parkhill, "Scarlet Sister Mattie" (typescript), p. 9. Parkhill does not elaborate on the publicity Maynard received after installing cash registers in his brothels.

26. Ibid., 28: 55075, from the RMN, September 12, 1909.

27. The New York activities of John W. Mahan (Jack Maynard) are in the DP, January 27 and 28, 1924, and the RMN, January 27, 29, February 2, 1924.

28. Elliott West, "Dirty Tricks in Denver," *Colorado Magazine* (summer 1975), pp. 225–243. The article provides valuable insight regarding one of Denver's most corrupt elections and the man who engineered it, Wolfe Londoner. James Connor's surname is variously spelled Connors and Conners.

29. Lawrence Lewis, "How Woman's Suffrage Works in Colorado," *Outlook*, January 27, 1906, pp. 167–178.

30. RMN, May 6, 1908.

31. SHS 27, clipping of November (date?) 1908, no clipping number or originating newspaper identified.

32. Ibid., 28: 54589, from the RMN, July 24, 1909.

33. Armitage and Jameson, *The Women's West*, p. 196.

34. For the rescue of youthful "slumming" girls from the wine halls, see SHS 26: 46884, 46885, from the RMN, September 4, 5, 1907. For an additional discussion of slumming, see Chapter 5. For the jail conditions, see the DP, May 27, 1917. The RD details additional characteristics of Denver's dreadful jail conditions and youthful offenders; see pp. 523–538.

35. Elliott West, "Of Lager Beer and Sonorous Songs," *Colorado Magazine*, spring 1971, p. 124, quoting Anna Wolcott Vaile and Ellis Meredith, "Woman's Contribution," in *History of Colorado*, James H. Baker and LeRoy R. Hafen, eds., 5 vols., vol. 3, p. 1107 (Denver: Linderman, 1927). Likens is discussed in the RD and other, briefer histories of the Denver Police Department. On July 3, 1923, a memorial fountain in Likens's honor, which still stands, was placed near the southeast corner of Colfax Avenue and Broadway in Denver. On February 13, 1999, a marker was placed at Likens's gravesite at Riverside Cemetery. See the RMN, February 14, 1999.

36. See Annette L. Student, "Sadie Likens, Patron of the Fallen," *Colorado Heritage*, summer 2001, pp. 20–31. Likens's July 1, 1889, appointment date—a year later than usually believed—is listed on an 1892 Denver police roster, copy in the possession of Ronald L. Samson. Both Sadie and daughter Belle, the assistant matron appointed at age twenty-two on May 6, 1891, are listed as five-feet-two and residing at 455 South Fifteenth Street (today's 1100 block of Acoma Street). For an account of Likens's departure from the matron's job, see the RMN, August 23, 1895.

37. SHS 26: 47659, from the DR, November 23, 1907.

38. Ibid., 27: 50354, from the DTI, July 21, 1908; 50365, from the DR, July 23, 1908, August 8, 1908.

39. Ibid., 29: 58130, from the DTI, June 14, 1910.

40. Ibid., 29: 58177, quoting the DR, June 19, 1910.

41. RMN, June 22, 1906.

42. DP, June 17, 1906.

43. RMN, May 7, 9, 1908. For Denver Detective Billy Green, see Lukas, *Big Trouble*, pp. 236–237.

44. The case of Eva Walker and Benjamin M. Borland is in the DP, November 18–20, 1899; January 30, 1900. Inquiry has failed to verify a "federal judge Riner" or to disclose his first name. He does not appear in listings of the 1899, 1900, or 1901 federal, state, or city judiciary. No lawyer by that name appears to have resided in Denver during those years.

45. Quoted in Stephen Crane, *Maggie: A Girl of the Streets*, Norton Critical Ed. (New York: W. W. Norton, 1979).

46. Parkhill, *The Wildest of the West*, p. 24; Parkhill, "Scarlet Sister Mattie" (published version), p. 26.

47. Evalyn Capps Walker, "The Strange Story," *Colorado Magazine*, summer 1977, pp. 294–311.

48. Petrik, *No Step Backward*, p. 42.

49. Harlan Jennings, "Grand Opera Comes to Denver, 1864–1881," *Opera Quarterly*, spring 1997, pp. 57–84; Jennings, "The Singers Are Not on Speaking Terms: Grand Opera in Denver, 1864–1881," *Colorado Heritage*, spring 1999, pp. 2–19. For an additional example of Denver prostitutes' unwelcome presence at a theatrical event, see Chapter 4.

50. DTI, October 4, 1886.

51. Parkhill, *Wildest of the West*, p. 18; Bancroft, *Six Racy Madams*, p. 14.

52. Perkin, *The First Hundred Years*, p. 371.

53. For the incident of Baby Doe Tabor entering Lizzie Preston's brothel, see Reiter, *The Women*, pp. 141–142; the event is repeated in other volumes on the Tabors. Betty Moynihan, biographer of Horace Tabor's first wife, Augusta (*Augusta Tabor, a Pioneering Woman* [Evergreen, Colo.: Cordillera, 1988]), supplied the author with copies of sworn statements from policeman Edward Newman and Baby Doe that detail their encounter with Harvey Doe inside Lizzie Preston's. The text of Harvey's letter to his parents is in Gordon Langley Hall, *The Two Lives of Baby Doe* (Philadelphia: Macrae Smith, 1962), pp. 91–92, and the letter is deposited at the Western History Department, Denver Public Library, as well. Tabor scholars believe the account of Baby Doe's "raid" of Lizzie Preston's bagnio is true, although scant verification has been found in newspapers. The DTR appears to be the only publication to have addressed the incident, and the *Tribune* account does not name Baby Doe and is at odds with other aspects of the story. Said the *Tribune* the day after the incident, March 3, 1880: "Quite an excitement was raised about 9 o'clock last evening by a lady, who, being suspicious that her husband was indulging in forbidden pleasures, started out to visit various immoral dens, in the expectation of catching the erring spouse. Failing to find him, and finding herself alone, and at night some distance from her residence, her courage forsook her, and

she called upon Officer Ed. Newman to escort her home. A large crowd followed her, evidently believing that some great sensation was on the tapis." That is the extent of the *Tribune* report.

54. See, for instance, Jacqualine [*sic*] Grannell Couch, *Those Golden Girls of Market Street* (Fort Collins, Colo.: Old Army, 1974), pp. 10–12. Aside from newspaper accounts, the Liz Preston/Essie Preston story seems to have first been related by Parkhill in *The Wildest of the West*, pp. 57–58. Parkhill, who utilized the quotations given here plus other particulars not found in newspaper stories of the Baby Doe raid and court case, says baby Essie May was adopted from St. Anne's Infant Asylum in the District of Columbia, but the DP, October 9, 1905, quotes the decision of Judge Lindsey as stating that the baby was "taken from" Sisters Hospital in Washington, D.C. The matter of whether Essie May was adopted or otherwise removed became central to the outcome.

55. Miller, *Holladay Street*, pp. 90–91. The DTI, October 9, 1905, carries the fullest account of Judge Lindsey's decision against Essie May Foster and verifies that Lizzie Preston "sent her [Essie] away in her early youth in order that the child might never learn the sort of life her mother led. The child grew up in ignorance of her mother." The DP article of the same date states that Essie May was "taken from" rather than adopted from Sisters Hospital in Washington, but the *Post* story never mentions that Hannah Foster and Lizzie Preston were the same person. The RMN account of October 10 dismisses the matter in one paragraph that adds nothing. The story of Lizzie and Essie May appears to be true because of its supporting newspaper accounts, but it smacks of what madam Nell Kimball classified in her "autobiography" as "whorehouse yarns" that "made the rounds" of bordello circles. Kimball gives examples: the "sporting man" who had "the reputation as a great whoremonger" who one night in a Cleveland bagnio discovered that his fourteen-year-old hostess was the daughter he had deserted years earlier. Or the "young college boy" who finds that the older woman entertaining him is his mother. "For the proper sense of skin-crawling," wrote Kimball, "it's all supposed to [have been discovered] *after* they have had their lay." Kimball relates other, more intricate stories. See Kimball, *Nell Kimball*, pp. 234–235.

56. Parkhill, "Scarlet Sister Mattie" (typescript), p. 10, and published version, p. 33. Supplemental details including Stella's name and the notice of her death are in Parkhill, *The Wildest of the West*, pp. 275–277.

57. Fowler, *A Solo in Tom-Toms*, pp. 211–226. There is no entry for a Grand National Market in the Denver city directories of the 1905 period, the time frame referenced by Fowler in the Trixie episode. Fowler is the only writer located during this study to refer to Jennie Rogers as "Sarah Jane Rogers."

58. Miller, *Holladay Street*, p. 77.

59. Sam Howe included this lengthy story in his Book 1, clipping 84, from the *Denver Tribune-Republican*, June 15, 1885. Howe erroneously identified the clipping as from June 14. Additionally, the *Tribune-Republican* spells the name as Gulden, whereas the Denver city directories of 1884 and 1885 spell the name Guldan. Howe accompanied the clipping with a mug-shot engraving of Gulden, taken from a tabloid newspaper of the day titled *Police News*, July 4, 1885. The city directories identify Gulden as an employee of the nearby Collender Billiard Parlor.

60. RMN, December 12, 1883; for the salaries see SHS 26: 59853, from the RMN, July 7, 1911.

61. Gilfoyle, *City of Eros*, pp. 44, 170, 214.

62. Parkhill, *The Wildest of the West*, p. 26.

63. SHS 1: 137, 1883 newspaper unspecified. The figures are outrageous, and the newspaper apparently gave the public no credit for being able to detect that these statistics could not possibly have been valid.

64. Ibid., 6: 1584, 1586, newspapers unnoted.

65. Not to be confused with "Creede Lilly." In *Creede: History of a Colorado Silver Mining Town* (Denver: Artcraft, 1949), Nolie Mumey wrote (p. 102): "Creede Lilly was a confirmed faro player, and often had a large bank roll. She had been among the down and out class before her death on the morning of June 8, 1892, the day Bob Ford [murderer of Jesse James] was killed [in Creede]. No one knew her real name. She had kept much to herself and did not drink or mix with those that got drunk. A sad-faced woman went around with a sheet of paper, asking people to contribute money to help bury Creede Lilly, who was found dead in her tent. [Confidence man] Soapy Smith contributed five dollars. Bob Ford gave ten dollars and under the amount wrote: 'Charity covereth a multitude of sins.' A reporter, Hugh Thompson of the *Daily Chronicle*, was asked to say a few words over the grave. He lifted his face and said: 'Dear God, we are sending you the soul of "Creede Lilly". Thou knowest the burdens she had to bear. Be merciful.'"

66. Mrs. A. H. Majors, "Life in North Creede in the Early Days," *Colorado Magazine*, November 1945, pp. 267–269.

Duane A. Smith wrote in "The San Juaner: A Computerized Portrait" (*Colorado Magazine*, spring 1975, pp. 137–152) that of the San Juan communities examined in his study, only Lake City (1880) and Ouray (1885) admitted presence of prostitutes in census statistics. In Lake City they were listed as prostitutes, in Ouray as sporting women. In those two towns the average prostitute's age, Smith reported, was 24.5; and 33 percent were married, widowed, or divorced.

67. DP, March 26, 1907. The *Post's* perception of Denver prostitution became suspect when the newspaper said in the same story: "Of the three most noted proprietresses of notorious Denver resorts, Lizzie Preston, Lillis Lovell, and Fay Stanley, but one survives. She is Fay Stanley." Lizzie Preston may have been a moderately prominent Denver madam; Lillis Lovell and Fay Stanley never were. Conspicuously absent from the *Post's* assessment were Mattie Silks and Jennie Rogers.

68. DR, March 25, 1907. The *Republican* reporter apparently was unaware of the plans for cremation and not burial of the body.

69. Lillis Lovell's will, death certificate, and property inventory are from the Mazzulla collection, box 48A, "Prostitution" folder, ex–Amon Carter Museum, Fort Worth, Texas, now at the Colorado Historical Society, Denver. Copies are in the author's possession. The story of Lillis and Lois Lovell appears to originate with Parkhill in *The Wildest of the West*, pp. 54–55, and is repeated in Dallas, *Cherry Creek Gothic*, p. 241. Although Colorado historians today regard Parkhill as a reasonably reliable resource (although he seldom lists any sources in his writings), in this case he misstates Lillis's death date by a year and a day; her death certificate lists it as March 22, 1907, at St. Joseph Hospital. Lillis Lovell's only sister who was said to be in Denver, Mary Nirene Quigley Wilder, is listed in Lillis's papers as residing at 221 West First Avenue. No "Lois Lovell" is mentioned in Lillis's papers. A 1901 liquor license was issued to Lillas Lovell (note spelling), 2020 Market Street (see record of liquor licensing, Colorado State Archives). Lillis Lovell's will spells her name as both Lillis and Lillas; the former is generally used and preferred.

70. See Butler, *Daughters of Joy, Sisters of Misery*, p. 61.

71. SHS 28: 52619, from the RMN, January 11, 1909.

72. Armitage and Jameson, *The Women's West*, p. 202.

73. Miller, *Holladay Street*, p. 176. This interview was probably obtained by Miller's coauthors Fred and Jo Mazzulla, who did considerable research during the late 1940s, 1950s, and 1960s regarding early prostitution in Colorado.

74. SHS 4: 910, from the DTI, October 25, 1886; 10: 3603, from the DTI, July 12, 1889.

75. The so-called triplet murders of prostitutes Lena Tapper, Marie Contassot, and Kiku Oyama were extensively covered by the RMN, DP, DTI, *Times-Sun*, and DR. A subsequent retrospective was in the *Post* on December 31, 1903, and the dream of Diana Fouchet was in the RMN, March 15, 1895.

76. SHS, 16: 11698, from the *Denver Evening Post*, February 14, 1896.

77. The author appreciates the efforts of Joan Golden, G. K. Elliott, and Annette L. Student in researching contemporary Denver newspapers and compiling notes regarding the death of Mabel Brown.

78. SHS, 22: 31364, from the DR, July 6, 1903.

79. Ibid., 12: 5779, from the DTI, October 3, 1891.

80. Ibid., 12: 5805, from the DR, October 15, 1891. The phenomenon of seizing hats or other apparel from men as a method of prompting them to enter a bordello may have been practiced especially by black prostitutes. Researcher Timothy Gilfoyle reported in *City of Eros* (p. 209) that in New York City, "by the early 1900s, West Thirty-sixth to Forty-first street between Eighth and Ninth avenues was filled with black women. . . . West Thirty-seventh Street residents remarked that female neighbors stood in front of their houses from early evening to as late as four in the morning with little clothing, 'speaking to all men who pass (especially white men) and then taking them up to their flats.' . . . On Fortieth Street . . . [clergyman] Adam Clayton Powell, Sr. observed prostitutes snatching the hats off men, forcing men to run into hallways after them."

81. *Sam Howe Murder Book*, p. 200.

82. Ibid., pp. 110, 356. For accounts and statistics of female inmates at the Colorado State Penitentiary, see Benham, "Women in the Colorado State Penitentiary." For the interviews with Warden, Lemmon, Smith, and Gates, see the *Denver Tribune-Republican*, December 27, 1884. Very brief accounts are also in the DTI, December 26 and 27, 1884. The victim Fitzgerald plus perpetrators Warden, Lemmon, and Gates were black; "Nigger Charley" Smith was white. Policeman Phillips's recollections of the Belle Warden case are in Walling and Kaufmann, *Recollections of a New York Chief of Police*, p. 653.

83. RMN, August 21, 1880.

84. SHS 22: 31956, from the RMN, July 16, 1903.

85. RMN, May 4, 1889; DR, May 5, 1889.

11

"All Ze French Ladies Vill Be Glad"

THE WORKING WOMAN'S LIFE ON DENVER'S ROW as the twentieth century approached was not one of merriment. Not only did the madams have the police and tough customers to worry about, but the landlord could be heartless to a *demimondaine*.

In April 1889 John J. Gorman, a slumlord who owned the properties at 2006, 2008, and 2010 Market Street, tried to pull a fast one on the spirited Frenchwoman Josephine Getze, who conducted her business out of one of Gorman's houses and sublet the other two to fellow Frenchwomen. Gorman wanted to increase the $20 monthly rent from each property, and he especially wanted Getze out of there.

She refused to vacate, and Gorman had no grounds for eviction. So he paid policeman Pat Lewis $20 to toss the three working women out and to deposit them in jail if necessary. The ladies refused to open their door, so Gorman, Lewis, and "a few colored men" broke down the door, threw the women in the paddy wagon,

and hauled them to jail just long enough for Gorman to toss their belongings into the street and expropriate the $865 in cash he discovered inside.

None of this occurred with the benefit of warrant or any legal process, so when the highly regarded local lawyer Edgar Caypless heard of the matter, he brought it to the attention of the grand jury. Gorman, Lewis, and the "colored men" found themselves accused of burglary. Remarked Getze, as quoted by the newspapers: "Ze brute, ze wretch, he take all de tings out of my house and he tink he could bulldoze me, but he has got in ze zoup himself. He no bargain on ze French woman for what she be worth, and ven he go to ze penitentiary, all ze French ladies vill be glad."[1]

No less scandalous was the ongoing dilemma of Deputy Sheriff William Wogstrom, court clerk Edward Hitzler, and "special deputy" John Schlottman, all of whom were caught trying to "shake down" madam Ethel Lamar. The scandal even spread to a crooked justice of the peace, John E. Harper. It became one of the most outrageous scenarios of late-nineteenth-century Denver jurisprudence.

On the night of December 22, 1895, Wogstrom and Schlottman went to Lamar's Market Street establishment, arrested her and three boarders, and set out for police headquarters. The sixsome, Lamar later told authorities, got as far as "the first saloon, and halted." The account preserved by Sam Howe continues the story:

> At this saloon, she says she was told that if she would pay $8 for bonds she and her three companions would be released until the next day, when cases would be called in court. Preferring not to go to jail, she paid the $8 and returned to her house with the three other women. Ethel had not been told why she was arrested, and regarded the incident as "unexpected but not unusual." The next day, she went to court as ordered, but was told by clerk Hitzler that the case had been continued to the day following. That night, Wogstrom and Schlottman appeared again at her house and told her they thought they could "square" the whole situation for forty dollars—ten dollars per defendant. Otherwise, they said, she would stand trial for keeping a lewd house, and the others for being inmates of a lewd house. She paid the forty dollars and was given a release by clerk Hitzler.
>
> After some thought, Lamar deduced that she had been preyed upon by corrupt officers and reported the entire matter. The situation quickly reached the district attorney, who brought charges of blackmail.[2]

The outcome is unrecorded, and the matter may have been dismissed in favor of what the district attorney considered a stronger case against those who had preyed on the women. Court clerk Hitzler, it appears, could not refrain from trying to fleece the Market Street working women. Subsequently, Hitzler, now identified as "ex clerk" of the justice court, was tried for conspiracy to defraud Minnie Hill, 1952 Market Street, of $100 on November 25, 1896. Lawyer and Justice of the Peace John E. Harper plus Deputy Schlottman were implicated as well and were indicted with Hitzler. The scam was substantially the same as that in the Ethel Lamar case.[3]

Following a one-day trial, Hitzler was convicted of obtaining money from Hill by false pretenses. The defense presented no testimony.[4] The result of the case against Schlottman is not recorded, and charges were dropped against Harper because he "did not know what was going on in his court." Harper, however, was indicted by the county grand jury on April 29, 1896, for allegedly embezzling proceeds from fines paid to his court over a two-year period.[5]

Judge Harper was indicted again, along with Schlottman and Hitzler, on January 31, 1897, on charges of swindling several madams under threat of prosecution. The headline over the story in the *Denver Republican* was "Harper and His Harpies."[6] And six months later he had additional difficulties with the law. This time, acting as an attorney, he was accused of extorting $15 from a defendant with the offer to "fix it with the officials."[7]

The outcome was not recorded by Sam Howe, but Judge Harper was arrested yet again for cohabiting with a married woman, Myra Edison, age twenty-eight, whom Harper was representing in a divorce action. A complaint against the pair was sworn out by her husband, Alvin E. Edison, a wagon driver, who told authorities he had been happily married until "seven months ago, when she began to show fondness for other men."[8] Harper was certainly among the more colorful characters in turn-of-the-century Denver jurisprudence.

The prostitutes of Market Street had the usual business concerns in addition to dealing with grouchy landlords, recruiting new inventory, pleasing the bureaucrats, keeping the police at bay, taking care of crooked clerks and judges, and trying to turn a profit all at the same time. The parlor houses not only offered feminine companionship to the visiting miner, farm lad, or portly business visitor but also served up fine cigars and the best continental brandies. Certain licensing procedures thus came into play. Liquor licensing was not to be toyed with. City hall was dedicated to maintaining this revenue source. The bagnios themselves were not subject to licensing (although the possibility was mentioned on occasion over the years), but the madams were careful to make certain their liquor licenses were in order.

Just as the more prominent madams regularly exchanged real estate in the bordello district, they also traded in liquor licenses. Microfilm records in the Colorado State Archives preserve some of these transactions. On March 5, 1885, for instance, Rose Lovejoy transferred her retail liquor license at 525 Holladay Street to Pauline Blair, and at the same time Clara Dumont was a retail liquor licensee at 570 Holladay Street. Mattie Silks deeded her retail dispensing license at 502 Holladay Street to Alice Cole on December 4, 1884, and on February 5, 1885, Jennie Rogers transferred her license for 527 Holladay Street to Eva Lewis and apparently opened up shop across the street at 516 Holladay. Other liquor licenses during the same period were granted to Mary Kingsleys, 530 Holladay; Deanie Handley, 449 Holladay; May Robin (a marvelous nom de plume!), 520 Holladay; and Laura Beaucamp, 440 Holladay.

In the 1884 city licensing book Mattie Silks's name is listed adjacent to that of the stuffy, pudgy, and thoroughly corrupt Wolfe Londoner, pioneer merchant and soon to be (1889–1891) mayor of Denver. Londoner was securing a retail liquor permit for his mercantile store at 265–267 Blake Street, six blocks from the Row.[9]

In April 1894 Hamilton Armstrong became chief of the police department, the first of an impressive four terms in that office. Small in stature but big in fortitude and blessed with a marvelously profane vocabulary, Armstrong had his own procedure for dealing with gambling, especially when Capitol Hill society was involved. A memorable instance is recalled when Armstrong

> flecked a lonely speck of dust from his left coat-sleeve, and borrowed an ax from the fire department. Then he proceeded to the house at 1346 Sherman Street, where Mrs. William Sexton lives. The windows were gaily lighted and there was the sound of revelry. The chief entered, unannounced, and walked to the middle of the room . . . [where he] raised high the ax above his head and brought it down with shattering emphasis on an unusual bit of furniture. It was a roulette wheel.
>
> The society women present screamed and ran. The wheel, of elegant inlaid mahogany and black walnut, was in smithereens. Armstrong gathered the fragments, and returned to city hall, where he gave them to the janitor tending the furnace.[10]

Denver's liquor licensing laws as they applied to the city's madams came into question in 1901 when the city auditor determined that these businesswomen lacked the proper licenses. Thus the ladies and one man were cited in court to resolve the matter. The defendants were Mattie Silks, 1916 Market Street; Rose Lovejoy, 2005 Market Street; Littie Sargent, 2301 Market; Lizzie Preston, 1942 Market; Louise Crawford, 1952 Market; Minnie Hall, 1950 Market; Grace Jabine, 2000 Market; Albert Montell, 1917 Market; Lillas Lovell, 2020 Market; Mrs. R. L. Hathaway, 1504 Curtis Street; and Retta Malloy, 925 Eighteenth Street. Hathaway and Malloy were so-called massage house operators.

The defendants were defiant, and they obviously had influence at city hall. The Fire and Police Board ruled that they *should* buy the proper licenses, but the city did not force the issue, which was allowed to quietly drop.[11]

With the arrival of the new century, any hopes that Denver was maturing were confronted by moral conditions as degenerate as ever. Vices remained out of control. Gambling halls and saloons were open twenty-four hours a day, and prostitution ran virtually unrestricted within its geographic boundaries. From Nineteenth to Twenty-third Streets, said the *Denver Republican*, there was a display of vice "not to be seen in any other city in the country." The girls displayed names and signs, many of them suggestive. "Brazen" women were allowed to appear "half-clad" on the sidewalks and to call out to pedestrians. The women snatched the hats of passing men and rushed, giggling, into their cribs, followed by the owners of said hats.[12] The *Denver Post* said:

> It is a well known fact that the city is overrun by as tough a class of citizens as has ever assembled in a Western city. Whether because they are protected, or because the purblind police are not aware of their presence, or because the fire and police board is more concerned about the politics of its business than it is about public morals or public safety, these delectable gentry are permitted to work their own sweet will and practically go as free as the air which blows across the prairies.[13]

In April 1901 the *Denver Times* began questioning yet another breakdown in law enforcement along Denver's streets of vice, noting that the "drinking holes, dance halls and wine rooms were holding high carnival long after the hour fixed by law for sweeping out their patrons and closing their shutters" while the police "looked on complacently." The paper asked the city authorities to do something.[14]

The following November the *Republican* again began harping that the Fire and Police Board was nothing but a political machine devoted only to working for the Democrats who controlled the state government and denounced Denver's police system as "a disgrace to the whole state." A few months later, in January 1902, fifteen policemen including Sam Howe were dismissed because they were "adverse to doing political work." Howe was reinstated the following June. The newspaper supported Police Chief Armstrong, pointing out that whenever he tried to punish an incompetent policeman he was laughed at because the policeman had been appointed by powerful friends on the city council.

The city council designated a committee to investigate the police and fire matters. The committee validated what the *Republican* had reported and added more: gamblers made generous contributions to the Democratic Party election funds, prostitutes walked the streets openly, Market Street was as "brazen a theatre of crime and degradation" as had ever been seen in Denver, and the city council could do nothing about all this because the Fire and Police Board was still responsible only to the governor.[15]

Denverites' patience with the their police department was fully expended, and the citizens organized a vigilance group called the Committee of Safety, sending out 1,000 men to patrol the town. Most were armed and were provided with special badges so citizens could recognize them. They were instructed to hand crooks over to the police or take them to jail, but the effort did not last long.[16]

But changes loomed. No longer would the citizens allow city hall and the police to wink at Old West mining camp vices. In 1904 home rule became law, allowing Denver citizens to draft their own city charter, control their own police force, and establish a civil service system to free the fire and police departments from local political influence.[17]

Home rule was the beginning of the end of more than thirty years of official corruption and rampant vice in Denver, although the process was slow. As late as 1912, for instance, policemen were so intrigued with the brothel district that they were restricted from that neighborhood unless in full uniform. Detective Sam Howe recorded the proclamation:

> In the future, no patrolman in citizen's clothes may visit the district upon pain of instant discharge. If he is in uniform and wishes to visit the district on police business he must report to one of the two patrolmen detailed to watch the district, state his business and secure permission. Report has it that some members of the force have found the district an attraction and have spent more time there than is good for them.[18]

An additional example of vice's hold on Denver after the turn of the century occurred on June 8, 1902, when Sheriff David D. Seerie closed two dozen gambling houses. The next morning the sheriff was summoned to a meeting with the president of the Fire and Police Board, the state insurance commissioner, and a state senator, who reminded the sheriff where his allegiances lay. The gamblers were back at their tables that afternoon, and the sheriff apologized for his hasty action.[19]

Public officials responsible for momentary lapses in licensing procedures, however, risked discovery by a snoopy press. Under a headline that screamed "Fraud Most Colossal," the *Denver Republican* on May 16, 1891, exclaimed that the city treasurer "forgot" to collect $45,000 in liquor licensing fees from Market Street's bordellos: "There are a large number of these places from which the city has not received a cent for years. As to how much the owners of these resorts paid to be allowed to keep open without a [liquor] license will never be known, but they were not given permission by those who had charge of the licensing department for nothing."[20] It was, as scandals went, fairly interesting. Arrested four months later were the by-then-resigned city treasurer, W. M. Bliss; his former deputy, James P. Hadley; and ex–deputy city auditor George R. Raymond. The *Republican* had misstated

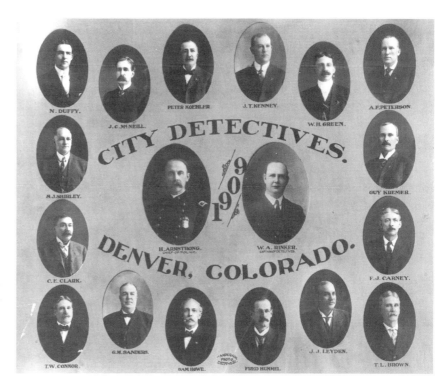

In 1909, Sam Howe was seen in this rare hatless view, and many of his old comrades were still working alongside him in the detective bureau. Pete Koehler, Billy Green (part cop, part pimp), John Leyden, and George Sanders. Ham Armstrong is once again chief, and Washington Rinker is captain of detectives.

the amount missing, which was closer to $26,000, but the press referred to the accused trio as the "City Hall Boodlers."[21]

The *Colorado Graphic*, a short-lived newspaper, compiled a set of law enforcement statistics in 1890. The Denver Police Department consisted of eighty personnel: a chief, an inspector, two lieutenants, five sergeants, two jailers, two clerks, twelve detectives, four patrol wagon drivers, one police court bailiff, and fifty patrolmen. Twenty-five patrolmen in each of two shifts covered 10,000 acres containing 370 miles of streets and 190 miles of alleys, giving each policeman 22.4 miles of roadways to cover by "foot, wagon, or horseback." With a population of 130,000, the newspaper figured, "each man gets 5,000 souls." Arrests between May 1, 1889, and July 30, 1890, totaled 13,779, or 275 per patrolman.[22]

The corrupt police regime of Henry Brady (see Chapter 7), which was responsible for Denver's peacekeeping during this period, ended with Brady's resignation and his statement that he did not really want the job. Brady was replaced by John Farley, generally a capable and conscientious police chief, although his hands were often tied by the political system under which he worked—including that of "Boss" Speer. Within a year, however, Denver was so grateful for Farley and his police department that the business community took up a collection to purchase the chief a magnificent custom-made, twelve-pointed star badge of gold and diamonds. The badge is currently owned by Farley's descendants.[23]

Chief Farley, in his four-year tenure, did not attempt to eradicate gambling and prostitution because the community did not want them eradicated, but he did reinforce controls and constraints. Under Farley, police historian Eugene Rider wrote, "women of easy virtue were no longer permitted to solicit patronage openly or to hail persons with vile and indecent remarks as they had done under Mayor [William Scott] Lee's [and Henry Brady's] administration." Within a month after Farley took over in April 1889, the patrol wagon in one evening made five trips to Twentieth and Market Streets. Four wagon loads returned French women to jail, and the fifth carried "Negro women."[24] A similar raid, described in Chapter 10, had taken place two weeks earlier.

Policeman-turned-gambler Thomas W. Baird saw the opportunity to become an extortionist. Baird's scam was referred to in Sam Howe's scrapbook as "shaking the plum tree" and involved $110 in blackmail payoffs from "Negro gamblers" J. B. Moore and Tom Klingman (or Clingman). Policeman Ike Gilmore was investigated as the go-between who passed Baird's

Reminiscent of the August 13, 1899, slayings of Denver Patrolmen Thomas C. Clifford and William E. Griffith. From an old engraving.

protection demands to gamblers who were told that if they made payoffs, they would be immune from prosecution.[25] Baird supposedly represented himself as an agent of the district attorney and was accused of obtaining money under false pretenses. To District Attorney Daniel Prescott's chagrin, Baird was acquitted.[26]

While gambling and prostitution showed no abatement in the new century, neither did the abuse of liquor. In 1904 one in four arrests was for drunkenness (2,345 of 9,540), a sizable ratio. Additional 1904 arrest statistics were disturbance, 776; murder, 15; assault to commit murder, 61; "deserters from Fort Logan," 26; burglaries, 76; and burglary suspects, 38. The difference between the final two categories is not known. Again, as was historically the case, prostitution and gambling statistics were not included, but Police Chief Michael A. Delaney assured the populace through a police department propaganda publication:

> Repressive measures against houses of doubtful repute heretofore unknown in Denver have been taken up. "Denver shall be a clean city," is the motto of Chief Delaney, and he is living up to it. Complaints of citizens receive prompt attention, and disreputable dives have been suppressed.[27]

An account follows of how Mike Delaney suppressed things and how he nearly sunk Boss Speer in the process.

The dangers of Market Street at times transcended the occasional fight, poisoning, suicide, or police raid. On March 19, 1895, Detective Alpheus J. Moore was slain at Nineteenth and Market Streets, and on August 13, 1899, Patrolman Thomas C. Clifford was shot and killed during a saloon disturbance a block away

at Twentieth and Market. In the latter incident Patrolman William E. Griffith heard the shots and chased assailant Wellington C. Llewellyn to the Sixteenth Street Viaduct, where Griffith was shot and killed.[28] In perhaps the oddest twist in early Denver crime annals, Llewellyn proceeded to a secondhand store where he purchased "farmer clothes," ducked down alleys to a barbershop where his hair and moustache were cut, and proceeded to the southern outskirts of town where he enlisted in the army under a fake name and was dispatched to the Philippines for Spanish-American War duty. From there, his trail vanishes.[29]

The killings of policemen Clifford and Griffith had two immediate consequences. A week after the deaths, the Reverend Dr. F. T. Bayley of the Plymouth Congregational Church, observing that the chain of events had begun in a saloon, spoke from the pulpit:

> Society is the chief victim of the saloon, and it has drugged us all. Its fearful work goes on under our eyes constantly. The saloon is the tap root of the drink habit, and the drink habit is a public evil of measureless dimensions. The saloon is a robber. It robs [the victim's] children of their bread; his wife, his mother, of their heart-rest. The saloon is a murderer, too. It killed our two policemen last Sunday morning.

According to the handwritten memo from Detective George Sanders, Chief John Farley wanted Sam Howe to utilize his crime books to research the murderer of policemen Thomas C. Clifford and William E. Griffith. "Keep this Quite" [sic], admonished Sanders. The circumstances regarding the escape of the killer, Washington C. Llewellyn, were among the oddest in Denver crime history. While fleeing, Llewellyn stopped in a barbershop to alter his appearance, changed clothes, dashed to an army recruiting office, signed up, and was shipped almost immediately to the Philippine Islands to help fight the Spanish-American War. He was never returned to Denver to face charges of killing the two policemen.

> POLICE DEPARTMENT.
>
> DENVER
>
> DETECTIVES' OFFICE.
>
> _____ 190_
>
> Report of Goods Stolen
>
> Name Sam Howe
> Address the Chief Wants
> Phone You to look up
> Report the case of the
> Killing of Clifford
> and Griffith. He wants
> the names of the
> Partys who was with
> Llewellin the night
> of the Killing, the
> date and give it
> to me when I come
> down this morning
> Keep this Quite
> Geo Sanders

The killings prompted the Fire and Police Board to observe that both Clifford and Griffith were shot near the heart. The *Denver Evening Post* wrote:

> The fire and police board have about decided that the big silver star policemen wear of the left breast is a dangerous target at night, the bull's-eye being the officer's heart. The big star catches and reflects enough light at night . . . and on the background of the dark blue coat the star becomes doubly apparent. . . . It is understood that the police board will order that in the future police officers shall not wear the badge outside the coat at night. The helmet and uniform are thought to be sufficient insignia and at night the star will be worn under the coat.

Moreover, the Fire and Police Board noted that the killings of Clifford and Griffith illustrated another problem. The officers had fired no fewer than twelve shots at Llewellyn, missing each time. "It is probable," the *Post* wrote, "that some of the officers of the force have not fired a pistol in years . . . the city has never provided for target practice. . . . Half the men [are] armed with weapons fit only for a second-hand gun store, not even useful as clubs." Further, rules required that policemen keep their revolvers *under* a buttoned coat. If the board took any actions as the result of its observations, they are not recorded. Denver's police, however, did not move their badges inside their coats.[30]

As the new century approached, Denver was finally witnessing the decline of some of its early reckless ways. The city did not become pure, but as Denver embarked on the twentieth century it showed signs of growing up, despite its obstinacy. The city was now forty years old.

Notes

1. SHS 10: 3311, from the RMN, April 28, 1889. Ethnic presence along Denver's Row in the late nineteenth century generally seems to have been of little importance. Exceptions were the French prostitutes (and their notorious French pimps) who were identified in both the Denver and Leadville press by their nationality. Other prostitutes of Denver's *demimonde* were almost never described by nationality. The situation was different on the New York City brothel scene. In *Fighting the Traffic in Young Girls* (p. 187), Ernest A. Bell observed criminal ethnic classes among the New York City *demimonde:* "[Irish saloon keeper] Jimmie Kelly manages one or two high class pugilists, but around his saloon are to be found many preliminary boxers. These men cannot make a living as preliminary boxers and must depend on something else to eke out a livelihood. Through their connection with men like Kelly they are given the protection necessary to enable them to conduct immoral resorts or to keep women soliciting on the streets, without interference from the police. In return for this immunity they help Kelly deliver the illegal vote necessary to keep the corrupt Tammany machine in power. The Italian because he is more prone to crimes of violence pays for his political protection in votes, while the Jew largely pays cash. The Italian, unlike the Jew, very rarely puts women of his own race into the awful life; there are relatively very few Italian prostitutes. The Italian [flesh] traders seem likely to displace the French, as they are kinder to the women and they adapt themselves to the political environment in a way that the French do not understand."

2. SHS 16: 11509, from the DR, January 16, 1896.

3. Ibid., 17: 14588, from the DTI, June 22, 1897.

4. Ibid., 17: 14591, from the DR, June 23, 1897.

5. Ibid., 16: 12135, from the DR, April 30, 1896; 17: 14588, 14607, newspapers not identified.

6. Ibid., 16: 13674, from the DR, February 1, 1897.

7. Ibid., 17: 15098, from the *Denver Evening Post*, August 25, 1897.

8. Ibid., 17: 16333, from the DR, May 22, 1898.

9. "Transfer of Saloon Records," Denver city treasurer, 1884 and 1885, Colorado State Archives, Denver.

Registration numbering soon was applied to liquor licenses. Jennie Rogers, then at 2005 Market Street, was issued "Bottled Goods" license number 32 on July 18, 1894, but she transferred it to an unlisted party the following April 1. License number 36 was awarded to Cora Totty, 2009 Market, on July 25, 1894; license 37 went to Minnie A. Hall, 1950 Market, on the same date; license 38 went to Lola H. Pennington, 2015 Market, on August 1, 1894; and license 41 was awarded to Mattie A. Silks, 1916–1918 Market Street, on August 28, 1894. Jennie Rogers obtained the license at 1942 Market on May 11, 1895, and Ethel Lamar had a permit at 1923 Market, issued August 19, 1895 (four months before her attempted shakedown by the crooked judge, court clerk, and sheriff's deputies). As of January 1, 1894, Denver had 21 establishments licensed to sell bottled goods (liquor stores) and 362 licensed retail liquor dealers (saloons), respectively producing for the city treasury $4,200 and $216,000 in fees annually. "License Register of the Treasurer's Office," City of Denver, 1892–1897, Colorado State Archives, Denver.

10. SHS 30: 62185, from the DR, October 13, 1911.

11. Hanna, "The Art of American Policing," pp. 52–53.

12. RD, pp. 517–518.

13. RD, p. 518, quoting the DP, July 10, 1901.

14. DTI, April 25, 1901.

15. RD, pp. 519–521.

16. Ibid., pp. 521–522.

17. Readers concerned with the impact of home rule on crime and policing in Denver are referred to the RD, which devotes an entire chapter to the matter, pp. 539–575.

18. SHS 31: 65828, from the DR, December 4, 1912.

19. Hanna, "The Art of American Policing," pp, 53–54.

20. SHS 12: 5367, from the DR, May 16, 1891.

21. Ibid., 12: 5826, from the DR, October 24, 1891.

22. The *Colorado Graphic*, August 16, 1890.

23. John Farley is the subject of a privately published biography: Farley and Dillon, *The Farley Scrapbook*, copy in the author's possession.

24. RD, pp. 333–334. The roundup of the "French women and Negro women" occurred the night of May 15, 1889.

25. SHS 18: 18646, from the DR, July 5, 1899; 18660, from the DR, July 6, 1899.

26. Ibid., 18: 19000, from the RMN, September 22, 1899.

27. Arvine W. Sowers, William R. Collier, and John H. Phillips (comps), *Denver Fire and Police Departments Illustrated* (Denver: Smith-Brooks, 1905), p. 81.

28. Samson, "Chronological History," p. 3; author's conversation with R. L. Samson, November 25, 1994.

29. Jack Ganzhorn, *I've Killed Men* (New York: Devin-Adair, 1959), p. 114.

30. For the Reverend Bayley's observations, see the DR, August 21, 1899. The article on police badges and guns is from the *Denver Evening Post*, August 22, 1899.

12

"Mayor Speer Was a Wonderful Man. He Kept Market Street Open."

DENVER WAS ORIGINALLY PART OF Arapahoe County, Kansas Territory, becoming Colorado Territory (still Arapahoe County) on February 28, 1861, and the new state of Colorado (Arapahoe County) on August 1, 1876. The city's next geopolitical change came in 1902 with the birth of the City and County of Denver.

Citizens hoped Denver's new organizational sophistication would cleanse the city of its long-established vices. As it happened, the city's reformation took longer than the residents wished. The process might have been quicker if Denver had not had to endure two and a half terms of Robert Walter Speer as mayor.

Speer came to Denver in 1878 as a recovering tubercular and entered politics. Six years later the board of aldermen appointed him city clerk. In 1885, having learned the value of political connections, he was appointed Denver postmaster by President Grover Cleveland, and in 1891 he became a Denver fire and police commissioner. Speer used that position to provide jobs for fellow Democrats, and in the process he quickly learned that people wanted liquor and saloons and, further, that they wanted gambling and prostitution—so long as those vices were kept under control.

Those realizations served Speer well. He quickly learned that keeping vice under control provided him with another tool for graft and shakedowns. In 1901 Speer became Denver's chief of public works, a position that controlled nearly half the city's budget and introduced him to the most powerful men in town.

Denver was maturing and needed a city charter that would set policies and procedures, but the correct sort of charter was paramount in the minds not only of Denver's vice lords but also among the politicians and czars of public utilities and corporations. After a 1903 defeat at the polls (a subsequent investigation revealed a thousand dead or untraceable "voters" on the polling registration lists), in March 1904 a revised charter and a home rule form of government favorable to Speer and his cronies were finally approved.

Two months later Robert W. "Boss" Speer became mayor. In his inaugural address he told Denverites:

No effort will be made to make a puritanical town of a growing western city. An administration should always stand for what is right, but you must take the people as you find them. Vice will not run riot, but wherever found will be promptly controlled or suppressed. Social evils that cannot be abolished will be restricted and regulated so as to do the least possible harm.[1]

The mayor's words meant the parlor houses and crib girls would continue to be confined, just as they had been for more than forty years, to the upper reaches of Market Street, where they would not bother the "decent" folks. Madam Laura Evens later remarked: "Mayor Speer was a wonderful man. He kept Market Street open."[2]

Reformers did not give up easily, however, and maintained an ongoing clamor against Speer and his pals. Harvard-educated lawyer Edward Costigan was a special irritant to Mayor Speer's machine. Costigan visited the wine rooms of Denver and announced that he observed "girls being enticed into them, given knock-out drops, and sexually assaulted, only to finally end up in houses of ill fame."

The night of Sunday, August 11, 1906, the notorious saloon-smashing antibooze crusader Carry Nation hit Denver for the first time. Under the auspices of the Colorado Anti-Cigarette League and with a gaggle of newspaper reporters in tow, Carry cut a wide swath through the Market Street vice district, knocking cigars and cigarettes out of the mouths of men and entering several cheap cribs. At 1920 Market she encountered Blanche Carpentier, who was astonished by the presence of the black-clad figure in the Quaker bonnet. Proclaimed Carry:

You poor, degraded wretch. I pity you. I have hatred for you. You are the victim of bad, bad men, rotten heredity, and a terrible environment. The police are living off you. How much do you have to pay every month to continue your awful life of sin? I am your friend, and I have come to help you. Do not fear these men in blue coats. They can scare you, but they cannot scare me.

Bonnet askew, gray hair waving in the wind, face drawn and white, and eyes shining fiercely and belligerently, she turned to Patrolman George Kaylor, spotting his badge number 23. In a shrill voice she exclaimed:

Number 23! Skidoo, Mr. Policeman, don't you interfere with me. I am Carry Nation. I am trying to save these girls and I will see at least twenty-three of them tonight, just to show you that your number doesn't frighten me! I have come to Colorado to teach the people of this state how to smash saloons. No man can stop me. I am a woman, but I am also a forerunner of the great future. I am a prophet. God has inspired me. I am the Almighty's instrument in carrying out his glorious work. I will smash every saloon I see. I will visit the fallen women and warn them of their awful fate. I will make converts among the prostitutes by the score. I have done it in other cities and I can do it here. (*Denver Post*, August 12, 1906)

By now a sizable crowd had assembled, composed, the *Post* reported, of every saloon man and pimp on the Row plus "thinly clad girls in bizarre dress, their scarlet skirts and rouge smeared faces glistening beneath the glare of the arc light. The strangest thing of all was that there was no laughter." Officer Kaylor, seeing trouble ahead, placed Nation in the paddy wagon for a trip to jail. There Captain Robert Carter detained her for about an hour, releasing her after advising her to behave herself or she would be prosecuted. She then made speeches in Greeley, Fort Collins, Loveland, Longmont, Boulder, and back to Denver.

Boss Speer had many friends along Market Street and among the liquor interests, and the man he named as police chief to maintain certain sensitive balances was Michael Delaney—soon known as "Third Degree" Delaney. Delaney was an ongoing problem for the mayor, and not just because of his heavy-handedness. In 1907 Mrs. T. F. Rowland publicly called the chief a "cold-blooded murderer" after the police auto in which he was riding struck her son Charles while speeding to a burglar alarm. She said her son was tossed into an ambulance "like a sack of flour," and authorities at Speer's County Hospital lied to her about his grave condition. He died.[3]

The *Rocky Mountain News* on September 12 leveled harsher allegations against Delaney and his police department:

> The police department is rotten. It is rotten from circumference to core. . . . Criminals may rob and steal and plunder if they will. . . . Denver is syndicated to a gambling combine. Its members are authorized to rob the public, debauch its morals and ruin its young, if they will only do it in the manner prescribed by the mayor and his chief of police. The redlight district is run upon the same plan. All of this means graft, graft contaminating the executive department of the city through and through. IT IS ROTTENNESS. It is a known fact that Chief Delaney is in compact with thieves and crooks under pledge from these, the vilest of human sputum. Has anybody tried to learn why it is that Mayor Speer holds on to Delaney as his chief of police?

Delaney eventually exhibited his own idea of justice: when an accused burglar denied wrongdoing, Delaney kicked him in the head until the man confessed to something he had not done. A court tossed out the confession. Speer and Delaney survived that crisis, but Delaney was later accused of conflicts of interest and became the source of many problems for Speer. Finally, Delaney, who was married, seized a man he saw emerging from his (Delaney's) girlfriend's house and beat the man, only to learn that he was an innocent plumber.

That was it. Speer fired Third Degree Delaney, and the mayor announced for reelection in 1908. During that campaign a thousand businesspeople signed a petition in Democrat Speer's support, Market Street entrepreneurs and Republicans among them. The cooperative Republicans sent Speer's supporters a list of possible opposition candidates with the message: "Pick the man you think you can beat, and we'll nominate him."

Speer had been holding hands with Denver's vice lords and ladies for so long that as cries for reform intensified throughout his first mayoral term (1904–1908), he had a difficult time responding. Market Street, as he acknowledged, was still there and was pretty much confined within its prescribed geographical boundaries, but those who wanted to clean up the town kept picking at the mayor and his philosophies. And he repeated the same old line, although citizens were now realizing there was something hollow about Bob Speer discussing morals. His biographer, Charles Johnson, quoted Speer:

> I want to see Denver become one of the foremost cities of the country as regards moral cleanliness. I believe the only way to exterminate the vices that have been practiced for so many hundred years, and which, I am sorry to say, will continue for many hundreds of years more, is to take the matter up along practical lines. The only way vice can be controlled is to segregate it from all other parts of the city and not spread it around.

This lame old platitude was not working the way it once had, and the Speer machine knew it. A week before the 1908 election, former judge N. Walter Dixon made accusations that in Denver, crime and vice were rampant, all because of the iniquity of Speer. Speer won the election, but his foes were not finished.[4]

The year 1909 evidenced an increasing move toward police professionalism in Denver despite Mayor Speer, who had learned to stop asking the city police to collect his graft payments from the liquor and bordello interests. This was a new century, and the people of Denver had new expectations about the ethics of their policemen.

Whereas Denver's earliest law enforcers had no physical, educational, or training requirements, by 1909 prospective policemen were tested, according to a city publication, on "spelling, penmanship, arithmetic, general duties, city information, physical development, strength, experience and mental qualifications." Each officer was to serve six months' probation and was to measure between five-feet-eight and six-feet-four and weigh between 145 and 235 pounds. (Sam Howe, at five-feet-four and 135 pounds, would not have qualified.) Patrolmen were paid $85 a month; the chief got $250. Clean uniforms "and linen" were required, and officers were reminded that "a kind word and a smile go further with most people than a cuff and a club."[5]

As early as the 1870s, women had been periodically banned from Denver's saloons—in theory at least—and even as Denver was finally coming of age the city occasionally exhibited a Victorian attitude regarding women in public drinking places. Even in 1909—with the bordellos still operating on Market Street—the city council tried to keep unescorted women out of saloons, and even out of restaurants that served alcohol, during certain evening hours.

Although their mothers may have accepted such ultimatums without question, the women of 1909 were not about to be trod upon in such a manner. Under the headline "About Unescorted Women," the *Denver Municipal Facts* civic publication noted that some resistance had arisen to "the order recently issued which forbids women unaccompanied by escorts to enter liquor-serving restaurants after 8 o'clock at night," and "it is the contention of the [Fire and Police] Board that it is only in rare instances that a respectable woman will desire to enter" such an establishment.[6]

A week later the same publication noted that some "club women" had attacked the rule as discriminatory and that to circumvent the new restriction, management of some of the off-limits bars and cafés were offering in-house "escorts." The city was not fooled by such subterfuge. The Women's Rights Club, the Women's Civil Service League, and even the Women's Christian Temperance Union joined the uproar against the "Escort Rule." City officials were astounded at this resistance, having believed "the rule would meet with the hearty approval of all the good women of the municipality on account of the fact that its enforcement would undoubtedly lessen the evil consequences attendant on the public self-degradation of the lower class of women, so common here as well as in all other centers." It did not happen that way, with the women's clubs persisting in their outcry that the order "was simply another evidence of man's brutal tyranny over woman." Boss Speer was forced to enter the fray, writing an open letter stating that "the order is in no way intended to reflect on the host of good women of Denver."[7]

Now that the issue of women visiting liquor outlets had been attended to, it was time to proclaim that gambling was under control. In 1909 Police Chief Hamilton Armstrong announced in the *Denver Municipal Facts* that aside from a kitchen poker game here and there, "Denver is more free from gambling at the present time than it has ever been in the history of the city," adding:

> It is an impossibility to entirely suppress poker playing because all the tools required are a deck of cards, a table, some chips and a few chairs—just the furnishings that are to be found in any kitchen or dining room. We are constantly on the lookout for public games and I do not think that any of them manage to run more than two or three nights before they are tipped off to us and raided. We have never invaded a private home to raid a poker game unless we have had at least reasonable evidence showing that it is a public game. By this is meant a game participated in by gamblers who contribute so much to the proprietor for the privilege of playing.
>
> Faro, roulette, and other "bank" games require paraphernalia that takes up considerable room and these games are therefore easier to detect and weed out than are poker games. Crap shooting is probably indulged in between negroes and whites, too, for that matter, in alley or in rear rooms. But there are no regular or established crap games running in Denver, and we do not intend that there shall be any.[8]

Speer was in office at the time, and there is a defensive tone to Armstrong's remarks, particularly regarding the suggestion that his men had been raiding private poker games.

By 1910 Speer was still committed to protecting the prostitutes, although old-timers such as Mattie Silks were nearing retirement and organized prostitution in Denver was waning. During 1910 only 63 girls were jailed for occupying a disorderly house, and only 6 madams and pimps were arrested for administering the houses. Another 84 arrests were made for soliciting. A factor in these totals was the emergence of the "two-maid system" by which hotels could, with the implied approval of authorities, keep on the premises two such women—one a maid, the other not a maid. The total arrests that year in a city of 213,381 population were 14,200, including 4 for "escape from a chain gang," 7 for "fast driving," 109 for gambling (perhaps other than the kitchen-table variety), 6 for "insulting women," 1 for "contributing to an opium joint," and 83 for "spitting in street cars"—a genuine concern because it contributed to the spread of tuberculosis.[9]

Reform was gaining momentum in 1912, and its activists set their sights on Market Street and its protector, Mayor Speer. The mayor's opponents charged him with "unlawfully, knowingly and willingly permitting certain common, ill-governed and disorderly houses, to the encouragement of idleness, gaming, drinking, fornication and other misbehavior." Anticipating defeat, Speer chose not to run again, although he would be back on the ballot—as a winner—four years later, in 1916, as a more mellow and honest mayor. He died in office in 1918.[10]

Speer's replacement in 1912 was Henry J. Arnold, the former county assessor whom Speer had fired when Arnold demonstrated that Speer's financial backers had been undertaxed. Arnold refused to vacate the assessor's office, so a Speer henchman, George Collins, broke into the office in the middle of the night and evicted Arnold. Collins thereafter was known as "Crowbar" Collins.[11]

Arnold, at least initially, was a foe of wrongdoing and selected as his police commissioner George Creel, who had written for Frederick G. Bonfils's and Harry Tammen's *Denver Post* and also for Senator Thomas Patterson's *Rocky Mountain News*. Upon joining the *News* in 1911, Creel, Patterson, and their supporters had pledged to "kick out Mayor Bob Speer." Creel as a newspaperman laid the city's vice problems at the doorstep of Boss Speer. The Speer administration, Creel declared, "drew its votes and money from the vileness that it encouraged and protected," adding that Arnold had inherited "a condition of social evil unsurpassed by any city in the nation."[12]

Arnold and Creel pledged not to "persecute the individual prostitute; women who are nothing more than the victims of society." Instead, they would address the prostitution district as an entity that could be fixed up and painted up, making the longtime houses of ill fame "tenantable" for respectable people.[13] Creel's autobiography described Market Street, even in 1911, as

an artificial street lined on both sides with cubicles in which half-naked women sat for sale beside a soiled bed and a dirty washbowl. When a customer mounted the short flight of steps, a corrugated shutter was pulled down. Every night the street was packed and jammed with milling crowds, men for the most part,

but with a high percentage of veiled women, and even more distressingly, many teen-age boys and girls. . . . I wrote to the police authorities in other cities, asking what they were doing.[14]

Mayor Arnold, however, turned weak-kneed, gravitating toward the more permissive stance of the *Post*'s Bonfils and Tammen who believed plans for a greater Denver were being blocked by "a bunch of wild-eyed reformers." Arnold and Police Commissioner Creel experienced a major split: with Creel out of town, Arnold returned to policemen their nightsticks, which Creel had banned, and rescinded Creel's order prohibiting liquor sales in the bordello district.[15]

Creel persisted. Each night, he directed, a certain number of prostitutes would be taken into custody, arraigned, and examined at County Hospital. The resentful women were reminded that these actions were not just another moral crusade but were taken in their own interest. The *Post*, *Times*, and *Republican* cried out against "tax dollar waste," but despite the protestations the atmosphere of Denver was changing.[16]

Momentum for reform increased. By early 1912 the all-night saloons were conforming to new rules; increased political and police pressures and paint-up campaigns were driving the madams and their girls out of town; and Denver's long-present second-story gambling walk-ups were shutting their doors.

But perhaps the most telling evidence of Denver's moral awakening was the case of police patrolman Charles T. Power. When police payday arrived on May 1, 1912, Bob Porter, political graft collector for the city and county Democratic Party, was routinely sent around to collect the regular fifteen-dollar "donation" from every policeman, despite the fact that this practice was now a violation of civil service regulations. Power tore up his assessment form, threw it in Porter's face, submitted his resignation, turned in his badge and keys, and told his captain that if he could not keep the job on his merits and without contributing to a campaign fund, he did not want it. The scene may have seemed small, but it represented a new attitude in Denver.

After twenty-eight years of protection by Robert Speer as city commissioner and mayor plus twenty-five years of tolerance by city administrations before him, Denver's *demimonde* began disappearing under a new civic conscience that had grown weary of the Old West image of unrestrained merriment. The year 1913 had barely dawned before the word was issued—and this time it was not simply the empty statement of a police chief operating with a wink at the behest of his friends at city hall—that a new morality was arriving at Market Street.

Denver had heard the words before, but this time they were for real. The *Rocky Mountain News* of February 23, 1913, made the pronouncement, and it had an air of finality:

> Denver's redlight district was abolished by the fire and police board late yesterday afternoon. Two hours after the board had commanded Chief of Police [Felix] O'Neill to close every house in the restricted district, the word had been sent along that the restricted district was to go. There was a hurried exodus by women when the word came. All were told that the word was final and there was to be no dallying. "Move or be arrested. Tonight is the deadline."

Josephine Roche, a twenty-six-year-old Coloradan who graduated from Vassar and took a master's degree in social work at Columbia University, interrupted work on her doctorate and answered her friend George Creel's summons and returned to Denver in October 1912 as "inspector of amusements." She had full police powers—she was Denver's first full-fledged policewoman—enabling her to monitor the public places where young people congregated and got into trouble.

In her master's thesis Roche had established the chief cause of prostitution to be economics, and in Denver she determined that half of the prostitutes had chosen their profession for its wages. She pleaded for better jobs and higher pay for all women. She further spoke out against the decades-long city policy of confining the brothels to their own geographic district, alleging that this did not control anything; instead, it made the city a partner in vice.

Roche, who had learned much sociology theory in the classroom, met with only marginal successes in her attempt to clean up the Denver youth problem. She found she could not enforce a curfew for persons under age twenty-one, and her crusade to ban inti-

mate dancing and the tango failed. Roche was more successful in reaching fallen women and raising money to return them to their family homes.

As sometimes happens with reformers, Creel got into trouble. He berated his boss, Mayor Arnold, whose dedication to reform was evaporating, and Arnold fired Creel in February 1913. Roche publicly censured Fire and Police Board president A. A. Blakely for helping his pals avoid liquor regulations. Blakely responded that he was tired of Roche's advice on how to raise children when she had no children and knew nothing about them. A month after Creel was kicked out, Roche was informed she was being discharged because of a so-called lack of funds.

She continued her interest in social causes, became involved in her father's Rocky Mountain Fuel Company where she strove for improved working conditions for miners, and during the New Deal became an assistant secretary of the treasury in charge of public health. Many years later, as an elderly lady, she confessed to relishing the days when she invaded the red light district and took fourteen-year-olds home to their mothers.[17]

Roche and Juvenile Court judge Ben Lindsey had estimated that 300 full-time prostitutes remained in the Market Street district and that 2,000 women in rooming houses between Market Street and Broadway were "semi-prostitutes." Despite Roche's absence, the police persisted in ridding Denver of its brothels. Purity crusaders could scarcely believe what they were seeing.

It was happening elsewhere, too, as the eve of World War I approached. In *City of Eros*, his history of prostitution in New York City, Timothy J. Gilfoyle enumerates forces through which the open prostitution of the brothels, the streetwalkers, and concert saloons were finally driven underground, becoming diluted in the process:

♦ Changes in governmental policies. Federal and state governments for the first time cooperated to effectively define prostitution and take measures to eradicate open commercial sex. For instance, the Mann Act of 1910 made illegal the transportation of women across state lines for purposes of prostitution.

♦ Prohibition's effects on prostitution. (Colorado went dry on New Year's Day 1916, followed three years later by national Prohibition.) This outlawed many of the venues of prostitution: the saloons, the concert taverns, and the wine halls.

♦ The "medicalization" of prostitution. The public was exposed to educational programs explaining the relationship between open prostitution and venereal diseases. Such awareness campaigns were augmented by a new open attitude toward the public discussion of sex.

♦ The improved situation of women. Better wages and working conditions for women made prostitution less necessary for many women.

♦ Changes in sexual habits. American heterosexual behavior witnessed significant changes following 1900, manifested by increases in premarital sex and in sexuality within marriage. Thus the allure of prostitution was lessened.[18]

It was the end of a long tradition, a leftover from the wild and woolly days of the Old West. In Denver, Detective Sam Howe pasted the Josephine Roche–Judge Lindsey edict into his thirty-second crime scrapbook. He might have been recalling the days when painted ladies winked at prospective clients from the porch steps of the Denver Row—the most famous district between St. Louis and San Francisco.[19]

The Denver policemen moved in, and Market Street became known as "Padlock Alley."[20] By 1916 the *Denver Times* was able to report that the old Alcazar Theater at Twentieth and Market, where the dime-a-dance girls made fifty cents a night, was now a warehouse. The opposite corner, where "king of the red lights" Jack Maynard held forth, was a $7,000 automobile repair garage. "The improvement of business conditions in Denver," the *Times* said, "is shown by the gradual transformation of the old 'prohibited district' where the night life of the city once held sway."[21]

Prostitution still existed, but its form was changing. After decades of visibility up and down both sides of McGaa and then Holladay and then Market Streets and in places such as Ed Chase's Palace, the "call girl" was now available only in her apartment or cheap hotel room along "uptown" Arapahoe, Curtis, or Champa Street. She no longer openly plied her trade from her window or the porch step or saloon.

Long traditions, however, perish with difficulty. Some of the crib girls, pushed from the habitat where they had been allowed to languish safely for so many decades, now used alleys or even park benches, whereas the fancier parlor ladies joined out-call services. Increasingly, some hotel chambermaids were genuine; others were not.

Whether Denver was better off with Market Street finally closed was doubtful to some. Prostitution, everybody knew but only some would admit, could not be eradicated; the clientele still existed, and the girls were there to provide the services. As the city shut down the long-controlled atmosphere of Market Street, matters threatened to get out of control. The *Denver Post* on June 9, 1913, told on page 1 that the women of Denver's netherworld, driven out of their protected district, had taken to the streets. During the twenty-four hours prior to the story's publication, twenty-four women had been arrested for soliciting on the streets, been fined ten to twenty-five dollars each, and been warned by Justice of the Peace Ben Stapleton that on repetition they could get ninety days in County Jail. The *Denver Republican* wrote the same day:

> Among those arrested was Rosie Hart, 24, who came in the limelight on the night of May 12 when she engaged in a struggle with Sheriff [Daniel] Sullivan and escaped from him after having blackened his eye and scratched his face. She was arrested shortly after 10 o'clock last night at Seventeenth and Tremont streets. . . . A fight ensued during which she was thrown to the sidewalk. She got to her feet and taking advantage of an opportunity, struck the sheriff across the face with a mesh purse. She then escaped, and hailing a passing automobile got into it and rode to police headquarters and sought protection.

When Market Street was open, some people argued, such violence never would have occurred at a location as respectable as Seventeenth and Tremont.

Certain municipal officials had long argued that it was wiser and easier to segregate prostitutes than to try to eliminate prostitution. Now, distressingly for the reformers, that philosophy was emerging again: only five months after the crib and brothel crackdown, the city grand jury recommended—probably at the behest of the convention and visitor business interests—

that the "segregated district be re-established until a time when vice can be eradicated."[22]

Denver knew better, and the grand jury's recommendation was rejected. Legitimate merchants were becoming increasingly nervous: with the gigantic convention of 30,000 Knights Templar members approaching in August 1913, 300 prominent businessmen petitioned to the city administration that Denver was becoming known among conventioneers as an "inhospitable city" that was so quiet that its downtown was "the best-lighted cemetery in the country." The press agreed that conditions were becoming a bit severe, complaining that new rules trimming the operations of formerly twenty-four-hour saloons constituted an "ill-timed order." The business interests asked Judge Charles C. Butler to intercede, but he declined.[23]

One young man believed booze, not driving the prostitutes underground, was the problem. Frank Krbetz, age fifteen, became weary of his father spending most of the family money on liquor, so he took a revolver, pinned on a deputy sheriff's badge, and started out to single-handedly close all the saloons in Denver. "You'll have to close up your shop and do it right now," he told the astonished saloon men. "I'll be back in five minutes and there'll be something doin' if you're not locked up. Dad spends most of his money in these places and I'm not goin' to stand for it." The barkeeps were amused until Frank pulled the gun. Patrolman Edward A. Benbow and Special Officer John S. Phillips of the Juvenile Court escorted Frank to the boys' detention home.[24]

In 1916, after four years out of the mayor's chair, a mellower Robert Speer, who acknowledged Denver's new morality, ran for office again and won. It was an age of Prohibition. Posted in the window of R. Schwartz's saloon at 1636 Curtis Street, to be sung to the tune of "It's a Long Way to Tipperary," was the lyric

> *It's a long way to California,*
> *It's a long way to go.*
> *It's a long way to California,*
> *To the wettest place I know.*
> *Good Bye Tom & Jerry,*
> *Good Bye Rock & Rye.*
> *It's a long way to California*
> *When Denver goes dry.*[25]

With Prohibition the law, Denver fretted over how to slake its historically unquenchable thirst. At least the citizens no longer had to worry so much about their city's scarlet ladies and eyeshaded gamblers.

Or did they?

Notes

1. For Mayor Robert W. Speer, see Johnson, *Denver's Mayor Speer*; Leonard and Noel, *Denver: Mining Camp to Metropolis*, pp. 132–136; Dorsett, *The Queen City*. Speer's inaugural address is quoted in the RD, p. 563.

2. Hanna, "The Art of American Policing," p. 64.

3. For the case of Mrs. T. F. Rowland, see the RMN, September 12, 1907.

4. Johnson, *Denver's Mayor Speer*, pp. 144–154, especially p. 147. Students of Denver's reformist movements during the first dozen years of the twentieth century should consult the winter 1968 issue of *Colorado Magazine*. In this important publication, historians chronologically and methodically examine various plans to cleanse Denver politics and coincidentally rid the city of its long-standing vices. The articles are Roland L. DeLorme, "Turn-of-the-Century Denver: An Invitation to Reform," pp. 1–15; J. Richard Snyder, "The Election of 1904: An Attempt at Reform," pp. 16–26; J. Paul Mitchell, "Municipal Reform in Denver: The Defeat of Mayor Speer," pp. 42–60; and Charles J. Bayard, "The Colorado Progressive Republican Split of 1912," pp. 61–78.

5. *Denver Municipal Facts*, April 3, 24, 1909. *Municipal Facts* was created as a mouthpiece for Speer's administration, a publication that would print the "good news" about what the city government was doing. Speer had long felt the newspapers were unduly criticizing him and were not dispensing positive stories about Denver's (or his) accomplishments. Despite its rose-colored-glasses function, *Municipal Facts* was well received by the populace and is a valuable resource for historians, as it contains information and photographs that exist no place else. The Colorado Historical Society library and the Western History Department of the Denver Public Library maintain files of *Municipal Facts*.

6. Ibid., April 24, 1909.

7. SHS 28: 54129, from the DR, June 12, 1909.

8. *Denver Municipal Facts*, August 7, 1909.

9. Ibid., February 4, 1911.

10. Noel, *The City and the Saloon*, pp. 108–109.

11. Leonard and Noel, *Denver: Mining Camp to Metropolis*, pp. 135–136.

12. George Creel, *Rebel at Large: Recollections of Fifty Crowded Years* (New York: G. P. Putnam's Sons, 1947), p. 97.

13. RMN, August 22, 1912.

14. Creel, *Rebel at Large*, p. 104.

15. Ibid., pp. 108–109.

16. Ibid., pp. 110–111.

17. Elinor M. McGinn, unpublished ms., "My Hobby Is Humanity: The Story of Josephine Roche" (Lafayette, Colo., 2000); Marjorie Hornbein, "Josephine Roche: Social Worker and Coal Operator," *Colorado Magazine*, summer 1976, pp. 243–260.

18. Gilfoyle, *City of Eros*, pp. 306–311.

19. SHS 32: 66580, from the RMN, February 23, 1913.

20. Noel, *The City and the Saloon*, pp. 108–109.

21. In the August 9 edition.

22. SHS 32: 67621, from the DR, July 19, 1913.

23. Ibid., 32: 67450, 67451, from the DR, June 27, 1913.

24. Ibid., 32: 68169, from the RMN, September 20, 1913.

25. James E. Hansen II, "Moonshine and Murder: Prohibition in Denver," *Colorado Magazine*, winter 1973, p. 3.

13

That Is Good

ORLD WAR I MARKED THE END of organized and controlled prostitution, not only in Denver but also in other U.S. urban centers that housed federal facilities where young men were stationed. At the insistence of authorities at central Colorado military installations, prostitution and gambling were stringently suppressed throughout the war years. When the war ended, however, both vices reappeared in the twelve-block Denver area bounded by Eighteenth, Twenty-second, Champa, and Larimer Streets—just southeast of what had been the long-protected district centered at Twentieth and Market. Behind heavy curtains, ladies of the night again worked rooming houses or migrated to the nearby low-rise downtown hotels.

In his colorful book *Fighting the Underworld*, the crusading district attorney Philip S. Van Cise reported that in post–World War I Denver, gambling houses and bootleg joints were running with the full knowl-

edge of the police, and prostitutes were occupying parts of the old section of the city, although their activities were less brazen. Sixty houses were operating, in addition to the prostitutes working in small downtown hotels.

As in the bad old days, city hall and the police department were involved. A man named Abe Silver, who held the quasi-police office of "city constable," worked quietly on behalf of the municipal government to offer a measure of protection to the prostitution operations and small gambling halls. It was the Row all over again—less boisterous, certainly, but larger geographically.[1]

By 1920 venereal disease in Denver was so out of control that the U.S. government dispatched investigators to the city. Federal health administrator David Robinson met with Mayor Dewey C. Bailey, Safety Manager Frank M. Downer, and Police Chief Hamilton Armstrong. Like so many mayors before him, Bailey

311

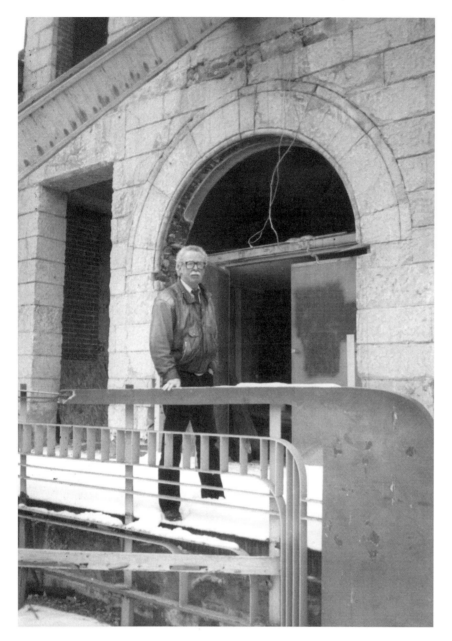

a whiskey. The city hall publication *Denver Municipal Facts* in April 1919 wrote:

> Nearly all the states have enacted legislation to suppress venereal diseases, and about all the large cities have passed ordinances to cope with this problem. Secretary of the Navy Josephus Daniels says: "One of the compensations for the tragedy of war is the fact that an enlightened opinion is behind the organized campaign to protect the youth against venereal disease." The campaign begun in war to insure the military fitness of men fighting is quite as necessary to save men for civil efficiency. Colorado has passed a venereal bill and the same has been signed by the governor. Denver anticipated the movement over a year ago and was one of the first among the large cities to take action and pass an ordinance.

said Denver's problem was no worse than elsewhere. Robinson responded that if Denver did not get rid of its vices, the feds would.

Denver was finally ready to clean up its act. Citizens were anxious to shed the Old West image of motherly madams and their happy hookers, of gamblers like Doc Holliday and Big Ed Chase, of gunfighters striding through the saloon's swinging doors to order

Denver authorities called for a grand jury investigation of the problem. The results were fifteen indictments of underworld characters and the closing of twenty hotels as public nuisances. Van Cise targeted twenty-two additional hotels and rooming houses plus about fifty women who worked there, twenty-five "alleged men parasites," and fifteen prominent businessmen who owned the properties. Even in the more respect-

The restoration of the House of Mirrors disclosed the outline of the original staircase to the second floor, trod with great anticipation by many a wealthy business magnate or hardscrabble prospector just down from the hills, ore pouch in hand.

able uptown hotels where the bogus two-maid system had persisted for many years, at the outbreak of World War II the army prevailed on the city to prohibit that subterfuge as well.[2]

The abundance of military personnel at Lowry and Buckley Fields and Fitzsimons Army Hospital during World War II provided a substantial consumer base for female companionship, however, and the love-for-sale merchants became difficult to eradicate once again. A cooperative federal-state study in 1944 proclaimed:

There was prostitution in the Denver area in and prior to 1941. A well-defined "district" comprising about 20 square blocks in downtown Denver was in operation. Streetwalkers, taxi drivers, bellboys and others were engaged in the trade and suffered only occasional interference. When the soldiers first began to arrive at Lowry Field, it was a common sight to see them lined up before the well-known "houses."[3]

Even in 1950 a prostitution ring was discovered operating within the walls of Fitzsimons. Willie C. Carter and William Robinson were charged with recruiting

Rosajine Wilson and June Blaney to provide sex for tuberculosis patients at the hospital. An immediate federal cleanup was ordered.[4] As in 1859 when the newly widowed Ada LaMont first set up shop on Indian Row, rental companionship was a commodity in demand, and the community tried to do something about it.

Clutching her blanket to her neck, "Blind Sadie" Doyle, eighty-six, sat in her apartment above a hardware shop at 1923 Arapahoe Street, May 21, 1949, recalling the halcyon days when Market Street was the first place a man headed when he hit Denver. Sadie remembered when she first arrived in 1893 and proceeded straight from Union Station to the most crimson street in the West. She remembered the manhunt when Wellington Llewellen killed policemen Thomas Clifford and William Griffith at Twentieth and Market. She remembered when Annie Ryan, a Market Street girl, shot former cop Maurice Lyons. Sadie was in the room during the shooting, but she was blind and could not witness it, so the judge set Annie free. Sadie recalled the rich and powerful men she had known, and she remembered the night in 1901 when she was tossed into jail at city hall, Fourteenth and Larimer, and how she cursed that old building and wished it would disappear. Later that night it caught fire. "Ain't it beautiful?" she observed as the flames licked the third floor. Sadie remembered how she had saved all the money she made on Market Street so she would not have to go on welfare.

Three months later, August 20, 1949, District Judge Joe Cook signed an order restraining Blind Sadie from using her room on Arapahoe Street as a den of prostitution. Doyle's longtime caretaker, Frank "Toughy" Keith, fifty-one, had been renting Sadie's bed to Anne O'Neil, who in turn had been renting out her favors there.

Sadie Doyle died in a convalescent home, October 1, 1950. Fifty friends but no curiosity seekers went to the funeral. A tenor sang "The Old Rugged Cross," and the prayers spoke of immortality. And forgiveness.[5]

Twentieth and Market was a place Denver had not been proud of. Twentieth and Market is now within a baseball's throw of Coors Field, home of the Colo-

rado Rockies ball team. It is a handsome structure, and the city is proud of it. Next door are $750,000 condominiums, ritzy brew pubs, and upscale nightspots. Where Big Ed Chase's notorious Palace Gambling Hall once robbed girls of their virtue and prospectors of their gold dust stands the Palace Lofts luxury condominium project, which brags that millions of dollars are still exchanging hands there. Next to where Mattie Silks knocked Katie Fulton down and broke her nose and where Cort Thomson was shot on that whiskey-sodden night in 1877, a spacious auditorium named after a soda pop beckons famous entertainers and sports stars. The old neighborhood of Jennie Rogers, Mattie Silks, and the murderous Black Ide is the swankiest address in town.

Whiskey flows copiously in the clubs and bars. Jennie and Mattie would approve.

The only gambling in sight is a dollar a pocket in the oak-paneled billiard parlors or a more substantial whispered wager over the baseball game. Jennie and Mattie and Ed Chase would approve of that, too.

A police officer on the take is doubtful, and of that Boss Speer and his city hall henchmen would decidedly disapprove.

The visitor probably need not search far for certain controlled pharmaceutical products, but they are not laudanum, raw morphine, or Rough on Rats, all of which once produced death with a dime's worth. Right here on this streetcorner.

And within the stadium and auditorium and oak-and-brass barrooms and the chandeliered dining parlors and loft condos with indirect lighting and sunken tubs and stretch limousines waiting outside, there are probably women of joy.

Jennie Rogers and Mattie Silks would say that is good.

Notes

1. Hanna, "The Art of American Policing," pp. 78–80. For Van Cise, see *Fighting the Underworld* (Cambridge, Mass.: Riverside, 1936).

2. DP, March 22, 1922; Hanna, "The Art of American Policing," pp. 78–80. The papers of Fred Mazzulla, Colorado Historical Society boxed collection 1231, ff. 140, con-

tain a letter dated July 4, 1967, to Mazzulla from Carl J. Cox of Yreka, California. Mazzulla had just published *Brass Checks and Red Lights*, and Cox suggested the following for inclusion in any second edition: "You might add a little something from the early '20s of Denver about a couple of sporting gals on Larimer Street, Mabel Wilson and Frances Daws. Frances got religion, joined the church, and preached all along the streets in lower Denver. One day she ran into Mabel and asked her what she was doing now-a-days. Mabel said she was still in the racket and was doing O.K. Frances said, 'Honey why don't you see the light and take God into your heart. Forget about this terrible life you are leading and come with me and walk down the straight and narrow path. Believe me, you will discover a new, beautiful way of life. Tonight I am preaching at the corner of 15th and Larimer Street at 7 o'clock. Please Honey, come down and join me.' Mabel had a pretty good day and that evening was flying higher than a homesick angel but had run out of refreshments, so about 7 o'clock she staggered down to her bootlegger. At 15th and Larimer she spotted the little group on the corner, and Frances on a box preaching to the bunch. Frances said, 'Once I was a lost woman. I drank. I smoked. I used the name of the Lord in vain. I have lain in the arms of the chief of police. I have lain in the arms of the mayor, and I have lain in the arms of half the men in Denver, but tonight thank God, I am going to lie in the arms of Jesus!' Mabel, swaying in the back of the crowd, yelled, 'Atta Boy, Frances, fuckum all!'"

3. Denver Metropolitan Planning Project Final Report, "Preventing Prostitution, Promiscuity and Venereal Disease in the Denver Metropolitan Area," June 1944. Copy in the Denver Public Library, Western History Department.

4. DP, October 25, 1950.

5. For Sadie Doyle, see the DP, May 22, August 20, 1949, and October 24, 26, 29, 1950; and the RMN, August 20, 1949, and October 5, 27, 1950. She is buried in Mount Olivet Cemetery.

Appendix A:
The Howe Methodology

THE FOLLOWING TABLE lists the Sam Howe Scrapbooks utilized in this study, giving the volume number, applicable dates, and the clipping numbers contained in that volume. Chronological gaps or inconsistencies can be attributed to missing entries or vagaries of Howe's methodology. An asterisk (*) alongside the volume number means Howe prepared an index, generally fairly thorough, located in the front of that volume. In the case of Volume 12, the index applies loosely to several adjacent volumes as well. The Howe Scrapbooks are preserved in the rare book and document storage rooms at the Colorado Historical Society, Denver. They are recognized as unique in the national literature of criminology.

Detached indexes were prepared for some books by Sam Howe and are in separate thin volumes relating to these years: 1901, 1902, 1903, 1904, 1906, 1907, 1908, 1909, 1910, and 1911. Front indexes exist for Howe books 14 (March–July 1894), 15 (July 1894 through 1895), 16 (January 1896–April 1897), and

17 (April 1897–July 1898). Additional Howe indexes exist. One marked "Murder Index" (not to be confused with the Howe *Murder Book* index) applies to a scrapbook of murder clippings dating between 1921 and 1941 prepared by other police personnel following Howe's retirement. These clippings, unfortunately, do not employ Howe's discipline of organization and numbering. Because of their dates, they are outside the scope of this study.

Howe's *Murder Book*—a remarkable volume detailing many years of pre-1921 murders in Denver—is indexed alphabetically by Howe at the front of the volume. The *Murder Book* is still the only one of the Howe Scrapbooks available to researchers on microfilm.

Detective Sam Howe's indexes are unsophisticated and are scribed in the characteristic flowery script of the day but can be functional to the researcher who has patience.

Aside from use of an index, the easiest way to locate entries in a Howe Scrapbook is to search by date for a particular crime. Once the initial clipping is located, it often will contain Howe's inked-in reference numbers to subsequent clippings regarding the same crime. This procedure generally applies only to crimes Howe regarded as particularly important or interesting, but the system can be useful in tracing a crime from its commission through the court and appeals system and on to its conclusion by imprisonment, parole, pardon, or execution. The author has frequently succeeded, with perseverance, in locating data on obscure crimes and criminals using the Howe indexes.

In addition to his scrapbooks, Sam Howe maintained his *Murder Book*, which is a Colorado state treasure. Not only is it unique among Howe's books, but it may be unique among the crime literature of any state. The standard volumes in the Sam Howe Scrapbook series have maroon covers, are generally 11 by 18 inches in page size, and are 1 to 10 inches thick. They contain indexed copies of published newspaper clippings. The *Murder Book* departs from the concept and format of the Howe Scrapbooks and was maintained by Howe roughly during the time period of the scrapbooks. Unlike the scrapbooks, it contains criminals' photographs, photographs of murder scenes, and handwritten (rather than published) accounts, penned by Howe, of Denver murder cases. The book is 4 inches thick, has a white fabric cover, and its page size is 9 by 14 inches. Unlike the Sam Howe Scrapbooks, which because of their fragile condition are under restricted use at the Colorado Historical Society Library, the *Murder Book* is available to researchers on microfilm through the courtesy of retired Denver police sergeant Ronald L. Samson.

Table A.1—Dates and Clippings

Howe Volume	Dates	Clip Numbers
1	April 1883–November 1885	1–196
2	November 1885–February 1886	202–427
3	February 1886–July 1886	430–746
4	June 1886–October 1886	753–962
5	October 1886–February 1887	965–1208
6	January 1887–September 1887	1212–1892
7	October 1887–February 1888	1896–2226
8	February 1888–August 1888	2241–2748
9	September 1888–March 1889	2751–3238
10	March 1889–July 1889	3255–3634
11	July 1889–December 1889	3637–3999
12*	January 1890–December 1891	4000–6044
13	January 1892–March 1894	6045–8650
14	March 1894–July 1894	8651–9144
15	July 1894–December 1895	9146–11417
16*	January 1896–May 1897	11418–14099
17*	April 1897–July 1898	14100–16508
18	July 1898–February 1900	16511–19574
19	January 1900–July 1901	20000–23000
20	July 1901–November 1901	23001–26457
21	January 1902–December 1902	26500–29999
22	January 1903–January 1904	30000–33500
23	January 1904–January 1905	33501–37228
24	January 1905–February 1906	37200–40657
25	January 1906–August 1907	40700–44459
26	January 1907–January 1908	44600–48171
27	January 1908–July 1909	48257–52542
28	January 1909–May 1910	54504–56476
29	June 1910–November 1911	56401–60094
30	January 1911–February 1912	59801–62812
31	January 1912–February 1913	62802–66165
32	January 1913–March 1915	70675–71258

I N 1990 A DRAWER CONTAINING TWELVE LONG-UNSEEN Denver police annual reports was found in an old desk at central Police Headquarters. They were dated 1916 to 1929 inclusive—1917 and 1919 were missing—representing most of the Prohibition period in Colorado. Research for the first edition of this book was under way, and police technician Mark Shonk, who discovered the reports, graciously offered their data to the author. Even though those years fall beyond the scope of this study, crime statistics contained in the reports are included here, augmented by data located in the archives of the Denver manager of safety's office, for their sociological importance and for the benefit of future researchers.

Colorado enacted Prohibition in 1916, four years before nationwide Prohibition became the law. Although Colorado's Prohibition had a restrictive effect on local imbibing, it did not eliminate it: during that year police arrested 566 scofflaws for Prohibition violation—5 percent of the year's total arrests (10,045).

A further tabulation of the 1916 Denver crime picture includes these arrest figures: assaults, all categories, 37; adultery, 2; beating a board bill, 3; bunco, 4; burglary, 47; burglary and larceny, also 47; carrying a concealed weapon, 46; contributing to juvenile delinquency, 16; cruelty to animals, 21; cruelty to children, 8; deserter, 17; discharging firearms, 11; keeping a disorderly house, 15; disturbance, 733; drunkenness, 1,605 (or 16 percent of the year's total arrests); false pretenses, 12; fraudulent checks, 15; forgery, 25; "found dead," 17; gambling, 348; keeping a gambling house, 18; contributing to a house of prostitution, 4 (it is assumed these were arrests of clients); keeping a house of prostitution, 6 (this classification included the madam and pimp); inmate of a house of prostitution, 10 (this figure represents the girls themselves); harboring vicious dogs, 2; "insane," 150; indecent exposure, 10; indecent language, 1; "investigation" (a catchall term used to detain anybody for scant reason; it would not be tolerated today), 823; larceny, 203; murder, 7; "riot,"

5; reckless [auto] driving, 63; soliciting, 64; vagrancy, 1,246; and traffic violations, 403.

The year 1917 is missing from the Shonk find. Arrests and incidents for 1918 included intriguing new crime classifications, including "seditious utterances" (a World War I infraction), for which there was 1 arrest that year, and "refusing to work for U.S.," which accounted for 2 arrests and probably was also war related. Additionally, there were 2 apprehensions for "violating window cleaning ordinance," which may or may not have been related to a still-active Denver ordinance prohibiting placement of pies, flowerpots, or other potential missiles on windowsills because of the danger of them falling and striking an unsuspecting pedestrian on the head. The remainder of the 1918 police blotter included: assaults, 32; burglaries, 38; burglary and larceny, 28; carrying concealed weapons, 53; contributing to juvenile delinquency, 19; cruelty to animals, 25; cruelty to children, 8; "deserter," 27; discharging firearms, 19; keeping a disorderly house, 24; disturbance, 517; drunkenness, 1,423; "drowned," 4; deserted children, 3; escaped convict, 5; embezzlement, 4; fraudulent checks, 21; forgery, 26; fugitive, 162; "found dead," 28; fornication, 1; gambling, 740; keeping a gambling house, 23; keeping a gambling game, 46; keeping a gambling device, 9; contributing to a house of prostitution, 2; keeping a house of prostitution, 37; inmate of a house of prostitution, 45; "insane," 123; "insulting women," 5 (*see note); indecent exposure, 5; investigation, 998; "injured," 754; jumping on moving [trolley] cars, 10; "killed," 12; larcenies, 215; lost persons, 103; loitering, 11; murder, 9; mayhem, 1; "out nights," 16 (a juvenile offense tantamount to today's curfew violations); operating auto, no permit, 8; "slackers," 3; speeding, 138; and soliciting, 182.

By 1920 the officially stated tally of saloons in Denver had dropped from 410 a decade earlier to zero (Noel, *The City and the Saloon*, p. 116). To accommodate law-abiding citizens who still wished to gather socially, Denver began issuing licenses for the enjoyment of soft drinks, ice cream, and billiards. The license fee was twenty-five dollars. Probably a holdover from the liquor licensing days was the provision that no soft drink license could be awarded within a half-

block of a school, according to records housed in the offices of the Denver manager of safety. It is evident from those records that at least some ice cream and billiards parlors were fronts for illegal booze. The soft drinks and billiards license of one M. Engbar, 3472 West Colfax Avenue, was suspended for "violating the prohibition law," and there are similar citations as well. These records also reflect instances of police officers being suspended or dismissed for Prohibition violations or drunkenness. The text of this book details many such accounts.

Prohibition during 1920 appears to have been increasingly ignored, with 655 liquor arrests that year. One citizen was charged with "buying government property"—a new classification that cannot be interpreted today. The remainder of the 1920 list of 12,947 arrests and incidents was: assaults, 35; adultery, 2; abortion, 2; beating a board bill, 3; burglary, 33; confidence game, 1; concealed weapons, 91; contributing to juvenile delinquency, 27; cruelty to animals, 34; cruelty to children, 2; deserter, 27; discharging firearms, 10; keeping a disorderly house, 14; disturbance, 715; drunkenness, 1,847; draft evader, 1; embezzlement, 8; fraudulent checks, 16; forgery, 24; "found dead," 49; gambling, 648; keeping a gambling house, 25; keeping a gambling game, 54; keeping gambling paraphernalia, 9; frequenting a gambling home, 9; contributing to a house of prostitution, 30; keeping a house of prostitution, 21; inmate of a house of prostitution, 17; "insane," 151; illicit distilling, 5; indecent exposure, 10; indecent liberties, 5; investigation, 1,319; jumping on moving cars, 6; kidnapping, 2; larcenies, 216; murder, 19; "masher," 3; "out nights," 27; "profane letters," 1; rape, 16; reckless driving, 152; speeding, 421; soliciting, 21; tampering with auto, 3; vagrancy, 2,111; violation of fortune telling ordinance, 4; violation of pool room ordinance, 1; violation of traffic ordinance, 203.

Following are Denver police incident statistics through much of the remainder of Prohibition in Colorado.

1921

Total arrests, 19,649. Assaults, 31; auto theft, 3; abandoned baby, 1; burglaries, 45; breaking in house,

4; concealed weapons, 122; contributing to juvenile delinquency, 13; counterfeiting, 2; cruelty to animals, 3; cruelty to children, 9; deserter, 26; discharging firearms, 7; drowned, 2; keeping a disorderly house, 4; disturbance, 883; drunkenness, 3,163 (double the 1920 figure); dog bite, 1; flaging [*sic*] cars, 6 (meaning not known); false ambulance call, 2; fast driving, 91; fraudulent checks, 11; fell in flood water, 1; fighting, 2; gambling, 525; keeping a gambling house, 48; contributing to a house of prostitution, 88; keeping a house of prostitution, 50; inmate of a house of prostitution, 33; insane, 174; indecent exposure, 16; indecent language, 1; investigation, 1,882; insulting women, 2; killed in auto accident, 1; larcenies, 167; murder, 26; masher, 10; picketing, 10; poisoning, 24 (this category appears fairly regularly from this point on and may signify cases to which ambulance patrols responded); purse snatching, 1; rape, 18; reckless driving, 27; disorderly rooming house, 3; running a gambling game, 2; ticket scalping, 1; vagrancy, 3,637; violating Prohibition law, 271; violating traffic ordinance, 936.

1922

Total arrests, 18,667. Assaults, 46; adultery, 4; auto theft, 5; bunco, 9; burglary, 57; burglary and larceny, 98; bigamy, 1; burned, 2; contributing to a disorderly house, 52; crimes against nature, 3; concealed weapons, 118; contributing to juvenile delinquency, 15; cruelty to animals, 41; cruelty to children, 7; deserter, 20; discharging firearms, 11; keeping a disorderly house, 61; disturbance, 772; drunkenness, 4,031; demented, 157; drowned, 4; electrocuted, 2; fraudulent checks, 12; forgery, 34; found dead, 67; gambling, 468; keeping a gambling house, 60; contributing to a house of prostitution, 30; keeping a house of prostitution, 8; inmate of a house of prostitution, 25; insulting women, 4; indecent exposure, 37; indecent language, 1; interfering with an officer, 26; investigation, 1,815; incorrigible, 2; injured, 1,217; impersonating an officer, 6; juvenile delinquency, 18; killed, 14; larcenies, 195; loitering, 19; malicious mischief, 45; murder, 32; mashing, 5; manslaughter, 1; nonsupport, 8; poison[ing], 40; picketing, 25; rape, 12; resisting an officer, 4; refusing to move, 6; robbery, 19; highway robbery, 12;

runaway, 52; running a disorderly house, 1; sodomy, 3; stealing, 45; shot, 62; soliciting, 181; vagrancy, 2,806; violating Prohibition, 887; violating narcotics laws, 140; traffic violations, 1,291; violating fortune telling ordinance, 220.

1923

Total arrests, 17,288. Assaults, 50; auto theft, 9; bigamy, 2; beating a board bill, 1; blackmail, 1; burglary, 33; burglary and larceny, 23; crimes against nature, 2; concealed weapons, 105; contributing to juvenile delinquency, 17; cruelty to animals, 46; cruelty to children, 11; deserter, 12; discharging firearms, 13; keeping a disorderly house, 19; disturbance, 892; drunkenness, 3,111; demented, 249; drowned, 6; dope, 1; escaped convict, 2; embezzlement, 2; disorderly conduct, 1; fraudulent checks, 22; forgery, 16; found dead, 103; gambling, 436; keeping a gambling house, 49; harboring a vicious dog, 3; inmate of house of prostitution, 73; inmate of a disorderly house, 9; indecent exposure, 34; interfering with an officer, 30; investigation, 1,749; incorrigible, 4; injured, 1,453; juvenile delinquency, 42; killed, 7; larcenies, 148; mashing, 9; malicious mischief, 34; murder, 13; "murdered," 4; nonsupport, 21; nuisance, 1; poison, 10; peeping tom, 1; rape, 16; resisting officer, 26; refusing to move, 2; robbery, 5; highway robbery, 11; runaway, 58; running a disorderly house, 86; shot, 45; soliciting, 98; vagrancy, 2,292; violating Prohibition, 1,144; violating narcotics law, 68; violating traffic ordinance, 2,084; violating fortune telling ordinance, 2; wrongs to children, 7.

1924

Total arrests, 19,825. Assaults, 38; adultery, 2; abortion, 2; arson, 2; abandoned children, 2; burglary, 36; burglary and larceny, 37; breaking glass on highway, 15 (the first appearance of this classification and suggesting a new proliferation of automobiles and the dangers posed by even small shards of glass to the thin tires of the day); bribery, 1; bigamy, 3; burns, 2; confidence game, 3; crimes against nature, 1; concealed weapons, 128; contributing to juvenile delinquency, 9;

cruelty to animals, 32; cruelty to children, 4; contributing to disorderly house, 151; deserter, 41; discharging firearms, 16; keeping a disorderly house, 64; disturbance, 902; drunkenness, 3,003; demented, 195; dround [drowned], 9; fraudulent checks, 5; forgery, 8; found dead, 81; gambling, 295; keeping a gambling house, 37; homicide, 6; contributing to house of prostitution, 64; keeping a house of prostitution, 15; inmate of a house of prostitution, 35; harboring a vicious dog, 11; indecent liberties, 1; indecent exposure, 31; indecent language, 1; interfering with officer, 28; investigation, 2,299; injured, 1,566; juvenile delinquency, 30; kidnapping, 3; larcenies, 131; malicious mischief, 23; murder, 13; manslaughter, 1; mashing, 7; nonsupport, 43; poison, 154; rape, 9; resisting an officer, 33; refusing to move, 2; robbery, 5; highway robbery, 14; runaway, 41; running a disorderly house, 33; reckless driving, 97; stealing, 22; shot, 34; shoplifting, 7; short checks, 7; soliciting, 90; vagrancy, 3,142; violating fortune telling ordinance, 1; violating barber ordinance, 3; violating Prohibition, 1,303; violating narcotics law, 39; violating traffic ordinance, 1,798; violating dance ordinance, 4.

1925

Total arrests, 20,356. Assaults, 36; abortion, 1; auto theft, 18; beating a board bill, 1; burglary, 39; burglary and larceny, 55; breaking glass on highway, 44; bigamy, 2; bribery, 2; crimes against nature, 1; concealed weapons, 87; contributing to juvenile delinquency, 10; cruelty to animals, 16; cruelty to children, 5; confidence game, 13; deserter, 29; discharging firearms, 24; keeping a disorderly house, 62; contributing to a disorderly house, 218; disturbance, 1,080; drunkenness, 2,982; demented, 172; dround [drowned], 1; embezzlement, 1; false call, fire, 1; fraudulent checks, 10; forgery, 21; found dead, 87; harboring a vicious dog, 7; gambling, 476; keeping a gambling house, 61; harboring a nuisance, 9; contributing to a house of prostitution, 37; keeping a house of prostitution, 25; inmate of a house of prostitution, 19; hold for juvenile court, 279; indecent exposure, 28; investigation, 1,841; incorrigible, 1; injured, 1,772; indecent liberties, 5; juvenile delinquency, 28; joy riding, 2; killed,

auto accident, 1; larcenies, 173; loitering, 47; malicious mischief, 13; murder, 7; mashing, 33; nonsupport, 20; manslaughter, 3; operating a punch board, 1; obstructing streets, 12; poison, 123; rape, 6; resisting an officer, 70; refusing to move, 10; robbery, 14; highway robbery, 15; runaway, 34; running a disorderly house, 131; reckless driving, 276; stealing, 25; sick, 716; shot, 33; shoplifting, 7; soliciting, 81; selling fireworks, 4; vagrancy, 3,161; violating Prohibition law, 1,360; violating narcotic law, 68; violating automobile ordinance, 565; wrongs to children, 7.

1926

Total arrests, 18,109. Assaults, 36; abortion, 1; arson, 1; auto theft, 15; beating a board bill, 3; bunco, 6; burglary, 31; burglary and larceny, 42; breaking glass on highway, 43; crimes against nature, 1; concealed weapons, 103; contributing to juvenile delinquency, 20; cruelty to animals, 15; cruelty to children, 2; confidence game, 14; destroying city property, 2; deserter, 31; discharging firearms, 14; keeping a disorderly house, 38; contributing to a disorderly house, 26; disturbance, 1,069; drunkenness, 2,916; demented, 154; driving auto under influence of liquor, 40 (this is the first notation of alcohol-related traffic offenses and is entered in pencil); embezzlement, 5; false call, fire, 7; fraudulent checks, 5; forgery, 21; found dead, 131; fishing in City Park [Lake], 1; gambling, 322; keeping a gambling house, 72; contributing to a house of prostitution, 12; keeping a house of prostitution, 10; inmate of a house of prostitution, 25; harboring vicious dogs, 14; incest, 4; indecent exposure, 12; indecent language, 1; indecent liberties, 3; interfering with an officer, 29; investigation, 1,964; injured, 2,240; juvenile delinquency, 7; larcenies, 158; loitering, 24; malicious mischief, 18; murder, 6; murdered, 2; mashing, 8; poison, 112; peeping tom, 10; rape, 7; resisting officer, 69; refusing to move, 14; robbery, 16; highway robbery, 10; running a disorderly house, 104; shot, 5; shoplifting, 3; short checks, 8; soliciting, 50; vagrancy, 2,237; violation of probation law, 1,147; violation of narcotics law, 71; violation of traffic ordinance, 2,269; violation of automobile ordinance, 23; traffic, ordered in, 728; white slavery, 1; wrongs to children, 6; zoning law, 3. (Several traffic classifications including "ordering in"—akin to today's traffic summons—reflect the growing presence of automobiles and resulting problems.)

1927

Total arrests, 18,485. Assaults, 24; adultery, 2; arson, 3; auto theft, 3; burglary, 17; burglary and larceny, 25; breaking glass on highway, 20; bigamy, 1; crimes against nature, 1; concealed weapons, 69; contributing to juvenile delinquency, 25; counterfeiting, 1; cruelty to animals, 7; confidence game, 23; destroying city property, 13; deserter, 34; discharging firearms, 8; keeping a disorderly house, 40; contributing to a disorderly house, 200; disturbance, 1,079; drunkenness, 2,835; demented, 57; driving auto under influence of liquor, 181; drowned, 1; escaped convict, 2; embezzlement, 6; fraudulent checks, 3; forgery, 13; found dead, 144; gambling, 286; keeping a gambling house, 74; homicide, 1; contributing to a house of prostitution, 36; keeping a house of prostitution, 14; inmate of a house of prostitution, 22; harboring vicious dog, 11; indecent exposure, 30; interfering with officer, 19; investigation, 2,658; injured, 2,645; juvenile delinquency, 4; kidnapping, 1; larcenies, 72; loitering, 46; malicious mischief, 10; murder, 5; mashing, 6; murdered, 1; nonsupport, 2; poison, 137; peeping tom, 5; rape, 7; resisting an officer, 54; robbery, 3; highway robbery, 5; runaway, 37; running a disorderly house, 43; shot, 4; shoplifting, 4; soliciting, 60; vagrancy, 2,164; violating narcotics law, 40; violating Prohibition law, 1,390; violating traffic ordinance, 1,162; violating traffic ordinance, ordered in, 3,534; wrongs to children, 5.

1928

Total arrests, 20,459. Assaults, 28; auto theft, 13; burglary, 55; burglary and larceny, 14; breaking glass on highway, 64; crimes against nature, 1; concealed weapons, 107; contributing to juvenile delinquency, 2; counterfeiting, 4; cruelty to animals, 10; confidence game, 29; deserted baby, 1; deserter, 39; discharging

firearms, 25; keeping a disorderly house, 49; contributing to a disorderly house, 261; disturbance, 1,380; drunkenness, 3,690; demented, 44; driving auto under influence of liquor, 281; embezzlement, 13; false call, fire, 5; forgery, 11; found dead, 172; gambling, 220; keeping a gambling house, 85; possession of gambling devices, 3; contributing to a house of prostitution, 27; keeping a house of prostitution, 24; inmate of house of prostitution, 37; harboring vicious dog, 25; indecent exposure, 20; investigation, 2,560; injured, 2,721; juvenile delinquency, 6; joy riding, 2; larcenies, 141; murder attempt, 10; malicious mischief, 21; murder, 9; mashing, 13; murdered, 2; poison, 93; peeping tom, 6; resisting officer, 101; robbery, 7; highway robbery, 13; running a disorderly house, 52; shot, 34; soliciting, 92; uttering [threats], 1; vagrancy, 3,053; violating narcotics law, 73; violating tobacco ordinance, 2; violating bad pictures, 2 (the nature of this category is unknown); violating fortune telling ordinance, 4.

1929

Total arrests, 19,450. Assaults, 26; abortion, 1; auto theft, 12; bunco, 1; burglary, 34; burglary and larceny, 16; breaking glass on highway, 39; burglary tools in possession, 1; concealed weapons, 90; contributing to juvenile delinquency, 14; cruelty to animals, 15; confidence game, 19; clairvoyant, no license, 19; deserter, 32; discharging firearms, 44; keeping a disorderly house, 19; contributing to a disorderly house, 151; disturbance, 1,368; drunkenness, 3,343; demented, 45; driving auto under influence of liquor, 212; drowned, 3; escaped convict, 7; embezzlement, 6; false call, fire, 1; forgery, 33; found dead, 135; gambling, 193; keeping a gambling house, 44; keeping a gambling device, 37; homicide, 29; keeping a house of prostitution, 4; contributing to a house of prostitution, 4; inmate of a house of prostitution, 8; indecent exposure, 28; investigation, 2,371; injured, 2,512; juvenile delinquency, 8; joy riding, 16; kidnapping, 3; larcenies, 103; malicious mischief, 3; murder, 7; mashing, 10; murdered, 3; nuisance harboring, 1; pickpocket, 1; poison, 107; peeping tom, 4; resisting an officer, 90; robbery, 26; highway robbery, 25; running a disorderly house, 43; shot, 44; violating narcotics law, 87; violating Prohibition law, 1,581. (The steady yearly increases in liquor violation arrests demonstrate that Prohibition was not functioning effectively in Denver.)

Note

*The offense categorized in the 1918, 1921, and 1922 crime statistics as "insulting women" calls for explanation. Sam Howe Scrapbook 22, clipping 32968, dated November 1903, contains the notation under the headline "Insulting Women" that "three colored girls were insulted last night at the corner of Ninth and Larimer streets by three white men who addressed indecent remarks to them." That appears to have been the extent of the offense. The brother of two of the girls, fireman John Martin, went to the scene with his shotgun, the butt of which he used "with terrific effect" on one of the insulters, electrician James J. Ryan. Ryan was severely beaten, arrested, and then hospitalized. His accomplices escaped.

Appendix C:
A Market Street Prostitution Census

THE FOLLOWING TABULATION OF DENVER'S Market Street prostitutes, listed by name, working address, and state or country of origin, was discovered in the back of a file cabinet at Denver Police Headquarters in March 1992 by police technician Mark Shonk. The figure "1916" was typewritten atop the document in a type style much newer than the rest of the document. The figure could not be the date of the document for at least two reasons: (1) the document includes names of madams not active in that late year, most notably Mattie Silks (misspelled "Silk") and Verona Baldwin; and (2) by 1916 the Market Street bordellos were essentially gone. This figure may have been a later attempt to guess the date of the document.

Entries suggest the list is from the very early 1900s because Mattie Silks's boyfriend and second husband, "Handsome Jack" Kelley (real name John Dillon Ready), is listed (as "Joe" Kelley) at 1950 Market Street, and he joined Mattie at about that time. The figures in the left-hand column are street numbers of the brothels; the figures in parentheses may be alternative or subsequent business addresses of the prostitutes. "LL" designates "landlady"; the male names are those of housemen, bouncers, piano players, or pimps.

Inclusion of the geographic place of origin seems almost census oriented, although it is doubtful that these women remained in one place long enough—or would have been sufficiently forthright—to have been included in a census. The listing is revealing on several counts. The figure seven or eight boarders is seldom exceeded, suggesting the capacity of the larger establishments—although several accounts in this book refer to as many as twenty boarders. The smallest house had just one girl; the filthy three-girl cribs, crowded close together, are readily identifiable (e.g., 2038, 2042, 2044). Asians did not deserve having their names listed (2115); the French bordellos, mentioned in the text of this book, are readily identifiable; and at least one probable set of sisters is included.

Table C.1—Location and Names of Prostitutes on Market Street, Denver, Colorado

Street Number	Name	Geographic Origin
1907	Trixie Gauhen (LL)	Utah
	Edna Hamilton	United States
	Mable Fisher	
1908	Margaret Smith (LL)	New York
	Evelyn Ryssell [*sic*]	Seattle
	Eva Smith	Colorado
	Della Perry (2032)	Canada
	Julia Brown	New York
1911	Hellen [*sic*] Wroth (LL)	United States
	Violet Ahl	Sweden
	Zeke Stauder	United States
1912	Mamie Riesner (LL)	Austria
	Goldie Smith	Hungary
	Lilly Bogosefsky	Globeville, Colorado
	——— Smith (1908)	
1915	Ellis Boschell (LL)	United States
	Leonia Watkins	Colorado
	Laura Ciswell	Iowa
	Anna Delilly	Pennsylvania
	Bertha Clement	France
1917	Vesta King	Pennsylvania
	Avon Diamond (1907)	United States
	Violet Williams (1907)	United States
	Gail Keith	United States
	Lulu Warham	Arkansas
	Nellie Ray	Arkansas
1922	Eva Marshall (LL)	United States
	Dot Smith	Omaha
	May Howard	United States
	Maud Sager	Pennsylvania
	Maud Thompson	Virginia
	Elizabeth Howard	Minnesota
	Sadie Louis	Nebraska
	Grace White	United States
1923	Tessie Davis (LL)	United States
	Jennie Carlson	United States
	Dollie Mason	United States
	Alice Hinsley	United States
	Mattie Smith	United States
1929	Beth Rice (LL)	United States
	May Ray	Omaha
	Babe Wilson	Denver
	Goldie Clark	Missouri
	Verne Ekstrom [?]	Sweden
1931	Rita	
1933	Edna Benett [*sic*] (LL)	Illinois
	Ruth Reid	New York
	Emily Walsh	Philadelphia
1934	Pearl Rogers (LL)	United States
	Ray Morris	United States
	Ella Gallagher	United States
	Hellen [*sic*] Williams	Illinois
	Dora Long	Indian Territory
1938	Lillian Dumont (LL)	Germany
	May West	Denver
1939	Ruth Campbell (LL)	Alabama
	Millie Hoffman	Germany
	Edith Brown (2043)	United States
	Alice Holmes	Nebraska
1942	May Wilson (LL)	United States
	Gertrude Smith	United States
	Catherine Clark	United States
	Peggy Taylor	United States
	Frances Baker	United States
	Helen Tripe	United States
	Dorothy Thompson	United States
1943	Mildred Martin (LL)	United States
	Lillie Rogers	Michigan
	Dora [?] Roberts	United States
	Tex Price	Texas
1945	Pearl Marshall (LL)	United States
	Glen Harris	United States
	Mildred Walker	United States
	Hazel Smith	United States
1949	Gladys Ford (LL)	United States
	Lillie Wood	Denver
	Mabel Clark	United States
	Vic Linton	United States
1950	Mattie Silk [*sic*]	United States
	Joe Kelley	United States
	Annie Rice	United States
	Pearl Patterson	United States
	Hattie Marshall	United States
	Florence Lunt	United States
	Ray Cleason	United States
1953	Yetta Imberman (LL)	Poland
1954	Leona Decamp (LL)	United States
	Virginia Vernon	United States
	Cecil Gordon	United States
	May Sullivan	United States
	Flo Berry	United States
1957	Ida Montrose (LL)	Colorado
	Selma Vohs	Germany
	Mertyl Grant	United States

1958	Helen Traynor (LL)	United States			Ellen Brown	United States
	Medeline [*sic*] Santree	United States			Lona Wright	Nebraska
	Paulett Monot	United States			Mamie Sullivan	Iowa
	Ruth Clark	United States		2030	Annie Reid (LL)	United States
1960	Lucile [*sic*] Miller (LL)	United States			Josephine West	Kansas
	Trixie Earl	United States			Babe Murphey	Colorado
	Evlyn [*sic*] Williams	United States			Florence McCoy	Montana
	Clara Cooper	United States		2032	Minnie Williams (LL)	United States
	Thelma Russel	United States			(2038)	
2004	Julia Puppet (LL)	France			Mildred Ackley	United States
	Jack Porter	Nebraska			Mamie Schmidt	New York
	Grace Misel	Nebraska			Gladys Kean (2052)	United States
	Marie Grand	Kansas			Nancy Brown	
	Lillian Morris	United States			Della Perry	
	Leon Simmons	United States		2038	Rose Atwood (LL)	United States
	Marcel Smith	France			Minnie Smith	United States
2005	Fay Stanley (LL)	United States			Mildred White	United States
	Frankie Arnold	United States		2042	Lena Schwartz (LL)	Roumania
	June Desmont	United States			Flora Blackmen	New York
	Gladys Hufflnan	United States			Rose Gold	New York
	Clo Ward	United States		2043	Yeeta Rosen (LL)	Russia
	Juanita Mischard	United States			(2 girls)	
	Grace Ray	United States			[Under this address in pencil are the names Hazel	
	Rose Dellmore	United States			Davis, Eva Brody Raymond, Tillie King, Edith	
2009	Lillie Fox (LL)	New York			Brown.]	
	Nellie Hanes	Kentucky		2044	Sadie Brown (LL)	Russia
	Billie York	South Dakota			Molly Schwartz	Austria
	Maxine Melrose	South Dakota			Mary Fisher	Austria
	Blanch Debare	Louisiana		2045	Dixie Patrick (LL)	United States
2010	Evlyn [*sic*] Reed (LL)	United States			Eva Hamilton	Denver
	Faye Belinder	United States			Madge Williams	Iowa
	Stella Pitt	United States		2048	Irene West	United States
2015	Tillie Rosen (LL)	New York			Ida Taylor	Iowa
	Julia Silvia	United States			Pearl Lirnond	Colorado
	Margaret Silvia	United States			Ethel Burgess	United States
	Lorris Matthews	United States			Edith Edwards	
	Evylin [*sic*] Hass	United States		2051	Florence Miller	Kansas
	Fay Linch	United States			Flora Moore	Ohio
2016	Verona Baldwin (LL)	United States			Ruby Dale	United States
	Mae Wagner	United States		2052	Blanch Davis (LL)	United States
	Gladys Parker	United States			Bertha Collins	United States
	Dora Sharp	United States			Cora Lorens	United States
	Carmine Green	United States		2059	Madge Freemont	United States
	Elsie Smith	United States			Irene Love	Texas
	Hazel Wilson	United States			Georgie Allis	Colorado
2020	Mary Evans (LL)	United States			Beatrice Earl	United States
	Vernie Mitchell	United States		2060	Dottie Morgan (LL)	United States
	Inda Hamilton	United States			Nellie Mitchell	United States
	Pearl Lee	United States		2063	Kittie Murray (LL)	United States
2024	Marie Little (LL)	United States			Mary Richards	United States

	Stella Van Gilder	United States	2134	Jeanne Kaundolf (LL)	France
	Queenie Burns	United States		Lucile Lacourt	
2101-3-5	Dick Howe (LL)	Indiana		Blanch Laduc	France
	Billy Hyde	United States		Bertha Delacroix	France
	Florence May	Ohio	2138	Stella Sterling (LL)	United States
	Nellie Wilson	Missouri		Annie Nelson	South Dakota
	Sammy Gordon	Missouri		Mabel Lewis	United States
2109	Jennie Smith (LL)	Nebraska		Myrtel [*sic*] Smith	United States
	Clara Smith	Nebraska		Rose Sweeney	United States
	Esther Smith	Indiana	2154	Florence Rockowitz (LL)	Austria
2115	3 Japanese women			Jennie Smith	Austria
2119	Jimmie Monroe	United States		Jessie Emerson	Chicago
	Eva Wilson	United States		Josephine Larkins	New Orleans
	Myrtle Ray	United States	2160	Myrtle Wilson (LL)	Germany
2122	Laura Wilson (LL)	United States		Thelma Anderson	Atlanta
	Anna Wills	United States		Rose Harris	United States
	Irene Lynch	United States	2161	Madge Gilmore (LL)	United States
	Raymon Kellog [*sic*]	United States		Bessie Stevens	Nebraska
2126	Margaret O'Keefe (LL)	United States		Pearl Adams	Nebraska
	Marie Cavois	France		Florence Hamilton	Illinois
	Mamie Herbert	Canada		Sadie Samuels	Austria

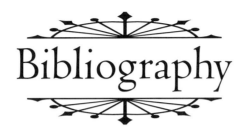

Bibliography

Materials in this bibliography are confined to sources actually consulted in preparation of this book, unless noted.

Published Materials

BOOKS

Allen, Mary Wood, M.D. *What a Young Woman Ought to Know.* Philadelphia: Vir, 1898.

Armitage, Susan, and Elizabeth Jameson. *The Women's West.* Norman: University of Oklahoma Press, 1987.

Bancroft, Caroline. *Six Racy Madams.* Boulder: Johnson, 1965.

Barnhart, Jacqueline Baker. *The Fair but Frail: Prostitution in San Francisco, 1849–1900.* Reno: University of Nevada Press, 1986.

Barry, Kathleen. *Female Sexual Slavery.* New York: New York University Press, 1984.

Bell, Ernest A. *Fighting the Traffic in Young Girls, or War on the White Slave Trade.* N.c.: G. S. Ball, 1910.

Bellocq: Photographs from Storyville, the Red-Light District of New Orleans. New York: Random House, 1996.

Best, Hillyer. *Julia Bulette and Other Red Light Ladies.* Sparks, Nev.: Western Printing, 1959.

Best, Joel. *Controlling Vice: Regulating Brothel Prostitution in St. Paul, 1865–1883.* Columbus: Ohio State University Press, 1998.

Bettmann, Otto L. *The Good Old Days—They Were Terrible!* New York: Random House, 1974.

Blair, Kay Reynolds. *Ladies of the Lamplight.* Leadville, Colo.: Timberline, 1971.

Breslin, Jimmy. *Damon Runyon.* New York: Ticknor and Fields, 1991.

Butler, Anne M. *Daughters of Joy, Sisters of Misery.* Urbana: University of Illinois Press, 1985.

Coel, Margaret. *Goin' Railroading.* Boulder: Pruett, 1991.

Cohen, Patricia Cline. *The Murder of Helen Jewett.* New York: Alfred A. Knopf, 1998.

Collier, William Ross, and Edwin Victor Westrate. *Dave Cook of the Rockies.* New York: Rufus Rockwell Wilson, 1936.

———. *The Reign of Soapy Smith: Monarch of Misrule.* Garden City, N.Y.: Doubleday Doran, 1935.

Cook, General David J. *Hands Up, or Twenty Years of Detective Life in the Mountains and on the Plains.* Norman: University of Oklahoma Press, 1958 [1882].

Couch, Jacqualine [*sic*] Grannell. *Those Golden Girls of Market Street.* Fort Collins, Colo.: Old Army, 1974.

Crane, Stephen. *Maggie: A Girl of the Streets.* New York: n.p., 1893. Consulted here was the W. W. Norton Critical Edition (New York: W. W. Norton, 1979), which contains useful background/source citations, contemporary reviews, and criticism.

Creel, George. *Rebel at Large: Recollections of Fifty Crowded Years.* New York: G. P. Putnam's Sons, 1947.

Cunningham, Eugene. *Triggernometry: A Gallery of Gunfighters.* N.c.: Caxton, 1941.

Dallas, Sandra. *Cherry Creek Gothic.* Norman: University of Oklahoma Press, 1971.

Dary, David. *Seeking Pleasure in the Old West.* New York: Alfred A. Knopf, 1995.

DeArment, Robert K. *Bat Masterson: The Man and the Legend.* Norman: University of Oklahoma Press, 1979.

———. *Knights of the Green Cloth.* Norman: University of Oklahoma Press, 1982.

Denver City Directories. Denver: Ballenger and Richards, 1873–1921.

Denver Police Department Pictorial Review and History, 1859–1989. Denver: Denver Police Department, 1985.

Denver Red Book: A Reliable Directory of the Pleasure Resorts of Denver. Denver: n.p., 1892. Copies in the Colorado Historical Society Library, Denver, and in the Western History Department, Denver Public Library.

Dial, Scott. *The Saloons of Denver.* Fort Collins, Colo.: Old Army, 1973.

Dill, R. G. *Political Campaigns of Colorado with Complete Tabulated Statements of the Official Vote.* Denver: Arapahoe, 1895.

Dodds, Joanne West. *What's a Nice Girl Like You Doing in a Place Like This? Prostitution in Southern Colorado, 1860 to 1911.* Pueblo: Focal Plain, 1996.

Dorsett, Lyle W. *The Queen City: A History of Denver.* Boulder: Pruett, 1977.

Drago, Harry Sinclair. *Notorious Ladies of the Frontier.* New York: Ballantine, 1969.

Dwyer, Jim (ed.). *Strange Stories, Amazing Facts of America's Past.* Pleasantville, N.Y.: Reader's Digest, 1989.

Etulain, Richard W., and Glenda Riley (eds.). *With Badges and Bullets: Lawmen and Outlaws in the Old West.* Golden, Colo.: Fulcrum, 1999.

Farley, Mary M., and Marcella E. Dillon. *The Farley Scrapbook: Biography of John F. Farley.* n.c., n.d., n.p. Copy in the Colorado Historical Society Library, Denver.

Feitz, Leland. *Myers Avenue.* Colorado Springs: Little London, 1967.

Fetherling, Dale. *Mother Jones: The Miners' Angel.* Carbondale: Southern Illinois University Press, 1974.

Fischer, Christine (ed.). *Let Them Speak for Themselves: Women in the American West 1849–1900.* Hamden, Conn.: Archon, 1977.

Fowler, Gene. *A Solo in Tom-Toms.* New York: Viking, 1946.

Friedlander, Lee (ed.). *Bellocq: Photographs from Storyville.* New York: Random House, 1996.

———. *E. J. Bellocq: Storyville Portraits.* New York: Museum of Modern Art, 1970.

Ganzhorn, Jack. *I've Killed Men.* New York: Devin-Adair, 1959.

Gerboth, Christopher B. *Address Unknown: The Human Face of Homelessness.* Denver: Colorado Endowment for the Humanities, 1995. This volume is based on a paper delivered to the Colorado History Colloquium on January 27, 1994, by Gerboth and Marcia Kehl: "Address Unknown: Notes on an Ongoing Historical Study of Homelessness and General Poverty in Colorado and Denver, 1858–1990."

Gilfoyle, Timothy J. *City of Eros: New York City, Prostitution, and the Commercialization of Sex, 1790–1920.* New York: W. W. Norton, 1992.

Gladden, Sanford Charles. *Early Boulder Series No. 5, "Ladies of the Night."* Boulder: n.p., 1979.

Goodstein, Phil. *Denver Streets: Names, Numbers, Locations, Logic.* Denver: New Social Publications, 1994.

———. *Denver's Capitol Hill.* Denver: Stuart MacPhail, 1988.

———. *The Seamy Side of Denver.* Denver: New Social Publications, 1993.

Greenwood, Grace. *New Life in New Lands.* New York: J. B. Ford, 1873.

Griswold, Don, and Jean Griswold. *History of Leadville and Lake County, Colorado.* Denver: Colorado Historical Society and the University Press of Colorado, 1996.

Guerin, Mrs. E. J. *Mountain Charley, or the Adventures of Mrs. E. J. Guerin, Who Was Thirteen Years in Male Attire.* Introduction by Fred Mazzulla and William Kotska. Norman: University of Oklahoma Press, 1968.

Hafen, LeRoy R. *Colorado and Its People,* 4 vols. New York: Lewis Historical Publishing, 1948.

Hafen, LeRoy R., and Ann W. Hafen (eds.). *Reports from Colorado: The Wildman Letters, 1859–1865.* Glendale, Calif.: Arthur H. Clark, 1961.

Hall, Gordon Langley. *The Two Lives of Baby Doe.* Philadelphia: Macrae Smith, 1962.

Hanchett, Lafayette. *The Old Sheriff and Other New Tales.* New York: Margent, 1937.

Hell's Belles of Tombstone. N.c. but probably Tombstone, Ariz.: Red Marie's Bookstore, 1984.

Hill, Alice Polk. *Colorado Pioneers in Picture and Story.* Denver: Brock-Haffner, 1915.

Horan, James D. *The Authentic Wild West.* New York: Crown, 1980.

Hoyt, Edwin P. *A Gentleman of Broadway.* Boston: Little, Brown, 1964.

Johnson, Charles A. *Denver's Mayor Speer.* Denver: Green Mountain, 1969.

Kaufmann, A. *Recollections of a New York Chief of Police, and Historic Supplement of the Denver Police.* N.c.: Caxton, 1887.

Kimball, Nell. *Nell Kimball: Her Life as an American Madam.* New York: Macmillan, 1970.

King, Clyde Lyndon. *The History of the Government of Denver with Special Reference to Its Relations with Public Service Corporations.* Denver: Fisher, 1911.

King, William M. *Going to Meet a Man: Denver's Last Legal Public Execution.* Niwot: University Press of Colorado, 1990.

Lackmann, Ron. *Women of the Western Frontier, in Fact, Fiction, and Film.* Jefferson, N.C.: McFarland, 1997.

Larimer, William H.H. *Reminiscences of General William Larimer and of His Son William H.H. Larimer, Two of the Founders of Denver City.* Lancaster, Pa.: New Era, 1918.

Larsen, Lawrence H. *The Urban West at the End of the Frontier.* Lawrence: Regents Press of Kansas, 1978.

Lavender, David. *Bent's Fort.* Garden City, N.Y.: Doubleday, 1954.

Leonard, Stephen J., and Thomas J. Noel. *Denver: Mining Camp to Metropolis.* Niwot: University Press of Colorado, 1990.

Limerick, Patricia Nelson. *The Legacy of Conquest.* New York: W. W. Norton, 1987.

Look, Al. *Sidelights on Colorado.* Denver: Golden Bell, 1967.

Lukas, J. Anthony. *Big Trouble.* New York: Simon and Schuster, 1997.

Madeline ———(pseud.?). *Madeline, an Autobiography.* New York: Harper and Brothers, 1919. Reprint, New York: Persea, 1986.

Martin, Cy. *Whiskey and Wild Women.* New York: Hart, 1974.

Mazzulla, Fred, and Jo Mazzulla. *Brass Checks and Red Lights.* Denver: authors, 1966.

Miller, Max. *Holladay Street.* New York: Signet, 1962.

Mosher, Clelia Duel, M.D. *The Mosher Survey: Sexual Attitudes of 45 Victorian Women.* New York: Arno, 1980.

Moynahan, Jay. *Red Light Revelations: A Glimpse into Butte's Sinful Past.* Spokane, Wash.: Chickadee, 2000.

Moynihan, Betty. *Augusta Tabor, a Pioneering Woman.* Evergreen, Colo.: Cordillera, 1988.

Mumey, Nolie. *Creede: History of a Colorado Silver Mining Town.* Denver: Artcraft, 1949.

Murphy, Emmett. *Great Bordellos of the World.* London: Quartet, 1983.

Noel, Thomas J. *The City and the Saloon.* Lincoln: University of Nebraska Press, 1982.

———. *Denver's Larimer Street.* Denver: Historic Denver, 1981.

Odem, Mary E. *Delinquent Daughters: Protecting and Policing Adolescent Female Sexuality in the United States, 1885–1920.* Chapel Hill: University of North Carolina Press, 1995.

O'Reilly, Harrington. *Fifty Years on the Trail: A True Story of Western Life.* London: Chatto and Windus, Piccadilly, 1889.

"O. W." *No Bed of Roses: The Diary of a Lost Soul.* New York: Sheridan House, 1930.

Parkhill, Forbes. *The Law Goes West.* Denver: Sage, 1956.

———. *The Wildest of the West.* New York: Henry Holt, 1951.

Perkin, Robert L. *The First Hundred Years.* Garden City, N.Y.: Doubleday, 1959.

Peterson, Rachel Wild. *The Long-Lost Rachel Wild, or Seeking Diamonds in the Rough.* Denver: Reed, 1905.

Petrik, Paula. *No Step Backward: Women and Family on the Rocky Mountain Mining Frontier, Helena, Montana, 1865–1900.* Helena: Montana Historical Society Press, 1987.

Phelps, Alfred C. (comp.). *The Charter and Ordinances of the City of Denver.* Denver: Denver Publishing House, 1878.

Prassel, Frank Richard. *The Western Peace Officer.* Norman: University of Oklahoma Press, 1972.

Reiter, Joan Swallow. *The Women.* Alexandria, Va.: Time-Life, 1978.

Robertson, Frank C., and Beth Kay Harris. *Soapy Smith: King of the Frontier Con Men.* New York: Hastings House, 1961.

Roe, Clifford G. *The Great War on White Slavery, or Fighting for the Protection of Our Girls.* N.c., n.p., copyright 1911 by Clifford G. Roe and B. S. Steadwell.

Rosa, Joseph G., and Waldo E. Koop. *Rowdy Joe Lowe, Gambler with a Gun*. Norman: University of Oklahoma Press, 1989.

Rose, Al. *Storyville, New Orleans*. Tuscaloosa: University of Alabama Press, 1974.

Rosen, Ruth. *The Lost Sisterhood*. Baltimore: Johns Hopkins University Press, 1982.

Rosen, Ruth, and Sue Davidson. *The Maimie Papers*. Old Westbury, N.Y.: Feminist Press, 1977.

Scamehorn, G. N. *Behind the Scenes, or Denver by Gaslight*. Denver: Geo. A. Shirley, 1893.

Schlissel, Lillian, Byrd Gibbens, and Elizabeth Hampsten. *Far from Home: Families of the Western Journey*. New York: Schocken, 1989.

Schlissel, Lillian, Vicki L. Ruiz, and Janice Monk. *Western Women: Their Land, Their Lives*. Albuquerque: University of New Mexico Press, 1988.

Schuller, Gunther. *Early Jazz: Its Roots and Musical Development*. New York: Oxford University Press, 1968.

Seagraves, Anne. *Soiled Doves: Prostitution in the Early West*. Hayden, Id.: Wesanne, 1994.

Selcer, Richard F. *Hell's Half Acre, the Life and Legend of a Red-Light District*. Fort Worth: Texas Christian University Press, 1991.

Shikes, Robert L., M.D. *Rocky Mountain Medicine*. Boulder: Johnson, 1986.

Shores, C. W. "Doc." *Memoirs of a Lawman*, Wilson Rockwell, ed. Denver: Sage, 1962.

Smiley, Jerome C. *History of Denver*. Denver: Times-Sun, 1901.

Smith, Gene, and Jane Barry Smith. *The Police Gazette*. New York: Simon and Schuster, 1972.

The Social Evil in Chicago: A Study of Existing Conditions, with Recommendations by the Vice Commission of Chicago. Chicago: Vice Commission of Chicago, 1911.

Sowers, Arvine W., William R. Collier, and John H. Phillips (comps.). *Denver Fire and Police Departments Illustrated*. Denver: Smith-Brooks, 1905.

Stone, Wilbur F. *History of Colorado*, 4 vols. Chicago: S. J. Clarke, 1918.

Szarkowski, John (ed.). *E. J. Bellocq: Storyville Portraits, Photographs from the New Orleans Red-Light District, Circa 1912*. New York: Museum of Modern Art, 1970.

Tanner, Karen Holliday. *Doc Holliday: A Family Portrait*. Norman: University of Oklahoma Press, 1998.

Tong, Benson. *Unsubmissive Women: Chinese Prostitutes in Nineteenth-Century San Francisco*. Norman: University of Oklahoma Press, 1994.

Travelers' Night Guide to Colorado. n.c., n.d., n.p. Copy in the author's possession.

Utley, Robert M. *Cavalier in Buckskin: George Armstrong Custer and the Western Military Frontier*. Norman: University of Oklahoma Press, 1988.

Van Cise, Philip S. *Fighting the Underworld*. Cambridge, Mass.: Riverside, 1936.

Villard, Henry. *The Past and Present of the Pike's Peak Gold Regions*. Reprinted from the 1860 edition. Princeton: Princeton University Press, 1932.

Walling, George W., and A. Kaufmann. *Recollections of a New York Chief of Police and Historical Supplement of the Denver Police*. New York: Caxton, 1887.

Washburn, Josie. *The Underworld Sewer: A Prostitute Reflects on Life in the Trade, 1871–1909*. Lincoln: University of Nebraska Press, 1997.

Weiner, Ed. *The Damon Runyon Story*. New York: Longmans, Green, 1948.

West, Elliott. *The Saloon on the Rocky Mountain Mining Frontier*. Lincoln: University of Nebraska Press, 1979.

Wharton, J. E. *History of the City of Denver from Its Earliest Settlement to the Present Time*. Denver: Byers and Dailey, 1866.

White, Richard. *It's Your Misfortune and None of My Own: A History of the American West*. Norman: University of Oklahoma Press, 1991.

Whiteside, Henry O. *Menace in the West*. Denver: Colorado Historical Society, 1997.

Whitmore, Julie. *A History of the Colorado State Penitentiary 1871–1980*. Cañon City, Colo.: Printing Plus, 1984.

Willison, George F. *Here They Dug the Gold*. New York: Reynal and Hitchcock, 1946.

Wilson, Samuel Paynter. *Chicago and Its Cess-Pools of Infamy*. Chicago: Samuel Paynter Wilson, n.d.

Wiltz, Christine. *The Last Madam*. New York: Faber and Faber, 2000.

Wolle, Muriel Sibell. *Stampede to Timberline*. Denver: Poertner Lithographing, 1949.

Zamonski, Stanley W., and Teddy Keller. *The '59ers*. Denver: Stanza-Harp, 1967.

ARTICLES

"Address of General Frank Hall at the First Annual Reunion of the Colorado Pioneers, Held in Denver, January 25, 1881." *The Trail*, October 1922: 92.

Barnacle, Barkalow. "'Soapy' Smith, the Gambler." *The Trail*, January 1920: 5–11.

Battles, E. R. "Denver's Volunteer Fire Department." *The Trail* (part 1) January 1917:12–16, (part 2) February 1917: 11–17.

Bayard, Charles J. "The Colorado Progressive Republican Split of 1912." *Colorado Magazine*, winter 1968: 61–78.

Bender, Norman J. "Crusade of the Blue Banner in Colorado." *Colorado Magazine*, spring 1970: 91–118.

Bennett, Eve. "Shady Ladies of the '80s." *Rocky Mountain Life*, April 1947: 12–13.

Bloch, Don. "The Saga of the Wandering Swede." *1954 Brand Book* of the Denver Posse of the Westerners. Boulder: Johnson, 1954: 6–10.

Brandenstein, Sherilyn. "The Colorado Cottage Home." *Colorado Magazine*, summer 1976: 229–242.

Burg, B. Richard. "Administration of Justice in the Denver People's Courts, 1859–1861." *Journal of the West*, October 1968: 510–521.

Burroughs, John Rolfe. "As It Was in the Beginning." *Colorado Magazine*, summer 1969: 185.

Carey, Raymond G. "The 'Bloodless Third' Regiment, Colorado Volunteer Cavalry." *Colorado Magazine*, October 1961: 279–286.

Cochran, Alice. "Jack Langrishe and the Theater of the Mining Frontier." *Colorado Magazine*, fall 1969: 324–337.

Cox, George W., M.D. "The Social Evil." *Transactions of the Colorado State Medical Society at Its Twelfth Annual Convention.* Denver: Edwin Price, June 1882: 65–80. Copy in the periodicals department, Colorado Historical Society Library, Denver.

Danker, Donald F., and Paul D. Riley (eds.). "The Journal of Amos S. Billingsley." *Colorado Magazine*, October 1963: 241–270.

DeArment, Robert K. "Bat Masterson and the Boxing Club War of Denver." *Colorado Heritage*, autumn 2000: 28–36.

DeLorme, Roland L. "Turn-of-the-Century Denver: An Invitation to Reform." *Colorado Magazine*, winter 1968: 1–15.

"Denver's Efficient Police Department." *The City of Denver*, October 25, 1913: 3–7.

Eby, Cecil D. "'Porte Crayon' in the Rocky Mountains." *Colorado Magazine*, April 1960: 108–118.

Eisele, Wilbert E. "Gun Men of the Middle West." *The Trail*, April 1925: 15–18.

Fielding, K. J. "James Thompson's Colorado Diary." *Colorado Magazine*, July 1954: 202–216.

Giddens, Paul H. "Letters of S. Newton Pettis, Associate Justice of the Colorado Supreme Court, Written in 1861." *Colorado Magazine*, January 1938: 3–14.

Goodykoontz, Colin B. "The People of Colorado." *Colorado Magazine*, November 1946: 241–255.

Gower, Calvin W. "Vigilantes." *Colorado Magazine*, spring 1964: 93–104.

Grace, Mrs. L. W. "Harry L. Baldwin." *Colorado Magazine*, November 1944: 208–212.

Hafen, Ann Woodbury. "Frontier Humor." *Colorado Magazine*, September 1947: 177–188.

Hafen, LeRoy R. "Colorado's First Legislative Assembly." *Colorado Magazine*, March 1943: 41–50.

———. "Lewis Ledyard Weld and Old Camp Weld." *Colorado Magazine*, November 1941: 202.

Hansen, James E., II. "Moonshine and Murder: Prohibition in Denver." *Colorado Magazine*, winter 1973: 1–23.

Harvey, James R. "Cebert Alexander Trease, Engineer." *Colorado Magazine*, November 1939: 221–231.

Hewett, William L. "The Election of 1896: Two Factions Square Off." *Colorado Magazine*, winter 1977: 44–57.

Hornbein, Marjorie. "Josephine Roche: Social Worker and Coal Operator." *Colorado Magazine*, summer 1976: 243–260.

———. "Three Governors in a Day." *Colorado Magazine*, summer 1968: 243–260.

Hubbell, Sue. "Polly Pry Did Not Just Report the News: She *Made* It." *Smithsonian*, January 1991: 48–57.

Jennings, Harlan. "Grand Opera Comes to Denver, 1864–1881." *Opera Quarterly*, spring 1997: 57–84.

———. "The Singers Are Not on Speaking Terms: Grand Opera in Denver, 1864–1881." *Colorado Heritage*, spring 1999: 2–19.

Jensen, Billie Barnes. "Entertaining the 'Fifty Niners.'" *Journal of the West*, January 1966: 82–90.

Krauser, Minnie Hall. "Brinker Collegiate Institute–Navarre Café." *Colorado Magazine*, March 1947: 79–85.

Lambert, Julia S. "Plain Tales of the Plains." *The Trail*, February 1916: 5–12, March 1916: 6–13.

Latta, Robert H. "Denver in the 1880s." *Colorado Magazine*, July 1941: 131–136.

Leonard, Stephen J. "Judge Lynch in Colorado, 1859–1919." *Colorado Heritage*, autumn 2000: 3–10.

Lewis, Lawrence. "How Woman's Suffrage Works in Colorado." *Outlook*, January 27, 1906: 167–178.

Lintz, Rebecca, and Clark Secrest. "Mr. Sanborn's Maps: Colorado Neighborhoods of the Past." *Colorado Heritage*, spring 1997: 38–47.

Majors, Mrs. A. H. "Life in North Creede in the Early Days." *Colorado Magazine*, November 1945: 267–269.

McConnell, Virginia. "A Gauge of Popular Taste in Early Colorado." *Colorado Magazine*, fall 1969: 338–350.

McGrew, A. O. "Denver's First Christmas, 1858." *Colorado Magazine*, January 1937: 15–25.

McMechen, Edgar C. "Father Kehler, Pioneer Minister." *Colorado Magazine*, May 1934: 97–101.

Mills, Fred C. "A Boy's Hike in the '70s." *The Trail*, October 1924: 17–18.

Mitchell, J. Paul. "Municipal Reform in Denver: The Defeat of Mayor Speer." *Colorado Magazine*, winter 1968: 42–60.

Morrison, Sidney B. "Letters from Colorado, 1860–1863." *Colorado Magazine*, May 1939: 92.

"Nathaniel P. Hill Inspects Colorado." *Colorado Magazine*, October 1956: 261.

"Newton Vorce, Frontiersman, Passes Away." *The Trail*, June 1924: 21–22.

Norton, Nancy Fitzhugh. "Christmas in Denver in 1859." *The Trail*, December 1920: 11–15.

"An Old Landmark Disappears." *The Trail*, August 1916: 28–29.

Ourada, Patricia K. "The Chinese in Colorado." *Colorado Magazine*, October 1952: 273–278.

Parkhill, Forbes. "Scarlet Sister Mattie." *1948 Brand Book of the Denver Posse of the Westerners*, 1949: 21–36.

Parsons, Eugene. "Important Events in Early Colorado History." *Sons of Colorado*, April 1908: 13–15.

"Passing of the Pioneer." *The Trail*, November 1927: 23–24.

Perrigo, Lynn I. "Law and Order in Early Colorado Mining Camps." *Mississippi Valley Historical Review*, June 1941: 41–62.

Pierce, James H. "With the Green Russell Party." *The Trail*, May 1921: 14.

Rainsford, George N. "Dean Henry Martyn Hart and Public Issues." *Colorado Magazine*, summer 1971: 208–210.

Sanford, Albert B. "How the Prospectors of '59 Lived." *The Trail*, December 1925: 10–19.

Shoemaker, Arthur. "Hard Rope's Civil War." *Civil War Times Illustrated*, September–October 1990: 52–55.

Smith, Duane A. "The San Juaner: A Computerized Portrait." *Colorado Magazine*, spring 1975: 137–152.

Snyder, J. Richard. "The Election of 1904: An Attempt at Reform." *Colorado Magazine*, winter 1968: 16–26.

Sopris, S. T. "Fifty Years Ago." *The Trail*, April 1909: 8.

Sprague, Abner E. "My First Trip to Denver." *Colorado Magazine*, November 1938: 218.

Stanton, Frederick J. "The Founders of Denver and Their Doings." *The Trail*, May 1922: 3–12.

Stern, Mort. "In Search of Major Anderson." In *mem-ber-a-bil-ia*. Georgetown, Colo.: Historic Georgetown, August 1997: 1–12.

———. "Mattie Silks in Georgetown." *Georgetown/Silver Plume National Historic Landmark District Journal*, April 1996: 3.

Student, Annette L. "Sadie Likens, Patron of the Fallen." *Colorado Heritage*, summer 2001, pp. 20–31.

Thom, William B. "In Pioneer Days." *The Trail*, October 1926: 2.

———. "Stage Celebrities in Denver Theatres Forty Years Ago." *The Trail*, April 1927: 8–13, May 1927: 8–14.

Thomas, Chauncey (ed.). "Sheriff of Elbert." *The Trail*, November 1927: 18–20.

Thompson, Thomas Gray. "Early Development of Lake City, Colorado." *Colorado Magazine*, April 1963: 92–105.

"'Uncle Billy' Maine: His Own Story of Experiences in Crossing the Plains in 1858 and of Coming to Denver in 1858." *The Trail*, April 1926: 3–11, May 1926: 4–6.

Vaile, Anna Wolcott, and Ellis Meredith. "Women's Contribution." In *History of Colorado*, James H. Baker and LeRoy R. Hafen, eds. 5 vols., vol. 3: 1075–1147. Denver: Linderman, 1927.

Vaille, Howard T. "Early Years of the Telephone in Colorado." *Colorado Magazine*, August 1928: 121–133.

Van Evra, T. E. (related by). "One Man's Experience in Early Leadville." *The Trail*, December 1918: 20–23.

Walker, Evalyn Capps. "The Strange Story." *Colorado Magazine*, summer 1977: 294–311.

West, Elliott. "Dirty Tricks in Denver." *Colorado Magazine*, summer 1975: 225–243.

———. "Of Lager Beer and Sonorous Songs." *Colorado Magazine*, spring 1971: 108–128.

Whiteside, Henry O. "The Drug Habit in Nineteenth Century Colorado." *Colorado Magazine*, winter 1978: 47–68.

Wortman, Roy T. "Denver's Anti-Chinese Riot, 1880." *Colorado Magazine*, fall 1965: 275–291.

PERIODICALS
(DATES AND USAGE CITED IN THE TEXT OR NOTES)

Aspen Weekly Times
Boulder Daily Camera

Colorado Evening Sun [Denver]
Colorado Graphic [Denver]
Colorado Magazine
Denver Daily Gazette
Denver Municipal Facts
Denver Post
Denver Republican
Denver Times
Denver Tribune
Denver Tribune-Republican
Gunnison Review
Madison County [Montana] *Monitor;* data provided by the Montana Historical Society
Mississippi Valley Historical Review
Piqua [Ohio] *Daily Call*
Polly Pry [Denver]
Pueblo Chieftain
The Road [Denver]
Rocky Mountain News [Denver]
Weekly Commonwealth and Republican [Denver]

CATALOGUED COLLECTIONS

Mazzulla Collection, ex–Amon Carter Museum, Fort Worth, Texas, now at the Colorado Historical Society, Denver.

Mazzulla Collection 1231, Colorado Historical Society, Denver.

UNCATALOGUED COLLECTIONS

Denver Public Library, Western History Department, loose newspaper clippings of police chief reports, unidentified as to newspaper or date.

Loose newspaper clippings of prostitution reports issued by Frederick J. Bancroft, M.D., Denver city physician 1872–1876, assembled by Caroline Bancroft and provided to the author by Robert L. Shikes, M.D.

Unpublished Materials

GOVERNMENT DOCUMENTS

The Charter and Ordinances of the City of Denver to Oct. 31st, 1862, Inclusive, Together with an Act Concerning Warrants of Cities and Towns. Denver, Colorado Territory: City Council, city attorney J. Bright Smith, comp., 1862. Copy in the author's possession.

Denver County Court probate case 12912, box 53293, regarding the estate of Leah J. Wood. Colorado State Archives, Denver.

Denver Metropolitan Planning Project Final Report. "Preventing Prostitution, Promiscuity and Venereal Disease in the Denver Metropolitan Area," June 1944. Copy in the Denver Public Library, Western History Department.

National Archives report dated January 11, 1895, by Adjutant General George A. Ruggles with regard to Civil War pension application by Sam Howe (Simeon Hunt). Copy in the author's possession.

CERTIFICATES

Promissory note secured by real estate deed, Sam Howe to L. N. Greenleaf and G. G. Brewer, December 3, 1860, documents collections, Colorado Historical Society.

Soldiers and Sailors Benevolent Society certificate to Samuel Howe, May 27, 1908, Denver Public Library document no. Minus M-371.

DISSERTATIONS AND THESES

Benham, Marjorie A. "Women in the Colorado State Penitentiary, 1873 Through 1916," master's thesis, University of Colorado at Denver, 1998.

Hanna, R. L. "The Art of American Policing, 1900–1930," master's thesis, University of Colorado at Denver, 1990.

Hogan, Richard Lawrence. "Law and Order in Colorado: 1858–1888," Ph.D. diss., University of Michigan, 1982.

Knapp, Anne Curtis. "Making an Orderly Society: Criminal Justice in Denver, Colorado, 1858–1900," Ph.D. diss., University of California at San Diego, 1983.

Rider, Eugene Frank. "The Denver Police Department, an Administrative, Organizational, and Operational History, 1858–1905," Ph.D. diss., University of Denver, 1971.

MANUSCRIPTS

Dawson, Thomas F. "The Sporting Side of Denver," interview with Edward Chase, July 11, 1921. Mss. IX-4, Colorado Historical Society Library, Denver.

Freudenburg, Betty D. "Overland Correspondent, Alva Adams?" Estes Park, Colorado, 1991.

Mazzulla, Fred. Undated (circa 1951), uncatalogued interview with Laura Evens. Ex–Amon Carter Museum, Fort Worth, Texas, now at Colorado Historical Society Library, Denver.

McGinn, Elinor M. "My Hobby Is Humanity: The Story of Josephine Roche," Lafayette, Colo., 2000.

Miller, Max. "A Salute to the Frontier Madames of Colorado," circa 1971, copy in Mazzulla collection 1231, ff. 30, Colorado Historical Society Library, Denver.

"The Non-academic Approach to History with Sight and Sound," copy in Mazzulla collection 1231, ff. 129, Colorado Historical Society Library, Denver.

Parkhill, Forbes. "Scarlet Sister Mattie," bound typescript, Denver, July 1948; copy in the Colorado Historical Society Library, Denver.

Samson, Ronald L. "Chronological History of the Denver Police Department," Denver, 1991. Copy in the author's possession.

Sanford, A. B. "Silver Heels," fictionalized treatment of the Silverheels saga, n.d. Typescript (qR Sa 57s) in the Colorado Historical Society Library, Denver.

SCRAPBOOKS

Farmer Lawton Scrapbooks. Western History Department, Denver Public Library.

Howe, Sam. *Sam Howe Murder Book,* 1883–1920, Colorado Historical Society Library, Denver.

———. Sam Howe Scrapbooks, 1883–1915, Colorado Historical Society Library, Denver.

RECORDS

"License Register of the Treasurer's Office," City of Denver, 1892–1897, Colorado State Archives, Denver.

Records of liquor permits issued in the City and County of Denver, circa 1880–1890, Colorado State Archives, Denver.

Records of prostitute census, circa 1895, Denver Police Department, Denver. Copy in the author's possession.

"Transfer of Saloon Records," Denver city treasurer, 1884 and 1885, Colorado State Archives, Denver.

INTERVIEWS

Author's interviews with James Oda, Piqua (Ohio) Historical Society, November 7, 1991; December 6, 1991.

J. T. Kearns interview with Yuma County judge Irving L. Barker, 1935, Colorado Historical Society Pam. 352/23, Colorado Historical Society Library, Denver.

Elinor Kingery and Nancy Denious interview with Arthur Bawdin, Denver, February 3, 1967, oral history interview no. 119, typescript, Colorado Historical Society, Denver.

CORRESPONDENCE

Correspondence and documents submitted to the author regarding William Henry Corwin from the Ohio Historical Society, April 28, 1995, and from the Warren County (Ohio) Historical Society, May 17, 1995.

Denver Police Department memorandum donating Sam Howe Scrapbooks to the Colorado Historical Society, November 21, 1939. Copy in author's possession.

Sam Howe to W. J. Phillips, February 10, 1920, W. J. Phillips Collection, box 493, Colorado Historical Society Library, Denver.

Index

Page numbers in italics indicate illustrations.

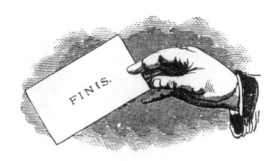